CULTURAL
Anthropology
Understanding Ourselves & Others

Richley H. Crapo received his Ph.D., with an emphasis in cultural and linguistic anthropology, from the University of Utah in 1970. He is presently an associate professor at Utah State University where he has taught the introductory course for over 15 years. **Cultural Anthropology: Understanding Ourselves and Others** was conceived and developed in his classroom. Beginning as handouts that his students used as supplements, it grew over a period of ten years into an integrated text that has been rewritten, class-tested, reviewed and revised into its present form—a coherent, comprehensive and interesting introduction to anthropological understanding of all cultures, including our own.

To Sharon: With love and gratitude for your patient helpfulness

About the Cover

Design by Dulcianne Vye.
Left: Dakota (Sioux) woman, North American Plains (source: American Museum of Natural History)
Center: Dakota (Sioux) man (source: American Museum of Natural History)
Right: Makah man, Northwest Coast (source: *Art of the Northwest Coast Indians,* University of California Press)
Background: Mandan (Sioux) shield (source: American Museum of Natural History)

CULTURAL

Anthropology

Understanding Ourselves & Others

Richley H. Crapo

Utah State University

DPG

The Dushkin Publishing Group, Inc.

Credits & Acknowledgments

Chapter 1 2 United Nations photo; 5 Napoleon A. Chagnon; 6 De Vore—Anthro Photo; 10 The Granger Collection; 11 The Bettmann Archive, Inc.; 13 The Bettmann Archive, Inc.

Chapter 2 18 Cleveland Museum of Natural History; 21 H. B. D. Kettlewell; 22 Mike Eagle; 26 Mike Eagle; 29 American Museum of Natural History, Neg. No. 120801; 34 Drawing by Luba Dmytryk Gudz from *Lucy: The Beginnings of Humankind* by Donald C. Johanson and Maitland A. Edey ©1981; 36 Mike Eagle; 37 Eric Mose, previously published in *Scientific American*, May, 1969 ©1969 by Scientific American, Inc. All rights reserved; 38 American Museum of Natural History, Neg. No. 333193; 40–41 Mike Eagle

Chapter 3 44 American Museum of Natural History, Neg. No. 33113; 50 J. Kirschner—American Museum of Natural History, Neg. No. 34834; 54 Dr. F. Rainey—American Museum of Natural History, Neg. No. 2A3793; 55 United Nations photo; 57 Courtesy Southeastern Peanut Farmer; 62 Brian Spykerman

Chapter 4 66 United Nations photo; 70 Courtesy Royal Thai Embassy; 71 United Nations photo; 73 ©Michael Hanulak—Photo Researchers, Inc.; 77 United Nations photo; 78 The Bettmann Archive, Inc.; 81 United Nations photo; 86 Charles Vitelli; 91 United Nations photo by Louise Gubb; 95 Library of Congress

Chapter 5 100 United Nations photo; 102 George Holton—Photo Researchers, Inc.; 111 American Museum of Natural History, Neg. No. 32101; 113 Rene Burri—Magnum Photos, Inc.; Keystone Press Agency, Inc.; 117 H. Terrace—Anthro Photo; 118 The Gorilla Foundation; 128 Mike Eagle, after Salzmann

Chapter 6 134 Bill Aron—Photo Researchers, Inc.; 142 ©Katrina Thomas—Photo Researchers, Inc.; 146 George Rodger—Magnum Photos; 149 Mike Eagle; 150 Mike Eagle; 151 Mike Eagle; 153 United Nations photo by John Isaac; United Nations photo; 155 Sid Schuler—Anthro Photo; 159 ©Jill Hartley—Photo Researchers, Inc.

Chapter 7 162 ©Marc and Evelyne Bernheim—Woodfin Camp and Associates; 164 Konner—Anthro Photo; 170 United Nations photo; 175 Cheryl Kinne—DPG; 181 Napoleon A. Chagnon; 183 M. Shostak—Anthro Photo; M. R. Harrington—Museum of the American Indian; 186 Elaine M. Ward; 188 The Peabody Museum of Salem; 189 American Philosophical Society; Smithsonian Institution; 190 Courtesy Embassy of Indonesia

Chapter 8 194 Brian Spykerman; 198 James Holland—Black Star; American Museum of Natural History, Neg. No. 292759; 199 Brian Spykerman; 201 Kit Porter; 202 Carmelo Guadagno—Museum of the American Indian; 205 Brian Spykerman; 207 Courtesy Australian News and Information Bureau; 209 American Museum of Natural History, Neg. No. 312384; 211 American Museum of Natural History, Neg. No. 2A3648

Chapter 9 220 John Lewis Stage—Photo Researchers, Inc.; 225 Mike Eagle, after Mellaart; 229 American Museum of Natural History, Neg. No. 319377; 232 Walter Fairservis; 234 The Brooklyn Museum, lent by Robin B. Martin; 236 Courtesy Mexico Ministry of Tourism; 238 Mark Lusk; 240 Noxon and Marcus

Chapter 10 242 Napoleon A. Chagnon; 244 Terry Pearce—Canadian Government Film and Video Centre; 247 American Museum of Natural History, Neg. No. 328745; Marc and Evelyne Bernheim—Woodfin Camp and Associates; American Museum of Natural History, Neg. No. 2A3751; 248 Mike Eagle; 249 Israeli Tourist Office, NYC; 253 DeCost Smith—Museum of the American Indian, Heye Foundation; 260 Leonard Freed—Magnum; 264 American Museum of Natural History, Neg. No. 326597

Chapter 11 272 United Nations photo by Antoinette Jongen; 275 The Granger Collection; 278 Charles Vitelli; 279 Charles Vitelli; 281 United Nations photo by John Isaac; 282 United Nations photo by John Isaac; 283 United Nations photo by Ida Pickerell; 285 United Nations photo; 289 Charles Vitelli

Chapter 12 292 United Nations photo by Milton Grant; 295 ©Arthur Tress—Photo Researchers, Inc.; 297 UPI/Bettmann Newsphotos; 299 Charles Vitelli; 302 Cheryl Kinne—DPG; 306 United Nations photo by Doranne Jacobson; 309 George Hunter—Canadian Government Film and Video Centre; United Nations photo by Paulo Fridman; 311 UAW Solidarity photo; 312 Courtesy Florida Division of Tourism; 313 Courtesy Minnesota Office of Tourism; 314 Courtesy Bermuda News Bureau; 315 Charles Vitelli; 320 Courtesy New York State Department of Commerce

C U L T U R A L

Anthropology

Understanding Ourselves & Others

Printed in the United States of America
Library of Congress Catalog Card Number: 86–73095

International Standard Book Number (ISBN) 0–87967–637-X

First Printing

The Dushkin Publishing Group, Inc., Sluice Dock, Guilford, Connecticut 06437

Preface

Anthropology, like its study, humankind, is a tremendously diverse subject. This diversity at once creates its richness and excitement as well as providing a challenge for anthropologists to present to students a coherent and meaningful introduction. While no text is likely to fulfill the hopes of all teachers, I believe *Cultural Anthropology: Understanding Ourselves and Others* will provide the basic insights into our field which a thoughtful student ought to have as part of a liberal education. These include not only facts and theories but most importantly the anthropological attitude: a commitment to understanding and appreciating cultural diversity.

CONTENT AND ORGANIZATION *Cultural Anthropology: Understanding Ourselves and Others* is an integrated text. I have tried to avoid fragmentation by building systematically from one concept to the next. In the process, I cover the wide range of interests which comprise the field of anthropology. Each of the four major subfields—physical anthropology, archaeology, cultural anthropology, and linguistic anthropology are discussed—with primary emphasis on cultural anthropology.

The book begins with a succinct discussion of the rich, yet complex subject of anthropology itself: its uniqueness among the social sciences, the breadth of its content, its history and contemporary forms, its methods, and its ethics. Chapter 2 surveys topics in the biological evolution of the human species: the mechanics of evolution and clues to our primate past. Chapter 3 introduces the concept of culture, including discussions of both ideology and technology, as well as issues on how different cultures respond to and influence each other.

Building on these basics, the next five chapters discuss aspects of the broader cultural system: social organization, with institutionalized inequalities (Chapter 4), learning and communication (Chapter 5), life cycle stages and ceremonies (Chapter 6), cultural shaping of personality, psychological disorders, and altered states of consciousness (Chapter 7), and cultural patterns in religion (Chapter 8). The next three chapters approach culture historically: Chapter 9 looks at the archaeological record of early societies, Chapter 10 examines the process of evolution from small-scale bands to large-scale states, and Chapter 11 discusses the contemporary mix of vanishing nonstate societies, peasant cultures, developing countries, and industrialized societies. The book ends with a special chapter about the United States, interpreting its characteristics in all these areas from the unique anthropological point of view.

I have attempted to write clearly and logically, and the vocabulary and the level of writing that I have adopted are appropriate for the serious student. I have found that when one addresses one's students with respect and dignifies them with the assumption that they possess more than a modicum of intelligence, it pays off. Students, like anyone else, live up to or down to one's expectations of them. I believe that after a decade in which the conventional wisdom has been that basic texts should be written down to their audiences, the trend is now to recognize this as a tragic error for our educational system. The classroom is a place of education and the purpose of teachers and students and their texts should be the perpetuation of wisdom and intellectual skills.

LEARNING AIDS A variety of learning aids has been systematically incorporated into the text. Each chapter begins with an *outline* to aid students in recognizing the main concepts and in understanding how they will be organized. To facilitate students' learning of the basic concepts of each chapter, all *terms* are defined in context and *underlined* for easy recognition. Each chapter ends with a list of these terms in the order in which they occur, with page numbers indicating where they are defined. These technical terms are also defined in a *glossary* at the end of the book. Since learning the subject matter of a new field also involves acquiring a new vocabulary, students should be encouraged to use these glossaries as a valuable learning review. By testing their knowledge of the meaning of each term, they can readily determine which parts of each chapter need further study in preparation for tests.

Major concepts are often illustrated by *extended narrative examples* integrated with the text. These provide concrete, down-to-earth examples of the material under discussion. For instance, in chapters that concern cultural anthropology, the extended narratives introduce students to appropriate aspects of cultures using an ethnographic record, from the practical reasons for India's sacred cows to attitudes toward conformity in Germany, Japan, and the United States. A number of these narratives describe aspects of Native American cultures, reflecting current interest in these peoples and my own fieldwork among the Shoshoni. These narrative examples are marked with a bullet (•) in the table of contents and are identified within the text by vertical color rules.

All cultures to which students are introduced that might be unfamiliar are located on a map at the beginning of the book and are included in the index. All references cited within the body of the text have been compiled into a single bibliography placed immediately before the index. For teachers using the text, I have prepared an instructor's resource guide: *Teaching and Testing from Cultural Anthropology: Understanding Ourselves and Others.*

ACKNOWLEDGMENTS   I deeply appreciate the help of many people who contributed their knowledge, skill, and time in ways that generally enhanced the quality of this book: Carol J. Loveland, who repeatedly shared her expertise in physical anthropology; Edna H. Berry, who was an invaluable source of demographic data; and Gordon Keller, Pamela J. Riley, Brian Spykerman, Mark Lusk, Deborah Marcus, and John Noxon for the original photographic materials that they made available.

I am also indebted to those who gave constructive criticism and expert advice as reviewers of this book:

Elvio Angeloni, Pasadena City College; James Eder, Arizona State University; Robert C. Harman, California State University, Long Beach; Robert A. Randall, University of Houston; Professor Jay Sokolovsky, University of Maryland, Baltimore; Linda M. Whiteford, University of South Florida; Scott Whiteford, Michigan State University.

Special thanks are also due John Holland, Managing Editor of The Dushkin Publishing Group for his careful attention to detail and for the high level of competence that he expected of those who worked on this text; to Mary Pat Fisher for her exceptional skill as a developmental editor and for her many useful suggestions, to Kathleen Burns and M. Marcuss Oslander who copyedited the text, to Pamela Carley Petersen for finding the right pictures, and to Bill Ferneau for bringing the publisher and myself together. I wish also to thank Sharon Cannon-Crapo for her patience and for her useful criticisms of the manuscript as it evolved.

Richley H. Crapo

Table of Contents

Note: Bullet ● placed in front of an item indicates an extended narrative example.

This map shows the approximate location of the cultures introduced in this book. You will find page references to these cultures in the index.

Chapter 1

Anthropology: A Unique Approach To Understanding

Figure 1.1 *Anthropology This young girl lives in Bamako, the capital of Mali, a country on the southern edge of the Sahara. Anthropology is the holistic study of diverse human societies both of the past and the present.*

Many of the sciences and humanities study humankind, but anthropology is a special way of understanding our species. In a sense, it incorporates all other ways of studying human societies. This chapter introduces what anthropology is, how it has evolved as a discipline, how it gathers information about human behavior, and how it tries to keep its work on an ethical basis with respect for all its subjects. The chapter ends with an overview of this textbook, defining its unique aproach to the study of anthropology.

The Breadth of Anthropology

Anthropology excites me because it is something new in the history of the world. Anthropologists want to understand human nature, as do members of several other fields, but anthropology is an approach to studying the human condition that differs from any other discipline. Classified by subject matter, our field is one of the humanities, so anthropologists share some of the interests of philosophers, literary and art critics, translators, and historians. By aspiration, anthropology is a science and shares a great deal with sociology, psychology, political science, economics, linguistics, geography, paleontology, and biology. Wolf (1964) claims that anthropology bridges the gulf between the sciences and the humanities:

Anthropology is both a natural science, concerned with the organization and function of matter, and a humanistic discipline, concerned with the organization and function of mind. Its subject matter is man, who is both part of the ecology of nature and an improbable departure from what one might expect to find in the natural realm. He is the animal with culture, that is, an animal equipped with the ability to create and use symbols to devise new, artificial worlds of his own making. Just as the subject matter of anthropology is dual, so the concern of the anthropologist is dual: he must mediate between human biology and

3

ecology on the one hand, and the study of human understanding on the other. Necessarily, he must be both outside observer and participant in the internal dialogues of his informants. By definition, therefore, anthropology is less subject matter than a bond between subject matters, and the anthropologist will forever find himself translating from one realm to another. (p. 13)

This breadth in the subject matter and goals of anthropology has created an extremely diverse field that brings together specialists whose topics of study might be central to other fields. Consider this diversity: In the past decade, the major American anthropological journals have included articles on the changing role of the family in Iran, the definition of religion, the nutritional implications of cannibalism, the origins of agriculture in Southeast Asia, the political and educational implications of creationist theology in the United States, the problems of Third World economic development, the discovery of three-and-one-half-million-year-old fossil ancestors of the human species in Tanzania, the effects of different foods on the wear patterns of teeth, the relationship of diet to human fertility, and the origins and diversity of human languages. Nevertheless, anthropology manages to unite these diverse topics by taking as its goal a unified understanding of the human condition.

One difference between anthropology and other fields in which human beings are the topic of study is that anthropology is broader in its scope. Our purpose is to paint a holistic picture of the human condition, that is, one that shows how different aspects of being human relate to and influence one another. For instance, an anthropologist who is especially interested in human economic life is likely to study how the economic customs of a society influence and are influenced by that society's physical environment, political system, religious customs, family patterns, or even its artistic endeavors. An anthropologist who is concerned with human biology might attempt to demonstrate that different frequencies of fractured vertebrae may result from different hunting practices. An anthropologist studying the language of a Na-

tive American society may attempt to determine the location of its ancestral homeland by comparing its words for plants and animals with those of other related languages and by considering the geographical distributions of those specific plants and animals for which the related languages share words.

In addition to being more holistic than other fields, anthropology tends to be broader in scope because anthropologists develop their ideas about what is typical of human beings by comparing a broader range of different human groups before drawing their conclusions. For instance, most of the ideas set forth in a contemporary textbook on abnormal psychology are based on research that has been carried out in Europe or North America in societies whose people differ relatively little in upbringing and life experiences. By contrast, a typical anthropological textbook about the nature of mental illness will include comparisons between peoples as diverse as Ituri Forest pygmies, Canadian Inuit, traditional Chinese villagers, and Swedish city dwellers. Anthropologists want their ideas about human nature to be based on as wide a spectrum of human ways of life as possible. For this reason, anthropologists study people in all parts of the world in both simple and complex societies. Their perspective, in other words, is based on cross-cultural research— research that draws data from many diverse ways of life rather than just one.

Anthropology's scope extends through time as well as space. Anthropologists try to uncover as much as possible about societies of the distant past as well as about life in contemporary societies. The artifacts and fossil remains of ancient peoples are studied for clues to how people lived in the past and how we became what we are today.

Kinds of Anthropology

There are four main types of anthropologists: cultural anthropologists, archaeologists, anthropological linguists, and physical anthropologists. Generally speaking, cultural anthropologists are interest-

Figure 1.2 *Ethnographical Anthropologist*
One way an anthropologist gathers information about the culture he or she is studying is to live with and participate in the daily activities of that culture. An important part of the research is the accurate gathering and reporting of the observations made as Napoleon Chagnon is doing on his solar-powered computer.

ed in understanding the rules that govern ways of life, or <u>cultures</u>. They study the customs of human societies to answer questions about what leads to the similarities and differences in how various peoples go about their lives. As a part of their training, students who are becoming cultural anthropologists are usually expected to spend a prolonged period of time—often a year or more—living in a society that practices customs very different from those of their own, participating in that way of life, and recording the customs of that society as accurately as possible.

Cultural anthropologists who continue to specialize in recording the customs of human societies are called <u>ethnographers</u>. Their descriptions of human ways of life are called <u>ethnographies</u>. Other cultural anthropologists known as <u>ethnologists</u> study the ethnographies of many different ways of life in the attempt to unravel the gener-

al laws that guide the development of human ways of life. Ethnologists have their own specialties, such as people's economic life, political systems, marriages, family and childrearing practices, art, religious practices and beliefs, or psychological traits. The specializations within this branch of anthropology tend to overlap with the interests of professionals in the other behavioral and social sciences within a university. Yet, cultural anthropology has a distinctive contribution to make in a university: to show how each part of human life, be it language, politics, economics, family life or religion, fits into a way of life as a whole. In a sense, other social and behavioral scientists study the various parts in isolation from one another, while the cultural anthropologist is interested in how each part of human life relates to the broader context of human life.

<u>Archaeologists</u>, like cultural anthropol-

ogists, are interested in understanding ways of life. However, the peoples studied by archaeologists ceased to exist before they were studied. While the cultural anthropologist studies ways of life described by researchers who lived among the people to observe their customs, the archaeologist reconstructs the history and the culture of a people from the things they left behind during their lives. The fieldwork of the archaeologist involves the careful, painstaking excavation of places where people have been. The skills required for the work of excavating a site that has been occupied or used by human beings include knowledge of surveying, map making, photography, and others necessary for the preservation of information about each object unearthed, including exactly where it was located compared to every other object discovered.

To analyze the materials obtained in an excavation, the archaeologist may use skills similar to those of botanists, zoologists, geologists, physicists and other laboratory scientists, since the original environment of the site must be reconstructed. The archaeologist at this stage may seek to answer questions such as what plants and animals were being eaten and whether these foods were domestic or wild, what the native plants and animals suggest about the climate of the site, or how the materials left behind may provide clues about the age of the site. After such questions have been answered, the work of the archaeologist becomes much like that of the historian and the cultural anthropologist. The goal at this point becomes the description of a way of life and its history.

Anthropological linguists are interested in the role of language in human life. They may be concerned with the origins of language, the biological characteristics of human beings that make it possible for them to use language, the ways in which languages change, or how they are used in daily life. Unlike linguists in other fields, anthropological linguists are chiefly concerned not with language for its own sake, but with the relationships between language and the human condition. Like cultural anthropologists or archaeologists, anthropological linguists may devote their

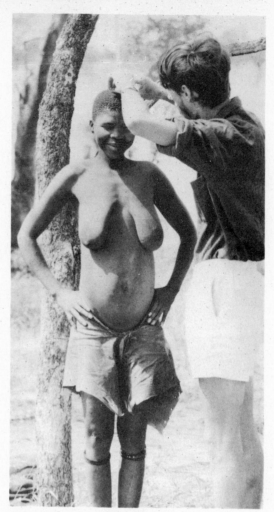

Figure 1.3 *Physical Anthropologist*
The physical or biological anthropologist studies the causes of physical variations in human populations by focusing on evolution, heredity, and environment. In this photo John Yellen is measuring the length of a San woman's hair.

efforts to fieldwork. In the field, the anthropological linguist may record the little-known languages of the world, the oral traditions, the music, the poetry, the styles of speaking, or the social and geographical dialects that are characteristic of a people. Other anthropological linguists with more theoretical interests may study the data from many related languages, much as the ethnologist compares descriptions of the customs of different societies.

Physical anthropologists are also sometimes called biological anthropologists. The purpose of their research is to answer a variety of questions concerning the origins of the human species, its evolutionary history, and the current biological variation among the peoples of the world. Some physical anthropologists study the fossilized skeletal remains of our early human ancestors and their close relatives, with the goal of developing an accurate picture of the evolution of our species. Others have a more specialized interest, such as learning about the diseases from which ancient peoples suffered. Some physical anthropologists specialize in studying how the biological characteristics of contemporary peoples differ from one another and how these differences may have come about. There are even physical anthropologists who devote themselves to the study of the biology and behavior of our close nonhuman relatives, such as the chimpanzees, gorillas, and monkeys, to learn more about the similarities and differences between us.

As diverse as the specialized interests of different anthropologists may be, what unifies them is their common desire to better understand the nature of humans and to relate their research to the broader picture of the human condition. It is this integrating tendency and holistic viewpoint that is characteristic of the anthropological enterprise and differentiates it from other disciplines that study the human condition.

Methods of Anthropological Research

As a science, anthropology has its own distinctive research methods. These involve fieldwork and the comparative method. In cultural anthropology, these take the form of participant observation, and cross-cultural comparison.

Fieldwork

The essential method of anthropological research that is shared by anthropologists regardless of their specialization is <u>fieldwork</u>—study carried out in the field for firsthand observation. Biological anthropologists may spend time in search of fossil remains of human ancestors or observing primates such as chimpanzees or baboons in the wild to learn about the behavior of

species closely related to our own. Archaeologists spend time in the field examining and excavating sites once occupied by human beings. Anthropological linguists work with native speakers of diverse languages to gather data firsthand about these languages and how they are used in real life situations. Ethnographers spend prolonged periods of time living in isolated non-Western societies, in developing countries, or in a variety of settings such as rural villages, religious communes, or central city slums in Western societies to gather data about the life and customs of those they observe.

Direct observation in natural settings is the common factor in data collection by all kinds of anthropologists. This feature contrasts with the work of other social and behavioral scientists, who have traditionally collected their data in artificial laboratory settings or through indirect data-gathering techniques such as questionnaires or polls. Consider, for example, the differences in approach of a psychological anthropologist and a psychologist or sociologist interested in social psychology. Most research by psychologists who study social psychology is conducted in laboratories. For instance, a psychologist who is interested in human aggression might advertise for volunteer subjects and then have these volunteers administer what they are told are electric shocks to confederates of the researcher, ostensibly to study the effects of punishment on learning but actually to study human willingness to follow aggressive role models and authority figures. Volunteers who were exposed to a staged argument on their way to the laboratory might be compared with those volunteers who were not. Despite the insights thus gained, there are significant limitations on the usefulness of such studies. Subjects are limited to people who volunteer to come to the laboratory to participate in the research. Whether people who volunteer for such activities are typical members of society is always questionable in such research. Furthermore, it is not always clear what a subject's willingness to administer an electric shock in a research setting when told to do so by a psychologist wearing a lab smock reveals about the same person's likelihood of participating in a riot during a blackout, getting into a bar fight, volunteering for military service during a national crisis, or committing homicide.

An anthropologist interested in human aggression would be more likely to carry out research in the social environments in which violence occurs. The research would most probably be carried out over a period of months, while the anthropologist lives among the people being studied, interacting with them in their normal, day-to-day settings and recording fortuitous examples of real aggression as they spontaneously occur. Based on repeated observations over long periods of time, the ethnographer might then suggest some general conclusions about the situations or patterns of interaction that are most likely to trigger aggressive behavior in the particular society being studied.

Participant Observation

Most ethnographic research is also carried out using what is called participant observation. The anthropologist does not study people from afar as a sociologist might, relying on secondary data such as census records or data collected by questionnaires sent to subjects through the mail. Rather, he or she goes to the subjects in the field and remains living among them for a long enough period to earn the trust that people require to behave in the ways they usually do when strangers, tourists, or "outsiders" are not present. Ideally, the ethnographer would like to become skilled enough at following local customs to be accepted as a functioning member of the group, while maintaining sufficient objectivity about the way of life to be able to describe and analyze it fairly and impartially. In practice, complete acceptance as a member of the community being studied is rare. After all, anthropologists are usually born and reared according to customs and values different from those of the peoples they study. Nevertheless, the goal of respect for the local community's standards and customs gives the anthropologist the greatest possible chance of inspiring

enough trust in the community members that they will feel comfortable and behave spontaneously even when the anthropologist is present. The goal of observing the normal behavior of people is another reason why anthropologists expect to spend months or even years carrying out their participant observation research. Even if the researcher never comes to be seen as a true insider, his or her prolonged presence can breed sufficient tolerance for the people's behavior to return to the routine normally followed when true "outsiders" are not present.

Anthropological observation is called *participant* observation because it is not limited to passive watching and note taking. Anthropologists try as much as possible to practice local customs to gain a "feel" for the way of life that helps them understand it as the people themselves do. Thus, anthropologists expect to learn the native language of the people they study. This is not merely to become better able to understand what is being said around them, but also to give anthropologists a more accurate perception of the native way of life, since a language is a kind of record and model of a people's understandings of themselves and their environment.

Learning the native language of a people also facilitates the direct questioning of informants about their customs and the meanings that those customs have to people. Direct questioning is an important part of participant observation as opposed to simple observation. Anthropologists carry out their questioning in ways that are systematic enough to uncover hidden and implicit but not normally discussed aspects of ways of life that might otherwise remain undiscovered. Systematic questioning requires asking the same questions of many different informants. This is done partly to verify the accuracy of what the researcher is told—after all, anthropologists are outsiders, and they may be considered fair game to informants who may resent their presence or simply enjoy the humor of deceiving them. Asking the same questions of many informants also insures that the information obtained is typical of the ideas expressed in the community at large.

Cross-Cultural Comparison

The third component of anthropological research is cross-cultural comparison—examination of the varied ways a certain aspect of human life is treated in many different cultures. For instance, an ethnologist who is interested in the general rules that relate to aggression in any society might compare the ethnographic data from a broad range of human societies to determine what social factors are consistent predictors of specific forms of aggression.

Anthropological fieldworkers are especially skilled at providing insights into the relationship of a custom to its broader social context. Their in-depth exposure to a particular way of life allows them to notice in detail how one part of a culture influences another. Yet, to develop truly useful generalizations about the ways in which culture functions, it is necessary to demonstrate that relationships that appear to be valid in one culture will hold true for others under like circumstances. Cross-cultural research is the strategy that anthropologists use for this purpose. By comparing a sufficient number of historically unrelated cultures from different parts of the world, it is possible to determine, for instance, whether warfare is more likely in societies in which there are large differences in wealth between families than in societies in which all families have about the same level of wealth, or whether sexual inequality is more likely in societies where warfare occurs between neighboring peoples who belong to the same culture than in societies where warfare occurs between members of very different cultures.

Currently, the most sophisticated collection of data on many different societies is one which was begun about 40 years ago by George Peter Murdock and several colleagues (1961). This collection of cross-cultural data is known as the Human Relations Area Files (HRAF). It now contains over half a million pages of information on over 1,000 different ways of life, each of which has been coded for the presence or absence of characteristics on a standard list of about 800 cultural and environmental traits. Use of data from the HRAF has made it possible for researchers to determine what cultural traits or environmental factors are the best predictors of the presence or absence of various customs, thereby testing their ideas about the effects of one part of a cultural system on another.

History of Anthropology

Although anthropology is a relatively young discipline, it has its roots in earlier attempts to learn about unfamiliar cultures. Even after anthropology became systematized as a science, it evolved through many forms.

The Prescientific Period

Anthropology owes its birth to European expansionism of the fifteenth and sixteenth centuries. Exploration and colonization brought Europeans into contact with many peoples of diverse racial characteristics and ways of life. Government officials who wished to exert political control over native peoples and missionaries who desired to convert them to Christianity both had reason to learn about the peoples they were trying to influence. Missionaries, in particular, were active in recording and studying the languages of native peoples. The religious beliefs and practices of native peoples were also of interest to writers of this period.

As knowledge of other cultures grew during this epoch, ideas about the origins of non-Western peoples were dominated by the European religious view that all people were the product of the divine creation described in the Bible. The world itself—indeed, the entire universe—was generally held to be only a few thousand years old. Irish Archbishop Ussher (1581-1656) had set the date of creation as 4004 B.C. by studying the ages reported in the genealogies of the Book of Genesis. In the European view, cultures had degenerated from the way of life that had originally been established among human beings by God. This degeneration was thought to be especially evident in the ways of life of non-Western peoples who were viewed as savages. European civilization, by virtue of its presumably superior way of life, was obligated to bring order and morality to the rest of the world.

The Evolutionary Period

Out of the contrast Europeans saw between simple and complex societies grew the idea that cultures had evolved from simple beginnings to eventually more complex civilization. During the eighteenth century, as a more secular view of the world became prominent, cultural evolutionism, the idea that cultures had evolved from savagery to civilization, became the dominant view among scholars.

Toward the end of the eighteenth century, scholars began to consider seriously the idea that biological species might also be evolving. In 1735 Carolus Linnaeus had published the *Systema Naturae*, which classified plants and animals into a hierarchical system based on their degree of similarity to one another. Although Linnaeus's purpose had been simply to demonstrate the divine order of God's creation, his systematic categorization of humans and other living things made it easy to suggest that living forms had achieved their current differences through evolution. The discovery of ancient fossils of extinct animals also contributed to the idea that animals had not been simply created all at one time as fixed forms in a single act of divine creation.

Ideas about human racial differences were also growing more sophisticated during the eighteenth century, and they too contributed to the gradual rise of an evolutionary view of biology. Linnaeus's classification of living things is still accepted today as essentially correct for most animals. His views, however, about the human races were highly distorted by tales from travelers and adventurers about the presence of bizarre human types in far-flung parts of the world. Linnaeus included in his system categories of headless humans, four-footed humans, and other strange human types that were later recognized as nothing more than inventions of the human imagination. This aspect of Linnaeus's work was corrected by Johann Blumenbach, who is cited by some as the father of physical anthropology.

In 1775 Blumenbach published *On the Natural History of Mankind*, in which he divided the human species into five racial types based on skin color and other phys-

Figure 1.4 *Charles Darwin*
Darwin was the first scientist to propose the controversial theory of natural selection or the evolution of a species through change.

ical characteristics. Blumenbach's views about human race were still not entirely secular, but they admitted the possibility of change within the species. According to Blumenbach, the Caucasian represented the form created by God, and other human varieties had developed by degeneration from the original Caucasian type.

In the nineteenth century, the belief became popular that the races differed in their natural abilities. This idea was used to explain the differences in people's way of life. Meanwhile, interest in the concept of biological evolution continued to grow. Geology contributed evidence that the world was millions of years old and this made it easier to imagine that species could evolve from earlier, very different forms. Then in 1859 Charles Darwin published *On the Origin of Species*, in which he set forth the first successful theory of the mechanisms by which evolutionary change occurs. About the same time, the discovery of the first known fossil remains of ancient

Figure 1.5 *Edward Burnett Tylor*
Tylor postulated, in the 19th century, that culture evolved uniformly and progressively, thus making possible the idea of progress for all societies.

Figure 1.6 *Franz Boas*
The first-hand observation of other cultures and careful collection of data about them was Franz Boas's greatest contribution to modern anthropology.

humans added dramatic support to the applicability of Darwin's ideas to the human species.

In the nineteenth century, archaeology was also providing support for the idea that ways of life evolved. Excavation of the remains of prehistoric societies was showing that earlier human cultures were simpler than later ones that developed from them. In 1871 Sir Edward Burnett Tylor published *Primitive Culture* in which he developed a theory of the evolution of religion and discussed the concept of survivals, remnants of earlier social customs and ideas that could be used as evidence for reconstructing the evolutionary past of societies. In 1877 a contemporary of Tylor, Lewis Henry Morgan, published another strong argument for the evolution of cultures, *Ancient Society*, a book that has remained influential to this day. In 1883 Tylor became the first anthropologist to hold a position at a university, and anthropology as a professional field of study was born.

The Empiricist Period

The American brand of anthropology developed its own distinctive flavor about the beginning of the twentieth century under the leadership of Franz Boas. Originally trained in physics, Boas brought to the field of anthropology a scientific emphasis on empiricism that greatly influenced its history in America. Boas stressed the importance of fieldwork by anthropologists. Since his day it has become the rule for students to spend a period of time studying a non-Western way of life by personally living in the society. Boas taught his students that the careful collection of accurate information about other ways of life was as important as the building of theory. He also vigorously condemned armchair theorizing—the building of grandiose theories based on speculation rather than on research. Boas was, in other words, an empiricist who viewed science as a discipline dedicated to the recording of fact. During his career, Boas published over 700 articles

11

dealing with topics as diverse as changes in the bodily form of descendants of American immigrants, Native American mythology, geography, and the relationships between language and thought.

It was Boas and his students who established anthropology as a field of study in major universities throughout the United States. Boas set the tone of the distinctive form that American anthropology cultivated for half a century. Beyond stressing the importance of fieldwork data collection, Boas and his students strongly rejected the idea that cultures were determined by race or that races differed from one another in their ability to learn any way of life. Well ahead of their time, Boas's students became the most outspoken adversaries of racism in the early twentieth century. Similarly, Boas avoided comparing cultures in ways that carried any implication of ranking them. Instead, he stressed the importance of cultural relativism, the idea that it is invalid to try to evaluate other cultures in terms of Western standards and that each way of life is best understood by its own standards of meaning and value. This idea remains a fundamental concept in anthropology to this day.

During the first half of the twentieth century, interest declined in the development of ideas about cultural evolution. Many of the earlier theories of cultural evolution fell into disrepute because of the tendency of earlier scholars to judge non-Western ways of life to be primitive simply because they failed to use Victorian standards of propriety. During the period dominated by Boas, anthropologists commonly adopted the concept of diffusion—the spread of customs, artifacts, and ideas from one society to another—to organize their ideas about how ways of life influence each other. In the United States, the concept of diffusion led to the idea of culture areas, relatively small geographical regions in which different societies, such as the Plains Indians societies of the United States, had come to share many similar traits through diffusion. The idea of culture areas suited the need of museums to find ways of organizing their displays to show the lifeways of peoples from various parts of the world.

During the period of the first half of the twentieth century while diffusionism was the dominant view in America, European anthropologists were also abandoning their interest in cultural evolution and turning to their own brand of diffusionism as a means for reconstructing social history. European diffusionists felt that earlier anthropologists had placed too much emphasis on the independent invention of social traits and underrated the role of the diffusion of ideas. They traced the spread of social traits and ideas around the entire world from a small number of centers in which they believed those traits had been originally invented.

The Functionalist Period

In England the diffusionist viewpoint took on its most simplistic form. The British diffusionists contended that all important inventions had occurred but once, in ancient Egypt, and spread from there to other parts of the world. By the 1930s this overly simple view of human history had been replaced by an approach known as functionalism. Functionalists turned away from a concern with history or the origins of customs. Their interests were in the mechanics of society, the way in which it functioned. In their view, a society was able to continue to exist because its customs were adaptive and made it possible for people to cope with their environment and with one another. Therefore, a society's customs can be analyzed by their functions, their contribution to maintaining the unity and survival of the society. The main proponents of this view were Bronislaw Malinowski and Alfred Reginald Radcliffe-Brown. Both Malinowski and Radcliffe-Brown stressed the importance of field work and rejected evolutionism and diffusionism. Malinowski emphasized that societies survive by making it possible for their members to meet seven biological and psychological needs: nutrition, reproduction, bodily comforts, safety, relaxation, movement, and growth. He analyzed the functions of a society's customs by how they helped the individual to meet these needs. Radcliffe-Brown, on the other hand, was concerned with social functions, the mechanisms that operate within society to

Figure 1.7 *Ruth Benedict*
Benedict was instrumental in establishing the importance of studying cultures and their behavior in comparison to other cultures.

Figure 1.8 *Margaret Mead*
Mead is best known for her study of culture and personality. The book Coming of Age in Samoa *is her influential study of adolescent development and behavior.*

maintain an orderly social life among its members.

While functionalism was on the rise in England, one branch of American anthropology was becoming more interested in the role of psychology in ways of life. Many of the anthropologists of this tradition were students of Boas who were influenced by his interest in human psychology and worldview. The best known of these anthropologists were Ruth Benedict and Margaret Mead. In 1934, Benedict published *Patterns of Culture*, which is still among the most widely read of American anthropological works. In this book, she argued—like the functionalists—that ways of life are integrated wholes. Unlike the functionalists, however, she found this integration in the unity of a people's mentality and values. Margaret Mead stressed the importance of childrearing practices on personality development. During the 1930s, students of culture and personality, as this new subfield of anthropology came to be known, were

greatly influenced by Freudian views of developmental psychology. Following World War II, their influence declined. The early practitioners of culture and personality studies have been faulted for their tendency to overgeneralize about cultural patterns based on impressionistic stereotypes that ignored variations in the behaviors of the peoples they studied.

The Period of Specialization

After World War II, two major earlier interests—the symbolic aspects of culture and the material and social conditions to which human life must adjust—continued to be the major divisions within cultural anthropology, but many specialized subfields have developed within both of these approaches to culture. For instance, in response to criticism of their earlier lack of methodological rigor, culture and personality studies have matured into what is now most often called psychological anthropology. Psychological anthropology has adopted an emphasis on the use of statistical comparisons of data from many different societies. By doing so, psychological anthropologists hope to develop valid general descriptions of the functional relationships between personality and various aspects of society such as its economic, political, and social organization, as well as childrearing customs.

Other cultural anthropologists with training in symbolic interests have created new subspecializations that they believe better fill the niche of earlier culture and personality studies. Ethnomethodology, for instance, has borrowed the methodological rigor of linguistics as a tool for analyzing the symbolic patterns within ways of life. Structural anthropology, also influenced by linguistic models of finding patterns in language, has focused on the less conscious patterns in lifeways in a search for universal symbolic patterns in human cultures. Symbolic anthropology also views culture primarily as a system of meanings that gives unity to a society, but focuses primarily on the analysis of myths, rituals, folklore, and the meaningful aspects of kinship as the basis for understanding the rest of human social life and custom.

Anthropologists whose interests center on the more practical factors underlying the creation of customs have also created new and exciting subspecializations. For instance, the changes in anthropology during this period have included a rebirth of the study of cultural evolution—neoevolutionism—as well as the development of new interest in the rules that govern how people adjust to their natural and social environments. These specialized subfields include: cultural ecology, the study of the adjustment of ways of life to different habitats; Marxist anthropology, which emphasizes the role of class conflict in social and cultural change; and neofunctionalism, which carries on the tradition of functional analysis while stressing the role of conflict within society as one of the mechanisms by which stability is maintained.

Finally, an entirely new emphasis on the application of anthropology outside the academic setting has developed within this period. Applied anthropology is the attempt to use anthropological skills and in-

sights to solve the thorny issues of cultural development in nonindustrialized parts of the world. And practicing anthropology is the growing use of anthropological expertise in various occupations within the private economic sector. Practicing anthropologists are employed in a diverse set of circumstances outside the traditional educational settings in which most anthropologists have been employed. Practicing anthropologists work for law firms, for cultural resource management companies, in human management and data management consulting firms, and in a host of other nonacademic positions in which their training in a holistic approach to human systems and in participant observation techniques and cross-cultural communication skills are particularly useful.

The increasing number of specialized areas of study within anthropology reflects the rapid social, economic, and political change that has characterized our society during most of this century. It also reflects the increasing contact between anthropology and other disciplines since World War II. In a climate of change, the predominance of functional analysis with its emphasis on stability has given way to more change-oriented theories. Perhaps the dominant viewpoint that crosscuts the specializations within anthropology today is an eclecticism that is willing to select its theories from a wide variety of sources.

Ethics in Anthropological Research

Since the subjects of anthropological research are human beings, there are important ethical considerations in doing fieldwork. It is generally agreed that the first loyalties of an anthropological fieldworker must lie with the people being studied. Our work must be carried out and reported in ways that cannot be used to harm the peoples whose ways of life we are investigating. When an anthropologist lives for extended periods of time with a people to thoroughly absorb the details of their lives and customs, it is almost inevitable that the researcher will become privy to information that might be harmful to the welfare and dignity of the host people were it to become public knowledge. Such knowledge is expected to be held in confidence, and anthropological research is reported only in ways that insure the anonymity of individual informants and the welfare of the communities studied.

Since anthropological research carried out among living peoples is a matter of skilled observation and inquiry, anthropologists generally have no qualms about informing their subjects about the purposes of their research. There are, of course, situations in which the gathering of specific information about people's behavior would be made more difficult by an explicit indication of what the anthropologist is seeking, either because the informants' knowledge would make them self-conscious—thereby causing them to alter their normal behavior—or because informants may sometimes say what they think the investigator would like to hear. Thus, anthropologists may be open about their general topic of interest without compromising their ability to observe the specific behaviors that are relevant to learning about that topic. The real issue here is that anthropologists endeavor not to deceive their subjects or carry out research that serves interests that differ from their own. Clandestine or secret research is frowned on by most anthropologists. When anthropologists are hired or supported by government agencies to study a people's customs, they do so only with the understanding that their research is not intended for purposes that will be harmful to their subjects or that will conflict with the values and goals of those subjects. One way of avoiding conflicts of interest over allegiance to the people studied and to others with differing political aims is a commitment to avoid accepting research assignments that the funding agency requires to be carried out in secrecy.

The anthropologist's second allegiance is to the expansion of a scientifically respectable body of knowledge about the human condition. Thus, anthropologists seek to do everything in their power to collect accurate information and to make it openly available to others in a form that does not violate their informants' rights or dignity. This mandate for open publication of research data is a further barrier to undertaking clandestine research for agencies or employers who would prevent researchers from submitting what they learn about a people to the scientific community at large. Anthropologists believe that their work should be carried out and reported in a way that can be shared with the people being studied as well as with others. It is common practice for anthropologists to see to it that copies of their research reports and publications are made available to the communities they were studying. This openness insures integrity in the research process and loyalty to the values of the subjects, and it also makes it possible for the fruits of anthropological research to be used by the research subjects for their own benefit.

The Goal of this Book

The goal of this textbook is to share some of the understandings of that broader picture of the human condition that has been built up by the work of many different anthropologists. To this end, the chapters that follow will begin by exploring the physical origins of our species and the nature of culture, the distinctive human component of our life as a social animal. The relationship between human biology and human culture will then be discussed, followed by an examination of the role of symbols and communication in human life. The following chapter will outline the major life events that commonly occur in human societies throughout the world. The next two chapters deal with the effects of culture and social life on human personalities and with religion, the central symbolic preoccupation in human ways of life. The final four chapters of the text will outline the evolution of culture from its simplest to its most complex forms. These chapters will begin with a discussion of the evolution of human cultural life, examined by exploring the prehistory of human ways of life through the rise of the early civilizations of the world. This will be followed by chapters about contemporary primitive societies, the peasant cultures of the developing world, and

American culture as seen from an anthropological perspective.

This book is intended to provide an overview of anthropological knowledge rather than method. It is not designed to train students in the techniques they will need to learn if they choose to become anthropologists. The purpose here is to characterize the anthropological view of humankind in a general way that may benefit and enlighten the inquiring student whether or not he or she elects to pursue a professional career in anthropology. The emphasis in this text is therefore on understanding how and why people live their lives in a variety of different ways. This text is devoted primarily to cultural anthropology and its various areas of knowledge. In support of this emphasis, anthropological linguistics is examined in terms of the nature of human communication and the relationship between language and human social life. Archaeology is addressed only in terms of its contribution to our knowledge of the evolution of human social life and the origins of civilization. Biological anthropology is also considered, but only its concern for human origins, since this aspect of the subfield provides important background about our species's cultural capabilities and also because human evolution is a major topic of controversy in our society today.

Summary

Anthropology is the broadest of the disciplines studying the human condition, for it draws on fields as diverse as philosophy, art, economics, linguistics, and biology for its conclusions. The major fields of anthropology itself are cultural anthropology, archaeology, anthropological linguistics, and physical anthroplgy. They operate by the same basic anthropological method: fieldwork and comparative studies. In cultural anthropology, these take the form of participant observation, and cross-cultural comparison. These fields and methods have evolved from prescientific European interest in the customs of unfamiliar cultures. As a science, anthropology has developed historically through attempts to show that cultural complexity has evolved, to gather data on varying cultures in the field, and to demonstrate that customs and ideas have survival value to a society. Today the two main models for understanding—culture as a symbolic system and culture as an adaptation to the environment—are represented by a number of new specialized subfields in anthropology, including psychological anthropology, ethnomethodology, structural anthropology, symbolic anthropology, neoevolutionism, cultural ecology, Marxist anthropology, and neofunctionalism. While most anthropologists continue their work through universities, applied and practicing anthropologists are bringing their skills to nonacademic settings. Even when working for governmental or commercial employers, anthropologists try to maintain an ethical approach that safeguards the interests of the people they are hired to study. This book draws on the findings of all branches of anthropology, with a focus on cultural anthropology.

Key Terms and Concepts

holistic 4
cross-cultural research 4
cultural anthropologists 4
cultures 5
ethnographers 5
ethnographies 5
ethnologists 5
archaeologists 5
anthropological linguists 6
physical (biological) anthropologists 6
fieldwork 7
participant observation 8
cross-cultural comparison 9
Human Relations Area Files (HRAF) 9
cultural evolutionism 10
Systema Naturae 10
survivals 11
empiricism 11

cultural relativism 12
diffusion 12
culture areas 12
diffusionism 12
functionalism 12
functions 12
culture and personality 13
psychological anthropology 13
ethnomethodology 14
structural anthropology 14
symbolic anthropology 14
neoevolutionism 14
cultural ecology 14
Marxist anthropology 14
neofunctionalism 14
applied anthropology 14
practicing anthropology 14

Annotated Readings

Agar, M. H. (1980). *The professional stranger: An informal introduction to ethnography.* New York: Academic Press. A good general overview of field research.

Angeloni, E. (Ed.). (1987). *Annual Editions: Anthropology.* Guilford, CT: Dushkin Publishing Group. An annually revised collection of significant articles on contemporary issues in social and cultural anthropology.

Bohannan, P., & Glazer, M. (Eds.). (1973). *High points in anthropology.* New York: Alfred A. Knopf. A thoughtfully selected collection of the classic writings by the major names in the history of anthropology.

Casagrande, J. B. (Ed.). (1960). *In the company of man: Twenty portraits by anthropologists.* New York: Harper & Row. Discussions of fieldwork experiences by ethnographers.

Chagnon, N. A. (1974). *Studying the Yąnomamö.* New York: Holt Rinehart and Winston. An in-depth report of the fieldwork experience by one of the top contemporary American ethnographers.

Crane, J., & Angrosino, M. V. (1974). *Field projects in anthropology: A student handbook.* Morristown, NJ: General Learning Press. A short book of projects illustrating various types of research characteristic of anthropological fieldwork.

Harris, M. (1968). *The rise of anthropological theory: A history of theories of culture.* New York: Thomas Y. Crowell. An authoritative and comprehensive history of cultural anthropology by a leading figure in contemporary anthropology. Must reading for students who have decided to major in anthropology.

Lawless, R., Sutlive, V. H., Jr., & Zamora, M. D. (1983). *Fieldwork: The human experience.* New York: Gordon and Breach, Science Publishers. Aspects of fieldwork explored by 12 anthropologists.

Lowie, R. H. (1937). *The history of ethnological theory.* New York: Holt, Rinehart and Winston. The traditional view of the history of cultural anthropology in a readable style.

Pelto, P. J., & Pelto, G. H. (1978). *Anthropological research: The structure of inquiry* (2nd ed.). New York: Cambridge University Press. A discussion of techniques of anthropological research. Especially important for the anthropology major.

Spindler, G. D. (Ed.). (1970). *Being an anthropologist: Fieldwork in eleven cultures.* New York: Holt, Rinehart and Winston. Thirteen anthropologists discuss how they and their families adjusted to life in a variety of cultures. Especially useful to the anthropology major.

Spradley, J. F. (1980). *Participant observation.* New York: Holt, Rinehart, and Winston. A step-by-step overview of how ethnographic research is conducted.

White, L. A. (1949). *The science of culture: A study of man and civilization.* New York: Farrar, Straus and Giroux. A classic text that argues that culture can be validly interpreted only as a system that is made possible by human biology but that follows its own rules in how it functions and changes.

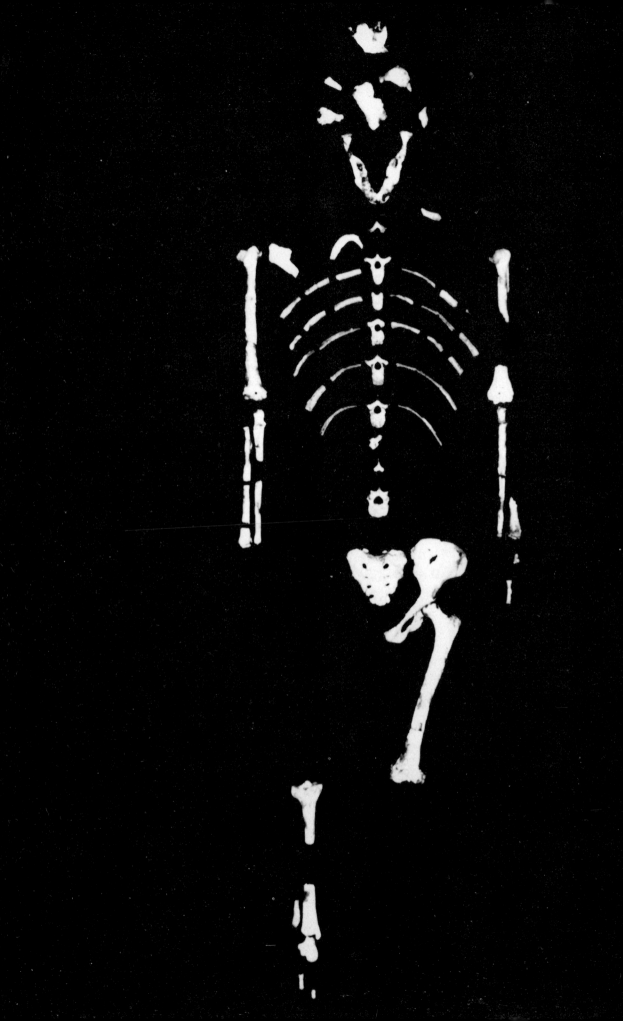

Chapter 2

Our Biological Evolution

Figure 2.1 *"Lucy"* - Australopithecus Afarensis
Found by Donald Johnson in the Afar region of Ethiopia in November, 1974, Lucy is the oldest, most complete, best-preserved skeleton of any erect-walking human ancestor yet discovered. Nearly 3.5 million years old, Lucy gets her name from the 20th century Beatles song, "Lucy in the Sky with Diamonds."

One of the areas we can study in trying to understand ourselves is our biological heritage. We humans are quite distinct from other animals in our abilities to use tools and symbolic language and to pass our innovations and beliefs from one generation to the next as the culture of our group. Yet there is evidence that we evolved from apelike beings who did not have these abilities. Anthropological explanations of how we came to differ from other animals are based on an understanding of the mechanisms of evolution, explained in the first part of this chapter, and on comparisons with contemporary apes and the study of fossils of our changing apelike ancestors. Fossil evidence of our origins is still quite skimpy. Many details have to be inferred from very fragmentary clues, such as the patterns of wear on teeth and the presence of stone chips that were used as crude tools. Since our ancient ancestors left no written history, we have few clues of when they developed language. Because of these limitations, anthropologists do not agree on all aspects of our prehistoric evolution, but this chapter will describe the stages that appear to have led to our species, now known as Homo sapiens *(literally, "wise man").*

The Mechanisms of Biological Evolution

We will consider first how evolutionary changes occur in an animal species—a population that can interbreed and produce fertile offspring. Biological evolution is cumulative change in the inherited characteristics of a species over successive generations. Biological evolution is not something that happens to the individual animal. It is a process that influences the characteristics of the species as a whole, that is, of the system of interbreeding individuals. The mechanisms known to produce change at the species level are natural selection, mutations, genetic drift, and gene flow. Together these processes gradually create separate species, groups so different that they can no longer interbreed and produce fertile offspring.

Natural Selection

The first mechanism of biological evolution to be described here is known as natural selection. Natural selection is the outcome of the struggle for survival in any given environment. Individuals' survival and reproductive rates differ depending on the nature of the environment and of their own traits. The concept of natural selection was first suggested by Charles Darwin in 1859 in *On the Origin of Species*. His own description of the process of natural selection is as follows:

> Owing to this struggle for life, any variation, however slight and from whatever cause proceeding, if it be in any degree profitable to an individual of any species, in its complex relations to other organic beings and to external nature, will tend to the preservation of that individual, and will generally be inherited by its offspring. The offspring, also, will thus have a better chance of surviving, for, of the many individuals of any species which are periodically born, but a small number can survive. (p. 61)

In any environment there are natural limits to the total number of individuals in animal populations. These limits are set by such factors as the availability of food and water, the presence and effectiveness of predators, and the natural hazards of the area. Because of such factors, in every generation more offspring are born than ever reach maturity and reproduce. In effect, animals in any population are engaged in a competitive struggle with one another to survive. Since biological traits are passed on to the next generation through reproduction, the traits that increase an individual's chances of succeeding in this competition for survival until reproduction are those that have the greatest chance of being passed on into future generations. As new generations continue to arise, beneficial traits will increase in frequency within a breeding population, while harmful traits will be weeded out. It should be kept in mind that "beneficial" and "harmful" as used here do not refer to absolute qualities of the traits themselves. Rather, they are relative terms: A trait that is beneficial in one environment may be detrimental to its carrier in another habitat.

Due to the environmental pressures that determine which kinds of traits will im-prove their carriers' chances of survival, the overall makeup of any population will change in ways that gradually increase the adaptation of the whole population to the environment. The changes that occur in a species through time are not, therefore, simply random. Natural selection is the guiding mechanism in the evolutionary process. It controls the direction of biological change in an interbreeding population.

The effects are of the same types as those accomplished by any stockbreeder, although the process of natural selection is much less efficient. The stockbreeder selects traits that he or she desires to emphasize in a herd and sees to it that animals with those traits reproduce. At the same time, the stockbreeder prevents the reproduction of animals with traits that he or she wishes to eliminate. The environmental pressures of nature also "select" various traits, in the sense that natural conditions will facilitate or make more difficult the survival (and therefore the reproduction) of animals that possess different traits. Natural selection lacks the conscious intent of the stockbreeder; it simply occurs because the individuals that make up any group are not identical to one another. Since the members of any group differ from one another in many ways, some individuals in any group must necessarily have a greater likelihood of surviving and reproducing, as a result of the advantages that their genetic traits confer on them in their particular environments. The process by which the frequencies of biological traits that are found in an animal population gradually change in response to the natural conditions of the group's environment is called *natural* selection, in contrast to the conscious selection of the stockbreeder.

Although natural selection guides the direction of changes in a population through time, it should not be viewed as a straight-line process that must continue in the same direction. On the contrary, an evolutionary trend continues only so long as the selective pressures in that direction are maintained. Natural selection is completely opportunistic. A change in environmental conditions or the introduction of new traits to the group (through processes

Figure 2.2 *Peppered Moths*
The light-colored moth is more visible to predators than the dark-colored moth on a dark tree trunk. When trees in England became coated with black soot from industrial pollution, natural selection favored dark-colored moths. This is one example of natural selection occurring in a relatively short period of time.

such as mutation, described later) may change the traits being furthered.

If the environment changes or a part of the population moves into a new area, the selective pressures on the group will change. A classic example of how natural selection may pull a species now in one direction, now in another as a result of changes in the habitat is the case of the peppered moth of England (see Fig. 2.2). It was reported by the British naturalist H. B. D. Kettlewell (1959). Before the Industrial Revolution, the peppered moth had light-colored, speckled wings. This pattern camouflaged it well against the background of lichen-covered tree trunks, providing protection from insect-eating birds. Occasional mutants with black wings were clearly visible, easy prey for birds. As a result, such moths were extremely rare; the first specimen of the black variety was not observed until 1848. Then the habitat began to change. Due to the increasing burning of coal and wood during the Industrial Revolution, soot and smoke began darkening the trees. On the blacker background, the rare black-winged

mutants became favored by natural selection as the light-winged insects became more visible to their predators. In just 50 years, peppered moths with speckled wings constituted only 2% of the population, the remaining 98% being the black type. In another 50 years, the speckled variety was almost completely absent from the peppered moth population—only a century after the discovery of the first black specimen! But since smoke-control laws came into effect in England in the 1950s, the trees have begun to lighten gradually and investigations have indicated a rise in frequency of the speckled peppered moth once again.

In the peppered moth example, coloration was changed by natural selection because of the varying protection provided by the camouflaging effects of different colors (see Ford, 1964). Any biological trait can potentially be so influenced. If the traits being altered by natural selective pressures happen to be ones that affect sexual reproduction itself, isolated groups of a species may so change that they become incapable of interbreeding successfully. When this happens, they will have become separate species.

The Mechanisms of Heredity

Natural selection operates on the overt characteristics of the members of a species, the characteristics that actually interact with the environment. The overtly observable characteristics of an organism— technically called its pheno-type—are the product of the interaction of its inherited biological traits, its heredity, with its environmental circumstances. The inherited constitution of an organism is called its genotype, which is composed of many individual units of inheritance, known as genes. The exact number of genes found in members of the human species has not yet been determined, but there are certainly tens of thousands of genes in each human individual, and a figure near 100,000 is not thought to be unreasonably high.

The genes that make up an individual's inherited constitution are actually sequences of molecules arranged in long strands known as <u>DNA</u>. DNA strands are contained in large bodies called <u>chromosomes,</u> of which there are 46 in the human species. These are grouped into 22 pairs plus two individual chromosomes determining our sex. In controlling the development of a given inherited characteristic, genes also act in pairs. Each gene of a particular chromosome is paired with another gene that is situated at the same location on the other chromosome of the pair. Of the 46 chromosomes each of us possesses, 23 come from each parent. At conception, the 23 chromosomes of a sperm cell unite with those of an ovum to produce the 46 chromosomes.

A gene for a particular trait may occur in several forms known as <u>alleles.</u> Since corresponding alleles at the same location of a pair of chromosomes come from two different parents, any given pair of alleles may contain different instructions about the development of the characteristic for which it is responsible. In such a case, one of the two alleles may be <u>dominant</u> over the other in determining the actual phenotypic trait that shows outwardly. Thus, in spite of our outward appearance, we may be carriers of many genes that we do not manifest. These dominated alleles that are carried by an individual but that do not show up externally are referred to as <u>recessive</u> alleles. Although they do not affect the phenotype when paired with a differing dominant allele, recessive alleles may be passed on to offspring. The quality that is controlled by those recessive alleles will only be manifested in our phenotypic qualities if we receive identical recessive alleles from each parent.

The difference between dominant and recessive alleles can be illustrated by an example taken from the work of Gregor Mendel, an early nineteenth-century Czechoslovakian monk. Mendel found that if he took a pure-breeding sweet pea with a red flower and one that belonged to a strain that bred true for white flowers and cross-pollinated them, the resulting offspring were

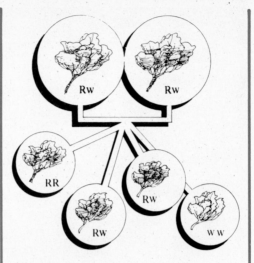

Figure 2.3 *Mendelian Inheritance*
Gregor Mendel's experiments with cross-breeding plants resulted in the discovery of dominant and recessive traits. See text for discussion.

not pink. Instead, they had all red flowers. When they were allowed to self-pollinate, however, the next generation consisted of plants with either red or white flowers in a ratio of three red-flowered to one white-flowered plant. The white-flowered plants, when self-pollinated, produced only white-flowered offspring. These results are most easily explained if the color of the flower is thought of as being determined by the interaction of various possible combinations of an allele for redness and an allele for whiteness. (The allele responsible for the development of a red flower may be indicated with the symbol R, upper case indicating the dominance of this trait, and the allele for white flowers with the symbol w, lower case indicating the recessiveness of this genetic trait.) Each purebred red plant would have two dominant red-controlling alleles, RR, and each purebred white-flowered plant would have two recessive alleles for whiteness, ww. If an RR plant were crossed with a ww plant, all offspring would have genotypes of Rw, but phenotypically they would all produce red flowers since the R allele would be dominant in determining the color of the flower. When an Rw plant is crossed with another Rw plant of this generation, however, four possible combinations could occur: The R of the first Rw plant could combine with either the R or the w allele of the second, resulting in an RR or an Rw offspring; and the w gene allele of the first plant could similarly combine with the R or w allele of the second plant, yielding another Rw combination or a ww combination. In total there would be one white-flowered ww plant and three phenotypically red-flowered plants. Of the latter, only one would be genetically RR, while two would have an Rw gene pair. (see Figure 2.3)

Although most human traits may be controlled by the combined effects of more than one gene pair rather than by the simple action of one pair of genes, the sweet pea example does illustrate that individuals may be the carriers of recessive alleles that are not outwardly manifested. Therefore, recessive traits are influenced by natural selective pressures only when they are inherited in double doses and manifest themselves in the phenotype of their bearer. Dominant traits are more readily accessible to the pressures of natural selection, since they always have a phenotypic manifestation. The effects of natural selection operate very slowly in altering the characteristics of a species. Even if natural selection permitted only red-flowered plants to reproduce, the presence of recessive white-flower alleles would continue to cause pure white individuals to crop up (in decreasing numbers) for many generations.

Mutations

New traits are constantly arising in all animal and plant populations, providing the new materials on which natural selection operates. Such new traits come into existence when the DNA sequences undergo a change, influencing the way the offspring grow to maturity. Offspring may thus grow up with traits that were absent in their parents. Changes in the hereditary material of an organism that bring new traits

into existence in a species constitute the second major mechanism of evolution. Such changes are called mutations.

How Mutations Occur. In sexually reproducing animals, mutations occur as random changes in the molecular structure in the DNA of the chromosomes of the parents' sperm and ovum cells. After the sex cells of the parents have combined and begun to grow into a new individual, the traits of that individual will be determined by the altered DNA structure of the chromosomes it has inherited. The specific change that occurs as a result of a mutation depends on where the actual molecular change occurs along the strand of DNA, since each gene in the DNA strand has a different function in an individual's heredity.

Mutational changes may occur spontaneously in any of the genes of a chromosome for no apparent reason. Other mutations are known to be caused by external agents such as ultraviolet light, cosmic radiation, exposure to X-rays, some chemicals (such as mustard gas, phenol, formaldehyde, and caffeine), and other events that can alter the arrangement or structure of the molecular chains that make up the chromosomes of an organism. Since these molecular chains serve as the code that guides the growth of new individuals, such changes may make the individuals who carry them a little taller or a little shorter, a little faster or a little slower, a little more or less keenly sighted, a little better or more poorly adapted to survive than they would otherwise have been.

Mutations and natural selection. Mutations occur constantly in all animal groups. Natural selection therefore has a constantly replenished supply of new and different traits to draw on in guiding the evolution of a species through time. Estimates for the typical rate of mutations in the human species range from one per 10,000 to one per 100,000 genes, which amounts to saying that each of us is likely to carry from one to ten mutations from birth. Thus, mutations are not so rare and drastic as they are sometimes portrayed in science fiction. On the contrary, they are a normal occurrence that are usually so insignificant that they go unnoticed. Mutational changes in a population occur at a more or less constant rate, but, unlike natural selective changes, they are random in the direction of their influence and individually unpredictable in their occurrence. However, since the hereditary material of a species must already be more or less adaptive for it to be coping with its environment, mutational changes in the hereditary code tend to result in traits that are less adaptive, and occasionally even fatal, for their bearers. In the majority of these cases, natural selection eliminates the less useful mutation. When mutations are fatal, we can say that natural selection eliminates the trait immediately. Harmful but nonfatal mutations are eliminated more slowly by the natural selective processes. However, not all mutations are harmful or fatal. Those few that give their owners some advantage in survival and reproduction will be favored by natural selection and will influence the future evolution of the population.

The mechanisms of mutation and natural selection influence one another during a population's evolutionary history. Mutations constantly and randomly serve as a source of new variations in a population, changes that natural selection can draw on as the population adjusts to its environment over the generations. Consequently, breeding populations are always changing around the world, diversifying to fit their differing (and changing) environments.

Genetic Drift

Genetic drift is a catchall term for random or "accidental" changes in the total genetic makeup of a breeding group. Unlike mutation, these processes do not add new traits but simply alter the frequency of existing traits in random ways. The most important way in which genetic drift operates is through a kind of "sampling error." If, for example, two small groups were to split off from a single parent population and migrate to separate areas, it would be statistically improbable that the frequency of the traits in these groups would be identical to each other or to those of the parent group. Their future evolutionary history will be correspondingly different, since natural selection will have different traits available in each group on which to operate.

A somewhat different example of genetic drift is that of literal accidents (such as drowning, death in a rockslide, falls from trees, or capture by predators). In a small breeding group such accidents could, by sheer chance, eliminate all those individuals from the group who shared some adaptive trait. Selective pressures would then favor some other trait that otherwise would have been less favored. As a result, the evolutionary course of that group would change.

In recent years many researchers have come to believe that the effects of genetic drift are much more important than had been thought and that a great many evolutionary changes may be a matter of random alterations in traits. Genetic drift may be as important as, or even more important than, natural selection in the evolutionary history of a species.

Gene Flow

The process of gene flow is the transfer of hereditary characteristics from one breeding group to another of the same species as a result of hybridization. This process introduces new traits into a breeding group, thus increasing its variability and, thereby, its chances of surviving when environmental changes occur. Gene flow therefore must be considered as playing a potential role in preventing the extinction of populations. Hybridization of distinct varieties within a species commonly results in offspring with greater fertility, strength, and viability than was found in either parent population. This fact has been noted and made use of frequently by plant growers and stockbreeders. The effect is known as *hybrid vigor*. Contrary to the idea that interracial mating leads to biological degeneration, the phenomenon of hybrid vigor is no less apt to occur in the human species than in any other animals.

Speciation

A species is a population of animals whose members are able to successfully interbreed and produce fertile offspring. In some species, isolated subpopulations in different environments may gradually change in different ways, each being molded by natural selection towards an increased adaptation to the characteristics of its particular environment. Given prolonged isolation, the gradual accumulation of different mutations in each group, different selective pressures, and the random effects of genetic drift, the two subpopulations may eventually change so much in factors that govern sexual compatibility that they are no longer capable of interbreeding successfully or producing fertile offspring. When the two groups become too different to successfully reproduce, the two populations are said to have speciated, that is, to have become two new species of animals.

It seems logically possible that speciation might occur as a result of gradual changes in an isolated part of an original species, changes that build up over a long period of time by the processes of biological evolution. This is the traditional view of speciation. However, careful study of the fossil record indicates that this is not the usual process by which new species arise (see Eldridge & Gould, 1972). The fossil remains of ancient species indicate that most species, being reasonably well adapted to their environments, remain more or less stable over long periods of time, sometimes for millions of years. By contrast, speciation usually occurs in a relatively brief period, such as 100,000 years or so. This may occur when there is a radical change in an environment, when a part of a species invades a new environment, when mass extinctions open new environments to be exploited, or because a variety of other factors dramatically changes the selective pressures. Evolution seems more often to proceed by spurts and stops than by a smooth gradual change from one form to another. The suddenness with which evolutionary change and speciation usually occur explains why it has been so difficult to find examples of fossil forms that are transitional between two related species. The period of time in which the transitional forms existed is relatively short, due to the rapidness of the transition from one form to another, so they represent only a tiny fraction of the total fossil record.

Primate Evolution

Our own species seems to have evolved by such mechanisms to its present characteristics. Its origins extend back far before recorded history, so we must infer our past from various clues. Some involve our common ancestry with living creatures of other species, especially other members of the group known as primates; some involve attempts to piece together our own line of ascent based on fossils of our predecessors.

Classification Clues to Evolutionary Relationships

Classifying contemporary animals by how similar they are to each other can give some clue about their evolutionary relationships. By comparing the human species with other animals, we find that it belongs to a group of animals called the primates: apes (chimpanzees, gorillas, orangutans, and gibbons), Old World monkeys (leaf-eating monkeys, baboons, and macaques), New World monkeys, and prosimians (composed of a variety of small, tree-dwelling primates), and *Homo sapiens*. If the degree of biological similarity of these species is assumed to reveal their degree of evolutionary relationships, then the rough "family tree" in Figure 2.4 indicates how these various modern primates are evolutionarily related.

Fossil forms of ancestral animals might be expected to bear degrees of similarity to modern forms depending on their genetic closeness to those forms. Fossils that were ancestral only to humankind (called fossil hominids) would be expected to have more in common biologically with modern humans than with any of the other living primates. In those traits that set modern human beings apart from modern apes, fossil hominids would fall consistently on the same side of the fence as human beings. However, hominid fossils and fossil apes would be more and more similar to one another as one approached the point of divergence between humans and the apes. Before this point, ancestral forms would be expected to have had traits that modern human beings and apes still share. As a group, humans, apes, and their ancestors back to

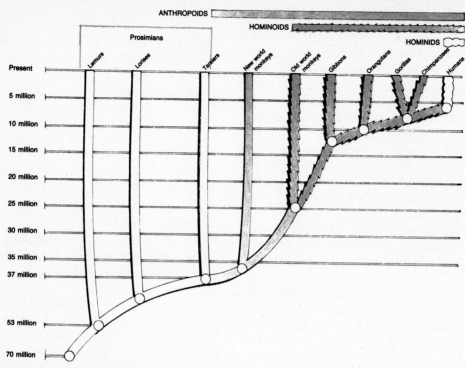

Figure 2.4 *Evolutionary Divergence of the Primates*
This chart shows the ancestry of modern primates. The evolutionary trend toward hominid traits which include being ground dwellers, being omnivorous, and having more or less upright posture can be traced back at least 70 million years.

and including their common ancestors are technically called <u>hominoids.</u> The traits that all hominoids share include being ground dwellers, having more or less upright posture, and being omnivorous (eating both plants and animals).

Evolution of Primate Traits

The original primates were probably small tree-dwelling plant-eaters. From such beginnings, according to Clark (1971), 13 evolutionary trends have characterized the primates as a group:

- retention of five digits on both hands and feet
- nails instead of claws
- flexible hands and feet with a good deal of grasping ability
- a tendency toward erectness (especially in the upper body)
- retention of the collarbone
- a generalized rather than specialized dental pattern
- a lack of specialization in diet
- a reduction of the snout and the use of smell

- an increased emphasis on vision
- expansion and increased complexity of the brain
- an increasingly efficient means of fetal nourishment
- an increased dependency on flexible learned behavior with lengthened periods of infant dependency
- permanent association of adult males with the group.

In the lineage that gradually led to *Homo sapiens*, the following changes are believed to have occurred in the original primate pattern: (1) a move from an arboreal habitat to a ground-dwelling forested habitat and then later to an open grassland ground-dwelling habitat, (2) an increasing body size, (3) an increasing brain size, (4) a more and more upright stance, and (5) more emphasis on an omnivorous diet with the development of hunting among early human ancestors.

The technique of comparing humans with other modern primates allows us to predict what traits are to be expected in the fossil record at periods of time corresponding to different parts of the primate family tree. The discovery—in the appropriate chronological sequence—of fossils that have the characteristics that these comparisons lead us to expect serves as important evidence for the utility of the concept of biological evolution.

Dating Fossil Remains

Determining the age of fossil material is an important part of the reconstruction of our evolutionary history. Several different dating techniques exist. Potassium-argon dating, carbon 14 dating, and fission-track dating permit absolute dating of fossils, dating that assigns a specific age to those fossils. Paleomagnetism, stratigraphy, and biostratigraphy are methods for the relative dating of fossils, that is for determining whether particular fossils are older or younger than other fossils.

Absolute dating techniques. Potassium-argon dating is based on the fact that potassium 40, a radioactive isotope of potassium, decays at a known rate into argon 40. By determining the ratio of potassium 40 and argon 40 trapped in basalt, a volcanic rock, scientists can compute the length of time since the potassium was originally trapped in the lava. Thus, the age of fossil material can be determined by calculating the age of volcanic rock immediately above or below it. This method is useful for dating material from about 100,000 years old to about 4.6 billion years old. Similar techniques based on the radioactive decay of uranium 238 (into lead 208), uranium 235 (into lead 207), and rubidium (into strontium 87) can be used to measure the age of materials from 10 million years old to 4.6 billion years old.

For younger fossil material, carbon 14 dating is useful. As nitrogen in the atmosphere is bombarded by natural radiation, a certain percentage of the nitrogen is converted into carbon 14, a radioactive isotope of carbon. This is taken into the bodies of living things as carbon dioxide which contains the radioactive carbon. Carbon 14 emits beta particles as it slowly decays into nitrogen at a known rate. After an organism dies, the amount of nonradioactive carbon in its body remains stable, but decay of the radioactive carbon 14 into nitrogen continues. Measuring the rate of emission of beta particles from a sample of organic material with a known weight of carbon allows us to calculate the amount of time since the organic material, (e.g., bone or wood) died and stopped absorbing new carbon. However, studies of organic materials such as wood that can also be dated by techniques like tree ring counting have demonstrated that the amount of radioactive carbon in the atmosphere at earlier periods has not remained constant. Current levels, for instance, have been changed during the past century by the tremendous outpouring of carbon dioxide into the atmosphere by industry around the world and by the testing of atomic weapons. Scientists doing carbon 14 dating of wood samples that are also datable by other means have been able to adjust for carbon 14 dates by taking these changes into account. Carbon 14 dating can now be used to measure the age of material from the near present to about 50,000 or 60,000 years ago. It is most accurate for materials between 500 and 40,000 years old.

Fission-track dating makes use of the decay of uranium 238. By counting the microscopic tracks left in certain minerals by particles given off in the decay of uranium 238 atoms, it is possible to determine the ratio of decayed to undecayed atoms in the sample. From this ratio, the age of any sample from 20 years old to 4.6 billion years old can be calculated.

Relative dating techniques. Relative dating techniques do not provide an age in years for an individual fossil or the environment in which it was found. Instead, relative dating allows us to determine whether a particular fossil or group of fossils is younger or older than other fossils. These techniques allow us to construct a chronological sequence that shows the age of each fossil relative to others in the sequence.

One of the relative dating techniques, paleomagnetism, makes use of the fact that the earth's magnetic field has undergone numerous changes in its orientation, so that what we now call the north magnetic pole was at some times in the south rather than the north. Magnetically charged particles trapped in sediments have an orientation that is aligned with the direction of the magnetic field of the earth at the time the sediments were laid down. By carefully measuring the orientation of the magnetic particles in a sample from a fossil site it is possible to establish the location of the earth's magnetic north pole at the time the sediment was laid down. As the sequence of the changes in the earth's magnetic field is being worked out for the past several million years, paleomagnetism is becoming an increasingly useful tool for dating the age of sites at which fossils are found.

In stratigraphy, fossils found in deeper strata, or layers, of earth are judged to be older than fossils taken from higher layers. This is so because in the normal processes by which different strata of earth are deposited, the oldest strata are laid down first and are therefore the deepest.

Biostratigraphy is the use of fossil animals at an archaeological site as a source of information about the age of the site. Sequences of changes in certain animals' evolution have been worked out and dated with other techniques. These sequences can now be used to establish the date of a site at which animals of a known form are found.

Our earliest primate ancestors can be traced back to the rise of small, tree-dwelling primates some 70 million years ago. Their next 40 million years of life in an arboreal habitat provided effective natural selective pressures in favor of semi-upright posture, grasping hands (and feet), stereo-

scopic vision, and larger, more complex brains. These biological traits were the foundation that made possible the eventual evolution of the human species with its complex social, technological, and intellectual life.

Many ground-dwelling mammals have a posture in which the trunk is horizontal and parallel to the ground. Such a posture is well suited for supporting a four-footed animal on a horizontal surface. A semi-upright posture, on the other hand, is more efficient for maintaining balance among the branches. In a semi-upright posture, the center of gravity is shifted toward the rear limbs, and the forelimbs become freed from the sole task of body support. The forelimbs can then be used in exploration, manipulation, and feeding activities—a foretaste of the highly skillful use of the hands by *Homo sapiens*. Grasping hands provide a surer hold on an animal's perch and help insure its survival in an arboreal environment. Stereoscopic vision—integration of the images seen by each eye into a single three-dimensional image—is also a useful trait for an animal that lives in the trees and scampers and jumps from branch to branch. Stereoscopic vision, possible only for animals with eyes located on the front rather than the sides of the head, makes it easier to accurately judge how far away that next branch is, a skill that can help keep active primates alive. Those with less effective depth perception were more apt to be weeded out by natural selection: falling out of the trees. Greater intelligence is also a useful asset in such a precarious habitat. An increasingly large and complex brain is favored by natural selection as a necessary support for the efficient coordination of physical abilities, such as grabbing for a handhold and manipulating objects. A larger brain also helps in the accurate evaluation of visual information, such as effective depth perception.

While certain primates evolved in these directions, the least changed descendants of these early tree-dwelling primates continued to survive in the Eastern Hemisphere. They are the modern prosimians: lemurs, loris, and tarsiers. By 58 million years ago, these small tree-dwelling prosimian creatures had also given rise to the earliest fossil monkey forms, now known only by their skeletal remains. In the Western Hemisphere, the early prosimians were completely replaced by the monkey forms that may have evolved from them. The earliest fossil hominoids, now-extinct creatures with traits that we would expect in the common ancestors of both humans and apes, date from about 25 or more million years ago and have been found exclusively in the Eastern Hemisphere. Some earlier fossils with the beginning of hominoid-like traits existed more than 30 million years ago.

The Fossil Record of Human Evolution

Discoveries of the remains of the bones, skulls, and teeth of thousands of individuals who bear varying resemblances to modern humans have allowed physical anthropologists to piece together a tentative evolutionary history of our species. It begins where we shared a common ancestor with the apes and concludes with prehistoric peoples who used stone tools and drew on the walls of their caves. For the oldest periods, many millions of years ago, evidence is still too fragmentary for anthropologists to agree on precisely which fossil forms were directly ancestral to *Homo sapiens*.

The Dryopithecines

The dryopithecines have been thought by many to occupy the position on the primate family tree where the human and ape lines branched apart. These fossil apes included several species, some of which were ancestral to the modern great apes and possibly to human beings. Dryopithecines have been found in Asia, Europe, and Africa and are thought to have lived from about 23 to about 14 million years ago. The traits they share include a distinctive number and arrangement of cusps on their lower molar teeth, known as the Y-5 pattern. In the Y-5 arrangement, the molar teeth have five cusps, or points, on the biting surface, and the intervening fissures between these cusps are connected in a "Y" shape. This

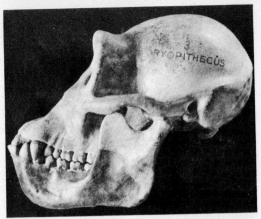

Figure 2.5 Dryopithecus
Dryopithecus *took several forms and may be the ancestor of monkeys, apes, or orangutans. Whether one of these forms is a human ancestor is still subject to debate primarily because fossil remains are difficult to obtain from the tropical forests these beings inhabited, where the acid soil and bacteria eat away any remaining bones.*

pattern is still found in modern gibbons, great apes, and humans.

There is currently great variation in opinions on how to classify the dryopithecines. For the sake of simplicity, we will follow the typology of Brace and Montagu (1977) who group the dryopithecines of Africa into three species: *Dryopithecus africanus*, *Dryopithecus major*, and *Dryopithecus nyanzae*. *Dryopithecus africanus* may have been the ancestor of the modern chimpanzee and possibly also of human beings. It weighed about 30 to 40 pounds. Its teeth and arm bones resemble those of modern chimpanzees, and its skull is very similar to that of a pygmy chimpanzee. Its wrist bones and elbow joints indicate that it was capable of supporting and swinging itself from its arms. *Dryopithecus major* is a possible ancestor of modern gorillas. This large species occupied the highland tropical forest areas on the slopes of the numerous volcanoes of the region where it was found. *Dryopithecus nyanzae* is intermediate between the other two forms in size, but seems to be somewhat closer to *Dryopithecus major* in some of its dental characteristics. *Nyanzae* is closely similar to a European form of dryopithecine, *Dryopithecus fontani*. Both *nyanzae* and *africanus* occupied lowland savannah areas. Like *africanus*, *nyanzae* is a potential candidate as a human ancestor.

Which, if either, will eventually be viewed by most anthropologists as occupying that position must await further research.

Ramapithecus

Once humans and apes begin to go their separate ways, the human branch of the primate evolutionary tree is known as the hominid branch. There is disagreement about precisely when this occurred. In the traditional view, the first fossil that may be a hominid is known as *Ramapithecus*. The ramapithecines belong to the time from 15 to 8 million years ago and may have evolved from a dryopithecine about 15 million years ago. *Ramapithecus* has left us only scant fossil material: upper and lower jaw fragments and teeth and a few facial and cranial materials, found in China, India, Europe, and Kenya, and possibly some upper limb bones from Greece (Andrews & Tobias, 1977; L. S. B. Leakey, 1962; Pilbeam, Meyer, & Badgley, 1977; Rukang, 1981.

Many researchers believe that *Ramapithecus* was most likely a three- or four-foot-tall, ground-dwelling, bipedal creature, but others point to similarities with tree-dwelling primates. Unfortunately, since ramapithecines have not left us many fossil remains, our knowledge about them is sketchy. They are believed to have lived on the grassland borders of tropical forest areas, and they may have been the first of our ancestors to begin leaving the forested regions to forage in the open grasslands (Andrews & Evans, 1979; Pilbeam, 1979). *Ramapithecus* tooth wear patterns are similar to those of contemporary primates who eat a gritty diet of grassblades and grass rhizomes, insects, reeds, and other hard spherical items which must be crushed by the molar teeth (Jolly, 1970). There is no evidence of their having used tools, so they were probably not hunters like later hominid forms. But they may have begun to scavenge the meat remains of other predators and kill and eat an occasional young, sick, or crippled animal that they happened to find.

In a small, non-tool-using primate, social cooperation and increasing intelligence would have served a useful purpose in the pursuit of meat as well as in providing group protection against the larger predators of those grassland areas. A greater reliance on adaptive intelligence and social cooperation, rather than on biologically controlled behavioral responses, is implied by some of the characteristics of the fossil teeth that *Ramapithecus* left behind. Wear patterns indicate that, as in modern humans, the molar teeth of *Ramapithecus* erupted one at a time. This delayed eruption indicates that maturation was a prolonged process in *Ramapithecus*, as it is in modern humans, and that *Ramapithecus* infants experienced a prolonged period of dependency within which social learning could occur. Decreased biological controls over behavior would have been furthered by such a period of early learning, during which new mechanisms of social behavior could have been passed on to the infant.

Another characteristic of *Ramapithecus's* teeth reinforces this view. Like human beings, *Ramapithecus* had rather small canine teeth instead of the sharp, protruding canines found in most primates. Among meat-eating animals, the large canine is a useful weapon in fighting and is also an effective tool for piercing and tearing. Among later tool-using and meat-eating primates, an increased use of stone implements as tools and weapons would reduce selective pressures for large canines, such as those found in the apes. However, the smaller canines of *Ramapithecus* (for whom there is no evidence of tool use) were possibly influenced by another mechanism. Holloway (1970) has suggested that the mechanism that led to smaller canines in the early hominids was natural selection in favor of cooperation within the social life of the group. In modern ground-dwelling primates the social role of the large canines is their use in aggressive display behavior which serves to regulate interaction by establishing dominance in social relations. In the apes the canines are especially enlarged in males (who form the basic dominance hierarchy of primate social groups) through the influence of sex hormones. Thus, there may have been changes in hormone functioning that reduced the role of aggressive biological dominance in structuring the social life of early hominids; these changes may also have led to canine reduction in *Ramapithecus* and the hominids that followed.

Dating Hominids by Molecular Biology

Just how long ago did the hominids separate from the line of the great apes? The dryopithecines appear to have lived immediately before the split between human and ape lines of descent. *Ramapithecus* has characteristics that lead us to believe it may have been the first hominid. The earliest *Ramapithecus* fossils have been dated to approximately 14 million years ago, and the dryopithecines from which *Ramapithecus* may have arisen lived about 20 million years ago. Thus, judging from dated fossils, the consensus among physical anthropologists is that the hominid line arose between 15 and 20 million years ago.

In addition to the fossil evidence, researchers studying molecular biology have developed techniques for measuring the degree of genetic difference between modern human beings and other animals by comparing their hemoglobin, serum proteins, and occasionally the actual DNA molecules that make up the entire genetic code. DNA comparisons indicate that about 98.2% of the DNA sequence in humans and chimpanzees is identical. Humans and chimpanzees differ by about only 1.8% of their genetic material. Gorillas and humans differ by slightly more, about 2.3% of their genetic makeup. These direct genetic comparisons are complex and difficult to perform. Simpler methods of assessing the relative distances between humans and other animals involve the comparison not of the genetic code itself but of various proteins such as hemoglobin and serum proteins, which are directly produced by DNA.

One such technique has been developed by Vincent Sarich and Allan Wilson (1967). By measuring how readily a specially prepared antiserum reacts against the serum protein of different animals, they are able to measure the relative degree of difference—called the antigenic distance—between those animals. Their work has resulted in a family tree that in most respects confirms the traditional family trees that were created by comparing the overt physical similarities and differences between animals. Sarich and Wilson have improved this work by devising a means for calculating the length of time required for a particular antigenic distance to develop between two animals with a common ancestor. In effect, they can assign dates to the branchings on the evolutionary family tree. The dates assigned by Sarich and Wilson agree well with those established by traditional methods for dates older than about 20 million years. The serum protein date for the separation of humans and chimpanzees is about 4 million years; for the separation of humans and gorillas, about 5 million years. This is much more recent than the estimated 15- to 20-million year age of the hominid line based on traditional evaluation of fossil materials. If the serum protein dates are correct, *Ramapithecus* would not be the first hominid. The first hominids would be the fossil forms immediately arising from *Ramapithecus*.

Some researchers now think that the rate of evolutionary change in serum protein albumin is slower in gorillas, chimpanzees, and humans than in other primates. If this is correct, then the serum protein dates for the divergence of the hominid, gorilla, and chimpanzee lines would be underestimates.

The Australopithecines

The next major groups of ancestral hominids lived from about 5 to 1 million years ago. These early hominids are known collectively as australopithecines. In contrast with *Ramapithecus*, the australopithecines are quite well represented by fossil remains.

Australopithecus afarensis. The earliest of the currently known australopithecines are called *Australopithecus afarensis* after the Afar

Depression, an area of land in eastern Africa where many *afarensis* fossils have been unearthed by Donald C. Johanson and his colleagues (1981). *Afarensis* fossils date from perhaps as early as 5.5 million years ago to about 2.9 million years ago, although the fossil material older than about 3.9 million years is fragmentary. A site in the Middle Awash River Valley in north central Ethiopia has yielded the upper part of a thighbone and skull fragments of an individual slightly more than four feet tall, dated about 4 million years old. At one site, Laetoli in northern Tanzania, the remains of 13 individuals were found, along with tracks of hominid footprints that have been dated at 3.7 million years. These footprints were made by individuals who clearly walked with an upright gait like that of human beings today.

At another site, Hadar in northeastern Ethiopia, over 20 australopithecine individuals have been unearthed, including one individual known as "Lucy," 40% of whose skeleton was intact. This site, dated at between 3.1 and 2.6 million years, included the remains of a group of 13 individuals including 4 infants who seem to have died at the same time, possibly in a flash flood. This group, known as the "First Family," possibly did represent a single family or social group.

The sites of the Afar Depression reveal a group of hominids who were quite variable in size. They ranged in height from about three and one-half feet to five feet and weighed from 60 to 150 pounds. The thickness and scope of their bones shows that they were heavily muscled, and they were probably stronger than modern humans in spite of their smaller size. Although they were fully upright and walked erect on two legs like modern humans, they still had arms that were longer for their body size than those of humans today. This was probably a carry-over from their ancestors who had not yet achieved upright posture and had used their arms to carry part of their weight in a semi-upright posture. *Afarensis* also had hands similar to those of modern human beings, but the fingers tended to curl slightly more than ours do today. This may be because *afarensis*'s own ancestors

had been adapted to a "knuckle-walking" form of locomotion before the development of truly upright posture. *Afarensis* had a small brain, about the same size as that of a modern chimpanzee, and no chin. This creature was most apelike from the neck up. For instance, the arrangement of the teeth formed two parallel rows, unlike the gradual curve along which modern human teeth are arranged. There is no evidence yet that *afarensis* made or used stone tools as did some later fossil forms.

Australopithecus africanus. *Afarensis* is followed in time by a fossil form that was given the name *Australopithecus africanus* by its discoverer, Raymond Dart. *Africanus* lived between 2.9 and about 1.3 million years ago in South Africa and East Africa. These hominids were smaller than later australopithecines, being about four feet tall, and weighing between 50 and 70 pounds. But, like their descendants of later times, they had an upright posture and bipedal locomotion (walking on two feet rather than four). Their brain was already about the size of modern chimpanzee and gorilla brains. The cranial capacity of *africanus* fossils varies from about 428 to about 485 cc (cubic centimeters). In contrast, modern human cranial capacity averages about 1450 cc. Yet, like our brain today, the *africanus* brain had longer frontal lobes than those of modern nonhuman primates.

Dart (1925) believed that *africanus* possibly made simple tools of stone, bone, tooth, and wood because simple stone tools known as pebble tools were found in the South African caves in which *africanus* remains were also found. The stone of which these pebble tools were made is not native to the caves, and the tools were clearly modified in a deliberate way. Dart believed he also saw evidence of toolmaking in some of the animal bones found in the caves. The South African australopithecine caves yielded bones of antelope, water turtles, birds, hares, pigs, and other small game, as well as of some larger animals such as giraffes, hippopotami, rhinoceroses, and horses. These remains included a disproportionate percentage of antelope thighbones, especially of the heavy, double-headed end that could have served as useful clubs. Interestingly, baboon skulls were also found in these caves, almost all of them fractured by what might have been violent blows to the head. Sometimes the wound has two main points of fracture, as might be left by the end of an antelope leg bone if it were used as a club. The limestone caves in which *africanus* was found in southern Africa also contained many antelope jaw bones. Dart argued that these would have served as useful cutting tools. On the basis of these facts, Dart contended that *africanus* was an early toolmaker. He was also convinced that if *africanus* made tools of bone, tooth, and stone, it is likely that wood would not have been overlooked as a useful material for making tools as well.

Unfortunately, the evidence for toolmaking by *africanus* is ambiguous and is not accepted today by most physical anthropologists. Studies by Brain (1975) of bones discarded by contemporary peoples have shown that the animal bone and tooth accumulations similar to those associated with *africanus* can result naturally without any modifications intended to produce a tool. As useful as they may have been as clubs, knives, and scrapers, the *africanus* bone and tooth "tools" may simply be unmodified material carried into the caves by other predators. What then of the baboons that seem to have been killed with antelope leg bone clubs? It is possible that wounds like those in question could have been inflicted by the teeth of a leopard.

In the view of Brain (1970) and Klein (1977), all the bones in the South African caves, including those of *africanus* were dropped there by carnivorous animals. If this view is correct, the few stone tools at these sites must have been left by some later toolmaking hominid. Unfortunately, the nature of the South African cave deposits does not lend itself to determining the relative ages of the material deposited in them. It is possible that the stone tools in question are not as old as the *africanus* remains in the caves. On the other hand, the earliest stone tools at other sites where dating is possible appear to be about 2.5 million years old. Stone toolmaking therefore began about halfway between the oldest and youngest *africanus* specimens.

Australopithecus robustus. Another australopithecine species, called *Australopithecus robustus*, is also known to have existed in South Africa from perhaps as early as 3 million years ago to about 1.3 million years ago. Members of this species may even have extended their range as far as Java in later times. *Robustus*'s body weight was between 100 and 200 pounds, and *robustus* approached modern humans in height. Yet the brain size of *robustus* was only about 500 cc, not much greater than that of *africanus*. The *robustus* skull is more apelike in appearance than the skull of *africanus* due to the presence of heavier brow ridges and a slight "sagittal" crest along the top of the head. It has been suggested that both of these traits are only superficial changes that occurred during the growth of individuals from childhood in response to the demands of large jaw muscles that required more surface area for their attachment than the small *robustus* skull provided. If this is correct, these more apelike traits may not be the direct result of any significant evolutionary change, and the major physical difference between *africanus* and *robustus* may be merely the greater body size and somewhat larger brain of *robustus*.

Robustus also appears to have had larger back teeth and smaller front teeth than *africanus*. Studies of the teeth of these two forms also have revealed differences in their wear patterns. They suggest that the diet of *africanus* included significantly more meat, while that of *robustus* consisted primarily of vegetable foods, which normally contain a fair amount of grit. This apparent difference between the diets of *africanus* and *robustus* suggests that these two australopithecines occupied somewhat different environmental niches. *Africanus* is believed by many anthropologists to have been at home in dry savannah areas, while *robustus* may have resided in more vegetation-rich forest areas (see Clark, 1967; Pilbeam, 1972; Robinson, 1972).

A third australopithecine of this same period is known as *Australopithecus boisei* (see Fig. 2.6). *Boisei*, whose fossils date from about 2.2 million to about 1.1 million years ago, has many characteristics in common with *robustus*. Indeed, some authorities ar-

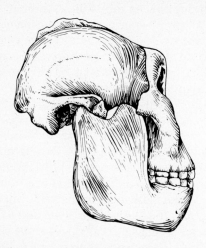

Figure 2.6 Australopithecus Boisei
Found by Mary Leakey in 1959, "Zinj" was the first Australopithecine skull discovered outside South Africa, specifically in the Olduvai Gorge, East Africa. This skull was also the first to be reliably dated at 1.8 million years.

gue that *boisei* is simply a super-robust geographical variant of *robustus*. This australopithecine occupied dry open country in East Africa north of the areas occupied by *robustus*. The habitat of *boisei* had low rainfall and was not the forest area that is characteristic of modern ape territory. *Boisei* had enormous teeth, a large broad face, and a sagittal crest like that of *robustus* along the top of the skull. The cranial capacity of *boisei* was around 530 cc, about the same as that of *robustus*.

Much debate is going on among physical anthropologists in search of the best interpretation about the relationships between these three australopithecines who occupied areas of Africa at about the same time. Views regarding *africanus* and *robustus* have included the idea that they represent a single variable population, *robustus* simply being large individuals. A variant of this idea is the suggestion that the differences between *africanus* and *robustus* are nothing more than differences of sex, *africanus* being the smaller female and *robustus* the larger male of the species. But since it seems that *africanus* and *robustus* fossils have tended to be found at different locations, this hypothesis generally has not been accepted. Since the discovery of *boisei*, who is so clearly similar to *robustus*, the dominant

view seems to be to regard *robustus* and *africanus* as distinctly separate species. Most physical anthropologists now see *africanus* as a direct descendant of the earlier *afarensis*, with *robustus* and *boisei* as separate but closely related species who both evolved either directly from *afarensis* or from an early *africanus* shortly after its development.

Most authorities do not regard either *robustus* or *boisei* as being ancestors of modern human beings in spite of their hominid status. These lines are now believed to have become extinct by about a million years ago. Of the australopithecines, *africanus* is the most likely ancestor of our human line.

Homo habilis

After decades of searching through the Olduvai Gorge in East Africa, Louis B. Leakey (1961) and his co-workers recovered the remains of a much larger-brained hominid who was contemporary with the later australopithecines. This form is now known to have existed from at least 2 million years ago to 1.5 million years ago. Leakey has described these fossils as being members of the genus *Homo*, the same general group to which our present human species belongs, and has given them the name *habilis*.

Early technology. Leakey regards *Homo habilis* as the maker of the world's oldest stone tools, tools of the kind originally attributed to *Australopithecus africanus* by Dart. Current evidence suggests that although some of these tools were deposited in the same limestone caves as the australopithecines, they were made more recently than 2 million years ago. Most now agree that *Homo habilis* was the maker of these tools.

Habiline tools are currently undergoing reevaluation. Keeley (1977) has developed a technique for determining how stone tools were used. By examining the different kinds of polish given to stones by different uses, it is possible to distinguish between uses such as cutting meat, scraping skins, whittling wood, or cutting plants. Using Keeley's approach, Toth (1985) has examined 2-million-year-old artifacts from East African habiline sites for evidence of their use as tools. His studies suggest that the flakes that *Homo habilis* was knocking from these pebbles were the primary tools. Although the cores that were left behind by removing several flakes may also have been used as tools such as choppers, they seem now to have been the discarded material rather than the intended tool. This conclusion is supported by an examination of marks on animal bones at habiline sites (Lewin, 1984). Most often these marks are the results of slicing motions, rather than the kind of breakage associated with the use of heavy chopping tools. Thus, the earliest demonstrated stone tools now known appear to have been simple, knife-like flakes of stone removed from pebbles about 2 million years ago.

Preferential Right-Handedness Among the Habilines

Toth (1985) has compared the stone cores that remained after removal of flakes by *Homo habilis* with cores from the one habiline site at Olduvai Gorge and has found surprising evidence that a preference for the right hand had already become a trait of the species.

Among contemporary apes, individuals may have a hand that they habitually prefer for manipulating objects. However, the preference of the right or left hand is equally distributed within the entire species, so that about half the individuals prefer the left hand and half the right. Among humans, about 90% of individuals are right-handed.

Where flakes are struck from a rock core is determined partially by hand preference and partially by the shape of the core itself. Toth has determined that when right-handers remove a series of flakes from a core, they tend to rotate the core in a clockwise direction as they proceed. Left-handers follow the opposite procedure. Because of the angle of the blows and the direction that the core is turned, right-handers tend to produce a larger number of flakes with the original external surface of the core on their right side. Toth examined 2-million-year-old tools from habiline sites in Kenya and found that 57% showed a right-handed bias, almost identical to the 56% that he found in a series of 1,569 flakes that he—a right-hander—produced himself.

Our *Homo habilis* ancestors have left us one other interesting evidence of their ability to modify the environment to make their lives easier. One habiline site at Olduvai Gorge has yielded what may be the world's oldest shelter or windbreak, a 14-foot-diameter ring of stones set up about two million years ago with higher piles of stone about every 2 feet that may have supported poles at one time.

Relationships with the australopithecines. The brain of *Homo habilis* was much larger than that of the australopithecines. The average cranial capacity of *Homo habilis* was 686 cc. Physically, *Homo habilis* is difficult to distinguish from *Australopithecus africanus*, except for its much larger brain size. Some anthropologists describe *habilis* as physically transitional between *africanus* and a later hominid known as *Homo erectus*. If this theory is correct, then *Homo habilis* may have evolved from an early *africanus*. Since *habilis* coexists with later australopithecines, the australopithecines would have to be viewed as having become extinct after the rise of *habilis*. Leakey himself believed that older *habilis* fossils remain to be found, and that the *habilis* line continues back to an earlier period before the rise of the australopithecine line from a common ancestor. Since there are currently no *habilis* fossils before 2 million years ago, this view is, of course, hypothetical. A few physical anthropologists are convinced that the late *africanus* fossils form a single variable population with the *habilis* forms, but this remains a minority view. Since *Homo habilis* and *Australopithecus* existed at the same time, the larger-brained hominid may represent the main line of evolution between *Australopithecus africanus* and later humans, while *robustus* may have been a separate descendant of *africanus* that continued for a time as a specialized side branch of the hominid family tree and finally became extinct (see Fig. 2.7).

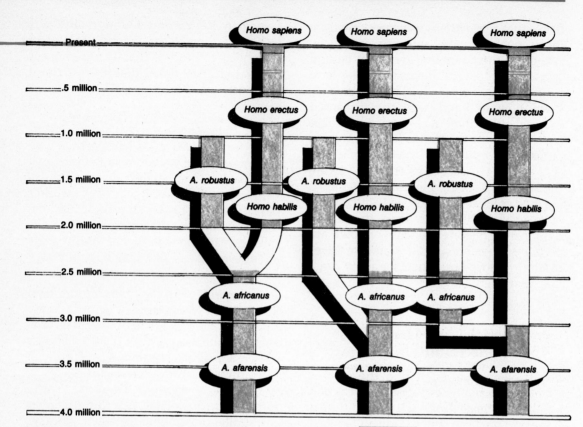

Figure 2.7 *Alternative Interpretations of Relationships between Australopithecines, Habilines and Later Hominids Researchers differ on the relative placement of evolutionary forms on the family tree. These are the most commonly held views, and differ basically in the placement of the* africanus *form.*

Homo erectus

In the next stage of hominid evolution, from about 1.5 million to 300,000 years ago, beings now called *Homo erectus* lived throughout the Old World, even into the colder areas bordering the glacial ice sheets of northern Europe and Asia. This move into the colder, glacier-dominated Northern Hemisphere was made possible by the control of fire. The hearths of *Homo erectus*, dated 500,000 years old or older, have been found in both Asia and Europe. *Homo erectus* is also known to have built large huts such as the ones found at Terra Amata, France. Along with fire, these shelters would have been useful in a cold climate.

Homo erectus also manufactured more sophisticated stone tools, which physical anthropologists call hand-axes. *Homo erectus* hand-axes were core tools that were carefully chipped into a teardrop or pear shape with a point at one end and an edge running around the entire silhouette of the

tool. *Homo erectus* was a true big game hunter. In *Homo erectus* living sites archaeologists have found not only the remains of fallow deer, sheep, antelope, roebuck, hyenas, horses, and camels but also remains of elephants, rhinoceroses, bison, water buffalo, large cave bears, and saber-toothed tigers.

Homo erectus had a slightly larger brain than *Homo habilis*. The average cranial capacity of *Homo erectus* was about 1000 cc, about twice that of the australopithecines and equal to the lower limits of the brain of modern humans, which measures from 1000 to 2000 cc and averages 1450 cc. With a brain this large, *Homo erectus* may well have had recognizable language ability. In fact, there are enough data available from fossil materials to speculate about the language-learning abilities of *Homo erectus*.

Grover Krantz (1961) has pointed out that, in contemporary humans, children do not begin to acquire language until their

Figure 2.8 Oval Huts
A reconstruction of the type of hut built at Terra Amata by Homo erectus. *The walls were made of stakes set as a palisade in the sand and braced by a ring of stones. It is thought some larger posts were set up to form a roof, but how they were connected is unknown. The hearth was protected by a small pebble windscreen.*

brain reaches a volume of about 750 cc, at about one year of age. He suggests that this is the minimum volume in which the necessary neurological organization is possible for true language abilities. By this standard, the average brain size of a mature *Homo erectus*, about 1000 cc, is large enough to permit language. However, the brains of *Homo erectus* children did not reach a size of 750 cc until they were five or six years old. Krantz suggests that if language acquisition occurred at the same maturational stage then as it does today, *Homo erectus* children would not have begun to make use of language before five or six years of age. If Krantz's speculations are correct, this might help to explain why the cultural materials left behind by *Homo erectus* changed so little over a period of almost half a million years. Unlike modern human children, for whom language facilitates the learning of a way of life from the beginning of their second year of life, *Homo erectus* children would have had a period of time to learn their culture between the acquisition of language and puberty, when they would be more on their own. This much shorter period for the

efficient transmission of culture from one generation to the next would make change through the accumulation and transmission of ideas more difficult than it is today, when children have many more years to learn an increasingly complex cultural system. Nevertheless, *Homo erectus* was a cultural animal, and the way of life of *Homo erectus* can probably be differentiated from that of modern humans only in its degree of complexity.

Neanderthal

As far as we know, the major biological difference between *Homo erectus* and *Homo sapiens* lay in brain size. By 125,000 years ago, the hominid line had evolved a brain size of 1500 cc. The fossil form that achieved this modern level is commonly called Neanderthal. Neanderthal lived from 125,000 to 40,000 years ago. Neanderthal is now judged to have been a member of the same species as modern human beings, but different enough from members of our species today to be considered racially distinct from contemporary humans. The distinctive traits that separate Neanderthal from

Figure 2.9 Homo Erectus *(see page 36)*
Homo erectus *was the name given to early hominids who walked upright. In both Java and Peking specimens the skull was long, low, and thick with a flat frontal area and prominent brow ridges. The teeth were relatively small and arranged as in modern humans. This photo shows an* erectus *skull with restoration work done by McGregor.*

modern humans include heavy brow ridges, a skull that protruded at the back, the absence of a chin, and a heavier bone structure than is found in modern humans. Because of these distinctive traits, we give Neanderthal a separate racial designation—*neanderthalensis.* However, these differences from modern humans are clearly smaller than differences that we find in a single species alive today, so we have no reason to suspect that Neanderthal was of a species other than our own. Thus the full technical name *Homo sapiens neanderthalensis* distinguishes Neanderthal from modern human beings, *Homo sapiens sapiens.*

Investigation of the reconstructed vocal tract of one Neanderthal fossil by Lieberman, Crelin, and Klatt (1961) indicates to them that the speech abilities of Neanderthal may have been somewhat limited. The vocal apparatus of Neanderthal does not appear to have been effective enough to permit Neanderthalers to speak as rapidly as modern human beings do. Nevertheless, Neanderthal had a brain that was actually slightly larger than the modern human average. It is therefore generally believed that Neanderthal was able to communicate symbolically—to use one thing to refer to another, the basis for language. In fact, Brace (1967) has suggested that the rise of Neanderthal corresponded with the period in human evolution during which the symbolic capacity began to have a greater impact on survival than did the other biological abilities of these early humans. If this is correct, then it would be understandable why the culture of Neanderthal at the beginning of this period was characterized by sudden expansion and diversification. Neanderthalers manufactured many new types of tools, including blades, scrapers, and knives made from stone flakes, instead of only the earlier tools made out of the central core of a stone. Neanderthalers also made points, some of which they hafted as spears. Their dwellings included not only cave entrances and other natural shelters but also perhaps lean-to types of shelter or huts made of brush or skins.

Archaeological evidence suggests the presence of religious beliefs and practices among Neanderthalers. These people prepared graves and buried their dead carefully. Like many of the world's peoples today, they covered the corpse with red ochre, a practice that gives the corpse a life-like color. Often they also included in the grave a supply of tools, food, and flowers. Such practices imply belief in an afterlife where the tools and food could be used by the deceased. Besides burial practices, Neanderthalers engaged in another practice that seems to have had a religious significance: the ceremonial arrangement of cave bear skulls within specially prepared storage areas. In caves in both Switzerland and France, archaeologists have found cube-shaped chests that were made by lining a pit with stone and covering it with a massive stone lid. The skulls and other bones of cave bears had been placed within these chests in a carefully arranged way that indicates the significance this creature must have had to these early hunters. Within the Swiss cave, other cave bear skulls were left in niches along the cave wall. Since the cave bear was a powerful and dangerous predator and less formidable game were available to Neanderthal hunters, it is unlikely that the cave bear was hunted simply for its food value. A stronger religious motivation is suspected to have guided the hunt and ritual disposition of these trophies, perhaps as a symbol of spiritual control over animals as a source of food. Such ceremonial treatment of the cave bear by the Neanderthalers has parallels in ritual practices among several northern hunting peoples of the world today.

A Bear Sacrifice Ceremony Among the Ainus

Although ritual arrangement of cave bear skulls by Neanderthal does not tell us how they were used, ritual use of bears by the Ainus, the aboriginal inhabitants of Japan, illustrate how a powerful animal may play an important role in the religious life of a hunting and gathering people. Ainu hunters stalked animals as large as bears and walruses, and Ainu fishermen even caught whales. Fishing allowed the people of this now-extinct culture to live a rather sedentary life in autonomous villages.

The Ainus kept the skulls of the animals they hunted in a sacred spot near each family hut. Occasionally the Ainus sacrificed an animal and shared it in a kind of communion service. This was sometimes done with birds and other animals; when a bear was used, it was an especially important occasion, since the bear was the Ainu supreme deity (see Ohnuki-Tierney, 1972). The bear that was sacrificed was one that had been captured as a cub and tamed. It was allowed to play with the children of the family and was suckled by the mother like a child. When it grew larger, it was kept in a cage, and people continued to treat it with great respect.

According to Ohnuki-Tierney (1969) the bear ceremony was performed to signify the beginning of the cold season, when the bear provided its meat to Ainu hunters. Guests were invited to attend. The people drank alcohol and made offerings to the family deities. The women and girls danced around the cage. The men offered *sake*, Japanese rice wine, to the cub. The bear was spoken to respectfully about the honor it was to receive by being sacrificed. It was asked not to be angry. Then the bear was led from the cage by a rope. It was shot with blunt arrows and yelled at to excite it. A piece of wood was forced into its mouth, and it was strangled with two poles. After the bear was dead, its blood was drunk by the men, who also smeared the blood onto their beards. The body of the bear was skinned and given offerings of food and drink. After this, the meat was boiled and eaten in a ritual communion service. The head of the bear was placed on a pole in the sacred spot near

1. *Dryopithecus*   2. *Australopithecus afarensis*   3. *Australopithecus africanus*   4. *Homo habilis*

Figure 2.10 *Hominid Evolution*
This drawing depicts the traditional view of the evolution of physical traits in the hominid.

the family home. The purpose of this ceremony, according to the Ainus, was to return the bear deity to the mountains which are its home.

Ancient *Homo sapiens sapiens*

Humans of completely modern biological type, *Homo sapiens sapiens*, existed by 40,000 years ago, according to the fossil record. These people with modern characteristics began to occur at that time throughout Africa, Europe, and Asia. The glacial period during which these early modern forms lived had its beginnings during the times of Neanderthal and began to terminate about 10,000 years ago.

This prehistoric period of human evolution was characterized by a greatly increased rate of change in technology, with more and more specialized tools and a tremendous number of local varieties and traditions within the tool kit. A major technological focus of this period was the manufacture of long, thin blades struck from a prepared stone core. Such blades were used as both knives and scrapers.

Another common type of blade was the burin, a chisel-like tool used for engraving bone, ivory, and similar materials. It seems to have originated in the plains areas of central and eastern Europe where wood suitable for making tools was lacking or at a premium. It was employed in the manufacture of the famous carved and engraved art works of this period and also made possible the carving of bone needles, wire pins, and detachable barbed harpoon heads.

The spear-thrower seems to have appeared toward the beginning of this period. It was a device for increasing the leverage of the human arm to propel a spear or dart to a greater distance and at a greater speed. The bow and arrow, an even more efficient device for use in hunting, came into being in this early Ice Age period. It was invented about 30,000 years ago, possibly in the Sahara—which was not a desert but a grassland region occupied by human hunters during the peak of the last glacial period. The new and highly efficient bow and arrow device was borrowed gradually and spread throughout most of the inhabited world, reaching the Western Hemisphere about 2,000 years ago.

5. *Homo erectus*   6. *Homo sapiens neanderthalensis*   7. *Homo sapiens sapiens*

The final outstanding trait of this period of early modern *Homo sapiens* was their now-famous art works, which included stone and bone carvings and modeled clay figures, engravings, and paintings found in caves like those at Altamira, Spain, and Lascaux, France. The central theme of this cave art was the portrayal of animals. The artistic tradition of these people emphasized the animals they hunted, which were generally portrayed in a realistic style. Often they were depicted as pregnant or with darts aimed at or entering their bodies. These two traits suggest that the pictures had magical functions for the early hunters: increasing the fertility of the animals that served as the basis for their survival and insuring the success of the hunt. This interpretation is supported by other indications that it was the act of creating the image itself, rather than the pure aesthetic value of portrayals, that was most valued. For one thing, vegetation and other aspects of the background were not portrayed. Second, individual animals were portrayed at different scales; they were generally not arranged in any mural depiction as a group. Third, individual portrayals were created at very differ-

ent angles to each other, often overlapping earlier—apparently no longer important— ones. Finally, the paintings and wall reliefs were generally located in the darker, less accessible, recesses of the caves, rather than in the inhabited cave entrances where they might have been mere decorations. These facts make sense if the creation of each portrayal were part of a religious ritual in which it was the creative act itself, rather than the aesthetic value of the end product, that was most valued.

Humans were rarely depicted and then only in a highly stylized manner that almost never seemed to attempt to capture the unique traits of an individual person. That is, this art work was not portraiture but seems to have served other purposes. The most outstanding examples of human representations are small figurines of modeled clay, stone, or ivory, known commonly as "Venus" figurines. These female figurines are found in the Northern Hemisphere from France to Siberia. Most are found in eastern Europe and all date from 20,000 to 27,000 years ago. They are generally fat and have exaggerated sexual features with large, pendulous breasts, pro-

41

truding abdomens—sometimes suggesting pregnancy—and large hips and buttocks. The legs, on the other hand, tend to dwindle to a point, with no apparent feet. Similarly, the hands and arms are underemphasized, often being portrayed as mere lines on the body. The head may display hair but never has facial abstract representations of femininity in general. Like the cave paintings, these figurines may have had a religious significance in magical rituals intended to insure fertility.

Summary

In attempting to reconstruct the evolution of our species, we looked first at the mechanisms by which evolution is known to occur: natural selection, mutation, genetic drift, and gene flow. When such processes lead to substantial changes, subgroups of a species may become so different that they can no longer interbreed successfully, at which point they are said to constitute distinct species. For humans, this process seemingly originated among those primates who left their arboreal habitat to live on the ground in the grasslands of Africa, Asia, and Europe: the hominoids. Past evolutionary relationships between humans and other living primates can be inferred by differences in their current biological makeup. The point at which the line that led to humans split off cannot yet be definitely pinpointed. According to the fossil record, the dryopithecines may have been ancestors to apes and humans. *Ramapithecus*, who may have evolved from one of the dryopithecine lines, may have been the first hominid, ancestor only of humans and not of apes. The australopithecines who followed had a fully upright posture and may have made tools, although evidence of tools found with australopithecine fossils is now usually attributed to the next known hominids: *Homo habilis*. Ancestral beings now known as *Homo erectus* followed. They knew how to use fire and build shelters and were able to migrate northward even during the glacial periods in the Northern Hemisphere. The Neanderthalers who were next in our family line differed only slightly from us in biological terms, with brains as big or perhaps even bigger than ours. They may have evolved early symbolic systems with religious rituals as well as new toolmaking technologies. These were elaborated by our most recent prehistoric ancestors, *Homo sapiens sapiens*, whose art work gives us some insight into their lives as tool-using hunters.

Key Terms and Concepts

species 19
biological evolution 19
natural selection 19
phenotype 21
heredity 21
genotype 21
gene 21
DNA 22
chromosomes 22
alleles 22
dominant 22
recessive 22
mutation 23
genetic drift 24
gene flow 24
speciation 25

Annotated Readings

Campbell, B. G. (1985). *Humankind emerging* (4th ed.). Boston: Little, Brown and Company. A comprehensive and up-to-date introduction to human origins.

Darwin, C. (1958, originally published 1859). *Origin of species*. New York: New American Library. Darwin's account of the facts and logic that led to his revolutionary interpretation of the mechanisms of change in species.

Johnson, D. & Edey, M. (1981). *Lucy: The beginnings of humankind*. New York: Warner Books. An engrossing and highly readable account of the discovery and interpretation of the earliest known hominid.

Lawick-Goodall, J. van. (1967). *My friends the wild chimpanzees*. Washington, DC: National Geographic Society. A readable look at the field experience of a biological anthropologist who specialized in the study of living primates.

Nelson, H. & Jurmain, R. (1982). *An introduction to physical anthropology*. St. Paul, MN: West Publishing. An exceptional introductory account of biological anthropology.

Pfeiffer, J. E. (1978). *The emergence of man*. New York: Harper & Row. A readable introductory-level account of human origins.

Schaller, G. B. (1963). *The mountain gorilla*. Chicago: University of Chicago Press. A superb account of the behavior of the gorilla in its natural setting.

Chapter 3

Culture

Probably unlike other animals, we humans have a persistent tendency to try to make sense of our existence and to share those understandings with others of our group. We also feel a necessity to alter the environment so that we can survive more comfortably and predictably. These ideas and survival strategies are institutionalized and perpetuated as culture, the subject of this chapter. After analyzing the systematic patterning of beliefs, feelings, and ways of surviving, we must note that these patterns differ from one society to the next, commonly resulting in misunderstandings and mistrust between human groups.

Figure 3.1 *Intercultural Influences*
The dress of these Samoan women, both in style and manner, demonstrate the influence of European culture on their traditional, native garb.

Culture Defined

All human groups develop complex systems of ideas, feelings, and survival strategies and pass them from one generation to the next. Anthropologists call the system of ideas, feelings, and survival strategies of a particular human group the culture of that group. Great diversity exists among anthropologists' definitions of culture, but according to Kroeber and Kluckhohn (1952) the concept of culture has always centered on the idea that there is a pattern to the ideas and feelings that unify a human group and give it an identity as a society. Those who share this way of life may be explicitly aware of some parts of the pattern. Other parts of the pattern of a culture may be implicit in a people's customary behavior without their being conscious of it.

Culture is not biologically predetermined. Instincts, innate reflexes, and other biologically predetermined responses are not a part of culture. Behaviors that are guided by culture are learned, rather than acquired through biological inheritance. Some parts of a culture are taught explicitly. Other parts are learned by observation of the behaviors of others.

In learning the customs of their culture, people are taught that they share some "common understandings" with one another and that others expect them to follow those customs. In this sense, much of a way of life is like a set of rules about how one ought to live. These parts of culture, like the rules of a game, give structure and

45

continuity to the social life of each human group. The predictability that culture lends to a people's behavior gives them security since it allows them to anticipate the behavior of others, including those they are meeting for the first time. Therefore, the parts of culture that are explicitly taught are often thought of as the *proper* ways of behaving.

Participating in a shared and traditional system of customs also gives life a sense of meaningfulness. The customs (and products of those customs) that are acquired culturally have meanings for the participants and may be thought of as symbols of the culture: as objects and events whose meanings have been created by their users. Clothing, for example, is chosen not only to protect our bodies from the elements—what we wear also conveys symbolic messages that are interpreted by others according to the shared meanings of our culture.

North American Clothing as a System of Meanings

The clothes we wear convey many meanings to those of our culture. In the United States and Canada, the patterns of clothing are complex and express many different kinds of information (Sahlins, 1979). Our choices of what to wear reflect the part of the country we live in, where we happen to be, the time of day or night and the season, and our age, sex, and social class. Clothing expresses the differences defined as meaningful within each of these categories.

A major distinction exists between clothing worn at home and in public. In public, we even tend to dress more formally to go downtown than to stay in our own neighborhood. Time is also important. We distinguish in our dress between the time of day, the day of the week, and the season. We begin the day with a change from nighttime clothes into those of the day. Greater formality exists in "evening wear." Weekdays and weekends also differ in style of dress, with sacred days generally being set off by more formal dress than other days.

Although contrasts are minimized in some settings and social groups, North American fashions generally include differences in the dress of men and women. Clothing manufactured for men tends to be made of heavier, coarser, and stiffer materials, such as denim and wool. Lighter, softer, more supple fabrics, such as cottons and silks, are more common in women's clothes. Class differences can be seen in fabrics as well. Wools and silks are high-status fabrics, whereas denims and cottons were not chosen by the wealthy until nostalgia for a simpler life elevated these fabrics to high fashion. The colors of clothes may also differ by class, with muted colors and minimal contrasts preferred in higher-status clothes.

Patterns in North American clothing include many more distinctions than the few mentioned here. For instance, many differences in clothing reflect occupation, ethnic group, or the specific activity being undertaken. However, this brief discussion has illustrated that clothing is not merely designed for sheltering us from the elements; the clothes we wear are also symbols that communicate categorical distinctions as they are understood by North Americans.

Ideology

Within any culture, there are regularities in how people act, think, feel, and communicate, but people are not conscious of all of them. They may never explicitly state an underlying rule to which they seem to be conforming. Yet the regularity in their behavior may be obvious to an outsider. Imagine that we noticed that the members of a certain society always took care to lock the doors and windows of their homes and automobiles when leaving them, that they never left their bicycles unlocked when they entered a store, that they never left valuable items unattended or in open view even at home. We might conclude that these people believe that some of their fellows are likely to steal, even if they never say so directly. We would include in our description of their culture the implicit rule of maintaining the security of one's own possessions, even if these people do not explicitly refer to such a rule when speaking among themselves.

A culture, then, includes both conscious, formally stated beliefs and feelings—called the ideology of the culture—and unconscious, informal, or implicit beliefs and feelings. A culture includes all the rules that govern a way of life, while an ideology is that part of a culture of which its practitioners are most fully conscious.

Ideological Communication

Given the regularities that culture produces in all areas of human life, people in every society will probably become conscious of many of their shared feelings and ideas. As people communicate about themselves and their environment, they build a consensus about the nature of humankind and the universe in which it exists, as well as how one should live in one's corner of the universe. Ideological communication is an important way in which people identify themselves as members of a group, since expressing common sentiments and assenting to the central ideas of the group makes it clear to others that one belongs to the group. Much of the communication about ideology is not a transfer of information but a declaration of group allegiance. While ideological rituals have the outward form of communication, their predictability precludes any new information from being expressed (Wallace, 1966).

Ideological communication reaffirms those things that give identity to the group. It frequently takes the form of highly ritualized acts, such as a pledge of allegiance to a flag or some other symbol of the group, recitation of articles of faith, or singing of hymns that glorify the doctrines of the group. Ritual affirmations of one's social solidarity with others may, of course, be less formally structured, as in so-called ''small talk,'' the content of which is nonetheless highly predictable. For instance, North Americans recognize that the greeting ''How are you?'' is not a request for infor-

mation but simply the opening gambit of a ritual communication of friendship and willingness to interact. The more or less predictable response—''I'm fine, thank you''—is not a measure of one's actual state of health but an affirmation of the same willingness to interact and a declaration that one shares the same cultural code of symbolic behavior. Such ritual reaffirmations of mutuality may be interspersed throughout an entire conversation in stereotyped communications, as in a discussion of the weather.

Beliefs

An ideology has two main interacting components: a subsystem of beliefs and a subsystem of feelings. Beliefs are the means by which people make sense of their experiences; they are the ideas that they hold to be true, factual, or real. By contrast, feelings are a people's inner reactions, emotions, or desires concerning experiences. These two systems interact. Although beliefs are judgments about facts, they are not always the result of rational analysis of experience. Emotions, attitudes, and values—aspects of the feeling system—may determine what people choose to believe. Within limits set by the necessities of survival, persons may choose to believe what is pleasing to believe, what they want to believe, and what they think they ought to believe. On the other hand, once people are convinced of the truth of a new set of beliefs, they may change some of their previous feelings to make it easier to maintain those new beliefs. Recognizing these interactions, we will nonetheless examine beliefs and feelings separately, beginning with beliefs.

Conformity to a belief system. The beliefs of a culture are the intellectual subsystem of its ideology. They are the consensus of a people about the nature of reality. Beliefs are those things that the members of a culture regard as true: ''God exists''; ''The sky is blue''; ''Geese fly south for the winter''; ''Spilling salt causes bad luck.'' Each culture has its own distinctive patterns of thought about the nature of reality.

As children, we learn that the other members of our society share a system of

47

thoughts, a pattern of thinking about the nature of the world. The knowledge of a society is taught to its children either implicitly or explicitly, as *the proper way* of understanding the world. North Americans grow up under a formal educational system in which mechanical models sometimes are used to demonstrate the plausibility of the idea that the moon is a sphere, the apparent shape of which depends on the relative positions of the sun, the moon, and the earth. By contrast, the Shoshoni Indians of the western United States Great Basin area traditionally founded their explanations of the phases of the moon on the idea that the moon was shaped like a bowl or basket rather than a sphere. The phase of the moon was thought to be simply a matter of which side of the moon was facing the observer: A crescent moon was a side view, and a full moon was the outside convex bottom.

We obtain full acceptance as members of our group by conforming to the ways in which others think. Cultural ideas are imposed on us through rewards for conformity and punishments for deviance. Individuals who violate their culture's rules for proper thinking are likely to experience punishment ranging from a mild reproof or laughter to severe sanctions such as banishment, imprisonment, or death. In the contemporary United States, normal people do not "hear voices." Those who do may find themselves placed in mental hospitals "for their own good" or "for the safety of others." In other times and places those who heard voices have been honored as spiritual teachers. North American school children are rewarded for believing that the moon is a sphere and punished for believing otherwise. During my fieldwork on an isolated Shoshoni reservation in the late 1960s, I discovered that my attempt to describe the moon as a sphere evoked either argument or skeptical looks, and my desire for acceptance soon silenced my expression of deviant views.

Widespread adoption of a system of beliefs gives people a sense of identity as a group. A people's knowledge that they share a set of beliefs gives them a feeling of security and a sense of belonging. As people discuss their beliefs, they may begin to think of their shared ideas as a symbol of their identity as a people. When people become self-conscious of their shared beliefs, especially if they assign a name to their system of beliefs, this part of their ideology may begin to function as an active, driving force in their lives. Such conscious systems are particularly common in complex societies. They are most dramatically illustrated by the named religions and political factions that can command the loyalties of great masses of people.

Types of belief systems. Each society tends to develop two different kinds of belief systems: scientific beliefs and nonscientific beliefs. The former occurs because a certain degree of practical insight into the nature of the world and its workings is necessary for any society to survive. Beliefs about such matters as how to obtain food and shelter or how to set broken bones must be based on pragmatic rather than emotional judgments if they are to be useful. These beliefs that are based on the desire to solve the practical day-to-day problems of living may be referred to as the <u>scientific beliefs</u> of a society.

The second basic type of belief found in every culture grows out of a people's feelings about their existence. These <u>nonscientific beliefs</u> are often formally <u>organized</u> within the framework of religious and artistic philosophies. These philosophies have the important task of portraying the universe and of expressing (sometimes in the guise of descriptions of reality) deeply valued feelings about the world in which people find themselves. Strong emotional commitments may also exist in political or recreational institutions. These, too, are often guided by beliefs that express the members' deeply held feelings.

Feelings

Feelings and beliefs tend to strengthen each other. Our feelings may be the motivation for believing things for which no objective support exists. Beliefs may, in turn, validate our feelings. When we believe that our feelings are the same ones that other people experience in the same situations, we are more confident in our judgments. Recognizing that our feelings are shared by others also supports our sense of belonging to a definable group.

Three major kinds of feelings find their idealized expression within an ideology: emotions, attitudes, and values.

Emotions. An <u>emotion</u> is a reaction to experience as pleasant or unpleasant, to varying degrees. As we mature, we learn many subtle variations on the two basic emotional themes of pleasantness and unpleasantness, such as delight, elation, affection, love, mirth, happiness, surprise, or exultation, and contempt, anger, distress, terror, or grief. Which emotions we learn to experience in various circumstances depend on the culture in which we are raised.

Each culture trains its members to associate certain emotions with certain situations and to experience each emotion at differing intensities in different settings. For instance, the situations in the dominant North American culture wherein unpleasant feelings such as disgust or fear are considered appropriate are not the same as those in which Navajo culture encourages the same emotions. In Navajo culture, it is appropriate to fear the dead, strangers, witches, and lightning. The dominant North American culture has, at times, considered it normal to fear Communists, homosexuals, spiders, and snakes. What excites or fascinates one people may bore or disgust another.

Cultures differ in how strongly or mildly feelings should be expressed and in which emotional experiences are most commonly emphasized. For instance, Ruth Benedict, author of one of the most widely read anthropological books ever printed, *Patterns of Culture* (1934), cited the late nineteenth-century Kwakiutl culture of Vancouver Island as one in which the expression of strong emotion—especially feelings of extreme self-worth bordering on megalomania—was encouraged. She described their religious ceremonies in the following words:

In their religious ceremonies the final thing they strove for was ecstasy. The chief dancer, at least at the high point of his performance, should lose normal control of himself and be rapt into another state of existence. He should froth at the mouth, tremble violently and abnormally, do deeds which would be terrible in a normal state. Some dancers were tethered by four ropes held by attendants, so that they might not do irreparable damage in their frenzy. (pp. 175-176)

Benedict contrasted the Kwakiutl with the Zuñi of the early 1900s. The Zuñi, who lived in the southwestern part of the United States, had a culture that encouraged moderation in the expression of all feelings. Zuñi rituals were monotonous in contrast with those of the Kwakiutl. They consisted of long, memorized recitations that had to be performed with word-perfect precision. The Zuñi had no individualized prayers; personal prayers were also memorized and recited word for word. As an illustration of how Zuñi culture required moderation in emotion, Benedict cited the case of a woman whose husband had been involved in a long extramarital affair. She and her family ignored the situation, but after she was exhorted by a white trader to take some action, the wife did so by not washing her husband's clothes. In her words, "Then he knew that I knew that everybody knew, and he stopped going with the girl" (p. 108). No argument, no yelling and crying. Just a mild indication that her wifely status was in question. For a Zuñi husband, this message was strong enough.

For the Dobuans, a people of Melanesia whose culture was studied in the early 1900s by Reo Fortune (1932), the dominant feelings were animosity and a mistrust that bordered on paranoia. These feelings permeated their customs. For instance, even husband and wife would not share food for fear that they might poison each other. All deaths were regarded as murders. In deaths that other people might ascribe to natural causes, black magic was the assumed weapon, with the surviving spouse the most likely suspect as the murderer. Dobuans assumed that their spouses were unfaithful whenever the opportunity existed, so they bribed their children to spy on each other. According to Benedict (1934),

Figure 3.2 *Cultural Influences in Clothing*
One aspect of a culture's influence is apparent in its style of dress. The Somoan woman on the left is dressed in a traditional way while the Tahitian woman on the right shows the effects of acculturation in her European style of dress.

The formula that corresponds to our thank-you upon receiving a gift is, ''If you now poison me, how should I repay you?'' That is, they seize upon the occasion to mark by formula to the giver that it is not to his advantage to use the universal weapon against one who is under obligation to him. (p. 166)

Attitudes. Our attitudes are statements of our preferences, our likes and dislikes. More generalized than our specific emotional reactions to situations, our attitudes are our general tendencies to seek or avoid types of experiences. Skydiving, for instance, may create conflicting emotions: fear and exhilaration. A general attitude toward high adventure—liking or disliking it— determines which way the scales will tip. Attitudes need not correspond to the pleasantness or unpleasantness of the emotions associated with an activity. Probably in every society individuals are taught to dislike or feel neutral about some situations that lead to pleasant emotions and to like other situations in which they experience unpleasant emotions. Athletes may learn to

crave the exercise that their goals demand, even though they dread the pain that attends each workout; soldiers may be taught to seek the very situations of battle that arouse their deepest fears; and the pious may steadfastly insist that they now dislike the bodily pleasures in which they had once indulged.

Values. The third part of the feeling subsystem of an ideology is values: feelings about what should or should not be, what is good and bad. Values include the moral imperatives in dealing with other humans: ''Thou shalt not steal!'', ''Love thy neighbor as thyself!'' They also include feelings about right and wrong that do not directly affect interpersonal relations but may affect one's relationship with nature or the supernatural. For instance, Jewish dietary laws, Mormon rules against drinking alcohol or coffee, and the Blue Laws outlawing sales on Sundays fall into this category.

The values of different cultures can be amazingly diverse, to the extent that what is held to be supremely desirable by the members of one society may be despised by another. That which one people hold dear as a religious or moral obligation of the most sacred kind may be viewed as sacrilegious or immoral by another. When the Samoans were first met by Europeans, women did not cover their breasts in public. Indeed, to do so would have been considered highly improper and immodest by the traditional Samoans. In contemporary European culture, an opposing set of evaluations prevails concerning public exposure of the breast; yet, the European woman is quite unconcerned about exposing the back of her neck in public, an act that would have resulted in strong disapproval in traditional Chinese society.

The Toda of India, who have no word for adultery in their language, consider it highly immoral for a man to begrudge another man his wife's sexual favors, but they have strong rules against being seen eating in public. Among the Dobuan islanders, being happy was not a valued emotional state. Yet, the American Founding Fathers declared the pursuit of happiness to be one of the three fundamental values of society. In the United States today, competitiveness seems fundamental to much of day-to-day life, while the early nineteenth-century Hopi of the southwestern United States carefully taught their children that it was wrong to shame others by excelling over them in competitive situations. The child who finished a race first was expected to take care not to do so the next time around.

Ideal vs. real culture. It is important to note that culture is a system of *ideals* for behavior. People do not always follow the guidelines of their culture. Sometimes individuals violate cultural ideals about proper communication behavior, as North Americans do when they behave rudely to show their anger at a slight. Sometimes people violate their culture's ideals for personal gain at the expense of others, but most of the time their failure to conform to cultural ideals is not consciously intended. For instance, only about 2% of United States drivers make technically legal stops at stop signs, but most do not think of themselves as breaking the law as they make their near-stops and proceed. People also tend to say

that dinner is eaten about six o'clock in the evening, unaware that the most common dinner time in the United States is closer to seven o'clock.

In studying culture, one must recognize that there is a difference between what is called ideal culture and real culture. The former refers to the ways in which people describe their way of life; the latter refers to the actual behaviors they engage in as a people. The disparity between the Zuñis' ideal and real behaviors provides a good example of this distinction. If people's actual behavior did not vary from the ideals embodied in their culture, if all members of a society conformed exactly to one another's expectations, then cultures could never change.

Ideal and Real Culture Among the Zuñi

Descriptions of the ideals embodied in a culture's rules for living are not always the same as descriptions of the people's actual behavior. Ruth Benedict's portrayal of the Zuñi of the United States Southwest, and presumably their portrayal of themselves to her, was one of a culture in which emotional excess and individualism were held to a minimum. The Zuñi avoided selecting as leaders people they believed sought the office. They carefully taught their children to avoid competition and conflict. Their ritual life idealized emotional restraint. Benedict (1934) claimed of the Zuñi that "Drunkenness is repulsive to them" (p. 82), that violence was so rare that only a single case of homicide could be remembered in village history, and that "Suicide is too violent an act, even in its most casual forms, for most Pueblos to contemplate. They have no idea what it could be" (p. 117).

These cultural ideals do not give an accurate picture of the realities of Zuñi life. Deviance occurred among the Zuñi as it occurs in all other societies. According to Ruth Bunzel (1952), the Zuñi were often split into factions that disagreed about whether anthropologists should be accepted in the village. There was rivalry along religious lines as well.

Li An-Che (1937, p. 69) claimed that "A strife of immense magnitude took place between the Catholic and Protestant elements." Zuñi initiation of children into adult life, like initiations at other pueblos, involved severe whippings (Roth, 1963). Village ceremonies were often marred by drunkenness (Barnouw, 1963). Violence was not nonexistent in Zuñi life, and although Pueblo culture might foster a reticence to discuss it, even suicides did occur (Hoebel, 1949).

Culture provides guidelines that mold people's behavior, but there are conditions under which deviance from the guidelines may be more common than conformity to them. One of these conditions is the effect of contact with other societies and their customs. Was Zuñi life more emotionally constrained before its political and economic subordination within the United States nation-state? This may well have been the case, since contact with more powerful societies can be especially disruptive to the internal harmony of a way of life. Certainly the alcoholism must be understood, at least in part, as a result of disruptive outside influence on Zuñi life. Probably we will never know how much pre-contact Zuñi behavior deviated from Benedict's portrayal, but we should remember that ideal culture and behavior are never identical.

The Cultural System and Human Adaptation

While much of culture exists in the symbolic realm of ideas—the beliefs and feelings of an ideology—there is also a practical aspect of culture that makes it possible for a people to survive physically. Each culture, as a system of common understandings, serves not only as a form of social bonding but also as the action plan by which a human society interacts with its natural environment to fulfill its survival needs. The following sections offer three different approaches to understanding cultures as adaptive systems: Malinowski's list of human needs met

by culture, the four major cultural patterns determined by groups' ways of getting food, and Harris's categories of cultural behaviors.

Human Needs

Bronislaw Malinowski (1939), the best-known anthropological fieldworker of the 1930s, outlined seven basic human biological and psychological needs that must be dealt with by every culture: nutrition, reproduction, bodily comforts, safety, relaxation, movement, and growth. Malinowski's list is probably an incomplete summary of human survival needs, but it can be used to illustrate that cultural variation is constrained by the practical necessities of human survival. A culture can only survive if it responds effectively to its members' survival needs.

As cultural creatures, we human beings do not meet our biological and psychological needs directly. Instead, we fulfill our needs as the culture of our social group prescribes. In no society do people eat every edible plant or animal available to them. People eat only those things their culture defines as "foods," and they exclude from their diets other items of equal nutritional value. For instance, in parts of the Orient dog meat is considered a delicacy, while the Western custom of eating cheese and yogurt is considered disgusting.

Similarly, in no society is the need for reproduction fulfilled by allowing all people to mate indiscriminately. In every society, sexual acts are controlled by cultural rules, such as those determining appropriate partners, when and where sexual acts may occur, and how those acts should actually be performed. For instance, among the Navajo of the southwestern United States, sexual intercourse is forbidden between any persons of known familial relationship, no matter how distant. The pre-Conquest Quechua Indians of the Andes, on the other hand, expected their emperor, the Inca, to mate with his full sister.

The need for bodily comforts is dealt with in each society by forms of housing and clothing. These cultural patterns provide each society with a plan for making minor improvements in the individual's immedi-

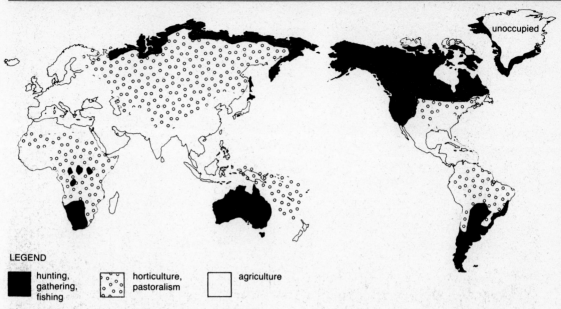

unoccupied

LEGEND

■ hunting, gathering, fishing

○ horticulture, pastoralism

□ agriculture

Figure 3.3 *Subsistence Technologies of A.D. 1600.*
This map shows the worldwide range of subsistence technologies in A.D. 1600.

ate environment, such as changing the temperature or humidity in which a person must work, rest, or sleep.

Each culture also includes plans of action for insuring greater safety in dangerous situations. These include such guidelines as rules for conduct during a fire, when lost, or when attacked by an animal or by a human enemy. Human skills in coping with danger vary from culture to culture.

The needs for relaxation, movement, and growth are met in culturally patterned rhythms of work and sleep, exercise and rest, recreation and practical activities. Each society trains its young in the way of life of its people and teaches its members the skills they must acquire at each stage of their lives.

Technology

To fulfill the human needs, every culture must include valid ways of coping with the natural environment. The natural environment is the source of energies and raw materials used to fulfill group and individual needs. Tools and the knowledge and skills evolved for fashioning them and extracting resources are called the technology of the culture. In every society, objects are manufactured and used in undertakings ranging from recreation and worship to basic survival. Technology provides ways in

which the forces of nature, be they physical or biological, are captured, transformed, and utilized for the preservation of human life and comfort. In fact, a human society might well be described as the organized patterns of human interaction through which the energies of nature are channeled from person to person.

The anthropologist Leslie White (1971) has suggested that those activities that are most related to survival—the provision of food, shelter, and defense—have the biggest influence on how the rest of a cultural system is organized. Regardless of how simple or how complex a society is, its tool kit and technological know-how include the means for solving these problems of nutrition, bodily comfort, and safety. And of these, the nature of a culture is most directly influenced by its subsistence technology— the tools and techniques by which the people obtain their food. In the long history of human cultures four basic types of subsistence technology have evolved: foraging, horticulture, pastoralism, and agriculture.

Foraging. The oldest and simplest of these subsistence technologies is foraging: hunting wild animals and gathering wild plant foods. Human beings have subsisted by foraging for more than 99% of their existence. Thus, foraging has been a very suc-

Figure 3.4 *Inuit Whale Hunt*
Foragers of the far north, Inuits continue to hunt the whale for food. Here, they are cutting up the whale meat.

cessful and adaptable way of surviving. Depending on their environments, foragers place different relative emphasis on the gathering of plants, hunting, and fishing. Those foragers who emphasize plant collecting have the least specialized subsistence technology and the least emphasis on separation of the roles of men and women.

The principal subsistence tools in those few remaining cultures that still live by foraging are such items as digging sticks, clubs, spears, bows and arrows, fishing devices, traps, fire, and containers for storing, cooling, and transporting food. Tools are few in number and general purpose in use, since they must be made on the spot when needed or transported as the people move from place to place in the quest for food. According to Lomax and Arensberg (1977), who surveyed the subsistence systems of 1,308 societies, "The emphasis is on hand skills rather than tools" (p. 668). Since individual skill is critical to success in the quest for food, foragers generally socialize their children to be independent and assertive and to rely on their own initiative rather than to be compliant to the demands of others.

Since hunting and gathering technologies rely on naturally occurring wild foods, foragers are unable to live year-round in groups as large as those supported by food domestication. Therefore, social mechanisms more complex than the family are not necessary for organizing the political and economic lives of foragers. Foragers lack governments and warfare. They tend to be highly mobile, especially when hunting provides a major portion of their food supply.

Considering the small size of their social groups, it is hardly surprising that foragers generally have been less politically powerful than food domesticators. In competition with food domesticators, foragers have usually been at a disadvantage. As a result, they continue to exist primarily in those areas of the earth of marginal interest to the plant and animal domesticators: the arctic wastes (the Inuit of the Arctic), the tundras (the Chuckchi of Siberia), deserts (the southwest African !Kung Bushmen and Hottentots and the Shoshoni Indians of the Great Basin in the United States), and tropical environments (the Mbuti pygmies of the African Ituri Forest).

Horticulture. Domestication of plants and animals began about 13,000 years ago. The earliest form of food domestication technology was horticulture, or primitive farming. Horticulture differs from true agriculture in that such factors as the plow, draft animals, soil fertilization, crop rotation, and irrigation are largely absent. The most common

Figure 3.5 *Horticulture*
The subsistence technology of horticulture provides people with food in a simple uncomplicated way. This African woman in a village on the Ivory Coast is pounding grain into flour.

tools used in primitive labor-intensive horticultural societies are the digging stick and the hoe. Most horticulturalists have some domestic animals with which they supplement their diets, but animals are never the source of the bulk of their diet.

A horticultural technology provides a more reliable subsistence and produces more food per acre than does a hunting and gathering technology, so peoples with horticultural technologies live in larger communities than do foragers. Their denser populations give them correspondingly greater political power than foragers have, so horticultural societies are much more widespread. Today, they are found primarily in the tropical forest areas of South America, in many parts of North America, in most areas of Africa, throughout the islands of the Pacific, and in some of the Asian mainland. Nevertheless, the simple tools of horticulturalists give them relatively little control over the productivity of the land they cultivate, so there are natural limits on their distribution throughout the world. They are found in areas with warm or temperate climates favorable to the domestication of plants.

In the tropical forest areas, root crops tend to be the staple foods, while in drier, more open areas, cereal crops are more important. Forest-dwelling horticulturalists commonly practice a form of farming called slash and burn cultivation. A small garden plot is prepared near the residence by cutting down the trees and clearing the garden plot by burning. Especially in tropical forests where horticulture rapidly depletes the soil, it is necessary to build new gardens each year, so that each farmer has several plots in various stages of soil depletion. Farming proceeds through a cycle in which garden plots are allowed to sit idle for several years after they become too unproductive to warrant another planting. After several years, these plots may be cultivated again, since they are easier to clear than the virgin forest. Ultimately, after several cycles of use and abandonment of plots, entirely new gardens must be prepared. The soil will have become so depleted that the forest does not grow back. Eventually, gardens may be so far from the original village that an entire settlement of several hundred people may be relocated to a more convenient area.

In nonforested regions where cereal crops predominate, the settlements of horticulturalists may be more permanent than those of tropical forest farmers. Particularly in drier climates, horticulturalists may engage in some hand watering of plants or limited irrigation of fields, but irrigation is not so common or complex as in agriculturally based societies.

Control over the food supply allows horticulturalists to live in larger local groups than foragers. Villages of several hundred people may live together throughout the year. Housing is more permanent and house construction more elaborate than are the temporary shelters of foragers. Village life necessitates greater accommodation to the presence of others, so childrearing necessarily emphasizes compliance and responsibility over independence and assertiveness in children. Family organization tends to be more elaborate among horticulturalists than among foragers, since a large number of family members may reside in the same location over many generations.

The authority of the family organization in the lives of its individual members is great, since the family is the basic governing institution in horticultural villages. Each family organization may be a politically autonomous component of the village except in matters that affect the common welfare. Such matters tend to be dealt with by a council of family leaders from the entire village who seek to achieve a consensus on how to handle the problem.

The greater numbers and more complex social organization of horticulturalists and the need for control of the land as a source of income makes warfare a common element of life in horticulturally based societies. Nevertheless, just as horticulturalists have tended to be more politically powerful than foragers, horticulturalists have tended to be politically less powerful than agriculturalists. For this reason, they tend now to be restricted to arable areas of the world that are less desirable to the agricultural societies.

Pastoralism. A more specialized form of domestication technology is pastoralism, which focuses on animal husbandry as the major source of food. It tends to be found in areas unsuited to agricultural pursuits and is probably of more recent origin than horticulture. Indeed, it is commonly argued that pastoralism in most parts of the world developed as farming peoples expanded into environmentally less productive zones and adjusted by relying more heavily on domestic animals as their basic source of income. Most pastoralists do supplement their diets with food grown in simple gardens, but plant growing is always subordinated to the demands of their animal husbandry. Examples of pastoral peoples are the reindeer herders of the Northern Scandinavian Subarctic, the yak herders of the Central Asian Steppes, the camel nomads of the Sahara, and the cattle herders of the East African grasslands. Like the hunters and gatherers, pastoralists tend to be mobile, following their herds to a new pasture, usually twice a year.

Since they occupy territory that is often marginal and unproductive, pastoralists are generally unable to produce everything they need. Therefore, they must obtain some goods from neighboring horticultural or agricultural peoples. This is often accomplished by trade, but sometimes it is more profitable to raid their more sedentary neighbors to meet some of their needs. Especially when the animals they keep, such as horses or camels, give them great mobility, these peoples can carry out their raids rapidly with little warning and leave quickly afterwards.

According to Lomax and Arensberg (1977), "Pastoralists overproduce as a guarantee against famine and a sign of prosperity and pride, but large herds overgraze, and pastoral overgrazing has created deserts where gardens once were" (p. 676). Since the herds of pastoralists are vulnerable to theft, pastoralists must be constantly with their herds and live in perpetual readiness for conflict. Warfare is a prominent fact of life in pastoral societies. Thus, childrearing emphasizes obedience, deference to authority figures, competition, and male dominance over women.

Agriculture. Agriculture is more intensive than horticulture in the use of land for food production. The greater productivity of agriculture is made possible by the use of tools and techniques like the plow, irrigation, soil fertilization, and animal traction. Agriculture is much more recent than horticulture, being a scant 6,000 years old. An agricultural way of life creates large food surpluses. This surplus permits a much larger population to develop and makes it possible for large numbers of specialists to devote their full-time labor to nonagricultural pursuits. These features, in turn, greatly increase the political power of agricultural societies relative to those with a simpler technological foundation. Therefore, agriculturalists have become the largest, most widespread, most dominant peoples in the world and occupy the most productive parts of the world's surface.

Traditional agriculture. Traditional agriculture includes a heavy reliance on non-industrialized tools and techniques for increasing the productivity of the land. Human labor supplemented by the use of draft animals is the major source of energy for the work of food production, but use of the

Figure 3.6 *Industrialized Agriculture*
An extremely efficient method of food production is an agriculture that utilizes the mechanization of industry such as this peanut harvester.

plow and animal or human fertilizer to enhance the productivity of the soil makes agriculture more land-intensive than labor-intensive. Horticulturalists can expand their populations only by opening new land to cultivation. However, land-intensive agriculture can allow farmers to support population growth by increasing the output of their fields. The towns occupied by agricultural peoples commonly number in the thousands or tens of thousands. Such large groups require a high degree of specialization and the presence of a system of government that is not based solely on the authority of the family organization. Agricultural societies frequently have class distinctions with inherited differences in political power and wealth within the local communities.

Industrialized agriculture. The most recent innovation in food production technology is industrialized agriculture. In this subsistence system, productivity is greatly increased by using tractors, harvesters, and other machinery along with chemical fertilizers and pesticides. These, together with an industrialized system of transportation to carry the produce over great distances, have made possible the rise of farms of tremendous acreage. An industrialized agriculture nevertheless operates at great costs, when one measures the amount of energy required to produce its food output. But it is so productive that in the United

States, for instance, less than 3% of the population is involved in food production.

Societies whose subsistence technology is industrialized agriculture invariably support full-time governments that monopolize political power. The populations united under a single central government commonly number in the millions or hundreds of millions. Indeed, individual cities in industrialized societies may number in the millions.

Behavioral Categories

A third way of looking at culture's adaptive significance has been suggested by Marvin Harris (1979). Harris has summarized the major behavioral categories within which culture is manifest and then proposed that all are ultimately linked to practical responses to the world. The first of these behavioral categories is the mode of production, the technology and practices by which people expand or limit their basic subsistence production in their specific habitat. A culture's mode of production includes its subsistence technology, technological relationships to ecosystems, and work patterns. The second category is the mode of reproduction, the technology and practices by which a people expand, limit, and maintain their population. Discussions of mode of reproduction would touch on matters of demography; mating patterns; fertility, natality, and mortality; nurturance of infants; medical control of demographic patterns; and contraception, abortion, and infanticide.

Domestic economy—the organization of reproduction and basic production, exchange, and consumption within the family or household—comes next in Harris's model. This is the realm of family structure, domestic division of labor, domestic socialization, age and sex roles within the family, and domestic discipline. Next comes the category of political economy—the organization of reproduction, production, exchange, and consumption outside the domestic setting. Here one finds the political organization of society, its factions, clubs, associations, and corporations. Here also is nondomestic division of labor, taxation, and tribute, as well as public education, class, caste, urban and rural organization, and the mechanisms of social control and warfare. The final category, according to Harris, is the <u>behavioral superstructure,</u> the realm of art, music, dance, literature, advertising, rituals, sports, games, hobbies, and science.

Each of these behavioral categories has a corresponding component within the system of culture. The last, the behavioral superstructure, is most intimately centered within ideology, the symbolic core of culture, and the furthest removed from the mundane influences of practicality. A link exists, nonetheless. Harris contends that the modes of production and reproduction have a major influence on the characteristics of the domestic and political economy, which in turn influence the behavioral superstructure of a culture. In brief, the means by which a people survive and maintain their population within an environment influence their social customs and even the more purely symbolic parts of human life.

Practical Reasons for Dobuan Paranoia

According to Reo Fortune (1932), the Dobuans had a fierce mistrust of one another, a mistrust that bordered on paranoia. Their life was filled with sorcery. Food never grew without magic and neighbors engaged in magical theft of one another's crops; the winds did not blow except by magic; sex occurred only when one was bewitched; and all death was believed to have been caused by sorcery, with the surviving spouse the probable sorcerer. It would have been a mistake, though, to interpret Dobuan ideology as rampant mental illness. When the Dobuan outlook on life, nature, and their fellow Dobuans was seen as a cultural adaptation to their unhappy circumstances, it made a great deal of sense.

The Dobuans lived on islands that were much less productive than those of their Melanesian neighbors. They were rocky, volcanic islands that had only sparse pockets of soil. The Dobuans lived in extremely small villages which never numbered more than about 25 people. They made their living with gardens they cut from the jungle. Their staple food was the yam, but the meagerness of their environment made hunger a constant threat, even though they lived in small and scattered groups. There was never enough food to allay the worry about food, and everyone went hungry for several months before each planting time to make sure there would be enough seed yams. Eating one's seed yams was the ultimate mistake, for not even a person's own family would provide new ones to someone who had proven to be such a failure. Dobuan economic life was characterized by fierce and secretive competitiveness, even within families. Husbands and wives maintained separate gardens and, although they worked together and pooled their food, they did not share seed yams.

The death of a Dobuan created severe economic obligations for the in-laws. During the period of mourning, a surviving husband had to work the gardens of his deceased wife, her parents, and her brothers and sisters, while his own brothers and sisters had the added work of caring for his. After the burial, the kin of the survivor had to make a large payment of food and yams to the relatives of the deceased. At the death of a man, his wife's children were required to cook a mash of bananas and taro, a starchy root plant, and deliver it to the relatives of their father. After the mourning period was over, the children were never again permitted to enter the village of their father or to eat food from his garden.

Is it any wonder that with conditions of economic hardship such as these, the Dobuans were not a trusting people? The Dobuans lived in a world of limited resources, and their concept that one could prosper only at the expense of another was not unrealistic. This unhappy outlook on life was exaggerated by the Dobuans when they tried to gain a symbolic modicum of security in an insecure life. Like peoples the world around, the Dobuans sought security in religion. To the Dobuans, nature was not the kind provider; it was magic alone that assured the growth of crops. Yams, the Dobuans believed, would only grow with the aid of incantations inherited from one's mother's family. When hunger still occurred each year, the Dobuans salvaged the emotional security that religion brings at an awful cost—by attributing their poor harvest to the sorcery of their neighbors. They thus affirmed that their magic did work, and in fact was so powerful that it could be used to steal the yams of others. In simplest terms, the Dobuans traded the fear of possible starvation for a mistrust of their fellow humans.

Cultural Differences

Cultures differ greatly in their ideologies and practical responses to their varying environments. What happens when very different peoples come in contact with each other? In some cases, contact between groups changes one of them, usually the one with less political and economic power. Even when both maintain their integrity, members of differing groups may find it difficult to understand and appreciate each other's ways. In this section, we will look at intercultural influences, intercultural prejudices, ethnocentrism (the attitude that one's own culture is the only proper way of life), and cultural relativity (understanding and appreciating other cultures in relationship to their own unique context).

Intercultural Influences

Contact between cultures can bring tremendous change. This is especially true when the two societies differ greatly in economic and political power. Sometimes the extinction of native populations has been carried out by systematic acts of war. Even in less extreme cases, the transition from the original way of life to a socially dependent status is never without turmoil. Cultural subordination of one way of life by another, even when it occurs peaceably, can be a shattering experience both psychologically and culturally.

Time and time again, anthropologists have described the tragic effects on the world's nonagricultural peoples of contact with the industrialized nations of the world. Diseases introduced from the more densely populated societies sometimes decimate the local population, in which there is less resistance to the diseases of the civilized world. The awareness that other peoples are more powerful and more blessed with luxuries is a blow to the cultural pride that unifies a society. Often, contact is followed by a rise in the rate of internal conflict and other forms of deviance, such as alcoholism and suicide. For the Kwakiutl, contact with Europeans may have led to exaggerated—and destructive—attempts to display wealth and power.

The Kwakiutl Potlatch: A Reaction to European Contact?

The Kwakiutl, the indigenous population of Vancouver Island and the British Columbia coast, were described by Franz Boas (1967), who visited them first in 1886, and by Ruth Benedict (1934), one of Boas's students. When Boas observed them, the Kwakiutl were a people whose culture encouraged emotional extremes, channeled into fierce competition for status between individuals and groups. According to Benedict, ''The object of all Kwakiutl enterprises was to show oneself superior to one's rivals. This will to superiority they exhibited in the most uninhibited fashion. It found expression in uncensored self-glorification and ridicule of all comers'' (p. 190).

The expansiveness in the Kwakiutl personality was seen at the great giveaway *potlatches*, ceremonial feasts at which gifts were lavishly given to guests as part of a public announcement of an important event in the life of the host, for instance the host's claim to having achieved a higher social status. The most dramatic of the potlatches were those at which the Kwakiutl sought to shame their rivals with demonstrations of the unmatchable superiority of their wealth. Kwakiutl potlatch hosts proved their wealth with lavish gifts of food, blankets, and other valuable property. Gallons of fish oil were poured by "slaves" through the smoke-holes of their longhouses onto the fires to make the fires blaze higher. Blankets were ripped to shreds, and holes were chopped in the bottoms of boats to show the host's disdain for surplus wealth. Sometimes entire villages were burned by a chief and the slaves put to death in the extremes of conspicuous consumption. At potlatch feasts, a chief's retainers sang hymns of praise such as the following one reported by Benedict (p. 190):

> I am the great chief who makes people ashamed.
> I am the great chief who makes people ashamed.
> Our chief brings shame to the faces.
> Our chief brings jealousy to the faces.
> Our chief makes people cover their faces by what he is continually doing in this world,
> Giving again and again oil feasts to all the tribes.

What are we to make of such extremes? To Benedict, the Kwakiutl behavior simply illustrated the diversity of culture, but later anthropologists placed this behavior in better perspective. The Kwakiutl described by Boas and Benedict had long been in contact with the Europeans. Intensive trade for almost forty years before Boas's first visit had greatly affected their culture, and many of the extremes he observed were exaggerations of their earlier customs—exaggerations that arose as attempts to adjust to the effects of European contact. Helen Codere (1950) points to the core of the problem: Smallpox and other diseases introduced by contact with Europeans decimated the Kwakiutl population, which had fallen to less than a tenth of its original size by the time Boas first met the Kwakiutl. Marvin Harris (1974) believes that this population shrinkage and the loss of many working-age people to employment away from the Kwakiutl villages greatly intensified the competition for labor; at the same time, European wages brought unexpected wealth into the Kwakiutl economy, which was also being flooded with blankets and other trade goods in return for native furs. The native practice, common in many small-scale societies, of holding communal feasts at which food is redistributed by the chiefs to the poor, was modified into celebrations of material wealth by which the chiefs tried unsuccessfully to attract people back to the villages.

Intercultural Prejudices

When cultures meet, people may have little understanding or appreciation of groups whose ideologies and adaptive strategies differ from their own. People grow up under the nurturance of their group and learn to fulfill their needs by living according to their group's culture. As people learn their way of life, they generally identify themselves as members of the group that has cared for their early needs and has taught them the rules for living. Simultaneously, they generally develop positive feelings toward this reference group and its behaviors. Often, the training of children in the ways of the group is communicated expressly by contrasting them with the supposed behaviors of outsiders: "Other parents may let their children come to the table like that, but in our family we wash our hands before eating!" Such expressions teach children the patterns of behavior expected of group members, but they also communicate a disapproval of outsiders.

In complex societies with large populations and many competing groups, prejudices between groups within the society may become a common element of daily experience, varying from good-natured rivalry to direct antipathies. In the United States, we may think of our own state as "God's own country," our politics as the only rational way of doing things, or our religion as the only road to salvation. Even such group symbols as hair length and the kinds of clothing we wear have served as grounds for suspension from school, public demonstrations, and interpersonal violence.

The extreme form of allegiance to one's own group is the feeling that the culture of one's entire society is superior to the ways of life of all other societies. The attitude that one's own culture is the naturally superior one, the standard by which all other cultures should be judged, and that cultures different from one's own are inferior is such a common way of reacting to alien customs that it is given a special name by anthropologists. It is called ethnocentrism, meaning centered in one's *ethnos*, the Greek word for a people or a nation. Ethnocentrism is found in every culture. Everywhere, people allow their judgments about human nature and about the relative merits of different ways of life to be guided by ideas and values that are centered narrowly on the way of life of their own society.

Ethnocentrism serves a society by creating greater feelings of group unity. When individuals speak ethnocentrically, they affirm their loyalty to the ideals of their society and call forth in other persons echoed feelings of agreement about the superiority of their social body. This enhances their sense of identity as bearers of a common culture and as members of the same society. A shared sense of group superiority— especially during its overt communication between group members—can help the members to overlook internal differences and conflicts that could otherwise decrease the ability of the group to undertake effectively coordinated action.

For most of human history, societies have been smaller than the nations of today, and most people have interacted only with members of their own society. Under such circumstances, the role of ethnocentrism in helping a society to survive by motivating its members to support one another in their common goals has probably outweighed its negative aspects. However, ethnocentrism definitely has a darker side. It is a direct barrier to understanding among peoples of diverse customs and values. It enhances enmity between societies and can be a motivation for conflict among peoples whose lives are guided by different cultures.

Ethnocentrism stands in fundamental conflict with the goals of anthropology: the recognition of the common humanity of all human beings and the understanding of the causes of cultural differences. To many students, much of the appeal of the field of anthropology has been its intriguing discussions of the unending variety of customs grown out of what, from the viewpoint of the uninitiated, may seem like strange and exotic, unexpected, and even startlingly different values. A people's values generally make perfectly good sense when seen and explained in the context of their cultural system as a whole. Yet, from the viewpoint created by the symbolic understandings of another culture, they may be unexpected and seem, therefore, strange or even morally incomprehensible. It is often difficult to make sense out of customs that belong to another cultural tradition on the basis of symbolic meanings that similar acts might have in one's own culture. A negative reaction to customs alien to one's own society is therefore easy for people to adopt. But such ethnocentric reactions to other people's customs must be guarded against by the student of anthropology.

Cultural Relativism

The alternative encouraged in anthropology students is cultural relativism, the idea that the significance of an act is best understood by the standards of the actor's own cultural milieu. When we try to understand the meanings of an alien custom in a culturally relativistic way, we search for the meanings that those customs have in the actors' own culture instead of in our own. Relativism is not an idea unique to anthropology. In every culture, people interpret the meaning of a thing depending on the context in which it occurs. In the United States, for instance, most people would not be alarmed by a masked stranger who appeared at their door at night if it were October 31st and that person were holding a Halloween trick-or-treat bag. The symbolic basis of all cultural systems invariably leads to variations in the meanings of things from situation to situation. People who share the same culture learn to take the context of one another's acts into account when they are trying to communicate. Of course, intergroup prejudices sometimes interfere with people's efforts to understand one

Figure 3.7 *Cultural Relativism*
Subsistence technologies differ from culture to culture depending on its needs and natural environment. This Burmese woman carries her wood in a traditional manner.

another, even within the same culture, and relativism is even less used by people in thinking about the customs of other societies. In contrast to ethnocentrism, cultural relativism is an uncommon way of viewing other cultures.

Nevertheless, anthropologists have come to value cultural relativism as a first step toward understanding other cultures. A relativistic view of other cultures holds all ways of life to be equally valid sources of information about human nature. This does not imply endorsing customs such as infanticide or cannibalism, but merely accepting that they, too, are a part of the human condition that we wish to explain. Relativism, as a research tool, reminds us that even customs that seem inhumane or irrational by our own values must be described and analyzed as objectively as possible if we wish to develop scientifically valid understandings of human behavior. Relativism reminds

us that all cultures have customs that seem bizarre or repugnant to outsiders. For instance, both electroconvulsive treatment for depression and the use of machines for measuring heartbeat, blood pressure, and respiration to determine whether a person is lying might well seem inhumane or irrational to people whose cultures do not include these practices.

Cultural relativism is easy to reconcile with the anthropological goal of understanding the human condition in a way that is valid for all humankind. In support of this goal, anthropologists historically have elected to conduct most of their research among less complex non-Western societies. Such societies have cultures that differ greatly from those with which Western anthropologists would have been most familiar. In devoting their efforts to the study of diverse ways of life, anthropologists have hoped to maximize their data about the limits of diversity within and between human cultures. Also, they hoped to preserve for future generations knowledge about ways of life that were rapidly becoming extinct as complex industrialized societies expanded their influence throughout the world.

As a result of working among peoples with ways of life very different from their own, anthropological fieldworkers commonly find that the preconceived notions they bring with them do not help them understand what is going on in the culture they are studying. Cut off from their own people and their accustomed way of life, it is they who must learn to understand the meanings of the symbols of the people they are living with, rather than the other way around. The anthropological imperative is "Respect or fail!" Learning to understand the language and the customs as they are understood by the insiders of the group is often a clear and basic necessity for survival in a foreign culture. It can also be prerequisite to the work of gathering accurate information about a culture or of developing insights about how it might have come to be the way it is and why it functions the way it does. The necessity of interpreting the meaning or value of an act within the culture in which it is found, that is, from a cultural relativistic viewpoint, has been long recognized within anthropology as a fundamental first step in learning to understand a culture as a coherent system of meaningful symbols.

Doing Fieldwork Among the Yąnomamö

The difficulties of adjusting to life in an alien culture where language and customs differ greatly from one's own can be tremendous. Even brief isolation in a foreign culture can be a bewildering experience. Finding oneself in an environment where the symbols of one's own culture fail to provide the secure orientation we all need to maintain a sense of psychological well-being can lead one quickly into an extremely distressing state that anthropologists call culture shock.

Napoleon Chagnon (1968), an anthropologist who conducted his research among the Yąnomamö Indians of Venezuela, has described his initial reaction to that people. The Yąnomamö are an extremely fierce and warlike people who value and cultivate extremes of aggressive behavior unequaled in many parts of the world. Their use of hallucinogenic drugs in their religious rituals adds to their distinctive cultural configuration. Although it is certainly not typical of an anthropologist's first day in the field, Dr. Chagnon's uncommonly frank revelation of his feelings on first exposure to a non-Western culture gives some sense of the psychological effects of radical changes in one's symbolic environment and the ease with which ethnocentric prejudices might arise and preclude even the first steps towards the objective study of other ways of life.

We arrived at the village, Bisaasi-teri, about 2:00 p.m. and docked the boat along the muddy bank at the terminus of the path used by the Indians to fetch their drinking water. It was hot and muggy, and my clothing was soaked with perspiration. It clung uncomfortably to my body, as it did thereafter for the remainder of the work. The small, biting gnats were out in astronomical numbers, for it was the beginning of the dry season. My face and hands were swollen from the venom of their numerous stings. In just a few moments I was to meet my first Yąnomamö, my first primitive man. What would it be like? . . .

My heart began to pound as we approached the village and heard the buzz of activity within the circular compound. Mr. Barker commented that he was anxious to see if any changes had taken place while he was away and wondered how many of them had died during his absence. I felt into my back pocket to make sure that my notebook was still there and felt personally more secure when I touched it. Otherwise, I would not have known what to do with my hands.

The entrance to the village was covered over with brush and dry palm leaves. We pushed them aside to expose the low opening to the village. The excitement of meeting my first Indians was almost unbearable as I duck-waddled through the low passage into the village clearing.

I looked up and gasped when I saw a dozen burly, naked, filthy, hideous men staring at us down the shafts of their drawn arrows! Immense wads of green tobacco were stuck between their lower teeth and lips making them look even more hideous, and strands of dark-green slime dripped or hung from their noses. We arrived at the village while the men were blowing a hallucinogenic drug up their noses. One of the side effects of the drug is a runny nose. The mucus is always saturated with the green powder and the Indians usually let it run freely from their nostrils. My next discovery was that there were a dozen or so vicious, underfed dogs snapping at my legs, circling me as if I were going to be their next meal. I just stood there holding my notebook, helpless and pathetic. Then the stench of the decaying vegetation and filth struck me and I almost got sick. I was horrified. What sort of a welcome was this for the person who came here to live with you and learn your way of life, to become friends with you? They put their weapons down when they recognized Barker and returned to their chanting, keeping a nervous eye on the village entrances.

We had arrived just after a serious fight. Seven women had been abducted the day before by a neighboring group, and the local men and their guests had just that morning recovered five of them in a brutal club fight that nearly ended in a shooting war. The abductors, angry because they lost five of the seven captives, vowed to raid the Bisaasi-teri. When we arrived and entered the village unexpectedly, the Indians feared that we were the raiders. On several occasions during the next two hours the men in the village jumped to their feet, armed themselves, and waited nervously for the noise outside the village to be identified. My enthusiasm for collecting ethnographic curiosities diminished in proportion to the number of times such an alarm was raised. In fact, I was relieved when Mr. Barker suggested that we sleep across the river for the evening. It would be safer over there.

As we walked down the path to the boat, I pondered the wisdom of having decided to spend a year and a half with this tribe before I had even seen what they were like. I am not ashamed to admit, either, that had there been a diplomatic way out, I would have ended my fieldwork then and there. I did not look forward to the next day when I would be left alone with the Indians; I did not speak a word of their language, and they are decidedly different from what I had imagined them to be. The whole situation was depressing, and I wondered why I ever decided to switch from civil engineering to anthropology in the first place. I had not eaten all day, I was soaking wet from perspiration, the gnats were biting me, and I was covered with red pigment, the result of a dozen or so complete examinations I had been given by as many burly Indians. These examinations capped an otherwise grim day. The Indians would blow their noses into their hands, flick as much of the mucus off that would separate in a snap of the wrist, wipe the residue into their hair, and then carefully examine my face, arms, legs, hair, and the contents of my pockets. I asked Mr. Barker how to say ''Your hands are dirty''; my comments were met by the Indians in the following way: They would ''clean'' their hands by spitting a quantity of slimy tobacco juice into them, rub them together, and then proceed with the examination.

Mr. Barker and I crossed the river and slung our hammocks. When he pulled his hammock out of a rubber bag, a heavy, disagreeable odor of mildewed cotton came with it. ''Even the missionaries are filthy,'' I thought to myself. Within two weeks, everything I owned smelled the same way, and I lived with that odor for the remainder of the fieldwork. My own habits of personal cleanliness reached such levels that I didn't even mind being examined by the Indians, as I was not much cleaner than they were after I had adjusted to the circumstances.[1]

1. From *Yanomamö: The Fierce People* (pp. 9–10, 10–12) by Napoleon A. Chagnon, 1983, New York: Holt, Rinehart and Winston, Inc. Copyright 1983 by CBS College Publishing. Reprinted by permission.

Summary

Culture consists of the learned ideas and survival strategies that unify members of a particular human group. Group members are conscious that some of their beliefs and feelings are shaped by the ideology of their culture. Cultural ideas also subtly influence us in ways of which we may not be aware but which the study of anthropology may bring to our attention. An obvious manifestation of our culture is our subsistence technology, with foraging, horticulture, pastoralism, traditional agriculture, and industrialized agriculture being the major patterns in existence today. Our subsistence technology tends to shape all other aspects of our culture, including its rules about reproduction, its economic organization, and the ideological patterning of nonsubsistence behaviors. Facing different environments with differing ideas about how one should live, cultures have evolved along different lines. Variations are often so extreme that people from different cultures have a hard time understanding each other's ways. When interpreted ethnocentrically, other cultures seem bizarre. But there is another approach, one long used by anthropologists and promising better understanding among all peoples: cultural relativism, in which we try to make sense of the values and behaviors of other cultures within their contexts, rather than our own.

Key Terms and Concepts

culture 45
symbol 46
ideology 47
ideological communication 47
beliefs 47
feelings 47
scientific beliefs 48
nonscientific beliefs 48
emotions 49
attitudes 50
values 50
ideal culture 51
real culture 51
biological and psychological needs 52
technology 53
subsistence technology 53

foraging 53
horticulture 54
slash and burn cultivation 55
pastoralism 56
agriculture 56
traditional agriculture 56
industrialized agriculture 57
mode of production 57
mode of reproduction 57
domestic enonomy 57
political economy 57
behavioral superstructure 58
ethnocentrism 61
cultural relativism 61
culture shock 63

Annotated Readings

Geertz, C. (Ed.). (1971). *Myth, symbol, and culture.* New York: W. W. Norton. An important collection of essays on culture as a symbolic system.

Harris, M. (1974). *Cows, pigs, wars and witches: The riddles of culture.* New York: Random House. An exciting popular illustration of the cultural materialist approach to explaining human customs.

Kaplan, D., & Manners, R. A. (1972). *Culture theory.* Englewood Cliffs, NJ: Prentice-Hall. A simple and straightforward discussion of the major theoretical orientations of cultural anthropology.

Kroeber, A. L., & Kluckhohn, C. (n.d.). *Culture: A critical review of concepts and definitions.* New York: Random House. A survey of definitions and uses of the word "culture" from the beginning of anthropology to the 1950s.

Lévi-Strauss, C. (1963). *Structural anthropology.* New York: Basic Books. Seventeen articles by the founder of structural anthropology, the application of linguistic techniques to the study of culture.

Sahlins, M. (1976). *Culture and practical reason.* Chicago, IL: University of Chicago Press. A critique of the materialist view of culture as the product of practical activity, in which the author argues for an understanding of culture as a system of meaningful symbols, the structure of which determines people's perceptions of what is and is not practical action.

Chapter 4

Social Organization

Figure 4.1 *Status
By his position in his tribal
society, this Ghanian chief
is accorded a high ranked
status. At his installation
ceremony in Accra, he is
surrounded by his family
and tribal members.*

Nowhere are all people treated equally. In every society, people are organized into groups and levels of honor and social power. Categorizing people on the basis of distinctions such as the kind of work they do or their relationships to each other has the benefit of making social life efficient, orderly, and predictable. But some ways of categorizing people lead to inequalities that are unrelated to people's innate abilities. Among these problems in social organization are discriminations made on the basis of race and sex. In this chapter we will first look at the patterns of social organization and then consider the complexities of racial and sexual distinctions between people. The anthropologist's view of these distinctions is that they often mirror culturally learned rather than biologically inherited individual differences.

Organizational Patterns

Throughout human history, cultural continuity has been maintained by symbolic communication among members of a particular society. The pattern of their communication is determined by how their society is organized. The social organization of a society consists of (1) the various groups from which the society is built, (2) the statuses that individuals may hold, (3) the division of labor, the way in which the tasks of society are distributed among individuals and groups, and (4) the rank accorded to each group and status.

Groups

Every human society is itself a group. Its members perceive their common identity because of the culture that binds them together. All human societies that have ever been studied have been subdivided into smaller groups that coalesce from time to time for specialized activities. When a group gets together, it has geographical boundaries, specifiable members, a common activity engaged in by its members, and a division of labor. Football fans scattered across the country are not a group, but football spectators at a specific game are. When a group is formally organized, it may have an explicitly formulated ideology, a goal-oriented "game plan" or set of procedures for carrying out the activity that brings its members together.

The members of social groups generally identify themselves symbolically with a name or some other emblem of their group identity. Commonly, the identifying emblem indicates the activity that draws the members together or represents some other important aspect of the group's characteristics. Thus, the group identity of the United States of America is symbolized by a flag that portrays the political unity of that society's 50 states by a group of 50 stars. The Great Seal of the United States of America contains the image of an eagle clutching an olive branch and arrows, symbols of peace and war, which suggest that the major purpose of the nation as a political entity is to maintain internal order and to defend the group. A smaller, more face-to-face group, such as a religious congregation, may identify itself as a unified body by naming the congregation and by symbolizing its religious purpose with some symbol of its religious ideology, such as the Star of David, a church spire, a cross, or a denominational flag.

There will also be structured relationships between groups in every society. Interactions by groups are culturally patterned, and there may be a hierarchical ranking of groups, giving them different degrees of honor and social power. Groupings and group relationships are sometimes called the social structure of a society, to distinguish this aspect of social organization from other aspects such as individual statuses and roles (Service, 1962).

Statuses and Roles

Besides groups, each pattern for social organization also includes several kinds of relationships. Each such relationship that a person may have with others is called a status. Statuses are the kinds of things we can be for one another: government official, doctor, lawyer, teacher, taxicab driver, husband, lover, mother, child. Since each status is actually part of a relationship, the statuses of any society exist in pairs, such as doctor and patient, husband and wife, parent and child, or friend and friend. The status pairs of a society are of two types:

those in which the holders of the statuses are expected to behave in different but compatible ways and those in which the holders of the statuses are expected to behave in a similar way towards one another.

Status pairs in which both parties are expected to behave in different but compatible ways are called complementary statuses. Neither status in such a pair can function without the other, and the complementarity of their relationship is symbolized by referring to each status in such a pair by a different word. The status of doctor requires the existence of the complementary status of patient, that of parent implies that of offspring, and without the status of student there could be no teacher. In each of these cases, the holder of one status of the pair is expected to behave differently from the holder of the second status.

Statuses such as friend, neighbor, enemy, colleague, or ally, on the other hand, imply the existence of two or more holders of the same status who are expected to act toward one another in similar ways. Statuses paired in this way are called symmetrical statuses. One cannot be an enemy unless there is someone who will respond in kind as an enemy, too (Watzlawick, Beavin, & Jackson, 1967).

In every society, each person may be involved in many different kinds of relationships. Each person therefore has many different statuses. The same person may be a wife, a mother, a student, an employee, a friend, and a political activist. The statuses that we are allowed to have are often based on our age or sex and, in some societies, on the family or racial groups into which we were born. Such statuses, known as ascribed statuses, are assigned to us at birth. Other statuses must be acquired during our lifetimes. These statuses, such as team captain, college student, or club member, are known as achieved statuses.

The ways in which the holder of a status is expected to behave are called the roles of that status. Every status has several different roles, each of which is considered appropriate for certain times and places. In a culture in which emotional reserve and independence are valued, a mother may be expected to play the role of comforter to a distressed 10-year-old in private, but to maintain a more detached supportive role toward the child in public, particularly when his or her friends are around.

By conforming their behavior to the role expectations of others, holders of a particular status symbolically communicate that they hold that specific status and that they wish to be responded to in a manner appropriate to it rather than to some other status that they might also hold. The team captain is expected to direct action without discussion on the field; off the field, the same person may be expected to listen to and respect the opinion of another with whom he or she shares the status of friend.

Because each status has its own role expectations, the various status pairs of a society form a pattern of predictable relationship expectations that guide the interactions of society's members with one another. Due to this pairing, the process of communicating to others that one possesses a particular status simplifies the establishing of a social relationship since it also communicates the nature of the role that one wishes them to play in return. When team members accept another's status as team captain, they know that during a game their appropriate relationship to the leader is that of followers. Without such role agreements, ball games—and social life—would be somewhat chaotic.

Division of Labor

The day-to-day work that must be done in any society is allocated to people through their statuses. By playing their various roles, people accomplish that work. This makes it possible for the members of society to be organized efficiently into a clear-cut, well-known, and effective division of labor by which all the tasks of life are accomplished.

Even in the simplest of human social systems, where few specialists exist, there is some division of labor. In those societies that have the simplest social organizations—those in which people survive by foraging for wild foods—age and sex are the primary bases for assigning the work of life. Even though tasks may overlap and distinctions may not be strictly enforced, males and females in all societies are generally expect-

ed to specialize in somewhat different economic activities, as are the members of different age groups. Typically in the foraging societies, men are assigned the status of hunters, while women specialize as gatherers of wild plants. Children may provide some help around the campsite, fetching water or gathering branches for the fire. Older members of the group may be relied on for their experience in interpersonal and intergroup relations to mediate disputes, negotiate with strangers, or arrange marriages. In more complex social systems other forms of specialization develop, and the division of labor may become much more intricate. For instance, in societies in which people grow their own food, individuals or entire villages may specialize in the growing of a particular crop or the manufacture of woven goods or pottery. These are traded to other people or villages in return for their specialties. In industrialized societies, there are so many specialized occupations that a monetary system is needed to organize the exchange of labor. In these divisions of the work of life, some kinds of work are valued more highly than others, introducing the social effects of rank.

Rank

Rank is a measure of the relative importance accorded to groups and statuses. Holders of highly ranked statuses and members of highly ranked groups generally have more ready access to whatever is valued in their culture than do other members of their society. That is, depending on whether the rank is high or low compared to other groups, the rank of a group aids or hinders its members' quests for attaining the most valued goals of their culture.

Power and honor. Rank has more than one component. According to Kemper (1978), the two characteristics of a status that determine its social rank are the amount of social power and honor[1] associated with it.

---

1. Kemper uses the word "status" to refer to what is here called "honor." This reflects the lack of standardization in the terminology of the social sciences. Kemper (1978, p. 378) defines status as ". . . relationship in which there is *voluntary compliance* with the wishes, desires, wants and needs of the other" [italics in original]. To avoid confusion I will continue to use the word "honor" in this discussion wherever Kemper uses "status."

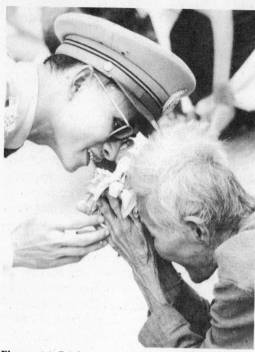

Figure 4.2 *Rank*
A status pair consists of two individuals who relate to each other in a way that depends on their rank in society. In Thai society the military has a higher ranked status than a peasant or laborer.

Power and honor are measures of one's ability to influence others successfully. Power is the ability to exercise coercion in obtaining what is sought and to punish the failure of others to comply. Someone is honored if others freely choose to give benefits to that person.

Groups, too, may be ranked in the degree of power and honor that they command. For instance, secret societies and vigilante groups are often characterized by high access to power, but their level of honor may be judged low by others. Service associations may have little power to obtain social benefits for their members coercively, but they may be high in the honor accorded their members.

Like groups, individual statuses may be ranked. Within a status pair, one status may be thought of as the superior of the two and may have access to a greater amount of honor, social power, and/or wealth. Thus, parents are expected to train and control their children rather than the other way around, and it is the teacher who tests and assigns grades to the student. Statuses that

are not part of the same status pair may also be ranked with respect to one another. In the United States, the occupational statuses of doctor or senator are generally considered more desirable and their holders given more social power and greater incomes than are the holders of the less valued occupations of teacher, mail carrier, or carpenter.

Societies differ in which statuses are most highly ranked. For instance, in industrialized nations where many of the important relationships in life are based on jobs, occupational status is a major determinant of the rank most people hold. In these societies, the loss of income that comes with retirement is often accompanied by a loss of rank. In socially simpler societies in which kinship relationships determine the most important roles, it is common for rank to increase with age and experience.

Class. Ranking of diverse statuses is more common in those societies that have large populations and many differentiated, highly specialized statuses. These societies are organized into a hierarchical structure that sometimes is subdivided formally into ranked classes of statuses. A class is a broad stratum that cuts across society and is made up of unrelated families that have more or less equal access to income and prestige. The larger and more complex a society is, the more likely it is to distinguish between the holders of various statuses on the basis of a system of ranked classes. Sometimes class membership is determined by birth and the statuses that individuals may hold during their lifetimes are limited to those of the class into which they are born. In such a case, when people are not permitted to move from one formally demarcated class to another by acquiring a new status, the classes are called castes.

Caste in India

Caste in India has been described by many anthropologists, including Beals (1974, 1980), Dumont (1978), Kolanda (1978), and Mandelbaum (1972). The system of organizing people socially by grouping them into castes is an ancient practice that is couched in religious concepts. The system of castes is complex

Figure 4.3 *Caste*
The caste system in India is a complex social and religious system of ordering the members of its society. The highest rank is the Brahmin caste and the lowest, the Sudra. Beneath these are the Untouchables, not considered a part of the caste system.

and differs somewhat in various parts of India. In simplified terms there are four major kinds of castes. The first of these, the Brahmin caste, is ranked highest in ritual purity and closeness to God. Members of this caste are priests in theory, although in fact most practice other occupations. Socially, members of the Brahmin caste are accorded greater honor than are those of the lower castes even though they have less power and wealth than many members of other castes. The Kshatriya—warrior-rulers, nobles, and landowners—are next in honor. They are thought to be less ritually pure than the Brahmins and are subject to fewer dietary and ritual restrictions than the priestly class. Next come the Vaisya, the commoners, and, finally, the Sudra,

who are the farm artisans, servants, farmers, and laborers. Below all these are the people of no caste, the so-called Untouchables who perform the ritually polluted tasks of life such as removing dead cattle from the village, tanning hides, working leather, and removing human waste.

Although Indian society accords greater honor to the higher castes, it does not link freedom with this honor. Members of the higher castes are hedged about by various restrictions, most notably dietary restrictions. The Brahmins and Vaisya are expected to be strict vegetarians, although the Kshatriya may eat goat, considered a relatively clean animal, and may drink liquor. The Sudra may eat chicken (a less pure animal) as well as goat, and the Untouchables may eat any meat, including beef and pork. The members of higher castes also are expected to avoid physical contact with the members of lower castes in varying degrees.

Within each caste there are many occupational subcastes or jatis that are also ranked by ritual purity. Members of each jati have rights over and responsibilities to the members of other jatis. For instance, potters of the artisan class are expected to make pottery for the farmers, while the farmer is expected to present the potter with a traditional portion of his harvest. The relations between the jatis are most noticeable when a ritual is performed. For instance, Brahmins must officiate, using bowls made by the Potter jati and wearing clothes provided by the Weaver jati and washed by the Washer jati. Such rituals portray the interdependence of the various jatis and reassert the rights of each jati to belong to the community, since all public rituals require the cooperation of all jatis involved. In everyday economic life, few people in modern India actually make their living on the basis of their jati occupation. Washers often do so, and a local artisan may provide services in return for a portion of the harvest. However, many people may provide services for a fee or follow an occupation different from their traditional jati occupation, since most jatis have more members than are necessary for performing the service. Thus, jati occupations represent a system of ritual rather than economic ranking.

Hostilities sometimes arise within the system because the different castes have access to different amounts of honor, power, and wealth. The Hindu religious ideology helps to minimize these conflicts by asserting that individuals who conform well to the rules that govern their position in life will be rewarded by future rebirth into a higher caste. By accepting the caste system and following its rules, one may eventually attain a sufficient spiritual development to avoid being reborn into the world and

its misery. Those who rebel against the rules of caste purity will be reborn at a lower position, thereby prolonging the cycles of reincarnation and human suffering.

In socially less complex societies, statuses are not ranked into complex hierarchies, but a given status may outrank others. For instance, a person may be the best basketmaker or the chief hunter, the firstborn child, the head of the largest family, or the spokesperson for the group. However, widely differing statuses are not ranked with respect to one another as they are in all industrialized societies.

Contextual Cues

No matter how simple or complex a society, each of its members will hold more than one status. Each role of each status has a particular situation in which its manifestation is considered appropriate. In other words, people learn to play each of their numerous roles as they are directed by culturally defined contextual cues. These contextual cues might be the location in which the actors find themselves, the date and time of day, or the statuses of other persons who are present. Thus, in the United States and Canada, holders of the status of student who find themselves in the context of a classroom during a scheduled class meeting time are expected to play one of their student roles that is appropriate to that set of cues. Elsewhere, students may continue to relate to a teacher through another of their student-appropriate roles, but one that is more appropriate to the nonclassroom setting. When the teacher leaves, their behavior may shift radically as they begin to play the roles of entirely different statuses.

Sometimes conflicting contextual cues occur in the same situation, calling for behaviors appropriate to different statuses. In such circumstances, depending on how different those statuses are from one another, the individual may experience an extreme degree of psychological disorientation and confusion technically called role conflict. For instance, the first time a newly married couple is visited by their parents in the couple's home, a degree of awkward-

Figure 4.4 *Master Status*
Certain social conditions change the usual pattern of determining status. In the situation above, the pimp at the right displays a master status to his prostitute.

ness may arise when the young couple attempt to play the role of heads of household in the presence of their parents, who have previously had a monopoly over that superior status.

Master Statuses

The usual pattern in which the setting determines which of a person's statuses may be manifested is violated by a few unusual statuses, called master statuses. Master statuses are those that are so strongly imbued with importance in the minds of people that it is difficult to forget or ignore them, even in situations where they are not the most appropriate statuses for their bearers to manifest. Either the status in question is so highly valued by others that it outshines its holder's other statuses or it elicits such a negative valuation that it overshadows its

possessor's other more positively valued statuses. Thus, a master status may be said to carry its own context with it. If the Chief Justice of the United States Supreme Court were to appear in a college classroom on a parents' visiting day, this visitor would not be treated as just another parent in the audience. More likely, instead of the situation's defining the status of the visitor, the situation itself would be redefined to fit the visitor's master status, and the classroom hour would be radically altered.

When people's statuses have significantly different degrees of rank, they will tend to adopt the highest status that is appropriate to the situation. The greater the importance that ranking has in a society, the more its members will attempt, wherever possible, to avoid appearing in roles of subordinate statuses. The exception to this rule is that a person who is very clearly of a high master status, such as a senator or a Nobel Prize winner, may play the role of a much lower status as a way of showing respect for his or her subordinates. United States presidents have been photographed in their shirt sleeves on tractors, and Diana, Princess of Wales, has driven a tank while visiting a British military base as ways of "humanizing" themselves in the public eye.

Another category of people who may not follow the usual pattern of adopting the highest status appropriate to the situation is those with low-ranked master statuses. They may have formally acquired other more highly ranked statuses, but their master statuses bar them from access to a higher degree of social power. Because of their lack of social honor and power, the master statuses of low social rank are sometimes given the special designation of minority statuses. Minority statuses of the United States society include such ascribed statuses as female, black, Chicano, or Native American, and achieved statuses such as drug addict, prostitute, ex-convict, physically handicapped person, or mental patient.

Even though these statuses are commonly called minority groups, the minority status is not a matter of numbers. In the United States, for instance, females make up slightly more than 50% of the population, and blacks constitute large numerical majorities in many cities and counties. Yet, irrespective of numbers, birth into either of these statuses may bar acquisition and successful use of highly ranked social statuses. Thus, women currently hold only about 8% of elective offices in a society in which they compose over half of the total population, and adult black males in the United States suffer from an unemployment rate that is twice the unemployment rate of the adult male work force as a whole.

The Education of Dr. Poussaint: A Study in Master Status[2]

Alvin Poussaint, a black psychiatrist, has given a powerful account of the black experience in a white-dominated

2. From "A Negro Psychiatrist Explains the Negro Psyche" by Alvin F. Poussaint, August 20, 1967, *The New York Times*, pp. 52–53, 80.

society. The following passage illustrates that despite his professional status, in the 1960s his master status as a black in the United States sometimes called forth strong expectations that he should adopt a subordinate role in interacting with whites.

Once last year as I was leaving my office in Jackson, Miss., with my Negro secretary, a white policeman yelled, "Hey, boy! Come here!" Somewhat bothered, I retorted: "I'm no boy!" He then rushed at me, inflamed, and stood towering over me, snorting, "What d'ja say, boy?" Quickly he frisked me and demanded, "What's your name, boy?" Frightened, I replied, "Dr. Poussaint; I'm a physician." He angrily chuckled and hissed, "What's your first name, boy?" When I hesitated he assumed a threatening stance and clenched his fists. As my heart palpitated, I muttered in profound humiliation, "Alvin."

He continued his psychological brutality, bellowing, "Alvin, the next time I call you, you come right away, you hear? You hear?" I hesitated. "You hear me, boy?" My voice trembling with helplessness, but following my instincts of self-preservation, I murmured, "Yes, sir." Now fully satisfied that I had performed and acquiesced to my "boy" status, he dismissed me with, "Now boy, go on and get out of here or next time we'll take you for a little ride down to the station house!" (p. 53)

Biological Traits and Social Statuses

In every human society, some of the statuses that people hold are assigned on the basis of biological facts. Factors such as sex, degree of biological maturation, physiological handicap, or skin color have been commonly used as the grounds for assigning statuses and role expectations.

Statuses Based on Biological Distinctions

In all human societies that have been studied by anthropologists, the physiological differences between males and females have been the basis for expecting individuals to adopt life-work and ways of acting thought to be appropriate to their gender. For instance, in the simplest and oldest form of human society, survival is based on the search for nondomesticated foods. In such societies, the status of hunter is commonly assigned to the males of the group, while the gatherers of wild vegetable foods are usually females.

Similarly, all human societies have used differences in the biological aging process to place individuals into different statuses. Everywhere, social distinctions involving different behavioral expectations, rights, and responsibilities have been made between infants, children, adults, and the aged.

The blind, deaf, mentally retarded, and other individuals considered to have unusual physiological characteristics are also often set apart in status. They may be expected to behave differently from other people because of these characteristics, even if their biological characteristics might not force them to do so.

In many societies today, racial differences are also used as an important fact of social life, and persons may be categorized and given different statuses on the basis of race. Holders of these different racial statuses may then be expected to play vastly different roles from one another. The behavioral expectations that are placed on them may be highly arbitrary, with no basis in the actual physiological characteristics that differentiate the status holders.

Innate Differences vs. Socially Learned Roles

We humans may differ from one another in behavioral capacities or generalized tendencies, such as activity level, aggressiveness, or responsiveness to stimuli. Such differences are present when we are born and may result from biologically inherited hormonal and neurological factors. However, social roles are not inherited biologically. As cultural phenomena, social roles are learned. Our inborn predispositions may influence the style with which we play

a role, but they do not determine the content of our roles.

The roles that we learn to play, even those that are expected of us on the basis of our biological characteristics, depend on the statuses assigned to us. So, although we may be given a status on the basis of our biological characteristics, the roles that we must learn as holders of that status may involve qualities that would not otherwise result from those biological facts. Because a role is a cultural phenomenon, it need not reflect biological facts. For instance, an active female child may be subject to intensive social training that leads her to conform to a more passive and nonaggressive role because her society considers these traits attributes of the female status. Similarly, Scott (1969) has described an interesting process by which persons with poor vision may acquire the status of blind persons. Having been labeled blind by legal criteria, such persons may begin to interact with various care-giving agencies. In the process of providing their services, these agencies may unwittingly encourage their poorly sighted clients to learn to perceive themselves as helpless. Learning to play the blind role inhibits the use of what vision the clients actually possess.

When statuses are assigned to people because of biological characteristics, the role that they are expected to play commonly comes to be thought of as a natural and inherent result of those biological conditions. In societies where men hold the powerful statuses, the culture is apt to contain beliefs that men are somehow naturally more dominant than women. Where one racial group dominates another in the same society, the race whose members tend to hold the more highly ranked statuses will generally be described as inherent leaders, while the subordinate race will be commonly portrayed as naturally lazy, less intelligent, and in need of guidance. This practice of attributing differences in role expectations to the supposed biologically inherited qualities is especially widespread in views commonly held in many parts of the world about racial and sexual differences. The belief that differences in the role expectations of members of different racial groups are actually hereditary characteristics is known as racism. The case in which role differences between women and men are held to be biologically caused has a parallel name, sexism.

Racial Inequality

Race is a social concept rather than a clear biological distinction. As a socially designated status in most countries, it is often rationalized as a biological category but in ways that are scientifically unjustifiable.

Belief in Distinct Races

The ideologies of many societies include the idea that the human species contains distinct biological subdivisions called races. Although some scientists who are interested in the biological diversity within our species also use the concept of race, the popular idea of races incorrectly views them as discrete subdivisions of humankind that have little overlap with one another in their biological traits. Scientific studies of human diversity actually reveal something quite different: *Homo sapiens* is a species in which great diversity exists in every local group and in which the frequencies of traits vary gradually from region to region across the face of the earth. Furthermore, the peoples who originally occupied different regions of the earth—such as Subsaharan Africa, Europe, the Orient, Australia, and the Americas—differ from one another in only 0.2% of their genetically inherited traits. Thus, the so-called "races" referred to by popular culture are not nearly so different from each other as people imagine.

Throughout most of history, people interacted only with neighbors who differed little in their average biological characteristics. Even if their cultures differed radically, their different statuses were not likely to be defined in biological terms. Thus, in early times the status of a nonmember of one's own society was more likely to be framed as a nonbiological concept such as *foreigner* or *stranger*. Those who held such statuses might be treated ethnocentrically as social inferiors and be expected to play an inferior role. But it was not until the peoples of distant parts of the world began

to interact that the idea of race became a common way of maintaining social contrasts between peoples.

The belief that humankind is divided into several major races began during the age of European colonial expansion. Travel to far-flung parts of the world brought people together from places where the most frequently observable biological traits such as skin color or hair texture differed enough to be readily noted by the travelers. These contrasts were the basis for creating racial statuses when the political need arose. An ideology that distinguishes one "race" from another and thereby creates separate racial statuses implies the expectation that the different "races" will play different social roles. The purpose of colonial expansion was not to discover people of foreign lands and treat them identically to members of the colonialists' homeland. Colonial expansion was undertaken to obtain economic and political benefits for the homeland. Expecting members of the colonized societies to play different roles from the colonizers supported this goal. The racial ideology helped to maintain the distinction between "us" and "them."

The criteria by which "races" are defined vary from culture to culture. Usually, the criteria are easily observable traits such as skin color, the shape of facial features, hair color and texture, or body stature. Less observable traits such as blood type would not allow quick and easy decisions about what social roles should be played between people. In North America, skin color and hair texture are the most powerful determinants of the "race" to which one will be thought to belong. In Bolivia, on the other hand, nonbiological facts such as clothing and dialect or accent may greatly influence other people's beliefs about one's "race."

In societies where the concept of race exists, the ideology may recognize as few as two socially relevant racial categories. In other societies a multitude of different racial subdivisions may exist. How individuals are racially categorized in any given culture is a matter of social consensus. Where race is a concept, people are often dealt with on the basis of the qualities that are culturally attributed to their race instead of the qual-

tal needs such as supporting the political and economic goals of various segments of society.

Racial discrimination. Racism goes a step beyond the mere belief that different races exist. Racial discrimination states that people of different ''races'' differ in behavioral abilities and that they therefore should play different social roles. The differences in those roles, of course, generally reflect the ethnocentric prejudices of the racist, the superior roles being reserved for those who belong to the racist's group.

The racist approach to describing the races of a society is predicated on a confusion of biological heredity with the learning of culturally assigned roles. In the United States, nearly everyone has heard such racist stereotypes as ''White people are natural leaders,'' ''Blacks are natural athletes and have rhythm in their blood,'' and ''Jews are born businessmen.'' The continued existence of such stereotypes that contend that certain ways of acting are inherited through one's biological race readily supports a society's ongoing practice of treating the holders of different racial statuses in different ways.

Such publicly held racist ideas tend to inhibit social change by supporting current discriminatory policies. Even the so-called minority groups may use racist stereotypes—''Whites are naturally racist''—to gain more power by uniting members of their group in opposition to the status quo. Racism of this type also serves as political leverage when applied against the guilt that many people of the dominant status groups feel about the inequitable past treatment of minority groups.

Whether serving the values of the dominant or subordinate members of a society, racist stereotypes are frequently based on the prejudices of the group that is doing the labeling and may be highly inaccurate. For instance, when Jackie Robinson was attempting to become the first black to enter major league baseball in the United States, newspaper editorials throughout the country contended that to allow blacks to play in the major league teams would lower the quality of the game. In that day, blacks were regarded as naturally inferior athletes. Now

Figure 4.5 *Racial Discrimination*
In the Republic of South Africa, Apartheid became official State policy when the National Party took power in 1948. A ruling coalition of Dutch-speaking Afrikaaners and English-speaking Europeans allowed the meetings of whites for political purposes, but denied those of nonwhites.

ities that they possess as individuals. The prevalent racist stereotypes thus help to maintain the current way of organizing people and of distributing power within societies.

Racism

Any definition of race that fails to distinguish the great difference between biological structure and its genetic inheritance on the one hand and the functioning of an individual within the constraints of a symbolically learned social role on the other cannot be expected to provide valid insight into the real nature of human beings. Defining a race in ways that include culturally defined role expectations as if they were a part of the biological attributes of the group is given the special name of racism. Though inaccurate and demeaning, racism has evolved because it serves a variety of socie-

77

Figure 4.6 *Slavery*
This engraving from a drawing by Matt Morgan, 1887, portrays the exploitation of blacks by plantation owners. In exchange for work the slaves were given food, shelter, and the supposed benefits of a superior white culture.

that it has become commonplace for blacks to be recruited to professional sports, one is more likely to hear the equally racist idea that blacks are inherently superior athletes.

Slavery and racist views.   In ancient times, peoples who had alien customs and values were often condemned by ethnocentric standards as "outsiders." But the most common intergroup rivalries were between neighboring peoples who differed more in customs than in physical appearance, and ethnocentric epithets were a more handy symbolic weapon under such circumstances. Use of racism has been primarily a modern phenomenon. The modern racist way of reacting to "outsiders" by claiming that they are biologically inferior, unable to learn the "superior" customs of the racist's own group, came into existence as a way

of protecting the eighteenth- and nineteenth-century institution of slavery when voices began to speak out against it. Defenders of slavery even claimed the institution was divinely willed. For example, in 1772 the Reverend Thomas Thompson published a work entitled *The Trade in Negro Slaves on the African Coast in Accordance with Humane Principles, and With the Laws of Revealed Religion*, and in 1852 the Reverend Josiah Priest published *A Bible Defense of Slavery*.

When use of Africans as slaves began in the United States, there was little need to justify it with racist arguments. Ethnocentric values sufficed more commonly as rationales for the institution. Slave owners could claim that their slaves were better off as slaves than as free persons in their own allegedly inferior cultures. It was supposed that they had been given the chance to learn a superior way of life, higher moral values, the true religion, and a more enlightened way of thinking, in addition to enjoying a higher standard of living, better medical knowledge, and a longer life expectancy than if they had been permitted to remain in their former supposedly savage state. It could also be contended by the ethnocentrist that one could not simply discharge a slave after a few years of service because releasing a slave to his or her own devices in a complex society would be ''inhumane.'' According to this argument, the complexity of the ''superior way of life'' would be more than a person taken into slavery as an adult could learn to cope with. Olmsted (1904) quotes one Alabama farmer who shortly after the Civil War said:

> It wouldn't do no good to free 'em, and let 'em hang 'round, because they is so monstrous lazy; if they hadn't got nobody to take keer on 'em, you see they wouldn't do nothin' but juss nat'rally laze 'round, and steal, and pilfer, and no man couldn't live, you see, war they was—if they was free, no man couldn't live. (pp. 218–219)

By this argument, it was the slaveholders' burden to take care of these ''innocents'' the rest of their lives in order that they might enjoy the benefits of a superior civilization while being protected from the dangers of making their own way as free but naive persons. And, of course, it was only fair—so the argument ran—for them to work for the ''benefactors'' in return for these acts of ''kindness.''

Ethnocentric rationales such as the foregoing are not so useful when applied to the second generation of slaves. If a slave's children are exposed from infancy on to the way of life of the slave owner, this second generation of slaves cannot be described as any less aware of how to live ''properly'' than any other member of the society unless one adds a new rationale to the old ethnocentric one. The new rationale is the racist contention that something ''in the blood'' of the enslaved peoples makes them incapable of adequately learning the ''superior'' way of life. To continue to rationalize slavery into the second and third generations, the slave-owning group had to

develop the view that the group they held in bondage was somewhat inferior in that its members were genetically unable to learn the new way of life adequately to participate on an equal footing in a ''civilized'' society.

With this change from a simple ethnocentric argument to a concept of an inherent incapacity of some nonwhite ''races,'' the old claim took on an even stronger aura of inevitability. Although the old institution of slavery no longer may be used as the vehicle for the domination of one group by another, the concept of differences in the capacities of different ''races'' lives on as a rationale for the dominance of one culture over another or of one segment of a society over its other members. The following excerpt from Putnam (1967) is a contemporary example of this kind of thinking, which denies any merit to indigenous, long-lived nonindustrial cultures or any capacity for intelligent self-government to their peoples:

> The dissolution of the colonial system among backward peoples throughout the world, which the United States has done so much to encourage and which had produced such growing confusion and violence, stemmed from the assumption that these peoples had the innate capacity to maintain stable, free societies. . . .
> Running away from reality was not kindness. Wrecking time-tested colonial systems of control among backward peoples and substituting systems which produced increasing misery and bloodshed were not acts of brotherhood. (pp. 6–7)

Rationalizing social inequality. The racist way of looking at human differences fits the traditional Western tendency to portray the primary causes of human behavior as being traits that lie within the person. Such inner traits include willpower, determination, ego, inborn potentials, capacities, and the like. This tradition has made it difficult to convince many people of the value in viewing behavior as being controlled by cultural factors that are outside the person. So the racist view was readily adopted by Western society at large, especially by those who had a vested interest in maintaining the existing social structure. Racist thinking served as a way of rationalizing the inequalities from which the dominant members of society were benefiting. The pseudoscientific language of the racist lent an aura of propriety to the inequities that existed within the social machinery. Within the context of a racist ideology, unequal treatment of social minorities could be perceived as the result rather than the cause of the differences between the various segments of the society. Being an effective way of supporting the status quo, the racist approach to explaining human behavior became such a common way of reacting to human behavior differences that it remains unquestioned by large segments of society today, two centuries after it originated.

Racism has become so deeply rooted in many societies' basic assumptions about human nature that many rationales have developed that make it easy for well-intentioned people to accept racist beliefs, even though they feel no ill will toward members of other races. Customs based on racist beliefs, as we will see later, may have devastating effects, however, even when they are not directly motivated by racial prejudices.

Early European biological scientists and other scholars were given to expressing the ethnocentrism of the day in the veiled form of racist descriptions when they examined the human species. Carolus Linnaeus (1758) was the author of an eighteenth-century classification of the animal world that was so carefully done that it remains the basic system used even today by biologists. Yet, his description of the human species is an excellent example of how an otherwise careful and methodical analysis can become biased by ethnocentric prejudices in studying one's own species. In Linnaeus's classification of the human races, the "European race" was described not only in such biological terms as "white, ruddy-complexioned, muscular, blue-eyed, and yellow-haired," but also in behavioral terms such as "governed by rites." Thus, Linnaeus's classification of the human species is not simply a biological classification but a racist one as well. That his racist contentions about the human species were guid-

ed by his European ethnocentrism is clear in his behavioral characterization of the "Asiatic race" as "governed by opinion" and the "African race" as "governed by whim."

The same kinds of pseudoscientific characterizations have continued to be found in publications of apparently educated Western writers. For instance, Charles Ellwood (1931), a past president of the American Sociological Association and the author of a once-popular sociology text, *Sociology and Modern Social Problems*, wrote in that text concerning the racial heredity of blacks:

> The African environment of the ancestors of the present negroes in the United States deeply stamped itself upon the mental traits and tendencies of the race. For example, the tropical environment is generally unfavorable to severe bodily labor. Persons who work hard in the tropics are, in other words, apt to be eliminated by natural selection. On the other hand, nature furnishes a bountiful supply of food without much labor. Hence, the tropical environment of the negro failed to develop in him any instinct to work, but favored the survival of those naturally shiftless and lazy. Again, the extremely high death rate in Africa necessitated a correspondingly high birth rate in order that any race living there might survive: hence, nature fixed in the negro strong sexual propensities in order to secure such a high birth rate. (pp. 233-234)

The clothing of public prejudices in the pseudoscientific language of racism lent the weight of scientific prestige to biases that supported discriminatory hiring policies that commonly denied blacks access to any but supervised laboring occupations. It also reinforced the whites' desire to maintain social segregation of blacks and whites.

More recently, Arthur Jensen (1969), a prominent American educational psychologist, presented a carefully worded but controversial argument that biological inheritance is more important than environmental experiences as a determinant of human behavior. Jensen contended that human intelligence has a substantial genetic component and that race governs intellectual capacities as well as other biologically inherited traits. Thus, the concept that the ability to live successfully in a society may differ from race to race on the basis of biological heredity is not simply an idea of historical interest. On the contrary, it is still espoused strongly by persons of influence today.

Legalized racial distinctions. Often the racism of the politically dominant segments of a society receives official sanction through legislation. Since the politically dominant segments of the United States generally have been composed of whites, laws about supposed racial differences have often been prejudiced by ethnocentrism that was flattering to whites. The "white way of life"—that is, northern European-based, industrialized, capitalistic culture—was assumed to be the superior way of living and therefore the most deserving of protection by law. Insofar as the ability to participate in a way of life was thought to be "in our blood," it followed that the most effective way of preserving the "white civilization" would be to maintain as much separation of the races as possible. Thus, over three quarters of the states in the United States eventually passed laws prohibiting interracial marriages. That is, those of nonwhite racial statuses were forbidden to marry whites, although nonwhite races were not consistently forbidden to intermarry with one another. Nineteen states still had such laws in 1968, when they were struck down by the Supreme Court of the United States as unconstitutional.

A contemporary example of a society built on the principle of racial segregation is the Republic of South Africa, a nation in which the force of law maintains barriers that prevent a nonwhite majority from achieving social equality with the dominant white minority. South African law recognizes the existence of four "races": Whites, Africans, Coloureds, and Asians. Whites are those of European ancestry, mostly descendants of Dutch Boers and English settlers. Africans are native African blacks. Asians are people of Indian descent whose ancestors came to South Africa in the nineteenth century. Coloureds are peoples of mixed descent. Africans make up over 71% of the population but lack voting rights that would give them a corresponding influence over

Figure 4.7 *Apartheid*
Apartheid is a policy of political and economic discrimination against non-Europeans in South Africa. The white ruling class has made the tyranny of racism legal for many years and is gaining worldwide attention for its unjust practices.

the government. The government defines Africans as citizens of various Homelands, reserves that have been set aside for their occupation. South African cities, on the other hand, are set apart by law for white residents only. Nonwhite laborers who work in the cities reside in Townships located outside the cities. Although whites represent only 16% of the population, they receive by far the greatest social benefits. For instance, while the African unemployment rate may be as high as 30%, White unemployment is below 10%. This is partly because the white-dominated government is the single largest employer of whites, 40% of whom work for the bureaucracy. Thus, through control of the government, South African whites maintain a system of political and economic privilege based on race. Until recently the rigid separation of the "races" has been maintained by laws forbidding interracial marriages, the legal requirement of segregated residence, separate systems of education, and unequal voting rights. These barriers to social equality between the races are beginning to be eroded, but it is unclear whether the South African government will be able to achieve a peaceful resolution of the conflicts that stem from growing dissatisfaction among both nonwhites and whites for the racially elitist system under which they have lived in the past.

Germany under Nazi rule is another example of the extremes to which a racist ideology can lead. In the name of purifying the Aryan "race," Hitler's regime systematically exterminated about six million Jews and other peoples of southern and eastern European ancestry. In fact, ideas of racial purity are no more than myths. Neighboring human groups are constantly exchanging genes through intermating, and no human groups are really isolated from their neighbors, even when rigid taboos exist against mating between the groups. It has been estimated by Stuckert (1966) that approximately 23% of persons classified as white in the United States in 1960 had at least one ancestor of African origin. Truly separate races in the sense of really distinct and biologically pure strains have never developed in the human species. Perhaps the tenacity of the idea of racial purity in spite of these facts is due to the role that myth plays in lending validity to the economic and social segregation of people on the basis of race, a practice that helps to perpetuate control by those of the dominant social statuses.

Economic and political roots of racism. That such social applications of racism have consistently represented nonscientific and arbitrary judgments that serve the changing, often ethnocentric values of society is evidenced by three scientifically untenable characteristics of these racist standards. First, standards of racial classification have been highly arbitrary in biological terms; rather, they are socially directed to supporting the supposed "purity" of the dominant group. For instance, in the United States, anyone who admits having even one black ancestor is commonly classified by others and treated socially as a black—regardless

of physical appearance. It would be just as logical to classify someone who has a small proportion of "white blood" as a white. But the function of racial classification in the United States has been to deny economic and political power and honor to those of other than northern European ancestry.

The second major evidence that racism, far from being scientific, grows out of the predominant social values of the day is that racist ideas about the behavioral tendencies of the "races" change with the shifting winds of public and political sentiment. Thus, in the United States of 1935, the Japanese "race" was commonly viewed as progressive, intelligent, and industrious. Only seven years later, in 1942, the Japanese were widely viewed as an inherently cunning and treacherous "race." In 1950, as political allies of the United States, they once again became "progressive by nature"! Similarly, when there was a labor shortage in California during the construction of the transcontinental railway line, the Chinese who provided cheap labor were described as a frugal, sober, law-abiding "race." Then, when competition for jobs became severe and it became economically desirable to exclude further immigration of Chinese laborers, the Chinese "race" suddenly became described as dirty, unassimilable, and even dangerous.

A third evidence that the racist approach to human differences is the handmaiden of societal rather than scientific values is the double standard commonly used by racists when evaluating different social groups. For instance, when two groups of white children differ in IQ scores, the explanation of the difference is commonly sought in factors such as differences in the quality of their schooling, in their social environments, or in the socioeconomic positions of their parents. But when minorities and whites differ from one another in precisely the same way, it is apt to be labeled as a "racial difference."

The racist approach has consistently failed to be of any scientific value. On the contrary, it supports social prejudices by claiming that socially created group differences are biologically determined and therefore unchangeable. Such an argument provides a rationale for people to oppose attempts to change the current limitations in access to social prestige and political and economic power on the basis of race. For that reason, the racist argument has persisted for several centuries, even though it has never proven itself to be of any scientific value in explaining human social difference.

Economic and health costs of racism. Maintenance of different ways of treating the socially designated races is not without its cost. Consider this example based on information from the *Statistical Abstract of the United States 1969* and *Statistical Abstract of the United States 1986* (U.S. Department of Commerce, 1969 and 1986): In 1900, the life expectancy of males classified as white in the United States was 150% that of males classified as black! The difference can be attributed to a higher infant mortality rate among blacks, a differential access to adequate medical treatment and hospital facilities, and the debilitating effects of the lower-class jobs available to black men. By 1940, the gap had closed somewhat with a general rise in the standard of living, but the white male population could still look forward to an average of 10 more years of life than was available to the black male population. By 1981, the white male life expectancy reached 71.1 years, 6.7 years more than that of black males. Thus, in effect, in every generation of 71.1 years, 6.7 years of life were denied to the 12.6 million United States males classified as black, an equivalent of 84,500,000 years of human life wasted needlessly. If the method of racial discrimination were death by execution rather than barriers to health and wealth, approximately 22,384 18-year-old black men would have to be executed each year to depress the overall life expectancy of the black male population of the United States as much as actual discriminatory conditions of life seem to have been doing as of 1981.

Effects such as these take their toll on other groups as well. For instance, Native Americans today are so culturally disenfranchized in the United States that three quarters of this group have incomes below the officially designated poverty level. The Native American unemployment rate is about 50%; on the average, Native American life expectancy is only about 63 years.

It is in effects such as the lowered life expectancies and living standards among those who hold minority racial statuses that racism makes itself felt in its most harmful way. To those who feel its effects, even more abhorrent than ethnocentrism or racial prejudice is the fact that these attitudes may become the basis of social policies, supported by the weight of law or custom, that perpetuate arbitrary and harmful inequalities between peoples. Great harm may be done even without any outward show of prejudice or violence.

Race, Cultural Ability, and Intelligence

Discriminatory treatment of socially defined "racial" groups is rationalized by the racist idea that the different races are biologically endowed with different cultural abilities. Yet there is no scientific evidence that any racial group is superior or inferior to any other in its innate cultural abilities. Neither is there any evidence of racial differences in individuals' abilities to learn and adequately participate in any cultural system when they are given an equal opportunity to learn the necessary skills.

Anthropological researchers who have studied human lifeways around the world have reported again and again that biological differences seem to be no barrier to sharing a way of life. They report that common ways of living, customs, and values are sometimes spread over regions occupied by peoples of different biological backgrounds. Such research has yielded no evidence that the different races are any less equipped to carry on a way of life so long as society does not use the concept of race as a criterion for abridging education, rights, or access to high-ranked occupation. How people go about their lives is determined by their experiences in life and their opportunities to implement that experience. A child of British parentage whisked away at birth and raised by adoptive Asian foster parents will learn and value the customs of his or her Asian peers and speak an Asiatic language with the same accent as his or her Asian playmates. Nothing in the racial biology of such a child would impel him or her to value the British political system or to speak with a British accent.

Yet the argument continues to arise that some races are inherently less capable of full participation in a particular society. Indigenous peoples of desert areas might conclude that other peoples are biologically incapable of using their sense of smell to locate water, since they cannot. In the United States, the form of logical thought that is measured by intelligence tests is a highly valued social skill, and much has been made of the fact that some "races" seem to score higher on these tests than others. There is a difference of approximately 15 points between the average IQ (intelligence quotient) scores of blacks and whites on most tests of intellectual skills commonly used in the United States. In this section, we will look closely at nonbiological factors that may influence these test scores, including differences in education, language, socioeconomic background, and motivation, and cultural biases in the tests themselves.

Educational Effects on IQ Scores

Most people cannot smell fresh water from a distance because their society has not trained them to do so. They have not learned to develop a sensitivity to the scents of plants and trees that grow near water. Similarly, performance on IQ tests is strongly influenced by cultural training.

In the United States persons are socially categorized by their "race," and holders of these socially designated racial statuses have different life experiences, including differences in the quality of the schools that are available to them. Blacks in some northern states score higher on IQ tests than do whites in some southern states, a fact that correlates with the amount of education received by residents of these states and with other socioeconomic differences between them. This was first shown during World War I, when the United States Army carried out a massive intelligence testing program of personnel from many civilian backgrounds (see Kroeber, 1948). In such cases, a white racist is likely to concede that the difference between the groups is best

understood as an environmentally influenced one. But contributing environmental factors such as education differences are disregarded in racist interpretations of tests in which their own group does better than others. In general, the educational opportunities for people of African heritage in the United States have been inferior to those available to people of northern European descent. To ignore this fact when evaluating differences in the performance of these groups on intelligence tests is scientifically indefensible.

Contrary to popular belief, an individual's IQ score is far from a stable measure of an unchanging trait. Several studies have demonstrated that environmental factors are able to affect IQ scores by much more than 15 points in individual cases. In one study of 12-year-old New York City black school children, most of who had come from southern states, it was found that those children who had lived in New York City for more than seven years scored 20 points higher on IQ tests than those who had lived in the city for two years or less (Downs & Bleibtreu, 1972). It has also been demonstrated that our IQ continues to rise while we attend school and begins to decline again when we leave the academic setting. The school environment keeps students actively engaged in the use of precisely those skills that are called on when they take an intelligence test. A group's average IQ score is therefore influenced by the quality and length of its education, both of which factors differ for socially designated racial groups in the United States.

Language Effects on IQ Scores

Language or dialect differences may be another important variable affecting the average intelligence test scores of different groups. The effect of language on intelligence test scores is easy to understand, since such examinations may test one's knowledge of such language traits as spelling and grammar. However, even when these are not the specific topics examined in such tests, the taking of intelligence tests also requires the use of language skills by the individual to read any written instructions or questions. It is only to be expected that immigrants to any country would perform poorly on such tests, regardless of race.

The Ellis Island Project: A Study in the Misuse of Intelligence Tests

In 1913, Henry H. Goddard (1913, 1917; see also Chase, 1977) a psychologist who believed that "social diseases" such as immorality, criminality, and insanity were biologically inherited, carried out a research project for the United States Public Health Service on Ellis Island. After testing the ability of European immigrants who were entering the United States through Ellis Island, he reported that there was an especially high incidence of "feeble-mindedness" among Southern and Eastern European immigrants. For instance, he contended that 87% of the Russian immigrants, 83% of the Jews, 80% of the Hungarians, and 79% of the Italians were feeble-minded! Since it was believed that these immigrants' inability to score well on these tests would be inherited by their descendants, admitting them to the United States was considered potentially dangerous. As a result, in following years there was a great increase in the deportation of immigrants who scored poorly on intelligence tests.

Incredible as it may seem today, these judgments—and the policy decisions that were affected by them—were made on the basis of English-language tests, administered orally through an interpreter. Goddard assumed that immigration officials would already have prevented the most obviously mentally defective from entering the United States. Therefore, to evaluate the intelligence of the European peoples in question, he purposely had his assistants pick out and test people who appeared to them to be "feeble-minded," to make up for those who already would have been culled out by immigration officials. The immigrants who were so tested were not even a random sample of all immigrants but were selected from those who arrived by third-class passage, most of whom had little or no formal education. The effects of such testing methods are aptly portrayed in the words of Stephen Jay Gould (1981):

> Consider a group of frightened men and women who speak no English and who have just endured an oceanic voyage in steerage. Most are poor and have never gone to school; many have never held a pencil or pen in their hand. They march off the boat; one of Goddard's intuitive women takes them aside shortly thereafter, sits them down, hands them a pencil, and asks them to reproduce on paper a figure shown to them a moment ago, but now withdrawn from their sight. Could their failure be a result of testing conditions, of weakness, fear, or confusion, rather than of innate stupidity? Goddard did not think so. Incredibly, he attributed the low scores of these immigrants to a biological deficit in their intellectual capacities rather than to problems in the testing procedures.

Chandler and Plakos (1969) clearly demonstrated the language bias in intelligence testing in one California school district by reevaluating the intelligence test scores of its Spanish-speaking children with a Spanish-language intelligence test. Most of the children who had previously been classified as "educable mentally retarded" on the basis of the earlier English-language tests achieved a normal score, and some of them achieved above-average scores. In the United States, the centuries of social segregation of blacks from whites has led to the development of a distinctive Black English dialect that differs greatly from the Standard American English dialect that is rewarded with high grades in schools and invariably used in tests of intelligence. Since the Standard American English has much more in common with the dialects spoken by most whites than it does with the Black English dialect, there is a strong linguistic bias against black students built into intelligence tests used today.

Social Background and IQ Scores

Holders of different racial statuses in the United States also have had unequal oppor-

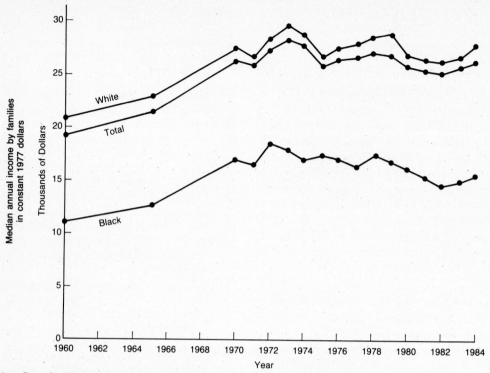

Note. From *Statistical Abstract of the United States: 1979* p. 436, by U.S. Bureau of the Census.

Figure 4.8 *U.S. Socioeconomic Status by Race*
Racial groups in the U.S. have a different rank status in social position and occupation due to such factors as language bias which influence learning, IQ scores and opportunities for advancement.

tunities to achieve highly valued social positions and high-income occupations. As a result, races are socially and economically stratified in the United States. According to the United States Bureau of the Census, whites possess a disproportionate share of the higher socioeconomic statuses and nonwhites are disproportionately relegated to low socioeconomic positions (see Fig. 4.8). Note, too, that intelligence tests are generally designed by well-educated, well-paid professionals, such as psychologists with doctoral degrees from universities. Those who do best on such tests are generally those who share the most in common with the authors of the tests, namely, well-educated individuals of high socioeconomic class background. Thus, social groups who have been strongly segregated and otherwise denied participation in the mainstream of United States culture will tend to receive lower scores on such tests. The lower average scores of such groups reflect their unfamiliarity with the kinds of experiences that are familiar to and valued by test

designers and incorporated into these tests.

If socioeconomic class differences are held constant when evaluating IQ scores—that is, if persons of similar social, educational, and economic backgrounds are compared—all socially designated races achieve equivalent IQ scores. For instance, Zena Blau (1981) carried out a study of 579 black and 523 white mothers and their fifth- and sixth-grade children in Chicago area communities. The two groups she studied differed by 10 IQ points, but when black children were compared with white children of similar social and economic rank, the scores of the white children averaged only 6 points higher than those of the black children.

Religious background also influences the intellectual development of a child. For instance, Hofstadter (1963) has discussed the anti-intellectualism of the evangelical fundamentalist churches—their opposition to science, modern secular education, and the secularization of life that has resulted from industrialization and urbanization. Since a fundamentalist religious background is much more common among blacks than among whites in the United States, this influence on black-white IQ differences is an important one. In Blau's sample (1981), for instance, two thirds of the black students were of a fundamentalist religious background. When she compared black and white students of similar socioeconomic *and* religious backgrounds, the difference between the average IQ scores of the two groups dropped to only 4 points. Among high socioeconomic status Protestants and nondenominational and nonreligious children there were no IQ score differences between black and white children at all.

Motivation and IQ Scores

Besides environmental factors that discriminate against some test takers, the motivation of the test taker will also have an effect on the IQ score he or she achieves. If individuals are not motivated to do well on examinations, their scores will not validly reflect their abilities. It is certainly possible that social factors may create a higher level of motivation in one social group than in another in a testing situation. For example, many minority groups have a heritage of social and political subordination in the United States. This being so, it is possible that students from these groups might be less motivated to do their best on tests administered to them in an academic setting that is generally dominated by white teachers, administrators, and testers. Indeed, a study by Canady (1936) of just this fact demonstrated that blacks who are given an intelligence test by a black tester will score an average of several points higher than a similar group of blacks given the same test by a white tester.

These examples of environmental and motivational influences on intelligence test scores indicate that it is insupportable to attribute the average differences in IQ scores of supposed racial groups to racial heredity. Although the discussion has focused on black-white differences in intelligence test performance, the concepts involved apply equally well in the cases of other minority groups. For instance, the long segregation and economic deprivation of Native Americans has minimized their acquaintance with mainstream Anglo-American ideas and values. Considering that Anglo-American intelligence tests evaluate one's skill at participating in Anglo-American society, it is not surprising that persons brought up in another cultural tradition, and perhaps speaking natively a language other than English, might fare poorly on such tests.

Cultural Bias in IQ Tests

IQ tests themselves are not flawless. For most of their history, intelligence tests have been popularly perceived as scientific measures of an individual's innate intellectual potential. Yet, from the beginning, they have contained questions that assumed a knowledge of societal experiences, practices, values, and ways of thinking that were characteristic of the higher socioeconomic classes. For instance, an intelligence test once used to measure the mental abilities of grammar school children included the question: "Pick the word that doesn't belong: (a) cello, (b) harp, (c) drum, (d) violin, (e) guitar." Some 85% of the high socioeconomic class children recognized that they were all musical instruments and that "drum" was the item that "did not belong" in that it was the only nonstringed instrument in the list. However, 45% of the low socioeconomic class children who took this test failed to answer this question in the way the testers perceived as correct. By virtue of their different social experience— not by virtue of any difference in brain structure—lower-class children were not so likely to have learned the characteristics of all these musical instruments. Yet, because of their "wrong" answers, they were said to be less intelligent than the children who, by virtue of their life experiences, were more likely to have been exposed enough to all the items to select the "correct" answer.

Similarly, during the economic depression of the 1930s elementary school children of poor families in the United States were said to be less intelligent than children of families with higher incomes when in response to an intelligence test question, "The color of milk is: (a) white, (b) black, (c) red, (d) blue," they selected the answer "blue." According to the psychologists who prepared the test, that was an incorrect response. Yet these children were simply describing reality as they had experienced it: from economic necessity, poor families during the Depression were apt to be consumers of skim milk that does, in fact, have a slightly bluish cast. In the dialect of the day, it was called "blue John." Their answer was not incorrect in their own experience, but intelligence tests really are measures of the degree to which one shares experiences in common with the authors of the tests.

A few years ago, a colleague working in the African state of Malawi found the following item on a test that was being used to assess the intelligence of students: "If ten crows are sitting on a fence and you shoot one, how many will be left?" The response "nine," based on the arithmetic operation of subtracting one from ten, was scored as the correct response and was considered evidence of a student's intellectual skill. It was finally noticed, however, that many of the children who were tested failed to answer this seemingly simple arithmetic problem correctly and that they tended to respond with the same "incorrect" response of "zero." The reason for their "error" was their rural background. It gave them a more realistic appraisal of the behavior of birds—who would fly away if shot at—than was held by the author of the test, who had selected the answer on the basis of a purely academic frame of reference. One could not ask for a better example of the effects of different life experiences on the ways in which one might interpret a test question.

The Dove Counterbalance Intelligence Test

Adrian Dove has presented an interesting illustration of the cultural biases of intelligence tests. Imagine for a moment that your own economic status or the future educational quality and social opportunities for your children depended on an "intelligence" score achieved by taking an "intellectual capacities" test that was biased in favor of those who had an experience in life different from what is built into those tests currently in use. Consider how you or your children might fare on a test

composed of questions such as the following:[3]
If they throw dice and "7" is showing on the top, what is facing down? (a) 7, (b) Snake eyes, (c) Box-cars, (d) Little Joes, (e) Eleven.
Cheap "chitlings" (not the kind you purchase in the frozen food counter) will taste rubbery unless they are cooked long enough. How soon can you quit cooking them to eat and enjoy them? (a) 15 minutes, (b) 2 hours, (c) 24 hours, (d) 1 week (on a low flame), (e) 1 hour.
What are the "Dixie Hummingbirds"? (a) A part of the KKK, (b) A swamp disease, (c) A modern Gospel group, (d) A Mississippi Negro, para-military strike force.
Which word is most out of place here? (a) Splib, (b) Blood, (c) Gray, (d) Spook, (e) Black.

The cultural bias is evident in these questions. It has been no less real in questions in intelligence tests actually in use, although the biases favored the segments of society from which test authors, administrators, and evaluators themselves came and were, therefore, easily overlooked by those with the social power to define intelligence.

These examples illustrate that intelligence tests are not measures of some unchanging, inborn, genetically inherited intellectual potential, but of how much the person tested has in common with the author of the test in social experience, values, and arbitrary ways of communicating directions for the completion of tasks. The built-in biases of such tests will tend to make it more difficult for children of lower-class families, females, nonwhites, and members of other minority groups to achieve a high score. Thus, intelligence tests, in the guise of being scientifically valid descriptions of the intellectual adequacies of these groups, serve the function of giving an official negative label and

3. From "Taking the Chitling Test" by Adrian Dove, 1968, *Newsweek*, p. 52. Copyright 1968 by Newsweek, Inc. The answers, incidentally, are a, c, c, and c.

its attendant handicaps to segments of society that generally have less access to social power and prestige to begin with.

Intelligence Labeling as Self-fulfilling Prophecy

Scores achieved on tests of intellectual skills are often used as criteria for making judgments concerning schoolchildren that may influence their future academic careers. Judgments based on such testing may, for instance, lead to the assigning of students to accelerated classes or classes for "slow learners." Once assigned, the original categorization of students as "superior" or "slow" in their supposedly native intellectual endowment may continue through the years. Later teachers may be swayed in their own expectations about students on the basis of the reputations that grow out of the original labeling by a prestigious test that is commonly thought of as a measure of inborn capacities.

Rist (1970) described a three-year observational study of a class of ghetto children that illustrated how the school system may unwittingly reinforce the class differences between the families from which the children come. The kindergarten teacher of these children made judgments about their intellectual skills and assigned them to different groups within the class. This categorization was reflected in the seating arrangement of the students. Those placed at the first table were those whom she described as "fast learners," while those at the last two tables "had no idea of what was going on in the classroom." Rist contends that the criterion for assigning the children to these groups, which the teacher believed to be different in their intellectual abilities, was actually the degree to which the children conformed to several middle-class American characteristics. That is, the real differences between the children consisted of such things as the degree to which they used Standard American English, their neatness and cleanliness, and whether their parents were educated, employed, and living together.

Rist further noted that this initial place-ment of the students—based on the kindergarten teacher's impressions during the first eight days of class—persisted into later grades. The students' achievement was influenced by the way the teachers acted toward them, which in turn corresponded to the expectations for their behavior that were implicit in the original classifications. The initial perception of each succeeding teacher was influenced by preconceptions based on knowledge of how the students were categorized and how they performed in the previous grade. This example illustrates the possibility that socially biased judgments about supposed differences of innate ability may be a *cause* of later differences in the performance of students, differences that are used to justify the "accuracy" and even propriety of the original practice of classifying the students.

It is not difficult to imagine how labels such as "slow learner" or "superior student" may hinder or aid their bearers through the rest of their school careers. Students who are labeled "above average" are apt to receive endless encouragements to "live up to their potential" and enroll in intellectually valued subjects that lead to a college career and highly valued occupations. Students labeled "below average," on the other hand, are more likely to be encouraged to enroll in subjects that are intellectually less stimulating; when they fall behind in their work, they are less likely to be pushed so as not to "frustrate" them by demanding more than they are capable of doing. These latter students are likely to end their scholastic careers earlier and with less training.

Intelligence tests on which labeling and expectations are based may thus serve as vehicles for inhibiting social and economic mobility. By reflecting the social experience and values of the higher socioeconomic segment of society, intelligence tests distinguish members of this sector from other members of society and function as an impressive rationale for providing a less adequate educational experience to members of the socially less powerful segment of society. As a result, of course, intelligence test scores given at an early age in the school system are good predictors of a schoolchild's later academic success. This is not because they measure biologically inherited and unchanging abilities of the child, but because the scores achieved at an early age can readily influence the way the children are treated throughout the remainder of their educational experience.

The Impossibility of Culture-free Testing

Recently, psychologists and educators have attempted to salvage the use of intelligence tests to measure innate differences in intellectual abilities by redesigning the tests to minimize their most obvious cultural biases, such as the inclusion of idioms and ideas shared by only one segment of society. They have hoped thereby to create so-called "culture-free" intelligence tests, that is, tests that are unbiased in favor of the values and life experiences (the "culture") of any one segment of a society. However, even if the specific items in a test do not reflect knowledge available to the members of only one part of society, the differences in the life experiences of different segments of a complex society will lead to differences in the ways people respond to the tasks. Cultural learning affects the way we perform any task. If one style of response is regarded as more appropriate than others, even a "culture-free" test will serve as a vehicle for assigning higher scores to members of the segment of society that most prepares its members to respond in that style, just as older so-called "intelligence" tests have always done. It is impossible to create a measure of pure, environmentally uninfluenced, biological intelligence, since all human beings are raised in a social environment that will influence their behavior as inevitably as their genetically inherited biological qualities will.

Sexual Inequality

Like the racial distinctions that deprive many social groups of power on the basis of observable physical traits, many cultures also apply a low-power master status to many of their members simply because they are females. Sexism is the contention that sexual biology is the cause of the different behaviors of males and females that are embodied in the socially complementary roles of men and women.

According to Friedl (1975), men may be hunters, warriors, diplomats, and politicians, but in all cultures women are defined primarily by their kinship relations. Whatever else they may be in fact, women are perceived primarily as daughters, sisters, potential mates, wives, mothers, and widows. Their other life occupations tend to be perceived as secondary to these family-based roles. The honor accorded these roles varies among cultures, but they typically involve little of the direct social power that is associated with male roles.

Female "Circumcision" and the Subordination of Women

Many cultural practices serve to keep women in subordinate roles, restricting their freedom. Some societies keep women in restrictive clothing, for instance, or under veils. Certain others in which male dominance over women is an important fact of life mutilate the genitals of female children, a practice called female circumcision. Hosken (1980) describes the most common forms of female circumcision, their effects, and the cultural settings in which they occur.

Infibulation—an operation by which the sides of the vulva are closed over the vagina—is particularly common where the virginity of wives is especially important, since this childhood operation insures virginity. Following infibulation, sexual intercourse is not possible until the barrier created by the operation is cut by the husband. Excision—removal of the pleasure-sensitive clitoris—is performed to reduce a woman's sexual sensations and, thereby, her interest in sex. This is thought to increase her fidelity in marriage, especially in societies where polygyny (where men are permitted to have more than one wife) is practiced and legitimate opportunities for heterosexual intercourse are less common for wives than for husbands. Excision is sometimes thought

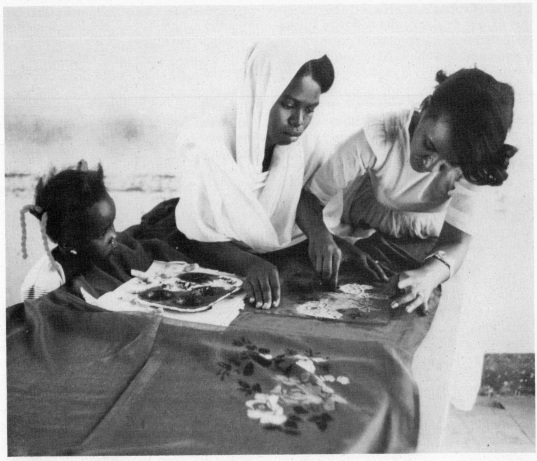

Figure 4.9 *Female Roles*
One aspect of racism is the subtle discrimination against females. While males are generally identified by their position in the workplace, females are more often identified by their kinship roles.

to increase female fertility, so it is also practiced to insure that a woman will have many children.

Female genital mutilation is most common today in the most populous areas of East, Central, and West Africa, in some Middle Eastern countries including Egypt and the southern Arabian Peninsula, and in some parts of Indonesia and Malaysia. Though these mutilations are particularly common today in Moslem areas of these parts of the world, they should not be thought of as Moslem practices. Excision, for instance, is practiced by Christian Copts in Egypt as well as by Egyptian Moslems and by non-Moslem groups in the 26 African countries where it has been documented. Furthermore, although infibulation was not a traditional Western practice, excision was practiced by European and American surgeons into the twentieth century (Barker-Banfield, 1983) as a supposed cure for masturbation and "nymphomania," a negative label for sexual desire in females.

The basic biological characteristics of men and women are the same in all societies, so biological differences between the sexes do not explain why women in some societies have statuses of equal rank to those of men, while in other societies women's statuses are of low rank. Friedl (1975) argues that the rank of women—as manifest in a society's sexual division of labor, the differential allocation of power and recognition to men and women, and the quality of the relationships between the sexes—grows largely out of the society's subsistence technology and political organization. In every society, the right to distribute and exchange valued goods and services to non-relatives is the major source of social power and honor. Friedl believes that women are subordinated to men in those societies where women's roles do not include the right to distribute goods and services outside the family. Women are more likely to have social equality with men if they both participate in subsistence activities, including the production of goods, *and* have opportunities to distribute and exchange valued goods and services outside their own domestic group.

The political realm, particularly warfare, is the second major influence on women's societal rank. Since women bear the children who will constitute the next generation of a society, any population can survive the loss of males more easily than the loss of females. So men consistently are more involved in political alliances and warfare. In preindustrialized societies where population pressures cause conflict over limited resources and warfare between neighboring peoples who share the same language and culture—a form of warfare known as internal warfare—women are systematically subordinated to men (Divale & Harris, 1976). Harris (1974) has summarized the impact of this form of warfare on male and female roles:

> Male supremacy is a case of "positive feedback," or what has been called "deviation amplification"—the kind of process that leads to the head-splitting squeaks of public-address systems that pick up and then reamplify their own signals. The fiercer the males, the greater the amount of warfare, the more such males are needed. Also, the fiercer the males, the more sexually aggressive they become, the more exploited are the females, and the higher the incidence of polygyny— control over several wives by one man. Polygyny in turn intensifies the shortage of women, raises the level of frustration among the junior males, and increases the motivation for going to war. The amplification builds to an excruciating climax; females are held in contempt and killed in infancy, making it necessary for men to go to war to capture wives in order to rear additional numbers of aggressive males. (p. 87)

Since female children are often unwanted in these societies because they lack social power but still need to be fed, female infanticide has been the major means of population control in most societies throughout human history. Divale (1972) studied foraging and horticultural societies that practiced warfare and found that the ratio of boys to girls aged 14 and under was 128 to 100. Since throughout the world about 105 boys are born for every 100 girls, the extra 23 boys per 100 girls in Divale's sample indicates a higher death rate among girls in these societies.

The female subordination that occurs with internal warfare does not accompany external warfare, in which men are absent from home for prolonged periods while fighting with distant enemies whose languages and customs are different from their own. Under conditions that lead to external warfare or prolonged absence of men for other reasons such as long-distance trade, the rank of women is likely to be much higher. It is women who make the day-to-day economic and internal political decisions of the village while the men are away. In such societies, the gardens and houses are often the property of women, female infanticide and polygyny are likely to be uncommon, and inheritance is usually through the line of female ancestry. In societies of this kind, the power of men over their wives is minimized by their lack of ownership over their wives' home and gardens. Their power is also limited by their lack of authority over their wives' children, who are members of their mothers' families, not their fathers'. The male head of the household will not be a woman's husband but her brother, who belongs to her own family.

With industrialization, the means of subsistence have shifted for most families increasingly toward sources of income other than food production. In many societies, including European countries during the rise of industrialization and, more recently, in other parts of the developing world, men have been drawn more quickly into the industrialized sector of the economy than have women. This situation has increased the economic dependence of women on men. This need not be a feature of industrialized economies, however, as suggested by the rise in the status of women in the United States as the percentage of women in the labor force has increased in recent decades.

Male and Female Roles in Iran

For an in-depth example of socially patterned status differences between males and females, we can look at Iranian men and women. According to Behnam (1985), the traditional Muslim family traced its ancestry through the father, tended toward marriage between cousins, favored polygyny, and was male dominated. The Iranian family was an autonomous economic unit in production as well as consumption. This lent it great cohesiveness, and the decision making for the domestic group lay in the hands of the male hierarchy within the family. According to Nassehi-Behnam (1985), the economic role of the family made marriage an important union between two family lines, so marital choices were a matter of great importance, with preparations sometimes beginning at birth.

In wealthy Iranian families, the symbolic distinction between the private intimacy of the household and the profane external world of strangers was portrayed by dividing the house into two areas, the private (*andaruni*) interior of the home, the area of the wife, and the public (*biruni*) area of the man, the threshold between the home and the outside world. Although the men of the family could enter the private areas of the home, the women were excluded from the public areas.

The responsibility of the woman for the domestic work of life is emphasized by the Islamic religious traditions. The exemplary models of the division of labor within a marriage were Ali, the brother of Muhammad, and Ali's wife, Fatimah. In Islamic *hadith* or sacred tradition, Fatimah took responsibility for the domestic affairs, such as grinding the flour, baking the bread, and sweeping the house, while Ali took responsibility for all works outside the door of the house, such as bringing the firewood and obtaining food for the family. In the words of Allah as recorded in the *Qur'an* (4:34), ''Men are the protectors and maintainers of women because God has given the one more (strength) than the other, because they support them from their means.'' Men, in other words, are thought to excel women in natural strength, so it is their responsibility to support their wives. Since a son will bear the economic responsibility of supporting a wife, a daughter need not inherit as much as a son. The *Qur'an* (4:11) specifies that, ''God (thus) directs you as regards your children's (inheritance): to the male, a portion equal to that of two females.''

In the Islamic view, men and women differ not only in strength but also in temperament. The woman is thought blessed by God with a tender spirit and greater emotional sensitivity. This temperament is in harmony with her role as a nurturer of children and as the conscience of her husband, but in legal matters the objectivity of her judgment may be tainted by emotion. The *Qur'an* (2:282) therefore treats the testimony of two women as equal in weight to that of one man: ''. . . and get two witnesses out of your own men, and if there are not two men, then a man and two women such as ye choose for witnesses, so that if one of them errs, the other can remind her.''

The man is thought to be endowed by God with greater rationality and the natural ability to become a leader. In the words of the poet Iqbal, ''The virtue of man shines without any outside help; but the virtue of woman depends on another (i.e., man) to bring it out'' (as quoted in *Mahjubah*, November 1984, p. 19). Thus, the Prophet has said: ''The most honoured women before Allah are those who are obedient to their husbands and remain within the boundaries of their homes'' (as quoted in *Mahjubah*, November 1984, p. 18).

Industrialization has created many strains on the traditional Iranian family structure. Urbanization has drawn many people away from rural areas. This shift has created higher divorce rates, especially as men have left their families in search of work in the cities. The older extended family networks that controlled the economic life of families have been undermined by the move of couples away from their parents into the cities. Housing problems in the cities make it difficult for extended families to maintain a common residence, further fragmenting the earlier family hierarchies. Industrialization also created increasing opportunities for women to be employed. This opportunity has made divorce easier, since employment permits women to support themselves following divorce. Thus, the divorce rate is three times as high in urban areas as in rural areas (Nassehi-Behnam, 1985).

The revolution of 1979 brought attempts to reestablish the old male/female distinctions, with an increased application of Islamic religious principles in family law and values and repeal of the Family Protection Laws passed in 1972 that granted women the right to divorce, the right to an education and to work without their husband's consent, and the right to custody of the children, as well as restrictions on plural marriage. The wearing of the veil by women in public has become mandatory, women's employment has been restricted, and coeducational schooling has been terminated as contrary to Islam.

The war between Iran and Iraq has increased the death rate among men, so polygyny has been been officially encouraged to provide for the widows. Islam permits a man to have as many as four wives. This makes it unnecessary for women to remain without the support of a man and decreases the need for women's employment. Once again only the man has the legal right to divorce. Under Islamic law, a man may

declare himself divorced from his wife. A wife, on the other hand, cannot divorce herself from her husband without the decree of a judge, but even in civil law a divorce is more readily granted a man than a woman.

It is to be expected that Iranians who share the contemporary official Iranian view of men's and women's divinely instituted roles would have very different ideas about legal equality than are common in the West. For instance, the high percentage of employed women in Western countries is sometimes described by Iranians as a form of exploitation of women, in which women are expected to continue their ''natural'' responsibilities of childbearing and childrearing while taking on the duties of men as well. Thus, Western ''emancipation'' of women is seen as a clever device of men to overload women with work that the men should be doing themselves. According to the editors of *Mahjubah* (November 1984) an Iranian magazine for Muslim women, ''Islam has liberated woman from the turmoils and troubles of the outside world; so that she may concentrate on the duties of domestic affairs (p. 18).''

Women's Status in the United States

Another society making sexist distinctions between males and females is the United States. Women here are holders of minority status, a low-ranked master status that tends to overshadow the other statuses they may hold. Like racism, this sexism creates inequalities of opportunity.

Similarities between sexism and racism. Striking parallels may be found in the history of the treatment of women and blacks in the United States. Caroline Bird (1973), a contemporary feminist author, lists some of these parallels.

To begin with, neither women nor blacks could hide the respective facts of sex or race. Generalizations about blacks and women as workers relegated both groups to inferior status on the job. Both groups were regarded as a labor reserve, denied equal

Figure 4.10 *Woman's Status in the United States*
Historically, as holders of minority status in the United States, women have had to battle for basic rights and equal status with men. This parade for women's suffrage took place in New York City in 1912.

hiring, training, pay, promotion, responsibility, and seniority at work. Neither group was supposed to boss white men, and both were limited to jobs white men didn't want to do.

Blacks were supposed to be better able to stand uncomfortable physical labor; women, boring details. Both had emerged from a "previous condition of servitude" that had denied them the vote, schooling, jobs, apprenticeships, and equal access to unions, clubs, professional associations, professional schools, restaurants, and public places. Strikingly similar rationalizations and defense mechanisms accommodated both denials of the central American ideal of equal opportunity. (p. 130)

Ashley Montagu (1974), one of anthropology's most outspoken critics of racism, has noted that:

In connection with the modern form of race prejudice it is of interest to recall that almost every one of the arguments used by the

racists to "prove" the inferiority of one or another so-called "race" was not so long ago used by the anti-feminists to "prove" the inferiority of the female as compared with the male. . . .

In the nineteenth century it was fairly generally believed that women were inferior creatures. Was it not a fact that women had smaller brains than men? Was it not apparent to everyone that their intelligence was lower, that they were essentially creatures of emotion rather than of reason—volatile swooning natures whose powers of concentration were severely limited and whose creative abilities were restricted almost entirely to knitting and childbirth? For hundreds of years women had played musical instruments and painted, but to how many great female musicians and painters could one point? Where were the great women poets and novelists? Women had practically no executive ability, were quite unable to manage the domestic finances, and, as for competing with men

Nine Jobs Where Men Are Scarce:

Occupation	Number	Percent Held by Men
Prekindergarten and kindergarten teacher	329,000	1.2
Dental hygienist	56,000	1.5
Secretary	4,059,000	1.6
Receptionist	679,000	2.4
Licensed practical nurse	402,000	3.1
Child-care worker	738,000	3.9
Welfare service aides	82,000	7.4
Textile sewing machine operators	760,000	9.8
Librarian	201,000	13.0

Six Jobs Where Women Are Scarce:

Occupation	Number	Percent Held by Men
Automobile mechanic	906,000	99.3
Surveyor and mapping scientist	22,000	98.7
Truck driver, heavy	1,838,000	97.9
Aerospace engineer	95,000	95.3
Police and detective	652,000	89.9
College and university teacher	643,000	64.8

Note. From *Professional Women and Minorities: A Manpower Data Resource Service*, by B. M. Vetter and E. L. Babco, 1986, Washington, DC: Commission on Professionals in Science and Technology.

Table 4.1 *U.S. Occupations Held Predominantly by One Sex, 1985*

in the business or professional world, such an idea was utterly preposterous, for women were held to possess neither the necessary intelligence nor the equally unattainable stamina. Man's place was out in the world earning a living; woman's place was definitely in the home. (pp. 186-187)

That the roots of the women's movement for freedom from such sexist stereotyping and the crusade for abolition of slavery are intertwined is not surprising. A good example of the interrelatedness of the problems surrounding the unequal treatment of blacks and women is found in the history of Sara and Angelina Grimké, two early nineteenth-century militant American feminists and abolitionists. Because they spoke out strongly for women's rights and for the rights of blacks to freedom from slavery, no less a figure than John Greenleaf Whittier urged them to stop their work for women's rights because it was undermining the antislavery campaign: "Why then, let me ask, is it for you to enter the lists as controversial writers in this question (of women's rights)? . . . Is it not forgetting the great and dreadful wrongs of the slave in a selfish crusade against some paltry grievances of your own?" (Barnes, 1934, pp.

223-224). To which Angelina, writing for herself and her sister, replied, "What then can woman do for the slave, when she herself is under the feet of man and shamed into silence?" (Barnes, 1984, p. 429).

Occupational discrimination. Several limitations have been formally placed on women in the United States on the basis of the idea that societal norms should reflect the biological differences of the two sexes. Among the strongest of these limitations has been the so-called "protective" legislation that is overtly designed to protect the female, thought of as the "weaker sex," from exploitation in the labor market. In many states, for instance, laws have forbidden employment of women in positions that require them to lift more than a nominal amount of weight. On the basis of such laws, many individual women who were perfectly capable of meeting the demands of a particular job have been denied employment "for their own protection," not because of evidence that they lacked the necessary skills, but because they were female. The fallacy of according rights and responsibilities to individuals on the basis of ideas about the average characteristics of the groups to which they belong was demonstrated long ago by a black freed woman named Sojourner Truth who told her own story at a woman's rights convention a century ago:

> "That man over there says women need to be helped into carriages and lifted over ditches," she began slowly. "Nobody ever helps me into carriages or over puddles or gives me the best place—and ain't I a woman?" Raising a great black arm Sojourner Truth went on:
>
> "Look at my arm! I have ploughed and planted and fathered into barns and no man could head me—ain't I a woman? I could work as much and eat as much as a man—when I could get it—and bear the lash as well! And ain't I a woman? I have borne thirteen children, and seen most of 'em sold into slavery, and when I cried out with my mother's grief, none but Jesus heard me—and ain't I a woman?" (Bird, 1973, p. 30)

Although traditionally male occupations are becoming increasingly available to women as a larger percentage of women enter the labor force in the United States, occupational differences by sex are far from nonexistent in industrialized societies.

Male/Female Role Expectations

Sexism, like racism, treats individuals as if they are by nature constrained by whatever traits are socially imputed to their group, often even after they have demonstrated that the stereotype that others have of that group does not fit them personally. People forget that the role expectations that society may place on a group may be arbitrary and socially learned rather than innate.

Such sexist concepts include the ideas that men are instinctively aggressive and females innately passive or nurturing. A father who chooses to remain home to care for his children or a mother who seeks employment outside the home may be thought of as "going against nature" and as somehow abnormal. The fact that individuals are capable of violating the traditional role expectations of their group is evidence that there is, in fact, no instinctive impulse for them to follow that role.

The well-known anthropologist Margaret Mead did fieldwork (1950) among three New Guinea societies in which the patterns of sex role expectations were quite different. Her description of these societies makes it clear that concepts of what it means to be masculine or feminine are highly variable and determined by culture rather than by any absolute dictates of biology. Among the Arapesh no temperamental differences were thought to exist between males and females. Neither men nor women were believed to be driven by spontaneous sexuality, and violence, although tolerated, was not linked with either sex. Men were expected to be gentle, unacquisitive, and cooperative, and women were taught to passively accept anything out of the ordinary without curiosity.

The people of a not-too-distant tribe, the Mundugumor, were quite different in their attitudes about the sexes. The Mundugumor were headhunters and cannibals, and their life was characterized by fighting and the competitive acquisition of women from their enemies. They assumed that there was a natural hostility between members of the same sex. As a result, inheritance crossed sex boundaries with each generation from father to daughter and from mother to son. Compatible with their way of life, both males and females were raised to have violent social personalities with no value on sensuality. For instance, breastfeeding of infants was done in a utilitarian way, with no hint of pleasure; nursing was carried out only to give food and never for comfort from fright or pain.

Finally, the Tschambuli, a third nearby group, did distinguish presumed personality differences between men and women, although these expectations differed radically from role expectations of men and women in North America. The Tschambuli preferred marriages in which a man had many wives and traced their ancestry through the men of the family, who owned the houses and the land and officially "owned" their wives. But in practice women held the main power in society, both in control of the economic system and in social initiative. Tschambuli women were socialized to be sexually aggressive, while the men, who were shy in adolescence, were thought to be not so urgently sexed.

Mead (1950) summarized her findings in these words:

Here, admittedly looking for light on the subject of sex differences, I found three tribes all conveniently within a hundred mile area. In one, both men and women act as we expect women to act—in a mild parental responsive way; in the second, both act as we expect men to act—in a fierce initiating fashion; and in the third, the men act according to our stereotype for women—are catty, wear curls and go shopping, while the women are energetic, managerial, unadorned partners. (p. vi)

These extremely contrasting examples demonstrate that the personalities of men and women in any one society are not unambiguous manifestations of inherent characteristics that are fixed by nature. Rather, they are manifestations of each society's culturally patterned role expectations.

Summary

None of us operates totally independently as isolated, self-sufficient individuals. Each of us lives within a society, and all societies organize their members into groups of various sorts and divide labor among their members. Our social life is also characterized by relationships with many people, each of which involves a status. Furthermore, each status carries various role expectations defined by our society. Statuses are ranked in power and honor by our society, with some—master statuses—considered so significant that their high or low rank outweighs that of all our other statuses.

Statuses are sometimes assigned on the basis of observable biological facts, such as age, sex, and skin color. The latter is one criterion popularly used to draw racial distinctions on the basis of "race," a concept that has little biological validity because variation among individuals prevents scientific grouping by uniform types. When people are socially grouped into low-ranked master statuses because such observable traits are thought to be linked with other traits that are not highly valued by the dominant culture, they are called "minority groups." Those who believe that such stereotyping reflects biological realities are called racists or sexists. Racist and sexist thinking bars minority group members from access to economic and political power with the rationalization that they cannot handle it. But the role expectations that accompany minority group status have little or no relationship to our innate characteristics; they are cultural phenomena, socially learned and enforced.

Key Terms and Concepts

social organization 67
group 67
social structure 68
status 68
status pair 68
complementary status 68
symmetrical status 68
ascribed status 68

achieved status 68
role 68
division of labor 69
rank 69
power 70
honor 70
class 70
caste 70

Annotated Readings

Dahlberg, F. (Ed.). (1981). *Woman the gatherer.* New Haven, CT: Yale University Press.   Six articles on women's roles from cross-cultural and evolutionary perspectives.

Dalby, L. (1985). *Geisha.* New York: Vintage Books, Random House.   A beautifully written and copiously illustrated description of geisha life.

Fox, R. (1967). *Kinship and marriage.* Baltimore, MD: Penguin Books.   Probably the best and most readable account of kinship systems available.

Friedl, E. (1975). *Women and men.* New York: Holt, Rinehart and Winston.   A brief but information-packed overview of sex roles and their relationships to variations in culture. Must reading for the major in anthropology.

Martin, M. K., & Voorhies, B. (1975). *Female of the species.* New York: Columbia University Press.   An examination of the status of women in societies of varying social complexity.

Montagu, A. (Ed.). (1980). *Sociobiology examined.* New York: Oxford University Press.   Sociobiology critiqued by 16 anthropologists.

O'Kelley, C. G. (1980). *Women and men in society.* New York: D. Van Nostrand.   An easy-to-read, introductory-level cross-cultural overview of male and female roles in a cultural evolutionary framework.

Rosaldo, M. Z., & Lamphere, L. (Eds.). (1974). *Woman, culture, and society.* Stanford, CA: Stanford University Press.   Discussions by female anthropologists of their observations of the status of women in a variety of societies.

Sanday, P. R. (1981). *Female power and male dominance: On the origins of sexual inequality.* Cambridge, NY: Cambridge University Press.   A cross-cultural examination of sex role inequality and the ways in which sex role differences are symbolized.

Service, E. R. (1975). *Primitive social organization: An evolutionary perspective.* New York: Random House.   An excellent and insightful interpretation of primitive social organization.

Wilson, E. O. (1975). *Sociobiology: The new synthesis.* Cambridge, MA: Harvard University Press.   A complex and controversial look at social systems from a biological perspective.

Wilson, E. O. (1978). *Human nature.* Cambridge, MA: Harvard University Press.   A sociobiological interpretation of the human condition. Controversial but worth reading.

Chapter 5

Learning and Symbolizing in Human Behavior

◀ **Figure 5.1** *Afghan School This instructor in an Afghan school in 1960 uses distinct language symbols to communicate lessons to his students.*

Human ways of life are far more varied and complex than those of other animals. Both the diversity and the complexity are possible, in part, because the human animal's ways of adjusting to its environment are readily modified by learning. We human beings are born with a tremendous capacity for learning any way of life to which we are exposed. The development of ways of life that are much more complex than those of other animals is facilitated not only by our remarkable capacity to learn but also by our distinctive ability to communicate the intricacies of these lifeways to other members of our group. Unlike other animals, we tend to portray our concepts by highly arbitrary but mutually accepted symbols, including languages. In this chapter, we will examine these two capacities, learning and symbolizing, which are so fundamental to the origin and perpetuation of the human pattern of life.

Learning and Conceptualizing

Like all organisms, we human beings interact with our environment. In the process, we gain experience and change our behavior to interact more effectively with our environment. Such changes in behavior are commonly called learning. In mammals, the process of learning is controlled by the neocortex, the newly evolved surface area of the brain. The neocortex gains information about the environment through the animal's senses. The senses enable animals to see, hear, smell, taste, feel pain, moisture, temperature and texture, judge whether they are lying or standing, and monitor several processes occurring within their bodies.

Building Concepts

In humans, and possibly in other mammals as well, information gained through the senses is gradually organized into mental models of things that are perceived. These models are called concepts. As mental models, concepts are the basis for memory. They also provide the organism with a knowledge of some part of its environment and help it to interact more effectively with its surroundings. We humans can manipulate concepts mentally to arrive at expectations about the behavior of things

Figure 5.2 *The Concept of Closure - Mbuti Pygmy Hunters*
The density of the forest environment for these Mbuti pygmy hunters necessitates the use of closure to accurately shoot their prey without seeing it entirely. This illusion is successful because of the conceptual idea of the animal in the hunter's mind.

in our environment. This ability increases our effectiveness in dealing with those things and therefore our ability to survive.

Each concept is built from many smaller bits of information called percepts. A percept is a perceived quality or attribute of the object or event. The more ways in which any object or event is perceived (e.g., from different angles, at different points in time, or with different senses) the more complete and useful the concept becomes. Consider the concept ''chair,'' for instance. When a child first sees a chair, the image cast on the retina of the eye is different at each angle from which the child might view the chair. In these original perceptions of the chair, if the child glimpses it at separate times from two different perspectives, this inexperienced being might not even recognize that what it has seen is a single object. Gradually, the learning child integrates the percepts into the concept ''chair,'' thereafter recognizing it to be the same object no matter from which side it is seen.

Correcting Incomplete Perceptual Data

Our conceptual models of the world can never be perfect or complete reflections of reality, for two reasons. First, the number of different perspectives from which perceptual data concerning any object or event may be obtained is infinite. Second, our senses are limited in their perceptual abilities. Thus our concepts are always to some degree incomplete or distorted, and no concept may be said to be correct in any absolute sense. The real test of a concept is not its truth but its utility; some conceptualizations are simply more useful to an organism than others in helping it cope with its environment.

Inasmuch as our experiences always suffer from some degree of incompleteness, we often fill in missing parts of the conceptual model, making it seem complete. This is necessary so that the model may be used to provide needed information about aspects of the thing with which we must deal even though we have not experienced them directly. Distortion occurs when some percepts are not integrated into a conceptual model because they do not dovetail neatly into the pattern formed by the other percepts.

The tendency to treat conceptual systems as if they were more complete, perfect, and correct than the incoming perceptual data is called closure (Wertheimer, 1938). Closure implies that a conceptual system has more parts and relationships than are actually perceived. Closure occurs when we build concepts based on assumptions such as the following: (1) when things occur together they belong together; (2) when things are similar they belong together; (3) when percepts can be combined into a single concept by the addition of a small amount of missing information, this is superior to an alternate combination that requires the brain to supply missing information; or (4) when we can group percepts so they match concepts that we already have, it is acceptable to do so.

Closure involves going beyond the available perceptual facts of experience and can, therefore, lead to errors and incorrect anticipations. Nevertheless, it does often convey some advantages by making it possible to make a necessary judgment before all the perceptual data are in. For instance, in the mid-1960s the Mbuti archers of the Ituri Forest of Zaire lived in a dense forest environment. It was often necessary for a hunter to fire an arrow quickly on hearing the sound of his prey before he was able to see clearly its outline in the foliage (Turnbull, 1965). To wait for a complete experience of the animal before acting would have made hunting an unprofitable business. In this case, the ability to make closure allowed the hunter to recognize the presence and approximate location of a game animal based on limited information. The hunter was then able to react quickly enough to obtain an adequate food supply.

Cultural and Environmental Influences on Perception

Since closure is often based on congruity with previous experiences, our cultural background and environmental setting have a great impact on how we interpret our experiences. An example of the impact of cultural differences on how people interpret experience has been reported by W. H. R. Rivers (1901, 1914), who showed the Müller-Lyer diagram to Papuan natives of Murray Island and to the Toda of South India. Both groups interpreted this figure more accurately than did English people. The Müller-Lyer figure consists of two horizontal lines of equal length, one of which terminates with diagonal lines pointing away from the center, while the other terminates in diagonals angled back towards its center. English subjects tend to report that the first horizontal line looks longer than the second.

The causes of this illusion have been investigated by many later researchers. In one interesting study by Segall, Campbell, and Herskovits (1966), 1,878 people from 14 non-European societies were shown this illusion. The researchers found that the lengths of the lines in this figure were most deceptive to people who lived in a ''carpentered world'' and whose way of life gives them experience with two-dimensional portrayals of things. In effect, the people who were fooled by the illusion lived where houses had flat walls that met at right angles, forming a straight

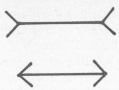

Figure 5.3 *Müller-Lyer Illusion*
The perception of visual illusions appears to be culturally and/or environmentally determined. In the figure above, most Europeans, for example, would judge the top line to be longer than the bottom one, whereas the natives of Murray Island and South India would interpret the line lengths as nearly equal.

line along their intersection, and especially where people were accustomed to judging flat pictures and diagrams as representations of three-dimensional forms. The perceptual habits developed in those societies led people to see the first line as if it were farther and the second as if it were nearer to the observer. Since the lines are of equal length, the one judged to be farther away will seem to be longer, as it would have to be for it to have the same apparent length on paper.

Another famous illusion is the full moon illusion. When seen near the horizon—even in pictures—the full moon seems much larger than when it is seen high overhead. Again, cross-cultural research has shown this illusion to be culturally and environmentally patterned. Segall et al. (1966) showed that this illusion was especially effective in environments that offer an open view of extended vistas. It fails to work with people who live in restricted environments, such as dense forests. The interpretation of this difference is similar to that of the Müller-Lyer illusion. People who have unrestricted views of the horizon become habituated to unconsciously judging the distance of things by how close to the horizon they are; they have the opportunity to learn that a distant object will appear to be the same size as a nearby object only if the distant object is larger. When they see a picture of an object such as the moon near a horizon and compare it with a picture of the same object with no horizon shown, the first is likely to seem larger, since it will unconsciously be thought of as a distant object.

Turnbull (1961) reports the interesting case of a Mbuti archer named Kenge who had grown up in a densely forested environment, where he had never had the opportunity to see objects at any appreciable distance. Turnbull took this individual on a drive out of the forest into the open savannah. When a herd of about 150 buffalo came into view in the distance, the Mbuti man asked what kind of insects they were. Turnbull unsuccessfully tried to explain that they were not insects: ''When I told Kenge that the insects were buffalo, he roared with laughter and told me not to tell such stupid lies'' (p. 253). After another passenger also claimed that the ''insects'' were indeed buffalo, Kenge ''strained his eyes to see more clearly and asked what kind of buffalo were so small. I told him they were sometimes nearly twice the size of a forest buffalo, and he shrugged his shoulders and said we would not be standing out there in the open if they were'' (p. 253). In an effort to convince his companion, Turnbull drove the jeep toward the herd. According to Turnbull:

> . . . as we got closer, the ''insects'' must have seemed to get bigger and bigger. Kenge, who was now sitting on the outside, kept his face glued to the window, which nothing would make him lower. I even had to raise mine to keep him happy. I was never able to discover just what he thought was happening—whether he thought that the insects were changing into buffalo, or that they were miniature buffalo growing rapidly as we approached. His only comment was that they were not real buffalo, and he was not going to get out of the car again until we left the park. (p. 253)

Generalizing Concepts

The ability to make closure—that is, to use incomplete data to build seemingly complete concepts—is possible only because concepts are by nature idealizations. If concepts were accurate models of real things, it would be necessary to have a different concept for each different thing, no matter how similar they were to one another. But concepts are idealizations of things, not one-to-one replicas of them. So two similar things also may be treated conceptually as if they were the same.

Since concepts are idealizations, a single concept may be created that refers to no one real or existing thing but to a class or category of nonidentical but similar things. Children need not see every existing cat before developing a generalized concept of cats; the concept is constructed out of those characteristics that they have perceived in most of the cats they have observed so far. Insofar as these perceived similarities are, indeed, traits shared by all cats, the abstract generalized conception will enable a person to recognize and appropriately respond to a new such animal on meeting it for the first time. This is so even though each cat is individually different in many respects from any other. Thus, the ability to develop a generalized concept from a limited amount of information increases the ability of the human being to function in spite of limited experience.

Perceiving Contrasts

Unfortunately, since we create concepts using limited information, we sometimes make erroneous judgments based on our concepts. Witness the classic anecdote of the child who, on seeing a skunk for the first time, tries to pet the ''pretty kitty.'' To be really useful, concepts must be set up and improved by noting relevant differences as well as similarities.

The kaleidoscope of patterns and colors perceived visually can be discriminated as ''objects'' and ''background'' because of visual contrasts that isolate the form of the object from the whole visual field. For instance, an object may be noticed when it moves: Some of the patterns and colors are seen to move as a group in contrast to the stable background. The necessity of contrasts in perception is illustrated dramatically by a process known as the ganzfeld phenomenon, the inability to perceive when contrast is not maintained (Cohen, 1957). For instance, when experimental subjects stare at a large, plain white wall or have two halves of a cut ping-pong ball taped over their eyes so that only a diffused white light can be seen, the visual centers of the brain have no contrasts to analyze. After about 20 minutes, persons who are experiencing no visual contrasts lose the awareness of vision itself. In such a state, subjects wearing ping-pong balls are no longer aware of the diffused white light and often even are unable to determine whether their eyes are open or closed. Control over eye movements is also lost, and the subjects cannot determine in which direction their eyes are looking.

Experiential contrasts are the building blocks of concepts. So the percepts out of which a concept is built can be described formally with a set of statements about the presence or absence of perceivable differences between objects. For example, according to Katz's analysis (1972) of the percepts that define the significance of the concept "chair," the recognition that an object is a chair requires that an observer be able to notice, among other things, that the object under observation is physical (rather than mental), nonliving (versus living), manufactured (versus natural), and that it has a backrest and a seating capacity of one. Such an object is conceptually contrasted by English speakers with a "stool," which is perceptually the same as a chair in all the above characteristics except one—the absence instead of the presence of a backrest.

The number of percepts required to define the boundaries of a concept is not fixed. Generally, the more in common that two things have, the smaller is the number of percepts necessary to distinguish them conceptually. The percepts needed to define depend on the context. For instance, an awareness of the absence of a backrest is relevant to distinguishing the class of things that are thought of as stools from those conceptually categorized as chairs, but no such perceptual fact is needed to distinguish between stools and tables. Similarly, the presence or absence of horns might be relevant in conceptually distinguishing between horses and cows, while the task of distinguishing cows from chickens would require a consideration of the presence or absence of such perceivable attributes as wings.

The conceptualizing process is different from the process of visualizing or mental imaging. Mental imaging involves a more complete remembering of a total experience. Concepts, on the other hand, are abstractions from experience and are composed of a limited number of percepts. A concept is built up with whichever percepts are relevant to its use in some particular problem-solving situation, such as thinking about, analyzing, or communicating.

Symbols and Signs

Analyzing one's experiences, whether internally in thought or externally in communication, involves the manipulation of concepts. In communicating, another capacity is also called into play. To transfer the information embodied in a concept from one person to another requires the use of an observable object or event to represent that concept, since one person's concept is not directly observable by another person. It is this ability to represent ideas in an external form that makes possible the communication of ideas from one person to another. The intense use of the process of communication is the most distinctive of all human behavioral attributes, and serves as the foundation for the extremely complex ways of life found in all human groups.

Most aspects of human cultures are transferred from one person to the next, through the generations, by intentional acts of communication. The process of communication is the use of objects and events to represent other objects and events so that the former may be manipulated in ways that transfer information about the latter. There are two different classes of communicative acts: those that use signs to transfer information and those that use symbols. Both humans and other animals communicate by means of signs, but humans are the only animals known to communicate naturally with symbols.

Distinguishing Between Signs and Symbols

A sign is an object or event used to represent some other object or event in a nonarbitrary manner. The meaningfulness of a sign is determined by factors of the communicator's biology or by the inherent physical properties of the sign itself (Cassierer, 1944). Thus, reflex acts and biologically inherited instinctive acts that convey meaning may be called signs. When a snarling dog bares its teeth, the act is highly expressive as a warning sign, and, in the context of muscles tensed and ready for sudden action, the meaning of the act is clear. Even when a sign is learned, the meaning is based on its intrinsic qualities, such as the sharpness of the dog's teeth. Sometimes an animal may have a biologically based predisposition to recognize the meaning of a sign, while in other cases it may have to learn the meaning of the sign by being repeatedly exposed to the sign and its referent.

The meanings of symbols, on the other hand, must be learned. A symbol is also an object or event that is used to represent another object or event, but the meaning of a symbol is arbitrarily created by its users (White, 1971). The relationship between a symbol and what it represents is not determined by the inherited biological tendencies of the communicator to relate the two to one another. Furthermore, a symbol need not share any physical similarities or physical proximity with its referent. There is, for instance, no reason dictated by human biology or the physical properties of the wavelengths of light that red had to be used to mean "stop" or green to mean "go" in traffic signals, nor is there any compelling reason in human biology or in geometric properties for a stop sign to be octagonal rather than triangular in shape. There may be causal factors in one's history or environment that influence the form of a symbol, but the meaning of a symbol is arbitrary in the sense that the meaning is not based on the intrinsic qualities of the symbol itself but exists solely because the users of the symbol agree to use it. Any symbol may be used to designate any referent.

Once a symbol comes into general acceptance, its meanings may seem as natural to its users as do the meanings of a sign. But, since the meanings of symbols are a matter of social convention or consensus rather than nature, those meanings can change quite readily even within the lifetimes of their users. It is the fact that humans can freely assign new meanings to objects or actions that allows people to communicate extremely complex and subtle messages to one another.

Human vs. Nonhuman Communication

Homo sapiens is not the only species of animal that communicates. Many nonhuman animals make use of both biologically innate and learned signs in communicative acts. However, the creation and use of symbols is characteristic of humans alone. Furthermore, we human beings are prolific in our constant use of symbols. When consciously attempting to communicate, human beings use symbols more frequently than we use signs. Even when acts do have rather natural meanings as signs, we often alter the meanings or the forms of these acts symbolically. In other words, we tend to transform almost anything with which we deal into symbols for other things.

In human beings, only the simplest of meaningful signs—those that communicate simple feelings in nonconscious or nonintentional ways—are biologically preprogrammed. For instance, we express heightened interest in whatever we are observing by an increase in the dilation of the pupil of the eye, a change controlled on an unconscious level by the autonomic nervous system (the part of the nervous system that controls the functioning of nonvoluntary actions such as the beating of the heart). This sign, though unintentional, is communicative, and other persons perceive the change and respond appropriately to it as evidence of personal interest. Similarly, the increased muscle tension that signals rising anger is often communicative enough to cause an observer to begin acting more carefully.

In some other animals, even complex communications may be governed by biologically controlled behavioral tendencies. For instance, a fighting timber wolf may indicate its submission by freezing its stance and exposing the vulnerable area of its throat to the attacking fangs of its opponent. This act might seem highly inappropriate and dangerous in the heat of battle, yet the timber wolf has a biological predisposition to signify its acceptance of defeat in this way. And the sign is responded to appropriately: Although the victor grasps the throat of its victim with its mouth as if to bite, its muscles tremble as if strained by the effort to control its enraged attack, and it does not bite to kill. If the submitting wolf remains rigid and unmoving, it will not be bitten, and the victor will continue to strain as if it desires but is unable to bite until, finally exhausted, it releases its hold and begins to walk away. Even now, if the submitting wolf starts to move, a renewed attack will begin until the sign of submission is given again. The process may be repeated several times until the loser manages to escape from the repeated attacks of the gradually tiring dominant animal.

In humans, on the other hand, all complex messages are transmitted by symbols. This tendency to create symbols—to continually use one thing to represent something else and to alter the meanings again and again after they have once been created—distinguishes humans from all other animals. Other animals, to be sure, are capable of learning to react to one item as if it were another, but only if these separate items are in some way similar to one another or are always experienced together at the same time or in the same spatial location. Humans alone seem to have a tendency to create meaningful relationships between things that do not share great physical similarities or occur together in nature. We humans live in a world of symbols.

Human Communication With and Without Symbols: The Case of Helen Keller

The dramatic impact that symbols have on human behavior is well illustrated by the case of Helen Keller, a person in whom the acquisition of symbols and, hence, the ability to communicate symbolically was delayed until she was almost seven years old. Stricken by illness at the age of 19 months, Helen was left both blind and deaf. Helen lacked the senses through which we normal-ly learn the arbitrarily agreed-on meanings of our communicative acts and through which we usually perceive those symbolic acts themselves. Nevertheless, she needed to communicate and did so by her own signs, acts whose meanings were implicit in the quality of the acts themselves. In her own words:[1]

My hands felt every object and observed every motion, and in this way I learned to know many things. Soon I felt the need of some communication with others and began to make crude signs. A shake of the head meant ''No'' and a nod, ''Yes,'' a pull meant ''Come'' and a push, ''Go.'' Was it bread that I wanted? Then I would imitate the acts of cutting the slices and buttering them. If I wanted my mother to make ice cream for dinner, I made the sign for working the freezer and shivered, indicating cold. . . .

I do not remember when I first realized that I was different from other people; but I knew it before my teacher came to me. I had noticed that my mother and my friends did not use signs as I did when they wanted anything done, but talked with their mouths. Sometimes I stood between two persons who were conversing and touched their lips. I could not understand, and was vexed. I moved my lips and gesticulated frantically without result. This made me so angry at times that I kicked and screamed until I was exhausted. . . .

Meanwhile the desire to express myself grew. The few signs I used became less and less adequate, and my failures to make myself understood were invariably followed by outbursts of passion. I felt as if invisible hands were holding me, and I made frantic efforts to free myself. I struggled—not that struggling helped matters, but the spirit of resistance was strong within me; I generally broke down in tears and physical exhaustion. If my mother hap-

---

1. From *The Story of My Life* by Helen Keller, 1954, Garden City, NY: Doubleday & Company, Inc. Reprinted by permission.

pened to be near I crept into her arms, too miserable even to remember the cause of the tempest. After awhile the need of some means of communication became so urgent that these outbursts occurred daily, sometimes hourly. (pp. 27-28, 32)

About three months before Helen's seventh birthday a teacher, Miss Anne Sullivan, arrived to attempt to train her to communicate by finger spelling. Gradually, Helen learned to spell several words, but she simply used these as she had previously used her own self-invented signs. That is, she had not yet recognized the essence of symbols: Since their meaning is arbitrarily assigned by their users, a symbol may be created to refer to anything. In the words of Anne Sullivan:

Helen has learned several nouns this week. ''M-u-g'' and ''m-i-l-k,'' have given her more trouble than other words. When she spells ''m-i-l-k'' she points to the mug, and when she spells ''m-u-g,'' she makes the sign for pouring or drinking, which shows that she has confused the words. She has no idea yet that everything has a name. (p. 253)

In a month of intense teaching, Helen learned only 25 nouns and 4 verbs. Here is her own description of this period of her slow learning of the finger-spelling signs:

The morning after my teacher came she led me into her room and gave me a doll. The little blind children at the Perkins Institution had sent it and Laura Bridgman had dressed it; but I did not know this until afterward. When I had played with it a little while, Miss Sullivan slowly spelled into my hand the word ''d-o-l-l.'' I was at once interested in this finger play and tried to imitate it. When I finally succeeded in making letters correctly I was flushed with childish pleasure and pride. Running downstairs to my mother I held up my hand and made the letters for doll. I did not know that I was spell-

ing a word or even that words existed; I was simply making my fingers go in monkey-like imitation. In the days that followed I learned to spell in this un-comprehending way a great many words, among them *pin, hat, cup* and a few verbs like *sit, stand,* and *walk.* But my teacher had been with me several weeks before I understood that everything has a name. (p. 35)

Helen's slow rate of sign learning was superseded by a remarkably accelerated rate of learning that began when her inborn symbolic abilities became activated in a single dramatic incident. This change was recorded by her teacher in two letters:

April 5, 1887.

I must write you a line this morning because something very important has happened. Helen has taken the second great step in her education. She has learned that everything has a name, and that the manual alphabet is the key to everything she wants to know.

In a previous letter I think I wrote you that ''mug'' and ''milk'' had given Helen more trouble than all the rest. She confused the nouns with the verb ''drink.'' She didn't know the word for ''drink,'' but went through the panto-mime of drinking whenever she spelled ''mug'' or ''milk.'' This morning, while she was washing, she wanted to know the name for ''water.'' When she wants to know the name of anything, she points to it and pats my hand. I spelled ''w-a-t-e-r'' and thought no more about it until after breakfast. Then it occurred to me that with the help of this new word I might succeed in straightening out the ''mug-milk'' difficulty. We went out to the pump-house, and I made Helen hold her mug under the spout while I pumped. As the cold water gushed forth, filling the mug, I spelled ''w-a-t-e-r'' in Helen's free hand. The word coming so close on the sensation of cold water rushing over her hand seemed to startle her. She dropped the mug and stood as one transfixed. A new light came into her face. She spelled ''water'' several times. Then she dropped on the ground and asked for its name and pointed to the pump and the trellis, and suddenly turning around she asked for my name. I spelled ''Teacher.'' Just then the nurse brought Helen's little sister into the pump-house, and Helen spelled ''baby'' and pointed to the nurse. All the way back to the house she was highly excited, and learned the name of every object she touched, so that in a few hours she had added thirty new words to her vocabulary. Here are some of them: *Door, open, shut, give, go, come,* and a great many more.

P.S.—I didn't finish my letter in time to get it posted last night; so I shall add a line. Helen got up this morning like a radiant fairy. She has flitted from object to object, asking the name of everything and kissing me for very gladness. Last night when I got in bed, she stole into my arms of her own accord and kissed me for the first time, and I thought my heart would burst, so full was it of joy.

April 10, 1887.

I see an improvement in Helen day to day, almost from hour to hour. Everything must have a name now. Wherever we go, she asks eagerly for the names of things she has not learned at home. She is anxious for her friends to spell, and eager to teach the letters to every one she meets. She drops the signs and pantomime she used before, as soon as she has words to supply their place, and the acquirement of a new word affords her the liveliest pleasure. And we notice that her face grows more expressive each day. (pp. 256-257)

Helen herself recalls this same episode through which she was introduced for the first time into the human world of symbols:

One day, while I was playing with my new doll, Miss Sullivan put my big rag doll into my lap also, spelled ''d-o-l-l'' and tried to make me understand that ''d-o-l-l'' applied to both. Earlier in the day we had had a tussle over the words ''m-u-g'' and ''w-a-t-e-r.'' Miss Sullivan had tried to impress it on me that ''m-u-g'' is mug and that ''w-a-t-e-r'' is water, but I persisted in confounding the two. In despair she had dropped the subject for the time, only to renew it at the first opportunity. I became impatient at her repeated attempts and, seizing the new doll, I dashed it on the floor. I was keenly delighted when I felt the fragments of the broken doll at my feet. Neither sorrow nor regret followed my passionate outburst. I had not loved the doll. In the still, dark world in which I lived there was no strong sentiment or tenderness. I felt my teacher sweep the fragments to one side of the hearth, and I had a sense of satisfaction that the cause of my discomfort was removed. She brought me my hat, and I knew I was going out into the warm sunshine. This thought, if a wordless sensation may be called a thought, made me hop and skip with pleasure.

We walked down the path to the well-house, attracted by the fragrance of the honeysuckle with which it was covered. Some one was drawing water and my teacher placed my hand under the spout. As the cool stream gushed over one hand she spelled into the other the word water, first slowly, then rapidly. I stood still, my whole attention fixed on the motions of her fingers. Suddenly I felt a misty consciousness as of something forgotten—a thrill of returning thought; and somehow the mystery of language was revealed to me. I knew then that ''w-a-t-e-r'' meant the wonderful cool something that was flowing over my hand. That living word awakened my soul, gave it light, hope, joy, set it free! There were barriers still, it is true, but barriers that could in time be swept away.

I left the well-house eager to learn. Everything had a name, and each name gave birth to a new thought. As we returned to the house every object which I touched seemed to quiver with life. That was because I saw everything with the strange, new sight that had come to me. On entering the door I remembered the doll I had broken. I felt my way to the hearth and picked up the pieces. I tried vainly to put them together. Then my eyes filled with tears; for I realized what I had done, and for the first time I felt repentance and sorrow.

I learned a great many new words that day. I do not remember what they all were; but I do know that *mother*, *father*, *sister*, *teacher* were among them—words that were to make the world blossom for me, "like Aaron's rod, with flowers." It would have been difficult to find a happier child than I was as I lay in my crib at the close of that eventful day and lived over the joys it had brought me, and for the first time longed for a new day to come. . . .

I recall many incidents of the summer of 1887 that followed my soul's sudden awakening. I did nothing but explore with my hands and learn the name of every object that I touched; and the more I handled things and learned their names, and uses, the more joyous and confident grew my sense of kinship with the rest of the world. (pp. 35-37)

Cultural Complexity and Symbolic Communication

Since the meanings of symbols are arbitrarily assigned, they are not fixed but may be changed whenever doing so can aid the communication process. For example, a teacher might explain, "In this discussion, when I say *money*, I mean anything used by people as a medium of exchange, not just officially issued currency." Similarly, new symbols can be created readily whenever they are needed to express new ideas. Fifty years ago, English lacked the words *quark*, *smog*, and *ethnocide*. Because of this ability to change the meanings of symbols and to create new ones at will, human symbolic communication can transfer information about complex and subtle details of experience, including new insights concerning the external world and inner experience that have never before been expressed. Such uses of symbols make human communication far richer and more complex than the sign communication of any other animal. With their symbolic communication abilities, humans have been able to develop a much more complex form of social life and cooperation than is found in any other species.

Since symbols may be physical objects that are arbitrarily endowed with meaning, a people's socially shared beliefs and values can be portrayed in long-lasting form, such as monuments, works of art, flags, and written documents. Such symbols can help to preserve information and public tradition over long periods of time. This makes possible the gradual accumulation and reevaluation of information over many generations. The total body of shared human knowledge may gradually become larger and more sophisticated than any one individual or group of cooperating individuals could hope to create. Thus, the human symbolic ability makes possible a growing degree of complexity that is not possible in any other social animal.

Nonverbal Communication

The two most active forms of interpersonal communication are nonverbal communication and language. Nonverbal communications, the subject of this section, are messages we convey to each other without words. Often these messages are unconscious expressions of our emotions and may not even be intended as communications. They range from grins and hugs to the spaces we place between ourselves in conversation and our handling of time (as in arriving early or late for an appointment).

Nonverbal Signs

The simplest forms of nonverbal communication are physiological signs, not symbols. For instance, blushing, which communicates embarrassment, is a direct reflection of one's emotional state and is controlled by the autonomic nervous system. Smiling, although it can be consciously controlled and assigned other symbolic meanings in special contexts, is also more generally a direct reflection of happy feelings. As such, it can be observed in deaf-blind individuals as well as in others. Slumping posture will signal submission or defeat without conscious effort; prolonged eye contact can indicate aggression or interest in maintaining contact; staring blankly while avoiding eye contact may signal fear or a desire not to interact.

Figure 5.4 *Andamanese Greeting and Parting Customs*
Andaman Islanders of either sex greet each other after absences of a few weeks by one sitting in the lap of the other and weeping. Since their etiquette demands crying as a means of expressing sentiment, the Andamanese learn to shed tears on demand.

Culturally Patterned Nonverbal Symbols

Nonverbal signs communicate the same meanings in every culture. Samoan, Navajo, or Chinese, we all express happiness with the same spontaneous smile, confusion with a distinctively human knit brow, and boredom with a yawn. Nevertheless, we humans have the distinctive tendency to play with meanings, and we sometimes take natural signs and give them an arbitrary cultural form or meaning. We make symbols even of signs. Our nonverbal symbols, such as parting gestures, flirtatious uses of the eyes, and hand gestures of contempt, vary from culture to culture. For instance, throughout Europe when people want to point out the location of something they gesture in the appropriate direction with their hand. The finger closest to the thumb, appropriately called the "pointing

finger" in colloquial English, may also be extended. Shoshoni Indians of the North American Great Basin use no such gesture unless they have changed their habits to accommodate imported European nonverbal symbols. Their traditional gesture, still used today, is with their lips. Many North Americans use a "thumbs up" gesture to express their feeling that things are going well. In Japan this gesture would likely be interpreted to mean "boss" or "father." The German who points to the side of his forehead communicates the same idea—"Crazy!"—that the North American may convey by tracing a circle next to the head with the index finger. North Americans point at their chests to indicate "self"; Japanese point to their noses with the same significance. Since such symbolic gestures have meanings that must be learned, we tend to be much more conscious of how we are using them and what we wish to communicate when we use them than we are of the multitude of meaningful nonverbal signs that we use spontaneously.

Our most common nonverbal symbolic communications tend to be performed with the highly visible upper extremities of the body—the hands, arms, shoulders, head, and parts of the face. They are often used in situations of purposeful communication: (1) where verbal communication is impossible, as when persons are too distant from one another to hear one another well; (2) where verbal communication is inappropriate, as when the actor wishes to send the message to only one member of a group (but knows others would overhear a verbal message), or when the sender feels that a verbal communication would be too direct or strong in impact; and (3) where their use will provide added emphasis while speaking verbal symbols.

Cultural variations in such symbols may inhibit full communication between people of different cultures, even on a nonverbal level. Greeting is not everywhere signified by a handshake: A kiss, an embrace, or a nose rub will do as well. Among the Toda of India, a woman indicates respect in greeting an elder kinsman by kneeling and lifting his foot to her forehead (Murdock, 1969). A wave of the hand that the European would interpret as a farewell might elsewhere be used as a request to approach. Such differences can lead to misunderstandings between well-intentioned persons from different societies who do not realize that their behaviors are only arbitrarily endowed with meaning and that the same behaviors might denote something different to people from another society.

Proxemics

Even the distance we place between ourselves and others conveys subtle nonverbal meanings. Edward Hall (1969) has studied the ways in which people symbolically structure their nonverbal manipulation of spatial relationships between themselves and others. He refers to the study of people's use of the space around them as proxemics. One finding of proxemic research is that the distances that people choose to place

themselves from others communicates how they feel about the interaction. According to Hall, there are four main distances to which North Americans adjust themselves in their business and social relations: intimate, personal, social, and public distances.

Intimate distance, which is reserved for occasions when caressing and touch are appropriate, varies in the United States from direct contact to one and one-half feet, where persons are still close enough to touch one another easily. We experience others in this zone intensely by many of our senses. They fill our field of vision, their breathing is audible, and we are aware of their presence by the senses of touch and smell as well. This intensified experience of the presence of another person in our lifespace brings a heightened awareness of how changes in ourselves result in changes in the other and vice versa. This intimate awareness often leads us to experience the other as an extension of our own self rather than as a separate entity. Intimate distance is normally regarded as too close a distance to be used by adults in public. In crowded situations such as elevators or subways, when one is forced to remain within the intimate distance of strangers, individuals communicate that they are not intentionally intruding on the intimate zone of others by focusing their eyes on infinity in an impersonal blank stare.

The second meaningful zone to which North Americans adjust themselves, called personal distance, indicates a close friendship relationship. It is the zone from one and one-half feet to four feet. A husband and wife generally place themselves within the first half of each other's personal zone from one another in public situations, while other friends will normally occupy the farther half of this zone in conversational situations. In many other cultures, the distances for this personal zone are somewhat closer than they are in the United States or northern Europe. This can make it difficult for persons of differing cultural backgrounds to communicate their interest in one another. An Anglo-American may feel ill at ease if a stranger from another society adopts a distance that in the stranger's homeland indicates friendship but which

A

B

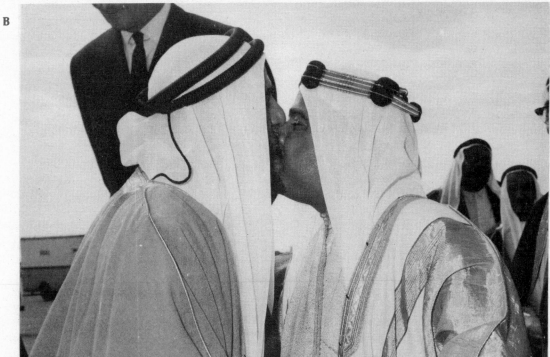

Figure 5.5 *Proxemics - Social Use of Space*
Specific social and cultural rituals determine how people use their individual space. The Taiwanese monks greeting each other, (A) are careful to observe a formal social distance. In other cultures (B) the greeting may include close physical contact such as a handshake or a hug.

to the Anglo-American seems overly intimate or pushy. When the Anglo-American backs away to a distance at which he or she feels comfortable among friends, the conversation partner may mistakenly interpret the nonverbal communication as disinterest. Such misunderstandings can be avoided only if one becomes aware that even the most habitual of human behaviors, being symbolic, have no universal meanings but vary in meaning from society to society.

Beyond personal distance is social distance of 4 to 12 feet, which is used in more impersonal interactions of a cordial type such as in business transactions. Public distance, which is greater than 12 feet, is the final zone. The usual distance placed between a teacher or public speaker and most audiences is 12 to about 25 feet. Distances greater than this are used to distinguish important public figures.

Hall (1969) has studied several societies and has found that the distances to which people adjust themselves for intimate, personal, social, or public activities are not the same in every society. For instance, among Germans personal space is expanded to include visible areas far beyond the North American's four-foot space. People are expected to greet formally anyone of their acquaintance who comes into sight and is within hailing distance. This difference shows up in the German preference for solid doors that clearly separate each room in homes and work places, a preference that contrasts with the common North American rooms connected by doorways that have no closeable doors. The closeable door allows the German to indicate more clearly his or her personal space with a definite boundary. Typically, the traditional German home or apartment has a lockable door on every room, including the kitchen. The North American walk-through floor plan with kitchen and dining areas open to and clearly visible from the living room would strike the traditional German family as strange, indeed. Arab homes, on the other hand, are much more open than those in North America. Privacy is obtained not by physical boundaries but by withdrawal from communication, which may simply

mean moving outside personal distance. To North Americans who identify their "selves" with their bodies, this intimacy might seem an invasion of their persons. Yet for Arabs, who have had to adjust to higher population densities in which contact with strangers is difficult to avoid, it is adaptive to learn to isolate their sense of personal identity deeper within their bodies than North Americans do.

Kinesics

Nonverbal communication often accompanies speech, providing the context within which speech is interpreted. Signs such as posturing of the body, gestures, and the use of the eyes communicate variations either in a person's interest and involvement in the others present or in the subject being discussed. Nonverbal communication is able to transfer information about emotions such as love, hate, fear, dependency, submission, dominance, interest, disinterest, or boredom that the actor feels about other persons or things. Nonverbal communication therefore defines and expresses the nature of the relationships of which the actor is a part. Without the maintenance of a successful nonverbal relationship between people, verbal communication may become impossible. For instance, if their body movements are too unsynchronized with each other or if they indicate hostility, successful verbal communication may be impossible.

The study of the body movements that complement speech as a means of communication is called kinesics. Ray Birdwhistell (1970) has developed a system for recording those movements with precise detail. He has discovered, for instance, that the human face can make a quarter of a million different expressions. For study purposes, 26 symbols are enough to record the basic facial positions. Birdwhistell's system for recording the movements of the entire body uses less than 100 symbols.

Birdwhistell has demonstrated that the ability of the human brain to process visual data on other people's body movements is astounding. He estimates that people are capable of processing as many as 10,000 bits of information or percepts per second. People's nonverbal interaction is subtle and complexly patterned. Birdwhistell's coding of the communicative body movements that people use and respond to involves a recording sheet of at least 100 separate lines for each participant. Each of these 100 recorded items is relevant in the normal communication process, and it requires about an hour's time to record all the information about body movement represented by one second of film. Children obviously have a great deal to learn in order to acquire the complex patterns of nonverbal behavior that are characteristic of their own society.

Some nonverbal signs can be brought under more or less conscious control and become overlaid with symbolic significance that will alter their basic significance as signs. Yet such nonverbal signs are not sufficiently free of their basic tendencies to reflect the emotional state of the actor for them to be used as a productive communication system. A true language is a system of verbal symbols that makes possible the easy translation of concepts into grammatical sequences of the symbols that represent the relationship between those concepts. This facilitates the transmission of complex messages. By contrast, nonverbal communication tends to be used for the sending of simple, often unconscious messages about one's feelings and about the ideas being expressed in language, if any (Watzlawick, Beavin, & Jackson, 1967).

Language

Language is a symbolizing system that does not rely on the expression or acting out of the meanings it represents. Language is therefore said to be an "open" system of communication because its subject matter is unlimited. New messages can be invented to express anything that can be thought. Language can be used not only to communicate emotional responses concerning things or persons being perceived at the moment of communication, but also to talk about nonexisting things and things that are not visible because they are displaced in space or time. Language is a meta communication system—one that can be used to communicate about the process of communication itself. In the following sections, we will examine the distinction between speech and language, the biological basis of humans' capacity for language, the structure of language, the interactions between language and culture, and the processes by which languages change and diverge from each other.

Language vs. Speech

Within the human supply of symbolic skills, language is the most singularly outstanding and systematically organized component. It is formally defined as a verbal system of symbolic communication. It should be noted that by this definition language is not the speech sounds uttered by speakers of a language (Chomsky, 1965). Speech consists of sounds used by communicators as symbols of their conceptual models of reality. Language, on the other hand, is the shared *system* that underlies the act of creating speech sounds in a patterned way. This system is made up of three sets of shared rules: (1) rules for forming the particular speech sounds used in the language, (2) rules for putting the sounds of speech together into words that symbolize concepts, and (3) rules for putting the words together into sentences that portray the relationships between concepts. The existence of a shared system for organizing speech symbols increases the amount of information that can be communicated with those symbols. If speakers could do no more than simply produce an unstructured list of vocal symbols, then a hearer could associate these utterances with a series of mental concepts, yet the hearer would have no way of deciding which relationship between the communicated ideas the speaker had in mind. Language enables the hearer to accomplish this—to share complex ideas.

When children begin learning language, they not only learn the vocal symbols of the speech which they hear uttered by others around them, but they also discover the meaningful pattern to the arrangement of these speech sounds. The number of sentences that can be spoken in any language is effectively unlimited. But the existence of a system that governs the organization of words into sentences makes it unnecessary for children to actually hear and memorize each separate sentence before they can communicate any idea they wish to express to someone else (Chomsky, 1971). They need only learn a finite number of words and a finite set of grammatical rules for arranging those verbal symbols into patterns that express relationships between the concepts for which they stand. They are then able to arrange and rearrange their words in ways that can communicate ideas and relationships which they had never heard expressed before. In summary, having a socially shared pattern for representing concepts by strings of vocal symbols makes it possible (1) to produce new sentences one has never heard before, (2) to communicate about new concepts, and (3) to interpret correctly new utterances that one hears for the first time. This is in direct contrast to the sign communication techniques of other animals, which set major limits on their communicative abilities.

Vocal Communication in the Nonhuman Primates

Is language unique to the human species? We are now attempting to understand the communication patterns and language potential of other animals including our own closest relatives. Biologically speaking, human beings are members of a group of animals known as *primates*. The other primates are the apes, the monkeys, and the small tree-dwelling prosimians. Biologically, these other primates are more like the human species than are any other animals. As a group, the primates also tend to be social and communicative animals. Nevertheless, the uniqueness of the human language capacity is apparent when one compares it with the communication systems of the other primates.

According to Altmann (1973), "For the most part . . . the social signals of monkeys and apes are not semantic: the messages do not stand for something else. They are simply social signals to which a response is given. In this they

are much more like the cry of a newborn infant than they are like the speech of human adults." Similarly, Marler (1965) observes, "It begins to appear that a repertoire of from about 10 to about 15 basic sound-signal types is characteristic of nonhuman primates as a whole. In some it may prove to be smaller or larger, but it is doubtful if the limits will be exceeded by very much. . . . Comparison with other highly vocal groups of vertebrates that have been closely examined reveals an approximately similar repertoire size." Thus, the nonhuman primates do not seem much different from other comparable animals in their vocal communicative abilities. Symbolic language seems to be a distinctively human trait.

In recent years, the limits of nonhuman primate communicative abilities have begun to be explored through attempts to teach various forms of language to chimpanzees (Mounin, 1976); possibly the most similar to human beings in their biological characteristics. These efforts have revealed a striking capacity in chimpanzees to expand their communication skills. One such study was started in 1966 by Allen and Beatrix Gardner (1969, 1985). A major problem in earlier attempts to teach a human language to chimpanzees (Kellog, 1968, Hayes & Nissen, 1971) had been the chimpanzee's difficulty in forming the sounds used in human speech. The Gardners overcame this problem by teaching a modified version of *American Sign Language (ASL)*, the gestural language of the deaf in North America. Chimpanzees naturally make use of a variety of gestures when communicating in the wild, and the Gardner's use of ASL proved to be a breakthrough. Within four years, Washoe had mastered more than 130 signs of ASL. In addition to using signs appropriately to name objects (e.g., dog, flower, or shoe), attributes (e.g., red, dirty, or funny), and actions (e.g., give, want, or drink), Washoe learned to combine signs into sequences such as "give" + "tickle." The Gardners and

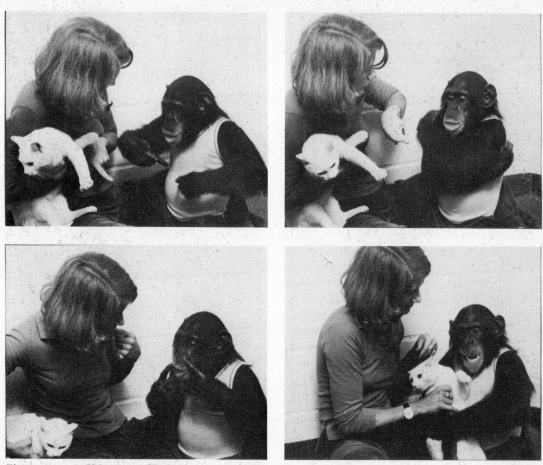

Figure 5.6 *A Chimpanzee Signing*
In several different experiments chimpanzees have been taught to converse with their trainers using American Sign Language. Here this chimpanzee asks to hug the cat and gets his wish.

Washoe's later trainer, Roger Fouts, claim that Washoe has mastered something equivalent to grammar in human language. In six successful studies they believe they have proven that chimpanzees have at least a basic ability to use language in the human sense. Others disagree. Terrace (1979) has worked with chimpanzees and has also analyzed videotapes of human/chimpanzee sign language interaction. He and several colleagues, Terrace, Pettito, Sanders, and Bever, (1979) claim that many of the apparent examples of chimpanzees' combining signs into grammatical sequences are not spontaneous but have resulted from the chimpanzees' responding to subtle cues that the trainers gave. Rumbaugh, Warner, and Von Glasersfeld (1977) began training

chimpanzees to communicate by pressing keys embossed with geometric signs. They agree (Savage-Rumbaugh, Rumbaugh, & Boysen, 1980; Savage-Rumbaugh, Pate, Lawson, Smith & Rosenbaum, 1983) with Terrace that chimpanzees can learn to associate signs with objects and actions and to use signs to make simple requests, but that the chimpanzees that have been taught ASL do not demonstrate a grasp of grammar. Rather, they merely string together any signs they know that are relevant to the situation in which they are making a request. Savage-Rumbaugh and her colleagues (1980:60) assert that the most important difference between chimpanzee communication and that of human children is that chimpanzees make requests but do not spontaneously begin to describe their environment. They make sequences like "give orange me give eat orange me eat orange give me eat orange give me you," but they do not make comments such as "The orange is cold" or "The orange juice is sticky" while they are eating the orange.

On the other hand, in more controlled settings, it has been possible to train chimpanzees to demonstrate some of the skills used in spoken language. Ann and David Premack (1972) have trained a chimpanzee, Sarah, to use colored geometric shapes to express herself. The shapes and colors were unrelated to the objects and processes they represented, and Sarah was able to master abstract concepts such as "same" and "different." She learned the meanings of about 130 geometric shapes and was able to arrange them into the order that words occur in English sentences. Rumbaugh (1977) and Savage-Rumbaugh, Pate, Lawson, Smith and Rosenbaum (1983) have reported that other chimpanzees, taught to communicate with their trainers using computer-linked keyboards, were able to learn to press the keys in correct sequences, and could recombine the keys into different sequences to express different ideas, both characteristics of human language. They were also able to communicate about things they were not directly observing. These studies suggest that chimpanzees do have many of the capacities that are important in human languages.

Another primate language training study has been carried out by Francine Patterson (1978; see also Hill, 1978) with a gorilla named Koko. Like Washoe, Koko has been taught American Sign Language. Her vocabulary is over 400 words. It includes words for emotions, such as sadness and shame, and Koko can communicate about her own feelings. She has spontaneously used descriptive phrases, such as "finger bracelet" for ring, to refer to things for which she had learned no word from her trainer, an ability that also had been

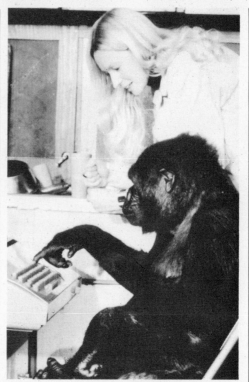

Figure 5.7 *Koko Communicating*
Koko, the gorilla made famous by her affection for kittens, has also been taught American Sign Language. Here she is using a computer which synthesizes human speech from symbols.

demonstrated by the chimpanzee Washoe. Koko has been caught lying, when she tried to blame a human for something she had broken. Koko has mastered sign language well enough to take an intelligence test designed for human beings and to score in the low-average range!

We have much to learn about nonhuman primate communication skills—what they have in common with and how they differ from human language. Considering the abilities that nonhuman primates have demonstrated, an intriguing question that remains to be answered is why they have not put these skills to use in the wild, where their communication with one another seems limited to a small number of signs that have very natural expressive meanings. One project now underway that may eventually help us answer questions like this one began at the Institute for Primate Studies in Oklahoma. There, a group of chimpanzees—including Washoe—who have learned American Sign Language were placed together on an island to see how they would use ASL with each other, whether they would learn signs from each other, and whether their skills would be passed on to the next generation (Linden, 1974). In 1980 the project was moved to Central Washington University where the study of communication between chimpanzees has been continued. Roger Fouts and his colleagues (R. Fouts, D. Fouts, & D. Schoenfeld, 1984) have reported that by 1984 Washoe's adopted offspring, Loulis, had learned 28 signs from her mother. By mid-1986 the number had reached 65 (D. Fouts, personal communication, July 15, 1986).

In evolutionary terms, chimpanzees and gorillas are our closest living relatives. Perhaps they do have the same basic symbolic capacities as human beings, but the controversy about how close their communication skills parallel our own continues. The communication skills of these nonhuman primates are tremendously impressive, but whether they can use the "languages" they have been taught as symbols and not just as systems of meaningful signs remains to be seen. So far none of the primates in these studies have demonstrated that they have Helen Keller's distinctively human insight that *everything* can be given a name.

The Biological Basis of Language

The exceptional human linguistic ability—an ability that has allowed the creation and perpetuation of complex cultures—is made possible by a biologically inherited, specialized set of structures in the brain. The human brain is a complex affair, as yet imperfectly understood. It consists of three major subdivisions: (1) the brain stem, which regulates involuntary processes such as breathing and heartbeat and controls basic drives such as hunger and anger; (2) the cerebellum, which coordinates muscular activity; and (3) the cerebral cortex, the largest and most recently evolved part of the brain, which monitors the senses, controls mental activities, and initiates voluntary activities (see Fig. 5.8).

The cerebral cortex is the area of the brain that analyzes sensory experiences and initiates conscious action. Seen from above, it is divided in half into two major components or hemispheres. Each hemisphere is creased by numerous folds. The specialized language mechanisms of the cerebral cortex are located on only one side of the cerebral cortex—on the left hemisphere for almost all individuals.

Below one of the major creases is Wernicke's area, an area of the cortex that receives incoming information about speech sounds. Wernicke's area seems to be the seat of comprehension of the meaning of speech, for it seems to perform the function of interpreting the meanings of words. This area also is involved in the formulation of verbal messages. Here concepts are apparently translated into their corresponding word representations.

From Wernicke's area, the word information is passed on to a larger region of the cerebral cortex called the association cortex. The association cortex coordinates information from various other parts of the cerebral cortex—such as the hearing centers, the visual centers, and the centers of physical sensation—with the vocal message by providing Wernicke's area with the conceptual information that guides its selection of the appropriate word symbols that represent those concepts.

From the association cortex, the linguistic message is sent forward to an area in the front half of the cerebral cortex known as Broca's area. In Broca's area, the message is organized grammatically. Broca's area also controls information about the sequences of movements necessary for the production of speech. Broca's area is directly in front of an important fold in the cerebral cortex known as the Fissure of Rolando, which controls the voluntary movements of various parts of the body. The part of the Fissure of Rolando directly next to Broca's area is the speech motor area. This area controls

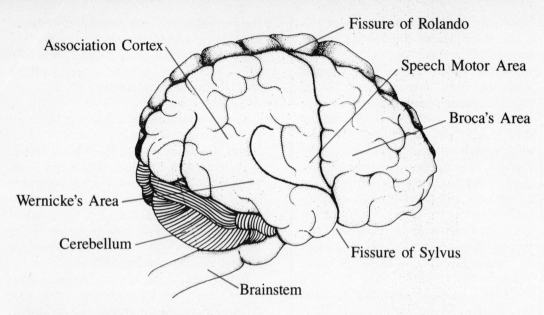

Figure 5.8 *The Speech Centers of the Human Brain*
Without the complex structures in the brain, humans wouldn't have the ability to transform sensory experiences into speech. The speech center is located in the left hemisphere of the cerebral cortex. Wernicke's area receives speech sounds and interprets them as meaningful. The association cortex coordinates information from other sensory stimuli to allow the brain to select a proper verbal response. Broca's area, including the Fissure of Rolando, controls the grammatical sequence of words and the physical movements necessary to produce speech.

the movement of the vocal cords, tongue, jaws, and lips. Thus, Broca's area seems to be directly in charge of causing this area of the brain to move the vocal apparatus in the proper sequences to produce the speech sounds of the message.

There are no *direct* connections between the parts of the association areas that deal with vision, those that pertain to hearing, and those that are related to the motor activities of speech. Lancaster (1968) has pointed out that in monkeys and apes the only way of making these connections involves another region of the brain known as the limbic system. The limbic system consists of some of the deeper and evolutionarily older areas of the cortex that deal with emotional experience. This may be why vocal communication in the nonhuman primates such as the apes and monkeys is limited to the expression of internal motivational states. In human beings, on the other hand, indirect connections that do not involve the limbic system (and emotion) can be made between the areas of the association cortex, which are connected with the other sensory centers, and the association areas connected to the speech centers

(DeVore, 1965). This gives humans the unique ability to withhold vocalizations in moments of emotional excitation and to communicate vocally about facts of no immediate emotional significance to the speaker, abilities of fundamental importance for symbolic communication.

The Structure of Language

Anthropological linguists who are interested in the structure of languages have shown that all languages have definite patterns in the sounds that their speakers use, in how those sounds are combined to form symbols, and in how those symbols are organized into meaningful utterances. These three structured parts of language are called phonology, morphology, and syntax.

Phonology. Phonology is concerned with the basic building blocks of a language. It is the study of the sounds that are used in speech and the rules for producing the various sequences of sounds that occur in a particular language. The human vocal apparatus is capable of forming a very large number of different sounds. However, the range of sounds actually produced in human languages is relatively small. Although there are at least 3,000 languages in the world, it is possible to record any human language using the International Phonetic Alphabet, a special alphabet that consists of less than 100 sound symbols.

The description of a specific language begins by using some of the symbols of this alphabet to record the phones, sounds made by speakers of the language. This record is called a phonetic description of the language. A phonetic transcription of a language records more sound detail than would seem necessary to native speakers. A simple phonetic transcription of verse from the well-known English poem, ''The Walrus and the Carpenter'' by Lewis Carroll looks like this:

ðə tʰāym hæz kʰʌm
ðə wɔlrʌs sɛd
tʰu tʰɔk əv mɛ̃ni θĩŋz
əv šuz æ̃nd šĩps
æ̃nd silĩŋ wæks
əv kʰæbəjə̌z æ̃nd kʰĩŋz
æ̃nd way ðə si iz bɔylĩŋ hat
æ̃nd wɛðər pʰɪgz hæv wĩŋz.

One important reason that a phonetic transcription of one's native language is difficult to read without practice is that it records more information than is needed by fluent speakers who are unconscious of many of the predictable sound patterns in their speech. In every language, it is found that some of the phonetically recorded sounds are not meaningfully distinct from one another. Instead, they are simply variants, or allophones of a more general sound called a phoneme of that language. For instance, a native English speaker is likely to say that the letter *t* in the words ''top'' and ''stop'' are the same sound. In fact, this is not the case. In the first word the pronunciation of the *t* ends with a definite explosion of air that is not present following the *t* in the second word. This difference can be demonstrated by pronouncing each word while holding the end of a strip of paper against the upper lip. The paper will flutter only when the word ''top'' is pronounced.

Once it is determined how the phones of a language are grouped into phonemes, it is possible to record the language phonemically using a smaller alphabet designed especially for that language. A phonemic alphabet is made using only one symbol for each phoneme of the language. The phonemes of such alphabets are the units of sound that native speakers of a language think of as different sounds. A phoneme is a psychologically distinct sound of a language in the sense that the meaning of a word will not be changed, in the opinion of native speakers, if one allophone is substituted for another, while substituting one phoneme for another can create a new word. The phoneme is the smallest meaningful unit of sound in a language, in the sense that substituting one phoneme for another can change the meaning of a word. Thus, if the word *stop* is pronounced so that the *t* is followed by the explosion of air found in its allophone in the word *top*, the word will still be heard by listeners as *stop*. However, substituting the phoneme *l* for *t* will create a different word, ''slop.''

A phonemic alphabet records the distinctions in sounds that are psychologically relevant to the native speakers of a language. It records their language in a way that native speakers are likely to describe as ''spelling words the way they sound.'' In a phonemic transcription of spoken English the word *hiss* would be written as *his*, and the word *his* would be written as *hiz*. Typically, only between 20 to 45 phonemes are necessary for writing a language. English, for instance, has 45 phonemically distinct sounds. Since the 26-letter alphabet used by English speakers for writing their language is not phonemically accurate, English speakers must learn a complex system of spelling to decipher the conventions they use in writing their language.

Grammar. Grammar is the analysis of the regular ways that the sounds of a language are combined to form meaningful utterances. Grammar has two subdivisions. The first of these is morphology, the study of how phonemes are combined into the smallest meaningful units, called morphemes. *Alligator, love,* and *Arkansas* are morphemes of English. These morphemes are called free morphemes because they can stand alone as words in sentences. English morphemes such as -s, meaning "plural," and pre-, meaning "before," are called bound morphemes because they cannot serve as words in sentences. Bound morphemes only occur as suffixes or prefixes of other morphemes. Sometimes several morphemes carry the same meaning, for instance -s, -z (written as an s in English), -en, and -ren—all of which mean "plural." Such morphemes are considered variants of one another, since it is predictable which will be chosen by English speakers as the suffix for another morpheme. Thus, child combines acceptably only with the plural morpheme -ren. Morphemes that carry the same meaning in this way are called allomorphs of one another.

Syntax is the second subdivision of grammar. It is the study of the rules for combining morphemes into complete and meaningful sentences. All languages do an adequate job of expressing meanings, but each language has its own distinctive rules that control how one goes about expressing those meanings. Although we each find the conventions of our own language quite natural, seeing how differently other languages operate can give us some idea of the fact that what seems natural to us as native speakers is merely one of many possible conventions.

Languages such as English use word order to indicate differences between the actor and the acted-upon. For instance, there is an important difference of meaning between the two English sentences, *The dog bit the child*, and *The child bit the dog*. In many languages, the distinction between subject and object is instead indicated by subject and/or object suffixes. For instance, in the Latin sentence *Canis infant-em momordit* (literally, "Dog child-object bit"), the suffix -em indicates the object. Languages that distinguish subjects and objects in this way can become quite free in their word order. Thus, in Latin *Infant-em momordit canis* also would be used to mean "The dog bit the child." Often, in languages that do not rely on order to indicate subject-object relations, differences in order may convey differences in emphasis. In the two Latin

sentences just used, the first might be translated as "The *dog* bit the child," while the second would be "The dog bit the *child*." Some languages have special ways of marking an emphasized word. For instance, in the Andean language Quechua the bound morpheme -qa indicates the emphasized topic of a sentence: *Alqu wawa-ta-a kʷanirqa* (literally, "dog child-object-topic bites"), which might be translated as "The dog bites *the child*," but *Alqu-qa wawa-ta kʷani-n* would be "*The dog* bites the child."

Quechua greatly elaborates the process of modifying single words with suffixes to express complex meanings. Thus, the two-word Quechua sentence *Mana kasu-wa-na-yki-chiq-ri-chu* (literally, "Not obey-me-for-you-plural-nicely-question") means "Is it not for you to obey me nicely?" Other languages such as Chinese use but one morpheme per word, so that the Chinese equivalent of "The dog bit the boy" would be *Gǒ yǎo le shǎohái*." (literally, "Dog child bite completed"), the time of the action being specified by a particular word *le* that indicates that the action of the verb *yǎo* is completed.

The many languages of the world differ tremendously in their phonologies and grammars. Despite the great diversity in how languages organize a small number of sounds into meaningful sentences, all languages seem equally able to express ideas. As natural as your own language may seem to you after years of use, it is no more fundamentally human in its workings than others. Like all symbolic systems, languages convey meanings effectively simply because their users have learned the same conventions for interpreting those meanings.

Linguistic Relativity

In their study of languages spoken in both simple and complex societies, anthropologists have not found a language that might be described as "primitive." All languages are equally able to be used as vehicles for the expression of complex and intricate ideas. Languages differ from one another simply in the superficial ways of organizing the verbal elements used to express concepts. Individual languages differ in the sounds they use for forming words, but in all languages it is possible to form a new verbal symbol whenever speakers wish to express a new concept. They differ in the order in which they arrange the subjects, verbs, and objects with which they express relationships between the things and processes that all human beings are capable of thinking about. They differ in that some use prefixes where others use suffixes and where still others use separate words instead of either prefixes or suffixes, but one of these methods is as effective as the others in getting the hearer to become aware of some finer aspect of form, quality, or process than the original word symbolizes.

The vocabularies of different languages also differ from one another, but this reflects no difference in the ability of speakers of one language to create, whenever the necessity arises, a new word for a concept already symbolized in the vocabulary of another language (Boas, 1966). Vocabulary differences are simply a reflection of current differences in what needs to be talked about in different social groups. Thus, the vocabulary of English includes terms for electron microscope, shortstop, and hero sandwich, while Navajo has a term *shosh* that means "to place slender stiff objects (like sticks or pencils) side by side (in a parallel position)" and a word, *hózhó*, for the beauty, harmony, good, happiness, and everything positive or ideal as embodied in the environment as a whole. As circumstances change and a social group acquires new things to talk about, the vocabulary of the language used by that group also changes.

Basic conceptual processes are universal in the human species, and the specific products of these processes, which differ from group to group, can be symbolically expressed in any language. Nevertheless, the vocabulary and grammatical differences of different languages do have an impact on (1) which things will be habitually noticed, labelled, and thought about in a highly conscious way and (2) how speakers will habitually organize their conscious expression of the relationships between these things (Sapir, 1949). The idea that language influences thought processes is expressed in the theory of linguistic relativity, sometimes called the "Sapir-Whorf hypothesis"

after two of its originators. According [to] [lin]guistic relativity, what a people habitua[lly] think about is a reflection of what the current vocabulary of their language impels them to notice, and at least some aspects of how people think will be affected by the grammatical relationships demanded by their language. Human thinking, in other words, is not simply a matter of universal biological cognitive processes. Human beings also habitually organize their thoughts in patterns guided by the grammatical structure of their own language. Although language structure does not *determine* how its speakers think, most anthropological linguists recognize that language does have some effects on what we think about most readily and on how we think much of the time.

Effects of Morphology. Benjamin Lee Whorf was an originator of the idea that the superficial and arbitrary grammatical patterns that distinguish one language from another influence the ways in which its speakers habitually think about the world. His strongest case is for the effect that the morphology of a language can have on its speakers' tendency to notice some things readily while failing to pay attention to others. For example, Whorf (1971) pointed out that one place in which industrial fires frequently begin is the room in which so-called "empty" containers are stored. The word *empty* is a symbol that refers to two somewhat different concepts: It is used to mean (1) "containing only residues, gases, vapor, or stray rubbish," and also, in a more basic sense, to mean (2) "vacuous, inert, or containing nothing." Those who label the room as a storage area for "empty containers" are using the word in its more specialized association with the first concept, but other persons are likely to behave around these containers of sometimes volatile residues and gases as if they were inert and vacuous. A worker who would never consider lighting a cigarette near a "full" gasoline drum might casually do so near an "empty" one, never stopping to think that the volatile gasoline fumes that remain in the empty containers are much more likely to ignite explosively than is the

... containers. Ac-
... of a single sym-
... different concepts
... zardous situations.
... that people's names
... ... how they behave
... even more than the
physical ... things themselves. He
cited the blower ... an example. Physically,
a blower is a machine that simply causes
air to move. Yet when it is used to make air
pass through a room—such as a room for
drying materials—because it is called a *blower* workers are likely to install it so that it
blows air into the room instead of *pulling* air
out of the room. The former method of installation is no more efficient and is much
more hazardous, since an electrical fire in
the machine itself will be blown into the
room where the contents may also ignite.
Once begun, the fire will be fanned by a
blower installed in this way as long as it
continues to function.

Sometimes labels are changed in the
hope of avoiding undesirable conditioned
responses or of calling forth some hoped-
for result. Thus, unpopular wars are called
"pacification programs" and the American
War Department was renamed the "Defense Department." Similarly, tuna did not
become a popular food in the United States
until one company began to label it "Chick-
en of the Sea." And those who wished to
support what they called more workable
"legal controls" over drug use or prostitu-
tion soon recognized that it was better to
use such labels for their legislative
proposals than to refer to them as attempts
to "legalize" these activities. Western
science provides a further example of con-
ditioning effects of verbal symbolic labels:
European scientists noted that when they
"added heat" to an object, its weight did
not change. So for years they searched for
evidence of other "weightless substances"
before they realized that heat, even though
it is labeled by a noun, is actually a process
rather than a substance.

Effects of syntax. Syntactical processes
may also affect how speakers of a language
think about the world and how they behave, although the influence of syntax is
probably not so great as the effects of mor-

phology. One finds numerous examples of
correlations between a society's customs
and values and the grammatical characteristics of its language. For instance, the Navajo language is highly verb-oriented; even
inactive verbs have a structure that implies
a state achieved by motion. The language
describes the universe as kinds of motion
to which subjects may attach themselves
but for which they are not causally responsible. This feature parallels perfectly the
Navajo world view, in which the universe
is seen as being in a state of dynamic flux
and humankind is seen as subordinate to
a more powerful nature, with which humans may interact and to which they may
adapt but never master. Similarly, in the
Navajo language, it is ungrammatical to use
a verb meaning "to cause to do" with a human object. The closest Navajo translation
of "I made him go home" would run something like "Even though he did not want
to go home, when I asked him to, he did."
This is in perfect parallel to Navajo social
values, in which coercion is strongly
rejected.

Harré (1984) cites examples of Inuit grammar that parallel Inuit ideology. If the Inuit
respond to the question "Who is preparing dinner?" their answer, *uva-nga*, does not
translate as "I am" but as "The being here-
mine." The English "I hear him" becomes
in Inuit *tusarp-a-ra*, literally, "his making of
a sound with reference to me." In general,
where English grammar portrays a person
as an entity who has attributes and intentions and who intiates actions, Inuit de-
signates a person as the location at which
qualities and relations occur. This characteristic of Inuit grammar mirrors and supports
Inuit social life, in which one's position
within the group is much more important
than one's characteristics as an individual.
Responsiveness to others is the hallmark of
Inuit social interaction: When one laughs,
all laugh; when one cries, everyone cries.
According to Harré, "At least with respect
to a large and varied catalogue of public per-
formances, individual feelings, intentions,
and reasonings play a very minor role"
(p. 88).

Such parallels between syntax and culture are best viewed as systems like that of

the chicken and its egg: It is not clear which came first. Syntax may change to reflect the culture in which the language is spoken, but the habits of thought embodied in that syntax may help to maintain conformity to the rules of the culture by making those rules feel very natural to those who speak the language.

An interesting parallel between grammar and ideas about the logical relationships between things in the universe is found in English religious literature concerning the existence of God. According to the believer, ''Creation itself demands a creator.'' If one examines this argument in terms of English grammar, it takes on a different significance than is intended when it is used as an argument for the existence of God. *Creation* is formed of two meaningful elements, the root *create* and the suffix *-tion*, which was borrowed from Old French into English. This suffix means ''that which has been — —ed.'' Indeed, many dictionaries define *creation* as ''that which has been created,'' forcing the reader to consult another entry for a complete definition. In English, a noun-focused language, no declarative sentence (one that makes a contention about the nature of some part of reality) may occur without a subject that can carry out the action of the verb used in the sentence. Therefore, the existence of the verb *create* (which is ''demanded'' by the existence of the noun *creation*) requires the existence of a noun that can serve as its subject in a declarative sentence. Many nouns can serve as the subject of the verb *create*. However, the noun that corresponds most closely to the verb *create* in the role of subject is the noun *creator*, which is formed of the same root and the Old French suffix *-tor*, which means ''one who ——s.'' Thus, what the argument ''Creation itself demands a creator'' really indicates is that the existence in English of a noun of the form *crea-tion* implies the existence of a verb *create* which, in turn, requires the existence for use in a declarative sentence of a subject noun of the form *crea-tor*. Whether the existence of the universe, which may arbitrarily be labeled with the symbol *creation*, ''demands'' the existence of a preexisting deity who brought it into existence is another matter entirely.

Although English speakers may be swayed by the ''logic'' of the sentence, this argument for the existence of God loses its impact when it is translated into many other languages.

Language, then, seems to have an effect on the way people relate to the world. It is a conscious vehicle of habitual thought. The vocabulary of any language selects out segments of reality of which its speakers must become aware when they learn to use their language. And the grammar is a built-in logic system that leads its users to relate the parts of the world to one another in the same way that the grammar organizes the relationships between the words that stand for those parts of the world.

Changes in Language

Since languages are symbol systems and much of the pattern of grammatical organization of a language's verbal symbols is itself arbitrary, languages are highly subject to change. Language change may occur as the language is passed, by learning, from one generation to the next. A language may also change as its speakers are influenced by their interaction with speakers of other languages. In the following sections, these processes of linguistic change will be described in detail.

Changes over time.   Since the sounds used to form the verbal symbols of a language have no necessary connection with the meanings of those symbols, it is possible for both the sounds used to build these words and the meanings attached to them to change as time passes. Likewise, the customary ways of organizing the verbal symbols into such meaningful grammatical patterns as word order to communicate relationships between the concepts may also change as time passes. Thus, with the passage of time, languages may change in their sound system, their semantic or meaning system, and in their grammatical system. Consider for instance, the differences between contemporary versions of the Lord's Prayer and this Old English version written before the year 1066:

Faeder ure, thu theube eart on heofonum, si thin nama gehalgod. Tobecum thin rice,

Gewurthe thin willa on eordhan swa swa on heofonum. Urne gedaeghwamlican hlaf syle us to daeg. And forgyf us ure gyltas, swa swa we forgyfadh urum gyltendum. And ne gelaed thu us on costnunge, ac alys us of yfele. Sothlice.[2]

Since language change involves change in the systems that comprise it, the changes show up in systematic or patterned ways. For instance, when the sounds of a language change from generation to generation, the change of one sound to a new sound expresses itself in every word of the language in which that sound occurs. Compare a list of Old English words of about 1,000 years ago with their modern English equivalents:

Old English	Modern English
hus	house
mus	mouse
ut	out
hu	how

In this list, the Old English *u* represents a sound that would be pronounced approximately as *uw*. Consistently, these same words are pronounced today by English speakers as the vowel sequence *ao*, variously written as *ou* or *ow* in contemporary spelling. That is, the Old English sound *uw* became *ao* in Modern English, consistently changing the pronunciation of all English words in which it occurs.

Subdivisions within a language. Such changes in language occur gradually with the passage of time. Yet, at any given time, the need to communicate effectively within a social group necessitates a certain degree of mutual sharing in the sounds used to form words, in the meanings of words, and in the grammatical patterns for combining them. So, as a language changes, it changes in the same way for all members of the group. However, when a group is subdivided, either geographically or socially, a characteristic of those divisions is the tendency for members of each group to communicate more frequently with members of their own group than with members of the

others. One result of such isolation is that new ways of speaking that arise in one of the groups may not pass over into the others. Thus, the language originally spoken in all these groups can gradually change until it is made up of separate dialects (Bloomfield, 1933). For instance, the English now spoken in England differs from the varieties of English spoken in the United States and Australia, although all three varieties developed from the same English that was spoken but a few hundred years ago by emigrants from Great Britain.

Dialects of the same original language can gradually become so different that their speakers are no longer able to understand one another. English and German are examples of two languages that were at one time in history a single language. This language, called Proto-Germanic by modern students of language, was spoken on the mainland of Europe in what is now northern Germany. The people who spoke this language were known as the Angles and Saxons. They left the mainland about 1,500 to 2,000 years ago to become a separate social group in the British Isles where their isolation allowed the language to change in different ways than it did on the mainland. Since the process of change was systematic in both groups, one finds a system of consistent parallels between the two "daughter" languages, German and English. Compare, for instance, the initial sound of the following word lists from German and English, and notice that the German *z* (written as upper case Z in the case of nouns), which is pronounced *ts*, is consistently a *t* sound in English:

German	English
zu	to
zwanzig	twenty
zwölf	twelve
zwitschern	twitter
Zinn	tin

Word-borrowing. Change in language also occurs when words are borrowed by the speakers of one language from other languages with which they come in contact, especially those spoken by their politically and economically more powerful neigh-

---

2. From *Old English: An Introduction* (p. 19) by Robert J. Kispert, 1971, New York: Holt, Rinehart and Winston. Copyright 1971.

bors. Such changes generally involve the borrowing of foreign words for items and activities that are introduced into society by speakers of another language or by interaction with more prestigious speakers of a foreign language. For instance, following the Norman invasion of England in 1066, English speakers began to be influenced by the Old French language of the more powerful Normans. Today, about half of the vocabulary of the English language traces its origins to borrowed Old French words. Approximately two and one half centuries after the invasion, an early historian, Robert of Gloucester (1300) described in his *Chronicle* the effects of the language of the Norman rulers on English:

Thus com, lo, Engelond in to Normandies hond; And the Normans ne couthe spek tho bote hor owe spech, And speke French as hii dude atom, and hor children dude also teche,
So that heiemen of this lond that of hor blod come Holdeth alle thulke speeche that hii of hom nome; Vor bote a man conne Frenss me to telp of him lute. Ac lowe men holdeth to Engliss, and to hor owe speche zhute.[3]

(Lo, thus England came into Normandy's hand; and the Normans speak nothing but their own speech, and spoke French as they did at home, and did so teach their children,
So that high men of this land that came of their blood Hold the same speech that they received of them; For except a man knows French men speak little of him. But low men hold to English, and to their own speech yet.)

Those English speakers who had the most contact with the Norman rulers began to adopt Old French terms for elements of Norman life, although the speech of the English commoners was less influenced. For instance, contemporary English has inherited a distinction between the cooked and live forms of several meat animals. *Mutton*, *pork*, and *beef* were adopted into English from Old French (*moton*, *porc*, and *boef*) for use when serving foods to the Norman rulers. When the animals were still alive and in the keeping of the English peasants they were called by their original English names, *sheep*, *swine*, and *cow*. These latter three terms have their counterparts, not in French, but in the German words *Schaf*, *Swein*, and *Kuh*, a derivation that reflects the recent separation of English and German from a common ancestral language. Similarly, the word *roast* represents a borrowing from Old French—*rostir*, a verb used by cooks when speaking about preparing meat for their Norman rulers. This aristocratic term did not, however, replace the original English word *bake*, which continued to be used in the peasant households for the same method of preparing meat. *Bake* itself stems from the same original word as the German word *backen*, which means ''to bake or roast.'' Notice that in modern English, one still ''roasts pork'' (both words being of Old French origin) or ''bakes ham'' (both Germanic words). Although the foods themselves and the cooking procedures may be identical, the two idioms reflect two socially different speech contexts (Leaf, 1971).

Basic Vocabulary

The tenacity of these Germanic words for things that were important in households suggests that domestic terminology may be somewhat more stable and resistant to externally induced language change than are other parts of a vocabulary. The part of a language that best reflects its internal history consists of those words that are learned by individuals early in their lives in their home setting. Such words are used with a high frequency in normal speech situations. The habit of their use is not easily overcome, and foreign terms are not likely to supplant them (Gudschinsky, 1964). The part of a vocabulary that has these qualities is known as the basic vocabulary of a language. It includes such words as *father, mother, brother, sister, head, hand, foot, eat, water, drink, fire, house, earth, sky, sun, moon, star,* and others that designate basic elements of people's social, biological, and physical environments.

By comparing the basic vocabularies of two languages, it is possible to determine whether they developed from the same

3. From *A Middle English Reader* (p. 210) by Oliver Farrar Emerson, 1923. New York: Macmillan. Copyright 1923.

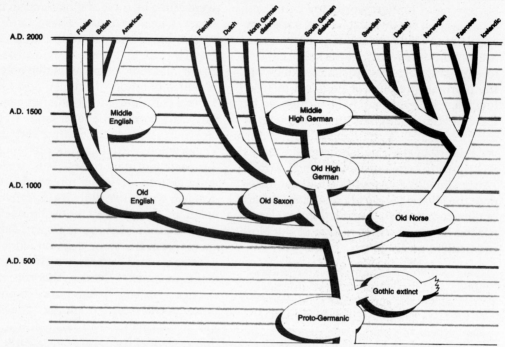

Figure 5.9 *The Family Tree of Northern European Languages*
The root or parent language of Northern European languages is Proto-Germanic which itself is derived from an earlier Proto-Indo-European common base.

common ancestral language, proof that may not be evident in comparing the entire contemporary vocabularies of the languages. For instance, although over 50% of the entire English vocabulary is derived from French, the frequency of French words in English does not indicate that French and English are languages that arose recently from a common ancestral language. This distinction becomes clear when one examines the English basic vocabulary. In this more stable part of the vocabulary, English words generally have their closest counterparts not in French but in the Germanic languages spoken in the region from which the Anglo-Saxon immigrants to England originally came. The recent common origin of English and German, for instance, is illustrated by the following short comparative basic vocabulary lists:

English	German
father	vater
mother	mutter
brother	bruder
sister	schwester

hand	hand
house	haus
mouse	maus
water	wasser
sun	sonne
moon	mond
fire	feuer

Language Families

Such lists of basic vocabulary terms make it possible to compare languages to find how many of these items they share. It is assumed that the more of these stable items two languages share in common, the more recently they began diverging from a single parent language to become separate languages in their own right. Using this assumption, it is possible to reconstruct a family tree of related languages. When one compares the languages of northern Europe by this method, a family tree results that looks like the one in Figure 5.9. The points of branching on this language family tree correspond to major occurrences in the histories of the societies that led to the separation of the speakers of the original language into socially separate subdivisions. Thus, the point of separation of Old English from the other branches that arose from Proto-Germanic reflects the migration of the Anglo-Saxons from the northern German coast to the British Isles about A.D. 500. After this time the islanders were no longer in intense enough communication with their mainland counterparts to maintain a language unity.

This process of language family tree construction has been used to demonstrate the common ancestry of most European languages and also to show that European languages are but one part of a larger family of languages stretching from Europe through India. This larger family of languages diverged from a single common ancestral language, called Proto-Indo-European by linguists today. It was spoken almost 5,000 years ago. The languages of other parts of the world also have been grouped into similar language families.

A method also has been developed to estimate the minimum number of years since the divergence of any two related languages. The method, called glottochronology, makes it possible to assign dates to the various branches in a language family tree. By comparing the basic vocabularies of languages that belong to different language families and have had long written histories, researchers discovered that about 14% of a 100-word basic vocabulary was replaced by new words every 1,000 years in all the languages that have been examined in non-isolated societies (Gudschinsky, 1964). Thus, the rate of change in the basic vocabulary, being a constant, can be used to compute the length of time that two languages have been diverging from one another. Since about 14% of the basic vocabulary of a parent language will be lost in any daughter language after a 1,000 years of change from that original state, each daughter language will maintain 86% of the original vocabulary. Therefore, 86% of whatever items any other daughter language has maintained from that original vocabulary will be found in the base vocabulary of any other daughter language. Consequently, if one compares lists of 100 basic vocabulary items for two contemporary languages and discovers that they share about 74 basic vocabulary items (86% of 86 items), then one may calculate that they were in fact a single language 1,000 years ago. Two languages will share about 55 (74% of 74) of the original 100 basic vocabulary items after 2,000 years of separation and about 41 items (74% of 55) after 3,000 years of separation (see Table 5.1).

Contemporary World Languages

It is estimated that there are at least 3,000 languages spoken in the world today. Some estimates are nearer 5,000. The exact number is difficult to determine because of dialects—geographical or social variants of the same language. The dialects that make up a language can be very similar to one another or so distinct that two linguists might not agree on whether they should be called dialects or separate languages. Consider German and Dutch. Although speakers of Bavarian German dialects would be unable to comprehend the dialect spoken in a German village in Schleswig-Holstein near the border of Denmark, the change from one local dialect to the next is too gradual to claim that there is more than one German language in the country. Similarly, the dialects spoken in small towns on either side of the German and Dutch borders may be so similar that the inhabitants of both towns can understand one another. Yet people speak of German and Dutch as if they were separate languages. In fact, some southern German dialects differ more from the nationally preferred way of speaking the modern standard German "language" (which is mostly based on northern German dialects) than some northern dialects in Germany differ from Dutch.

Some languages are spoken by relatively few native speakers. For instance, only a few thousand people speak Shoshoni today. On the other hand, some languages are spoken by many societies with very different cultures. Such languages may cross the borders of modern nation-states and be spoken by millions of people. For instance, English is one of the official languages of India as well as the native tongue of peoples as geographically distant from

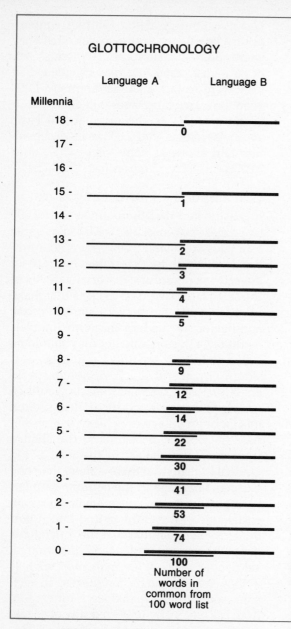

GLOTTOCHRONOLOGY

Table 5.1 *Glottochronological Change Human vocabulary shares a common ancestral language or protolanguage. After a period of one thousand years any given language will replace 14% of its vocabulary with that of another. This chart graphically portrays the divergence of languages over a period of time.*

one another as England, Canada, South Africa, the Falkland Islands, and Jamaica.

The languages spoken by the largest numbers of people today are those that have become the national languages of major nations. The Beijing dialect (formerly called Mandarin) of China is spoken by about 713 million people. English is the next most commonly spoken language of the world, with about 391 million speakers. Table 5.2 shows the 20 most widely spoken languages of the world as of 1981.

In some parts of the world, many different languages are spoken by people who differ relatively little in their culture. Canada maintains two nationally recognized languages, French and English; political speeches and advertising must be carried out in both. In Nigeria about 400 languages are spoken, of which only 3 have been designated as official languages. Such a diversity of spoken languages can create enormous political problems in administering governmental affairs throughout the country. The elevation of one or more languages to official status is intended to alleviate some of these problems. Since government business is largely conducted

Language	Speakers (in millions)	Language	Speakers (in millions)
1. Mandarin (China)	713	11. Malay or Indonesian	112
2. English	391	12. French	105
3. Russian	270	13. Urdu (Pakistan and India)	70
4. Spanish	251	14. Punjabi (India and Pakistan)	64
5. Hindi (India)	245	15. Italian	61
6. Arabic	151	16. Korean	59
7. Bengali (Bangladesh and India)	148	17. Telugu (India)	59
8. Portuguese	148	18. Tamil (India and Sri Lanka)	58
9. German	119	19. Marathi (India)	56
10. Japanese	118	20. Cantonese (China)	54

Note. From *The World Almanac and Book of Facts* (p. 164) by S. S. Culbert, 1982, New York: Newspaper Enterprise Association.

Table 5.2 *The World's Twenty Most Commonly Spoken Languages*
The use of one language by a great many people depends as much on population in a given area as it does on political and national status of the language.

in an official language, speakers of other languages are expected to learn one of the official languages or find an interpreter when they wish to deal with government administrators. Where national languages exist, they are likely to be the ones used in the school system, with the idea of teaching all citizens to use the national language. Although the selection of one of a society's languages as an official one may simplify some of the problems of governing a linguistically diverse country, the designation of an official language is not without its problems. For instance, speakers of a nonofficial language may find themselves at a political or economic disadvantage compared with others who speak the national language. Such circumstances can lead to political rivalries and conflicts that are difficult to resolve.

Summary

The basis for the complexity of human cultures is our ability to form and communicate concepts. Whereas signs are communications that express our feelings directly, symbols are forms of communication in which one thing is arbitrarily used to represent another, according to socially agreed-on and learned conventions. Human communication is highly symbolic and therefore extremely flexible. While some nonverbal messages such as our gestures, facial expressions, body language, and distances from each other are spontaneous signs of our emotions, even nonverbal communications may be symbolic. Verbal communication—language—is totally symbolic, for speech sounds, written words, and ways of arranging them are uniquely and arbitrarily assigned symbolic meanings within each culture.

The capacity for creating and using complex language systems seems to reside within certain areas of the human cerebral cortex. Research suggests that some non-human primates may have similar, though more limited, capacities but do not use them unless they are carefully taught to do so. Languages and cultures are so closely linked that the forms and patterns of our speech both affect and reflect how we perceive the world. Languages, like their cultures, change over time and with influences from other cultures and their languages. The part of a language that is most resistant to change is its basic vocabulary, which consists of household words taught and used from childhood. Differences and similarities in basic vocabularies allow linguists to trace the historical growth of language families into the many languages and dialects spoken in the world today.

Key Terms and Concepts

learning 101
neocortex 101
concepts 101
percepts 102
closure 102
ganzfeld phenomenon 104
communication 105
sign 105
symbol 106
nonverbal communication 110
proxemics 112
intimate distance 112
personal distance 112
social distance 114
public distance 114
kinesics 114
metacommunication system 115
speech 115
language 115
American Sign Language (ASL) 116
brain stem 119
cerebellum 119
cerebral cortex 119
Wernicke's area 119
association cortex 119

Broca's area 119
Fissure of Rolando 119
speech motor area 120
limbic system 120
phonology 120
International Phonetic Alphabet (IPA) 121
phone 121
phonetic 121
allophones 121
phonemic 121
phoneme 121
grammar 121
morphology 121
morpheme 121
free morpheme 122
bound morpheme 122
allomorph 122
syntax 122
linguistic relativity 123
Proto-Germanic 126
basic vocabulary 127
Proto-Indo-European 129
glottochronology 129
dialect 129

Annotated Readings

Birdwhistell, R. L. (1970). *Kinesics and context: Essays on body motion communication*. Philadelphia, PA: University of Pennsylvania Press. An exposition of the techniques used for analyzing body movement in nonverbal communication.

Blount, B. G. (1974). *Language, culture and society: A book of readings*. Cambridge, MA: Winthrop. A basic collection of articles on anthropological linguistics in the 1970s.

Burling, R. (1970). *Man's many voices: Language in the cultural context*. New York: Holt, Rinehart and Winston. A basic introductory text about anthropological linguistics.

Carroll, J. B. (1956). *Language, thought and reality: Selected writings of Benjamin Lee Whorf*. Cambridge, MA: M.I.T. Press. The primary writings of Whorf on the effects of language on thought and action.

Greenberg, J. H. (1968). *Anthropological linguistics: An introduction*. New York: Random House. A good nontechnical introduction to anthropological linguistics.

Hall, E. T. (1959). *The silent language*. Greenwich, CT: Fawcett Publications. An interesting look at the rules for nonverbal communications in a variety of cultures.

Hymes, D. (1964). *Language in culture and society: A reader in linguistics and anthropology*. New York: Harper & Row. A collection of seminal writings in the various subfields within anthropological linguistics. Somewhat dated, but still the most comprehensive collection of its kind.

Lenneberg, E. H. (1967). *The biological foundations of language*. New York: Wiley. The basic text on the biological basis of speech.

Linden, E. (1974). *Apes, men, and language*. New York: Penguin. A popular account of the history of work with chimpanzees and American sign language.

Mandelbaum, D. G. (1968). *Selected writings of Edward Sapir in language, culture and personality*. Berkeley, CA: University of California Press. A well-chosen collection of the classic writings of the father of American anthropological linguistics.

Chapter 6

The Life Cycle

Some of the social statuses we acquire follow one another in a definite sequence, a sequence that defines the typical course of life of an average member of society. This sequence of typical status changes from birth to death is known as the life cycle in a society. Many of the changes are gradual, such as our training in the ways of our society during childhood. But some are more dramatic shifts in status and may be dealt with through special ceremonies. These widely celebrated turning points in the human life cycle are birth, puberty, marriage, and death.

Rites of Passage

Arnold van Gennep (1960) has pointed out that as we move from one status to another within the life cycle, our changes in status and role expectations are commonly proclaimed to other members of society by formal rituals known as life crisis rites or rites of passage. Rites of passage symbolically dramatize how important status changes are in the eyes of society. Of all the possible changes in status that might be recognized with public symbolic rituals, four are commonly celebrated throughout the world naming ceremonies, which confer human status on the new member of society and proclaim the entry into parenthood of its caretakers; puberty celebrations, which confer adult status; marriages, which legitimize new sexual, economic, and childrearing obligations; and funerals, which proclaim the loss of human status by the deceased and restructure the ongoing social order.

There are many other status changes that are less widespread or peculiar to specific societies. The Navajo celebrate the first smile of a baby with ceremonial gift-giving (Kluckhohn & Leighton, 1946). In the United States, high school graduation is an important life change as is one's first full-time job. Divorce is found in every society, although in most, the majority of marriages do not end in divorce. Where the family organization is an important economic and political force, parents undergo a status change when their first child is born.

Rites of passage help to maintain stability and order in society while the social order adjusts to culturally sig-

Figure 6.1 *Bat Mitzvah At the synagogue of Kehilath Jeshurun in New York City, this girl makes her religious coming of age. During the ceremony devout Jews wear a skull cap called a yarmulke and a shawl called a tallis.*

nificant changes in people's lives. The acquisition of a new status is important. It calls for the successful adopting of a new set of roles by the person who is moving into the new phase of life. The formal dramatization of these changes in a ritual of status change may be psychologically beneficial to those who are beginning roles that they have not practiced before. Other members of society must also adopt new ways of relating to them. The rites reduce the potential stress of laying aside the old habits. This can make the change smoother, both for the individual and for society.

Our concept of who we are is intimately related to our ability to be comfortable in the roles we play. A rite of passage gives us dramatic encouragement to adopt a new set of roles and admonishes others to respect the change. Thus, a rite of passage may provide us with a greater sense of confidence in our new social identities. But in the dominant North American culture, rites of passage are relatively weak or sometimes lacking. For instance, few people in the United States experience any form of puberty ritual as they near adulthood. This lack often creates confusion about the roles we are expected to play and leaves individuals alone to wrestle with what in the United States are called ''identity crises.'' The existence of this expression in the everyday language is evidence of how extensive role confusion is in this society. It suggests the benefits that rites of passage may provide to a society's members by helping them maintain a greater sense of self-confidence as they undergo these normal changes.

Pregnancy, Childbirth, and Naming

The first life-cycle change we all experience is being born. Even before that obviously major event, our parents are experiencing the status changes of pregnancy. The biological facts of conception, pregnancy, and the birth process are interpreted differently among cultures. After birth, each society also has specific ways of raising us to behave as others think we should.

Pregnancy and Descent

In all cultures, people are awed by the mystery of a child's growth within its mother's body. This mystery is variously explained, and the subsequent birth is handled in varying ways.

The connection between intercourse and pregnancy. Most peoples believe that pregnancy is a result of sexual intercourse, but conception is explained in a variety of ways. Often the child is thought of as developing from semen, menstrual blood, or both. In many societies, both the mother and the father are believed to contribute to the conception and sometimes the growth of the child during intercourse. Sometimes, however, the role of one parent is given more weight in explaining the origin of the child.

The relative importance of the father and the mother in creating the child seems to be related to whether the emphasis in tracing ancestry is placed on the male or female descent line in the family. There are many possible ways of keeping track of ancestry. The three most common are patrilineality, matrilineality, and bilateral descent. In the patrilineal societies, where the line of descent is traced through the males of the groups, the father is likely to be believed to have placed the child within the mother's womb during intercourse; the mother is thought to simply carry it while it grows. Where ancestry is remembered matrilineally, that is, by a line of descent through the women of the group, babies may be considered something that women naturally produce after they have become sexually active. Bilateral descent involves tracing descent lines equally through males and females. In bilateral descent, both parents are likely to be perceived as playing an important role in the creation of the child.

How descent is traced is important because it determines the kind of groups that a child will experience as kin. In patrilineal and matrilineal societies each child is born into a preexisting kinship group, groups created by the fact of their common descent from a single ancestor. Where the ancestor is still remembered and all members of the kinship group can trace their specific genealogical ties to one another, the group is called a <u>lineage</u>. Where the kin assert common descent from an ancestor too far in the past to remember the specific ties that unite them, the group is called a <u>clan</u>. Both lineages and clans can play important social and economic roles in the life of a child, such as by owning the houses and means of livelihood or determining the child's potential future mates. In bilateral descent no such preexisting kinship groups exist, since the relatives of each child will share no common ancestor. The relatives of a particular child will function as a group only in respect to events that pertain to that child. Such a kinship group is called a <u>kindred</u>. Kindreds will exist only by virtue of their relationships to individual persons, so they cannot function to regulate marital choices or own property.

Conception Without Sex in the Trobriand Islanders' Ideology

Very few societies view spiritual causes rather than sex as the cause of conception. Most notable for such beliefs are the native peoples of Australia and the native inhabitants of the Trobriand Islands. Bronislaw Malinowski (1929), who contributed to the development of anthropological research and analytic methods, lived for years among the Trobriand Islanders during World War I. He reported their beliefs about conception in a book ethnocentrically entitled *The Sexual Life of Savages*, from which the following account is derived.

The Trobrianders' ideas about conception were related to their beliefs in reincarnation. The Trobrianders believe that after death the spirit, (*baloma*) of a person goes to Tuma, the Island of the Dead, where it enjoys a happier life than that of mortals. Periodically it rejuvenates itself until it decides to return to the world of mortals. Then it transforms itself into a small spirit-infant. The spirit-infant is brought to a human mother-to-be by an older controlling spirit, who usually appears to the woman in a dream to inform her that she is about to become pregnant. This controlling spirit is most often a maternal relative of the woman, or her father.

After revealing its intentions, the controlling spirit lays the child in the woman's head, causing blood from her body to rush there before descending to the womb with the spirit-child. Actual entry may be by way of the vagina, since the Trobrianders insist that a virgin is unable to conceive because of her "tightness." Although intercourse may open the way for the child, it is not thought to cause conception, which may occur thereafter without sexual relations. After conception the woman's menstrual flow is said to cease because the mother's blood nourishes the body of the infant and helps to build it.

According to Malinowski, the combination of mystical and physiological features of these pregnancy beliefs provided a complete theory of how human life originates. In addition, Malinowski notes, "It also gives a good theoretical foundation for matriliny; for the whole process of introducing new life into a community lies between the spirit world and the female organism. There is no room for any sort of physical paternity" (1929, p. 179).

Malinowski contrasted the Trobrianders' mother-oriented system of thought with the more male-oriented ideology of the missionaries who sought to convert them to a Christian belief system:

> We must realize that the cardinal dogma of God the Father and God the Son, the sacrifice of the only Son and the filial love of man to his Maker would completely misfire in a matrilineal society, where the relation between a father and son is decreed by tribal laws to be that of two strangers, where all personal unity between them is denied, and where all family obligations are associated with mother-line. We cannot, then, wonder that paternity must be among the principle truths to be inculcated by proselytizing Christians. Otherwise the dogma of the Trinity would have to be translated into matrilineal terms, and we should have to speak of a *God-kadala* (mother's brother), a God-sister's-son, and a divine *baloma* spirit. But apart from any

doctrinal difficulty, the missionaries are earnestly engaged in propagating sexual morality as we conceive it, in which endeavor the idea of the sexual act as having serious consequences to family life is indispensable. (pp. 186-187)

The Trobrianders vehemently opposed the idea of physiological paternity, a belief that is well suited to a society with a strong patriarchal ideology but not to their own. They characterized the missionaries' belief that sex is the cause of conception as an absurdity and the missionaries, therefore, as liars. For example, Malinowski quotes one of his informants as saying, "Not at all, the missionaries are mistaken, unmarried girls continually have intercourse, in fact they overflow with seminal fluid, and yet have no children" (p. 188). By native logic, if sex were the cause of pregnancy, the unmarried girls would become pregnant more often than older married women, since they engage in sexual intercourse much more often. Yet it is the older married women who have the most children. Another informant argued, "Copulation alone cannot produce a child. Night after night, for years, girls copulate. No child comes" (p. 189), contending thereby that the empirical evidence did not support the view of a relationship between sex and pregnancy. Malinowski also tells us that, "one of my informants told me that after over a year's absence he returned to find a newly born child at home. He volunteered this statement as an illustration and final proof of the truth that sexual intercourse had nothing to do with conception. And it must be remembered that no native would ever discuss any subject in which the slightest suspicion of his wife's fidelity would be involved" (p. 193).

According to Weiner (1976), the contemporary Trobrianders, who no longer disagree with Western ideas about procreation, continue to use the concept of "virgin birth" as a way of avoiding public shame over infidelity. Weiner, relying on myths and old people's beliefs, argues that the Trobriand ideas about

spirits causing pregnancy may have served this purpose even in Malinowski's day. She believes that the implicit understanding that both sexes are part of the process of reproduction existed in ideas that, although spirits cause the pregnancy, sexual intercourse is necessary for the development of the fetus *after* conception: "A man develops and maintains the growth of the fetus through repeated sexual intercourse with his wife" (p. 123).[1]

An ideology that denies any relationship between sex and pregnancy should not be confused with ignorance about the role of sex in reproduction. In any culture, there are things that people deny for ideological reasons even though they may intuitively be aware of what they refuse to affirm. Many United States citizens, for instance, described the building of the Boulder Dam near Las Vegas as a triumph of free enterprise, even though it was built with government funds, under government direction, by engineers who worked for the government. The prevailing political ideology made it unlikely that they would have described the dam as an example of the benefits of socialism. Similarly, after the Russian government completed work on the Trans-Siberian pipeline in the 1980s, using technology imported from capitalist countries, officials hailed the work as a triumph of socialist know-how. The Trobriand Islanders' denial that sex causes conception symbolically supported their emphasis on inheritance of both property and familial authority through the mother's line. The concept of a paternal role in the creation of a child would challenge the kinship system around which their political and economic life was built. The emotional intensity of the Trobriand rejection of the idea suggests that more was involved than a simple lack of knowledge.

1. From *The Sexual Life of Savages: An Ethnographic Account of Courtship, Marriage and Family Life Among the Natives of the Trobriand Islands, British New Guinea*(pp. 170–193), by Bronislaw Malinowski, 1929, New York: Harcourt, Brace and World, Inc. Copyright 1929 by Bronislaw Malinowski.

On the surface, some societies appear to be unaware of the link between intercourse and conception. Walter E. Roth claimed that the indigenous people of the Tully River of North Queensland, Australia, were ignorant of the role of sex in pregnancy:

> A woman begets children because (a) she has been sitting over the fire on which she has roasted a particular species of black bream, which must have been given to her by the prospective father, (b) she has purposely gone a-hunting and caught a certain kind of bullfrog, (c) some men may have told her to be in an interesting condition, or (d) she may dream of having the child put inside her. (quoted in Leach, 1969, p. 87)

On the other hand, Tully River people were aware that copulation causes pregnancy in animals. It is unlikely, therefore, that they were unaware that sex caused pregnancy in humans in a purely physiological sense. However, in any culture, people's ideas about humans are never straightforward descriptions of observed fact, uninfluenced by their values. Their denial of the role of sex in human pregnancy was not simple ignorance; it was a symbolic affirmation of their ideologically important values. According to Leach (1969), the pregnancy beliefs of the people of Tully River are ways of affirming that "The relationship between the woman's child and the clansmen of the woman's husband stems from public recognition of the bonds of marriage, rather than from the facts of cohabitation" (p. 87). The people of Tully River believe that pregnancy is "caused" by a woman's catching the right kind of bullfrog in the same sense that Christians believe that a wife's fertility is "caused" by the rice thrown at her at the end of her wedding ceremony.

Pregnancy rituals. Pregnancy is a time of potential anxiety, since it's fraught with possible negative outcomes such as miscarriage, physical defects in the baby, or death in childbirth for either the infant or the mother. Such anxieties cause people to turn to symbolic pregnancy rituals to protect the child and pregnant woman and to aid in a successful birth. These rituals are frequently expected to apply to the husband as well as the pregnant woman. They generally take the form of taboos against doing things that have some similarity to the feared outcomes. For instance, the Great Basin Shoshoni forbid a pregnant woman or her husband to eat either the mud hen, which they called the "fool's hen," or the trout, which flops about when one catches it, since the former might result in the child's being stupid and the latter in its becoming entangled in the umbilical cord during labor.

Among the Aztecs of Mexico, pregnant women were forbidden to look at an eclipse of the sun, which they called *Tonaltiu qualo,* meaning "The sun is being eaten," since to see this phenomenon might result in a lip defect, such as harelip, in the unborn child. As a prophylactic against the effects of accidentally seeing an eclipse, the Aztec mother-to-be might wear an obsidian blade over her breast to protect the child. Formerly, in many parts of the United States one heard advice against eating strawberries or raspberries during pregnancy, because they might result in birthmarks.

On the other hand, some pregnancy rules require behaviors that are similar to the characteristics of a good birth. The Shoshoni father was encouraged to hunt the otter, since this animal is known for its enjoyment of sliding down slippery riverbanks, much as the child was hoped to pass easily through the birth canal. In some groups in the United States, women are encouraged to involve themselves in artistic pursuits such as listening to classical music to increase the chances of the child's becoming artistically inclined.

Birth. In most societies, when the woman enters labor she is attended by one or more women who have already experienced childbirth themselves and who help her through the process. Most commonly, birth occurs with the woman assuming a kneeling or squatting position, a posture that facilitates the birth process more than the reclining position traditionally used in

139

many Western hospitals. These upright birthing positions have a beneficial effect on the angle of the birth canal and take advantage of gravity in aiding the passage of the infant.

It is only in recent years that Western medicine has begun to abandon its customary treatment of women in labor as if they were ill patients undergoing a surgical procedure. With pressure from women's groups, the role of the woman in her labor has been redefined as an active partner with others involved in the birthing process, and changes have begun to be made in the woman's posture during childbirth that facilitate her role and not simply that of the medical personnel.

Nisa's First Labor

Marjorie Shostak (1981) has written a fascinating biography of a !Kung woman, Nisa. The !Kung are foragers who occupy lands in Botswana, Namibia, Angola, and South Africa. !Kung women face childbirth without medical facilities or the help of traditional midwives, although they may be helped to give birth by their own or their husband's female relatives. About one woman dies for every five hundred births, and infant and child death is common. Nisa's account of her first birth is dramatic:

> I lay there and felt the pains as they came, over and over again. Then I felt something wet, the beginning of the childbirth. I thought, "Eh hey, maybe it is the child." I got up, took a blanket and covered Tashay with it; he was still sleeping. Then I took another blanket and my smaller duiker skin covering and I left. Was I not the only one? The only other woman was Tashay's grandmother, and she was asleep in her hut. So, just as I was, I left.
>
> I walked a short distance from the village and sat down beside a tree. I sat there and waited; she wasn't ready to be born. I lay down, but she still didn't come out. I sat up again. I leaned against the tree and began to feel the labor. The pains came over and over, again and again. It felt as though the baby was trying to jump right out!

Then the pains stopped. I said, "Why doesn't it hurry up and come out? Why doesn't it come out so I can rest? What does it want inside me that it just stays in there? Won't God help me to have it come out quickly?"

> As I said that, the baby started to be born. I thought, "I won't cry out. I'll just sit here. Look, it's already being born and I'll be fine." But it really hurt! I cried out, but only to myself. I thought, "Oh, I almost cried out in my in-laws' village." Then I thought, "Has my child already been born?" Because I wasn't really sure; I thought I might only have been sick. That's why I hadn't told anyone when I left the village.
>
> After she was born, I sat there; I didn't know what to do. I had no sense. She lay there moving her arms about, trying to suck on her fingers. She started to cry. I just sat there, looking at her. I thought, "Is this my child? Who gave birth to this child?" Then I thought, "A big thing like that? How could it possibly have come out from my genitals?" I sat there and looked at her, looked and looked and looked.
>
> The cold started to grab me. I covered her with my duiker skin that had been covering my stomach and pulled the larger kaross over myself. Soon, the afterbirth came down and I buried it. I started to shiver. I just sat there, trembling with the cold. I still hadn't tied the umbilical cord. I looked at her and thought, "She's no longer crying. I'll leave her here and go to the village to bring back some coals for a fire." (1984, pp. 193–194)[2]

---

2. From *Nisa: The Story of a !Kung Woman* (pp. 193–194) by Marjorie Shoshtak, 1984, New York: Random House. Copyright 1984 by Marjorie Shostak.

The *Couvade*

A few societies, most commonly gardening societies that occupy tropical forest environments, have a custom known as the *couvade* in which the husband acts as if he is going through labor while his wife is giving birth to their child. This ritual is often performed with the intent of providing religious protection for the newborn child by misdirecting any potentially harmful supernatural powers away from the actual birth that is in process elsewhere.

Why would such a practice be more likely in tropical forests? The groundwork for answering this question was laid by John Whiting (1964) who showed that in societies with protein scarcity—e.g., many tropical forest crops do not have all the amino acids necessary for protein building—children tend to be nursed for long periods. This protects the child from suffering from protein deficiency in its early developmental period. Prolonged nursing is facilitated by rules against sex between husband and wife for several years after the birth of a child, since a pregnancy would require weaning the first child. Since the sexual abstinence is to prevent the wife from becoming pregnant too soon, the sex taboo does not prevent the husband from having other wives and continuing his sex life during this period in their households. One result of this arrangement is that a male child spends his early years with no male role model in residence in his mother's household.

If male solidarity is extremely important—for instance, where warfare is common—painful male puberty rites may be one way of helping the boy finally break his sexual identification with his mother and prove clearly that he has entered the masculine domain. Munroe, Munroe, and Whiting (1973) have argued that the *couvade* was a possible alternative to severe male puberty rites in protein-deficient environments. Painful puberty rituals force the boy to prove his manhood by enduring pain. Where this is not done, the psychological identification with the female role is never fully lost, and the *couvade* occurs as a symbolic acting out of the female role at the time of childhood. Be this as it may, the link between the *couvade* and protein-deficient environments is clear. For instance, the *couvade* is not found in certain tropical forests such as those of Southeast Asia where pigs and chickens have been domesticated or where vegetable foods are grown that provide all the amino acids necessary for protein synthesis by the human body.

Although many do not accept Munroe, Munroe, and Whiting's rather Freudian interpretation of the significance of the *couvade* as a completely satisfactory explanation of its presence in protein-deficient environments in the absence of severe male initiation ceremonies, the custom does make sense in a rather pragmatic way: Since the father will be absent from the home in which his child will be raised, it becomes even more important than usual that his paternity be proclaimed publicly. This is symbolically accomplished through the *couvade* ritual. In this ritual the husband of a woman who enters labor affirms his new status as father of the child by acting as if he himself were experiencing the pains of labor and giving birth to his own new infant. Thereafter, there is no public doubt about who the legal father of a child is, even though the parents may have minimal contact during a period of many years.

Naming

The next important symbolic act in the life of a newborn baby is its naming ceremony. In this ritual the baby is officially received into the community of human beings and symbolically given a human status by the act of giving it a human name. In the birth or naming ritual, the infant is commonly brought into contact with those aspects of life that are of central concern to the members of the society into which it is being received. Thus, among the Samoans of Polynesia and the Yahgan of southernmost Argentina (Cooper, 1946; Murdock, 1934; Service, 1978), both of whom relied heavily on sea products as their main source of food, the newborn child was bathed in the sea shortly after birth. The Mbuti Pygmy of the Ituri Forest of Africa (Gibbs, 1965) grow no food but obtain all their basic needs from the uncultivated resources of the forest; they therefore speak of the forest as their parent and their provider. They initiate their children into the human group in a ritual in which vines from the forest are tied around the children's ankles, wrists, and waists, thereby bringing them into contact with their future livelihood.

In the industrialized societies of Europe and North America where millions live

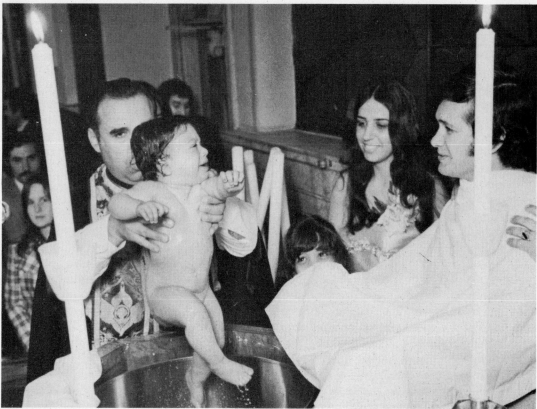

Figure 6.2 *Christening*
In this Greek Orthodox ceremony a newborn is named and initiated into the community with the ritual use of water as a symbolic cleansing. The baby will typically be sponsored by two people who then become its godparents or coparents and aid in its spiritual and sometimes financial upbringing.

together under single governments, many of life's problems relate less to uncertainties about control over the food supply and more to the difficulties of interacting daily with strangers with whom one has no close ties of kinship or residential unity. Strangers are more likely than family or co-residents to act against one another's interests and to violate each other's rights for their personal gain. So, in societies in which people must interact frequently with strangers to accomplish major goals, concern over issues of social morality are mirrored in the common practice of baptism, a ritual washing away of the effects of human sinfulness.

Enculturation, Childhood and Adolescence

From birth through adolescence, we humans are raised in some kind of family setting according to the dictates of our culture.

Our upbringing usually includes some restrictions on free expression of our sexuality, including taboos against intercourse with certain family members. In many societies, our attainment of sexual maturity is marked by special puberty rites honoring our passage into adulthood. Our culture may also have something to say about sex before marriage.

The Enculturation Process

As children grow, they slowly learn the way of life of their group. The process by which children learn the culture that guides the life of members of their society is known as enculturation or socialization. Even before they begin to communicate in the language of their society, those around them have begun to mold their behavior so that it will conform to the rules for living that make up their culture.

Anthropologists have long asserted that enculturation occurs partly by imitation and partly by direct teaching through language. According to Hall (1959) the psychological effect of enculturation on individuals depends on whether the learning of a custom is based mostly on imitation or direct teaching by language. In the latter case, the effect will depend on whether language is used primarily for admonition or for explanation when a custom is taught. Imitative learning, which Hall calls informal learning, results in a greater tolerance for individual stylistic variation and gradual adaptations of older ways of doing things to new situations. Much of what we have learned informally is done automatically, without awareness or concentration and with little or no feeling. When the informally-learned rules for doing things are broken, however, anxiety mounts rapidly in all present until someone acts to deal with the rule violation.

Learning that occurs when language is used to admonish us for violating a custom is called formal learning. In formal learning, customs are taught when we break a rule and are corrected by someone else. The teacher expresses disapproval of our behavior and suggests an alternative way of behaving as the proper, moral, or good way to act. We are conscious of the rules we are following if we learned them formally, since talking about the rule was part of the learning. When rules are learned formally, people expect them to be followed. Formal ways of doing things are endowed with deep feelings by the participants, and their violation leads to tremendous insecurity in those who rely on them to order and structure their lives. Since strong emotions are associated with practices learned through the formal method, adherence to the custom as taught is an important affair. Therefore, formally learned customs are slow to change.

It is also possible to teach a custom by talking about it but without expressing disapproval or disappointment of the learner's rule-breaking behavior. Instead, the new way of acting is explained by giving the logical reason that lies behind it. This form of learning has been called technical learning by Hall. Technically learned behaviors are those of which people are most highly conscious, since the learning included explanations of the reasons and benefits of the behaviors. Due to the emphasis on explaining the rationale, little emotion is associated with that which is learned in this way. Therefore, things learned in a technical way may be replaced readily by new technically learned ways of dealing with the same situation.

Childhood Sexual Socialization

Before we are able to play the role of adults with complete success, we must acquire knowledge of the sexual customs of our society. Most societies deal with this necessity in a fairly matter-of-fact way. According to Ford and Beach (1951), 34% of the 95 societies whose sexual customs they surveyed had little or no restriction on sexual experimentation in childhood. Examples of peoples whose attitudes toward childhood sexuality were permissive are the Lepcha, an agricultural society in the Himalayas, and the Trobrianders, who lived on one of the Melanesian islands. According to Ford and Beach (1951), the Lepcha believed that sexual activity is necessary in order for girls to grow up. Therefore, most girls were regularly engaging in full sexual intercourse by the age of 11 or 12. Among the Trobrianders, boys of 10 to 12 years of age and girls of 6 to 8 years are given explicit sexual training by older companions.

Fifty-one percent of the societies Ford and Beach studied were semirestrictive: Young people were expected to follow certain rules of etiquette in their exploration of their sexuality, although no severe punishments were imposed for violations. Only 15% of these societies were truly restrictive of childhood sexuality. Restrictions were most common where male solidarity was economically or politically important and where class distinctions or differences in wealth or the control of property were important matters. This is certainly understandable, since adults in such societies are likely to have a greater vested interest in the future marriage plans of their children. The more carefully the sexuality of unmarried persons is controlled, the greater are their parents' options in selecting the marriage partners of their children.

Incest Taboo

One rule regarding sexual behavior seems to be found in almost all cultures. This rule is the incest taboo, a rule that forbids sexual intercourse between parents and their children, between brothers and sisters, and frequently between other designated kin as well. There are a few cultures in which exceptions to this rule exist. For instance, the Hawaiian royalty, the kings and queens of ancient Egypt, and the Inca emperors were expected to perpetuate their lineages by brother-sister marriages. These persons were regarded as sacred and were therefore set apart from ordinary people by the expectation that they violate the incest taboo that applied to all others. Thus, their behavior was regarded as exceptional even in their own societies. Some studies have suggested that brother-sister and father-daughter marriages in ancient Egypt were not limited to the royal family but were actually common in the general population (Hopkins, 1980; Middleton, 1962) and that father-daughter, mother-son, and brother-sister mating and marriages may have been acceptable in ancient Persia as well (Slotkin, 1947). Even so, the incest taboo is the most nearly universal of all human cultural rules.

The inbreeding hypothesis. The near-universality of the incest taboo in human cultures has long been of interest to anthropologists. It is a commonplace that human cultures are extremely malleable. So the existence of a rule that is found in almost all cultures cries out for some kind of explanation. An early notion about why the incest taboo is universal was the idea that inbreeding is biologically harmful, so that those societies in which it was permitted died out, leaving only those societies where it was forbidden (Frazer, 1910; Muller, 1931). This hypothesis has been popular off and on for over a century, but it was strongly questioned by F. B. Livingstone (1969), who pointed out that inbreeding is not inherently detrimental. It does bring out genetically recessive traits that are only manifest overtly when they are inherited from both parents, since close inbreeding increases the likelihood that both parents will have the same recessive traits to pass on to their offspring. However, recessive traits may be beneficial or neutral as well as harmful. In human breeding groups, the number of harmful recessive traits that are brought to the fore by close inbreeding is not likely to endanger the survival of the group, since humans produce plenty of offspring each generation. Indeed, harmful recessive traits that are brought out in this way actually become eliminated from the group because they are harmful. Thus, in the long run, close inbreeding may actually provide a means for weeding harmful recessive traits from a group.

The "familiarity breeds contempt" hypothesis. Westermarck (1894), a proponent of the inbreeding argument, also contended that the taboo against sex between brother and sister merely recognized that children who grow up together are less likely to be sexually interested in one another than they are in outsiders with whom they are less familiar. In effect, he argued that there is a natural aversion to sex between children raised together or, in popular terms, that "familiarity breeds contempt." Bixler (1981, 1982) argues that the Westermarck hypothesis is still valid, and Lumsden and Wilson (1980, 1981) claim there are genetic influences in play in support of the human aversion to incest.

A few more contemporary researchers have lent support to this idea. Arthur Wolf (1966, 1969, 1970) studied arranged marriages in Taiwan. In these marriages the prospective wife was brought into the boy's household at an early age so that the husband and wife grew up together as a brother and sister might. Wolf found that a variety of measures—such as the frequency with which such husbands visited prostitutes, the frequency of adultery by both partners, and the rate of divorce and sexual intercourse in such marriages—all suggested that the level of sexual satisfaction in these marriages was lower than in nonarranged marriages. Studies of Israeli *kibbutzim* in which unrelated children were raised in communal sleeping quarters also have suggested that as such children reach maturity they express much more interest in developing intimate ties with persons who were not raised in their own group than with those who were (Shepher, 1971a, 1971b).

Two problems exist with this theory. The first is that the actual mechanism by which the aversion develops between children raised together has not been explained. The second problem is probably the chief weakness of the Westermarckian view: If siblings do tend to develop a natural sexual disinterest in one another, why should a rule against sex between siblings even be necessary, much less universal? A good theory of incest avoidance rules must account not just for the avoidance itself. It must also explain why the world's cultures have consistently developed rules that—sometimes vehemently—require such avoidance.

The family disruption hypothesis. Anthropologists like Bronislaw Malinowski (1927; see also Aberle, 1963; Bagley, 1969; Coult, 1963; Count, 1958) have argued that permitting incestuous relationships within the family would create jealousies, disrupt parental authority, and create confusion about what roles family members should play with one another. For instance, father-daughter relationships might foster jealousy between fathers and mothers as well as between fathers and sons. Role confusion also might arise over whether one should behave as a parent or a lover. Such problems would make it difficult to socialize children, since respect for parental authority is a prerequisite for effective socialization.

Opponents of this view point out that it is built on several assumptions that are unwarranted. First, sexual relations do not necessarily disrupt the authority of one person over another; otherwise, there would be no societies in which wives are subordinated to their husbands. Second, sexual relations do not necessarily engender jealousy. And if they do, jealousy does not necessarily undermine the family, for there are many examples of polygynous families in which co-wives live and work together, even under the same roof, in spite of jealousy. Certainly, incestuous relationships need not be considered inherently more disruptive to family life than are other forms of plural sexual relationships.

The family alliance hypothesis. Sir Edward Burnett Tylor (1888), another early anthropologist, based his views about the incest taboo on the "marry out or be killed out" rule. In his opinion, early families that allowed incestuous mating were likely to be politically and economically weaker than families that forbade incestuous matings and required their offspring to marry outside the family. The rule of marrying outside the family of one's birth created alliances between families that might otherwise be enemies, ties with in-laws who could be called on for aid in times of peril and deprivation. Families without in-law ties, he believed, have long since become extinct, having lost out in their competition with those more successful societies families that forbade incest.

This view has been criticized because incest taboos and rules requiring marriage outside the family of birth are not the same thing: The former govern sex; the latter govern marriage. Nevertheless, since marriage universally involves the establishment of a legitimate sexual union, Tylor's argument may be rephrased to account for the incest taboo: The prohibition of incest makes it necessary to establish sexual ties with persons outside the immediate family, which in turn increases the chances of the family's survival. That sexual unions outside the immediate family are formalized by marriage simply enhances the effectiveness of the incest rule at creating intergroup alliances. Since Tylor's theory includes a mechanism for explaining the universality of incest prohibitions, it still has strong advocates in this century.

Puberty Rituals

Near the time individuals reach biological maturity it is common for an adulthood ritual, commonly called a puberty ritual, to be held. This ritual signals the transition from childhood to adulthood and impresses on both the child and his or her community that the old roles of childhood are to be set aside and that others should treat him or her as an adult thereafter.

Not all societies practice puberty rituals, but they are quite common. In Cohen's examination (1964) of 65 societies, 46 had puberty rituals, while 19 did not. He divided these societies into two groups: those with nuclear families only (minimal families that consist only of parents and their children) and those with complex family organizations such as lineages and clans in which many related individuals participate in family affairs. He found that in societies based on the nuclear family—a situation in which children would be trained from an early age to be socially independent—the probability of puberty rituals was smaller. On the other hand, of those societies with more complex families—and in which children would have to be trained to play an interdependent, cooperative role with many other family members to become adults—almost all had puberty rituals.

Social circumstances that foster interdependent role playing can lock people into their current roles and make change difficult without the aid of a mechanism for transformation from one status to another. The puberty ceremony symbolically redefines the child as an adult in a dramatic, public fashion that is difficult for those involved to ignore. The ritual proclaims the changes in rights and responsibilities that everyone in the group must recognize for the change to occur. By symbolically transforming the child to an adult, the puberty ritual creates barriers against everyone's falling back into their previous habits of interaction.

Puberty rites for males. For boys, puberty rituals seem to be most dramatic when the transition from boyhood to manhood is potentially difficult. Under such circumstances, male puberty rituals are often severe and painful ordeals, involving ceremonies such as circumcision, scarification of the body (decorating the body with a pattern made of scars), tattooing, and the filing or knocking out of front teeth as indicators of adult status.

Whiting, Kluckhohn, and Anthony (1958) found that circumcision as a part of initiation rituals is especially associated with three social customs: a taboo on sex between husband and wife for a year or more after the birth of a child, the sharing of sleeping quarters by mother and child with

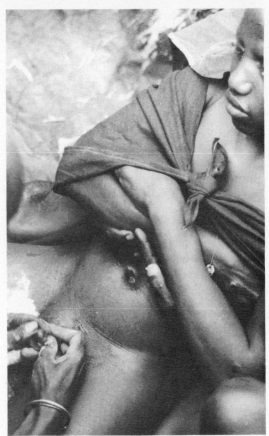

Figure 6.3 *Puberty Ceremony*
Circumcision is a ritual initiating the young male into adulthood. This Maasai shows no emotion throughout the ceremony. Afterward he will have a three month healing period during which he will wear black and the "Olemasari" headdress, will not wash, be seen eating, or have his food touched by a woman.

the father's quarters elsewhere, and the establishment of residence by a married couple near the husband's relatives. The first two of these customs make it more difficult for a male child to identify with the male role, since the most available adult role model is the mother. The third, residence of couples near the husband's relatives, is common where male solidarity is important among adults. The conflict between the need to identify with the male group as an adult and the relatively weak childhood tie between father and son make the transition from childhood to adulthood a stressful one. Hence the dramatic ritualizing of the status change by painful rites through which a boy proves to the adult male community that he is capable of adopting the adult male role.

Puberty rites for females. Brown (1963) found that about half of a sample of 60 societies practiced puberty rituals for girls. Girls' puberty rituals are most likely to occur in societies in which the residences of newly married couples are established near the wife's relatives. The more important a woman's labor is to the family food supply, the more likely it is that female puberty rituals will be practiced. According to Brown, female puberty rituals are painful in only 30% of the societies that practice such rituals. As with male initiation rituals, painful ceremonies are most likely in societies where mothers and daughters share sleeping quarters while the father sleeps elsewhere.

Sex Without Marriage

Following puberty, the majority of societies are quite tolerant of sexual experimentation before marriage. Ford and Beach (1951) found that of 95 societies surveyed, 81 had little or no restriction on premarital sexual relations. The least permissive societies are, as might be expected, those in which parents have the greatest interest in controlling the marital choices of their children, societies in which people are ranked by differences in wealth or class membership, and societies in which male solidarity is economically and politically important.

Courtship in Samoa

In traditional Samoa before contact with Europeans, children were unshielded from the facts of sex, birth, and death. Growing up sharing a house with no walls with 50 or 60 relatives, they did not develop the kind of shame that is connected with sex in societies where privacy is more common. Chastity in daughters was a mark of prestige for families, but as in all societies sexual experimentation occurred discreetly. Mead (1928) believed that both men and women were equally free to choose their partners, and her informants claimed that the European concepts of fidelity and jealousy were unheard of.

Etiquette required that a rendezvous be arranged through a go-between, called a *soa*. An unmarried woman might invite a suitor to spend the night with her in her family's home if she did not wish to meet him elsewhere. In such a case, the young man might remove his girdle and grease his body to make it slippery before entering the house after dark when other family members were already asleep. It was expected that he would be discreetly gone before others arose.

This form of courtship gave rise to a custom known as sleep crawling, in which an unpopular youth or jilted lover might sneak into the house of a young woman without invitation, in the hope that she might be expecting another lover and allow him to stay once she had discovered the deception. Freeman (1983) regards this as a form of rape and believes that a great deal of competition occurred among young men in this practice, due to the great emphasis that Samoan families placed on competition for status and on the chastity of their daughters as a symbol of their family honor. If the woman was not favorably disposed to the sleep crawler, she had the option of rousing her household to chase, ridicule, and beat the intruder for adopting such tactics. If he were publicly identified, a sleep crawler was disgraced and would not be entertained or considered for marriage by other women.

Informal clandestine love affairs in Samoa would eventually lead to the development of more or less permanent primary sexual liaisons between couples that were, in effect, a form of trial marriage. If the couple desired to formalize their relationship by marriage, a courtship process was required in which a go-between would accompany the lover to the woman's family and plead his case for him. After repeated visits, the actual proposal of marriage would be made by the go-between. If the marriage was acceptable to the family, a ceremony would be arranged in which elaborate gift giving took place between the two families.

Marriage and Kinship

Marriage is a publicly recognized union between two or more people that creates economic rights and obligations within the group, legitimizes their sexual relationship, and guarantees their offspring rights of inheritance. The rights of inheritance insure the continuity of the line of descent, through which property and social rights are passed from generation to generation.

The concept of descent is understood in most cultures as a biological relationship that exists between children and one or both of their parents. Children of the same parent through whom descent is traced are thought of as biologically related because they share a common descent line. In every culture there are rules that forbid sex and marriage between individuals who are closely related in terms of descent. Two effects of these rules are to minimize competition among close relatives and to increase the bonds of cooperation and friendship between neighboring groups. As a result of such prohibitions, a line of descent may be perpetuated only by sexual unions outside a defined circle of close relatives. Lines of descent are generally important in a variety of practical matters such as inheritance of property, settlement of disputes, and determination of the social rights and obligations that one person has concerning another. The sexual unions that make possible their continuity are therefore socially important in human societies. Because of their social importance, they are universally sanctioned by rituals which transform simple sexual liaisons into publicly recognized marriages.

Marriage makes official the sexual rights and obligations of sexual partners by publicly acknowledging them. Marriage also gives the partners a set of economic rights and obligations based on a cooperative division of labor. Finally, marriage also adds to the relationship a set of childrearing obligations that will come into play if children are born of the union.

In many of the world's societies, kinship groups—either individual families or groups of cooperating families—are politically autonomous and carry out the major activities of economic production. Where kinship groups perform governmental functions, such as the creation and enforcement of law, or where they are responsible for the production of the necessities of life, marriages are important not only for the persons to be married but also for their families. Marriage will create a new family group that will help to perpetuate the next generation of one or both of the parents' family lines. It also will unite the two kinship groups under an umbrella of reciprocal rights and obligations in matters of economics and intergroup politics. Under such circumstances, a marriage is likely to be created because the alliance benefits the families of the potential bride and groom.

Social Restrictions on Partner Choice

When marriages are of practical significance to a family, the culture often has formal guidelines about whom a person ought to marry. Such rules increase the likelihood that the practical well-being of the kin group will be fostered.

Exogamy. The most common example of such a rule is the rule of exogamy, a rule that requires marriage outside a designated group. Since marriage always involves legitimation of a sexual relationship, the existence of an incest taboo requires marriage outside the group of kin with whom sex would be incestuous. Except for the few societies or special social groups in which the usual incest taboo is not applied, the rule of exogamy always requires marriage outside the nuclear family, and usually it also prevents marriage with first cousins. However, rules of exogamy are more than mere extensions of the incest taboo. Incest taboos specifically govern sexual behavior. Rules of exogamy do more than this: They govern marriage rights. Therefore they may exclude from consideration for marriage a broad circle of persons with whom sex is not necessarily forbidden. Thus, rules of exogamy may require marriage outside one's own residential unit as well as outside one's own family. In some societies the local group is divided into two groups, or moieties, which are each exogamous—so that members of one moiety always marry per-

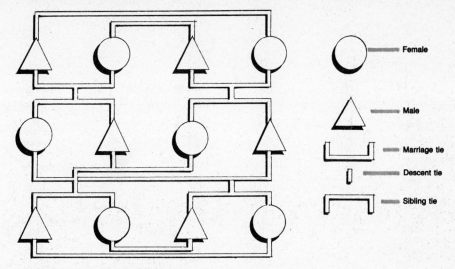

Figure 6.4 *Bilateral Cross-cousin Marriage*
Various clans or groups of people define their kinship by an elaborate system of descent. This diagram shows marriage occurring between cousins who are linked by parents of the opposite sex.

sons from the opposite moiety of their society. This arrangement divides each local group into two units that have reciprocal rights and obligations to one another. For instance, members of one moiety may host funerals when a member of the opposite moiety dies.

Endogamy. Rules of endogamy, on the other hand, require that both marriage partners be members of a certain kinship, social, or local group. For instance, a rule of endogamy may require marriage into one's own village, church, or social class. In the traditional castes of India, marriage partners were strictly limited to members of one's own caste.

Cousin marriages. Although the exogamy rules of most societies promote marriage beyond the circle of one's cousins, there are many that in fact prefer marriage between cousins. Most of these cultures have a rule of preferential marriage between cross cousins—cousins who are linked by parents of opposite sex, as children of a brother and sister. In both patrilineal and matrilineal systems of reckoning kinship, cross cousins belong to different lineages. With such marriages, members of each family gain in-laws outside their own lineage to whom they can turn for aid in times of need. A common form of cross-cousin marriage is one in which a brother and a sister marry cross cousins who are also sister and brother to

each other. In societies where the inequality of the sexes is marked, this is often described as two men exchanging sisters. In such cases, marrying one's brother-in-law's sister does create an added social bond between two men, a bond that may benefit them both politically and economically. Sister exchange or, more accurately, bilateral cross-cousin marriage, repeatedly links two lineages over many generations (see Fig. 6.4). This system is called "bilateral" because a man's wife is both his mother's brother's daughter and his father's sister's daughter.

A less intense pattern of intermarriage between two lineages is one in which a male of one lineage marries a woman from another lineage in one generation, and his daughter marries into that lineage a generation later. This permits his sister to marry into a third lineage, thereby extending the marriage alliances into an even greater circle of people. This system has been called patrilateral cross-cousin marriage because, from the male's point of view, the preferred marriage is with one's father's sister's daughter. Patrilateral cross-cousin marriage permits many lineages to be linked into a circle in which marriage partners flow in one direction in one generation and in the other direction in the next generation (see Fig. 6.5).

An even more common pattern is one in

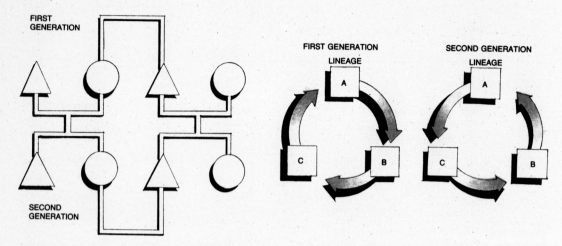

Figure 6.5 *Patrilateral Cross-cousin Marriage*
A circular type of lineage occurs in this form of marriage. In one generation the marriage partners are chosen in one direction on the diagram, and in the next generation they are chosen in the opposite direction.

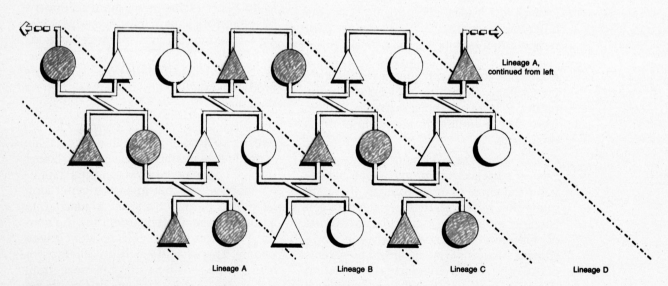

Figure 6.6 *Matrilateral Cross-cousin Marriage*
Similar to the patrilateral cross-cousin system, this type, however, does not alternate each generation. The women of each lineage marry someone in one direction as diagrammed on the chart, and their brothers marry into the lineage next to theirs but in the opposite direction.

which several lineages are linked into a circle in which the women of each lineage always marry in one direction around the circle, while their brothers marry into the lineage next to theirs in the opposite direction (see Fig. 6.6). This marriage system is like the patrilateral marriage system, but the direction of marriages is asymmetric and

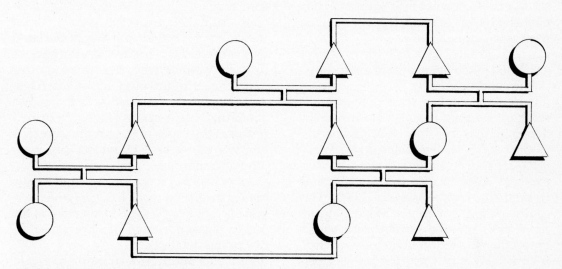

Figure 6.7 *Patrilateral Parallel Cousin Marriage*
This system of kinship maintains unity in a lineage because a man always marries his father's brother's daughter.

does not alternate each generation. This system also is known as matrilateral cross-cousin marriage, since a wife is always a mother's brother's daughter to her husband.

The rarest form of preferential cousin marriage is marriage with a parallel cousin (a cousin who is one's mother's sister's child or one's father's brother's child). Parallel-cousin marriage is found among many Arab societies. It is called *bint 'amm* or patrilateral parallel-cousin marriage, that is, marriage between a man and his father's brother's daughter (see Fig. 6.7). This rule is useful in maintaining solidarity within a lineage, since a man and his father's brother's daughter belong to the same lineage (Barth, 1954, Murphy & Kasdan, 1959). It is especially helpful, for instance, among Arab Bedouins where members of the same lineage may be dispersed from one another for long periods of time.

Levirate and sororate. The levirate is a more specialized marriage rule that requires the kin of a deceased man to provide his widow with a new husband, often a brother of the dead husband. A more or less opposite practice, the sororate, requires that the family of a deceased wife provide the

surviving widower with another wife from among the women of their own family. Both of these rules illustrate that in kinship-based societies, a marriage is actually a contract between two families who have continuing obligations to each other even after the death of a spouse. In matrilineal societies, a surviving wife may be expected to marry the heir of her deceased husband, generally the dead man's sister's son. This fulfills the same basic function addressed by the levirate and, at the same time, symbolizes that the dead man's heir has assumed not only his property but also his rights and obligations, including the obligation to care for the surviving wife.

Practical Negotiations

Negotiations before marriage between the two families will emphasize pragmatic issues, such as the size of the payment one family may make to the other, the work and domestic skills of the future spouses, and the like. Less rational matters such as the feelings of the prospective bride and groom for one another are not given as much weight as they carry in societies in which large kinship groups are not the major economic and political units of society. The feelings of the couple for each other need not be neglected, but they may play little role in such negotiations, for neither their sexual gratification nor their emotional compatibility is of greatest interest to their respective families. Rather, the couple to be married are a link by which those families are joined in the larger area of the society's politics and economics.

In perhaps three quarters of the world's societies, marriage negotiations involve the determination of how the prospective groom's family shall recompense the family of the bride-to-be for the loss of her productive and reproductive services (Coult & Haberstein, 1965; Murdock, 1957). This compensation may consist of gifts, known as the bride price or progeny price, a form of recompense found in 60% of societies. Alternatively, it may take the form of a period of work to be performed by the groom for his wife's family, in which case it is known as the bride service. The bride service has been reported in about 24% of societies studied. The amount of the compensation will reflect the importance of the bride's family compared with that of the groom's, since the bride's status as a married woman and the status of her children will be greater if the bride price or service is a high one.

The dowry is a payment that flows from the kin of the bride to the husband's family. The dowry is not the opposite of the bride price, since it is not intended as a compensation to the groom's family for his absence. Rather, the dowry is practiced in societies in which women are considered an economic burden. It compensates the groom and his family for accepting the responsibility of supporting the bride. Sometimes control of the dowry is in the hands of the wife, in which case it serves as a kind of advance on the inheritance to which she might be entitled at the death of her parents.

The Marriage Ritual

Once an agreement has been achieved between the families, the actual ritual of marriage may occur. Marriage rituals vary tremendously from society to society, but they generally involve symbolism dramatizing the union being created between the two families. They may also portray the relations, especially those of a stressful nature, that are expected to exist between the couple and their respective in-laws. For instance, among the Aztec of Mexico the bride was carried, like a burden, on the back of the old woman who had acted as her matchmaker to the place of the marriage. After lectures by the elders of both families about their new responsibilities as married persons, the capes of the couple were tied together into a knot by which they were joined in marriage.

An occasional form for marriage rituals to take involves a mock battle in which the bride is captured by the bridegroom and his family or friends from her unsuccessful, defending relatives. G. W. Stow (1905) described a South African !Kung marriage by mock capture. During the wedding feast the groom was expected to seize hold of the bride. Then the two families began to fight while the bride's family focused their attention on beating the groom with their digging sticks. The groom had to succeed in holding on to his bride during this beating for the marriage ritual to be complete. Had he failed, he would have lost his bride.

Postmarital Residence

Although marriage joins two family groups as allies, the couple joined by the ritual of marriage may be more involved in the daily life of one of their parental kinship groups than the other, depending on where they are most likely to set up their new residence. According to research by Murdock (1957), in about two thirds of the world's societies newly married couples are expected to set up residence in or near the residence of the husband's family. This form of residence, called virilocality or patrilocality, is most often found where the solidarity of the male group is very important. Naroll (1973) found that the best single predictor of virilocality was the man's predominance in food production. Its likelihood is increased by other factors that strengthen males' solidarity: e.g., where hunting is a primarily male activity; where food production requires heavy labor;

Figure 6.8 *Wedding Ceremony*
While marriage takes many forms, it is a universal phenomenon. In figure A the bride and bridegroom sit next to Brahmin priests in a typical high caste wedding in South India. The Togolese chief in figure B practices poly-gyny, here posing in a group with a number of his wives.

where warfare involves fighting between neighboring groups that share a common culture and language; where men have more than one wife; where men wield authority in a political organization that is a source of prestige; or where male accumulation of property is a sign of rank.

The second most common residence pattern is uxorilocality, formerly known as matrilocality. Uxorilocality is found in about 15% of societies and involves the setting up of a residence in or near the residence of the bride's family (Coult & Haberstein, 1965; Murdock, 1934). This is most likely to be practiced where food is provided by simple gardening in environments that do not require heavy labor and in warlike societies where belligerence is most common between distant groups.

A third residential pattern is bilocal or ambilocal: Residence may be in the home area of either the bride or the groom. This form of residence is practiced in 5 to 10% of societies. It permits flexibility of choice in societies in which cooperation within large kinship groups is important but in which it is useful to be flexible about which group a new couple joins, as in agricultural groups where land is limited.

In neolocality the couple sets up a residence in some new place apart from either family. This residence pattern provides maximum flexibility in electing a place to live and is most common when the nuclear family of two parents and their children is economically independent and responsible for its own survival. Only about 1 in 20 societies emphasizes neolocal residence. It is most common in industrialized societies.

Finally, in avunculocal residence the couple takes up residence in or near the house of the groom's mother's brother. This rare form of residence is common in less than 5% of societies and occurs only in matrilineal societies where the men of the matrilineage must stay together, as when warfare is common.

Marital Types

In form, marriages may be monogamous, polygynous, polyandrous, or group marriages. In monogamous marriages, one man and one woman are joined as husband and

wife. Monogamous marriages are the most common form of marital unit in all societies, even where other forms of marriage may be idealized as more desirable. Polygynous marriages were actually the preferred form of marriage in 83.6% of 185 societies surveyed by Ford and Beach (1951). In polygynous marriages, one man is joined to more than one wife. The most common form of polygyny is sororal polygyny, in which a man is expected to marry women who are sisters of each other. The highest frequency of actual polygynous families is found in societies in frontier areas, in societies where warfare is common, in societies in which the ratio of adult women to men is high (a condition that is common under either of the two preceding circumstances), and in groups where rapid growth of families is beneficial to family survival. Since the ratio of male and female children born is about equal in all societies, relatively few men actually are able to practice polygyny even in societies where it is the preferred marital form. Therefore, it is practiced most commonly by individuals of high social standing. Since it generally takes some time and effort to achieve the social standing that makes it possible for a man to have more than one wife, polygyny often involves an age differential between spouses, with older men taking much younger wives.

Polyandrous marriages, in which a single woman has several husbands, are rare. It is the idealized family type in probably less than 0.5% of the world's societies. The most common form of polyandrous union is one in which a woman is simultaneously married to several brothers, a form of polyandry known as fraternal polyandry. Polyandry is advantageous where resources are extremely limited and it is beneficial to keep the growth of the family at a minimum. Regardless of the number of her husbands, a woman is not likely to become pregnant any more often than she would in any other type of marriage. Polyandrous unions have been reported among Southern Indian and Tibetan peoples where land is at a premium and cannot easily be further subdivided from one generation to the next. It was practiced by the Shoshoni of the Great Basin—a man might temporarily

Figure 6.9 *A Polyandrous Wedding Ceremony*
One variation in the structure of marriage is the polyandrous in which one woman marries two men. This Nepalese woman, in the veil, is marrying the two brothers on the left.

share his wife with a younger brother until he was old enough to make his own way as an independent hunter with his own family. Like polygyny, polyandry is actually practiced by a minority of women in societies where it is the preferred marital form and gives evidence of a woman's high status. Group marriages, in which several males are simultaneously married to several females, are generally found in societies that also practice polyandry.

Polyandrous and Group Marriages Among the Toda of Southern India

The Toda of Southern India, described in detail by Rivers (1906), are one of the few peoples of the world where polyandry and group marriages were the rule. Marriages were arranged by parents when children were as young as two or three years of age. A marriage united the girl not only to the boy for whom she was originally selected but also to any brothers he might have, in-

cluding those born after the ceremony. Thus, a Toda wife typically had several husbands who were usually brothers, although she might also enter marriage with other men. Since a woman was considered to be the wife of any of the brothers of a man she married, if brothers entered into marriage with more than one woman, the result was a group marriage in which several women might be wives simultaneously to several men.

Both polyandry and group marriage made it infeasible to keep track of biological paternity, so this concept was unimportant to the Toda. However, since Toda families were patrilineal, fatherhood in its social sense was important. Therefore, the Todas employed a ritual of fatherhood, a ritual that designated a particular man to be the social father of any children a woman bore for a period of years thereafter, whether or not he was their natural father.

Since fatherhood was established by

a ritual act, the concept of adultery was irrelevant to the Toda view of family relations. Not only was sexual infidelity by a wife not grounds for divorce—since it would not have affected the legitimacy of a child's rights to inherit from the socially defined father—but it was also so unimportant a concept that there was not even a word for adultery in the Toda language.

The New Family

With marriage may come children, turning the social unit into a family. In many cultures, this family extends far beyond the parents and their children.

Parenthood

The relationship between spouses generally changes at the birth of the first child. Having a child creates new obligations for the husband and wife and new demands on their time and energy. Their domestic roles must be adjusted to accommodate their new status as parents. No longer will they have as much exclusive time for each other.

In societies in which the family organization is important economically and politically, entry into parenthood may be formally indicated by a change in the parents' names. By this custom, called teknonymy, a parent might be called Father of Lynn or Mother of Kay. Teknonymy is most often practiced by men in societies in which the couple takes up residence with or near the wife's family. It occurs for women as well, but in fewer societies. In either case, it reflects an elevation in the social rank of the individual, since because of the birth of the child he or she is no longer such an outsider to the family with which the couple resides. The name change calls to everyone's attention the greater bond that now exists between the new parent and the in-laws.

Family

Marriage legitimizes a sexual union and provides an institutionalized means for producing the next generation. Some group

must be charged with the responsibility for rearing the children born from the marriage union. The group in which children are raised is known as the family. This group need not be structured around the individuals who are united to one another in marriage. When the family does consist of parents and their children, it is called a nuclear family. This is the family type that is most familiar to peoples of Western societies in recent times. However, as the sole basis for households it is a rare family form.

Almost all societies throughout most of human history have had more complex family forms than the nuclear family. These more complex family forms, known collectively as extended families, include more individuals than a husband and wife and their children. They are formed when the postmarital residence rules are other than neolocal, since one spouse takes up residence with the relatives of the other. Extended families usually include three generations: either a pair of grandparents, their sons, the wives of their sons, and all the children of their sons, or a pair of grandparents, all their sons and daughters, and all the children of their daughters. These two basic types of extended family may be further elaborated, depending on the marriage forms involved, since the extended family may include plural spouses in the parental and grandparental generations.

Extended families may live under a common roof or in several closely assembled dwellings. Thus, they may make up a single household (residential unit) or several households. In any case, the number of individuals involved in childrearing responsibilities will be much larger in extended families than in nuclear families. Therefore, extended families are likely to have more formally established rules regarding the rights and obligations of various family members to one another than do societies in which nuclear families are the norm.

The Samoan Extended Family and Household

Ella (1895) and Mead (1928) described the traditional Samoan family system, which provides a marked contrast to

North American families and households. Among the Samoans, a single household was led by a *matai* or headman, a titled member of the family selected to act as their patriarchal head. The matai had life-and-death authority over members of the household and was responsible for carrying out religious rituals for the family. As family head, he also owned the land that was worked by the family members and assigned them their share to work.

Within the extended family group, children were tended by their older siblings. The mothers were thus freed for other activities and all adult relatives were viewed as having rights over the children of the group. Besides babytending, boys under eight or nine years of age and girls who had not yet attained puberty were expected to help adults in many other ways contributing to the work and welfare of the household. On the other hand, if the demands of the family became too great, children were free to leave home and take up residence with other relatives in another household that they found more congenial.

Divorce

Not all marriages last until the death of a spouse. In the United States, for instance, between 30% and 40% of marriages begun in 1987 are likely to end in divorce. Around the world, there are societies with higher and lower rates of divorce. Reasons for divorce vary, but impotence, infertility, infidelity, laziness, and simple incompatibility are common justifications. In probably three quarters of the societies that have been studied by anthropologists, women and men have been more or less equal in their right to divorce (Murdock, 1950).

Cross-cultural variations in divorce rates make it possible to discover some of the factors that make divorce less likely. The payment of a bride price to the bride's family gives her family a vested interest in the stability of the marriage, since the groom's family is likely to demand return of the pay-

ment if the marriage is dissolved. The dowry, a transfer of wealth in the opposite direction, has a similar effect of stabilizing marriage ties. When the couple lives in an extended family, relatives are also likely to have a stabilizing effect on their marriage. Matrilocality also is associated with a low divorce rate. Perhaps this is because the control over property this form of residence gives to women is associated with greater than usual social power and honor for women and little familial authority for the husband, who resides with his in-laws. Under these conditions, the frequency of abusive behavior by the husband is likely to be relatively low, a factor that is likely to foster stability in marriage.

Old Age

We all want to grow up, but we do not want to grow old. The negative feelings we have about aging are partly related to the loss of health and strength that accompany the biological process. Socially, aging may also bring a loss of our accustomed rank. What are the factors that contribute to the loss of social power and honor that old age brings in societies such as our own? Cross-cultural research sheds some light on this question.

When postmarital residence rules require a couple to live near one spouse's parents, it is easier for the parents to continue their roles as family heads into their old age. In societies in which the family is a cooperating economic or political group, the status of family head can be a major determinant of an older person's rank in life. According to a study of nonindustrialized societies by Lee and Kezis (1979), older people are more likely to have high ranked statuses in societies in which they live with related married couples and in societies in which descent is traced through only one of the parents (patrilineal or matrilineal societies) rather than through both. Nuclear families lack a family structure in which parents can maintain into their old age their role of family heads over their children and other relatives in the household. However, if an extended family is too large to be easily led by a single family head or couple, the family heads may govern in name only. When the political power or wealth of a family is not consistently related to a particular family line, parents' rank is not so likely to rise with age as in a system in which rank is intimately connected to a particular inheritance line.

In all societies, the elderly are accorded more respect if they are economically productive. Thus, in industrialized societies where rank is associated closely with wealth and income, the social rank of the elderly tends to decline markedly at retirement.

Death

Death is more than a simple biological process. It involves distinctive psychological and social changes as well.

Simple and obvious criteria such as the absence of breathing, heartbeat, or reaction to pain have been used in societies throughout the world to determine when biological death has occurred. With the development of a technology to measure brain functioning directly, in the United States and other industrialized societies, more emphasis seems to be directed toward defining death as the cessation of activity in the cerebral cortex of the brain, the center of intellectual and conscious processes. However, these criteria may not always agree with one another. For instance, the cerebral cortex may no longer be active while the heart and lungs continue to operate, or a person may be comatose and unresponsive to pain, yet later report having been fully aware of the surroundings.

Psychological death refers to the process by which people prepare themselves subjectively for their impending biological death. According to Elisabeth Kübler-Ross (1969), who studied dying patients' responses to their circumstances in United States hospitals, the initial reaction of most patients to learning that their illness is terminal is denial. Patients refuse to accept the correctness of the diagnosis, insisting that some error has been made or that their records have been confused with those of someone else. Their basic attitude might be summed up as "There must be some mistake; this cannot be happening to me!" When they finally accept that they are in

fact dying, denial is replaced by a period of anger, which is characterized by rage, envy, and resentment. In this period, the dominant question is "Why me, why not someone else?" The anger may be directed at anyone at hand—other patients, doctors, nurses, even family members who come to visit and comfort the person. The third stage is one of bargaining for more time. In this stage, patients seek a slight extension of their deadline—to allow doing something "for one last time" or some similar request, in return for which they vow to live a better life. In the fourth stage, depression predominates, while the dying person mourns because of the approaching loss of people and things that have been meaningful in his or her life. Finally, a stage of acceptance may be reached, a stage of quiet expectation. This is not a stage of happiness, but one of rest in which there are almost no strong feelings and in which the patient's interests narrow as he or she gradually withdraws from everyday life in preparation for what is about to happen. This may be a time of great distress for the patient's family, since they may feel rejected by his or her withdrawal and lack of interest in their visits.

Socially, death brings about the final change of status in the human life cycle—the change from a human status to a non-human one, such as spirit or ghost. Social death is the point at which other people begin to relate to a person with behaviors and actions that are appropriate toward a dead person. Like psychological death, social death may occur before biological death. W. H. Rivers (1926) reported that among the Melanesians, the word mate, which means "dead person," was applied not only to the biologically dead but also to individuals who were gravely ill, close to death, and to the very old who were likely to die soon. The Melanesians, of course, distinguished between biological mate and social mate. The purpose of referring to those who were close to death as mate was that they were treated socially as if they were dead. Such persons might be buried alive so that they could proceed to a more pleasant afterlife rather than linger among the living under the unpleasant circumstances of extreme

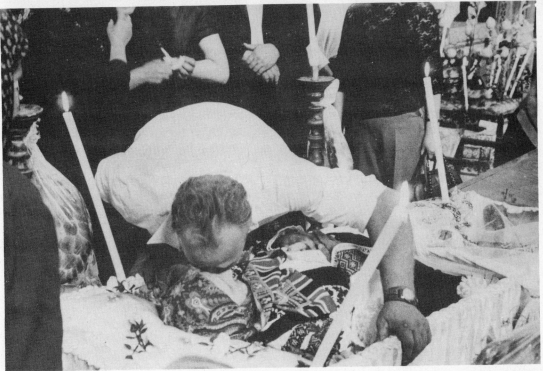

Figure 6.10 *Burial Ceremony*
A major change in a family or society is the death of one of its members. Many societies have elaborate rituals to help the spirit of the deceased in its journey in the afterlife as well as to help those left behind adjust to the loss.

age or terminal illness. Among the Inuit of the Arctic, the survival of hunting families would be endangered if they slowed their wanderings through arctic wastes in search of food to allow the aged or infirm to keep up. Eventually, at the urging of the afflicted party, the Inuit might hold a funeral ceremony and say goodbye to the one who had to be left behind to die so that others might live.

Since all societies must restructure their social relations so that the work of the world may be continued after the death of a member, social death is found in each society. The most dramatic aspect of this social custom is manifest in <u>funeral rituals</u>. Funeral rituals provide a mechanism for dealing with and disposing of the body of the deceased and, at the same time, provide a setting in which the survivors can be encouraged to adjust themselves to the person's now permanent absence. As a part of this second role of funeral rituals, issues of inheritance of property rights and of passing on the statuses of the deceased to new persons are dealt with in many societies during or immediately following the funeral.

The Mapuche Death and Burial Ritual

The Mapuche, a native people of southern Chile, believed, according to Louis Faron (1961, 1968), that death is caused by spiritual powers. The forces of evil known as *wekufe* were usually brought into play by a sorcerer-witch called *akalku*. When a person died, the corpse became dangerous to those who had to deal with it. One or two members of the household washed the corpse, clothed it in its finest garments, and laid it out for display on an altar in the house. After four days, the body was transferred to a canoe-shaped coffin that had been carved from a split tree trunk.

The relatives, especially the women of the family, mourned and lamented the loss, tore their garments, and promised revenge for the death which they believed to have been caused by sorcery. Then came the wake or "Black Gathering." First, the house was purified of evil spirits to prevent them from capturing the soul of the deceased. This was done by horsemen who surrounded the house and shouted at the evil spirits who invariably came in search of the souls of the dead. A four-day-and-night vigil by the relatives followed. This was important, since how the deceased spent eternity—either among the ancestors or in the underworld of witches—depended not on how he or she had lived but on how the mourners conducted themselves during the death ritual. It was their behavior that prevented the witches from stealing parts of the corpse for use in creating a new evil spirit.

After the four days of vigil, the corpse was taken to a bier in a field. There the deceased was praised in several speeches. The coffin was then painted black and decorated with cinnamon, apple, and the shrub maqui. A large wooden cross, a symbol borrowed from Catholicism, was placed at the head of the coffin, which faced toward the east.

When the chance that the spirit of the deceased would be captured by evil forces had been dealt with, the guests, who might number over 1,000, assembled in the mourning houses and were fed a ceremonial meal provided by the family of the deceased. The men were greeted by the host and the female guests by a female relative of the deceased, in separate groups. Although many feared to do so, it was customary for the guests to look on the face of the corpse. Small gifts, belongings, and a packet of food were dropped into the coffin to accompany the deceased on the journey to the afterworld of the ancestors.

Only the closest relatives finally accompanied the coffin to the graveyard. As they returned from the cemetery, ashes were scattered along the way to prevent the spirit from returning to bother the living.

Summary

We change in many ways through life, but some of our changes are not unique to us. Rather, they are signs that we are passing through predictable stages in the life cycle. The major stages discussed here are birth, socialization during childhood, marriage, family formation, old age, and death. Societies shape these changes in culture-specific ways, with only a few universals or near-universals such as the incest taboo.

Along the way, life cycle changes may be marked by customs such as pregnancy taboos, *couvade*, naming ceremonies, puberty rituals, marriage negotiations, marriage rituals, establishment of residence, divorce, and funeral rites, each of which has specific cultural meanings and purposes. Many cultures also have specific expectations about whom one can marry and with whose family the new couple should live.

Key Terms and Concepts

life cycle   135
rite of passage (life crisis rite)   135
descent line   136
patrilineality   136
matrilineality   136
bilateral descent   136

lineage   137
clan   137
kindred   137
pregnancy rituals   139
couvade   140
naming ceremony   141

Annotated Readings

Kenyatta, J. (1968). *Facing Mount Kenya: The tribal life of the Gikuyu*. New York: Random House. An excellent description of Kikuyu life by a Kikuyu anthropologist. Especially good chapters on life cycle rituals.

Pasternak, B. (1976). *Introduction to kinship and social organization*. Englewood Cliffs, NJ: Prentice-Hall. A brief introductory overview of kinship and social organization.

Shostak, M. (1982). *Nisa: The story of a !Kung woman*. New York: Random House. A fascinating account of the life history of a woman in a foraging society.

Simmons, L. W. (Ed.). (1942). *Sun Chief: The autobiography of a Hopi Indian*. New Haven, CT: Yale University Press. A fascinating autobiographical account of the life of a Hopi chief, Don Talayesva.

Stephens, W. N. (1963). *The family in cross-cultural perspective*. New York: Holt, Rinehart and Winston. A good discussion of family, sexual restrictions, mate choice, marriage, and related topics.

Van Gennep, A. (1960, originally published 1980). *The rites of passage* (S. T. Kimball, trans.). Chicago: University of Chicago Press. The classic discussion of the major changes in status that are celebrated in ritual.

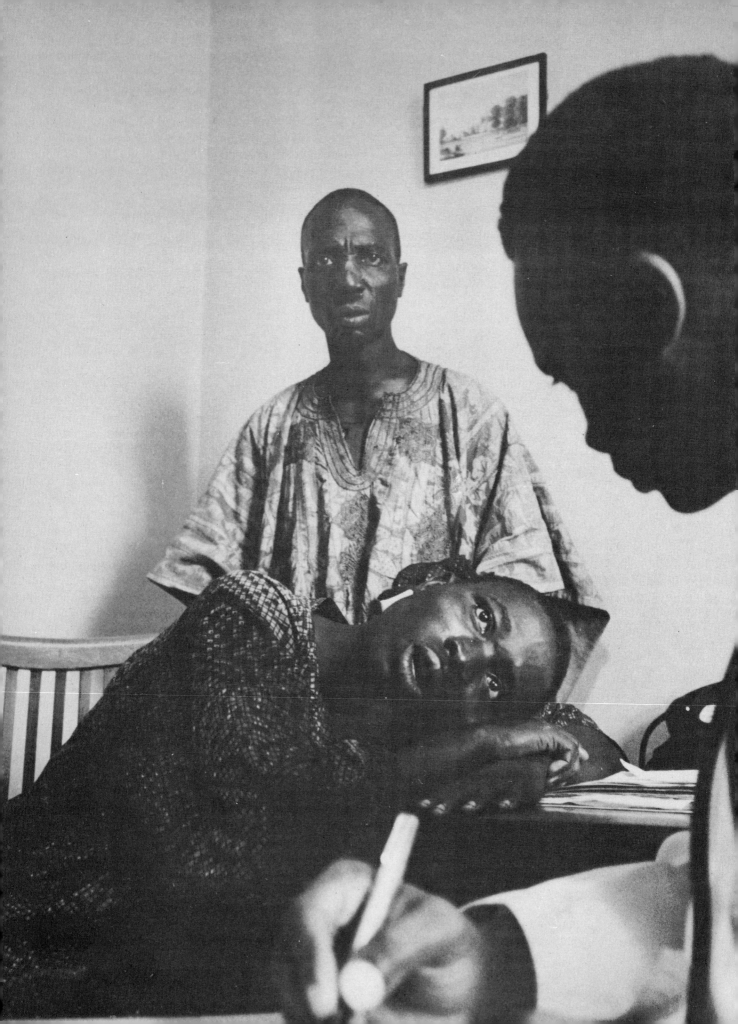

Chapter 7

Culture, Personality, and Psychological Processes

We like to think of ourselves as unique individuals, yet we tend to be somewhat similar to other people in our society. Our personalities are not merely our own. They are shaped to a great extent by our culture. In this chapter, we will look at how culture provides the limits within which we can express our unique qualities. Many of our actions grow out of attempts to relieve the stresses peculiar to life in our own society. If these attempts do not fit within the bounds of what others consider normal behavior appropriate for our roles, we may be labeled insane— or we may be playing, creating art, or having religious experiences.

Personality and Social Organization

In psychological terms, our personality may be defined as our consistent pattern of behaviors, resulting from a more or less enduring set of inner forces. Although we generally think of our personality as something located within ourselves, anthropologists are more interested in examining personality in relation to external cultural and social pressures. An anthropological view of personality portrays it as one part of a complex cultural system, most of which lies outside the individual. The governing mechanism of this system is culture, a network of assumptions, ideas, and feelings that guides the social life of a people who share them, much as the rules of a game guide its playing. Those who fail to follow the rules are subject to social pressure and personal emotional distress, sometimes to the point of being declared insane. Personality from this perspective is seen as an individual's pattern of behavior that results from the various social roles that he or she has learned to play. Whereas psychologists tend to be interested in the consistent ways of behaving regardless of the role being played, anthropologists are more likely to be intersted in how differences in the individual's style of behaving vary from role to role, depending on the time, place, or social context of the role playing.

Figure 7.1 *First Psychiatrist of Nigeria Tribal chief's son, Dr. T. Adeoye Lambo, runs a clinic at Abeokuta, Nigeria.*

163

Socialization and Modal Personality Types

Our culture is incorporated into our personality through socialization, the process by which a culture is passed from one generation to the next. Much of this socialization occurs during our childhood. Every society has its own customs by which children are raised toward adulthood. For instance, Margaret Mead (1950) pointed out that the warlike, aggressive Iatmul of New Guinea encouraged aggression in their children by allowing them to cry for long periods before feeding them and then frustrating their attempts to take food. The nearby Arapesh, on the other hand, having a peaceful way of life, indulged their children.

It is to be expected that the adults of each society, having personalities influenced by their culture's childrearing customs, will share many common personality traits. This fact is expressed in the concept of modal personality type—the idea that beyond individual differences a typical pattern of personality traits can be found in each society.

Institutions that affect personality. Kardiner (1946) held that children's personalities are most directly influenced by a society's primary institutions, those basic elements in social life that are most directly related to childrearing, and that out of people's personalities arise the secondary institutions of society, those most central to the ideology of a culture, such as religion, folk tales, and art. Just what are the primary institutions? According to Whiting and Child (1953, p. 310), "The economic, political and social organs of a society—the basic customs surrounding the nourishment, sheltering and protection of its members—seem a likely source of influence on child training practices."

Levine (1973) has elaborated these relationships. He contends that a society's adaptation to its specific environment determines its economic and social structure, what he calls the society's maintenance system. This system, in turn, determines the society's childrearing practices, which—mediated by the biological needs, drives, and capacities of these children—result in the development of child and adult person-

Figure 7.2 *Socialization*
Children in many parts of the world are nursed for three or four years, as is this !Kung child from the Kalahari Desert of South Africa.

alities. The prevailing child personality pattern determines how people work and play and is the basis of cultural products such as fantasy, sayings, forms of recreation, and basic understandings about the world. The modal adult personality, on the other hand, is reflected in crime rates, suicide rates, and leisure activities and is the basis of cultural traits such as religious beliefs, folk tales, and theories of disease.

Childhood socialization practices. During childhood, our personality is shaped by factors such as how we are fed and cared for, the degree to which we are touched and comforted, how long we are nursed, how we are weaned and toilet trained, and how and what we are taught about human sexuality. For instance, Cora DuBois (1944) reported that Alorese children in Indonesia received very inconsistent care from infancy. Mothers had to return to work in the fields within two weeks after the birth of a child, and infants received little attention until they were nursed when their mothers returned late in the afternoon. Once an Alorese child learned to walk, it received even less attention during the day. Weaning occurred before the birth of another child and was promoted by teasing, punishment, or even by sending the child to stay with relatives. As one might expect, Alorese children grew up to be suspicious and pessimistic, with shallow friendships. Alorese religion and art reflected their upbringing. Like parents, Alorese gods were not to be relied on. They had to be placated to avoid their anger. But this was done grudgingly, and religious art was only carelessly crafted, without devotion. Frustration and resentment were central themes of folk tales and stories.

The family setting also is influential in childhood socialization. Whiting (1959) has shown that societies composed of extended family households are more likely to punish aggression than are societies in which households are made up of nuclear families. When extended family members live under the same roof, aggression among children is more likely to constitute a problem that will be punished by adults. Similarly, Minturn and Lambert (1964) found that families who live in cramped quarters are the ones most likely to punish aggression. In such societies it is to be expected that children will experience greater anxiety about the control of aggression and that folk tales will reveal a preoccupation with aggression.

Subsistence patterns also seem to have a significant impact on personality development. Barry, Child, and Bacon (1959) compared agricultural societies with societies in which people survive by hunting and gathering wild foods. They found that the cultures of agricultural societies are more likely to stress compliance in children, while hunting and gathering people are more likely to teach their children to assert themselves as individuals. Whereas self-reliance is an important survival trait among hunters, following an established routine seems more important in the daily lives of agriculturalists. Children who play with and scatter the stored food reserves of agricultural peoples or who get underfoot in their more crowded settlements are not likely to be well tolerated.

The games that children make up and teach each other often contrast with instruction they receive from adults. Roberts and Sutton-Smith (1962) found that games of

strategy appear to be most popular where obedience is stressed in childrearing. A preoccupation with strategy may well reflect anxiety about powerlessness among children who lack the social power to achieve many of their goals directly. Games of chance, on the other hand, are more popular in societies in which duty and responsibility are stressed during socialization. Such games may represent a form of defiance of responsibility, a psychological release from anxiety about having to be responsible.

Personality and Social Roles

In guiding behavior, culture defines the nature of a society, the kinds of roles the participants may adopt, and, hence, the ways that people can interact. For instance, among the Cheyenne of the North American plains, the Contrary Warrior was expected to interact with others in a different way from other Cheyenne (Grinnell, 1961; Llewellyn & Hoebel, 1941). When Contraries wished to affirm something, they were required to say ''No''; to deny they said ''Yes''; when they were asked to go away it was anticipated that they would approach. Contraries were expected to be the bravest of warriors and possessed of visionary power, inspiring other warriors to fight their hardest. To set the status of Contrary apart from others, Contraries were expected to do all things backwards, displaying buffoonery even during otherwise solemn occasions.

Status-appropriate roles. Patterns for behavior are laid down in the culture's ideology as rules outlining the status-appropriate roles that people may play when interacting with one another and how those roles should be played. Personality therefore can be seen as a cultural phenomenon as well as an internal, psychological one—that is, as a culturally controlled pattern in an individual's role playing. Whenever people interact in settings where one of their statuses is appropriate, they normally manifest those parts of their personality that embody the roles of that status.

Each human group is made up of several statuses that the group defines as mutually compatible. When a person attempts

165

to enter a new group, members interact with the newcomer to determine her or his potential to hold an available status that the group recognizes as appropriate for its members. This process determines which roles of the group's various statuses the newcomer is capable of playing. In initiating the process, newcomers "present face," that is, communicate to the others the possible social value they claim for themselves. Once admitted to the group, individuals are expected to play a role that supports that face, or social standing. They will be evaluated by the others based on how well they continue to live up to that initial self-portrayal.

Sorority Rush: An Example of Establishing Face

Whether we are being interviewed for a job, discussing the news of the day with a group of potential new friends, or joining a sorority, our first interactions with others are an attempt to demonstrate that we can be of value to them. If we convince the group that we can fill a role that would benefit it and if the group convinces us that we have something to gain from playing that role, then we will be taken into the group. Depending on how formally the group is organized, the process may be more or less highly structured, but it is essentially the same in content wherever it occurs.

Consider the case of sorority rush, a more formal example of face-work. On the Utah State University campus, Greek Rush Week begins on Monday when the three sororities set up a registration table in the Student Center. Young women who wish to join a sorority pay a $5 registration fee to demonstrate the seriousness of their intent. They fill out an application giving their names, hometown, grade-point average, and interests, as well as identifying immediate relatives who have been sorority sisters. On Tuesday, applicants attend a movie that explains the Greek system: the "philanthropies" engaged in by each House, the intramural sports between the Houses, the parties and social events that each hosts, and the activities of Greek Rush Week that they are participating in as applicants. The applicants are then divided into groups of 30 or 40 for House Tours. Each group is guided through the three sorority Houses near the campus.

During the next three days of Greek Rush Week, the applicants and sorority sisters become more familiar with each other. The sisters must study all applicants' information, learning their names and as much as possible about them. On Wednesday they host half-hour "Halloween Parties" for each group of applicants. The activities include singing and dancing. The applicants and House sisters meet personally at this time. On the next day each House invites a smaller group to return to a "Beach Party." This group includes only those applicants in which each House is most interested. At this party, the sorority sisters talk with the applicants, trying to become better acquainted personally. After the party, the sisters meet to hold an open discussion and vote on each applicant.

On Friday an even smaller group of the most preferred applicants are invited to return to the "Preference Party." The selectiveness of the process works both ways, for even if the applicants are invited by all three Houses, they may attend only two events. Preference Day is the most intimate and emotional of the three days. The goal of the House at this party is to show the value of the sorority to its members, to communicate the closeness of the sisters and how they feel about each other. There is singing, and the senior sisters give talks about what the sorority means to them.

After the Preference Parties, the applicants must indicate their first and second choices of a House on a signed document. Once it is signed, their choices cannot be changed. The sisters of each house write the names of their top choices, and all applicants are ranked based on the total votes they receive. The Greek Council meets and compares the lists from each House with the preferences of the applicants, and each applicant is assigned a House.

On Saturday the applicants pick up the "bids" which inform them which house they have been assigned. They go immediately to the sorority House, where the sisters are waiting outside for them. They are greeted with song and a welcoming party. At a formal ceremony, applicants now become Pledges, a status they will hold for about eight weeks. At the end of that period, if the Pledge wishes to finalize her entry into the House, she will be initiated into the status of a full member.

Face-work. Much of our day-to-day social interaction is aimed at promoting and protecting our own face and the face of other members of our group. In general, the more highly ranked our social status, the more effort others will expend to protect our face. Erving Goffman (1955) has described as face-work the process by which we are maintained in the roles we have been assigned to play. Often, when one first behaves in a way that contradicts the face one has initially espoused, such violations are ignored, and no damage to face occurs. It is then possible for a person to return to the usual role, and social interaction continues according to the normal game plan. If, however, a violation of the norms is brought to public attention—that is, if it becomes publicly labeled as a violation of one's expected "normal behavior"—some work must be done to repair one's damaged face. This face-work is necessary if one is to be accepted again as a fully participating member of the group.

This repair process generally follows a definite sequence, which Goffman has characterized as (1) the challenge, (2) the offering, (3) the acceptance, and (4) the thanks. In the challenge, the person who has injured or threatened another's face is confronted with the warning that the threatened face will be defended. In the offering, the offender (or, occasionally, another person) is permitted to make amends for the offense, perhaps by indicating that the apparent threat was meaningless or unintentional, that it was only a joke, or that it had been unavoidable. The offering may also take the form of excusing the actor from responsibility for the act, as when one attributes an otherwise serious violation of rules to intoxication, fatigue, or illness. At the same time, compensation may be offered to the offended party, and the offender may take on a self-imposed punishment. The recipient of the offering may now indicate acceptance of its sufficiency for reestablishing the original symbolic balance of the group. If this is done, the forgiven offender expresses thanks for the forgiveness.

As individuals manifest their personal qualities in social interaction, their behavior is thus constrained by culturally defined rules for maintaining social order. The personality traits that are considered normal are those that can be integrated successfully into the interactions. Roles that consistently disrupt the recurring exchanges are likely to be seen as abnormal or deviant. Each society exists in a unique environment and has particular techniques for obtaining what its people need to survive there. Each society therefore has its own unique structure, with interactions among individuals guided by cultural rules that express that society's needs and values. Thus, the cultural ideals of "normal" interaction will be defined differently from society to society.

Inadequate Role Playing and Emotional Distress

Failure to play our roles as we are expected to may cause us personal distress. Every status has a culturally defined rank. To maintain face, the holder of each status is expected to use a particular amount of power and to receive a certain amount of honor. Failure to play one's roles in a way that uses the appropriate level of power or demands the appropriate amount of honor results in emotional distress for the role player.

The most basic form of this subjective distress is anxiety, a general sense of powerlessness and foreboding. Depending on the context in which the stress occurs and on how the individual interprets the situation, anxiety may alternate with more focused distressful feelings (see Table 7.1). Anxiety will take the form of the more concrete emo-

Emotional Responses of Inadequate Role Playing

Problem (Context of Stress)	Individual's Interpretation of the Role Playing Difficulty	Individual's Physiological and Behavioral Responses in Tension State**	Individual's Subjective Feeling
UNKNOWN DANGER, NON-SPECIFIC AROUSAL	"I need to act but I don't know what to do. I cannot cope with this."	generalized visceral tension, hyperventilation, breathlessness, tightness of chest, stomach spasms, diarrhea or constipation, rapid heart beat, respiratory distress, fainting, nausea, sweating, tremor and agitation	ANXIETY (includes frenzy, helplessness, inner conflict, worrying, feelings of loss of self-control)
KNOWN DANGER	"I have too little power."	*facial pallor, coldness of hands and feet, rapid and shallow breathing, rapid heart beat, immobilization or retreat	FEAR (includes terror, apprehension)
HARM TO ANOTHER	"I have used too much power."	head lowered (lower than in shame), gaze averted with only quick glances at other people, avoidance of eye contact, wringing of hands, face takes on "heavy" look with tightness around eyes, dryness of mouth, tightness of sphincter muscles, preoccupation with concepts of fault and wrongdoing	GUILT (includes self-reproach, remorse)
REJECTION, LOSS, ISOLATION	"I have too little esteem; I am worthless."	*sadness with or without tears, headaches, nasal congestion, swelling of eyes, feelings of hopelessness	GRIEF (includes loneliness, sadness, sorrow, pensiveness)
LOSS OF FACE	"I have claimed too much esteem, and others know of it."	*blushing, lowering or covering of face, gaze averted down and to one side, confusion, body curved inward on itself, curled up, makes self look smaller, eyes closed	SHAME (includes embarrassment, shyness, contriteness, sheepishness, mortification)
FRUSTRATION	"Someone/something stands in my way."	*violence of movement or speech, repetitiveness	ANGER (includes hate, rage, annoyance)

*From "The Distancing of Emotion in Ritual," by T. J. Scheff, 1977, *Current Anthropology, 18* (3), 483–506.
**Alternatively, any of these may be realized as emotionless and/or distraction.

Note. Ideas of power and esteem adapted from *A Social Interactional Theory of Emotions* by T. D. Kemper, 1978, NY: John Wiley and Sons.

Table 7.1 *Emotional Responses of Inadequate Role Playing*
In a given situation, when we fail to respond in a manner appropriate to our status or role, we experience emotional distress.

tion fear if the sufferer feels that he or she is playing a role with insufficient power to remain safe from the noxious effects of some specific problem. Anxiety alternates with guilt when stress arises from an awareness that one is exercising more power than is personally acceptable. Grief or sadness may be present when the stress-causing situation is understood by the sufferer as the inability to obtain voluntary esteem from others. Alternatively, anxiety may take the form of shame or embarrassment when there is a possibility that the present esteem of others may be withdrawn, that is, when the stress stems from discovering that one is receiving more honor than one's skills deserve. Any of these four negative concrete emotions—fear, guilt, grief, and shame— may be avoided if the sufferer has learned to respond to others with anger instead. We feel anger when we hold another person responsible for causing our own distress.

Emotional Distress and Ritual

Stress is the body's attempt to prepare itself to take action against any problem, whether organic (e.g., a drug-induced change in brain chemistry), psychological (e.g., learned habits that make it difficult to interact successfully with others), or external (e.g., a major life crisis, such as a divorce). Normally, we prefer to channel the energy mobilized by stress into direct attempts to eliminate the problem. When such pragmatic action is not possible, either because we have not correctly identified the problem, we have not learned a means of dealing with it adequately, we lack the skill to take action successfully, or we have no opportunity to take action, we begin to experience anxiety, conscious awareness and preoccupation with the stress we feel. Depending on how we interpret the situation, anxiety may be a general, nagging sense of foreboding, or it may take on the more concrete form of one of the distressful emotions: fear, guilt, grief, shame, or anger. Some persons so control the expression of anxiety that they experience affectlessness, a kind of emotional lethargy. Prolonged or intense anxiety has two common effects: the subjective experience of altered states of consciousness (trances) and outward

changes in behavior. The behavioral changes that often accompany spontaneous trances begin with a breakdown of old patterns leading to residual rule breaking, behavior that violates the unspoken, taken-for-granted rules of our culture. Sometimes this less typical behavior may result in a creative new solution to the original problem. More often it does not. In such cases, our residual rule breaking settles down into highly expressive (''signalized'') actions that portray how we feel about the unresolved problem. Whenever it recurs, we are likely to respond with the same expressive acts. Thus, stress-induced residual rule breaking coalesces into ritual, stereotyped repetitive behavior that expresses problems by acting them out. Although ritual acts have no pragmatic effect on the original problem, they do have the psychological effect of reducing our anxiety.

Ritual and the Control of Anxiety

We all spontaneously use rituals when we experience stress that we have not learned to handle in any practical way. Many of our rituals are organized into culturally established patterns that are shared by many people and thought of as *religious* acts. In times of crisis, these religious rituals are available as a source of comfort. Rituals give us something to do when we feel that we must act but do not know what to do. They permit us to channel some of the excess energy of stress into physical action and thereby relieve some of the physiological problem of stress. An even more important role of rituals is to distract us from the stress sensation by focusing our attention elsewhere.

Religious rituals are especially effective in this, since they are supported by an ideology that asserts that they are a source of supernatural power that can help in the problems we face.

Following major disasters, such as the 1985 earthquake in Mexico, individuals often seek comfort from grief and fear through prayer, both privately and in groups. More idiosyncratic rituals also appear, spontaneously created and car-

Figure 7.3 *Ritual Prayer*
In this village in the populous highlands of Guatemala in 1976, the residents gather for mass after an earthquake that left one million people homeless.

ried out with the same emotional benefit of relief from anxiety. For example, people sweeping the steps of a now-demolished house reassure themselves that order can be maintained in the midst of chaos. Others gain solace after the death of loved ones by temporarily denying the loss in word and deed— by preparing food for them as usual at mealtime or even by talking to them as if they were still there. We reassure ourselves in much the same way when we bring flowers or gifts to the bed of someone in a coma, keeping alive the hope of recovery by ritual communication. When we understand the real benefits that rituals give us in emotionally trying situations, we can see that a phrase such as ''empty ritual'' overlooks the importance of rituals to our emotional well-being. Rituals may not solve the problems that cause us stress, but they help us continue to function in spite of that stress.

Sometimes, however, our rituals fail to sufficiently allay our worries. When this happens, we may elaborate the rituals in a vain attempt to gain control over the anxieties they have not succeeded in eliminating. Then our rituals can interfere with other parts of our lives and become part of a vicious cycle in which we function less and less effectively. It is these rituals that others are most likely to see as evidence for insanity. Nemiah (1975) has reported the case of a young man whose rituals began over his anxiety about not performing well but eventually interfered with his performance:

A man of 32 who worked on the assembly line of an electronic concern developed the following compelling ritual: before he could solder one piece to another, he had to tap on the workbench 3 times with his left hand and 3 times with his right, followed by stamping 3 times on the floor first with his left foot, then with his right. For a time this merely slowed down his work performance, and he was able to continue his job.

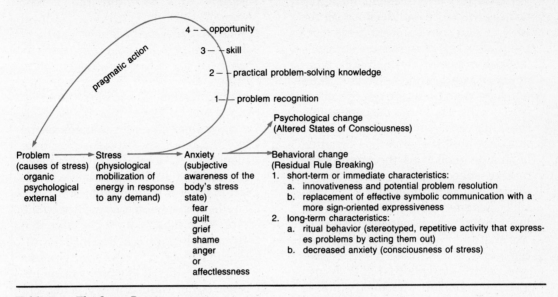

Table 7.2 *The Stress Process*
We tend to want to directly solve problems that cause stress. This may not be possible if 1) we fail to recognize the problem; 2) we haven't learned how to solve the problem; 3) we haven't the skill or 4) the opportunity for dealing with it.

Gradually, however, an element of doubt crept into his mind. After completing a sequence of tapping and stamping, doubting thoughts would flash into his consciousness: "Did I really do it right? Am I sure I tapped 3 times? Did I stamp with my left foot first?" In response to these questions, he had to repeat the ritual to make sure it was perfectly done; but, the more he performed it, the greater his doubt. Before long, almost his entire working day was taken up by his rituals, and he was forced to leave his job. (p. 1246)

Signalized behavior is behavior that has lost many of the communicative characteristics that are necessary for the exchange of symbolic information. Such communication remains highly expressive of feelings and intentions, but it is not very useful as a vehicle of abstract fact. Human communication generally consists of the use of symbols such as words and sentences and the simultaneous use of expressive signals such as the tone and volume of the speaker's voice, posture, muscle tension, and unconscious gestures. Normally, such signs provide a powerful context that helps us recognize which of the possible meanings of another person's symbolic behaviors are the intended ones. For instance, although the words are identical, the two sentences "That *dress* looks good on you" and "*That* dress looks good on you" will be interpreted in very different ways simply because of the sign difference in specifically which word is emphasized by greater volume and voice tenseness. When we are under stress, the usual contrast between symbols and signs breaks down and the significance of our words and other normally symbolic actions is less easily interpreted. At these times, our behavior, including our speech, becomes less clearly symbolic and portrays our feelings very expressively. Such behavior is best interpreted on the level of signs. Thus, as behavior is transformed into ritual, its significance as communication tends to take on meanings with more universal significance than the same behavior might otherwise have in its culturally defined symbolic role (see Table 7.2).

Signalized Speech
Since we normally pay attention to the symbolic aspects of speech, it is instructive to notice that when people are under stress the expressive element of their speech becomes more prominent. At such times, speech may fail to con-

vey facts very effectively. Its meaning-fulness will be best understood on the level of sign communication—as communication that expresses the speaker's feelings and needs through the connotation of words and the style of their delivery more than through the denotation of the words and the context that the other words provide. Since context does not limit the conscious meaning of an individual word, the words of signalized speech appropriately may be interpreted as representing all its possible meanings at the same time. The meaningfulness of signalized speech, like that of ritual behavior, may thus transcend its performance. The expressive nature of signalized speech also gives it a similarity to poetry that is often overlooked. Both are often best understood by considering the allusions of the words, the recurring themes, and the multiple meanings hidden in them, rather than by merely looking for the concrete story line.

Lehmann (1975) has reported the case of a schizophrenic secretary who wrote the following memo:

> Mental health is the Blessed Trinity, and as man cannot be without God, it is futile to deny His Son. For the Creation understands germ-any inVoice New Order, not lie of chained reaction, spawning mark in temple Cain with Babel grave'n image to wanton V day "Israel." Lucifer fell Jew prostitute and Lambeth walks by roam to sex ritual, in Bible six million of the Babylonian woman, infer-no Salvation. (p. 896)

We search in vain for a coherent message, but the expressive concerns leap out in repeated themes: health, religion, warfare, sex, sin, and punishment. Notice the plays on words that unite several themes: *Germ-any* represents concern about the nation involved in World War II and about germs, a cause of illness. *New Order* reminds us of the politics of Germany under Nazi rule but also can represent the mental patient's struggle for internal order. To *lie* is to deceive, but the word also has a sexual connotation. A *chained*

reaction calls to mind the atomic weapons born in World War II, but it is also true that the patient is "chained" as a reaction to her guilt. Like the Jewish prisoners of German concentration camps, the patient is confined—in a mental hospital. Is *mark* both the stigma of mental illness that she bears as a sign of her sin and the name of the illegitimate son she "spawned" and futilely tries to deny? In this signalized communication, it is possible with effort to find the remnants of a story line, but the information is so hidden by the expressive aspects of the message that any interpretation is at best a guess: After the patient "roamed" and became pregnant, she felt like a prostitute because of her wantonness. For her sin, she has been punished with a loss of mental health. She finds no solace in religion, for she is doomed to suffer pains of the *inferno*, and from her circumstances she can *infer no salvation*.

Social Stress and Deviant Personality

Besides feeling anxiety privately, we may be subject to social disapproval if we fail to play our roles properly. A person's personality will be seen as normal by others so long as she or he uses the amount of power and expects the amount of respect that the culture defines as appropriate for his or her statuses. An individual who exercises too much or too little power or expects too much or too little respect for rank will be seen by others as having a personality abnormality. The more often a person errs in the use of power or prestige, the more likely it becomes that the individual will be reassigned to a deviant master status such as that of "insane person."

Deviant statuses. A deviant is a person who has been labeled by others for his or her role-playing errors. The specific deviant status assigned will depend on the way in which a person misuses socially assigned power and prestige. The user of an excess of power will be seen as *hostile* and will be described as being prone to anger. The person who consistently uses less power than expected will be seen as *timid* or *fearful*. One who claims the right to an unrealistically high level of esteem will be viewed as *conceited* or *megalomaniacal*. The overly self-denigrating individual will be labeled as *depressive* or *insecure*. Each culture elaborates these four basic categories with labels for subtypes that occur with high frequency. For instance, in American culture there is a special term for the person who manifests the hostile use of power by insulting the rank of another person: Such a person is said to be *catty*. One who uses an excess of power to prevent another from terminating a conversation, while remaining overtly oblivious to his or her own violation, will be called a *bore*.

Categories of cultural rules. Rule violations in the use of culturally appropriate levels of power and prestige are common enough in all societies so that every culture is likely to specifically label and define realms within which violations of rules can be grouped. For instance, in the United States, rule violations will be seen as violations of *law* if they result in harm to persons or property. Violations of rules of prestige, which differentiate members of one class from another, are violations of *etiquette*. *Aesthetic* standards are those current values that determine which things may be compatibly organized together. As do all symbolic categories, aesthetic standards change. For instance, before the film *Flashdance*, wearing a torn sweat shirt in public was considered unaesthetic in most of America. Law, etiquette, and aesthetics are but three of a much longer list of formally labeled American rule categories.

The precise list of rule categories varies, of course, from culture to culture, and categories that are important in one society may be absent in another society. In most societies, for instance, there is no formal category of rules labeled *religious* rules, since the concept of religion as a separate aspect of human life is rare (Cohn, 1970). The one universal fact in categories of rules is that, regardless of how long the list may be, there will always be rules left over that belong to none of the categories. These left-over rules, which have nothing in common with one another except that none of them fits into the primary rule categories of the culture,

may be said to make up the *miscellaneous* or residual rules of that culture.

Violations of residual rules. Even if a residual category is not formally named, the violation of any of these rules elicits a similar reaction from members of society. Scheff (1966) has pointed out that it is the violation of the residual norms that results in the labeling of a person as *insane*. The violation of legal rules may be abhorred. But it is precisely because most members of society can conceive of situations in which they themselves might be tempted to violate the rights of others that such violations are deemed punishable. Likewise, violation of etiquette is undesirable, but this "poor taste" is understood as evidence of a failure to have achieved a desirable level of social ranking, something that not everyone is expected to be able to accomplish. The residual rules, on the other hand, are the rules that are taken for granted, conformity to which is assumed to come naturally to all normal individuals.

Residual rules are the prohibitions that need not be taught; it literally "goes without saying" that they are not to be done. Indeed, the prohibitions embodied in these miscellaneous rules could never be fully codified and formally taught since the list is, for any culture, an open-ended one that could be added to *ad infinitum*. It is doubtful that any Americans have ever been taught not to remove their shoes and juggle them while carrying on a conversation with a minister. Yet most if not all Americans would immediately recognize such behavior as a rule violation were they to witness it. If the actor, on being queried, failed to provide an acceptable rationale to American observers by the standards of their common ideology, the observers would be likely to judge the act and perhaps the actor as crazy.

Those who consistently violate the residual rules of their own culture are inviting others to assign them the master status of *insane person*. This is perhaps the most stigmatized of any master status, since its holder is, by definition, outside the group of normal humans. Holding this master status makes it difficult to relate to people on the basis of any other status one might have.

All other statuses are viewed as implying a level of normality in the holder while the master status of *insane person* is an affirmation of its holder's basic lack of normality, as normality is defined by the culture. From this perspective, it can be seen that insanity, the process of acquiring the master status of *insane person* or *residual rule breaker* may be viewed as a cultural process as well as a psychological one. In any society, insanity defines the limits of what is considered to be normal.

Stress and residual rule breaking. In the opinion of Scheff (1966), the causes of residual rule breaking are diverse. They include: (1) organic sources such as genetic, biochemical, and physiological problems; (2) psychological sources, such as problems in upbringing and training; (3) external stress such as drug ingestion, danger, lack of food and sleep, or sensory overload; and (4) volitional acts of innovation or defiance. The common denominator of all these causes is that residual rule breaking is likely to occur when the individual is experiencing stress, regardless of its sources. Stress is a physiological state that has been studied for years by Selye (1976), who defines it as the nonspecific response of the body to any demand. In the beginning stages of the stress state the human body is mobilizing itself for action. This state of readiness involves such general bodily changes as increased movement, heightened blood pressure, excess perspiration, and accelerated heartbeat.

In some situations leading to stress, the culture offers no practical avenues of acceptable action that will eliminate the cause of one's stress. In such a situation the energy inherent in the stress state may be channeled into ritualized behavior that expresses the stress feelings. Such behavior is repetitive since the stress that motivates it is not eliminated by the behavior. Yet it is associated with temporary emotional relief as the excess energy of the stress state is drained off by being put to use.

When one's culture has provided no normal response to a stressful situation, residual rule breaking does have the potential of being adaptive. By doing things that are not in the normal behavioral repertoire of the culture, the stressed person may discover a creative practical solution to the original stress-inducing problem. In such cases, residual rule breaking may be a source of cultural innovation and change when problems arise in a society. However, such innovations will be adopted by society at large only if enough other members of society are trying to cope with the same kind of problem and therefore recognize the benefit of the innovation (Wallace, 1961). When this is not the case, other members of society are likely to regard the residual rule breaking as a startling and undesirable form of deviance from the usual behaviors that they expect from one another. This is one reason why people labeled insane for their strange-seeming behavior are sometimes feared as potentially dangerous. When few others are experiencing the same stresses in life and society fails to recognize the adaptive benefit that residual rule breaking may have for the rule violator, the person runs the risk of being redefined by others as insane.

From childhood through adulthood, our personality is thus shaped by our society. The ways we behave when we are with others are guided by the roles considered appropriate for our statuses. We may feel considerable distress if we do not live up to our role expectations, sometimes leading to ritualized expressions of the feeling of stress. Each society has its own rituals for dealing with deviance, from face-work processes for restoring status to deviant labels for those who persistently err in the use of power and prestige. Behaviors that fall totally outside social expectations are neatly categorized as insanity.

Mental Disorders and Culture

Insanity is recognized in all cultures by its social inappropriateness. Edgerton (1976, p.63) has defined insanity as a situation in which ". . . a person's thought, emotions, or behavior appear to others in his society to be unreasonable or irrational, or when his ability to cope with the ordinary demands of life are impaired." As a case in point, Edgerton (1976, p.64) reports the example of ". . . an elder Sebei man of Ugan-

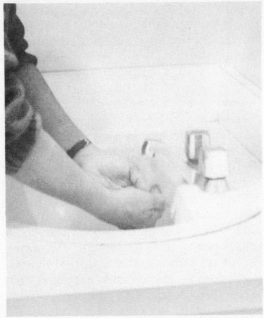

Figure 7.4 *Obsessive Compulsive Disorders*
An individual with an obsessive compulsive disorder may continually think about being contaminated by dirt. These obsessive thoughts may lead to compulsive acts such as constantly washing the hands or cleaning the house even when it does not need it.

da who for some years spent most of his waking hours hanging upside down from the limb of a tree or a rafter in his house. His only comments were: 'I have a chicken in my head' or 'I have countless wives.' Most Sebei easily agreed on labeling him psychotic.''

Many societies, including our own, recognize and label specific forms of insanity. Though they are culturally shaped, these categories share certain universal characteristics.

Psychiatric Categories

Contemporary psychiatric classification includes three categories of mental disorders that are held to be of psychological origin: schizophrenia, affective disorders, and neuroses. The various problems called schizophrenia are generally seen as disorders of thinking that result in bizarre forms of self-expression, often accompanied by hallucinations. In the terminology of this text, schizophrenic disorders may be defined as problems in the process of communication, especially in role acquisition and the presentation of face.

The affective disorders are defined as problems of feeling. Sufferers of the depressive variety of affective disorders characteristically experience deep emotional lows, attended by subjective judgments of personal inadequacy, loneliness, and worthlessness as well as by slowness of thought and movement. Depression refers, in other words, to problems related to the actor's sense of inadequate social value or esteem. Sometimes affective disorders begin with a brief period of mild depression that is replaced by a period of exhilaration and high activity known as a manic episode. It is believed that the manic episode helps the sufferer avoid experiencing the distress associated with depression.

The neuroses include a variety of problems in handling anxiety. From a cultural perspective, they may be seen as problems related to a sense of inadequate social power. The most commonly reported forms of neuroses are hysteria, phobias, anxiety states, hypochondriasis, and obsessive-compulsive neurosis.

In hysteria, an overwhelming anxiety, fear, or sense of powerlessness may be avoided by disassociating oneself from awareness of some aspects of the personality. For instance, in amnesia distressful memories are blocked out of conscious memory. This process occurs without the direct awareness of the afflicted individual. Hysteria may also take the form of conversion of anxiety into what appears to be an organic problem. Some part of the body ceases to function normally, even though there is no medical evidence of real organic impairment. For instance, in hysterical paralysis certain muscles can be used for some activities but not for others that are associated with emotionally stressful aspects of the individual's life. Tics, tremors, or an inability to speak are other examples of hysterical conversion reactions. As in amnesia, the failure of an organic function seems to occur without the person's conscious recognition or intent.

In phobias, conscious awareness of the true source of anxiety is avoided by displacing fear onto some object that is symbolic of whatever produces the anxiety. The overtly feared object is often something regarded as completely harmless by non-phobic individuals. Phobics may fear kittens, dirt, open fields, closed-in spaces—almost anything.

An anxiety disorder may involve a chronic state of tension and mild apprehension, or temporary but acute and terrifying panic-like reactions that are not associated with any real danger.

In hypochondriasis, there is an intense preoccupation with physical health and the body, a magnifying of sensations of normal bodily fatigue, aches, pains, and a recurring but unfounded fear that the sufferer's complaints are evidence of some dire disease.

In obsessive compulsive neurosis, consciousness of anxieties is avoided by engaging in repetitive thoughts and acts that distract the individual from the anxiety. However, the repetitive acts or thoughts generally have characteristics that are symbolically indicative of the underlying anxiety. Usually the person suffering from these obsessive compulsive reactions considers them undesirable but feels they cannot be controlled without the experience of great emotional stress.

Culture-Specific Forms of Hysteria

Although the basic psychological mechanisms by which schizophrenia, affective disorders, and the neuroses are produced may be common to all peoples throughout the world, the symbolic forms taken by the problems are molded by the shared meanings that behaviors have in particular cultures. Anthropological fieldworkers have reported a variety of culturally specific forms of mental disorders in traditional non-Westernized societies. The most commonly described examples have been hysterical disorders.

The hysterias. *Amok* is a disorder found in New Guinea (Langness, 1965; Newman, 1964). Only young men ages 25 through 35 seem to be afflicted by the disorder, which is an hysterical reaction of the dissociation type. After an initial depression, the victim enters a phase of anxiety and depression in which experiences take on an unreal quality, and the victim broods over offenses by others. Finally, in a burst of energy, the victim "runs amok," screaming and attacking people and their property. During this stage, the sufferer seems delirious and sometimes unable to hear what others shout at him. After exhausting himself, the victim returns to consciousness but has no memories of what he has done. Among the Gururumba of New Guinea, the individual who was affected by *amok* was not expected to recompense the losses he inflicted, for his behavior was believed to have been beyond his control, caused by the bite of an aggressive ghost or some similar factor that made him not responsible during the attack. Additionally, his susceptibility to the attack was seen as evidence of a weakness in his resistance to the normal stresses of Gururumba social and economic life. Therefore, payment of his previous economic debts was no longer vigorously sought by others. Disorders similar to amok were also reported in Malaya, Indonesia, Polynesia, and the Sahara.

Latah was found in Southeast Asia and Mongolia (Aberle, 1961; Van Loon, 1926). It is an hysterical dissociation brought on by a sudden startling encounter with things such as dangerous objects or even by tickling. After an initial fright reaction, such as tremor and collapse, the victim engages in compulsive imitation of the actions and speech of others. In Southeast Asia and Indonesia, *latah* was most common among women, but in Mongolia it was said to be more likely to afflict men.

Imu, which is perhaps simply a variety of *latah*, was found among the aboriginal inhabitants of northern Japan, the Ainu (Winiarz & Wielawski, 1936). Like *latah* in Southeast Asia, *imu* mainly afflicted women. Brought on by a sudden frightening experience, such as hearing a loud sound or being bitten by a snake, it begins with an aggressive or fearful startle reaction. This reaction is followed by automatic obedience or its opposite, negativism, and the compulsive imitation of sounds and gestures until the victim is exhausted.

A similar disorder, arctic hysteria or *amurakh*, was found among the the Yakut and Tungus of northeastern Siberia, where it also was most common among women (Czaplicka, 1914). Like its counterparts elsewhere, it involves compulsive imitation of sounds and gestures. At least in the form experienced by spiritual healers, or shamans, the original attack is brought on by a sudden fright.

Another hysterical disorder with dissociation characteristics was found among the native Greenlanders of northern Greenland (Foulks, 1972; Gussow, 1960; Wallace, 1972). This affliction is known as *pibloktoq*. It was found somewhat more commonly in women than in men. After a period of irritability and withdrawal, the victim becomes highly agitated, violent, and talkative. Some victims may tear off their clothing and run naked into the snowfields. Finally, after collapsing from exhaustion and falling into unconsciousness, the victim may recover from the attack with no memory of it.

Since *pibloktoq* was most common in the winter, increased life stresses caused by the work of coping with the rigorous arctic winter in small communities might be a triggering factor in this disorder. However, Wallace (1972) has argued that the basic cause of *pibloktoq* was the Greenlanders' calcium-deficient diet. Since vitamin D—produced by the body when it is exposed to sunlight—is necessary for the body to absorb calcium from food, the seasonal increase in *pibloktoq* could be explained by the decreased sunlight in winter. Calcium deficiency would impair the functioning of the central nervous system, producing the *pibloktoq* symptoms of nervous excitability and distortions in thought processes. Other researchers (Foulks, 1972) failed to find significant differences in the serum calcium levels of *pibloktoq*-prone and normal Greenlanders, so Wallace's calcium deficiency hypothesis remains controversial.

Hsieh-ping is an hysteria found in traditional Chinese societies (Wittkower & Fried, 1959). Sufferers, most commonly women, are believed to be possessed by spirits of dead relatives or of dead friends to whom they have failed to show the proper offerings of respect. This affliction includes symptoms of tremor and disorientation, with clouding of consciousness, delirium, speaking in tongues, and hallucinations.

Saka is an hysterical disorder found among the Wataita in Kenya (Harris, 1957).

Sometimes preceded by restlessness and anxiety, an attack begins with convulsive movements in which the upper body trembles and the head shakes from side to side. Occasionally, the victim may repeat actions or sounds thought to be in a foreign tongue. A trance or loss of consciousness and rigidity of the body may follow. Attacks may be precipitated by the sight, sounds, and smells of men or foreigners or even by things associated with them, such as the whistle of a train or the smell of a cigarette.

Social roots of hysterias. Each of these hysterical disorders is ideologically patterned in such a way that the people among whom it is found understand the symptoms according to their culture's unique system of meanings. Yet, all these disorders share several important characteristics with each other and with the varieties of hysteria described in the Western psychiatric tradition. For instance, in most of these cases, the affliction is more likely to strike women than men, a finding that may reflect women's traditional lack of socially granted power. In those cases where men are prominent victims, they are often failing in the goal-oriented masculine roles of their culture, roles in that power is expected to be exercised successfully. Attacks are often set off by a sudden frightening shock or by other stimuli that may call the victims' attention to how little power they have compared with others. Attacks are followed by great agitation and even violent behavior that is powerful in form, if not in fact. Alternatively, instead of violent agitation, one may find its opposite: behavior that dramatizes the powerlessness of the victim, such as automatic obedience or robot-like imitation of others' sounds and gestures. In either case, the hysterical behavior is generally performed in a mentally clouded, disoriented state of mind. Finally, after termination of this intense and ritualized drama of powerlessness, the victim, who may fall exhausted into a state of unconsciousness or sleep, is likely to experience amnesia concerning the attack itself.

Hysteria and culture. Hysterical disorders are most common in certain kinds of societies. Seymour Parker (1962) has summarized the traits common to societies in which hysteria is prevalent: (1) early socialization is not severe and there is a high level of gratification of dependency needs; (2) there is a corresponding emphasis on communalistic values and expectations of mutual aid; (3) the female role is ranked markedly below that of the male; and (4) the religious system often provides models of hysteria-like behavior in spirit-possession rituals. In other words, childrearing practices foster high expectations that others may be relied on to fulfill one's dependency needs; therefore, self-reliance does not reach a high level. Community values support these traits by providing a substantial level of support from others. At the same time, this communal orientation creates a strong emphasis on conformity to community values.

In certain areas of life, these expectations that one's needs may be met by others breaks down. The dependence on others rather than on oneself for fulfillment of one's needs implies that a person's self-esteem is contingent on the interpretation of his or her value in the eyes of others. Many times, this support for self-esteem is consistently available: children are not dealt with harshly, their wants are quickly fulfilled, and mutual aid among adults communicates their value. But in several areas of life, this system for gratifying the need for a sense of well-being breaks down. Women, for instance, are repeatedly reminded that their status is inferior to that of men in both esteem and power. By and large, women in these societies therefore carry a heavier burden of their day-to-day stress as private concern about their self-worth. They also are more likely than men to react to sudden dangers by fright reactions that lead to hysterical breaks with reality and that manifest their anxiety about having too little power to take care of themselves. Similarly, symbolic reminders of their inferior status may lead stressed women to fall into hysterical trances that manifest the same anxiety.

Social outcasts of either sex are not supported in their self-esteem by these societies. Rather, the communities use subtle and not-so-subtle sanctions to withdraw their support from deviant individuals. For the individual whose self-esteem is dependent on the support of others, this can be disastrous. For example, in traditional Chinese societies, the woman who failed, either out of laxity or poverty, to make the expected offerings to the dead could find herself losing the needed support of her community. This might lead quickly to great anxiety in a person not socialized to self-reliance. Since a married woman left her own family to reside with her husband and his kin, she lacked support from her own kin at times of emotional stress. The hysterical reaction that resulted was believed by those around her to be a manifestation of spirit possession. In performing a cure, the community would reintroduce her into its good graces and the hysteria would subside.

Men who are less active or who fail in the pursuit of the male goals in these societies also may develop anxiety about their inadequate personal power. This is likely in situations where they do not have others to whom they may turn for aid without denying the masculinity that they are expected to demonstrate by their independence. When arctic hysteria struck men, it usually struck those whom Edward Foulks (1972 p. 11) described as " 'nervous' young men aspiring to become shamans," that is, young men who were somewhat marginal in secular male pursuits and wished therefore to become spiritual healers.

Other Culture-Specific Disorders

Besides the hysterias, other disorders uniquely shaped by specific cultures have similar underlying patterns.

Kayak angst has been found among the native people of Greenland, especially those of western Greenland (Freuchen, 1935; Honigmann & Honigmann, 1965). It strikes males while they are alone and the sea is calm. The stress is that of physical immobility and environmental monotony in a potentially dangerous situation. The reaction begins with confusion, dizziness, and blurring of vision and depth perception. The victim becomes immobilized by fear of capsizing the kayak, a fear that is increased by a sudden chilling of his lower body, which he believes to be caused by water entering the kayak. These attacks may recur and be so incapacitating that the man may refuse to leave shore again, in spite of the economic importance of doing so. *Kayak angst* may be classified as a phobic disorder.

Susto, sometimes called *espanto* or *pasmo*, is most common in Latin America (Rubel, 1960). Following an experience of shame from failure to meet an important social obligation, the victim, whose soul is believed to have been lost because of a sudden fright or some other spiritual cause, becomes withdrawn, listless, and irritable. In addition, the victim loses appetite and experiences rapid heartbeat, nausea and vomiting, diarrhea, and restless sleep troubled by nightmares. *Susto* seems to combine some elements of depression with its primary symptoms as an anxiety reaction.

Koro has been associated most commonly with China and other parts of east and Southeast Asia (Hsien, 1963, 1965; Yap, 1963, 1965). Like many other neurotic disorders, *koro* attacks often follow a sudden fright. Male victims report that their penis feels cold, numb, and no longer a part of themselves. They fear that it is shrinking and being absorbed into their abdomen, leading to death. Among women, the fears center on the belief that their breasts are being similarly absorbed and that they will die. The cultural parallel of this anxiety about masculinity or femininity is clear: The traditional ideology of Chinese culture classified all things as masculine and feminine on the basis of the *yin* and *yang* or "female" and "male" essences they contain. In China, *koro* is believed to be caused by an imbalance of *yin* and *yang* in the victim. For instance, it is believed that koro can be brought on in men by the loss of semen through masturbation or frequent sexual intercourse, since semen is held to be a source of *yang*, which represents masculine vitality and strength. Like *susto*, *koro* is an anxiety reaction.

Frigophobia or *pa-ling* is a Chinese disorder that involves the obsessive compulsive need to change clothing repeatedly and to wear it in several layers to avoid heat loss from the cold and from winds (Kiev, 1972; Yap, 1951). The attendant fear of the cold and wind is rationalized by the victim of *pa-ling* by the belief that either of these may upset the balance of *yin* and *yang* necessary to health. It is believed that the resulting loss of vital essence may lead to death. In contrast to the normal use of layered clothing in China, sufferers of frigophobia may spend so much time changing clothes that they are unable to function in their normal responsibilities.

Anorexia Nervosa: A Culture-Specific Disorder in the United States

The unique social stresses of the modern United States also lead to culture-specific disorders, including one syndrome in which some young women literally starve themselves to death. Contemporary American culture emphasizes slenderness as a mark of beauty in women. Fashion models are much more slender than the average American woman. Advertisements and movies reinforce our image of a desirable figure. The stars of our motion pictures are rarely of average build, and the overweight actress is most often found in a comic role. Diet foods fill an entire section of our supermarkets.

United States culture also stresses the desirability of youth, another element in our concepts of beauty and attractiveness. In spite of an increasing awareness of the harm that sexism has in our practical and emotional lives, the word "girl" traditionally has been used as if it were a synonym for "youthful woman."

In a society in which youth and slenderness are highly valued, anxiety about weight gain and growing older is also common. As many as 1 in 250 American females between the ages of 12 and 18 years may suffer from a disorder called anorexia nervosa. The central characteristics of this disorder are an intense fear of becoming obese, an inaccurate body image, a significant loss of weight, and a refusal to maintain even a minimal normal body weight. Victims of anorexia nervosa are almost always female. They are frequently

179

described as perfectionistic "model children." The disorder usually starts in late adolescence. The patient refuses to eat and may lose 25 to 30% of her body weight. Although the most common pattern is a single episode followed by full recovery, some 15 to 21% of cases end in death by starvation.

Anorexia nervosa has been described as an obsessive-compulsive attempt to maintain a slender body build and an expression of fear of the transition from childhood to womanhood. Anorexics commonly feel inadequate in their social roles and incompetent in their work or school performance.

It is clear from these examples that the culture-specific disorders have much in common with one another. Indeed, the underlying psychological process seems to be the same. Individuals who are faced with stresses that they are unable to relieve by pragmatic action experience emotional distress about their inability to deal with their problems successfully and begin to show that stress by breaking the residual rules of their cultures. These various culture-specific disorders differ from one another mainly in their overt manifestations: The responses to stress are symbolic behaviors that are appropriate to the particular culture.

Altered States of Consciousness and Insanity

The subjective experience during stress-induced signalized ritual behavior is commonly called an altered state of consciousness. This experience may or may not be interpreted as a sign of insanity. After examining the characteristics of <u>altered states of consciousness</u>, we will look at some factors affecting whether those who enter altered states will be considered crazy.

Altered States of Consciousness

Psychologist Arnold Ludwig (1972) reports that the major characteristics of altered states of consciousness are: (1) alterations in thinking, (2) disturbance of the sense of time, (3) change in emotional expression, (4) change in body image, (5) distortions in perception, (6) change in the perceived meaning or significance of things, (7) a sense that the experiences cannot be described, (8) hypersuggestibility, and sometimes (9) a sense of loss of control, and/or (10) feelings of rejuvenation. Most of these changes may be results of stress, which may inhibit the usual role of the left hemisphere of the cerebral cortex in initiating action and controlling a person's behavior during symbolic interaction with others.

Biological explanations of altered states. To understand altered states of consciousness, we must first look at the effects of stress on the brain. In the discussion of a biological basis of language (see Chapter 5), we noted that the human cerebral cortex is divided into two major halves or hemispheres, and that the left hemisphere is more specialized than the right. The left hemisphere has specialized centers that make possible the symbolic skills embodied in language. Since normal human interaction is predominantly a series of symbolic interchanges, the left cerebral hemisphere tends to be dominant in initiating and controlling most human activities. Stress, however, interferes with the symbolic capacity of the human organism. This leaves the right hemisphere, the side of the cerebral cortex that takes the lead in non-symbolic behavior, to play the dominant role during the expressive acts that are common in rituals. This is a role to which it is well suited, since the right hemisphere's predominant way of operating involves communication by direct representation, that is, by signs.

The alterations in thinking that are common in altered mental states include increased difficulties in concentration, attention, and memory, all of which are understandable results of stress. There is also a shift away from thinking in terms of cause and effect—a left hemispheric way of organizing thought—toward a mode of thought in which opposites may coexist. The coexistence of opposite meanings is a hallmark of communication by signs: A smile may indicate friendship or sarcasm, tears may signal sorrow or joy, and laughter may express either relief from stress or mounting embarrassment.

It has been noted repeatedly in studies of differences between the left and right hemispheres that the ordering of information in a sequence, such as a chronological listing of events, is a left hemispheric trait. However, the experience of time as a passage of events one after another at a constant, measurable pace is alien to the way in which the right hemisphere orders its memory of events. Therefore, the disturbed time sense common in altered mental states may be a result of a shift away from the predominant influence of the left hemisphere's symbolic conceptualization of time.

The change in emotional expression in altered states may involve an increase or decrease in emotional reaction to events. This change may happen because the right hemisphere is more closely tied to the limbic system (which influences degrees of emotional reaction) than is the left hemisphere.

Body image change may occur because the left hemisphere's body image concepts are abstract symbolic representations of its body image ideals while the right hemisphere's body image information is stored in direct representations. Any clash between the two systems of body imaging is likely to be highlighted during periods of right hemispheric dominance, as during an altered state of consciousness.

Perceptual distortions take their most dramatic form as hallucinations, which are like vivid dreams in a waking state. According to Buchsbaum (1979), studies of how the left and right hemispheres communicate suggest that hallucinations may result from the failure of the left hemisphere to suppress incoming information about the fears of the right hemisphere. Normally, this suppression may involve an inhibitory chemical, serotonin, which is produced in the brain during waking hours (Goleman, 1978; Jacobs, 1978). Both dreams and daydreams are normally produced by brain stem stimulation of various brain centers on a 90-minute cycle (Krupke & Lavie, 1975; McCarley, 1978), and daydreams may be the waking state manifestation of dreams in a washed-out form. Under stressful circumstances, the levels of serotonin in the brain may decline, allowing daydreams to be ex-

Figure 7.5 *Drug-induced Altered States of Consciousness*
One means of inducing an altered state of consciousness is to ingest a drug. Here, anthropologist Napoleon Chagnon participates in a Yanomamö ritual of sniffing a hallucinogenic through a long tube.

perienced in the much more vivid form of hallucinations.

The change in the perceived meaning or significance of things often experienced during altered states is sometimes called the eureka experience. It is a sudden sense of deep insight into things "as they really are." This experience may occur because the right hemisphere analyzes experiences not by breaking them up conceptually into parts that are then related to one another by abstract logic, but by weighing the experience in its totality. The left hemisphere solves problems and discovers meaning by the symbolic process of analysis, while the right operates in a more holistic way that finds answers in sudden flashes of insight. Therefore altered state experiences may be described later as ineffable, that is, as not expressible in words, language being a left hemispheric means of communicating.

The hypersuggestibility of people in altered mental states may be because the right hemisphere is capable of understanding language and responding to simple commands or suggestions given to it in language. The experience of loss of control—which is not always present in altered states—may be nothing more than awareness that the logic-oriented, left hemispheric centers of decision making are temporarily subordinated to the more spontaneous and intuitive right hemisphere. This experience may or may not be distressful to individuals, depending on how important it is to them to keep their overt behavior in harmony with a preexisting, well-ordered set of conscious symbolic norms. Finally, the rejuvenation sometimes felt after altered states may simply be the cathartic sense of release from stress that is afforded by the sudden shift from an anxiety-laden state into an altered state of consciousness.

Creation of altered states. Ludwig (1972) reports five main ways of producing altered states of consciousness: (1) a prolonged reduction of sensory input and/or motor activity; or (2) the opposite conditions, namely, sensory and/or motor overload; (3) prolonged increased alertness or mental involvement; or (4) the opposite condition, a prolonged decrease in mental alertness or involvement; and (5) changes in body chemistry. The first of these may be exemplified by trances induced by solitary confinement, so-called "highway hypnosis," or the sensory deprivation associated with *kayak angst.* Examples of the second process are brainwashing, the trances of whirling dervishes, and the frightening encounter or tickling that leads to *latah.* Increased alertness as a path to altered mental states may be seen in the effects of fervent prayer or sentry duty. Decreased alertness is used in some forms of meditation to achieve a mystical mental state. Changes in body chemistry include all the drug-induced altered states of consciousness. The one thing that all these methods for bringing about altered states have in common is that they interfere with the normal functioning of the central nervous system in ways that create stress, the source of signalized ritual behavior.

Altered states and ideology. Interestingly, altered states of consciousness may play a part in the development of the ideology of a culture. Whenever people attempt to describe or account for the experiences they have had during an altered mental state, they must use the medium of language, a left hemispheric system of communication. Whatever the particular beliefs by which people make sense of altered state experiences, these beliefs share one thing in common: They invariably involve some degree of what Leslie White (1971) has called a confusion between self and not-self. This altered perception may take one of two forms: either (1) that which lies outside the individual is considered an extension of the individual, as when lightning is thought to be nature's response to a sinful thought; or (2) that which actually occurs within an individual, such as a dream or an hallucination, is spoken of as a truly external event. Ideas developed in this way are not pragmatic responses to the practical problems of day-to-day life. The function they perform is to relieve the personal effect of stresses. They do so not by eliminating the objective cause of the stress but by relieving the resulting inner feeling of distress.

Cultural Shaping of Altered States of Consciousness

To the extent that altered states of consciousness are responses to stress, they may be culturally shaped, in two dimensions. One dimension is the cultural nature of the stress itself; the other is the culturally molded responses to stress. Two areas in which the relationships between altered states and cultural patterns have been demonstrated are the use of dreams to control the supernatural and trance states.

Dream-control of the supernatural. D'Andrade (1961) compared societies in which people attempt to contact and control the supernatural with dreams with those societies in which dreams play no such role. He found that societies in which young men move far from their parents when they marry are more likely to make such use of dreams. And societies that have the capacity to store food are less likely to use dreams for supernatural purposes than are societies that are less able to preserve quantities of food. Since the latter type of society is also likely to emphasize independence and self-reliance as a natural consequence of its

Figure 7.6 *Altered States of Consciousness in Shamanism*
A Tapirapé shaman (A) in a tobacco-induced spirit travel trance is helped to walk by two companions. A Cayuga man (B) is dressed as a shaman who would perform rituals while under the influence of the spirit whose mask he wears.

low accumulation of foodstuffs, Bourguignon (1974) regards the use of dreams to control supernatural power as a response to stresses generated by the lack of human support.

Socialization and trance states. A relationship between socialization for independence and the nature of trance states also has been noted in cross-cultural research. Bourguignon and Greenbaum (1975) have noted that different cultural patterns lie behind two different forms of trance, which may be called spirit travel trance and spirit possession trance. The first is characterized by passivity or even unconsciousness during the altered mental state, which is interpreted as a "trip" in which the spirit leaves the body and communes with supernatural entities. Possession trances, on the other hand, involve a great deal of bodily activity thought to be under the control of a spirit visitor. These trances are often entered with the aid of repetitive chants and dancing. Unlike participants in spirit travel trances, people who engage in possession trances often experience amnesia about

what they said and did while possessed. In spirit travel trances, hallucinations may be vividly recalled and drugs are more likely to be used as an aid to entering the trance.

The spirit travel trances are most likely to be found in societies that place the heaviest stress on independence and assertion. Spirit possession trances, on the other hand, are most common where compliance is expected. Thus, Bourguignon and Greenbaum believe that the variety of trance that is more common in a culture is a kind of emotional safety valve for relief from the most common kind of stress in that culture. In cultures in which people normally are expected to behave in an independent way, spirit travel trances permit persons to be taken care of physically by others while they are on a spiritual trip. The spirits they visit offer help and assistance in a way that is not generally available in normal social settings, thereby fulfilling dependency needs that go unsatisfied in the participants' day-to-day social life. In contrast, in cultures where people usually play a more compli-

Social Class	Number of Persons in Each Social Class	Number of Schizophrenics in Each Social Class	Percentage of Social Class Under Treatment for Schizophrenia
I	358	6	1.67598%
II	926	23	2.48380%
III	2,500	83	3.32000%
IV	5,256	352	6.69711%
V	2,032	383	18.80216%
Total	11,077	847	7.64647%

*Adapted from August B. Hollingshead and Frederick C. Redlich, "Social Stratification and Psychiatric Disorders," *American Sociological Review* 18:163–169, 1953.

Table 7.3 *Social Class and Schizophrenia*
The higher a person's rank status in a complex society, the more he or she is allowed unusual behavior without being labeled as insane.

ant and dependent role, some may satisfy their normally unfulfilled desires for power and autonomy during a spirit possession trance in which they take on the personalities of the powerful, dominant spirits that animate their bodies. During these possession states they can behave in ways their normal roles do not permit, speaking boldly and acting powerfully. Later, they are not held responsible for behaving aggressively, since they did so in the role of a passive vehicle for the spirit that controlled them and may even claim no recollection of their own trance behavior.

According to Whiting and Child (1953), spirit travel trances were especially common in Native North America where they were found in 94% of the societies examined. In contrast, only 25% had spirit possession trances. In Sub-Saharan Africa, on the other hand, spirit travel trances were much less common: Only 36% had spirit travel trances. Spirit possession trances were about as common in Sub-Saharan Africa as in North America: 26% of the Sub-Saharan societies had this form of trance.

Insanity

Some people use altered states of consciousness as coping mechanisms for dealing with stress and then return to their normal behaviors; others get lost in altered states. What prevents some individuals from maintaining an acceptable social role while suffering from stress? The failure may be due in part to individual characteristics that make some people unusually suscept-

ible to the effects of stress. It may be due in part to the nature and level of the stresses involved. Finally, it also may be partly because the social reactions of others do not give each individual the same opportunity to escape from the anxieties that stress creates.

Individual susceptibility. Those who prefer to examine insanity from a psychological or biological perspective argue that insanity is at least partially a result of objective abnormalities within the sufferer rendering him or her incapable of dealing with stresses that most people can handle. Jane Murphy (1976) points out that one element of insanity in cultures around the world is the belief that those who are truly mentally ill are *unable* to control the spontaneous rituals and the onset of their altered states of consciousness. The developing trend in psychological literature, however, seems to be to regard individual genetically inherited differences as being predisposing factors that are insufficient by themselves to cause insanity. That is to say, genetic inheritance may play a role in setting an individual's level of tolerance for stress, but social stresses—which differ in form from culture to culture—are believed to be the critical triggering forces that precipitate episodes of insanity.

The social context. Those who prefer to apply a cultural perspective to the analysis of insanity reject the notion that it is an illness (Szasz, 1970). They assert, in other words, that it is not a problem that arises primarily due to some inherited inadequacy of the individual. The proponents of this approach believe that it is more enlightening to see insanity as a social process in which problematic situations force some members of society to play the role of sick or inadequate individuals. Those who maintain this position argue that the inability to control ritualized behavior and altered states of consciousness—used in many cultures as a criterion for judging a person to be insane—need not always be the result of a real biological incapacity of the individual who plays the sick role.

Another social aspect of insanity is that the same rule violation may be ignored when engaged in by one person, excused when done by another, and seen as evidence of "mental illness" in a third. What accounts for such differences in people's reactions to norm violations?

Research in complex societies has made it clear that the higher one's rank, the easier it is to behave in unusual ways without being labeled as insane. For instance, Hollingshead and Redlich (1953) examined data from New Haven and surrounding Connecticut towns. They found that there was an inverse relationship between social class and schizophrenia. The higher the class, the lower was the percentage of people being treated for schizophrenia (see Table 7.3). The lowest of five classes made up 17.8% of the community's total population but 36.8% of the psychiatric population. It appears, then, that one's social rank may be a factor in determining whether one enters into the role of a schizophrenic.

The situation in which a person deviates from the norms of the group may also influence whether or not the behavior is judged insane. For instance, the individual who engages in acts of autistic reverie will not be thought insane if this silent musing is confined to times when he or she listens to music. The person who carries on half of a dialogue with what seems to be an unseen partner will not be thought to be mentally ill if there are cues such as age or setting that suggest an alternative explanation—for instance, a child may talk to an "invisible playmate," and an actor or university professor may rehearse lines for a play or public address. Even the person who claims to hear voices that others do not hear or who "speaks in tongues" and makes unintelligible sounds need not be thought of as strange, if he or she does so only during the services of an appropriate religious organization. On the other hand, these same activities performed in other contexts may lead to the practitioner's being labeled insane.

Since the status of the insane is a master status with low access to both power and prestige, once people have been labeled insane they are likely to continue to be thought of as insane, irrespective of their future behavior. One American researcher, David Rosenhahn (1973), had himself and several other researchers admitted to a number of American mental hospitals as patients. He and his co-researchers discovered that once they had been admitted, even though they behaved normally, the hospital staff, including psychiatrists, psychologists, and psychiatric nurses, failed to recognize that they were actually sane.

The implication is that the researchers' predicament mirrored what happens in social life outside institutions. Once we are branded with a deviant status associated with an altered state of consciousness—such as "senile" or "insane"—others will assume that all our actions spring from an altered state of consciousness and therefore withhold power and prestige from us, severely restricting the roles we are allowed to play.

Play and Art

Stress-induced norm violation, ritualized behavior, and altered states of consciousness do not occur only in those labeled as insane. There are other nonstigmatized but stress-related roles with which these behaviors are associated. The most important of these are playing, engaging in artistic reverie, and behaving religiously. Of the three, religious behavior is the most socially approved as a trait that is expected to be part of the social life of every member of society. In the pages that follow, play and art will be discussed in counterpoint to insanity. Religion will be dealt with as a topic in its own right in the next chapter.

Figure 7.7 *Play as Stress Relief*
Children use play to gain practice in developing skills they lack and to control fears produced by certain events and objects. In either case, the knowledge that they are engaging in controlled behavior serves to reduce anxiety associated with these situations.

Play

Insanity and play are the two main ways in which an individual's behavior may deviate from the expectations of others and in which common judgments about reality are challenged. The primary distinction between insanity and play appears to be that participants in play seem to be in control of the behavior, and they describe the ways they challenge society's commonly held beliefs as fantasy. On the other hand, people are judged insane when they seem to lack control over their strange behaviors or insist on the truth of ideas considered socially deviant (Miller, 1974).

Play as stress relief. Like insanity, play releases stress through ritualized behavior and altered states of consciousness in which external things serve as extensions of the participant's own fantasy. In play, a broom may become a horse to ride, or a chair may become a castle. Unlike insanity, play does not imply a commitment to the objective reality of those fantasies. Rather, play is engaged in for the pleasure or emotional relief it provides. Since children lack the experience and skills necessary to adult functioning, they are likely to experience repeated stress related to their inability to perform many tasks that they attempt. Play provides the opportunity to practice various skills without experiencing anxiety about lack of skill.

The repetitive aspect of play activities helps children become proficient in motor activities, including complex sequences of acts. The mental component of play allows them to externalize their fantasies. Children can thus project into the outside world those things that are of current concern to them. How this process can help to alleviate stress is most clearly seen in the case of fears. For instance, when a child pretends that a pillow is a shark or a crumpled sheet a ghost, the signs of real fear may be evoked when the object is approached or brought closer. These fear signs usually alternate with laughter and a cathartic release from the tension of fear as the child suddenly retreats from the fear-evoking object. This cycle may be repeated many times, as the child alternately seeks to increase the level of fear and then to discharge the fear. The experience itself may involve real physiological fear. But, as long as the child is able to remember that the situation is only one of "make-believe," he or she is learning that fears are controllable. As the experience of controlled fear is generalized to the thing represented by the play object, the fear of that thing is gradually diminished. It becomes more difficult, in other words, for a child to continue to fear a thing that she or he has learned to *pretend* to fear.

Cain (1964, pp. 281-282) observed this process in a group of children who were mental patients:

> A considerable component of the erratic behavior of these children has a conscious element—that is, they are "playing crazy." Much, though by no means all, of the playing crazy centers around their past experiences of and continual concerns about "being crazy." Their playing crazy takes many forms. It may be very quiet and sub-

tle or blatant and obvious, identified as "pretend" by the child or exhaustively "defended" as crazy. Some of the varied forms are: "looking odd," staring off into space, or acting utterly confused; wild, primitive disorganized ragelike states; odd verbalizations; incoherencies; mutterings; alleged hallucinations and delusions; the child's insistence that he is an animal, goblin, or other creature; or various grossly bizarre behaviors. Most of the children show many of these forms of playing crazy. Most of the children make clear—though by no means reliable—announcements that they have played crazy or intend to do so, or speak of "just pretending."

At times, the child is quite consciously, deliberately, almost zestfully, playing crazy—he is under no significant internal pressure, is completely in control, and at the end is most reassured. For if one can openly *pretend* to be crazy, how can one really be crazy?

Note the conformity to the previously described pattern: Anxiety about being crazy is relieved by repeated ritual activity—in this case, play.

Play, of course, may be stimulated by stresses other than those derived from lack of skill, but reduction of the effects of stress is a consistent factor in play. Indirect release from the subjective aspects of stress accounts for another central quality: the pleasure that participants derive from it. Play is fun. Even though people report that they sometimes engage in play for the pure fun of it, this is tantamount to saying that when one plays, subjective distress—the opposite of pleasure—is decreased.

Games. Play that is formally structured into games has been examined by Roberts, Arth, and Bush (1959). They view games as models of the conflict-producing situations in society that create anxiety during childhood. Games provide both adults and children an outlet for the expression of these anxieties by permitting reenactment of these conflicts in a nonthreatening setting, as well as a safe chance to practice the skills needed in conflict situations. Societies with a simple social organization are unlikely to use games of strategy; games of strategy are usually present in societies with a complex social organization (see Table 4).

	Games of Strategy Present	Games of Strategy Absent
Societies with Low Social Complexity	5	18
Societies with High Social Complexity	14	6

Note. From "Games in Culture" by J. Roberts, M. J. Arth, and R. R. Bush, 1959, *American Anthropologist, 61*, p. 600). Copyright 1959. Adapted by permission.

Table 7.4 *Games of Strategy and Social Complexity Games are metaphors for social situations people are likely to encounter. Researchers have found that the more complicated a society is, the more likely it will be to engage in complex games of strategy.*

And games of strategy are preferred when obedience training is emphasized in childhood, whereas games of physical skill tend to be preferred when independence training is emphasized (Roberts & Sutton-Smith, 1962).

Art

Artistic acts, like play, are expressions of feeling and may be pleasurable and stress relieving. But, besides the characteristics that it shares with play, art makes an intentional statement. The artist gives conscious attention to how the artistic activity is carried out, since the acts and their products are thought of as meaningful. They are intended to be communications. Therefore, the element of skill has been held by many to be a fundamental quality of art. As long ago as 1916, Franz Boas, observed that "All art implies technical skill" (Boas, 1940, p. 535).

When play acts are performed with conscious attention because the acts or their products have become consciously meaningful to the participant, play has become art. Because art is intended as communication, it therefore implies an audience, real or at least potential. That audience may be only the artist, but art is intended as a communication. Like play, the acts of art are expressive of the hopes, fears, and desires of the actor, but in art, the expressive signs of the tension that exist between reality and desire are consciously refined. The artist transforms the raw, natural signs that are used intuitively by others, adapting them to the symbolic conventions of his or her own culture. Because symbols of art are derived from natural signs, commentators often speak of art as using a universal language or as making a statement that transcends the narrow confines of its society or time. Knowledge of the culture from which a work of art comes may be required to correctly interpret the meaning of its symbols. Yet, on the level of signs from which it was derived, a skilled work of art may be appreciated beyond its original cultural setting.

The artistic frame of mind has been described repeatedly in terms suggesting an altered state of consciousness. Artists frequently describe their creative ideas as if they come to them from somewhere outside themselves, like revelations. In general, all creative acts are intimately related to altered states of consciousness, which in turn are responses to the stress of life (Koestler, 1964).

Anthropological research has looked most intensely at the products of artists, since their works are more accessible to objective description and analysis than are their subjective mental states. The major categories of works of art with which anthropologists generally have dealt are visual arts, music, dance, and oral literature.

Visual arts. Three prominent types of visual arts are body decoration, pictorial art, and sculpture. People the world over decorate their bodies in a variety of ways. Common ways of decorating the body include tattoos, scars, painted designs, changes in the shape of body parts, and decorative clothing. These are used partly for the personal satisfaction such decoration brings, but body decoration is also invariably a means of symbolizing the individual's statuses and rank. Occupational statuses may be indicated by special symbols, such as uniforms. Men and women generally adopt different styles of body decoration. Within each sex, those of high rank usually engage in more elaborate body decoration than do those who are of low rank.

Pictorial art also may reflect social structure. Fischer (1961) compared the pictorial

Figure 7.8 *Body Decoration*
Tatooing, painting, and dyeing are various types of body decoration used as a means of marking status in society and/or as a means of sexual attraction. This Maori of New Zealand has used tatooing to designate his high ranking status in his tribe.

art of complex, socially stratified societies with the art of egalitarian societies (those that are usually organized into small, self-sufficient communities, with little differentiation of activities, statuses, or rank). He found that, regardless of the specific symbols used, art in egalitarian societies tends to use symmetrical designs and repetition of simple features. Much of the available space is left empty, and figures are not enclosed by a formal boundary. In stratified societies, by contrast, pictures tend to be asymmetrical and composed of dissimilar elements that are integrated into the full design. The tendency is for little empty space to be left within the field of works of pictorial art, and figures are often enclosed by well-defined boundaries.

Fischer speculated that symmetry may reflect the basic similarity of the generalized statuses within the egalitarian communities; repetition of simple elements may reflect the similarity of individuals. He suggested that the asymmetrical design of the art of stratified societies may reflect the specialized differences and ranking of statuses; the integration of inverse elements into the design may mirror the high degree of specialization and integration of diverse statuses in complex societies. Fischer also suggested that the greater use of empty space in the art of simple egalitarian societies may represent their relative isolation and self-sufficiency. By contrast, the filling of empty space in the art of complex societies may stem from the lack of isolation of individuals, who learn to find security through establishing a place for themselves in the network of statuses that makes up the community. Similarly, the enclosing boundaries may represent the imposition of controls on the behavior of individuals—since many rules imposed from above is a social trait most characteristic of the socially stratified societies.

Music and dance. Music was studied in great detail by Alan Lomax (1968), who found the songs of complex societies to be wordier than those of simple societies. He pointed out that precision in enunciation also tends to increase with social complexity. Lomax noted that choral singing is most common where cooperative labor is the hallmark of work. Polyphony, the singing of two or more melodies simultaneously, is most common in societies where women contribute at least half of the food. Counterpoint also is most common where women contribute the bulk of the food, especially among societies of food gatherers.

Lomax looked at dance as an art form that is culturally patterned. He found that "Movement style in dance is a crystallization of the most frequent and crucial patterns of everyday activity" (1968, p. 237). For instance, the postures adopted in work frequently are found in the dance style of a society.

Folklore. The myths, legends, folktales, stories, proverbs, riddles, and jokes people tell to one another have always interested anthropological fieldworkers. Folklore is the study of these parts of culture in terms of how they relate to the other parts of culture, customs, and the objects people make. In most of the societies traditionally studied by anthropologists, these were passed down from generation to generation by word of mouth. They are therefore sometimes called the oral literature of a society.

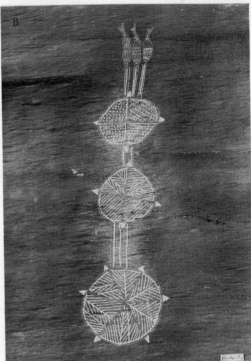

Figure 7.9 *Art and Social Complexity*
In this segment (A) of The Dresden Codex, the Opossum God carries the image of the Maize God to a shrine at the entrance of the town. This is an example of art produced by a stratified society. The bottom illustration (B), by contrast, is produced by an egalitarian society. Its design is simple, repetitive and surrounded by space.

Myths are the stories that recount the origins of things. They explain such things as the history of the gods, how the universe

189

Figure 7.10 *Javanese Dancers*
The dances of Java are divided into two categories, Putri and Wajang Wong, depending on the social status of the performers and the audience permitted to see them. These Wajang Wong dancers use precise disciplined motions of the body and head to depict set story motifs which symbolize social and environmental concerns.

came to be, how human beings, animals, and plants were created, how human ways of life began, the origin of death, and the nature of the afterlife. Usually myths are placed in the distant past and involve supernatural beings. For example, the Shoshoni of the Great Basin desert tell a myth of a time when the sun was so close to the earth that people were dying and the plants of the earth were burned up so there was no food to be found. Cottontail, one of the creatures of the earth, determined to kill the sun and set things right. He took some rocks as weapons and traveled toward where the sun rises until it got too hot for him. Then he began to burrow until he got to his destination. He made a hunting blind and waited until the sun came up. When the sun arose, Cottontail threw a rock at the sun and killed him. It was so hot that Cottontail was scorched, which left him brown, as he is to this day. After a while, the sun revived, but Cottontail removed the sun's gallbladder and told the sun that he must go up higher in the sky so that all people might have light to gather food, but not be

burned. Out of the sun's gallbladder, Cottontail fashioned the moon, which also went up to the sky. Since the moon turned out basket-shaped, it is not always round in the sky, but shows phases, depending on which side is facing the earth.

Legends are much like myths, and it is not always easy to decide whether a particular story is best classified as a myth or as a legend. In general, the distinction between myths and legends is that legends usually deal with a more recent period of time than myths, and the central characters of legends are heroes and heroines of great stature who are responsible for the beginnings of a particular society. Although they are usually regarded as real persons, these heroines and heroes are often thought to possess superhuman qualities and to embody the central values of their society. The legendary figures of American culture are noted for their individualism, self-reliance, strength, and cleverness. They stand up for their ideals against great odds, triumphing over adversity. George Washington is one American legendary figure who actually existed. Yet time has endowed him with stature somewhat above that of a real person. He is remembered in American folklore as being unable to lie even as a child. At one time, it was said that he was strong enough to have thrown a silver dollar across the Rappahannock. In many parts of the country, the river in this story has become the much wider Potomac. Other American legends are based on purely fictional characters, like Paul Bunyan, whose exploits included the creation of Puget Sound.

Folktales, commonly called fairy tales in the United States, are stories placed in a timeless setting and vague location. They portray the basic dilemmas with which people must grapple as they strive to attain the goals of their culture. For instance, many European folktales are built around the theme of a poor but beautiful young girl who is often mistreated by her evil stepmother or sisters but who, by supernatural intervention, is rescued from her life of drudgery and raised to high status as the wife of a handsome prince. Against the backdrop of European social systems in which the female role was traditionally one of domestic duties and economic dependence on an income controlled by fathers and husbands, such fairy stories can be seen as stress reduction through wish fulfillment.

According to Clyde Kluckhohn (1965), five themes seem to be universal in human myths and folktales: catastrophe (usually by flood), monster-slaying, incest (usually by brother and sister), sibling rivalry, and castration (in real or, more often, symbolic form). The list clearly deals with anxiety-related matters that must be dealt with by peoples the world around. George Wright (1954) has examined the less common theme of aggression and has found that it is most common in the tales of societies where children are severely punished for aggression.

Proverbs, like myths and legends, embody the basic values of a culture, but in a much shorter form. Their brevity makes it possible for proverbs to be inserted into conversations, where they can be used to cast light on the topics being discussed, comment on the propriety of a state of af-

fairs, call others to take action, or even mildly rebuke another person without direct confrontation. In accordance with the work ethic, Americans remind each other that "The early bird gets the worm." The Aztec leader who was informed about disputes among the commoners might have responded, "My task is to guard turkeys. Shall I peck at those who peck at one another?" He meant that it was no more his fault that the commoners contended among themselves than it was the fault of the turkey guardian that turkeys pecked one another. Those who leave their own culture may remember proverbs that they learned years before but be unable to recall the meanings of those proverbs, since they embody symbolism relevant to specific cultural contexts that are no longer present.

Riddles are mental puzzles told for entertainment. By describing common things in novel ways, they challenge hearers to exercise their ability to see similarities between common things that are not usually associated with one another. They are a source of information about the things that a people consider noteworthy in their environment, how they classify things, and what aspects of things they judge to be relevant. For instance, Aztec riddles about spindles often relate them to pregnancy. Perhaps the most obvious analogy in these riddles is that the spindle grows in size as it is filled, just as one does in pregnancy. However, a more subtle message carried by these Aztec riddles is one of classification: They reiterate the idea that the spindle is symbolically associated with the woman's role.

Jokes and other forms of humor have long been recognized for their role in helping people relieve the tensions to which their way of life exposes them. Since the major anxieties differ from society to society, so does the type of humor. Consider the Inuit of northern Alaska and Canada. They live in a harsh environment that challenges the limits of their skill. The ability to endure pain and to cope skillfully with potentially disastrous situations is necessary for survival in the far north. The people's reaction to many near-disasters is one of mirth. For instance, they might laugh uproariously at the tale of a party of travelers who are spilled into the wet snow and lose their dogs when their sled tips over, slides from the trail onto rotten sea ice, and breaks through the ice, immersing its contents in freezing water. In spite of the inconveniences involved, the disastrous possibility of the party's being thrown into the freezing sea-water has been escaped. Even the party that was involved in the situation might react with immediate laughter at their relief, before settling down to the unpleasant task of retrieving their dogs and damaged goods.

Summary

As children, we are socialized to fit into the patterns of our society. As we take on social roles, we learn the behaviors that are considered appropriate for them. If we do not play our roles as expected, however, we may feel emotional distress and may act it out in ritualized ways. If we stray too far from what society expects of us, we may be labeled deviant or even insane, especially if our actions become so unusual that no one had ever thought to create rules against them.

Although behaviors considered insane may not fit into society's patterns, mental illnesses tend to follow patterns that are so predictable that they can be classified. Even in our crazinesses, we are not unique. Western psychiatry recognizes specific forms of mental illness, including schizophrenia, affective disorders, and neuroses. They are found all over the world, shaped by the particular stresses and symbolic meanings of each society. Hysterias, for example, can be seen as attempts to relieve anxieties that are peculiar to a culture, through highly expressive ritualized acts that bring symbolic relief and help reduce the physiological stress response.

During psychotic episodes, one typically enters an altered state of consciousness. This state can also be created at will by people considered sane if they are playing, creating, using drugs, or seeking religious experience. Those labeled insane for entering altered states may be unable to avoid them—or they may be escaping from or reflecting the intolerable situation their culture imposes on them. Art and play offer safety valves of sorts: The tensions between our individuality and our social situation, our desires and social realities, can be externalized, attended to, and perhaps resolved on the level of fantasy if not in everyday life.

Key Terms and Concepts

personality (psychological definition) 163
personality (anthropological definition) 163
socialization 164
modal personality type 164
primary institutions 164
secondary institutions 164
maintenance system 164
Contrary Warrior 165
status-appropriate roles 165
face 166
face-work 167

anxiety 167
fear 169
guilt 169
grief 169
shame 169
anger 169
stress 169
affectlessness 169
ritual 169
signalized behavior 171
deviant 172
residual rules 173
insanity 174

Annotated Readings

Barnouw, V. (1985). *Culture and personality* (4th ed.). Homewood, IL: Dorsey. An introductory-level text on psychological anthropology.

Bateson, G. (1936). *Naven: A survey of the problems suggested by a composite picture of the culture of a New Guinea tribe drawn from three points of view.* Cambridge, MA: Cambridge University Press. The analysis of a Iatmul ritual that led to Bateson's revolutionary theory of schizophrenia.

Dundes, A. (1965). *The study of folklore.* Englewood Cliffs, NJ: Prentice-Hall. An exceptional collection of papers on the study of folklore.

Hsu, F. L. K. (Ed.). (1972). *Psychological anthropology: Approaches to culture and personality.* Morriston, NJ: Schenkman Press. A basic survey of the field of psychological anthropology for the advanced student.

LeVine, R. A. (Ed.). (1974). *Culture and personality: Contemporary readings.* Chicago: Aldine. A useful collection of papers on cultural and psychological aspects of the human condition, including cultural interpretations of the abnormal personality.

Marsella, A. J., DeVos, G., & Hsu, F. L. K. (Eds.). (1985). *Culture and self: Asian and Western perspectives.* New York: Tavistock Publications. A current examination of the experience of self from a cross-cultural perspective.

Price-Williams, D. R. (1975). *Explorations in cross-cultural psychology.* San Francisco, CA: Chandler and Sharp. A short but somewhat technical examination of cross-cultural psychology with emphasis on cultural relativism in the interpretation of human psychology.

Wallace, A. F. C. (1961). *Culture and personality.* New York: Random House. A short and insightful examination of culture and personality.

Chapter 8

Religion

Religion is an organized system of shared supernatural beliefs, which give meaning to perplexing parts of human society and its environment, and a system of rituals by which human beings strive for greater control over themselves and their social and natural environments. Psychologically, the beliefs and rituals of a particular religion symbolically express the kinds of stresses and anxieties that are common among the members of that society. The effects of stress on personality discussed in the preceding chapter are therefore relevant to an understanding of religious beliefs and rituals. Here, however, we are dealing with stresses that are typically shared by members of society at large. Religion is a group phenomenon. In this chapter we will examine both the psychological and the social aspects of religion.

The Definition of Religion

Religious beliefs and rituals take so many forms across the world that anthropologists have found it difficult to define religion in a way that encompasses them all. Aspects of a global definition of <u>religion</u> include belief in supernatural beings and power, symbolic expression of feelings, and ritualized behaviors.

Belief in Supernatural Beings

Over a century ago, Sir Edward Burnett Tylor (1871) attempted one of the first anthropological definitions of religion as the belief in supernatural beings, such as the soul, ghosts, spirits, and gods. It was Tylor's belief that religion served an important role in providing human beings answers to perplexing questions, such as the cause of unconsciousness, sleep, dreams, and hallucinations. Early humans, he contended, created the idea of the soul to account for such phenomena. Unconsciousness, fainting, sleep, and even death could be explained as the soul's departure from the body; dreams are memories of the soul's experiences as it travels outside the body during sleep; and visions or hallucinations are simply apparitions of souls and other spirit beings, for the idea of the soul implied the possibility of other spiritual entities,

Figure 8.1 *Avalokitśvara, Sovereign Lord of the Universe This image of Avalokitśvara is at the Buddhist Tikse Monastery in Ladakh, India. He represents compassion, one of the major aspects of Buddha—nature. His current incarnation is the Dalai Lama.*

such as ghosts, genies, angels, and gods.

Although Tylor's views were useful in pointing out the role that religion plays in providing people with ways of understanding parts of their experiences for which they have no pragmatic explanations, his perspective was narrow in its concern for the intellectual aspect of human functioning. For Tylor, a nineteenth-century Victorian scholar, religion was a product of the human intellect. Its relationship to human emotional life was of less interest to him.

Belief in Supernatural Power

An even greater limitation of Tylor's definition was its ethnocentric narrowness in excluding from the realm of religion the belief in formless supernatural powers. Robert Marett (1909) raised this criticism of Tylor and introduced the Melanesian word _mana_ to refer to the concept of spiritual power. _Mana_, which might be thought of as a kind of supernatural electricity, may reside in objects such as a rabbit's foot, a four-leaf clover, in powerful natural phenomena such as thunderstorms, or in anything strange, rare, or dangerous. In doses too large, it can cause harm, illness, or even death, but properly channeled it can be used by human beings to accomplish ends that are unattainable by other means. _Mana_ can increase one's luck, skill, and ability to gain knowledge of hidden things. _Mana_ is the force behind magic; it is the holiness in the ground around the burning bush; it is the sacredness of the Host in the Eucharist; it is Luke Skywalker's Force. As the embodiment of spiritual power in its rawest form, _mana_ inspires the sense of awe and reverence that people of every religion experience when they perceive themselves to be in the presence of the Holy. Though _mana_ makes things more powerful than they normally would be, it does not come and go of its own accord. Like its secular equivalent, electricity, it must be manipulated by human beings to benefit from its power. However, unlike electricity, the manipulation of _mana_ is accomplished through rituals.

Mana is one of the simplest and most widespread of religious ideas. Marett believed that the concept of _mana_ was a more primitive religious idea than that of spirits and asserted that it was therefore a more ancient religious idea, an idea that arose not from intellect but from the sense of awe and fear that is inspired by the unusual or the strange.

Where _mana_ plays a prominent role in religion, the concept of taboo is also likely to be important. A taboo is a rule that forbids contact with sacred or dangerous things, things filled with so much _mana_ that careless contact with them may harm the unwary. The term was derived from a Polynesian word, _tapu_ or _tabu_, which means both forbidden and sacred. Polynesian chiefs were sacred, and their bodies contained so much _mana_ that it was taboo for commoners to touch them, since to do so might kill an ordinary person. _Mana_ and taboo need not be immediately involved with beliefs about spirits or gods, so Tylor's definition failed to encompass an important aspect of religious practice and ideology. Marett broadened Tylor's definition to include _mana_ by defining religion as the belief in supernatural things in general.

The Ark of the Covenant

The protection afforded by taboos is well illustrated by a story in Exodus about the Ark of the Covenant. The ark was a sacred box of acacia wood overlaid with gold. Its top was crowned with a throne for God. In the ark were kept the most sacred things of the Israelites: the Tables of the Law, a pot of manna (food miraculously provided to the Israelites in the wilderness), and Aaron's staff. So sacred was the ark, so full of spiritual power, that it was not to be touched by human hands. The ark was transported by authorized priests who carried it with poles that were passed through rings mounted on the sides of the ark. On one occasion when the ark was being transported on a cart, the oxen stumbled and the ark began to fall. Uzzah, a soldier, tried to prevent the ark from falling, but when his hand touched the box he died. His good intentions offered no protection from the terrible sacredness of the ark which was taboo for good reason. His death followed his act, not as punishment for a sinful act in any moral sense but as effect follows cause in the world of *mana*.

Recently, a number of anthropologists have addressed the problem of clarifying some ambiguities of the word supernatural, which has almost always been a central element in Western anthropologists' definitions of religion. Traditionally, the supernatural has been understood to be a realm which transcends that of the natural senses. It consists of things that are believed to be very powerful but that do not seem to conform to the normal laws that govern the behavior of things in the world of everyday experience. Since the dichotomy between a natural and a supernatural realm has long played a central role in the distinction between science and religion in Western culture, few have felt that the term ''supernatural'' needed further clarification. However, Cohn (1967) has pointed out that the distinction between a natural and a supernatural realm is not made in most of the world's religions. Neither is there a word in most of the world's languages that translates as ''religion.'' How, then, have anthropologists decided to call behavior religious when they were studying cultures in which there is no word for religion and no explicit concept of a supernatural realm? To broaden the definition of religion beyond a system of beliefs and practices pertaining to the supernatural, other concepts may be added, as discussed below.

Symbolic Expression of Feelings

Emile Durkheim (1915), who gave French anthropology its impetus, extended the global definition of religion by emphasizing the role of feelings in stimulating religious ideas. Durkheim was concerned with the question of what lies at the roots of religious ideas and what maintains them through the generations. He suggested that religious ideas are symbolic representations, metaphors of those aspects of society and culture that inspire feelings of respect, fear, and awe. Durkheim believed that by maintaining and manipulating these feelings in symbolic form, religion perpetuated the sentiments that people must have toward

their society if it is to survive. Thus, for Durkheim, religion was society's symbolic worship of itself.

Ritual Behaviors

As anthropologists have become increasingly interested in the rituals of religion, behavior has been added as a component of definitions of religion. In the views of Anthony F. C. Wallace (1966), ritual is the central element of religion. He feels that the goal of religion is to use supernatural power to bring about or to prevent changes in human beings or in nature. These goals are achieved by means of rituals. Religious beliefs give meaning to the rituals by explaining and interpreting them and by directing the energy of the ritual performance.

Religion: A Definition

Guthrie (1980) has done a valuable historical survey of studies of religion and has shown that the common denominator in religious behavior is a form of anthropomorphism—assigning human qualities to that which is not human, especially in speaking to the nonhuman world as if it could and would respond to the symbols of speech as a human might be expected to do. With this and previous definitions in mind, religion may be defined as a system of (1) beliefs in which the nonhuman realm is portrayed as having humanlike qualities including the ability to respond to symbolic communication, (2) feelings related to those beliefs, and (3) ritual practices that elicit and control those feelings and that are carried out either to portray the beliefs or to influence the universe by symbolic communication.

Ideology in Religion

Religious ideology, the realm of religious beliefs and sentiments, has fascinated writers for centuries. The religious beliefs of different societies are extremely diverse, more so than any other aspects of cultural ideologies. Variability in nonreligious beliefs is directly constrained by their immediate practical results. An oar must be an effective tool for moving a small boat through the water, so ideas about how to build and

Figure 8.2 *Serpent-Handlers*
In trying to control the forces of evil in their lives some sects actually learn to handle venomous snakes. This serpent-handler in Appalachia, West Virginia, takes her power from New Testament Scripture which says the followers of Jesus will not be harmed.

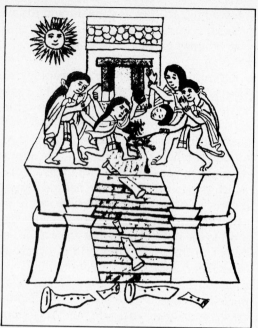

Figure 8.3 *Aztec Human Sacrifice*
Cannibalism may be one way for a society to impose order on chaos, to regenerate itself or to communicate with the supernatural. Recent evidence indicates that Aztecs sacrificed humans to placate their gods and engaged in ritual cannibalism. This shows the sacrifice of a captive warrior impersonating Tezcatlipoca.

use an oar do not differ greatly from one society to another. Feminine and masculine roles may vary across cultures and time, but all cultures must call attention to at least the biological distinction between male and female or become extinct. Cultures with automobiles may direct their drivers to drive on the left or the right sides of streets; simply allowing drivers to decide spontaneously how best to pass oncomers would probably be too costly to any society. Religious belief is more insulated from such pracical considerations, but variations between religions do seem to have some relationship to the people's varying social, technological, and environmental circumstances.

Diversity of Beliefs

Consider first some examples of religious diversity. Chastity, sexual fidelity, and even celibacy are venerated in some religious traditions. But if you were to visit a certain part of India, you would find people for whom sexual intercourse is a means of attaining the highest state of spiritual ecstasy and

among whom temple dancers share themselves sexually with the devotees as a sacred act. Not all witches fly on broomsticks. The Nyakyusa, a farming and herding people of Tanganyika, believe that there are witches living as pythons in the bellies of their human victims, whose insides they gnaw away to satisfy their cravings for flesh (Wilson, 1951). Cannibalism was a sacred act among several peoples in the not too distant past, notably among the Kwakiutl of the British Columbia coast where the Cannibal Society was the highest ranked religious association. Among the Aztec of Middle America, cannibalism may have played a role in the system of human sacrifice by which the Aztec gods were placated. Woodrow Borah (1977) has estimated that the Aztec sacrificed to the gods and then devoured about 250,000 people, or 1% of their population, every year.

Souls? They come in many sizes and shapes. Among the Shoshoni of the American Great Basin, the soul was thought to be shaped like a small ball of feathers that resided in the forehead. The Jivaro, who

Figure 8.4 *Thaipusam Ceremony*
One manner of honoring the gods in certain societies is by self-sacrifice. This man, with a skewer through his cheeks is participating in the Thaipusam festival at Kuala Lumpur, Malaysia, honoring the Hindu war god Subrahmanya.

were native to the forests of Ecuador, believed that a person might have three kinds of souls: the *nëkás*, the *arutam*, and the *muisak*. The *nëkás* was an ordinary soul that resided in the bloodstream and perpetuated the individual's personality after death. The *arutam* was a power-conveying soul that had to be acquired by prayer and fasting. It protected the possessor from death unless it was first lured away by magic. The *muisak* was an avenging soul that came into being only at the death of a warrior who had a power-conveying soul. Once formed, it sought to kill the murderer.

Many people have worshipped both female and male deities. Others have venerated animals or worshipped deformed children or other humans as deities. The adherents of some North American religions believe themselves immune to poisons, the bites of venomous snakes, or the weapons of enemies as long as they exercise sufficient faith, practice the rituals of their religion assiduously, or wear the proper charms. The possibilities of religious belief and obligation have been limited only

by the bounds of human imagination. From the unicorns of medieval European folklore to the cannibalistic stone giants of contemporary Shoshoni stories, if it can be imagined it has probably been a part of the religious ideology of some people somewhere.

The Adaptive Basis of Religious Beliefs

The view espoused in this text is that differences in religious ideologies must be accounted for as adaptations of culture to differing social, technological, and environmental circumstances. Religious ideology that conflicts too greatly with the nonreligious beliefs and values of a culture, including its survival strategies, will not be readily adopted by the people. For this reason there is a predictable degree of harmony between a people's religion and the rest of their culture.

One famous proponent of this view, Leslie White (1971), contended that the degree to which people view the world around them in religious terms is inversely related to the complexity of their technology. The more complex the technology, the more the world is related to in mechanistic rather than spiritual ways. In other words, as people develop direct, pragmatic control over their environment, they may become less likely to seek help from supernatural powers. Growth in technological complexity also tends to accompany growth in population and increasing social complexity and specialization. These factors make it increasingly likely that people will feel lost in a sea of strangers, lacking the power they would like to have in day-to-day social life. When such people are alienated from society, they are less likely to believe in the supernatural. Since religion is a system of rituals wherein people reaffirm their commitment to the fundamental goals and values of their society, stresses experienced by the socially alienated tend to be channeled into coping mechanisms other than the society's traditional religion.

Social structure also may affect religious ideology. Guy Swanson (1960) has tested the notion that religious beliefs are symbolic representations of what he calls the "sovereign groups'' of society, the groups that have ''original and independent jurisdiction over some sphere of life'' (p. 20) and, thereby, the power to inspire respect and compliance in their members. Using a sample of 50 societies from around the world, he found that strong statistical relationships existed between several common religious doctrines and social traits that could logically be expected to be symbolized by those doctrines.

Swanson found that monotheism, the belief in a high god, a supreme being who either created and ordered the universe or at least maintains order within it now, is most likely to be found in societies in which the sovereign, decision-making groups are organized hierarchically so that one of them is superior in rank to at least two levels of groups below it. In such societies, one sovereign group, like a supreme god, can create and maintain order between subordinates.

Polytheism is the belief in superior (but not supreme) gods who control major parts of the universe, such as the weather, the oceans, or agriculture. According to Swanson, polytheism reflects specialized purposes in human affairs. A society with many unranked occupational specialties is more likely to have a polytheistic religion than is a society with few such specialties. Similarly, societies with social classes are more likely to have polytheistic religions than are egalitarian societies, since the purposes of different social classes differ one from another. For instance, traditional Indian society with its hereditary social castes and numerous jati occupations had equally diverse specialized polytheistic deities.

According to Swanson's research, ancestral spirits remain active in human affairs when the kinship organizations that perpetuate the purposes and goals of their deceased members are more complex than the transitory nuclear family. Belief in reincarnation is most common in societies in which continuity from one generation to the next is maintained by small, isolated groups whose members are economically interdependent and occupy a common settlement smaller than a village. Belief in some form of human soul, the embodiment

of an individual's personality and personal memories, is almost universal. But Swanson distinguishes between societies in which the soul is believed to be lodged in the individual's body and those in which the soul transcends the body. People are more likely to believe in souls that are intimately tied to the individual's body if they live in societies that have: (1) many different sovereign groups to which everyone must belong, (2) situations in which individuals with conflicting objectives that cannot be reconciled by such means as courts must work together as a group, (3) situations in which groups of individuals whose relationship is not based on their common consent must function as a group to achieve the members' common goals, (4) large-sized settlements, (5) debts, or (6) no sovereign kinship group. All these social traits increase the degree to which each individual is set apart from each other.

Although all societies have moral and ethical rules that govern the conduct of individuals toward each other, not all societies use the threat of supernatural punishments for the violation of their moral rules. Supernatural sanctions for violations of moral rules are most common where interpersonal differences in wealth are prominent, that is, where different groups within society benefit unequally from those rules.

According to Swanson, sorcery—the use of rituals to harm another person supernaturally—is most common in societies in which individuals must interact with each other but in which socially approved means for one individual to control another do not exist. In an earlier study of sorcery, Beatrice Whiting (1950) showed that sorcery was most likely to be practiced in societies that lack ''individuals or groups of individuals with delegated authority to settle disputes'' (p. 90) and in which retaliation by peers is the main tool of social control. In addition, beliefs in sorcery and witchcraft—a related phenomenon in which the evildoer has an innate ability to harm others without using rituals—are most common in societies that engender severe anxiety about the expression of aggression or sexuality in children during their socialization (Whiting and Child, 1953).

Figure 8.5 *Sacred Cow of India*
The cow is sacred to Indians because it is economically and ecologically more sound to preserve it than to slaughter it. A curious sight to Westerners is the cow sharing the road with automobiles and the sidewalk with people.

India's Sacred Cow

Religious beliefs often serve practical purposes, though these purposes may not be obvious. Such is the case with the sacred cows of India.

Since the British colonial occupation of India, the English phrase "sacred cow" has stood for any custom that is maintained in spite of all rational reasons for its change. The zebu cow, held sacred by Hindus of India, symbolizes gentleness, life, and India itself. The cow is so greatly revered in India that its protection was written into the constitution. The cow may be neither killed nor molested as it wanders the streets. To the British, for whom cattle were an important food resource, it seemed the height of folly for a society in which hunger and even starvation were significant social problems to support cow reverence instead of cow eating. In spite of the thinly veiled ethnocentrism in this opinion, there is some intuitive merit to the idea that protection of the cow is irrational when its use as food might alleviate a major social problem.

Marvin Harris (1974), who believes that the material conditions of life have a greater impact on an ideology than an ideology does on those conditions, has argued that the custom of cow reverence is integrated with other facts of Indian life in such a way that using cows for food would create more problems than it would solve. Those whose only contact with cattle is the meat section of their local supermarket may be unaware of the great expenditure of resources that goes into the raising of cattle as food. In the United States, for instance, beef cattle are fed from farm-grown foods. Three fourths of the agricultural land in the United States is devoted to growing food for cattle. Since American farmers still are able to produce sufficient food for domestic consumption and export, this cost is well within their means. In India, though, the establishing of this kind of beef industry would remove acreage from the production of food for human beings. The result would be the displacing of millions of farmers and an increase in food costs and hunger.

Indian farmers pen their cows at night but allow them to wander the streets during the day, scavenging their own food. Eating the weeds and plants they find along the way, the cows consume as about four fifths of their diet things that are not edible to humans. The custom of permitting cows to range freely greatly reduces the amount of labor and feed that farmers must devote to the upkeep of their animals. Allowing cows to wander the streets to fend for themselves and fostering cow love especially benefits the poorest farmers who otherwise could not afford to own a cow or keep it during times of hardship.

Although the cow is not food for its owner, it is an important part of that farmer's means of food production. Teams of oxen are harnessed to pull plows. Cows are milked to provide a small amount of milk for their owners and a few milk peddlers. Cattle also produce dung, which is valuable as fertilizer and fuel in India, a country with little oil, coal, or wood. Cattle dung takes the place of expensive petrochemical fertilizers. It also is burned within the home. Finally, when cattle die from natural causes, the meat is not wasted, for most of it is eaten by members of the lowest castes. The custom of cow worship insures that the meat reaches the tables of those who could least afford

to buy it if it were a market item sought by all.

Perhaps someday beef will be routinely eaten in India, but under current circumstances beef-eating would not be cost-effective, whereas cow reverence is. Far from being a case of the irrationality of religious symbols, the sacredness of the zebu cow in India reflects the real importance of the cow as a resource and means of livelihood in India under the current economic conditions.

Ritual in Religion

Of the many cultural arenas in which ritual behavior is common, religion is the most publicly valued system for the ritual expression of people's concerns and anxieties. The rituals of the insane are strongly stigmatized, and even play and art tend to be somewhat restricted to special occasions, settings, or persons. But members of society usually are encouraged by their fellows

Figure 8.6 *Ghost Dance Shirt*
The Ghost Dance ritual originated among the Plains Indians in the 19th century as a response to the encroachment of the white man on Indian lands. In each version of the dance the idea was to destroy the white man and bring back to life the spirit of the dead Indians. The Sioux warriors wore Ghost Dance shirts in the belief they would be protection against bullets.

to participate in religion. Although play and art may be valued, societies rarely devote the energy to elaborating them as group activities that is routinely expended on organizing complex communal religious activities.

This section will examine the two main roles of ritual in religion: (1) to portray or act out important aspects of a religion's myths and cosmology, and (2) to influence the spiritual world and thereby the natural world for human beings or, conversely, to help human beings adjust to the conditions of the natural and spiritual realms. These two roles of ritual as symbolic communication may be present simultaneously in a single ritual and are not always clearly distinguished in the minds of the participants themselves.

Ritual as Portrayal

Religious ideologies always include myths, beliefs about the activities of spiritual beings and powers, especially at the beginnings of things. The symbolism of rituals often portrays several such stories simultaneously. For instance, the Christian ritual that is sometimes called the Sacrament of the Lord's Supper, in which wine and broken bread are shared by members of a congregation, may remind them of the final meal that Jesus and the disciples had together before Jesus's arrest and crucifixion. At the same time, the broken bread and the wine may symbolize or become the body and the blood of Jesus, who Christians believe died as a vicarious sacrifice on behalf of humankind. In addition, the ritual may represent purification and renewal of the spiritual bonds that unite members of the congregation with their religion as they receive and eat the sacramental meal. Similarly, the baptism by immersion that is practiced in some Christian churches simultaneously may represent: a washing away of sin; a portrayal of the death, burial, and resurrection from the dead that most Christians believe Jesus experienced; the spiritual death and renewal by which the individual enters the Christian religion; or the individual's own future death, burial, and hoped-for reawakening to a life beyond the grave. Part of the beauty of a ritual for its

participants lies in the multiplicity of meanings it may have for them, a characteristic that may give them the feeling that the ritual embodies meanings transcending those of ordinary symbols.

Ritual as Influence

In their attempt to influence the spiritual or natural worlds for the sake of human beings, some rituals are believed to be coercive in their effect. Others are thought to be more like requests for aid. Usually, rituals are more coercive in nature when people feel an urgent need for more control over events than they have by nonreligious means. The most coercive rituals are known as magic. Magical rituals are often performed with mechanical precision and careful attention to details, especially when the successful outcome of the magical act is crucial to the performers.

Sir James Frazer (1922) noted long ago that magic the world over seems invariably to make use of the same two principles: imitation and contagion. Magic that uses the principle of imitation (more often called the Law of Similarity by anthropologists) seems to be based on the idea that acts that are similar to the desired outcome increase the probability of its occurrence. Magical rituals that follow this principle imitate the thing that they are designed to bring about. Christians who immerse a convert in water to "wash away sin" and Pueblo who whip yucca juice into frothy suds to "bring rain" are both making use of the Law of Similarity. So is the American child who takes care to step over the cracks in the sidewalk, following the admonition in the childhood rhyme, "Step on a crack, and you break your mother's back"—in which there is a similarity in the sound of the words "back" and "crack" and in the appearance of the line of sidewalk blocks and the line of vertebrae in the spinal column.

Shoshoni Love Magic and the Law of Similarity

During my fieldwork on an eastern Nevada reservation, one 65-year-old Shoshoni informant described Shoshoni love magic or, as he called it, "girl medicine.'' His description made it clear that the concept of similarity was a rationale for the ritual actions involved:

> Weasel is used for girl medicine. It is good. You take the heart out before it is dead and talk to it. You take it off someplace by yourself and talk to it. . . . You put it under your pillow for five nights, to dream about girls. The heart is mixed with *pisappih* [red face paint clay] all ground up. If you don't dream something about girls, it won't work, so you throw it away. If you do, it will work.
>
> If you see a girl you like, but she won't pay attention to you, get a little piece of rock about half the size of your fingernail and put the medicine on the rock. Then go by her and hit her with it. When she feels it, that's a ghost. For half an hour or so, you walk around where she can see you. Then after a while she's getting worse and worse. After a while she follows you and talks to you. That's how you catch a girl, the oldtimers say.
>
> Weasels are pretty little things, especially in the winter. That's why they chose it to catch a girl.

The Law of Contagion involves the idea that once two things have been in contact with each other they remain in contact on a spiritual level, so that the magical manipulation of one will also affect the other. Contagious magic may be performed on anything that has had contact with the person to be influenced: A lock of the person's hair or a piece of his or her clothing are ideal; fingernail or toenail clippings, dirt from under the nails, or excrement will do just fine; even dirt from the bottom of a footprint will help. In magic designed to harm, the magical poison can simply be poured into the victim's footprint itself. The Law of Contagion is one reason why many people all over the world have two names, one for public use by others and a true, private name known only to themselves and perhaps a few close relatives. Since the name is an extension of the self, so the logic goes, to know someone's true name is to be able to use it as a form of contact in

speaking a magical spell. This is why in some parts of the world people customarily change their names as a part of the cure of an illness that is thought to have been magically induced, thus denying the sorcerer a chance for continued mischief by magical contact through the victim's name.

Often, magic employs elements of both the Law of Similarity and the Law of Contagion at the same time. My grandmother in Arkansas practiced the custom of protecting her children from tetanus by carefully washing the farmyard nail that had been stepped on, covering it with lard, and placing it on the kitchen windowsill. This magical ritual made use of the object that had inflicted the wound—the Law of Contagion—and treated it in a way that would prevent germs from reaching it—the Law of Similarity.

Obtaining hidden knowledge. An important use of rituals to obtain supernatural aid is divination, obtaining knowledge by supernatural means. People have been quite creative in developing methods of divination. Examining the entrails of animals for unusual signs, considering the flight direction of birds or the shapes formed by molten lead poured into water, or checking the lines on people's hands or the date of their birth have all been used as means to answer questions. Casting of the *I Ching*, spreading of *tarot* cards, and random selecting of Bible verses have served the same purpose. Methods of divination fall into two main categories: those in which the results can be easily influenced by the diviner and those in which the results cannot be readily influenced. The former include practices such as reading tea leaves or interpreting an astrological sign, since there is much latitude for subjective interpretation by the diviner. This category also includes methods such as trance-speaking and ''water witching,'' in which the movement of a willow branch held by the diviner is interpreted as evidence of water, since the diviner can influence the movement or speech, consciously or unconsciously. These methods permit the diviner's knowledge of the client's circumstances to play a role in providing answers that are psychologically satisfying to the customers.

Figure 8.7 *Divination*
By ritually manipulating a system of signs and symbols such as tea leaves or playing cards people hope to obtain information about the future as well as determine what might have occurred in the past. This Indian at Batu Caves, Malaysia, is reading a palm, a common method of determining a future course of action.

Methods that give responses that the diviner is unable to control include techniques such as casting lots or checking whether an object floats on water to answer a question. Like flipping a coin, these tend to randomize the answers. This approach to divination is especially useful when conflicting secular information or divergent opinions must be dealt with.

The Azande Poison Oracle

Evans-Pritchard (1937) described an interesting system of divination that uses poison. The Azande, who live in the Republic of the Sudan, Zaire, and the Central African Republic, consult the poison oracle on all important matters. They may use it to diagnose the cause of an illness, to decide how to most safely conduct vengeance by magic, or to determine who has used magic

against them. The poison oracle also is consulted to find out if a journey may be undertaken safely or to prepare for any dangerous or socially important activity.

Consulting the poison oracle usually occurs in the bush far from the homestead to maintain secrecy and to avoid people who have not observed the taboos necessary for the oracle to work. Participants must not have sexual intercourse or eat elephant's flesh and a number of other foods for several days before consulting the oracle. Smoking hemp will pollute the oracle as well.

The diviner, who with only rare exceptions is a male, scrapes a hole in the ground and places into it a large leaf to hold the *benge*, or oracle poison. He fashions a brush of grass to administer the poison to chickens, several of which are brought by each questioner. When everyone is seated, it is decided how each question will be framed to provide the most information. The diviner then pours water into the leaf bowl and adds the powdered poison. After mixing the paste with his brush, the diviner squeezes the liquid from the brush into the beak of one of the chickens. While several doses are given, the questioner asks the first question repeatedly, ending each time with a request for the poison to kill or to spare the fowl if the answer is affirmative. For instance, a question about whether adultery has occurred might be ended by the questioner's saying:

> Poison oracle, poison oracle, you are in the throat of the fowl. That man his navel joined her navel; they pressed together; he knew her as woman and she knew him as man. She has drawn *badiabe* [a leaf used as a towel] and water to his side [for ablutions after intercourse]; poison oracle hear it, kill the fowl. (Evans-Pritchard, 1957, p. 138)

The poison used is a red powder prepared from a jungle creeper. The alkaloid that it contains has effects similar to strychnine. Some chickens seem unaffected by it. Others die immediately or soon after it is administered.

In poison oracle divination, there are always two tests of each question, one framed positively and the other negatively. One chicken must die and another must survive to confirm an answer to a question. If both live or if both die, the oracle must be consulted at another time to obtain an answer to the question.

Affecting health. Influential magic also may be used to cause ill health. Illness is a problem with which people must cope in all parts of the world. Although health-related magic is most common in societies that lack complex secular medical technologies, one finds religious rituals for the cur-

ing and causing of illness in all the world's many societies.

According to Forest Clements (1932) there are six major theories of disease in the world's societies: natural causes, magic, the intrusion of disease objects into the victim's body, soul loss, spirit possession, and taboo violations. Each of these is associated with an appropriate approach to curing the illness.

Those diseases or infirmities that are thought to be the result of natural causes are treated by pragmatic techniques such as setting broken bones and the use of herbs. When magic is used to bring about illness or death in a victim, favored materials include things that have been in intimate contact with the victim such as hair clippings, nail parings, excreta, or pieces of the victim's clothing. Magic-caused illnesses must be cured by countermagic.

Sending a foreign object, called a disease object, into the body of a victim by magic is another favored technique of sorcerers and witches for bringing about illness or death. When a foreign object such as a barbed stick or a stone is believed to have been supernaturally projected into the victim's body, thereby causing pain and illness, the object is removed by massage and sucking.

The third spiritual cause of illness is soul loss. When a soul has left a person's body—whether dislodged from the body by a sudden fright, simply lost during its nightly wanderings, or stolen by another's magic—the body is left without the vitality it needs to survive. If this is believed to be the cause of the victim's ill health, a healer must coax the wayward soul back into the patient's body or recapture it and bring it back.

Spirit possession requires a ritual of exorcism to remove the offending spirit. Taboo violation is the only one of the six causes of illness in which magic may not play a role, but the rule breaker is not necessarily held morally responsible for the act, as in the Western concept of sin. In many cultures, it is believed that illness may come not as punishment but simply as a natural consequence of breaking a supernatural rule. Thus taboo violation includes willful breaking of the taboos but may also include rule breaking that was accidental or even done without the actor's awareness. For instance, Apache Indians of the southwestern United States believe that illness may result from using as firewood wood that has been urinated on by a deer, even though one is unlikely to know that this is the case. Furthermore, in some societies the illness that follows a taboo violation may strike someone other than the rule breaker. When taboo violation is thought to be the cause of illness, confession will play a role in the cure.

What determines whether people will believe that the malicious acts of others, such as sorcerers or witches, are the cause of illness or will attribute illnesses to other causes? As has been noted above, Beatrice Whiting (1950) and Guy Swanson (1960) cited the presence of societal conflicts in the absence of effective social means of resolving conflicts as a major cause of the belief in sorcery to work harm. The specific social conflicts surrounding sexual jealousy also have been suggested as a basis for witchcraft and sorcery. On the other hand, the two forms of belief that illness may be caused by nonhuman spiritual beings—that is, spirit possession or punishment for the violation of a taboo—are not related to the development of secular authority or to the severity of socialization anxiety. These beliefs may be found with the other four theories of disease, but they also are found in societies where the others do not occur. Bourguignon and Greenberg (1973) found that spirit possession is most common in societies in which people are expected to be submissive and compliant and that spirit loss is most common in societies in which people are socialized to be independent and self-assertive. In both cases, the supernatural concept of illness seems to symbolize anxiety about the kind of social role one is expected to play. Illness as a result of taboo violation is found in societies in which conformity to rules is important. For instance, taboo violation is an important cause of illness among the arctic Inuit, whose environment can be quite deadly if one is lax or careless in following the established rules of life.

Figure 8.8 *Bone Pointing*
A witch doctor in the Northern Territory, Australia, shows how the magic bone is pointed at a victim while he is being "sung." Somehow the victim learns of the ritual even though it is done in secret, and usually dies.

Death by magic. In some cases, victims of sorcery actually die. Anthropologists have tried for decades to understand the phenomenon of death by magic.

Cannon (1942) analyzed cases of so-called "voodoo death" and suggested that the actual cause of death in such cases may be prolonged shock induced by extreme fear. Cannon quotes Herbert Basedow (1907), who graphically described the terrifying effect of sorcery by bone-pointing (see Fig. 8.8) in native Australia:

A man who discovers that he is being boned by an enemy is, indeed, a pitiable sight. He stands aghast, with his eyes staring at the treacherous pointer, and with his hands lifted as though to ward off the lethal medium, which he imagines is pouring into his body. . . . His cheeks blanch and his eyes become glossy, and the expression of his face becomes horribly distorted, like that of one stricken with palsy. He attempts to shriek but usually the sound chokes in his throat, and all that one might see is froth at his mouth. His body begins to tremble and the muscles twist involuntarily. He sways backwards and falls to the ground, and after a short time appears to be in a swoon but soon after he begins to writhe as if in mortal agony, and, covering his face with his hands, begins to moan. After a while he becomes more composed and crawls to his wurley [hut]. From this time onwards he sickens and frets, refusing to eat, and keeping aloof from the daily affairs of the tribe. Unless help is forthcoming in the shape of a counter charm administered by the hands of the *"Nangarri"* or medicine-man, his death is only a matter of a comparatively short time. If the coming of the medicine-man is opportune, he might be saved. (Cannon, 1942, p. 181)

Normally, both fear and anger stimulate the sympathetic nervous system, which regulates the inner organs and the circulatory system. This stimulation prepares the body for prolonged muscular exertion by discharging adrenalin and accelerating the heart rate, by constricting blood vessels during the exertion, and by dilating the bronchioles within the lungs so that more oxygen may be available to the muscles and more carbon dioxide may be expelled. All of these changes prepare the body for the muscular action that may be necessary for the escape from danger. However, when the energy thus made available cannot be used for a prolonged period, the physiological stress of remaining in this state of preparedness for intense action will eventually result in exhaustion and damage to the bodily organs, which may result in death. As Hans Selye (1976) pointed out in his description of the stress response, which he termed the General Adaptation Syndrome: These are nonspecific changes that occur in the body as a result of any stress, and even adaptation to a stress-producing event eventually ends in a state of exhaustion. Adaptation to unusual levels of stress cannot go on indefinitely.

In fear-induced shock, the prolonged constriction of the small blood vessels occurs especially in the extremities and the abdominal viscera. The lack of an adequate supply of oxygen in the visceral capillaries causes their thin walls to become more permeable, and blood plasma escapes into the spaces surrounding these small blood vessels in the abdomen. This reduces the volume of blood available in the circulatory system until adequate circulation is no longer possible. The result is a lowering of the blood pressure, which in turn leads to

a deterioration of the heart and other organs that normally insure an adequate circulation of blood to the body. If the cycle is not broken, death is inevitable. The process by which it happens is often speeded by the fact that the victim may cease to eat and drink, thereby adding even greater stresses to the body. Recently Eastwell (1982) has argued that dehydration may be the actual cause of death. Since stress that is brought on by fear of sorcery cannot be eliminated by any practical action, death may indeed result unless the fear can be eliminated by a ritual cure.

Death by Sorcery in Dobu

R. Fortune (1963) gave a graphic account of the use of sorcery to kill among the Dobuans, inhabitants of a Melanesian Islands near New Guinea. The sorcerer and one or more assistants approached the area of the victim's garden in the forest. They rubbed their bodies with magically powerful herbs to make themselves invisible and then crept to the edge of the clearing where the victim was working in the garden. Suddenly, with a characteristic scream, the sorcerer jumped into the clearing. The victim, taken by surprise, would recognize what was happening from the cry and actions of the sorcerer. He or she would be overcome by fear and fall immediately into a faint. The sorcerer was then free to prance about and dramatically act out, in symbolic form, the surgical opening of the victim's abdomen and the magical removal of the entrails and vital organs. After closing the magical wound, the sorcerer would ask the victim, "What is my name?" The victim could not respond, insuring that the sorcerer would not be identified.

After the sorcerer departed, the victim gradually recovered enough to stagger home and crawl up the ladder to his or her house. Relatives, recognizing the expression of shock and fear on the victim's face, knew what had transpired and began to make arrangements for the funeral. The victim lost all appetite and could die from shock within the next few days.

Figure 8.9 *Iroquois False-Face Society*
These are samples of the kind of face masks worn by an Iroquois curing group known as the False-Face Society. Carved into the trunk of a tree and representing spirit forces, they were later worn by shamans who visited the victim's house to drive out the evil spirits causing illness.

Spiritual healing. Just as ritual is believed to play a prominent role in the causing of illness or even death, religious power is called on in many societies to cure illness. Curing illness is the primary concern of shamans, or inspired religious healers. In societies in which shamans are able to congregate in sufficient numbers, they may form organizations in which they discuss their practices, cooperate with one another in curing patients, and initiate apprentices into the shared secrets of the trade. For instance, among the Iroquois, a native American people who lived in northern New York and were described extensively by Morgan (1851), various illnesses were treated by the members of specialized medicine societies. Among these were the False Face Society, the Bear Society, the Pygmy Society, the Otter Society, the Chanters for the Dead, and the Eagle Society. Each specialized in the treatment or prevention of particular ills and had its own songs and rituals. Those who asked a particular society for a cure became members of that society if the cure was successful, as did persons who dreamed that they must join a society. Thus, following a cure, individuals acquired a new social sta-

tus and were expected to play a role in the curing of others who became afflicted by the same disease.

The Iroquois False Face Society

The False Face Society was a powerful religious curing society among the Iroquois of the northeastern United States. These cures were accomplished with the use of wooden masks representing various spirits that were worn by the members of the society during its ceremonies. The masks characteristically had distorted features and were created by carving the face into the trunk of a live tree (see Fig. 8.9). During the carving, prayers were made to the spirit force that it represented. After tobacco had been burned before the mask, it was cut free, painted, and decorated with hair made from cornsilk or horsehair.

Curing ceremonies took place at the request of the patient's family in the longhouse where they lived. The members of the False Face Society would don their masks and travel in a group to the patient's house. As they came, they mimicked the spirits represented by the masks. Upon entering the patient's house, they sprinkled the afflicted person with ashes and shook their turtle carapace rattles over him or her to drive away the illness. In return for their work, members of the False Face Society were paid with gifts and food.

The Social Organization of Religion

A hallmark of religion is ritual involvement with others. By participating in the religious rituals of their society, people express a sense of togetherness, unity, and belonging. This group aspect of religious practice fosters deeper loyalty to one's society. To be sure, all religions include rituals that individuals may perform for their own benefit: private prayer to petition the spirits and gods for aid, magic to achieve the same ends more coercively, taboos that are followed to avoid misfortune, and positive acts that foster luck, skill, and safety. However, no religious system is built solely from these individualistic ritual activities. All religions have at least part-time religious specialists who perform rituals for others, and some are organized into more complex communal or ecclesiastical religious groups (Wallace, 1966).

Ritual Specialists

Ritual may be performed by any adherent of a religion, but all religions also have some individuals who specialize in the use of spiritual power to influence others. These include shamans, sorcerers, and witches.

Shamans. The most common kind of ritual specialist in human societies is the medical-religious curer that anthropologists refer to as the shaman. The term "shaman" was originally borrowed from a seminomadic Siberian people called the Chuckchee, among whom shamanism was a male occupation. According to Waldemar Borgoras (1907) the Chuckchee shaman was a man who was socially withdrawn, listless, and prone to falling into trances before entering the shamanic career. Like healers in other societies, in other words, Chuckchee shamans tended to be social deviants. This fact was institutionally recognized: Shamans were expected to adopt the dress of women as a symbol of their deviant status. Having been chosen by another world, shamans were set apart socially by the transvestite role. In fact, those shamans who, besides adopting the clothing of women, took on the behavior of a woman and entered into sexual relationships or marriages with men, were thought to be the most powerful among the shamans.

Eliade (1964) has shown that the central feature of shamanistic practice is the ecstatic experience achieved in trance. In the trance state, shamans may send their spirits on errands in service to their clients, or they may invite powerful spirits to enter their bodies and give them power. In spirit travel and possession trances, shamans experience the ecstasy of visions of a world not seen by ordinary eyes. Noll (1985) has argued that the training that sets the shaman apart from other people in the skill of entering trances and experiencing visions is facilitated by practicing visual imaging. With practice the shaman's visions become more vivid and lively, and the shaman learns to control when the visions begin and end and what their content will be. Peters and Price-Williams (1980) describe the vivid shamanic trance as similar to waking dreams and guided imagery. Further, Price-Williams (1985) believes that the true shamanistic trance involves passing over from simple visual imaging into an altered state of consciousness in which the shaman experiences personal "participation and immersion in the imagery content" (p. 656).

Becoming A Shaman Among the Avam Samoyed

Where shamans are formally initiated by others of their kind, the initiation ceremony often enacts a kind of symbolic death, journey through the spirit world where the novice is trained and given the powers of a shaman, and rebirth into the human world. This formula is well illustrated in a story told by Popov (1936) about the vision of a Siberian Avam Samoyed man who received the power to cure. While lying near death from smallpox, his Sickness spoke to him on behalf of the Lords of Water and gave him the new name, Diver. After climbing a mountain, Diver met a naked woman, the Lady of Water, who took him as her child and suckled him at her breast. Her husband, Lord of the Underworld, gave him two guides who led him to the Underworld. There he learned of the diseases, both physical and mental, from which people suffer. Then he visited the Land of Shamanesses where voice is strengthened, since song is used in cures. On an island in one of the Nine Seas, he found the Tree of the Lord of the Earth. There he was given the wood for making three of the drums that shamans use in their ceremonies. After he received instruction in the medicinal use of seven herbs and in other techniques for curing, he was told that he must marry three women.

Then the initiate was led to another high mountain where he met two women clothed in the hair of reindeer. Each gave him a hair to be used when he used his power to influence reindeer. He crossed a great desert to another mountain. There he was dismembered, and his body parts were boiled in a great cauldron by a naked man who forged his head on an anvil that was used to forge the heads of great shamans. This man taught him to divine whether a cure would be successful, reassembled his body, gave him new eyes capable of seeing into the spirit world, and pierced his ears so they could hear the speech of plants. After all these things, he awoke and found that during the three days of his coma, he had been so close to death that he had almost been buried.

Sorcerers. The antisocial equivalent of a shaman is the sorcerer, a person who uses supernatural power to harm human beings. Sorcery may be used to cause misfortune, illness, and death. As dangerous as a sorcerer may be, acknowledged practitioners of the art may be tolerated by their neighbors, since their noxious powers may occasionally be sought by others. A sorcerer might, for instance, be hired by persons who believe themselves to have been wronged by others and who seek vengeance by sorcery. Since persons who discover that they have been cursed by a sorcerer may seek the removal of that curse by making amends for the wrong of which they have been accused, the sorcerer's role in society is sometimes similar to that of the law enforcers in complex societies.

Navajo Skinwalkers

Among the Navajo of the southwestern United States, it is said that a curer may be seduced by the dark side of power. No human being is all good or all evil. In the Navajo view, we each have both qualities or, more accurately, the capacity to do both good and evil. According to Witherspoon (1977), the goal of Navajo life is to bring one's impulses under control so that one grows and develops through a complete life in a condition of *hózhó*—the state of beauty, har-

Figure 8.10 *Navajo ''Sing''*
One way the Navajo counter the forces of evil in the universe or in man is to perform a ritual chant or ''sing.'' This Navajo mother is holding her sick child while sitting on a sand painting and chanting rituals intended to restore the child to health or a state of hózhó.

mony, good, and happiness—and then dies naturally of old age and becomes one with the universal beauty, harmony, and happiness that make up the ideal positive environment.

A person's *ch'indi*, or potential for evil, can be controlled by rituals that restore one to a state of *hózhó*. Although the state of inward beauty achieved through living in outward harmony with the ideal environment can be disrupted by contact with dangerous (*báhádzid*) things or by the sorcery of others, perhaps leading to illness or to death, such states can be countered by a traditional ritual chant, or ''Sing,'' of which there are over 60. Rituals channel supernatural power by reenacting the Navajo creation myths, which relate the deeds of the gods, both good and evil.

Navajo singers, the curing shamans of the Navajo, also can learn to use the power of ritual to harm other people. Initiation into the world of sorcery carries a high price: The initiate must consent to the death of a close relative. In using rituals to upset the ideal balance of life in others, the sorcerer's *ch'indi* grows stronger and may overwhelm him. Sorcerers live a life that inverts the ideals of the Navajo: They gather at night in places avoided by others to do their rituals; they dig up corpses to grind their bones into poisons; they don the skins of wolves and transform themselves into animals. Skinwalkers, as they are called, can travel great distances faster than ordinary humans can imagine. They cast their poisons into the smoke holes of their victims' hogans or magically shoot harmful substances into their bodies.

Witches. Witches share the world of supernatural power with sorcerers and shamans. Like sorcerers, they are believed to do evil to human beings. Unlike sorcerers, who must learn the rituals with which they work their harm, witches are thought to be born with the power to harm. The evil of a witch works so spontaneously that it may do its damage to others even without the witch's conscious intent. Witches are often viewed as the epitome of evil, and they may be described in terms that invert the normal qualities of human beings: Witches love the night; they commit incest and kill their own relatives; they may travel on their heads instead of their feet, and may fly as fireballs through the sky. Since witches are so different from ordinary humans, the very presence of persons who are believed to be witches may not be tolerated, and convicted witches are likely to be killed.

Shamanic Religions

Of all forms of religious organization, shamanic religions are the socially simplest and perhaps the oldest. Shamanic religions are based on rituals performed by nonspecialists for their own benefit and by the shaman for the benefit of nonspecialists. Shamans may perform rituals to divine the future or to gain answers to their clients' questions. As spirit mediums, they may be called on to increase the success of a hunt, the fertility of the game, or the growth of crops. The charms they make protect their clients from harm or increase their luck and skill. However, shamans are best known for their skill at manipulating the supernatural to cure illness. Their spiritual powers do not differ in nature from those that nonspecialists may use in their own behalf, but their special status grows out of their reputation for greater skill at manipulating these powers. In addition to their spiritual powers, shamans often possess an impressive body of knowledge about the natural medical effects of a broad range of native plants and other curative materials and techniques. Shamans also draw upon the awe and reverence of their patients for religious power, thereby increasing the patients' confidence in the likelihood of recovery.

A Shoshoni Shaman's Cure

On the reservation in Nevada where I did my fieldwork, a Shoshoni *puhakantee*, literally a "possessor of power," still cured the sick. The shaman's power to cure was not a human power but a spiritual power brought to him by a spirit partner, a *newe puha-pea*, the Eagle, who first appeared to him in a vision and gave him the power to cure.

When a prospective patient approaches this shaman, the first task is to determine whether he will be able to perform the cure. At the direction of his spirit partner, certain cases—such as those he diagnoses as cancer—must be referred to a medical doctor. To facilitate the diagnosis, the individual who has consulted him may be given an "eagle wing," a fan made of eagle feathers to place above his or her bed that night. That evening, the shaman consults his spirit partner for a diagnosis. On the next day, he will either accept or reject the petitioner as a patient, depending on the diagnosis.

A cure usually begins at sunset in the shaman's home. It is sometimes attended by other interested members of the community. Attendance at a curing ceremony is believed to foster good health in general among those who participate. The patient, who has bathed that morning at sunrise in a local hot spring, provides tobacco that is smoked by the shaman as part of the ceremony. After smoking, the shaman begins a chant that he was taught by his spirit partner in his virst vision. This chant is a call to the Eagle to come down from his mountain abode and enter the shaman to give him power to cure his patient's illness. He alternately smokes, chants, and massages the patient's body to remove the illness. Following the ceremony, the patient may be given some tasks to perform to complete the cure. For instance, a patient who is suffering from nosebleeds may be required to collect the blood and dispose of it on a red anthill. Patients are required to abstain from alcohol to insure the efficacy of the cure.

Communal Religions

A slightly more complex form of religious organization adds the practice of rituals by groups of nonspecialists to those found in the shamanic religions. These communal religions are found in more societies than are the shamanic ones. They tend to be found in societies that have slightly larger local groups than those in which shamanic religions predominate. In societies with larger social groups, communal rituals serve to celebrate the cohesiveness of the group or ease the transition of individuals from one status to another by publicly proclaiming that change in a rite of passage. Like shamanic religions, they are found in many societies where people survive by foraging wild foods. Communal religions also are found in societies where horticulture and pastoralism are practiced.

The group rituals permit broader social participation in the shared concerns of the community or of groups of specialists than do individual or shamanic rituals. They focus on matters that concern groups rather than individuals and increase the sense of social solidarity among those who participate. The group rituals that are most often celebrated in communal religions are: rituals to increase the fertility of game or insure success in hunting; annual rituals to influence the weather, the fertility of crops, and the harvest; social rituals to celebrate

changes in status or reinforce the importance of social divisions by sex or age; and ceremonies to reenact the mythology of the group or commemorate the memory of culture heroes, ancestral spirits, or particular deities.

The Rainbringing Ritual of the Jigalong People

According to Tonkinson (1974) the most important yearly ritual of the Jigalong people of the western Australian desert is the rainbringing ritual, called *Ngaawajil*. This ritual reenacts the story of Winba, an old snake-man ancestral being and other rainmaking beings, controllers of rain, clouds, thunder, lighting, hail, and other elements of the weather. If the people perform, the annual return of the rains is insured, as is the increase in the kangaroo and other game animals that depend on the rains for water in the desert environment where the Jigalong people live and hunt.

Since the ritual lasts for many days and consists of a number of ceremonies performed simultaneously in different locations, it requires the cooperation of five male and four female groups, each with its own name, insignia, and ritual responsibilities. Throughout the ritual there is a division of the participants into the two-generation-level moieties of Jigalong life, groupings that unite members of alternate generations (grandparents and grandchildren) and separate members of contiguous generations (parents and children). Thus, the ritual reinforces a major aspect of Jigalong social life by incorporating the moiety division into the structure of the ritual

The ritual activities occur at two locations, the Camp—where men, women, and children participate together in the ritual—and the "men's country" away from the camp—where only initiated males are involved in the ceremonies. At the Camp, men and women of appropriate status prepare food for the participants, and members of each moiety engage in chanting and

213

throwing water at members of the other moiety. Away from the Camp, the ritual requires two piles of sacred objects used to encourage the rainmaking ancestors to bring the rains: lightning, thunder, hail, and rainbow stones and other objects. These objects are sprinkled with blood symbolic of rain, covered with down feathers symbolic of clouds, and "fed" with ceremonial food and water. The desire for rain is communicated to the rainmaking ancestors by rainmaking snakes believed to live in the piles of sacred objects.

Ecclesiastical Religions

The ecclesiastical religions make use of all the previous ways of organizing some of their rituals, but they add to them a series of rituals performed by members of a professional clergy or priesthood. These religious practitioners are called priests to distinguish them from their more charismatic counterparts, the shamans. Whereas shamans serve individual clients when called upon to do so, priests perform rituals for a congregation on a full-time or at least regular basis. Priests may be organized into a bureaucracy which both organizes the activities of its members and regulates the ritual calendar of the congregations. Unlike shamans, who often are highly charismatic individuals who creatively follow the inspiration of the moment in modifying their ritual performance to fit the needs of their clients, priests tend to be much more concerned with the maintenance of the traditional forms of the rituals they have learned. Ecclesiastical religions tend to be found in agriculturally based societies, particularly in those with large enough populations to support a variety of full-time specialists. They are characteristic of the world's most complex societies.

Ideologically, the earliest recorded ecclesiastical religions had polytheistic beliefs in which a variety of high gods each required the service of special religious practitioners. Wallace (1966) has called these early ecclesiastical religions the Olympian religions to distinguish them from the later monotheistic religions in which the super-natural pantheon of ranked gods is superseded by one in which the highest deity is regarded as a truly Supreme Being, if not the only god in the pantheon. The ancient Greeks, Egyptians, Babylonians, and Romans followed the Olympian pattern, while monotheistic religions are represented today in Judaism, Christianity, Islam, and in modern philosophical Hinduism, in which all of the gods of earlier Hindu tradition are said to be merely various manifestations of a single, all-encompassing deity.

Mormon Priesthood and Pantheon

Mormonism was founded in 1824 in the eastern United States by a charismatic leader, Joseph Smith, following a series of visionary experiences, including a visitation by God the Father and Jesus. Today, this religion claims over five million members worldwide.

Mormonism is an ecclesiastical religion. Its priesthood, which is held only by male members of the church, is organized into a complex hierarchy, presided over by a president. The president of the church is also referred to as the *Prophet, Seer, and Revelator* of the church. As the presiding official of the church, the Prophet is believed to receive direct guidance from God whenever this is necessary for the work of directing the church. Below the Prophet is the Quorum of Twelve Apostles, which is presided over by its own president and two counselors. Below this level are intermediary officers down to the local congregations, called *wards*. The presiding official of the ward is the *bishop*. The bishop is a nonpaid minister, as are all local members of the priesthood. His responsibilities are not to deliver weekly sermons but to organize and preside over each Sunday's worship services and all other business of the ward. In this work he is aided by his own counselors and a series of priesthood quorums within the ward.

The local priesthood quorums are themselves organized into an age-graded system which is divided into two major components, the lower, or Aaronic Priesthood and the higher, or Melchizedek Priesthood. Boys are typically inducted into the Aaronic Priesthood at the age of 12 as Deacons. Their assignments include passing the Sacrament to members of the ward during the Sacrament meeting each Sunday. At 14 boys are ordained Teachers and are permitted to prepare the sacramental bread and water used in the service. Sixteen-year-olds become Priests, at which time they receive the authority to bless the Sacrament and to baptize. Eighteen-year-olds receive the full authority of the Melchizedek Priesthood as Elders, including the authority to confirm a baptized person as a member of the church and, by the laying on of hands, to give that person the right to receive direct and personal guidance through the Holy Ghost. At this time, it is expected that worthy males will spend a two year period as unpaid, full-time missionaries for the church. For most, the next major change occurs at age 45 when men are inducted into a High Priest's quorum.

The women's organization is an auxiliary program, since all policy-making and governing authority is vested in the priesthood. The men's and women's organizations are structurally equivalent, but they differ in authority and responsibility, with the women specializing in supportive service roles. Mormon ecclesiastical values reflect the secular differentiation of male and female roles. According to Shepherd and Shepherd (1984), Mormons are taught to idealize a family pattern in which the husband, as the family's sole source of income, plays a presiding role and in which the wife, as counselor to her husband, specializes in domestic responsibilities. In addition to a Father in Heaven, Mormon theology includes a divine Mother in Heaven (Heeren, Lindsey, & Mason, 1985). However, Her role in Mormon theology is an auxiliary one, like that of the women's organization within the church or of the wife within the idealized Mormon family. She is never explicitly mentioned in Mormon scriptures, She has no governing authority within the Godhead, and She is not approached in worship in any rituals of the church.

The recurring pattern of presidents and two counselors within the church structure mirrors Mormon theology, which includes a divine pantheon of many gods presided over by God the Father, Jesus Christ, and the Holy Ghost. Jesus, the firstborn spirit child of God, and the Holy Ghost, another spirit son of God, are believed to be fully separate individuals from the Father. Their role in the Godhead is much like that of the counselors to the earthly Prophet of the church. Thus, church organizational structure reproduces forms that Mormons think of as divine in origin and that reinforce the value of a presiding role for males.

Why Are People Religious?

Although cultures differ considerably in their religious beliefs, practices, and organizations, there is no known human culture in which religion is absent. There is archaeological evidence that religion has been practiced by our ancestors since at least the time of the Neanderthal, 125,000 years ago. In trying to explain the universal existence of religion in our species, anthropologists usually have considered the role that religion plays in making our social life more successful and the psychological benefits that religion gives us as individuals. The question of whether people also are responding to a true supernatural realm is, itself, not accessible to anthropological study.

The Maintenance of Social Order

Religion teaches people that they have a place in the universe and a relationship to it. Through the ideology of a religion and through its rituals, people gain a sense of identity and a feeling that life is meaningful. The practice of a religion creates greater solidarity among its participants, enabling them to work more effectively together and accomplish more.

Religion provides guidelines and values about how human life is properly conducted. In so doing, it motivates people to follow the customs of their society even in the absence of practical insights about how their actions may benefit their society. For instance, farmers suffering the effects of a prolonged drought may be too discouraged to dig yet another well after several failures until a ''water witch'' assures them of the presence of water at some location. Without such religious sources of motivation, the short-term costs of trying one more time in the face of the previous failures might seem to outweigh the potential long-term benefits.

Social rules that are necessary to the maintenance of order may be supported by the threat of supernatural punishments for their violation or supernatural rewards for their acceptance. This can be especially beneficial to a society that lacks secular means of insuring obedience to the rules. Viking men were promised the reward of Valhalla for valor in warfare, and Aztec warriors were assured that death in battle led to an eternity in the most glorious of the Aztec heavens, that of their war god, Huitzilopochtli. Among the Rwala Bedouin of northern Saudi Arabia, the pains of Hell awaited those who lied, and for the ancient Egyptians a similar fate was reserved for the stingy.

In situations in which disagreement might be divisive, religion may provide the means to achieve consensus without hard feelings. For instance, divination can be used to find the answer to a question about which the group is hopelessly divided. That solution then can be accepted by all without loss of face.

Finally, the rituals of religion provide emotional release from stresses that might otherwise lead to socially disruptive behavior. When Zuñi farmers blame their crop failures or illness on the malevolent activities of sorcerers in another town and take action to protect themselves through rituals, they may be sparing themselves the strife that might otherwise disrupt their own village if they took out their frustrations on neighbors or relatives.

The Reduction of Anxiety

In addition to benefits to society at large, there are psychological benefits for the individual in the practice of religion. People do not always have as much control over their lives or circumstances as they need to feel secure. When this is the case, the performance of rituals for control through supernatural means can alleviate debilitating anxiety. This is especially true when the anxiety stems from problems for which no secular remedies are known. More than one anthropologist has noted parallels between shamanistic curing rituals and Western psychotherapeutic practices.

In frightening situations, religion can be a source of strength to stand up to one's fears and overcome them. The prayer uttered privately or the blessing given by another before a dangerous act is undertaken may provide just enough confidence to insure success. Guilt can be overcome by acts of penance and sacrifice, and shame may be counteracted by demonstrations of piety that restore one's reputation. People who are unable to remove unjust obstacles in their lives can release their anger by acting it out with rituals that direct the power of magic against the source of their frustrations. At times of loss, religion may console the grieving. In these and other ways, religion helps people cope with troubling emotions.

The Cognitive Role of Religion

Religion's role in shaping beliefs also may be helpful to people. One important function of religious belief is to give people answers to important questions for which they have no scientific answers: Why do I exist? What will become of me after I die? What are the sun, moon, and stars, and how did the earth itself come into existence? Who were the first humans, and how did they originate? To such questions, religious ideology provides satisfying answers based on supernatural authority.

Some questions that religion answers, existential questions that deal with meaning and purpose, are questions with which science is not equipped to deal. However, others are questions that had no scientific answers at one time but which had come to be answered at a later time. The rise of scientific specialists in Western societies led to new answers to many questions that had been handled previously by religious leaders. This change resulted in social conflict between advocates of science and religious leaders, which gradually resulted in a major loss of social and political influence by religious professionals. Education, for instance, increasingly came under the control of secular educators. A natural byproduct of the conflict between science and religion was the evolution in Western culture of the idea that scientific and religious ideologies are fundamentally different, perhaps even irreconcilable. This idea is dramatically illustrated in the ongoing attacks on scientific knowledge about the age of the earth or about human evolution by Christian fundamentalist religious leaders in the United States who reject the notion that scientific insights should be allowed to influence their interpretation of scripture.

It is true that science and religion differ in the methods that they employ to create new ideas. However, it is an error to assume that the cognitive processes involved in religious thinking differ radically from those applied in science. Guthrie (1980, p. 181) has shown that "people hold religious beliefs because they are *plausible* models of the world, apparently grounded in daily experience" (emphasis added). Guthrie believes that anthropomorphism (using human qualities to explain the nonhuman realm) is fundamental to religion and that it is anthropomorphism that all religions have in common. He observes that our experiences are initially ambiguous, and we reduce this ambiguity by interpreting them. Whether we do so religiously or scientifically, we interpret our experiences by creating models for them, based on phenomena that seem to us to be analogous to the experiences we wish to explain. Humans make very plausible models for many of the things we experience for three reasons: (1) Humans are complex and multifaceted, so they have similarities to many phenomena; (2) human beings are likely to be found wherever the human observer may be; (3) humans are the most important factor in the human en-

vironment. Therefore, anthropomorphic models are readily used by human beings to interpret their experiences, and it is these models of the universe as created and governed by unseen humanlike beings that we call religion. Guthrie's view that there is nothing psychologically implausible about religious ways of interpreting experiences implies that when we ask why people are religious, we may be asking the wrong question. Perhaps we should be asking why people sometimes think in nonreligious ways.

Creationism: A Contemporary American Religion

Fundamentalist religious leaders in the United States have opposed scientific views about human evolution since Darwin first proposed them. In the nineteenth century, Darwin outlined the natural mechanisms that could guide evolutionary change in living things. Such mechanisms were a potential threat to religious ideas, since they did not require a role for God in the process, and incorporating them into a religious model would have required a major change in the fundamentalists' literal approach to interpreting scripture. Instead, they chose to oppose the introduction of evolutionary ideas into the United States school system. They successfully supported efforts to pass laws that forbade the teaching of evolution in states where their followers had sufficient numbers to command the respect of legislators. In 1925, John Scopes, an Arkansas high school teacher, was convicted and fined $100 for teaching his biology students that humans had evolved from simpler animals.

In the past decade, a new form of religious fundamentalism has developed in the United States, taking for itself the name *Creation Science*. The major creationist organizations are The Institute for Creation Research, which makes its home at Christian Heritage College, and the Creation Science Research Center. Creationist organizations do not carry out original scientific research in the traditional sense. Instead, they gather material published by scientists in any field that they judge relevant to their interests in creationism and use these within their argument for a creationist view of the universe. They also participate actively in lobbying to bring about legislation that forbids the teaching of evolution within the public schools without giving equal time to creationist ideas.

What do creation "scientists" believe? This is not an easy question to answer, since their views are not built up systematically as is usually the case within the sciences. Individual creationists differ in their opinions on specific issues, but some broad boundaries can be drawn that would probably surround them all. Generally, creationists are outspoken anti-evolutionists, refusing to believe that either life or the universe itself has evolved through time, even under Divine direction. They believe that the universe came into existence suddenly by the act of a Creator. Contrary to the dominant opinions of astronomers, physicists, geologists, biologists, and anthropologists, they believe that the universe, the earth, and all living things came into existence at about the same time, probably between 6,000 and 13,000 years ago. Individual creationists are divided on whether the process took six days or 6,000 years. They agree that the basic "kinds" of living things were created with essential-

ly the same traits that they have today. There seems to be no accepted definition of what constitutes a "kind," but creationists are in agreement that whatever it is, the only change that can occur in living things is within a "kind" and that one "kind" cannot evolve into another. Fossils of extinct living forms, creationists believe, were creatures that died suddenly as a result of a major, catastrophic, world-wide flood.

If creationist beliefs sound as if they were based on a fundamentalist religious interpretation of Genesis, it is probably no coincidence. To join the Creation Research Society, one must sign a statement that reads in part, "The Bible is the written Word of God, and because we believe it to be inspired throughout, all its assertions are historically and scientifically true."[1] The logo of the Creation Science Research Center surrounds the phrase, "In the beginning God. . . ." The religious basis for their beliefs seems clear, but their work of lobbying for the teaching of creationism within the public schools requires that they portray their views as "scientific" to sidestep the Constitutional prohibitions that prevent state supported schools from teaching or promoting sectarian religious doctrines.

1. From *Conference on Evolution and Public Education: Resources and References* (p. 80) edited by P. Zetterberg, 1981, St. Paul, MN: University of Minnesota Center for Educational Development.

Summary

Religion is found in all cultures but is subject to greater diversity than any other aspect of culture. Universal aspects that define religion in all societies are the belief in supernatural beings, the belief in supernatural power, the symbolic expression of feelings, and ritual behavior. The great diversity in belief systems may be related to variation in people's social, environmental, and technological contexts and may be seen as helping them adapt to those particular circumstances. Ritual religious behaviors may serve one or two general functions: portraying or influencing the supernatural. Rituals may be the province of solo practitioners—shamans, sorcerers, or witches—in small-scale societies. In somewhat larger societies, religion is often a communal matter, with group ceremonies. In large, socially stratified societies, religious specialists are commonly full-time practitioners, organized into hierarchical systems known as ecclesiastical religions. However organized, religion seems to help maintain social order, reduce individual anxiety, and help people make sense of the often puzzling world around them.

Key Terms and Concepts

religion 195
mana 196
taboo 196
supernatural 197
anthropomorphism 197
monotheism 200
polytheism 200
ancestral spirits 200
reincarnation 200
human soul 200
supernatural sanctions for violations of
 moral rules 200
sorcery 200
witchcraft 200
myth 203
magic 203
imitative magic 203
Law of Similarity 203
Law of Contagion 204
contagious magic 204

divination 204
disease object 206
soul loss 206
spirit possession 206
taboo violation 206
sin 206
voodoo death 207
bone-pointing 207
General Adaptation Syndrome 208
shamans 209
sorcerers 211
witches 212
shamanic religions 212
communal religions 213
ecclesiastical religions 214
priests 214
Olympian religions 214
monotheistic religions 214
creationism 218

Annotated Readings

Evans-Pritchard, E. E. (1956). *Nuer religion*. Oxford: Clarendon Press. Based on years of intensive study by one of the greats in British anthropology, this is a classic study of religion in an African society.

Furst, P. T. (Ed.). (1972). *Flesh of the gods: The ritual use of hallucinations*. New York: Praeger. A collection of articles on the use of hallucinogens to achieve altered states of consciousness in religious settings.

Howells, W. (1962). *The heathens: Primitive man and his religions*. Garden City, NY: Doubleday. An enjoyable, easy-to-read introduction to the basic concepts used by anthropologists in studying religion in non-Western cultures.

Kluckhohn, C. (1944). *Navaho Witchraft. (Papers of the Peabody Museum of American Archeology and Ethnology, Harvard University, 22(2))*. Cambridge, MA: Harvard University Press. An interesting look at a fascinating part of Navajo religious beliefs.

Lehmann, A. C., & Myers, J. E. (1985). *Magic, witchcraft, and religion: An anthropological study of the supernatural*. Palo Alto, CA: Mayfield. A thorough and up-to-date collection of articles on religion.

Lessa, W. A., & Vogt, E. Z. (Eds.). (1979). *Reader in comparative religion* (4th ed.). New York: Harper & Row. The classic comprehensive reader for the anthropology of religion. Must reading for the anthropology major.

Radin, P. (1937). *Primitive religion*. New York: Dover. A classic and insightful view of religion by an excellent writer.

Sharon, D. (1978). *Wizard of the four winds: A shaman's story*. New York: Macmillan. An insightful biography of a Peruvian shaman.

Swanson, G. E. (1960). *The birth of the gods: The origin of primitive beliefs*. Ann Arbor, MI: University of Michigan Press. An often overlooked, but important exploration of the Durkhe ian view of religious belief as a reflection of the anization of society. An important reference book r the anthropology major.

Wallace, A. F. C. (1966). *Religion: An anthropological view*. New York: Random House. Probably the most thorough and influential interpretation of religion as a psychological and a cultural phenomenon to have been written by an anthropologist. Must reading for the anthropology major, but worthwhile for any thoughtful student of religion.

Worsley, P. (1957). *The trumpet shall sound: A study of ''cargo'' cults in Melanesia*. London: MacGibbon and Kee. The classic comparative study of religious revitalization movements in Melanesia.

Chapter 9

The Prehistoric Evolution of Culture

On the whole, humans have moved steadily from a simple existence as hunters and gatherers of wild foods toward a settled life eating domesticated foods under the aegis of what we call "civilization"—large, complex, centrally regulated societies. In the final chapters of this book we will examine in detail the characteristics of contemporary groups that still embody stages in the emergence of civilization. But first, in this chapter, we will focus on the historical evolution of ancient civilizations, from foraging bands to towns to chiefdoms and states. Sometimes this process has involved the influence of one developing culture on another; sometimes civlizations have developed in isolation but along the same lines as cultural evolution elsewhere. And at the same time that humans were becoming more "civilized," they were spreading across the globe from the Near Eastern areas where Homo sapiens *had evolved as a species.*

Human Expansion

Before 30,000 years ago, the human species had spread throughout most of the Eastern Hemisphere, except for Australia and the Pacific Islands, and had developed a sophisticated hunting technology with numerous local variations. Soon thereafter, humankind began its expansion into the Western Hemisphere. This movement was possible because the great volume of water tied up in the vast northern ice sheets during the final Ice Age period resulted in a lowering of the sea level to about 400 feet below its present average (Beyers, 1957). Under these circumstances, much continental land now under water was exposed, and the shorelines were somewhat different from today's shorelines. The exposed land included the Bering Strait region between present-day Alaska and eastern Siberia. Consequently, the North American continent and

Figure 9.1 *Toltec Columns The Toltec, deriving their art from the Maya Indians, constructed commemorative stone shafts 5–25 feet high. Some of these stelae had bas relief figures surrounded by hieroglyphs.*

Siberia were connected during the final glacial period by a "land bridge" that was over 1,200 miles wide at some places.

Human movement across the land bridge connection from the East into the West was no purposeful and adventuresome migration. Rather, it was the result of the natural tendency to move, over the generations, in the direction in which game animals were least exploited. Ahead, game was more plentiful, since behind there was a far greater population of human hunters.

The natural pressures of growing human populations and shrinking animal resources drew humankind steadily into lands with untapped resources. The movement into the Americas may have happened in several waves, each one occurring at a different time when the shifting patterns of glacial ice left an open corridor of ice-free land between Siberia and North America. Some fragmentary evidence of early humans in the New World suggests that the first such movement into North America may have occurred about 30,000 years ago. A second wave of immigration, the one that left the most abundant and most definite archaeological evidences, seems to have occurred around 15,000 B.C. Martin (1967) has suggested that the extinction and near extinction of several American animals that began about 13,000 years ago were results of the arrival of early hunting peoples. These animals, including the musk ox, the saber-toothed tiger, the giant ground sloth, the horse, and the glyptodont, were unable to survive the effective hunting techniques that these people employed. A third wave of immigration into the North American arctic may have occurred more recently, beginning about 5,000 years ago as the ice sheets retreated. By 10,000 B.C., humans had reached the farthest tip of South America, where their remains have been found in seacoast caves.

By 10,000 B.C., humankind also had expanded into Australia, and the only major region of the world remaining unsettled was the Pacific islands, which were unreachable until an effective sea-travel technology evolved. The Pacific islands were gradually settled by waves of seafarers expanding out of southeast Asia from around 1700 B.C. to about the first century A.D.

The Origins of Food Domestication

At the same time that the human species was expanding across the globe, it also was developing new ways of providing food for its members. After the original pattern of hunting and gathering wild foods, many human groups turned to increasing reliance on food domestication, or intentional raising of plants and animals. This shift toward production also had significant effects on social structures, leading to greater concentrations of people and power.

The Benefits of Foraging

Although the shift of food domestication was traditionally viewed as progress, the current anthropological thinking is that foraging—the reliance on wild foods for survival—had its advantages. Judging from the few groups that still practice hunting and gathering, ways of life based on foraging are usually quite satisfactory in their ability to meet the needs of people. Population density is generally low, and the communities of cooperating individuals are never very large. Under these circumstances, it is simple for the local group to move quickly from place to place. As a result, food shortages are rare among hunters and gatherers. Nomadic or seminomadic hunters and gatherers do not live amidst their own refuse, one contributor to many of the diseases with which more sedentary peoples must contend. This factor, plus the low population densities that are characteristic of foragers, means that the epidemics that often plague peoples who live under crowded conditions are also rare. Furthermore, Marvin Harris (1977) has pointed out that foragers have a much shorter work week than do food domesticators. For instance, the southern African !Kung foragers need to work only about three hours a day to obtain a nutritious diet, even though their desert environment is not nearly so lush as most of the areas occupied by hunting and gathering peoples before the rise of farming.

The Trend Toward Food Domestication

Despite these advantages of foraging, as early as 20,000 years ago certain changes laid the foundations for the eventual domestication of plants and animals. About this time people practicing generalized hunting and gathering ways of life began to develop more specialized subsistence practices in the Near East: the gathering of different wild foods in different seasons and their preservation in storage pits for off-season use. This planning ahead made a more sedentary life possible even while exploiting wild cereal crops that were native to the area. These wild cereals could be harvested easily by lightly beating the stems so that the seeds would break loose and fall into a basket. After grinding with stone tools, the tough seeds could be prepared for eating in a variety of ways.

This use of the abundant wild grains in zones of sufficient rainfall along the hilly flanks of the mountains of the Near East resulted not only in a more sedentary life but also in population growth. Or population growth itself may have forced people to develop agriculture and animal domestication to better provide for their growing numbers (Boserup, 1965).

The rise of population that may have led to food domestication can be accounted for by the interplay between human fertility and sedentarism (a settled rather than nomadic life style). Rose Frisch and Janet McArthur (1974) and Rose Frisch (1975) have demonstrated that following the birth of a child, a woman will not again begin ovulation so long as less than 20 to 25% of her body weight consists of fat. This figure represents the approximate amount of calories that a fetus needs to develop full term to birth. That is, before a fertile woman will be able to conceive, her body must store enough calories of energy to nourish a developing fetus for a nine-month pregnancy. In active nomadic populations this threshold of body fat is more difficult to achieve than in sedentary populations, since the foragers burn more food energy themselves and their diets are likely to be lower in carbohydrates and higher in pro-

tein. Since nursing one child takes about 1,000 calories a day, it is unlikely that a woman will become pregnant so long as she is nursing if she lives in a semi-nomadic hunting and gathering society. Since nursing is likely to continue for at least three years in most societies, the level of fertility is, on the average, much lower in hunting and gathering societies than in sedentary societies using domesticated foods. The span of childbearing years is also shorter, for the onset of menstruation occurs later in hunting and gathering societies because a hunting and gathering diet is rich in protein. In demonstration of these theories, Richard B. Lee (1972) and Gina B. Kolata (1974) have reported growth in fertility and population among those !Kung hunter-gatherers who abandoned their native seminomadic way of life for a more sedentary food production economy.

Another explanation for the adoption of a comparatively sedentary way of life in the Near East is simply the availability of an abundance of native wild grains. Robert Sussman (1972) argues that such a change in the life style and diet of these early foragers would have resulted in an increase in the people's fertility and rate of population growth. Accelerated population growth, in turn, would have created pressure for even more effective control over the food supply. Specifically, population growth eventually made it necessary for people to move into less productive areas around the margins of the zones where wild grains grew in natural abundance. Lewis Binford (1968) and Kent Flannery (1971) believe that it was in these marginal zones that people found it necessary to seek more direct human control over their food supply. People began to keep near to the home base a few animals such as sheep, goats, dogs, and cattle, which had previously been hunted. This practice ensured a steady supply of meat as well as other useful products such as hides, milk, and milk products. By experimenting in how to plant seeds, people acquired grains as dietary supplements in areas where they had not been common previously.

Whatever the reasons for the growth of food domestication, by about 9000 B.C.

goats and sheep had been domesticated in the Near East, and barley and wheat were domesticated by 7000 B.C. in the same area. Cattle and pigs also were under human control by 7000 B.C. The domesticated grains differed from their wild relatives in that the crop domesticators favored larger seeds. As the seeds evolved to a larger size under human influence, the grain came to be more firmly attached to the stems and could no longer be harvested easily by shaking the stems over a basket. Thus, the domestication of grains required the simultaneous evolution of a new technology for use in the harvest, including knife-blades and sickles for cutting bunches of stems. Such tool kits were in use in the ancient Near East by 7000 B.C..

Early Towns

With the growing technology for food domestication, people who once had foraged in small nomadic bands soon began to settle down into more permanent encampments. Of the many large settled communities that developed rather quickly in the ancient Near East during the process of food domestication, three that have been excavated by archaeologists serve as good examples of what life was like in these early towns. They were Jarmo, Jericho, and Çatal Hüyük and seemed to share much in common, perhaps because of cultural contact among these early towns.

Jarmo

One of the best-known examples of early Near Eastern farming communities was at Jarmo in the hill country of Iraq. This early archaeological site dates from about 6750 to 6250 B.C. The site covered four acres but the habitation area itself was a cluster of about 50 huts, narrow alleyways, and courtyards. The population of Jarmo is estimated to have been from 150 to 300 people, who supported themselves by food production supplemented by a significant amount of collected wild foods.

The houses of the Jarmo settlement were multiroomed structures with hearths inside. These reed-roofed houses were often built on stone foundations and had walls plastered with mud. Grain was harvested with the aid of sickles, stored in silos, ground with stone mortars and pestles or on grinding slabs, and parched or cooked in ovens located outside the houses. Other artifacts found at the site include ground-stone axes or hoes and vessels, and chipped stone blades and burins (small stone chisel-like engraving tools). The people of Jarmo also used bone tools such as needles, pins, awls, pendants, beads, and round "napkin rings," whose function is unknown. Finally, there were anthropomorphic figurines of unbaked clay reminiscent of the great mother goddess of later times. Ceramic figurines and pottery were manufactured only in the latest periods of habitation at Jarmo. Domesticated animals probably included dogs and goats, possibly sheep, and, in later times, pigs.

Jarmo apparently had ties of trade with other areas. Archaeologists have found obsidian at Jarmo, which is not native to the area. The nearest source of obsidian was about 200 miles to the north. Seashells, which were probably used for decorative purposes, must have come to Jarmo from the Persian Gulf about 600 miles to the southeast.

Jericho

Another early town that left considerable archaeological evidence of its activities was Jericho. The site of the famous biblical town, it was excavated by Kathleen Kenyon (1957) in the 1950s. The earliest habitations at the site were clay-floored huts occupying about eight acres on soil just above the bedrock level near a spring. Burned remnants of the posts used to construct the huts were dated by the carbon-14 method at 7800 B.C., plus or minus 210 years. Over the generations, new dwellings were built on the debris left by earlier inhabitants. In more recent higher levels of the site, round houses were semisubterranean, with stone foundations and adobe walls. The roofs were domed, and they were plastered with mud as were the interior walls and floors. Eventually, the town covered nearly 10 acres and had perhaps as many as 3,000 residents. It was protected by a surrounding wall that was 6.5 feet wide at the base and

Figure 9.2 *Shrine at Catal Hüyük*
Wall paintings, plaster reliefs, animal heads and bull skulls decorate the interior of Catal Hüyük. Bull's horns were set into stylized heads of bulls or into benches and pillars and were thought to ward off evil.

12 feet high. The wall itself was surrounded by a ditch that was 27 feet wide and 9 feet deep. There was at least one stone lookout tower, the remains of which were still 30 feet high at the time it was excavated. This upper period of the settlement was dated at 6850 B.C., plus or minus 210 years.

There is some evidence of religious rituals among the people of Jericho, who often buried their dead beneath their dwellings. In at least some cases, skulls of the dead were removed, and the likeness of the deceased was carefully modelled onto them in clay. Cowrie shells were used to represent the eyes. Skulls of this kind were found buried separately in clusters.

The people of Jericho used serrated sickle blades to harvest grains and stone slabs for grinding them, but we lack evidence of exactly when agriculture began to be practiced. It is possible that in its early period this oasis settlement was supported by abundant wild grains, which were native to the area, and that the transition to plant domestication was a gradual one. There is some evidence that Jericho may have been set up as a fortified stopover on an ancient

trade route between areas to the north and south. Obsidian from as far away as the trade center Çatal Hüyük in Turkey has been found at Jericho.

Çatal Hüyük

Founded in what is now southern Turkey about 6500 B.C., the town of Çatal Hüyük survived until about 1900 B.C. (Mellaart, 1964). By 6450 B.C. the people of of this area were growing crops of barley, wheat, lentils, and peas. They wove cloth from the wool of domestic sheep. Their town was built of many windowless dwellings attached to one another by shared walls. Each dwelling was entered through an opening in the roof. This entrance also served as a smoke hole for the hearth and oven within. This construction made the dwelling complex into an easily defended structure of solid external walls that could be protected from the roofs.

Of 139 buildings excavated, 40 appear to have served as shrines. Clay cattle heads and statuettes of a great mother fertility goddess as well as a bearded male god seated on a bull were commonly found within the shrines. Painted murals on the white plastered walls of these shrines were occasionally renewed or replaced by replastering and painting a new mural. Scenes of life were painted in red on western walls and scenes of death in black on the walls to the east. A frequent death motif consisted of vultures devouring the flesh from decapitated corpses, possibly revealing something of the funerary customs of the people of Çatal Hüyük. The custom of allowing the body to be eaten by vultures still is practiced today by some peoples, such as the Parsis of India. After the body was eaten, the bones of the deceased were interred under the floors of dwellings. This practice and the removal of the head from the corpse are reminiscent of apparently similar rituals practiced hundreds of miles away at the site of Jericho.

Chiefdoms and States

Early communities participated in a well-developed network of trade and communication between far-flung areas. As these relations between neighboring groups intensified between 5000 and 3500 B.C., the world's first chiefdoms arose in Mesopotamia, the Southwest Asian region between the Tigris and Euphrates rivers (Flannery, 1972). To anthropologists, a chiefdom is a society that unites a number of villages under an incipient government. This government's authority is independent of family authority, but families still exercise a great deal of legal autonomy. Chiefdoms usually have differential social ranking of families and inherited political offices that often combine religious with secular authority.

It was in the period following 5000 B.C. that farming was carried down into the fertile river soil deposits of southern Mesopotamia. The soils were rich silts carried down the great valley system by the Tigris and Euphrates rivers, but the practice of agriculture here required the taming of the rivers. It was necessary to drain the overly wet soils to prevent flooding when the rivers were high and to irrigate the crops during the low-river period in the hot and dry summers (Service, 1975). The early farming inhabitants of this area began lay-

ing the foundations of irrigation by clearing natural river channels and digging small channels to water village crops. It was a natural step from there to increasing cooperation between neighboring groups to organize the work of digging larger and more efficient canal systems for drainage and irrigation. As the rivers were tamed, the governing agencies that coordinated the necessary labor gradually grew in power. Food surpluses, created and insured by a system of irrigation-based agriculture, added to the possibility of population growth and thereby to an even greater need for social control by governmental specialists. Chiefdoms continued to grow until about 3500 B.C., when they gave way to the even more specialized form of organization known as civilization.

During this period from 5000 to 3500 B.C., village specialization was common in Mesopotamia. A single village might specialize in the production of handsomely painted pottery or cold-hammered copper tools and trade them for the specialties of another village. Some settlements of this period had cobbled streets and wheeled chariots. Temple building, which began about 4500 B.C., was another trait of the period. Like the growing irrigation system, which probably involved higher-status labor organizations supervising lower-status workers, temple building suggests that there were full-time religious specialists of high status. The existence of inherited differences in rank is attested to more directly by variations in the material wealth present in burials, including the burial of statues and ornaments with some children. Burials of children whose rank was high enough for them to be more honored in death than were other children is particularly persuasive evidence of inherited differences in status, since, unlike adults, they would have had too little time to earn their distinguishing rank.

According to Wittfogel (1957), the upkeep of the canals and irrigation systems was directed by the temple priests, who were the first specialists who had managerial or administrative power. Towns were built around a central temple and marketplace. They had a redistributive economy con-

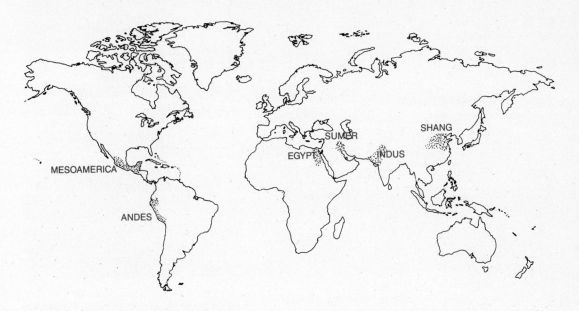

Figure 9.3 *The World's Early Civilizations*
This map illustrates the geographical areas of some early civilizations.

trolled by priests, who were in charge of the temple granary and supervised the temple weavers, clerks, and smiths. Other specialists were supported by the economic surpluses produced in the towns.

Eventually, some areas developed into states—political units in which centralized governments monopolize the right to exercise legal force and control the affairs of local communities—with power to levy taxes, pass laws, and draft people into work or war. Carniero (1970) has suggested that states arose in circumscribed environmental zones—zones surrounded by mountains, deserts, or other natural barriers to easy emigration—when population growth caused increased social competition for natural resources. This competition led to social stratification and the domination of some groups by others. Political centralization created powerful elites who were able to exact tribute and taxes from the dominated groups. Circumscribed habitats made it difficult for those who were losing in the competition to withdraw to other areas, since emigration to different kinds of environmental zones would have necessitated adopting different ways of making a living. According to Carniero (1979), once states developed they tended to expand at

the expense of less powerful neighboring peoples who lacked state organization.

Early Civilizations

It is generally held that by 3500 B.C. human society had crossed the threshold into the world's first civilization in southern Mesopotamia. This was followed shortly thereafter by similar developments in Egypt, India, China, and the Western Hemisphere. V. Gordon Childe (1950) has summarized the 10 fundamental characteristics of a civilization. They were generally present in all the world's earliest civilizations:

- population growth
- urbanization
- greatly increased full-time specialization of labor including nonsubsistence specialists such as specialists in trade
- long-distance trade in luxuries
- the emergence of class-stratification with a privileged ruling class of religious, political and military leaders
- the development of a political organization in which membership was based on place of residence rather than on kinship ties

Figure 9.4 *Ziggurat at Ur*
*The ziggurat, or temple tower, was the most prominent part of the temple compound in the Sumerian city at Ur.
On a massive base, 50 feet high, stand two successively smaller stages of which the uppermost served as a shrine.
About 270 feet high, it was intended to reach into heaven.*

- draft labor and monumental public works projects such as the building and maintenance of temples, palaces, storehouses, and irrigation systems
- the use of tribute and taxation to create a central store of surplus goods to support the process of social management
- the development of writing to facilitate the process of managing society (by helping in the necessary keeping of records of goods received and disbursed from the warehouses, and later, for the recording of laws, history, theology, and scientific ideas)
- the development of scientific techniques such as arithmetic, geometry, and astronomy that aided in the parcelling and allocation of agricultural land and in predictions regarding the agricultural cycle

The Sumerian state that developed in Mesopotamia was not alone as a center of civilization for long. The Egyptians achieved a centralized state-level government by about 3200 B.C. The Indus Valley of northwestern India was building planned cities by about 2500 B.C. Since some trade appeared to have existed between Sumer and these two areas, the stimulus for their move toward unified state-level governments may have been, at least in part, a response and adjustment to Sumerian influence. However, civilization seems most assuredly to have developed independently in at least two, perhaps three, other places in the world: in the Yellow River (Huangho) Valley of northern China by 1766 B.C., and in Central and South America by about 900 B.C..

Sumer

The civilization that arose in southern Mesopotamia about 3500 B.C. consisted of about a dozen independent city-states, cities that were organized around their own autonomous governments. The people of these various cities shared a common language and similar customs. Their society is known collectively as the civilization of Sumer. In the ideology of the people, each Sumerian city was the property of its own local god. The city was built around the temple of its god, which was set high on a step-pyramid or ziggurat (see Fig. 9.4). Scattered throughout the city were smaller satellite temples serving as storehouses for goods that the people tithed to their god for redistribution as needed in the name of the god. Cities were usually surrounded by a wall, with agricultural lands outside the

Figure 9.5 *City of Ur*
This diorama shows how religion dominated the life and architecture of the Sumerians at Ur. The plan of the city, with the ziggurat as its monumental nucleus, reflected the centrality of its god which was served as master.

walled area, and each city had several smaller satellite towns and hamlets that were economically and politically tied to it.

Sumerian government. The human government consisted of representatives of the god who owned the city. The god directed these representatives in how to manage the city. In other words, the government was a theocracy—political rule by religious leaders. The governing body was an assembly of elders and freemen who made decisions by discussing problems until a consensus was achieved. The assembly was presided over by a kind of city manager or governor of the god called an *ensi* who acted for the assembly or interpreted and carried out the commands of the god received through sacrificial divination or dreams. However, the *ensi* had no formal authority over other members of the assembly except during emergencies. Rather, in theory at least, the *ensi* was a kind of "first among equals" head of state.

In day-to-day matters, the *ensi* supervised the staff of the temple in which the god resided. This staff consisted of temple servants, diviners, musicians, temple prostitutes, and fieldworkers who cared for the crops in the god's fields. Temple lands were of three types: those that were worked to support the temple itself, those that were

worked to provide an income for the temple workers, and those that provided an income to support the official functions of the temple personnel. Land was allotted to citizens by the *ensi* for the god. A designated amount of what each allotment produced belonged to the god and was delivered to the temple storehouse for use by the state. The working family could then keep whatever was produced above this amount for its own use.

In times of crisis when strong, decisive leadership was needed, as in times of war between competing city-states, the *ensi* was given temporary authority to act as a commander-in-chief and give commands without consulting the assembly. Sometimes a temporary leader might be selected on the basis of his leadership and decision-making skills and installed as a temporary king or *lugal*, a name that literally meant "big man." At the end of the crisis, power would return to the hands of the more democratic assembly. With the passage of time, however, the *lugals* increased their power and influence based on their control of the military, so that over a period of about 400 years this Sumerian government was transformed from its earlier theocratic assembly form into a secular administration based on military power.

Politics in Sumerian City-States

Early Sumerian civilization was fragmented into many independent city-states, each with its own god and government. In the third millenium B.C., Sumerian government seems to have been relatively democratic, with decision-making power divided between a council of elders, the military, and the king, who was both head of state and commander-in-chief. The specific balance of power probably differed from city to city and from time to time depending on the circumstances and personalities involved. Certainly, the debates, politicking, and power plays that occur in contemporary governments were not foreign to ancient Sumer, as attested by some interesting historical documents.

Samuel Noah Kramer (1957) has translated and discussed some of the records of Sumer's political life. One of these records describes a war of nerves between the city of Kish, the traditionally paramount city of early Sumer, and the city of Erech, which came to rival Kish in power. In 2800 B.C., Agga, the ruler of Kish, threatened Erech with war unless its people acknowledged him as overlord. Gilgamesh, the greatest of Erech's kings who also was called the lord of Kullab, convened an assembly of elders to approve his wish to resist the dominance of Kish. In the words of the Sumerian scribe, as recounted by Kramer (1957, p. 32):

> The envoys of Agga, the son of
>   Enmebaraggesi,
> Proceeded from Kish to Gilgamesh in
>   Erech.
> The lord Gilgamesh before the elders of
>   his city
> Put the matter, seeks out the word:
> "Let us not submit to the house of Kish,
>   let us smite it with weapons."
> The convened assembly of the elders of
>   his city
> Answers Gilgamesh:
> "Let us submit to the house of Kish, let
>   us not smite it with weapons."

However, Gilgamesh was not satisfied with the counsel of the elders. To bol-ster his position, he convened the young fighting men for support:

> Gilgamesh, the lord of Kullab,
> Who performs heroic deeds for the god-
>   dess Inanna,
> Took not the words of the elders of his
>   city to heart.
> A second time Gilgamesh, the lord of
>   Kullab,
> Before the fighting men of his city put
>   the matter, seeks out the word:
> "Do not submit to the house of Kish, let
>   us smite it with weapons."
> The convened assembly of the fighting
>   men of his city
> Answers Gilgamesh:
> "Do not submit to the house of Kish, let
>   us smite it with weapons."
> Then Gilgamesh, the lord of Kullab,
> At the word of the fighting men of his
>   city his heart rejoiced, his spirit
>   brightened.

After pitting the hawks against the doves, Gilgamesh had his way, and the war was begun. The view of the prevailing side might be summed up by the 5,000-year-old Sumerian proverb, "The state weak in armaments—the enemy will not be driven from its gates" (Kramer, 1957, p. 125), an idea still expressed by some contemporary governmental figures. Erech won the war and became the dominant power in the region.

The people of Erech prospered politically under Gilgamesh, but his conquests also had their costs. The Sumerians also had a proverb that expressed the dangers of a ruler who exercised too much power: "You can have a lord, you can have a king, but the man to fear is the 'governor'!" (Kramer, 1957, p. 126). Gilgamesh was a tyrant. He drafted men and set them to work rebuilding the walls of the city, fought wars, caroused so wantonly that he "left no virgin to her lover," and so oppressed his people that they prayed to the gods for help. Perhaps their prayers were answered, for Gilgamesh finally wearied of conquest and worldly pursuits and departed the city on a quest for the tree of life that would give him immortality.

Sumerian religion. By about 3000 B.C., the Sumerians had developed a system of writing. Since they recorded their laws, their history, their customs, and especially their religion, we know a great deal about the Sumerians today (see Jacobson, 1946, 1948; Kramer, 1959; Moscati, 1962). We know, for instance, that Sumerian religion included a pantheon of many gods. Some were creators and rulers, others controllers of major forces and features of the world. The pantheon was presided over by a triad of creating deities: An, the god of the heavens beyond the dome of the sky; Enlil, the god of the air between the sky canopy and the earth; and Enki or Ea, the god of wisdom who presided over the great primeval waters on which the world was believed to float.

Next in prominence among the creating deities came Ninmah, the Exalted Lady, who was the Sumerian great mother goddess, the equivalent of Mother Earth. Her original name was Ki, Earth, and she was the consort of An. She was the mother of all living things and gave birth to human beings by fashioning them from clay. Humans were created so that the gods would have someone to serve them, bring them sacrifices and offerings of food and drink, and provide them with well-kept temples in which to dwell. In Sumerian belief, humans existed so that the gods might be freed from the labors of life.

Below the creating deities were those who did not create but who presided over the great forces and features of the universe, such as the sun, the moon, fertility, and warfare. Even lower were a multitude of demons, most of whom were evil. These roamed the earth and caused illness, plagues, and other misfortunes among human beings. The demons were not worshipped, but people attempted to counteract their harmful influence by magical rituals and exorcisms.

At death, the spirits of human beings departed to an underworld abode ruled by Ereshkegal, god of the dead, and guarded by a divine gate-keeper, a deity of the great river of the underworld that spirits had to cross before entering the kingdom of the dead, and ferrymen who helped them across. In the underworld, spirits of the departed led a dreary existence similar to but not so pleasant as life among mortals.

Historical shifts in power. As Sumerian cities grew in size, their need for agricultural lands increased, and competition between cities was magnified. This competition often escalated to open warfare and the conquest of one city by another. Over the centuries, minor empires were established only to fall when they were superseded by more powerful rivals. By about 2370 B.C. the center of Mesopotamian power had shifted from the southern end of the valley to the north, beyond the original boundaries of Sumer. A Semitic king, Sargon of Agade, rose to prominence and controlled much of the valley. By 2000 B.C. the cities of Sumer had achieved populations of a quarter of a million and more.

Babylon became the ruling city of all Mesopotamia about 1990 B.C. The impact of the Babylonians was felt throughout the Near East until they, in turn, were superseded by the Assyrians of northern Mesopotamia in about 900 B.C. In 612 B.C. the Babylonians overthrew Assyrian rule, but the final dominance of Babylon lasted only until 538 B.C. when it was conquered by Persians to the east of Mesopotamia.

Egypt

As the fortunes of the Sumerian city-states were rising and falling, another civilization was developing in Egypt. The earliest dated remains of a farming community in Egypt are west of the Nile from a lake area known as the Fayum (Caton-Thompson & Gardner, 1934; Johnson, 1979). The community has been dated at 5200 B.C. The farmers of the Fayum grew crops of wheat and flax and raised sheep, goats, cattle, and pigs. Their food domestication spread to the Nile itself, a river that flooded annually and laid down new layers of rich silt that the farming communities could readily use. By about 3700 B.C. there were large farming settlements on the flood plain of the Nile. Egyptian society at this time consisted of numerous small villages, called nomes, scattered mostly along the banks of the Nile. Each nome had a small temple and its own independent government. These

Figure 9.6 *Great Bath of Mohenjo-Daro*
The late third- and early second-millennia B.C. architectural remains such as the Great Bath in the Indus River Valley of Mohenjo-Daro suggest a modern commercial center with major avenues along a north-south orientation, streets as wide as 40 feet, multi-storied houses of fired brick and wood, and an elaborate drainage system.

Nile Delta communities were working with copper and silver by 3400 B.C. By 3300 B.C. they apparently were trading with Mesopotamia.

Around 3200 B.C. Egypt was united under a single government when the northern lowlands were conquered by occupants of the southern regions. Beginning about 3100 B.C. several innovations seem to have been imported from Sumer: monumental architecture of mud bricks, Sumerian art motifs, cylinder seals (engraved cylinders used to roll an impression on wet clay), and the idea of writing.

The famous pyramids of Egypt were built during the early period of Egyptian civilization. The largest pyramids were built during the first three dynasties, from about 2750 to 2350 B.C. The well-known Great Pyramid of Giza is made of about 2.3 million stones, weighing an average of over two tons each. It was built about 2600 B.C., taking about 20 years to erect. Mendelssohn (1974) believes that the building of the pyramids served the purpose of providing the people with work during the annual three-month flood season, while at the same time helping the government to create a centrally controlled economy in which local villages became more and more economically dependent on the government.

The ruler of Egypt was a divine king, believed to be a god. He was served by a vast bureaucracy of priests and tax collectors and an army of as many as 20,000 soldiers. The welfare of the land was believed to be dependent on the welfare of the divine king. His life, therefore, was carefully hedged about by tradition and ritual, which ruled his daily schedule in minute detail. In death, his remains were carefully embalmed and preserved in the massive pyramid erected during his lifetime or, in later times, in a mortuary temple.

India

In India, people were practicing farming by 3500 B.C. and possibly as early as 7500 B.C. (Hammond, 1973; Singh, 1971; Wheeler, 1968). Their crops included wheat, barley, peas, and the earliest domesticated cotton, which is likely to have been an important item of trade to other areas. Domesticated animals included cattle, water buffalo, asses, horses, and camels. An urban civilization known as the Indus Valley or Harappa civilization was developed between the subcontinent of India and the borders of present-day Iran by about 2500 B.C. (Fairservice, 1975; Wheeler, 1968). Since the 1920s, almost 1,000 sites have been found within the boundaries of the Indus Valley civilization, but it is best known from two great planned cities, Harappa and Mohenjo-daro. Each of these cities had a large fortified citadel and precincts of smaller houses along streets that formed rectangular blocks. Kiln-dried bricks were used in building, and there were a system of writing, standardized weights and measures, a ruling elite, and widespread trade.

The Indus civilization, like those of Mesopotamia and Egypt, had a system of writing, but it apparently was used only for keeping economic and ownership records and not for recording literature or histories. This writing occurs mostly on small soapstone and clay seals that also contain carvings of domestic and wild animals and people. These may have been used as stamps to mark items of trade. Some writing also occurs on pottery. The Indus Valley script, which is believed to record a language of the early Dravidian inhabitants of the area, is only now beginning to be deciphered (Fairservice, 1983). It gives suggestions of a society with well-defined social classes including governing leaders called chiefs, heads of guilds such as coppersmiths, overseers of warehouses, irrigation supervisors, landowners, drummers, and singers. Translations of the Indus Valley script also suggest a society in which kinship groups were still important. Lineages were associated with the sun, moon, stars, and possibly with the monsoon rains, and these in turn may have been subdivisions of larger groups such as clans. The clans of Indus Valley society also may have been divided into two major groups each with reciprocal rights and duties, such as marriage rights or economic obligations. There is much left to learn about the native Dravidian civilization of India as archaeological work proceeds and as the Indus Valley script continues to be deciphered.

The Indus civilization achieved its heights by 1900 B.C., when it covered a territory that extended 1,000 miles from north to south. Economic decline culminates in the abandonment of Mohenjo-daro by about 1700 B.C. This decline continued throughout the Indus Valley until about 1500 B.C., when the civilization ceased to exist as a unified culture. The causes of the decline of the Indus Valley civilization may have included deforestation and climatic changes. There is evidence from pollen studies that the territory was drying out from about 1800

B.C. (Singh, 1971). This period of decline also was one during which immigrants were moving into the region from the northwest. These immigrants, known as the Aryans, also may have contributed to the economic and political disruptions of the period. The Rig-Veda, the oldest surviving literature of the Aryans, includes reference to their conquest of large native cities of the Indus Valley area.

China

In China, farming began about 2500 B.C., with rice being the major domestic crop (Chang, 1977). Villages were fortified for defense of the inhabitants. Specialization and social stratification developed as the population grew. There is evidence of jade work, pottery making, and ritual practices such as divination by examining cracks formed on animal shoulder blades when they were heated. Just before 1850 B.C., Chinese civilization began in the lower Huangho (Yellow) River Valley and spread into other parts of China. The Chinese in these civilizations manufactured bronze artifacts, invented a calendar, and devised a system of writing from symbols on oracle bones that were used for divination by priests. The nobility was deeply concerned with ancestor worship, and the ruler, a god-king, served as intermediary between the people and the royal ancestors and the supreme god, Shang Ti. Palaces and temples were built under the nobles' direction.

The Chinese nobility controlled a standing army and carried out extensive trade. The society had numerous specialized statuses, ranked classes, and slavery. The kingdom was divided into several small feudal states, each comprising up to 40 towns ruled by a noble appointed by the king. The Chinese appear to have independently invented the craft of metalworking, and their bronze work reveals a distinctive major art tradition featuring mythological animals, such as the dragon, that remained characteristic of Chinese art until recent times.

The Western Hemisphere

As in China, the rise to civilization in the Western Hemisphere also was a long and gradual process, evolving independently of

Figure 9.7A *Artifact of LaVenta*
This jade figure of a priest holding a jaguar baby is typical of Olmec sculpture. Numerous figures combining the features of a human infant and a jaguar have been found, suggesting this creature was important in the Olmec pantheon.

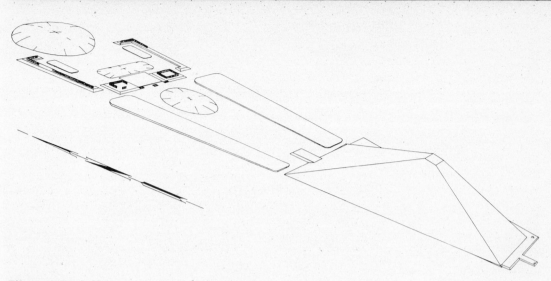

Figure 9.7B *LaVenta*
LaVenta was the heartland of the Olmec civilization. It was a ceremonial center with earthen platforms and columns of basalt marking out two large courtyards. Facing out from the courtyard were four huge human heads sculpted of basalt.

other early civilizations. Mexican foragers had domesticated squashes and avocados by 6700 B.C. (MacNeish, 1964). During the period from 6700 to 5000 B.C. they also were collecting wild beans, chili, the high-protein grain amaranth, and maize, the wild ancestor of modern cultivated corn. Corn, amaranth, and a variety of squashes and beans were domesticated between 5000 and 3500 B.C. By 3400 B.C. about one third of the food of these people was cultivated. They first produced pottery around 2300 B.C. Irrigation did not develop until about 700 B.C.

The Olmec civilization. The earliest American civilization may have arisen along the Gulf of Mexico. It was in existence by 1500 B.C., although it may have begun before that. These peoples, called today the Olmec, developed a calendar, their own system of writing, and a distinctive art tradition with a strong emphasis on jaguar motifs and portrayals of pudgy infants with claws and jaguar fangs. The Olmec had no cities, but they built impressive ceremonial centers surrounded by satellite villages. The largest such center, La Venta, was an island in a lowland swamp. It included a large pyramid and a series of smaller mounds, walled plazas, and carved stone pillars. The main pyramid alone is estimated by Michael Coe (1977) to have taken the equivalent of 800,000 human work days to

erect and involved transporting stone blocks, some over 40 tons in weight, onto the island from a location about 60 miles away (see Fig. 9.7). There is some disagreement among anthropologists over whether the Olmec represented a complex chiefdom or a true state-level society. In either case, the Olmec developed many of the important traits of civilization.

The Olmec expanded out of their heartland into the Maya lands of Guatemala and also founded colonies in the Valley of Mexico. Their civilization seems to have ended in their homeland area around 500 B.C., but their presence in the outposts in Guatemala and Mexico continued and may have stimulated the rise of those two areas to civilization. Like the Olmec, the Maya did not build cities, concentrating instead on erecting elaborate ceremonial centers surrounded by outlying hamlets. However, neighboring peoples influenced by the Olmec began to erect true cities in the Valley of Mexico at least 200 B.C., eventually eclipsing the Olmec influence in the area.

Teotihuacan. The most prominent of the pre-Columbian cities was Teotihuacan, northeast of what is now Mexico City. Beginning as a village of a few hundred inhabitants about 400 B.C., it became the dominant center of Mexico around A.D. 500 and even extended its power and influence

Figure 9.8 *Teotihuacán*
This "place of the gods" was laid out so that all of its temples were in symmetrical groups flanking a broad avenue. The pyramidal substructures that once supported a temple consisted of five tiers and one broad stairway alternately single and double, leading from the ground level to the top.

into the Mayan area which it dominated until about A.D. 650. According to Michael Coe (1977), Teotihuacan had at its height a population of 150,000 to 200,000 people (see Fig. 9.8). The ceremonial precinct was an impressive planned center with colorful buildings along a four-mile-long concourse known as the Avenue of the Dead that passed the 210-foot-high Pyramid of the Sun and ended at the famous Pyramid of the Moon. This route was bisected at its midpoint by another four-mile-long east-west avenue (Millon, 1973).

The priesthood of Teotihuacan seems to have been quite powerful, and it surely had great influence in the political affairs of its society. Wall paintings depict priests and gods in bright colors. The two major gods who were emphasized in the art of Teotihuacan were Tlaloc, the god of water, and Quetzalcoatl, creator of humans. The heaven of Tlaloc was depicted as a happy place where spirits of departed human beings were portrayed as singing, playing children's games, and chasing butterflies. The art of Teotihuacan lacked the militaristic emphasis of the art of later Middle American societies. The power and influence of the city over surrounding areas beyond the Valley of Mexico, therefore, may have resulted more from its role as an economic and religious center than as a dominating military power.

It is believed that the population pressure of having 200,000 people living in the same valley led to the decline of Teotihuacan. This large population became difficult to support by farming the surrounding valley. Economic competition with other regions may have added to the problems of Teotihuacan. Immigrants from the north also compounded the difficulties, and about A.D. 700, revolts among the Mayan people to the far south were successful. Teotihuacan was forced to retrench and withdraw its colonial influence to deal with the growing problems at home. In A.D. 750, the city of Teotihuacan was attacked and destroyed, leaving no unifying force among the civilized cities of Middle America.

Toltec and Aztec civilizations. A 200-year Dark Age period ensued with local city-states vying for power until a new dominant city arose. This new city, Tula, was located north of the Valley of Mexico. In A.D. 950 it became the capital city of the Toltec, an extremely warlike and militaristic people. The Toltec continued to spread their influence until they dominated most of Central America. Then in A.D. 1160, they in turn were overthrown. Almost two centuries later, the Aztecs rose to dominance in the Valley of Mexico, where they founded their famous capital, Tenochtitlan, in A.D. 1344 or 1345 at the site of present-day Mexico City. The Aztecs expanded their empire throughout Central America and ruled until their conquest by the Spanish in A.D. 1521.

Civilizations in the Andes. The final area of possible independent evolution of early civilization was in the Andes of South America. In the central Andes of Peru, beans were domesticated as early as 5600 B.C., followed by cotton, chili peppers, peanuts, manioc, and potatoes. The llama also was domesticated and used as a pack animal in the Peruvian area about this time. Later, the alpaca came under domestication as a source of wool. Between 4000 B.C. and 3500 B.C., peoples along the coast of Peru at a site called Pampas were supplementing their seafood diet with domestically grown squash. Between 3600 B.C. and 3200 B.C., gourds, guavas, chili peppers, and cotton were being cultivated at other coastal sites. From 2500 B.C. to 1800 B.C., temples and pyramids were being built and settlements were growing in size.

In the Andes highlands, food domestication occurred somewhat later than on the coasts. The earliest highland food domestication was at the site of Kotash in the eastern highlands of the Andes, a site that was built at least 2000 B.C. There is direct evidence of domesticated llamas, and it is believed that agriculture also would have been necessary to support the people who lived there. The site includes a masonry temple. Around 1800 B.C., pottery appeared.

About 900 B.C., features appeared in northern Peru that suggest a civilization: metalworking, temples on raised stone plat-forms in ceremonial centers surrounded by farming villages, and a distinctive art style that emphasized snake and jaguar motifs. In the latter, some have seen a potential Olmec influence in South America. The introduction at this time of maize of possible Mexican origin is in harmony with this possibility. This culture, known as Chavin, spread rapidly, and by 800 B.C. it extended over a large part of Peru.

By 200 B.C., the Chavin culture had improved agriculture by the expansion of irrigation projects to a size that would have required cooperation between several communities both to construct and to maintain. Temples were built that could have served more than a single community. The size of some of these religious edifices is striking, attesting to the power that the religious bureaucracy must have exercised. The political power of government must have rested largely in the hands of religious rather than purely secular authorities, since there is little evidence of military activity or fortifications. Particularly in the early years of the Chavin culture, this religious system seems to have emphasized the worship of a feline god, a striking yet perhaps coincidental similarity to the religion of the Olmec.

By 200 B.C., towns and various states existed in the Andean area, especially in the coastal valleys. States that at first dominated single valleys began to expand into neighboring areas. This growth first occurred in the north coastal area of Moche, from which the Mochican state expanded from A.D. 200 to about A.D. 1000 to encompass several valleys. Similar developments occurred in other coastal regions.

Around A.D. 500, the people began terracing the steep mountain slopes, and the increase in grains produced by this innovation led to rapid population growth. The development of a new local grain, quinoa, which is capable of growing at much higher altitudes than corn, accompanied this population expansion.

True urban centers began to grow up after A.D. 600 in the Andes. Around A.D. 800, the highlands saw the rise of the first Peruvian empire based on warfare, trade, and imposition of religious beliefs on conquered

Figure 9.9 *Machu Picchu*
Here, high in the Andes, lived the ancient Incas. Their architecture was famous for its dry-masonry techniques executed with extreme precision. These stones were sometimes laid horizontally, but more unusually, in a polygonal pattern.

peoples. This empire spread from Huari in the highlands and extended its influence by trade even into the southern coastal regions. Huari and other competing highland empires manifested increasingly secular and militaristic characteristics.

By A.D. 1300, the highland empires were in decline, and three major coastal states had risen to prominence. One of these, that of the Chimu, spread its planned walled cities into impressive empires from their principal city of Chan Chan, a city that covered at least ten square miles and had at least nine major walled precincts. The Chimu built an impressive network of highways between their cities and used these to expedite trade and the administration of their empire.

The final and dominant empire of the Andes was that of the Inca, who founded their society in A.D. 1200 and expanded by military conquest until they controlled most of Peru, Bolivia, and Ecuador as well as parts of Argentina and Chile. Governing six million people, the Inca emperors, divine rulers who claimed descent from the sun god, maintained one of the most strictly controlled societies the world has known. An elaborate bureaucracy controlled all of the society's labor and the flow of goods. Farmers, for instance, were allocated land based on their family needs and their productivity in the previous year. One third of their produce went to the state for use by the state religion. A second third was delivered to the state for secular purposes, such as road building, support of the military, and redistribution to widows and other needy. Farmers were permitted to use the final third of their produce for their own families. Messengers tied all parts of the vast empire to the capital, Cuzco, which was ruled by a divine monarch, the Inca, who was regarded as a direct descendant of the sun god.

The civilization of the Inca, impressive as

it was, lacked written records throughout its history. Its only notation system was the use of *quipus*, series of knotted cords that were used as memory aids in recording bookkeeping information such as the flow of goods into and out of the state storehouses (see Fig. 9.9).

When the Spaniards arrived in Peru in 1532, the Incan empire was in the midst of a bloody civil war between two sons of the previous emperor. Aided by the chaos of this civil strife and the support of outlying disgruntled factions who wished to throw off their Cuzco rulers, the Spaniards ended the most impressive empire of South America.

Archaeology: The Controlled Destruction of a Site

An archaeological site is a record of how people lived in the past. It contains valuable information that archaeologists wish to make part of our historical knowledge. There are many ways in which this information can be lost. Natural processes can take their toll: Wind, rain, ice, lightning-induced fires, or flash floods can destroy an archaeological site. But human influences damage the record of our past at an even greater rate. Archaeological sites may be bulldozed into nonexistence during the construction of a road or building. They may be covered by the lake created by a new dam. The Olmec site of La Venta is now an oil refinery. Losses to the process of technological development have been minimized in some countries by the cooperation of government and industry in efforts to recover archaeological data before the destruction of a site. In the United States, laws now require that the effects of development on archaeological resources be considered before building is undertaken on public lands.

More dramatic is the impact of deliberate vandalism. Archaeological sites of tremendous public interest been destroyed with increasing frequency in the United States in recent years. For instance, one of the most impressive prehistoric Native American rock art murals in the United States, a mural created at least 600 years ago in Butler Wash, Utah, has been severely damaged on two occasions by vandals using spray paint to cover the original paintings. Elsewhere, a brisk illegal trade in prehistoric artifacts still flourishes despite the efforts of many governments. For instance, remains of ancient Mayan artifacts not yet examined by professional archaeologists have been hacked apart by looters for sale on an international underground market.

Even the excavation of a prehistoric site by professional archaeologists destroys that site. However, there is an immense difference between the trained archaeological excavator and the "pothunter" who removes artifacts from their original location without regard to the information that is lost in doing so. Archaeologists proceed carefully and systematically to record the precise location of every artifact uncovered at a site, noting its relationship to other things around it, both natural and artificial. The archaeologist is as interested in a stain in the soil indicating the remains of an ancient fire pit or posthole as in the artifacts themselves. Grains of pollen in the soil, fragmentary bones of animals, or the charred remains of a fire may reveal much about the foods eaten, the uses of the artifacts, or the age of the material being excavated. An archaeological excavation is preceded by a careful survey of the site and methodical selection of the parts of the site to be excavated to gain the greatest amount of information with the least disturbance of the site. Detailed records are kept of everything done while the work is carried out. Even so, the archaeologist of today is likely to leave significant parts of a site untouched, knowing that techniques developed a decade or so in the future may be used to learn even more about the site if the entire site is not excavated today.

Figure 9.10 *Butler Washington*
Site of an impressive prehistoric Native American rock art mural, A, the view in B shows how vandals have destroyed this archaeological site by spray painting.

Summary

As humanity spread across the globe, it also developed ways of domesticating plants and animals to increase the amount of food that could be produced within a settled area. Organized settlements began with the early towns of Jarmo, Jericho, and Çatal Hüyük in the Near East. Population growth and specialization gradually led to the formation of chiefdoms and in some cases, states.

These centralized, socially stratified civilizations were able to carry on trade, monumental building projects, and war against neighboring peoples. The earliest examples of civilization appeared in Sumer, spreading to Egypt and India. Somewhat later, civilization developed independently in China and the Americas.

Key Terms and Concepts

food domestication 222
foraging 222
sedentarism 223
chiefdom 226
states 227
civilization 227
city-states 228
Sumer 228
ziggurat 228
theocracy 229
ensi 229
lugal 229
the Fayum 231
nomes 231
Indus Valley (Harappa) civilization 232
Harappa 232
Mohenjo-daro 232
Dravidians 233
Aryans 233
Rig-Veda 233

Huangho (Yellow) River Valley civilization 233
oracle bones 233
Olmec 235
La Venta 235
Maya 235
Teotihuacan 235
Tula 237
Toltec 237
Aztec 237
Tenochtitlan 237
Kotash 237
Chavin 237
Moche 237
quinoa 237
Huari 238
Chimu 238
Chan Chan 238
Inca 238
Cuzco 238
quipus 239

Annotated Readings

Adams, R. McC. (1966). *The evolution of urban society.* Chicago: Aldine. An analysis of the factors that may have led to the rise of cities in Mesopotamia and ancient Mexico.

Cohen, M. N. (1977). *The food crisis in prehistory.* New Haven, CT: Yale University Press. A discussion of the archaeological evidence for the role of population growth on the rise of agriculture in both the Eastern and Western hemispheres.

Cohen, R., and Service, E. R. (Eds.). (1978). *Origins of the state: The anthropology of political evolution.* Philadelphia, PA: Institute for the Study of Human Issues. Papers expressing various points of view about the origins of states.

Fagan, B. M. (1974). *Men of the earth: An introduction to world prehistory.* Boston, MA: Little,
Brown. A highly readable story of prehistory through the rise of civilization.

Jennings, J. D. (1974). *Prehistory of North America* (2nd ed.). New York: McGraw-Hill. An authoritative introduction to the North American past as revealed by archaeological research.

Kramer, S. N. (1963). *The Sumerians: Their history, culture and character.* Chicago: University of Chicago Press. Sumerian culture, based on an analysis of Sumerian writings.

Lamberg-Karlovsky, C. C., & Sabloff, J. A. (1979). *Ancient civilizations: The Near East and Mesoamerica.* Menlo Park, CA: Benjamin-Cummings Publishing Company. Illustrates the parallels in the rise of civilizations in Sumer, Egypt, the Indus Valley, and Mexico.

Chapter 10

The Process
of Cultural Evolution

Human cultural systems do not remain forever stable. In adjusting to the world around them, to the effects of population growth, and to the influence of other groups, human beings adopt new and different ways of manipulating their environment, of organizing themselves, and of thinking and communicating. As we saw in Chapter 9, cultural systems, over the millennia, have evolved from simple hunting and gathering ways of life to extremely complex ways of living based upon industrialized technologies. In addition to that historical picture of cultural evolution we can also reconstruct the process of cultural evolution on the basis of evidence provided us by the contemporary diversity of human cultural systems, the end product of their evolution. In this chapter we will explore the process of cultural change, the levels of cultural complexity, and the rules that govern movement toward greater complexity. The chapter ends with the question of whether technological progress is linked with progress in the psychological quality of life.

The Process of Change

Cultural traits are subject to many change-promoting influences, both internal and external. As one trait changes, others also shift, ultimately altering the nature of the entire cultural system.

Initial Cultural Change

No culture is completely static. Cultural changes may arise within a society, or they may result from the cultural influence of one society on another.

Innovations that arise within a society are of two types: discoveries and inventions. A discovery involves noticing something that has not been noticed before. Discoveries are made, of course, on the basis of what the current cultural pattern of thinking prepares people in the society to notice in their environment. Although they must be new and different from previous ideas, they must not depart too radically from the current way of thinking or they will seem bizarre. In such a case they will not be accepted. In a culture with a high degree of role specializa-

Figure 10.1 *Yąnomamö
Archer
The Yąnomamö, a fierce
tribe in the jungles of
Brazil, have so far resisted
the effects of twentieth-
century culture.*

Figure 10.2 *Diffusion*
One method of a society's cultural influence on another is that of diffusion. In this instance an Inuit woman shops for food at the Hudson Bay Store in Coral Harbour, Northwest Territory.

tion, it is possible for some members of society to have experiences that are so uncommon in society at large that the insights that they produce will be regarded as insignificant, foolish, or of no practical use. Gregor Mendel, a nineteenth-century Austrian monk, spent years cultivating plants and in the process developed revolutionary new ideas about genetics that were shelved for years. It was only much later that growing interest in evolutionary theory among biologists provided a place where Mendel's discoveries proved to be very useful and enlightening to the scientific community. Similarly, inventions, which might most simply be defined as putting previous cultural elements together in some new way, must be seen as valuable in terms of the prior values of a way of life or they will not be adopted by a people.

Cultural changes that occur as a result of the influence of one society on another are referred to as diffusion, the passage of a cultural trait from one society to another. Anthropologists generally distinguish between two forms of diffusion: direct borrowing of

traits and stimulus diffusion, in which the idea of the trait rather than the trait itself passes from one people to another. In both cases, the trait is likely to be modified in form, use, and meaning as it diffuses from one culture to another. Such adjustments allow it to fit into the ongoing way of life of the recipient society. But the greatest changes in a trait are likely to occur when the idea is borrowed and then the trait is created anew on the basis of the idea in the borrowing society.

Tobacco provides an example of changes in a directly borrowed trait. It was originally commonly used as an important religious ritual item in the Native American cultures. It was borrowed from one society to another until it is now found in all parts of the world. In the process, both the crop and methods of its preparation have been greatly modified. It is now used in many parts of the world as what might be called a recreational substance, smoked for enjoyment rather than for religious reasons (Linton, 1936). The development of writing in Egypt also illustrates how the form of a trait may be changed when it is borrowed. It is believed by many that the development of writing in Egypt was the result of stimulus diffusion from Mesopotamia, with transmission of the idea of writing rather than use of the actual visual symbols of Mesopotamia for portraying the Egyptian language. Entirely new pictorial forms were chosen.

When two or more cultures interact intensely so that they change in the process of adjusting to each other, anthropologists term the adjustments acculturation. In acculturation, two previously different cultures become more and more like each other. In general, when a society that controls a great amount of power interacts with one of much less power, the less powerful society is likely to change more than the more powerful society. The general long-term effects of the interaction of societies of unequal power have been formulated by David Kaplan (1960) as the Law of Cultural Dominance: "That cultural system which more effectively exploits the energy resources of a given environment will tend to spread in the environment at the expense

Cherokee Alphabet.

Ꭰ a	Ꭱ e	Ꭲ i	Ꭳ o	Ꭴ u	Ꭵ v
Ꭶ ga Ꭷ ka	Ꭸ ge	Ꭹ gi	Ꭺ go	Ꭻ gu	Ꭼ gv
Ꭽ ha	Ꭾ he	Ꭿ hi	Ꮀ ho	Ꮁ hu	Ꮂ hv
Ꮃ la	Ꮄ le	Ꮅ li	Ꮆ lo	Ꮇ lu	Ꮈ lv
Ꮉ ma	Ꮊ me	Ꮋ mi	Ꮌ mo	Ꮍ mu	
Ꮎ na Ꮏ hna Ꮐ nah	Ꮑ ne	Ꮒ ni	Ꮓ no	Ꮔ nu	Ꮕ nv
Ꮖ qua	Ꮗ que	Ꮘ qui	Ꮙ quo	Ꮚ quu	Ꮛ quv
Ꮜ sa Ꮝ s	Ꮞ se	Ꮟ si	Ꮠ so	Ꮡ su	Ꮢ sv
Ꮣ da Ꮤ ta	Ꮥ de Ꮦ te	Ꮧ di Ꮨ ti	Ꮩ do	Ꮪ du	Ꮫ dv
Ꮬ dla Ꮭ tla	Ꮮ tle	Ꮯ tli	Ꮰ tlo	Ꮱ tlu	Ꮲ tlv
Ꮳ tsa	Ꮴ tse	Ꮵ tsi	Ꮶ tso	Ꮷ tsu	Ꮸ tsv
Ꮹ wa	Ꮺ we	Ꮻ wi	Ꮼ wo	Ꮽ wu	Ꮾ wv
Ꮿ ya	Ᏸ ye	Ᏹ yi	Ᏺ yo	Ᏻ yu	Ᏼ yv

Sounds represented by Vowels

a, as a in father, or short as a in rival
e, as a in hate, or short as e in met
i, as i in pique, or short as i in pit
o, as aw in law, or short as o in not.
u, as oo in fool, or short as u in pull.
v, as u in but, nasalized.

Consonant Sounds

g nearly as in English, but approaching to k. d nearly as in English but approaching to t. h k l m n q s t w y. as in English. Syllables beginning with g. except Ꭶ have sometimes the power of k. Ꭺ Ꮝ Ꮆ are sometimes sounded to, tu, tv. and Syllables written with tl except Ꮭ sometimes vary to dl.

Sequoyah's alphabet, or syllabary, for writing Cherokee.
Smithsonian Institution.

Figure 10.3 *Cherokee Alphabet*
Language is fundamental to acquiring, storing and communicating knowledge and thus is crucial to the development of culture. Sequoia, the Cherokee chief, developed this alphabet for his tribe.

of less effective systems.'' Any interacting cultures have some effect on each other. But, since more traits flow from the dominant to the subordinate culture, the latter is the one more likely to be radically altered—if it survives the effects of contact with the more powerful society at all.

The Law of Cultural Dominance is not an invariable process. Cultures differ in their receptivity to acculturation on the basis of their degree of evolutionary adaptation. Some technologically simple societies have been remarkably resistant to the effects of cultural change at the hands of more powerful societies. Ruth Benedict (1934) pointed out long ago that the Pueblo Indians have had a long history of rather successful resistance to the effects of cultural traits of neighboring peoples. Nevertheless, in the general evolutionary scheme, societies with greater technological control over energy resources have fairly consistently expanded while technologically simple societies are becoming fewer each year.

Interrelationships Among Technology, Social Organization, and Ideology

Change may begin within any aspect of culture but is likely to then affect other aspects as well. The major goals of culture-guided behaviors are manipulation of the external environment (through technology), social interaction (the role of social organization), and symbolic expression of internal experiences (through ideology). These three major subsystems of culture—technology, social organization, and ideology—are related, and change within any one will affect the others (see Fig. 10.5).

Evolution through technological change. Technology—the means by which energy is drawn from the environment and used within a society—is considered by some anthropologists to be the area most likely to be the leading edge of cultural change. Leslie White formalized this idea as the Basic Law of Cultural Evolution: ''Other factors remaining constant, culture evolves as the amount of energy harnessed per capita per year is increased, or as the efficiency of the technological means of putting the energy

to work is increased'' (1949, pp. 368–369). Due to the extreme reliance of humans on tools to maintain life, changes in the tool kit of a society have profound effects on the nature of the society itself and on a people's understanding of the world.

The most immediate point of influence of technological change on the social organization occurs in the economy, for its structure determines the division of labor in the production and distribution of subsistence goods. Population size is affected too: The more effective a subsistence technology becomes at providing energy beyond the minimum necessary for survival, the larger the population will grow. As the population expands, there will be a corresponding increase in the complexity of the social organization and other parts of the technology. As the social organization grows more complex with increasing numbers of statuses and specialization—and interdependence of statuses—new and more complex means of political control will develop. Kinship statuses tend to become socially less important as new specialized political statuses take over roles previously fulfilled by kinship. Societies with the most complex technologies also tend to be those that are most highly stratified with ranked categories of statuses, some of which have access to greater amounts of power, prestige, and control over the material wealth of the society.

These technological changes will be reflected in ideological adjustments, first as new informal patterns of ideas and feelings arise and later as the formal, conscious ideology finally accommodates to the new circumstances. The ideology may reflect technological or social innovation by actually adding new beliefs. For instance, changes in a society's tool kit may provide people with added insight into the nature and functioning of the world around them. However, it is probably more often the case that ideological change involves the modification and replacement of earlier beliefs and feelings with newer ones, rather than the simple addition of new elements.

A classic example of the effects of technological change on social organization and ideology is the case described by Sharp

Figure 10.4 *Acculturation*
The process of two cultures interacting so they become more like each other is called acculturation. Here we see in A, a family of Tierra del Fuego Indians in primitive dress standing in front of their modern style house; in B, a Kikuyu tribal dancer on a Nairobi municipal bus; and in C, an Inuit on a whale hunt taking a break by reading a magazine.

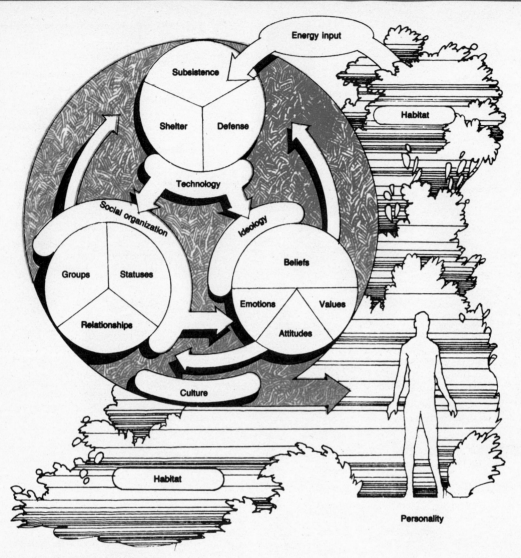

Figure 10.5 *Cultural Subsystems*
The chart shows the relationship of the cultural subsystems of technology, social organization and ideology. Change in any one will affect the others.

(1952) of the effects of the introduction of steel hatchets to the Yir Yiront, an Australian hunting and gathering society that previously had known only the stone axe. Among the Yir Yiront, stone axes were manufactured only by adult men and were the property of adult males only. They were, however, commonly used by women, by men who owned no axe of their own, and by children. Whenever these persons performed a task requiring an axe, they had to borrow one from an adult male kinsman. The process reinforced the authority of the kinship system that structured the society, and the axes served as symbols of masculinity and male dominance in the

social and economic system. Enter the European missionaries, who attempted to help the Yir Yiront "improve their conditions of life" by distributing or trading steel axes which, being technologically more efficient tools, were to help the natives "progress." Through the missions, it became possible for women, young men, and even children to possess their own axes. This change undermined the authority of the adult males of the society and eventually had a disruptive effect on the economic system of the Yir Yiront as well, since their trade with neighboring peoples was motivated by the need to acquire stone to manufacture stone axes. The festive annual

Figure 10.6 *Technological Evolution of Culture*
Technology is the leading edge of cultural change in a society. This Israeli stops to give water to his donkey at a gas station.

gatherings at which trade previously had occurred began to lose their social importance and excitement as trading partnerships weakened. A man might find it easier to obtain a steel axe from white men by selling his wife's favors than by traditional means, an outcome hardly foreseen by the European missionaries!

Evolution through social change. Cultural change may begin not only within the technological subsystem but also within the social organization. As a population grows, the number of social relationships increases, and new ways of coordinating society are needed. New statuses and institutions arise in response to these pressures. In very simple societies, the family is the fundamental institution of social control. It educates the young, produces food and other economic goods, carries out judicial activities when members violate important rules, and performs other "governmental" functions. As societies increase in population and density, new institutions arise to help coordinate human interaction. One important new institution is the special-interest nonkinship association—groups such as the local militia composed of all young men of the group, the voluntary fire brigade, or the harvest cooperative group. Larger-scale societies begin to develop full-time specialists and other new statuses and groups such as full-time governmental specialists, draft laborers, religious leaders, and standing armies.

As the social organization becomes more complex, these changes are reflected in the society's technology and ideology. For instance, when producers begin to specialize in the manufacture of the same item, wares tend to become more standardized in form.

Ideologically, as governmental specialization develops, members of the society increasingly value order and stability, even at the expense of individual autonomy.

Evolution based on ideological change. Adjustments in the cultural subsystems that are initiated in the ideological realm may be exemplified by processes such as the birth of a new religious or political philosophy. When successful, the new doctrine is proclaimed by a social body organized by the author of the new teachings. New ideologies thus give rise to new social structures, the presence of which, in turn, influences the functioning of the culture's technology.

An ideology may, on the other hand, slow the process of change. The Old Order Amish of Pennsylvania are a well-known example of a social body that for ideological reasons has remained highly resistant to the complex technological changes that have occurred among their neighboring Americans. The Amish have maintained a horse-and-buggy transportation system, a horse-drawn plow subsistence technology, and a home life unaffected by the presence of radios, televisions, and other common North American household appliances.

Levels of Cultural Complexity

As human technologies evolved historically from hunting and gathering through horticulture to agriculture, corresponding changes occurred in the social organization and ideology of human cultural systems. These changes will now be outlined using five societal types—bands, tribes, chiefdoms, agrarian states, and industrialized states—in order of increasing cultural complexity. All types still are present in the contemporary world, but the trend is toward industrialized states, with band and tribe forms becoming increasingly rare.

Bands

The oldest and simplest of human technologies is that which provides people with energy through hunting wild animals and gathering wild plant foods. This foraging technology forms the subsistence base of a societal type known as the band. According to Julian Steward (1955) and Elman R. Service (1962), the hunting and gathering technology places certain functional demands on the social organization of the band-level culture. Bands are typically small groups based on kinship, with labor divided only by age and sex, sharing of resources, temporary leadership roles, material possessions limited by nomadism, and ideals reflecting these features. Wild foods are a sparse resource for people with no other means of survival. The poor environments occupied by foragers in recent times are unable to support more than about one person per five square miles and in some places as few as one person per 500 square miles.

Group structure. Permanent social groups cannot be very large. The local group that works and lives together averages about 50 people in contemporary band societies and rarely exceeds 100 people. The local groups of band cultures may have been somewhat larger in earlier times, when bands occupied areas with more abundant resources than are now found in the marginal areas to which they have been restricted by the expansion of more powerful societies. Nevertheless, wild food resources cannot maintain large local groups except in very lush environments, since the larger the group is, the farther individuals must travel from their base of operations in their quest for food.

As a general rule, in the small, local groups of band cultures, all individuals will be related, either by descent or marriage. Kinship is the basic institution in a band society for organizing the education of children, social etiquette, and economic, political, military, and judicial practices. In these largely familial groups, family ties and ancestry are most commonly kept track of through the men.

Division of labor. The only specialization of labor in a band culture is that based on differences of sex and age. In a band society supported by the sparse resources of wild foods, the most economical division of subsistence labor usually assigns the work of hunting to the men, while the gathering of wild plants near the camp is done by the women and older children. The sexual aspect of this specialization of labor is an adaptation to pregnancy in the female and the need for prolonged nursing of infants. Although these two biological facts might hinder her as a hunter, the woman still can be an important provider of plant foods gathered locally during periods of pregnancy and lactation. Elman R. Service (1962), R. B. Lee and Ivan DeVore (1968), and J. Tanaka (1977), have estimated that women sometimes provide as much as 80% of the calories in the diets of people who survive by hunting and gathering. However, in circumstances where a rigid differentiation is not important for the survival of the group, men, women, and children may be allowed to play overlapping roles. In hunting and gathering societies in areas with plentiful wild foods, men may often gather wild plants as well as hunt; men, women, and children may frequently work together in cooperative hunting activities, even though hunting is thought of as more central to the male status.

Ernestine Friedl (1975) has suggested that the sexual division of labor in foraging societies takes one of four major forms. In the first, hunting is relatively unimportant, and both men and women are expected to gather their own plant foods. The main differentiation between the male and female roles lies in the fact that the male spends a small amount of time hunting in addition to the main gathering activity and the woman has the major responsibility for the children. In the second form, where cooperative communal hunting is more effective, men, women, and children all cooperate in hunting, gathering, and fishing. When hunting is undertaken, game is driven by the group to a central location where the animals are often entangled in nets or corralled and then killed by the men of the group. In the third form, where game must be sought individually, men are expected to specialize in hunting away from camp while women, who may contribute as much as 60 to 70% of the calories, specialize in gathering plants in or near the camp site while caring for the children. Finally, there are hunting and gathering societies in which large game, hunted by men, are the major available food. In these societies, women process the meat and skins and care for children, but they are almost completely dependent upon men for their survival. Usually in these societies men even make the tools that women use. As can be seen, these differences are largely a matter of the kinds and amounts of food resources that are available.

Since hunters are likely to become less efficient at this work if they move to a new, unfamiliar hunting territory, men generally remain in the hunting area where they grew up. It is women who leave home at marriage and go to live patrilocally in the hunting territory of their husband. This pattern, plus the role of men in warfare, creates a nucleus of closely related men through whom patrilineal ancestry is easily traced.

Economy. Beyond age and sex specialization, all persons are economic generalists. Without economic specialists, the band economy functions by a simple mechanism known as reciprocity, the mutual sharing of surpluses in the form of reciprocal gift-giving. The trait of generosity, so characteristic of band peoples, is actually a very effective economic device for insuring the survival of the entire group. For a hunter, the sharing of one's excess during times of successful hunts serves as a kind of insurance against his own future times of need. Every hunter is bound to experience some periods of poor luck in the chase. Generosity to others in one's own times of plenty is more than a mere act of good will; it is an investment. Those with whom a hunter has shared food or other useful goods in the past will make return gifts of their own later surpluses to insure the continuation of his good will in the future when they again are the ones in need. In the long run, the economic system of reciprocity maintains a balance in the distribution of goods. No one prospers at the expense of others, but neither does anyone need fear the specter of starving alone during the inevitable periods of personal failure or illness when one cannot hunt.

Leadership. As might be expected, band societies lack sufficient resources to support any full-time educational, economic, religious, military, judicial, legislative, or executive specialists. All leadership is charismatic. That is, a man or woman becomes a leader in some activity because of a personal talent in that area. Leadership also is unofficial; it is maintained only so long as a person demonstrates the qualities of excellence that draw a following. Charismatic leadership confers no authority, no power to coerce. A leader can only lend advice or take the initiative. Coming from a man or woman of respected abilities or wisdom, the advice or action is apt to be followed by others. As abilities decline, so does the following. The leader in the hunt is likely to be a man of proven ability in locating, tracking, and capturing game. A less effective hunter does not assert himself in matters of the chase but may nevertheless be a respected leader in political matters where his broad experience and proven wisdom bring greater attention to his judgments than to those of other members of the group.

Nomadism and material culture. Since the wild food resources near enough to be conveniently obtained from any given home base soon will be depleted or scattered too far to make their search and retrieval worthwhile, camp must be moved frequently. Without a domestication technology, people must follow their food supply. This semi-nomadic pattern has a feedback influence on the nature of a band society's material technology. The band society's tool kit is influenced by the number of things the group can carry when it moves on to a new hunting ground. Band-level peoples cannot afford to have as many different kinds of specialized tools as are commonly found among more sedentary peoples. Each tool must be able to serve many different functions. For instance, the Australian boomerang served not only as a throwing weapon used in the hunt but also as a flat working surface when making other tools, a digging tool, a club, a scraping tool, and a percussion musical instrument.

Ideology. Since a hunting and gathering technology has an impact on a band society's ideology, it is possible to outline ideological characteristics that are common to band cultures. Like members of all human

societies, band-level people learn to gain pleasure from their way of life; their likes and dislikes grow out of the experiences available in their own culture, as do their values. Perhaps the primary characteristic value of band cultures is that of generosity, for members of the group must adhere to the economic principle of reciprocity if all are to survive. Unlike the ideologies of settled horticultural and agriculture peoples, band ideology includes no concept of private ownership of land. Such an idea would be maladaptive to a society that must follow the game to survive. Of course, the belief system also must include accurate factual knowledge of subsistence and shelter techniques needed for survival by those who hunt and gather the wild products of nature.

The social organization of band societies also has an effect on their ideology. Some of these may be illustrated in terms of religious ideology. In an egalitarian society there is no hierarchical arrangement of the groups that initiate and control aspects of social life. In such societies, the supernatural realm will be equally unranked in its membership: There is no concept of a high god who rules over other lesser gods and spiritual entities. Hunters are more likely to be concerned with their personal spiritual relationship with animals and with spiritual entities and powers that may improve their hunting effectiveness.

In a society where a person's survival depends to a great extent upon her or his own talents and prowess, this autonomy of the individual is reflected in a belief in personal souls that reside in and animate the bodies of individuals. The ideologies of band societies also commonly include a belief in the reincarnation of the spirits of individuals. Reincarnation embodies the idea that the spirits of one's ancestors continue to be interested enough in the goals and purposes of the group that they return to it, thus symbolically expressing the continuity across generations of the personal interests and goals that are central to the life of the small local band.

Human health is another major concern of the religious ideology of the band. Since many illnesses lie beyond the control of the

Figure 10.7 *Shoshoni Winnowing*
The Shosoni wandered in search of their food supply from season to season. This woman on the Lemhi Reservation, Idaho, in 1904, is winnowing the wheat.

band-level medical technology, human anxiety concerning health is alleviated by the belief that such illnesses are caused by (and can be cured by) spiritual forces. The forces commonly believed to cause illness are witchcraft, spirit possession, the intrusion of a foreign spiritual substance into the body, or spiritual contamination due to the violation of some ritual rule.

The Great Basin Shoshoni: A Band Society

Steward (1938) described the native culture of the Great Basin Shoshoni. The Shoshoni occupied a territory that stretched all the way from near Death Valley, California, through central Nevada, northern Utah, and southern Idaho to central Wyoming. It generally is believed that the Shoshoni moved into the Great Basin from somewhere near the Death Valley area some 1,000 years ago. Throughout their territory, the Shoshoni spoke dialects of the same language, a language closely related to those of their Great Basin neighbors,

the Northern and Southern Paiute and the Ute, who practiced a similar way of life.

The Shoshoni were a highly mobile people who hunted game and gathered wild plant foods in a sparse desert environment. Variations in rainfall made the location and amount of plant and animal foods highly variable from year to year. The Shoshoni spent much of the year in search of food, wandering in small groups of one to three nuclear families. During the spring and summer months, their food consisted of foraged seeds, berries, roots, and small game such as insects, larvae, rodents, and other small mammals.

Occasionally, families who usually hunted separately would happen upon a large congregation of rabbits. If one of the families owned a rabbit net, a collective hunt would be held. The rabbit net was about eight feet high and several hundred feet long. It was laid out in a great semicircle, and everyone would fan out to drive the rabbits toward the net. When the rabbits became entangled in the net, they would be clubbed or shot. These hunts provided both meat and furs which, cut into strips and woven into capes, provided warmth in the cold winter season. Similar communal hunts were held when antelope were available. After the hunt was completed and the meat eaten, families would again go their own ways in the search for food.

In the late summer, Shoshoni families would move toward the mountain ranges where pine nuts would soon ripen. The best locations at which to gather pine nuts varied, so families would congregate at different locations each year as fall approached. They gathered pine nuts in the fall and stockpiled enough to feed themselves during the cold winter months.

During the winter months, 20 to 30 families would camp in the same vicinity. Winter was a time for socializing. Dances and gambling were popular recreations. The most common dance was a communal dance in which men and women arranged themselves in a great circle and sidestepped in one direction. This communal dance was believed to have some general health benefits for those who participated. Gambling took many forms. Especially popular was the handgame, played with two short sticks, one banded and the other plain. One member of each of two teams would alternately conceal these sticks, one in each hand, while a member of the opposing team would attempt to guess which hand concealed the banded token. Rapid singing was used to confuse the person who was guessing.

At the end of the winter, families began to disperse once again, some having added a new member or two by marriage. New wives left their families of birth and traveled with the family of their husband, for marriage among the Shoshoni was patrilocal. The Shoshoni were flexible about their marriage forms, which included polygyny, some polyandry, and group marriage as well as monogamous marriage. When a man

married several women, it was preferred that they be sisters. Young men frequently would marry each other's sisters, thereby cementing their two families more firmly together. Since winter encampments brought different groups together at different locations each year, marriages created kinship ties between families that were widely dispersed. This gave the nuclear family relatives in many different locations with whom they could cooperate whenever they met in their wandering quest for food.

Cooperation within and between families was the basis of Shoshoni economic and political life. There was no governing authority among the Shoshoni outside the family even during the winter encampments. Prior to European contact, there was no warfare among the Shoshoni. Property was limited to what people carried with them as they traveled, so there was little conflict over property rights. What few conflicts arose could usually be settled within the group on the basis of familial authority. Conflicts between different families were most often concerned with witchcraft accusations or wife-stealing. These might be settled by a feud, but the wandering way of life lent itself to conflict avoidance or even to settling of conflicts by each family's simply going its own way rather than pursuing the matter.

Shoshoni religion focused on the acquisition of spiritual power, called *puha*, which increased its possessor's skill, luck, and strength. *Puha* could be used to make love or gambling magic, to insure the success of a hunt, and to cure or to kill. Religious specialists, who devoted more time than others to the acquisition and use of *puha*, were known as *puhakanten*, "power possessors." Some *puhakanten* had the particular ability to attract antelope. Their skill was especially useful during communal antelope drives, since they could help draw the antelope into the corral. Other *puhakanten* devoted themselves to the curing of illnesses when called upon to do so. These spiritual healers were likely to have had a visionary experience in which they acquired a spirit ally known as a *puha newepea* or "power partner." During curing ceremonies, the healer would alternately chant and smoke tobacco until his spiritual ally would come and endow him with the power to cure.

Shoshoni religious beliefs included creation stories, known as Coyote Stories, in which anthropomorphic animals were the central characters. Coyote, the creator of human beings, was a Trickster, a deity who enjoyed playing practical jokes and whose own curiosity and lack of self-control often got the best of him. Coyote invariably refused to take good advice, almost always to his own detriment. Human beings entered the world by escaping from a bundle he had opened in spite of having been told to leave it closed. He later obtained pine nuts for the hungry Shoshoni by stealing this food from wealthier tribes to the north. He and his elder brother, Wolf, were instrumental in removing the teeth from women's vaginas, a problem that plagued people in mythological times. In addition to many tales of animals who, like Coyote, spoke and acted like human beings, there were stories of other creatures who bothered human beings. One popular story was that of the giant Rock Ghost who frequently would come down from her mountain cave home in search of Shoshoni children to eat. Coyote stories were enjoyed during the winter encampments but were generally not told at other times, since the telling of a Coyote Story could bring on a storm.

Tribes

When the hunting and gathering subsistence technology gave way to the domestication of plants and animals, functionally related changes came about in the social organization, in the ideology, and in other aspects of the technology, giving rise to a new societal type called the tribe.

In most tribal cultures, the subsistence technology emphasizes horticulture as the basic means for acquiring food. A horticultural technology is one with a capacity for gardening by the planting, weeding, harvesting, and storage of foodstuffs. Techniques for irrigating the gardens may or may not be present, but there is no use of the plow, fertilization of the soil, or crop rotation, all of which are characteristic of more complex agricultural technologies.

Group structure. Increased control over the food supply leads to understandable changes in the organization of society into a horticultural tribe. Population may grow to approach 10 people per square mile. Local groups must maintain more or less permanent residence near the planted gardens from which they draw their food. These groups can grow to be quite large in comparison with the local groups of hunting and gathering peoples. According to Marshall D. Sahlins (1960) the communities of contemporary horticultural societies have up to 200 to 250 residents. While the local groups in bands may be composed of anywhere from one to a dozen families that are loosely interrelated by ties of marriage, a tribal community may consist of as many as 20 residential families. Often, these families may be grouped into a number of lineages and clans, groups that are united to one another by ties of common ancestry. A lineage is a group of families that are descended from a common ancestor not more than five or six generations earlier than that of the present family heads. A clan is a larger group of families in which the common ancestor dates back more than six generations. The exact genealogical relationships between the contemporary families of a clan may no longer be remembered. Indeed, in some cases a mythological entity rather than an actual historical personage may serve as the symbolic common ancestor who represents the kinship unity of the families that belong to the clan. With the passage of time, clans may become so large that families belonging to the same clan reside in separate communities. Distant clan relatives may provide a source of refuge to a traveling member of the same clan from another community. As might be expected, such clans that are found in separate communities may easily play a role as natural channels for economic trade or political communication between communities.

Where clans exist, a rule of exogamy generally prevails; that is, clan members are not permitted to intermarry—although sexual liaisons between distantly related members of the same clan may be tolerated. Such rules of clan exogamy create mental ties between different clans—ties that may be renewed generation after generation, if it proves economically or politically beneficial to do so. According to Elman R. Service,

> The ultimate functions of clans vary greatly. In some societies they are land-holding, in others ceremonial only, and in others they operate only in the context of war and peacemaking. Yet in all some legal-like corporateness with respect to the defense of members occurs. Primarily a clan acts to preserve peaceful relations among its members; it thus has some effect on the relations of residential groups to each other, and acts to adjudicate or end disputes and punish wrongs in relations between members of different clans. (1962, p. 126)

Another common practice for helping to organize the activities of people is to divide all the families, lineages, or clans into two major groups, called moieties. Each moiety of such a society has reciprocal rights and responsibilities toward the other. For instance, members of one moiety may be expected to find their mates from the other moiety; one moiety may perform rituals such as funerals for members of the other moiety; or each moiety may specialize in performing the rituals of a particular season.

The increased specialization provided by the creation of lineages, clans, and moieties allows the institution of kinship to accomplish more as a means of organizing day-to-day human affairs than if it were limited to a mere extended family group. According to Robin Fox (1967), in societies where people are independent but sometimes need help, they are likely to create groups in which membership and obligations to help are based on having a kinship relationship. Such a group, which consists of all persons related in some way to a particular living individual who is not their common ancestor, is called a kindred. A kindred, consisting as it does of all the aunts, uncles, cousins, and other relatives of some particular persons, exists as a group only so long as the individual around whom it is focused is alive. It is a personal group and cannot function as a corporate entity like a clan, which may perform such tasks as owning land. It may, however, provide useful benefits to the individual around whom it is focused, such as helping him or her in work activities when called upon to do so.

Although family organization is still the basic institution around which most of daily tribal life revolves, even complex systems of kinship relationship such as the clan, the moiety, and the kindred are not adequate for dealing with the great variety of social problems that may arise in communities of several hundred members. In tribes, problems that concern more than one family may be dealt with by a number of nonkinship associations. These include such nonkinship groups as associations based on one's age, military and religious associations, secret societies, and other groups that draw their membership from all parts of a community. Such associations that have neither a kinship nor a residential basis are organized to carry out some basic activity that cannot be performed as effectively by the kinship organization of the tribes. These activities may be political, economic, or religious in nature, such as defense of the community, control of community members during group activities, conduct of trade, or the performance of curing ceremonies or other religious rites. In all cases, their uniting of members in a common cause forms the roots of an incipient system—though it may be generalized and diffuse—of secular government within the tribe. Most issues of law and polity, however, remain matters of legitimate familial concern at the tribal level of social organization, and tribes have no true centralized government.

As in bands, tribal leadership is charismatic. It is achieved by an individual's personal ability to convince others that it is in their own self-interest to follow his or her lead. Thus, leadership is a matter of skill rather than the power of an inherited status. By and large, tribal society is egalitarian like the band society in that every individual has more or less equal opportunity to obtain the necessities of life and the esteem of others in leadership activities.

Economy. Tribal society continues to make use of reciprocal sharing, both along kinship lines and between kin groups. But the division of labor in the realm of production is more highly specialized than in bands. In addition to having a division of labor along age and sex lines, tribal communities include among their residents individuals and groups who specialize in economic activities other than food production. These specialists can be freed from subsistence activities to engage in other occupations, since tribal communities have a more secure control over their yearly food supply than do band peoples.

Religion. Tribal religion involves a practice that is uncharacteristic of foragers: the ceremonial worship of gods—great spiritual beings who personify the major forces of nature that are of concern to food producers who must control the land from which they obtain their livelihood. These include gods of the wind, rain, plant and animal fertility, land, and war. The gods are not arranged in hierarchies. On different occasions, individual deities may rise in prominence and importance. Gods of war may be extremely important at times of war, and agricultural deities may be most important in times of drought. But the overall importance of the various deities balances out in the long run.

Pastoral tribes. Those tribes found in environments where gardening is too unproductive to support a sedentary tribal population make their living by pastoralism, a form of food production that emphasizes the herding of animals. The pastoral forms of tribal society are found mostly in arctic and subarctic areas, deserts, mountains, and grasslands. The animals herded include reindeer, horses, sheep, goats, camels, and cattle. Because of the marginality of their environments and the resulting specialized emphasis on animals as their basic food resource, pastoralists must often interact with neighboring agricultural peoples to secure materials that they cannot produce themselves, including foodstuffs. This may be accomplished by peaceful trade or, in some cases, by raiding the more sedentary agricultural peoples.

The Toda: A Tribal Society

Rivers (1906) described the Toda, a pastoral tribe of India. The Toda lived on a high plateau in southern India. They made their living by herding buffalo. Since they practiced no agriculture, the Toda supplied neighboring tribes with dairy products from their herds in return for farm products, pottery, ironware, and other goods and services. As might be expected, buffalo were extremely important to the Toda. Cows were individually named, and their pedigrees were carefully remembered. Some herds even were regarded as sacred. These herds were tended by special dairymen at sacred dairy temples. Their care involved elaborate rituals, and the dairymen who tended them lived the lives of priests, lives filled with rituals and special taboos. The ancestors of these sacred herds played an important role in the creation myths of the Toda, who believed that when the first 1,600 sacred buffalo were created by one of the gods, the first human appeared holding onto the tail of the last buffalo—an apt symbol of the Toda's economic dependence on their herds.

Socially, the Toda were divided into two endogamous moieties. The more highly ranked of these, the Tarthar, owned all of the sacred herds of buffalo and their dairies. The sacred dairymen who tended the herds all belonged to the second moiety, the Teivali. Both of these groups were further divided into exogamous patrilineal clans, each with its own territory. Clans served as land and herd-owning groups. The major villages and most sacred herds of buffalo were the property of entire clans rather than of the individual families that made up the clans.

Although families and clans were the main decision-making bodies among the Toda, the pastoral life of the Toda had created a population density that was too great for all problems to be settled without some mechanism that stood above clan membership. This mechanism was an incipient government organization, a tribal council known as the *naim*. Its five members always came from certain families of specific clans. Lacking the authority of the true governments of more complex societies, the *naim* had no voice in criminal matters. Its primary functions were to regulate ceremonies and to settle disputes between individuals, families, and clans when called upon to do so.

Population growth was limited by the Toda's location. Their land was bounded on all sides. In the southern directions, cliffs dropped from 3,000 to 5,000 feet. To the north were agriculturalists. With no room for expansion, the Toda had sought to solve the problem of population growth by limiting the number of women and therefore the number of children born in each generation. This was accomplished by the practice of infanticide in which unwanted infants, especially girls, were suffocated shortly after birth. This led to a surplus of men in each generation. To rectify this imbalance the Toda practiced polyandry.

Marriages were arranged, and they occurred between children as young as two or three years of age. The girl was considered to be the wife of the boy with whom the marriage ceremony was performed and of all his brothers, including those born thereafter. Until she was 15 or 16, the bride lived with her own parents. Shortly before puberty, she had to be initiated into sex by a man selected from the moiety to which her family did not belong, that is, to a man whom she would not be permitted to marry. If this ceremonial loss of virginity did not occur before puberty, the bride was stigmatized for life, and her marriage would be cancelled.

Since the Toda based their clan membership and inheritance on the principle of patrilineal descent, fatherhood was an important matter. But, since a woman had many husbands, fatherhood had to be designated on some basis other than the idea of biological paternity. Among the Toda, a man became a father by performing a fatherhood ritual. This was one of the most important rituals of the Toda. For a child to be born without its having been performed was a great scandal. In this ritual, a man and a pregnant woman went into the forest where the man carved a niche in a tree, placed an oil lamp into it, promised the woman a calf, and ceremonially presented her with an imitation bow and arrow. She held the bow and arrow to her forehead and watched the lamp until it burned out. Afterwards, he prepared a meal, and the two spent the night together. From this time forward, he would be the father of all children to whom she would give birth, until some other man performed the same ceremony with her to supersede him as father of her children. Although it was usual for one of a woman's husbands to hold the status of father of her children, it was possible for a man who was not one of her husbands to perform the bow-giving ceremony with her.

Chiefdoms

Another level of cultural complexity—the chiefdom—is typically found in the simplest agricultural societies. Chiefdoms are sometimes known as rank societies because their social systems are not egalitarian like those of the bands and tribes (Fried, 1967; Service, 1960, 1978).

Social, political, and economic structure. As in the bands and tribes, most day-to-day social life in chiefdoms revolves around the family, but the families in each local community are organized into broad social groupings that are ranked with respect to one another. Some families are more wealthy, prestigious, and politically powerful than others. Birth into these families conveys advantages not available to members of other families.

In addition to the family-based mechanisms of government that are found in bands and tribes, chiefdoms possess political specialists who have the right in at least some matters to exercise authority over persons who are not members of their own families. These specialists, called chiefs, generally derive much of their authority from religion. The power of the chief or governing council of the chiefdom is more limited than that of the governments of more complex societies, and families may legitimately exercise legal power in many areas of life, such as the contracting and dissolution of marriages or the punishment of individuals for minor thefts. However, the chief is normally called on for the adjudication of more serious infractions of law, such as major thefts or homicide. In some of these matters, the chief may be expected to play the role of mediator between the conflicting parties, with the goal of reestablishing peaceful relations between the members of the community. In other cases, the chief may have the authority to determine guilt or innocence and exact punishment for an offense without consulting the members of the offender's family. The position of chief is therefore a true office, and its holder has authority to legitimately wield power over others with whom the chief has no known kinship ties.

The office of chief is most often hereditary, although which relative of a deceased chief will inherit the office may be decided by the surviving family members. In some cases, the community as a whole may have some say in the selection of the new chief from the group of possible heirs.

Each community in a chiefdom is likely to have a chief who acts as its political head, and groups of villages within a chiefdom usually will be unified under a district chief of higher rank than the local village chiefs. The entire chiefdom, which may consist of several hundred thousand people in various districts, may or may not be unified under a central paramount chief, but the residents of the various districts will think of themselves as a single people in that they share a common language and culture.

Although the office of chief has definite political power, probably the most important function of the chief is the economic one of serving as a redistributor of goods and a provider of services. In a chiefdom, all families in a community are expected to contribute a portion of their annual produce to the chief's warehouse. The chief then sees to it that these goods are redistributed, generally at community feasts or festivals, to those most in need. It is often the case that a chief's power and prestige is maintained in direct proportion to the chief's generosity. Indeed, the level of gift-giving expected of a chief may exceed that which comes in from other families, so that the wealth of the chiefly family is gradually drained, to the benefit of other less prestigious families.

Specialists. In chiefdoms a high level of specialization of labor is common. Individuals and sometimes entire communities may specialize in the production of goods desired or needed by others. These goods are then exchanged for materials that the specialists do not produce or for labor that the specialists require but do not perform for themselves. Specializations may include crafts, such as pottery making or house building, and services, such as religious or military occupations.

Chiefdoms also generally have a system of drafted military personnel, partly as a result of two factors: (1) chiefdoms, compared to horticultural societies, have larger and more dense populations because agriculture is generally more productive than is horticulture, yet (2) agricultural societies are more likely to experience food shortages due to droughts than are horticultural societies (most of which are in areas of more reliable rainfall). Food shortages among people with dense populations are likely to result in intense military competition for control over land. The presence of a draft army reinforces the police power of the government and lends authority to the chiefly office. The trait of official authority is absent in the leadership positions of bands and tribes, where leaders must inspire their following but cannot compel obedience.

Chiefdoms generally have religious

Figure 10.8 *Bedouin Tent-dwelling*
Tribal Bedouins make their living herding camels. This 18-year-old boy lives on the men's side of the family tent in the Negev desert.

specialists who serve the entire community. Indeed, the chief may be the primary religious functionary. The religious ideology in chiefdoms reflects their social complexity. The gods are many and specialized in function, as are the social occupations of the human members of the chiefdom. Guy Swanson (1974) has demonstrated that in those societies in which decision-making power is organized hierarchically into at least three levels, the concept is very likely to be present that the gods are ranked in a hierarchy headed by a supreme deity. This level of social complexity is found in many chiefdoms throughout the world, as is the concept of a supreme god—a religious idea that is almost absent among tribal and band peoples.

The Rwala Bedouins: A Pastoral Chiefdom

According to Musil (1928), the Rwala had the largest and most powerful tent-dwelling Bedouin chiefdom of the northern Arabian peninsula. Although much of their life was organized around the concept of kinship, the Rwala also had officials whose authority was felt beyond the boundaries of their own kin. These chiefs or *sheikhs* were officers whose positions were inherited within particular patrilineal lineages. In addition to local *sheikhs* whose authority was felt throughout an entire camp, there also were regional chiefs whose authority derived from a lineage of greater prominence than those of the local chiefs. There also was a paramount chief or *sheikh*, often called a "prince," over all the Rwala. His main duties were the conduct of relations with the national government and with chiefs of other Bedouin peoples, but he had little power over the internal politics of the Rwala themselves.

Life in the camps was largely governed by kinship. Each man saw himself as the center of a group of relatives, or kindred, known as the *ahl*. A man's *ahl* consisted of all his patrilineal descendants and ancestors to the third generation. This group of relatives had strong obligations to him and could bear the guilt for his misdeeds. People also were organized into patrilineal clans, called *feriz*. Marriages were preferably within one's own lineage of the clan. In particular, a man was encouraged to marry his father's brother's daughter or his father's father's brother's son's daughter—his patrilineal first- or second-parallel cousin. This woman could marry no other without his waiving his prior claim. Since parallel cousin marriage was forbidden in many societies, anthropologists have debated the reason for this unusual preference. It has been argued that by marrying into their own patrilineage, the Bedouin kept inheritable property from being dispersed and increased the solidarity of the lineage which was divided most of the year into small wandering groups. The marriage preference system counteracted the fragmenting effects of the Bedouin pastoral adaptation to a desert environment (Barth, 1954; Murphy & Kasdan, 1959).

Although polygyny was permitted, few men had more than one wife. Divorce was quite common, and although it was the prerogative of the husband to divorce his wife or grant a divorce, he was expected to divorce his wife if she expressed love for another. Both spouses were free to remarry.

Rwala, like other Bedouins, had black servants who often have been referred to as "slaves." These persons formed a kind of separate caste within Rwala society, since they did not intermarry with the Rwala. They were expected to do much of the drudge work around the camp. These servants could not be bought, sold, or killed and could choose another master if they became disaffected with their previous one. They chose their own spouses, owned property of their own, and were entitled to take food from their master's larder.

The Rwala made their living by herding camels. Camels not only could be ridden but also provided milk for food and hides and hair out of which useful items could be manufactured. Camels were traded to merchants in return for cash, weapons, clothing, and other necessities. Trade was important, for the desert environment did not permit the Bedouins to be completely self-sufficient.

The yearly cycle of Bedouin life was made up of about 10 months of camel herding in the desert and about 2 summer months at the settlements on the edge of the desert where the Bedouins traded for needed goods. The basic work of life was caring for the camel herds. This was the duty of armed men, especially in the dry months when the herds were thinly dispersed to forage for food and were easy prey to raiders.

Stolen animals were the main reason for warfare, which consisted most often of surprise night raids on the enemy camp. Boys could accompany raids from the age of 12, but it was mostly the occupation of men from 16 to 40. War was enjoyed because it was an opportunity not only for booty but also for displaying one's skill and courage. Old age was rare for males, since over 80% of Rwala men died as a result of warfare.

Warfare was a central fact of Rwala life, and it tinged many other aspects of their culture. Weaker groups of Bedouins and villagers paid protection tribute (*khuwa*) to more powerful ones such as the Rwala. The receiver of this protection "tax" was bound to protect those who paid it and to restore any property that was stolen from them by raiders.

Since weapons had to be repaired, every camp of the Rwala had a blacksmith (*sane'*), as did those of other Bedouins. They did not marry the Rwala, but remained a caste apart. The blacksmiths' families lived with the Rwala and followed a way of life much like that of the Rwala, but, as outsiders, they did not participate in raiding or warfare. Their occupation, a necessary one for the Rwala, was protected by not being subject to the high death rate that Rwala warfare caused.

Blood feuds also were common among the Rwala. Kin were obligated to avenge the murder of a relative, and the murderer's kin shared the guilt to the third generation. The avengers therefore could take the life of a relative of the actual culprit should they happen on one before finding the murderer. Vengeance of this kind was legitimate, a matter of family law. Guilty parties were not permitted to defend themselves against avengers, but instead had to seek the protection of a powerful *sheikh* who aided them in reaching a traditional place of refuge, where they stayed until the avengers agreed to accept a blood price of horses, camels, and weapons to compensate them for the death.

As might be expected, the custom of hospitality was very strong. The power of a chief to protect those under his care was a matter of grave honor. Travelers who entered a Bedouin camp greeted the *sheikh* and were assured of his protection by his salutation of peace, which was binding on the entire camp. This custom helped to alleviate the negative effects of war, as did the custom of tribute "taxes" which obligated the receiver to protect those who paid them. Traders who traveled from group to group insured themselves and their own goods by having an acquaintance or "brother" (*akh*) in each group to whom they paid a fee in return for protection. Should the trader's property be stolen in a raid, it was the obligation of his *akh* in the raiding group to see to it that they were returned when claimed.

States

The most complex society is known as the state. This is an independent political unit in which a central government integrates and has considerable control over the many communities in its territory, theoretically monopolizing the right to use legal force within its boundaries.

Technology. The major technological difference between the chiefdom and the state is that the agriculture of the state society is more intensive than that of the chiefdom. The plow and draft animals are almost always present, and agricultural technology is generally much more complex than in chiefdoms. Irrigation systems play a major role in the agriculture of most states, so much so that one scholar, Karl Wittfogel (1957), has suggested that it was the necessity of controlling and regulating water resources that led to the rise of the world's first states. This view has not been accepted widely because it places too much emphasis on the single factor of irrigation at the expense of others, such as population growth, trade, diplomacy, and warfare. But it reminds us that irrigation was an important technological development that played a role in the increasing productivity of the state's subsistence activities.

Due to the effects of truly intensive agriculture, members of a state society may number in millions. They occupy densely packed towns and cities in which little or no agriculture may be practiced. They also occupy more rural communities of smaller size that specialize particularly in the production of food in return for the specialized nonagricultural products of the larger communities.

Market economy. The flow of goods over great distances between communities is facilitated by the rise in prominence of the market system. In a market economy, goods and services are made available to people at a common location where they are exchanged. In such a specialized economic system, the role of kinship in the production and distribution of goods is likely to become attenuated. By and large, productive work ceases to be a family activity, since production becomes more a matter of cooperation between groups of specialists. Similarly, the distribution of goods from where they are produced to where they are consumed easily becomes the work of specialists.

Centralized power. States differ from chiefdoms primarily in one important way: Whereas in chiefdoms the right to use force in matters of law is divided between the kinship systems and the political apparatus, in the state, the government monopolizes the right to use force. This difference is at least partly attributable to the growing need for a centralized coordination of society, especially in areas of potential conflict between individuals and groups. The need for centralized control of society is likely to grow as the number and density of people unrelated by kinship increases.

Social ranking. In the state society, statuses are ranked into broad social strata or classes that have differential access to prestige and power. These social classes may be recognized formally in the society's ideology or they may be present informally while the ideology may not recognize their existence. For instance, historically both American and Soviet ideologies have denied the existence of classes within their societies, although in both cases they are a definite part of the social system. In the Soviet Union, attempts have been made to eliminate class distinctions by legislation that forbids the children of individuals who hold political or other prestigious positions to hold the same status in the next generation. The effect, however, has not been to eliminate differences in power and prestige between families but simply to insure a change in occupations between generations within the same class. Children of a bureaucrat may become scientists or members of a university faculty, thereby maintaining the high rank of their parents.

The rigidity of classes differs even in those societies that recognize them. In some, the movement of individuals from one class to another may be possible, although not common. When changing one's class is not permitted, social scientists refer to the system as a caste system.

The Aztecs: A Nonindustrialized State Society

The Aztec capital Tenochtitlan, which was situated on an island in a lake in the Valley of Mexico, had a population of about 250,000 people when the Spanish arrived in 1519 (see Fig. 10.9). Aztec society was supported by agriculture that used corn (maize), beans, and squash as staple crops. Although the Aztecs lacked the plow, the farmers of Tenochtitlan were able to extend their fields into the lake surrounding their city first by driving piles into the shallow lake bottom to form a retaining wall around the new plot and then by filling in this piece of lake with dirt and refuse that formed new, rich soil to farm as it decayed. This innovative technique, called *chinampa* agriculture, was productive enough to support large populations and nonagricultural specialists who lived in the cities.

Tenochtitlan was connected to the mainland by a series of causeways, one of which contained an aqueduct that brought fresh water to the city. The city itself was divided into four great quarters, each with its own market, temple, schools, and local officials. Each quarter was occupied by a number of patrilineal clans (*calpulli*) that owned the lands of the district (Soustelle, 1961). Local affairs were controlled by a council composed of the heads of all families that belonged to the patrilineal *calpulli* district. The head of this council was the *calpullec*. He distributed the lands of the clans to the various families of each clan, according to need. These were to be worked by the families but remained clan property. Those who were lax in the use of the land allocated them would lose their right to work those lands.

Aztecs were strict in the upbringing of their children. Children were lectured frequently on the values of hard work and obedience. Laziness was considered to be among the greatest sins. Disobedient children were beaten, pricked with thorns, or held in the smoke of a fire containing chili pepper. At the age of 15, boys entered the clan boarding school (*telpochcalli*) where they learned the arts of war and government. The sons of nobles received their

Figure 10.9 *Tenochtitlan*
This Aztec capital was on an island in a lake in the valley of Mexico, now the site of Mexico City. It was connected to the mainland by a series of causeways. The four quadrants of the city each had its own group of markets, schools and officials.

training in a priestly school (*calmecac*) where they learned writing, astronomy, and religion. Since the Aztec had a written tradition before the arrival of Europeans, they recorded their own histories and continued to write about themselves after the Conquest (see Dibble & Anderson, 1950 to 1969).

Upon completion of their studies, sons of nobles chose entering the priesthood or the government. In Aztec society, a society of classes, the highest class was composed of military officials and priests. The military governed society, and the priesthood mediated between the people and the gods to ensure the growth of crops and success in war. The highest military leader was the king, or *tlacatecutli*. He presided over a council of 20 speakers or *tlatoani* who represented the 20 Aztec clans. It was they, along with other clan leaders, military officers, and high priests, who declared wars, mediated disputes between clans, and created new laws. The second most prominent official, next to the king, was the Snake Woman (*çiuacoatl*), the man who actually presided over the council of speakers and who was responsible for the administration of housing, tribute, and the judicial sys-

tem. Aztec priests dressed in black and lived a rigorous life of ritual and self-sacrifice, with self-torture and fasting. Seven times a day, they offered sacrifices of their own blood. It was the priests who educated the children of the nobility.

Although they were not part of the nobility, the traders (*pochteca*) were often among the wealthiest of the Aztecs. These traveling merchants carried on trade far beyond the borders of the Aztec empire and often acted as spies for the military. Any attacks on trading expeditions brought immediate retaliation by the military. At home, the *pochteca* had special privileges because of their particular value to society. They formed almost a separate society within Aztec society. Their occupation was hereditary, and the *pochteca* had their own gods and rituals as well as the right to their own court system. Yet, in spite of their wealth, traders often lived lives of outward poverty so as not to incite the anger of the king who might confiscate their property on some pretext if he thought they were becoming too powerful. A multitude of other occupational specialists existed, including metalworkers, jade carvers, feather workers, carpenters, stonemasons, weavers, potters, and farmers.

Below the class of commoners were propertyless laborers (*macehualtin*), who were mostly foreigners with no claim to land, and some Aztecs who had lost their clan rights. These laborers, whose position was much like that of the serfs of medieval Europe, did work such as carrying burdens or working a noble's land. At the very bottom of the social classes were slaves. Slaves were mostly debtors or the children of debtors but also included some younger people delivered to the Aztecs as part of the tribute paid by conquered people. Slavery involved rights over the work of the slave but did not include ownership of his or her person. A slave might own property, marry and raise children, or buy himself or herself out of slavery. For this reason, slaves included people who sold themselves into slavery to pay their previous debts.

War was a central preoccupation of the Aztecs. The chief god of the Aztecs, Huitzilopochtli, was the god of war and the traditional Aztec tribal god from the Aztecs' precivilized days. Valor in war was rewarded by knighthood in one of the two great military orders, the Eagles and the Ocelots. Persons so knighted held the privileges of nobility, although the status was not passed on to their descendants. Dying in battle insured a man a glorious afterlife in the heaven of the sun god. This fate was shared by women who died in childbirth, since every new child strengthened the Aztec nation. For the same reason, abortion was a capital crime. Marriage also was a legal obligation; refusal to marry was punishable by loss of clan membership, which placed one in the class of unpropertied workers.

The religion of the Aztecs was polytheistic. Atop the great pyramid at the center of Tenochtitlan was a temple dedicated both to Huitzilopochtli, the Aztec war god and the god of the nobility, and to Tlaloc, the god of rain and agriculture, a god of special import to the commoners. A third major god was Quetzalcoatl, the Plumed Serpent, god of wind and air and the patron deity of the priesthood. The great god Tezcatlipoca, or Smoking Mirror, chief god of the Mexicans prior to the Aztecs, also was revered as of great importance. Many lesser deities existed, each with specialized powers. The great gods of the Aztecs were honored in state ceremonies and were nourished with the blood of sacrificial victims who had been captured in war. Thus, warfare was to the Aztecs a sacred obligation and not just a means of expanding the empire.

Industrialized states. The most complex of the state societies are those with an industrialized technology, a technology that harnesses the power of fossil fuels, hydroelectric dams, or more recently tapped energy sources such as atomic energy, solar power, or geothermal power. Compared with nonindustrialized states, the industrialized are even more complex. The percentage of persons engaged in food-providing activities declines radically as new, highly specialized occupations come into existence.

Specialization of labor is the order of the day in state societies. For instance, in the United States—one of the technologically more complex of the contemporary state societies—there are specialists who make their living in these ways: driving trucks in which trash is collected from the individual households of a community, moving the trash from the households to the trucks, operating the machinery for burying the waste products so collected, and supervising the work of the trash collectors and disposers. The building of a simple house to be occupied by a single family may require the work of specialists who dig basements, specialists who lay concrete foundations, carpenters, dry-wall specialists, roofers, electricians, heating specialists, painters, glaziers, and a host of supervisory specialists. When it comes to health care, one must decide whether to visit a general practitioner, a specialist in internal medicine, a heart specialist, a specialist in problems of the digestive tract, a specialist in bone disorders, a skin specialist, or a surgeon, to cite but a few of the vast number of medical specializations. Even then, much of the actual work done when one visits a doctor will be executed by a variety of technical specialists who work for or with that doctor, such as X-ray technicians, laboratory technicians, and nurses. A government publication lists over 20,000 different occupations found in the United States (U.S. Dept. of Labor, Employment and Training Administration, 1977).

Secularism. Perhaps the most outstanding aspect of the ideologies of state societies is that relative to the socially simpler societies, state-level peoples see a much greater part of the world about them in nonreligious terms. The more complex technologies of state societies require—if they are to be used effectively—that their users think of the parts of the world that they are manipulating with tools in a more pragmatic and matter-of-fact way than do peoples who control less of their environment technologically. Crop rotation, the plow, fertilization of the soil, and efficient irrigation systems make it much less likely that their users will think of the growth of crops as being dependent upon mysterious spiritual forces than do peoples who rely on rainfall gardening for their food supply. Similarly, with an increasing degree of social specialization in state societies, religious ideology is likely to decline in importance, since specialists are likely to see their day-to-day activities in a matter-of-fact, blasé way due to their routine nature. State societies also foster a secular, pragmatic view of life because the interdependent contributions of humans—in contrast with the influence of deity—are quite apparent. The survival of each member of a state society is obviously dependent upon the services performed by an immense number of other specialists.

To take an extreme example, even the work of full-time religious specialists tends to become a matter of routine in state-level societies. Where there are full-time religious thinkers, religious belief tends to place more stress on organized rational theological doctrine, while characteristics such as religious

ecstasy and altered states of consciousness which are often found in simpler societies, are likely to be less common. The priests of ecclesiastical religions frequently forbid the performance of shamanistic activities, such as seances, faith healing, prophecy, and psychic readings by separate specialists. They also often frown on similar behavior in the lay congregation and may taboo such practices as spirit possession trances and the ecstatic speaking in tongues by members of the congregation. Thus, when there are full-time religious practitioners who specialize in the routine performance of rituals for the congregation, the role of the congregation moves toward less active participation. Their only active part may be to fit themselves into the ritual pattern, not spontaneously but in a highly predictable way on cue. For the most part, they may be but a passive audience to a ritual that is performed almost in its entirety by the religious specialist. For such a specialist the ritual behavior may become a matter of almost pure routine. Participation in these rituals may be largely motivated by a more or less secular desire to be accepted as a conforming member of society—that is, because people experience what Radcliffe-Brown (1958) has called ''secondary anxiety''— rather than because they feel an immediate personal need for the rituals for spiritual reasons. In state societies, even religion has a tendency to become somewhat secularized, in contrast to the religious behavior of people in simpler social systems where labor is less specialized.

Cultural Evolutionary Theory

The observable differences among tribes, bands, chiefdoms, and states have led a number of anthropologists to speculate about whether these levels constitute developmental stages in the advance toward civilization, how societies pass from one stage to another, and whether the changes actually represent improvements in the quality of life. In asking such questions, they have tried to formulate general laws that can be applied to the process of cultural evolution in all societies.

Stages in the History of Cultural Evolution

As indicated in chapter 9, the societies that became the earliest civilizations passed historically through less complex forms based on simpler technologies. In 1949 Julian Steward examined the developmental sequences of the early civilizations in Peru, Middle America (Mexico and the Mayan area), Mesopotamia, Egypt, and China. He found that there were important parallels in how complex societies evolved in each of these arid or semiarid regions. On the basis of these parallels, he developed a typology of five successive stages through which these societies tended to pass during the rise of civilization.

According to Steward (1949), the Pre-Agricultural Era was the period in which societies were organized into bands of food collectors. The Era of Incipient Agriculture was one in which increasingly sedentary bands supplemented their diets of wild foods with some farming. The world's first tribal societies developed during this era. During the Formative Era, chiefdoms arose. Irrigation was practiced on a small and local scale. The emergence of a system of social rank was reflected in a division of the technologies of this period into production of two kinds of goods: objects designed to meet the basic domestic and biological needs of people, and very elaborate and stylized objects symbolic of the higher status of their users. Ceramics, loom weaving, basketry, house building, and the erection of religious edifices were universal, and metalworking was developed everywhere except in Middle America during this period.

In the Era of Regional Florescence, local state governments arose under the control of theocratic leaders. Society came to be organized on the basis of class distinction rather than kinship. Warfare was generally less important than in later times. During this period, the priesthood developed a variety of full-time, nonproductive religious specialists who laid the foundations for the abstract sciences: writing, astronomy, the calendar, and mathematics. The development of the wheel was another hallmark of this era. It was in this period of early civilization that societies had the means to erect their biggest and most impressive monumental architecture. Finally, as population pressures reached, and in some cases perhaps overshot, the carrying capacity of irrigation-based agriculture, competition for arable lands increased, and large-scale militarism became increasingly prominent.

Thus began the Imperial Era of Cyclical Conquests. Theocratic governments gave way to secular, military-based authority, and empires were built as some regions expanded their political and economic domination over neighboring areas. Urbanization increased and walled fortifications became common. Several classes became rigid hereditary divisions in which upward mobility by means of achievement disappeared. These changes were reflected in the religions of the early empires, in that gods of war became the most prominent deities of the pantheons. In some cases this period began with the rise of a central and dominant empire, which then ended in collapse and a decline in population below the levels of the previous era as the agricultural base became overtaxed. This collapse was followed by a period of "Dark Ages" and then by a period of cyclical conquests between competing city-states during which first one and then another local region would rise to prominence, only to be supplanted by another. Elsewhere, the period of cyclical conquests followed the Florescent Era immediately with no unifying imperial military state initially dominating the rest.

Specific and General Evolution

The existence of extensive parallels in the development of early civilizations suggests that the evolution of ways of life is as lawful as biological evolution. Marshall Sahlins and Elman R. Service (1949) and Service (1971) have clarified the lawful regularity of cultural evolution by pointing out that cultures change in two fundamentally different ways: (1) through a process of specific evolution, or change in the direction of increasing adaptive specialization; and (2) through a process of general evolution, or change in the direction of increasing complexity. In the first form of change, a way of life becomes more adjusted to its specific environmental circumstances—in a word, more specialized. In the second, new parts of a total environment are drawn upon by the cultural system. As a culture becomes more complex, it relates to its environment in radically new ways, harnessing greater amounts of energy for new uses. Qualitative change is the hallmark of general evolution.

While biological changes cannot be passed from one species to another, the traits that arise in one culture may pass over into another. Thus, the evolutionary development of cultures must be seen in terms of the interplay of the specific and general evolutionary changes that occur within cultures and the interactions between cultures.

Stabilization vs. Evolutionary Potential

It is the interaction between cultures that makes possible an interplay between the forces of specific and general evolution. Acting alone, specific evolution leads ultimately to stability. If a culture were ever to achieve a perfect adaptation to its environment, any further change would be maladaptive. If a way of life is relatively inefficient in helping a society to deal with its environment, it is a simple matter for a people to improve their adjustment to the circumstances. However, the more efficient a way of life becomes in making use of the resources available to a people, the more expensive and difficult it becomes to implement each new increase in efficiency, so that change in the direction of greater adaptation gradually slows and a way of life becomes more stable. This fact has been referred to by Thomas Harding (1960) as the Principle of Stabilization. On the basis of this principle, Sahlins and Service (1960) have formulated what they call the Law of Evolutionary Potential, which states that a culture's capacity to move from one general evolutionary stage to another varies inversely with its degree of specific evolutionary adaptation.

If it were not for general evolution, interacting cultures would continue increasing their adaptations to their environments and to each other until a final stability would be achieved among them. But, as we have seen, under certain circumstances cultures may adopt radically new modes of adaptation and undergo a qualitative change in social complexity and power. General evolutionary change inevitably disrupts the previous balance of power between neighboring societies. As each new general evolutionary stage is achieved, societies at the new level expand at the expense of simpler, less powerful cultures. Some of these simpler societies may be absorbed. Others are driven out of their territory or annihilated as the more complex society expands in population and acquires new territory. Still others may adopt the new technology in order to defend themselves by entering the new level of general evolution. The latter will eventually need to improve the efficiency of their use of the technology that made the transition to the new stage possible. That is, they begin to improve their specific evolutionary adaptation to the new technology. As this process occurs, the earlier dominant societies of this stage are likely to achieve a high degree of social stability sooner than latecomers do.

Leapfrogging

When considered in light of the Law of Evolutionary Potential, the earlier stabilization of the first culture to make the transition from one general evolutionary level to the next makes it likely that this culture will be the first to move to an even more complex stage. Rather, it is the backwater cultures, those which are less specifically adapted to their current situation, that have the greatest chance to leap ahead in power and complexity by adopting and implementing radically new technologies. This fact has been formulated into another general law of cultural evolution, called the Law of Local Discontinuity of Progress. This law states that successive stages of general evolutionary change are not likely to be achieved in the same locality. General evolutionary change tends to occur in a kind of leapfrogging way with the dominant centers of world power shifting from one area to another over the centuries.

Elman R. Service (1971) believes that this leapfrogging process is likely to continue into the future. It is his contention that, should no unpredictable factor such as an accidental war intervene, the most likely course of future events is one in which Western civilization will be eclipsed by some of the currently underdeveloped nations. Service writes, ''Those nations that are now the most advanced in the present coal and oil complex have less potential for the full and efficient use of the industry of the future than certain hitherto 'underdeveloped' regions which could build a new civilization well-adapted to such a base'' (p. 42).

The forces of industrialization, of course, still are spreading gradually throughout the world. In Western Europe and North America, the process of industrialization was a gradual process that grew from quite small-scale industries to the large and complex international industrial corporations of today over a period of centuries. The social, political, and ideological life of these regions was gradually transformed to fit the needs of the developing industrial complex. Those areas of the world that are just now beginning the process of industrialization are naturally seeking to do so quickly. In Service's words (1971, pp. 44–45), ''They will begin with the latest and most advanced of the known technologies and attempt to create the complete industrial complex at once, skipping whole epochs of our development. This requires a high capital investment. The economy, therefore, must be socialistic; the government rather than private persons provides most of the capital by necessity.'' In the process of worldwide industrialization, Service expects that at least some of the developing nations will surpass the present status of the United States and Russia as the world's dominant powers, both politically and economically.

However, other factors besides a culture's ability to change readily must be considered in assessing current trends in cultural development. Part of the adjustment of a culture to its specific environment is its adjustment to other cultures with which it must interact. In the contemporary world, adjustment to the political and economic influences of the world's superpowers is a major factor in how the rest of the world's cultures are changing today. It is quite possible that the worldwide economic and political power of the superpowers is great enough to inhibit the traditional leapfrogging pattern of cultural change.

Progress?

Does technological progress also mean progress in the psychological quality of life? The major changes that occur in societies when technologies harness more energy are an increase in population, increases in the number of different statuses and groups, and an increase in the specialization of roles. Inherent in these changes is an increased dependence of everyone in society on each other. Individuals come to have less autonomy and less ability to fulfill their own needs by means of their own actions, since they must rely upon others to perform necessary tasks for which they themselves lack the skills. In general, the economic role of kinship declines. Family continues to play a role as an economic group in consumption but tends to lose its role as a production and distribution group. The role of kinship as a legitimate political force also declines. In the realm of ideology, more and more facets of life need to be understood in mechanistic rather than spiritual terms, for the role of religion as a source of explanations declines as a culture becomes more generally evolved. All of these trends tend to make the life of individuals less and less secure and stable, factors that have important psychological impact on the modal personality types at different stages of general cultural evolution.

The psychological effects of individuals' decreasing autonomy and control over their own lives is referred to as alienation. The concept of alienation is most strongly associated with Karl Marx (1961), who argued in 1844 that alienation develops when the work of individuals ceases to be carried out as a way of directly satisfying human needs and becomes instead merely a means of satisfying those needs indirectly. In the simplest societies, individual roles are highly generalized and each individual possesses most of the skills necessary for survival.

For instance, if a woman is hungry, she takes up a basket and a digging stick (often of her own making) and goes in search of food. This direct relationship between work and personal needs leads to a sense of fulfillment in work. As societies become more complex, however, persons work not to satisfy their immediate physical needs but merely to obtain some object such as money that can later be used to satisfy those needs. The labor is a step removed from the purpose for which it is ultimately performed. A telephone operator may spend the day pushing buttons in service of others, an activity that has no obvious connection with obtaining food or shelter or any other personal need. He or she may receive payment for this work only once a month and is not likely to feel the same personal satisfaction in that daily work as does the hunter in manufacturing the salmon spear or rabbit snare that will be used to obtain the day's meal.

As societies grow more complex and the work of individuals becomes more and more removed from the direct fulfillment of needs, alienation increases. The effects of alienation are multiplied when individuals must work for others in order to survive. Under such conditions, even the direct products of a worker's labor do not belong to him or her. This lack of control over the products of one's labor reduces the sense of satisfaction for having created some useful or aesthetic object.

High specialization of labor in which no individual has the skills to do everything necessary for personal survival also leads to competition between interdependent specialists. Each attempts to obtain the most possible from his or her goods or services at the expense of others. Such competition also increases the sense of alienation from society as a source of human security and meaningfulness.

The first anthropologist to emphasize the concept of alienation in the study of human cultures was Edward Sapir. He went so far as to suggest that cultures could be rated in terms of how "inherently harmonious, balanced, self-satisfactory" (1924, p. 410) they are, a view that has received little attention from other anthropologists. Although he did not suggest that there is a direct relationship between the complexity of a society and the degree to which its culture is "a spiritual hybrid of contradictory patches, of water-tight compartments of consciousness that avoid participation in a harmonious synthesis" (1924, p. 410), the parallel between his views and Marx's concept of alienation is obvious.

Summary

Cultures change—often in the direction of increasing complexity—through local discoveries and inventions, plus things borrowed from other cultures, including those to which they are politically subordinate. As changes occur within the realms of technology, social organization, or ideology, they affect the other realms so that the culture adjusts as a whole. The interrelated signs of increasing complexity are: harnessing of more energy per capita, increased specialization of labor, greater population density, greater status-ranking, decreasing emphasis on kinship, decreasing individual independence, more centralized political control, and more secular ideology. Four general levels of cultural complexity exist today—bands, tribes, chiefdoms, and states.

Historically, the great civilizations of the past are thought to have evolved according to a general pattern, categorized as the Pre-Agricultural Era, the Era of Incipient Agriculture, the Formative Era, the Era of Regional Florescence, and the Imperial Era of Cyclical Conquests. Another way of looking at the changes through which societies pass is to categorize them as specific evolution (adaptation and specialization) or general evolution (qualitative change toward greater complexity). The first tends to stabilize a society (the Principle of Stabilization), while the second moves a society toward increasing complexity, unless such change is inhibited by the effects of the society's previous adaptation (the Law of

Evolutionary Potential). Because those cultures that are already well adapted are less likely to change, new leaders in the movement toward complexity may emerge from the previously underdeveloped societies (the Law of Local Discontinuity of Progress). The features of increasing complexity may not be entirely desirable, for in the psychological realm they tend to cause a sense of alienation.

Key Terms and Concepts

discovery 243
invention 244
diffusion 244
direct borrowing 244
stimulus diffusion 244
acculturation 244
Law of Cultural Dominance 244
technology 246
social organization 246
ideology 246
Basic Law of Cultural Evolution 246
band 250
reciprocity 251
tribe 255
horticulture 255
lineage 255
clan 255
exogamy 256
moiety 256
kindred 256

nonkinship associations 256
pastoralism 257
chiefdom (rank society) 258
chief 259
state 262
market economy 262
nonindustrialized state 265
industrialized state 265
Pre-Agricultural Era 267
Era of Incipient Agriculture 267
Formative Era 267
Era of Regional Florescence 267
Imperial Era of Cyclical Conquests 267
specific evolution 267
general evolution 267
Principle of Stabilization 268
Law of Evolutionary Potential 268
Law of Local Discontinuity of
    Progress 268
alienation 269

Annotated Readings

Chagnon, N. A. (1977). *Yąnomamö: The fierce people* (2nd ed.). New York: Holt, Rinehart and Winston. An exceptionally well-written ethnographic account of a tribal society. Includes fascinating insights into the ethnographer's personal experience while doing fieldwork.

Sahlins, M. D. (1968). *Tribesmen*. Englewood Cliffs, NJ: Prentice-Hall. A short overview of tribal societies.

Sahlins, M., & Service, E. R. (Eds.). (1960). *Evolution and culture*. Ann Arbor, MI: University of Michigan Press. A thoughtful examination of various views on cultural evolution.

Service, E. R. (1979). *The hunters* (2nd ed.). Englewood Cliffs, NJ: Prentice-Hall. An excellent brief introduction to the basic characteristics of foraging societies.

Service, E. R. (1978). *Profiles in ethnology*. New York: Harper & Row. A well-written series of ethnographic descriptions of a variety of the world's traditional cultures. Must reading for the anthropology major.

Service, E. R. (1962). *Primitive social organization*. New York: Random House. A very useful reference work on the social organization of traditional societies written from an evolutionary perspective.

Steward, J. H. (1955). *Theory of culture change*. Urbana, IL: University of Illinois Press. A collection of the basic papers on cultural evolution by one of the most influential twentieth-century cultural evolutionists.

Thomas, E. M. (1959). *The harmless people*. New York: Knopf. A beautifully written account of life among the !Kung foragers of the Kalahari Desert of South Africa.

Turnbull, C. M. (1962). *The forest people*. Garden City, NY: Doubleday. A well-written, empathetic, and easy-to-read account of the Mbuti pygmies of Central Africa.

White, L. A. (1959). *The evolution of culture*. New York: McGraw-Hill. A review of cultural evolution as seen by the anthropologist who reawakened an interest in the subject in the twentieth century.

Chapter 11

Contemporary World Societies

THE VANISHING OF NONSTATE SOCIETIES

Acculturation

Ethnocide

Genocide

THE EFFECTS OF INDUSTRIALIZATION

Developed and Underdeveloped Societies

Economic Change

Urbanization

World Population Growth

Industrialization and the Quality of Life

PEASANT CULTURES

Feudal Peasantries

Colonial Peasantries

CONTEMPORARY PEASANTRIES

APPLIED ANTHROPOLOGY AND CULTURE CHANGE

THE FUTURE OF THE PEASANT WORLD

In the contemporary world, hunting and gathering cultures that have changed little over thousands of years coexist with rapidly modernizing industrial cultures whose trappings range from superhighways, heart transplants, and cable television to polluted air and water. Between these two extremes, the mass of humanity lives as peasants growing their own foods, with little income for other goods. Anthropologists are concerned about the fates of all three groups: the vanishing primitive peoples, the peasant cultures that cannot quite meet their own needs, and the industrial peoples threatened by problems such as overpopulation, strained resources, and disparities of wealth.

The Vanishing of Nonstate Societies

As the cultures of the world evolved, societies at each new general evolutionary level were technologically and socially more powerful than those of the preceding levels. Throughout the history of cultural evolution, societies with less dense populations have been displaced by those with technologies that have allowed their populations to grow increasingly powerful. Tribes have displaced bands, and chiefdoms have expanded at the expense of both band and tribal peoples. The process continues today as the state-level societies take control of territories that once belonged to nonstate peoples. As this happens, more and more of the nonstate societies of the world are becoming extinct. Today, relatively few bands, tribes, and chiefdoms still exist, and the number is declining each year. The expansion of state societies into territories once occupied by nonstate societies has given rise to a new class of people, called indigenous people, who are the native people of an area now controlled by a state political system within which they have little or no influence. Today, about 200 million people—4% of the world's population—have this status. As we shall see, however, not all indigenous people continue to live their ancestral way of life. Those who do are an even smaller minority.

There are three general ways in which indigenous cultures disappear: acculturation, ethnocide, and genocide.

Figure 11.1 *Indigenous People*
Many societies native to an area are becoming controlled by expanding state societies. In addition, they are losing their unique cultural characteristics. This baby wears her native Guatemalan bonnet.

In the latter, not only the culture but also the people are killed.

Acculturation

When two previously distinct cultures come in contact, they both change. In this process, called acculturation, each of the interacting cultures borrows traits from and adjusts to the other. Acculturation can change a culture so much that it soon has little in common with its own traditional characteristics.

The process of cultural change may begin before members of the two societies actually meet, as technological traits from one society are passed and traded through intermediary societies until they reach far distant groups. But acculturation occurs most dramatically when two societies are interacting directly. As each adopts the other's technological, social, and ideological traits, they become more like one another. When one of the societies is politically, economically, and technologically less powerful than the other, it will change the most. When this process is carried to an extreme, the subordinate culture can change so much that it is hardly distinguishable from the dominant one. As a more powerful society extends its boundaries and politically subordinates a less powerful people within its own native territory, the indigenous people generally come to have very little influence on the political decision making of the society that governs them.

The process of acculturation can take place forcibly, for instance, through military domination. It also can occur more peaceably through mechanisms such as trade. As members of the less powerful society seek to acquire materials they find useful from their more powerful trade partners, their own way of life changes in the process. Acculturation eventually can lead to the extinction of an entire culture even though its people survive.

Ethnocide

Sometimes the destruction of a traditional way of life is carried out by deliberate, systematic policies of the dominant culture. Such a process is called ethnocide. An example of the systematic attempt to extin-guish the traditional cultures of indigenous peoples has been the treatment of Native Americans in the United States. The political subordination of Native American peoples involved prolonged military campaigns as well as economic processes. Following military conquest, the native people often were forced to cede much of their original lands to the United States government. Initially, Native Americans lived as independent societies with whom treaties were signed that recognized their own rights to self-government on their own lands. Later, Native Americans were redefined by their conquerors as "dependent peoples" of the United States government, whose access to political power within the society that claimed to govern them was almost nonexistent. As more and more of their lands were taken for use by other nondependent citizens, Native Americans found themselves forced onto the least desirable lands, called reservations, and in some cases dispossessed of land altogether.

The Cherokee Trail of Tears

In the 1830s, the Cherokee, or *Tsalagi* as they called themselves, were a farming people who lived in what is now northern Georgia, western Tennessee, eastern North Carolina, and eastern Virginia, where they had lived since at least 1540. They had been greatly influenced by the customs of European immigrants and had adopted many of their ways. Many had attended college. Most had adopted Christianity. Their homes were generally built in the same manner as those in neighboring white communities. Their clothing was of woven cotton or wool. An 1825 census of the Cherokee Nation authorized by the Council of the Cherokee listed 10 sawmills, 61 blacksmith shops, 18 ferry boats, 31 gristmills, 2,493 plows, 8 cotton machines, 2,488 spinning wheels, and 762 looms. The United States government had signed a treaty in 1785 recognizing the Cherokee's right to perpetual occupancy of their lands. During the War of 1812, Chief Junaluska volunteered over 600 Cherokee scouts to aid the United States army in fight-

Figure 11.2 *Sequoia*
The Cherokee chief, Sequoia, created an alphabet unique to his nation. Utilizing only the idea of writing from the Europeans, Sequoia's symbols represented specific Cherokee syllables. (see page 245, Chapter 10)

ing the Creek Indians at the Battle of Horseshoe Bend. During this battle Chief Junaluska personally saved the life of Andrew Jackson. By 1821 the Cherokee Sequoia had developed a system for writing the language of his people, and within 10 years the literacy rate was greater among Cherokees than among U.S. citizens. In 1832 the Cherokee began printing their own newspaper in both Cherokee and English.

In 1828 a Cherokee boy at Ward Creek, Georgia, sold a gold nugget to a white trader, an act that one observer of its results said sealed the doom of the Cherokees. Cherokees began to be driven off their land by gold seekers. In 1830 the state of Georgia passed a law annexing a large portion of the Cherokee lands and declaring Cherokee laws and government null and void within Georgia. Cherokees were forbidden to mine gold within this area, a law enforced by the Georgia Guard. The Cherokees sought redress through the federal courts and sued the state to keep their lands. The case reached the United States Supreme Court, which was presided over by Chief Justice John Marshall. In 1832 the court ruled in favor of the Cherokees. However, Presi-

dent Andrew Jackson would not honor the Supreme Court's decision; he remarked, that "John Marshall has made his decision; now let him enforce it." Jackson instead became involved in the actual removal of the Cherokees from their lands. Chief John Ross sent Chief Junaluska as an envoy to plead with President Jackson for protection for his people, but Jackson rejected the pleas of the man who had saved his life. In 1835 the Treaty of New Echota, Georgia, made the evacuation of the Cherokees from all of their lands mandatory. Chief John Ross requested a two-year period for his people to prepare to leave their lands for land in what is now Oklahoma and Kansas.

The Cherokees continued their attempts to negotiate their right to remain. But, in 1838 while Chief John Ross was in Washington, D.C., attempting to work out an alternative to the removal of his people, 7,000 soldiers under the command of General Winfield Scott began immediate arrests of Cherokees wherever they were found. Men working in their fields were beaten and driven at gunpoint into stockades. Women were driven from their homes, and children were separated from their families. No time was allowed for people to take clothing, blankets, or food. Eighteen thousand Cherokees were housed in rat-infested stockades without sanitary facilities. From May until November of 1838, people with as much as one thirty-second Cherokee ancestry were arrested.

One of those evicted was John Ross, nephew of Chief John Ross, who was preparing to leave for Princeton. He was taken from his Georgia home, a two-story brick mansion, with his mother, a full-blooded Scottish woman, after his father was shot in an upstairs room. The mansion was burned as they left. During the fall and winter of 1838, the Cherokees were loaded into 645 wagons, and the 900 mile trek began. Four thousand died in the stockades or on the journey to Oklahoma Indian Territory.

Politically dominant societies may legally require that indigenous peoples send their children to schools that train them in the dominant culture and language of the nation. In some cases these are boarding schools where the children must live for long periods of time, far from their own families. Often the use of their native language is not only discouraged but also forbidden and punished. Removed from the normal process of socialization in their own native culture, they return home ill-equipped to carry on their parents' way of life. Missionary efforts also have contributed to the destruction of native ways of life. This has not been limited to attacks on traditional religious beliefs, for the missionaries often have sought to condemn as immoral other parts of native culture that differed from current customs in their own societies. For instance, Western religious leaders generally have worked for the abolishing of forms of marriage other than monogamy, even though their own religious heritage includes scriptural precedent for polygyny as a once-accepted form (Ribiero, 1971; Walker, 1972).

Genocide

Related to ethnocide, the destruction of a culture, is the practice of genocide, the systematic destruction of a people. Many of the indigenous people of the world have been and are being systematically exterminated. Military campaigns against native peoples have been only one way in which the extinction of whole societies has occurred. Biological warfare also has been used. In the earlier days of United States history, clothing and blankets infected with smallpox and other diseases were distributed to some Native Americans, ostensibly as gifts. Colonial people also have given gifts of poisoned foods to indigenous people and have sometimes hunted them for sport (Bonwick, 1870; Calder, 1874; Horwood, 1969). In the past decade in many parts of Latin America, Indians have been killed by settlers moving onto their traditional lands. This private warfare is carried out with guns, bombs, dynamite, and even rapid-fire weapons from helicopters by private individuals while the national governments have turned a blind eye to the killing. In some cases, government agencies have declared traditional native lands to be ''empty'' in spite of the presence of indigenous people and therefore legitimately available for settling by nonindigenous farmers, miners, and land speculators.

Gregor (1983) has reported the historical impact of the immigration of nonindigenous people into one Latin American country:

> In 1500 explorer Pedro Cabral landed on the coast of Brazil and claimed its lands and native peoples for the Portuguese empire. Since that time Brazilian Indians have been killed by European diseases and bounty hunters, forced off their land by squatters and speculators, and enslaved by ranchers and mine owners. Today the Indians, numbering less than one-tenth of the precontact population, inhabit the most remote regions of the country. (p. 1)

The effects of such violence have penetrated even into indigenous groups that have had little direct contact with outsiders. Gregor has described the Mehinaku, a single village tribe that lives in a vast protected reservation in the Mato Grosso of Brazil. Despite their official protection and relative isolation, contact with Brazilians has been sufficient to undermine the security of their lives. Gregor quotes one Mehinaku villager: ''Last night my dream was very bad. I dreamed of a white man'' (p. 1). According to the Mehinaku, such dreams portend illness. The symbolism is apt since, in the words of Gregor, ''In the early 1960s, almost 20 percent of the tribe died in a measles epidemic, and the villagers continue to suffer from imported diseases for which they have neither natural nor acquired immunity'' (p. 2).

The Effects of Industrialization

One fundamental factor sealing the doom of many nonstate societies and altering the nature of all the world's cultures has been industrialization. Beginning with the Industrial Revolution in Great Britain in the latter half of the eighteenth century, many cultures have joined the movement away from home production of goods to large-scale, mechanized factory production requiring great inputs of capital. This shift has brought profound alterations in all aspects of life, including changes in economic systems, growth of populations, and concentration of people around cities. Even those societies that have not industrialized are now defined and affected by their lack of industry.

Developed and Underdeveloped Societies

Societies may be categorized in a number of ways. One simple distinction commonly is made on the basis of industrialization. Developed countries are the industrialized nations of the world: the countries of North America, Europe, Japan, Taiwan, and the Soviet Union. Underdeveloped countries are the remaining largely nonindustrialized world societies, including all of Africa, Asia (excluding Japan, Taiwan, and the Soviet Union), and Latin America. The distinction between developed and underdeveloped countries is widely used, but the dichotomy is simpler than the reality it represents. For instance, the world's underdeveloped countries vary from extremely poverty-stricken societies in which hunger and starvation are daily problems to others that have incorporated a great deal of industrialized technology into their economy and will soon be viewed as having become developed countries. Those underdeveloped countries that are making major gains in industrialization are sometimes referred to as developing countries in recognition of the changes they are undergoing. As developing countries are drawn into the worldwide network of industrialized economies, they change in a variety of ways that are discussed in the following sections of this chapter.

As of mid-1985, three fourths of the human population lived in underdeveloped nations (Kent & Haub, 1985). Living standards are very low in these areas, and their current economies often will not support industrial development. Most underdeveloped countries suffer from severe shortages of land, capital, or labor. Land is often largely owned by a small, elite minority, with the remainder severely fragmented into plots too small to do more than meet the minimal needs of the families who farm them. The results of the absence of capital include roads that are impassable when it rains, schools that lack enough books, and per capita incomes that are extremely low. The average per capita gross national product of the underdeveloped nations is 700 U.S. dollars, compared with 9,380 U.S. dollars for the developed world. The population of the underdeveloped world is a more rural one than that of developed countries: While 73% of the people in developed societies live in urban areas, only 31% of the people in underdeveloped countries do so. These contrasts between the developed and underdeveloped parts of the world are results of the process of industrialization that began two centuries ago.

Economic Change

Industrialization has greatly influenced the economic and social life of societies in which it has occurred. Preindustrial economies are fundamentally matters of family-based production, and the food and other goods produced are used primarily by the producers themselves. Trade may exist, but mostly as trading of the surpluses from producing for one's own family and community rather than the specialized production of food or other goods for the purpose of trade. With industrialization comes a major increase in the number of specialized occupations. Industrialization has created a great demand for wage laborers at centralized locations, laborers who do not produce their own food. So industrialization is only possible if farming moves from being a family-oriented subsistence activity to a market-oriented enterprise.

Farming to raise cash crops is vastly different from farming to feed oneself. Farming peoples who produce for their own consumption are more likely to diversify their production into as many as 20 to 30 different kinds of crops and animals. This diversity minimizes their risks and maximizes their autonomy. Market-oriented farmers tend to invest in a smaller number of more specialized crops. Industry also fosters the production of nonessential food crops, such as cocoa and coffee, and non-

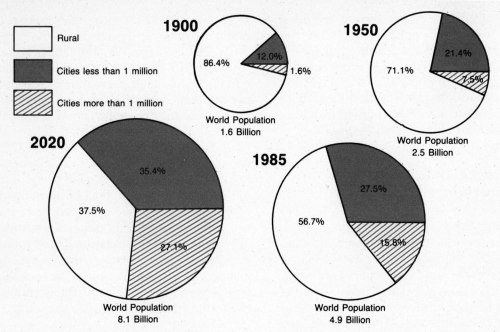

Sources: Kingsley Davis International Technical Cooperation Centre Review, July 1972; World Facts and Figures, 1979; UN Population Division; and Population Reference Bureau.

Figure 11.3 *Patterns of World Urbanization*
Industrialization has created the move to cities, increasing their size so that in 1985, eleven cities had more than 10 million people.

food products, such as wool for textiles or sisal for twine and cordage manufacture. So industrialization fosters a move of a large percentage of farmers away from staple food production. In an industrialized economy, the food-producing sector of farming becomes increasingly competitive, mechanized, expensive, and competitive, so that small-scale farms become less and less viable.

Urbanization

Agriculture created towns and cities long before industrialization began, but industrialization greatly fostered the growth of cities. Since the large-scale manufacture of marketable goods and trade go hand in hand as industrialization proceeds, industrialized centers of manufacture tend to be located in urban centers along the routes of trade. As industry produces a growing demand for labor, workers are drawn out of rural areas into the cities to find jobs, and urban areas grow in population.

In 1900 only 13.6% of the world's population lived in cities. By 1985 the portion of the world's population living in urban areas

had risen to 41% and it is expected to climb to 60% by the year 2020 (Murphy, 1985; see Fig. 11.3). Part of the process of urbanization has been an increase in the size of cities. In 1950 there were only 2 cities with more than 10 million inhabitants: the New York/New Jersey urban complex and London. In 1985 there were 11 such cities, the largest of which was Mexico City with 18.1 million people (Murphy, 1985; see Table 11.1).

World Population Growth

In addition to becoming more concentrated in cities, the world's population has grown in general as industrialization has increased our life expectancy, through factors described in the next section. The history of human population can be described as a long period of slow growth followed by a relatively recent explosion that reached its fastest rate of expansion in 1965, when world population was increasing at about 2% per year. The period of slow growth ended with the development of agriculture about 10,000 years ago, but the truly rapid explosion that we are still experiencing started with the Industrial Revolution.

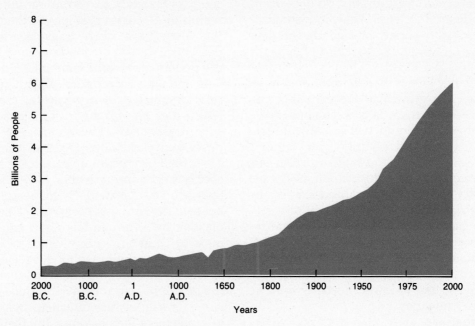

Figure 11.4 *World Population Growth Through History*
The growth of the population of the world has historically been a long, slow process until the Industrial Revolution, which initiated a rapid growth period.

A third of a million years ago, in the time of *Homo erectus*, the human population of the entire world was less than 1 million people. When food domestication began, about 10,000 years ago, there were still fewer than 10 million people in the world. By A.D. 1 the figure was about 300 million. It reached half a billion in A.D. 1650, and the first billion was achieved about A.D. 1800. By July of 1986 the figure had reached 5 billion. Using the same beginning point, a population of one billion required a third of a million years to reach. The second billion took only about 130 years, the third just 30 years, the fourth only 15 years, and the fifth a mere 11 years!

Industrialization and the Quality of Life

Industrialization does provide benefits. Its productivity is much greater than that of hand labor. This high productivity frees

1950	Population (in millions)	1984	Population (in millions)	2000	Population (in millions)
1. New York-N.E. New Jersey	12.3	1. Mexico City	18.1	1. Mexico City	26.3
2. London	10.4	2. Tokyo-Yokohama	17.2	2. Sao Paulo	24.0
3. Rhine-Ruhr	6.9	3. Sao Paulo	15.9	3. Tokyo-Yokohama	17.1
4. Tokyo-Yokohama	6.7	4. New York-N.E. New Jersey	15.3	4. Calcutta	16.6
5. Shanghai	5.8	5. Shanghai	11.8	5. Greater Bombay	16.0
6. Paris	5.5	6. Calcutta	11.0	6. New York-N.E. New Jersey	15.5
7. Greater Buenos Aires	5.3	7. Greater Buenos Aires	10.9	7. Seoul	13.5
8. Chicago-N.W. Indiana	4.9	8. Rio de Janeiro	10.4	8. Shanghai	13.5
9. Moscow	4.8	9. Seoul	10.2	9. Rio de Janeiro	13.3
10. Calcutta	4.6	10. Greater Bombay	10.1	10. Delhi	13.3

Note. United Nations, Department of International Economic and Social Affairs, 1985.

Table 11.1 *World's Ten Largest Cities*

many members of society to pursue the specialized occupations that do not exist in preindustrial societies. Thus, industrialization brings to society new goods and new services. Overall, the standard of living in industrialized societies is higher and the life expectancy longer than in traditional ways of life. The growth in life expectancy is influenced by many factors. The industrialization of food production can provide better nutrition and security from famine. Improved housing and sanitation also can be created through industrialization. The increased number of specialized statuses in industrialized societies represent new services that also can increase life expectancy. For instance, medical specialists—including doctors and other health care providers—can contribute directly to a declining rate of disease and to lower mortality rates in all age categories.

Industrialization also has its costs. Growth in industry is paralleled by growth in air and water pollution. As population grows, increased demand for goods can lead to the depletion of nonrenewable resources such as minerals and fossil fuels and to the overuse of potentially renewable ones. The urban growth that an expanding population fosters brings crowding and its attendant problems of unemployment, poverty, poor health and nutrition, and crime. It is an irony that industrialization can create both many new jobs and high unemployment, wealth and poverty, abundant foods and poor nutrition. Many of these problems grow out of the fact that although industrialization creates wealth, that wealth is not necessarily equitably distributed. Without exception, the process of industrialization has been accompanied by increasing disparities in the wealth, power, and honor of the social classes that are part of all state-level societies. At times, these inequities can be the source of major social problems.

Peasant Cultures

Since the beginning of urbanization, the contrast between urban centers of power and wealth and less influential rural food-producing areas has been a fact of human life. In some times and places, rural food producers have become so separated from sources of political and economic influence within the societies that govern their lives that they have been transformed into peasants. Peasants are food producers who use preindustrial techniques for producing food and who are economically and politically dominated by a governing class of which they are not a part. Peasants are a subordinated part of a larger society. They rarely control their own political destinies. Their food production is part of the larger society's economy, but they have little influence on its operation. Often, peasants do not own the land that they work. They rely on their own human labor and consume most of what they grow. Since peasants must produce their own food, they do not specialize in cash crops or crops that cannot be eaten. Peasants may produce some crops for sale or hire out their own labor to supplement their incomes, but their cash incomes are too low to change their material conditions or socially subordinate status.

Feudal Peasantries

In preindustrial times, peasants were part of political systems in which local aristocratic leaders who claimed ownership of the land granted the feudal peasants the privilege to use the land to grow their own food in return for rent or service. According to Dalton (1969), the relationship between peasant and lord in feudal times involved responsiblities and obligations on the part of the land owner as well as the peasant. For instance, the feudal lord provided military and police protection for the peasants, settled disputes among the peasants, and fed them in times of hardship. Feudal social forms are less common today but can, for instance, still be found in parts of India, El Salvador, and Guatemala. Peasants' lack of land ownership probably always has been a source of dissatisfaction in most feudal societies (Wolf, 1969), but the exploitation of peasants by feudal aristocracies was not so one-sided as that which followed industrialization, when contracted wage labor replaced the earlier paternalistic feudal system. In the industrialized economic system, the obligations of the propertied classes ended with the payment of the wage.

Figure 11.5 *Peasant Market*
Most peasant societies produce their own food and may sell some of their crops at market as these women in the delta region of St. Louis, Senegal.

Colonial Peasantries

Following the development of industrialized food production and transportation technologies, the subordination of peasantries intensified. Industrialization opened the door for colonial empires to spread into distant parts of the world, where inexpensive peasant labor made possible the cheap extraction of natural resources for the benefit of the colonial administrations and their homelands. Colonial peasants were encouraged, sometimes economically and sometimes by the pressure of military might, to move from food production to the production of nonfood export crops and to paid labor. As Lappé and Collins (1977) have pointed out:

Colonialism destroyed the cultural patterns of production and exchange by which traditional societies in "underdeveloped" countries previously had met the needs of the people. Many precolonial social structures, while dominated by exploitative elites, had evolved a system of mutual obligations among the classes that helped to ensure at least a minimal diet for all. A friend of mine once said: "Precolonial village existence in subsistence agriculture was a limited life indeed, but it's certainly not Calcutta." The misery of starvation in the streets of Calcutta can only be understood as the end-point of a long historical process—one that has destroyed a traditional social system. (p. 76)

The colonial subordination of peasantries can be seen as a process in which some societies have been underdeveloped to the benefit of others (Rodney, 1972). Colonial administrations encouraged the production of cash crops such as cotton, cocoa, coffee, sugar, and tobacco for export at the expense of the staple foods that had been produced previously. These export crops were selected for their high price value in the home market relative to their shipping costs and not for their value as foods. The methods used to bring about this shift to cash crop production included physical force and taxation. Since the taxes levied by colonial administrations had to be paid in cash, peasants were forced to grow cash crops. In some cases, foreign governments or private individuals claimed ownership of native lands and forced the native people to work the fields as slaves, wage laborers, or dispossessed tenant farmers. The profits of the export products grown remained in the hands of the foreign interests. Thus, through various means, previously self-sufficient farmers could no longer grow enough food to meet their own needs. Ironically, even though peasant peoples throughout the world are basically farmers, the peasant societies have had to become major food importers to feed themselves. This has locked them firmly into the world economy which today is dominated by the industrialized nations.

Contemporary Peasantries

Today, most of the people in the world can be classified as peasants, members of a social class of traditional, family-based food producers who are subordinate to an urban-based administrative class in each of their societies. The economies of these societies are, themselves, highly influenced by worldwide economic forces that are beyond their control. Because of the small volume of their specialized cash crops, the peasants lack the cash flow to pay for the equipment and services that would be necessary to industrialize their farming techniques. Neither is their economic base sufficient for state taxation to sustain the bureaucratic social benefits available in urban centers. Traditional credit and rental arrangements in peasant communities often are based on commodities rather than money, and exchange is centered on small marketplaces in which individual peasants act as ''penny capitalists,'' selling the few surplus products they produce at home or selling their labor on a piecemeal basis. Since in many peasant societies much of the most productive land is owned by a wealthy

Figure 11.6 *Irrigated Farmlands*
One type of peasant society typically works for an absentee landlord. This child works on an irrigated farm near Byanné on the southern edge of the Sahara.

elite—who long ago converted it to the production of cash crops—peasants find it difficult to produce sufficient foods on their ''postage stamp'' farms to meet their own nutritional needs. Much of their cash income is devoted to the purchase of food, and typically the cash incomes that they obtain prove insufficient to meet the expenses of life in an industrializing society.

The Varieties of Peasant Societies. Peasant societies are not all identical. They are found in various environments and use different subsistence technologies. Moris (1981) has outlined the basic contexts in which one finds peasant societies: pastoral and ranching areas, irrigation farmland, large-farm or estate areas, marginal lands and hill farming, intensive peasant small-holdings, organized settlement and frontier areas, labor reserve areas (remittance economy areas), tenancy and refugee farming, and peri-urban squatter settlements.

Pastoral and ranching areas have low-density populations that are spread over large territories. Sometimes the resources

Figure 11.7 *Pastoral and Ranching Societies*
The Maasai tribe of Kenya follow their herds in a pastoral tradition. They have great affection for their cattle, calling them each by name, and never slaughtering them.

they use must be owned communally rather than individually to be effectively utilized. Their need to migrate seasonally with their herds and the low population density make it difficult for them to form a power base to which the centralized government administrators will respond. This lack of political power is especially problematic since these people's needs differ from those of the more sedentary parts of a society with which administrators are likely to be familiar. Their special problems include stock theft and difficulties in establishing effective educational programs.

Irrigated farmlands often are worked by tenant farmers. There is heavy reliance on one or two major crops, such as coffee or hemp, grown for their market value. Tenant farmers may live in large villages near the land they work on behalf of absentee landlords. Peasant-landlord relations have many characteristics of the historically earlier forms of peasantry, since the land worked

by the peasant is owned by an elite whose good will the peasant must keep to maintain access to the land. Adequate medical facilities and other social resources are likely to be minimal in the peasant villages.

Large-farm or estate areas are common in the tropics. They are supported by foreign investment and typically grow export crops such as rubber or tea. Here the peasant is simply a laborer and lives in quarters provided by the management. In some cases, these estates may be owned by the local government rather than by members of the private sector. Estate settlements often have very differing social needs from those of neighboring towns, since the entire population of the estate settlement is made up of working-class persons.

Marginal and hill farming is found in isolated pockets of semiarid land and hill country where only hand techniques are usable in farming because of the steep slopes. Crops are limited to those relying solely on the yearly rainfall. Only the surpluses above the peasants' own needs can be marketed. Small stock supplement the subsistence needs of these peasants, but the animals often cause a gradual deterioration of communal lands where they are pastured.

Intensive peasant smallholdings are found where better soil and rainfall allow dairy farming or growing of perennial crops such as tea, coffee, bananas, and cassava. Farming in these areas is basically hoe farming done by hand. Since these areas are sometimes quite productive, hoe farming can yield enough to support population growth. This increase often is followed by a shift toward labor-intensive high-yield crops, such as irrigated rice, and smaller and smaller plots, until the equivalent of urban population densities are achieved in the rural peasant settlements. The people in these areas can become locked into increasingly impoverished conditions by division of land into intensively cultivated smallholdings.

Frontier areas develop when new lands are opened up to settlement by national governments that do not recognize the land claims of the indigenous populations there. The attraction of these areas is often the natural resources they contain, such as timber, gold, and other minerals useful to the industries of the nation. Land speculation is common in these areas, and what seems like a booming economy can lure farmers who are not aware of the riskiness of farming in these areas. Bank loans are made on the basis of the speculative value of the land, not its farm income value. Foreclosures gradually dispossess the farming populations, who become landless peasant workers or tenant farmers.

What Moris (1981) calls labor reserve areas should probably be called remittance economy areas, since they are "rural communities that depend on remitted earnings for cash income" (1981, p. 29). These are communities that experience high levels of out-migration as workers are forced to leave the communities to meet their economic needs. The local communities are thereby drained of younger working-age men. This lowers the productivity of community labor,

and what little income finally reaches the community from absent workers may accomplish little in improving conditions in the home community. Welfare costs of supporting the less productive members of the community who are left behind—the aged, the sick, and persons too uneducated to find employment elsewhere—further undermine the standard of living in the community. Absentee ownership of land may complicate matters in these areas, since those who reside in the communities often are unwilling to pay for improvements to land they do not own. Because of their stagnant economy and lack of services, these communities gradually gain a reputation as "backwards districts," to which young people are not likely to want to return.

Tenant or refugee farms worked by landless and dispossessed tenant populations may develop, according to Moris (1981), when the production system of a traditional society gives way to paid employment of tenant farmers. This change disrupts the traditional system of mutual obligations that gave peasant farmers the right to work land they did not own. After generations in which these rights have been recognized, the peasant farmers suddenly find themselves dispossessed and without any source of income. Modernization in these areas is difficult, since the lands that are worked are not owned by the peasant farmers. The officially recognized landowners are unlikely to be willing to bear the costs of such things as fencing or improved housing or farm structures, since these benefit the tenant farmers, not the owners. Similarly, the farmers are not motivated to make improvements on lands that belong to someone else.

Peri-urban squatter settlements are the final category of contemporary peasant-land relationships based on Moris's analysis. These are formed of people "who live in densely settled communities near rapidly growing cities" (1981, p. 30). Peri-urban squatters are especially common in tropical areas, where perennial crops can be grown and multiple cropping makes it possible to grow enough to support families on extremely small "postage stamp" farms. The unofficial settlements created by these

Figure 11.8 *Peri-urban Squatter Communities*
Squatter settlements are economically poor and politically without power. They exist near rapidly growing cities.
Residents support themselves by growing their own food and working at odd jobs.

peasants outside major cities may lack the recognition that would entitle them to public services or legal title to the land they occupy and work. Sanitary conditions are often extremely poor in these settlements, as are nutrition and health. Incomes are supplemented by petty trading, casual work, gardening, and other services performed for citizens of the nearby cities.

The difficulties of change in peasant societies. The economic limitations of peasant life are not easily overcome. Some observers feel that a major obstacle to change lies in the peasants' own attitudes. According to Foster (1967), life in peasant societies often leads to a rather fatalistic, dreary outlook in which the drudgery of life is not believed to bring much reward, since the achievement of one person can only be accomplished at the expense of another.

Foster has called this outlook the image of limited good. Because of this view of life, peasants are commonly jealous of success, and peasant life contains many social pressures not to excel over one's peers. Lewis (1966) saw this life style as fostering attitudes that cause peasants and other poverty-stricken people to think only of today, to spend and consume what they have right now since saving for tomorrow seems futile. Lewis called this approach to life the culture of poverty. Although this outlook certainly is not the underlying cause of the impoverished conditions of peasants in most parts of the world, it can make it difficult for peasants to take part effectively in opportunities for social change.

Wolf (1966) believes there are more substantial reasons why change is difficult in peasant circumstances. Peasants are slow to combine forces to overcome exploitation because they are individually bound into vertical political ties or ''patron-client'' relationships with more wealthy and powerful individuals on whose aid they depend in times of need. To work with other peasants for the common good is to sever these personally advantageous ties, so peasant communities are caught in a cycle of competition between individuals and factions.

Scott (1976) points out that the status quo does provide the peasant with a buffer from adversity. Peasant community expectations have a leveling effect that limits the poverty into which any one member of the society can sink. The maintenance of ''commons''— lands available to all, for instance as pasturage—is an example of the buffers against adversity that are built into the peasant community. Commercialization, according to Scott, is actually a threat to peasant security, since it undermines the mechanisms that provide that security in impoverished circumstances.

Nelson and Water (1984) argue that prices in peasant markets are quite unstable and seasonally variable, since peasants market only the surplus that their families do not need for food. Peasants tend to rely on relatives for credit and assistance. They lack sufficient cash incomes to support markets that sell factory-produced goods. Nelson and Water believe that this situation is self-perpetuating because reliance on family for labor and economic support leads to large family size and increased population growth leads to reduced savings and investment. This, in turn, necessitates greater reliance on family labor and traditional means of production.

Although there are many features of life in peasant societies that make change difficult, it would be a mistake to assume that peasant societies cannot change. Peasants have been ready to revolt against the system that maintains their landlessness and poverty when opportunities for successful uprisings have presented themselves. Many social scientists believe that peaceful improvement of peasant conditions is also possible. Popkin (1979) portrays the peasant life style as a rational response to the tight constraints that limit their production and to the high degree of risk they face in making a living. He contends that when markets and opportunities exist, peasants respond by increasing output.

Applied Anthropology and Cultural Change

As anthropologists have studied the problems of nonindustrial populations, many have felt a growing obligation to apply their insights to achieve constructive change in areas such as overcoming the cycle of poverty in peasant societies. This new subfield of anthropology is called applied anthropology. Applied anthropologists working in developing countries have pointed out that the problems of the developing world are not merely technological in nature. Technological change is intimately connected to social and ideological facts of life, and technological change can sometimes create unforeseen problems in these areas. Yet the social and ideological aspects of development often have been overlooked by the governmental administrators and technicians who have been given responsibility for improving conditions among peasant populations.

Fisher (1972) describes a number of reasons why government-sponsored development projects often fail. The list demonstrates that project failures are more typically social and ideological than technological in nature. Projects intended to improve the lot of the peasant poor often are designed by persons who are unfamiliar with life in the peasant community, and these projects are imposed from the outside. The governments involved sometimes fail to commit resources that are necessary for the projects to succeed. Goals and resource allocations may be revised in the middle of a project without regard to the effects on work in the community setting. Project planning sometimes is not economically sound, and the projects may not incorporate the incentives to which peasants respond. Erroneous assumptions are commonly made about the effectiveness or capabilities of the institutions involved in the project. Projects that look good on paper may not be targeted toward specific clienteles. Often, projects spread their resources too thinly to be effective in any one area. The human element in the real work of project implementation may not be fully taken into account. The various governmental ministries involved in the work may not coordinate their efforts. Finally, demand for the new product created by the peasants is often insufficient for the work to become self-sustaining, and the yield or output projections may be inconsistent with the level of management available.

The Masai Project: An Attempt at Planned Cultural Change

Moris (1981) has described the social and political problems that plagued a development project among the Maasai,[1] a Tanzanian seminomadic cattle-herding people. The 45,000 Maasai occupied a 14-million acre territory in northern Tanzania where they herded 1 million head of cattle and about 1.25 million sheep and goats.

Attempts at range management, planning for most effective use of land for raising livestock without depleting the environment, began about the time of Tanzanian independence in 1961. Following recommendations of an American range specialist, the Tanzanian government attempted to form a pilot project Ranching Association near the town of Arusha. Unfortunately, the choice of location for this pilot project was made without considering the social organization of the people who would form the Ranching Association. It necessitated cooperation between Maasai cattle herders and their rival neighbors, the Wa-Arusha, who herded goats and farmed small plots. The program therefore was plagued by political frictions and made little progress for its first three years.

In 1970 the Masai Project was begun with support from USAID (United States Agency for International Devel-

---

1. After the Masai Project began, Maasai became the preferred spelling for the people of Masailand because it better reflects their native language. The name of their territory maintains its historical spelling.

opment). Five technical experts were hired for work on the project: an animal production specialist, a range ecologist, a livestock marketing specialist, a water development engineer, and an anthropologist. The project took responsibility for range development in Masailand, an area of 24,000 square miles.

Within the first year and a half, four ranching associations had been formed. Cattle dips and range offices were being built, and technical data were being gathered on stocking rates. A vegetation survey was underway, and groundwork was being laid for the formation of a jointly owned breeding herd. Legal action was being considered to stop the spread of bean cultivation into grazing lands. But, at the same time, the Tanzanian government was sponsoring the formation of village-based farming—in what are called ''Ujamaa villages''— throughout the country, as part of its political policy of trying to create a socialist system of production. The regional government leaders began to see the Masai Project as interfering with their goal of teaching pastoralists to adopt farming in sedentary, government-sponsored villages.

As the Tanzanian government reorganized its system for administering local areas, Masai Project members were required to report daily to the local government office. Continual reporting of day-to-day matters through the hierarchy of district officials cut into the work time of project members and slowed routine decision making. According to Moris (1981), plans and personnel were continually in flux:

> The frequent changes and reassessments in the project took their toll upon staff and morale alike. As fast as Tanzanian staff were recruited as range officers, they were called up to do their national service or assigned to counterpart training. Of the initial five foreign experts, three finished their tours or otherwise left. In its first four years the team had had three leaders, reported to four successive regional heads, and worked under three District Livestock

Development Officers in Monduli. By the end of 1972 half the project vehicles were not running because of a lack of American spare parts.

The project was continuously under reconsideration, either by Tanzanian leaders or USAID. Among Tanzanians there were fears that the US experts might oppose the Ujamaa settlement program. When equipment was late in arriving, this was interpreted as a deliberate US action to impede Tanzanian development. Some USAID officials in Washington opposed the project's investment in a socialist country where land was not privately owned. (pp. 105–106)

By 1973 the ranching associations were becoming popular among the Maasai, partly because the Maasai could see that registered ranching associations received more government assistance than did other stock owners. However, instead of forming new ranching associations, neighboring Maasai moved into lands of the existing associations in order to obtain special livestock services. In cooperation with the Tanzanian government, the project then was reorganized and strengthened. Plans were laid to increase to 21 the number of ranching associations and to include a program for settlement of the Maasai into ranches equivalent to the government-sponsored villages.

By 1977 only one of the major issues of the Masai Project had not been solved. The remaining problem was how to integrate the government concept of socialist village settlements into the association structure. And team work time was being diverted into growing areas of responsibility, such as a land capability survey using remote sensing imagery, a U.S.-backed road-building program, and a livestock training center. The growing size of the project team, which had reached 10 technicians and 20 Tanzanian counterparts, and its expanded responsibilities led to internal stresses and disagreements over project priorities. By the middle of 1977, most of the more ex-perienced team members had left the project. Most of the replacements did not speak Kiswahili, the language used in almost all Tanzanian government meetings.

The Tanzanian government received assistance to establish a livestock marketing company. However, this commercial organization was unable to recover its operating costs in remote areas. All but a few dams in the water development aspect of the project washed out, roads deteriorated without maintenance, and the professional staff and equipment were gradually dispersed.

The Future of the Peasant World

In spite of the difficulties in planned cultural change, the life of peasant villagers, who make up the majority of the world's inhabitants, is changing. For village life in Asia, Hayami and Kikuchi (1981) report that the previous decreasing economic benefit to peasant farming, which resulted when population growth outstripped the ability of peasants to produce, is being counteracted by the introduction of irrigation systems, modern varieties of increased-yield food plants, and fertilizer technology. Where the application of new farming technologies is successful, the income differentials in rural populations are being reversed. In the view of Hayami and Kikuchi, the critical problem in peasant village development is achieving peasant labor productivity sufficient to counteract the strong population pressure on limited land resources. They believe this can be achieved by efforts to control growth, cultivate new land, and develop nonfarm jobs.

Critchfield (1981) has found that several important changes are occurring in peasant villages throughout the world. He believes that "Contraception and scientific farming are producing, at last, a change in the general human condition" (p. 320), and sees four changes in all the villages he has studied. First, contraception is now a fact of life in village culture, and "In places as scattered as China, India's Kerala and Karnataka states, Sri Lanka, and Java and Bali

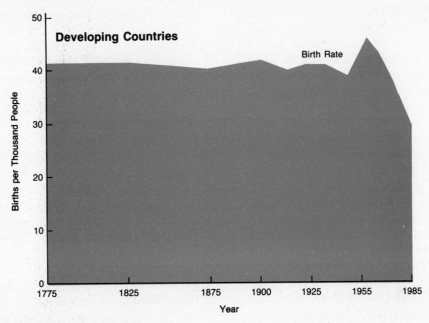

Figure 11.9 *Declining Fertility Rate*
Contraception and scientific farming have contributed to a declining birthrate in peasant villages in recent years.

in Indonesia, annual population growth rates have plummeted from 2½ percent—3 percent in the early Sixties to 1 percent—1½ percent now—mostly in the five years 1975 to 1980. Elsewhere, though less spectacularly, fertility [the number of children born per woman] has been declining for the first time in the modern era'' (p. 322; see Fig. 11.9). Second, high-yield, fertilizer-intensive, fast-maturing crops are spreading quickly into the world's villages along with year-round irrigation and multiple cropping. Third, the rural exodus to the cities is being replaced by a return of peasant workers to villages as they become able to feed them. Finally, the underdeveloped countries are becoming increasingly competitive in the world marketplace. Critchfield reports:

> During the 1970s more than one hundred and thirty developing countries joined in a new international network linking thirteen agricultural research centers, eight of them set up since 1971. They now pool knowledge and genetic material on all kinds of crops—wheat, maize, rice, sorghum, millet, cassava, potatoes, ground-

nuts, vegetables, legumes, tubers, and others. New findings are exchanged on livestock breeding, plant and animal diseases and farming systems. This new global scientific network cuts across all political boundaries and ideologies; scientists and trainees come from China, Russia, the United States, India, Pakistan, Cuba, Vietnam, Turkey, African and European countries, every nationality you can name. China's increasingly active role since the late 1970's, and its contributions of samples of basic genetic diversity developed only in China, now allows completion at last of the world's major plant germ-plasm collections. (p. 325)

From changes of these kinds, we may well expect major adjustments in the political and economic role of the currently underdeveloped countries in the next two decades as they move into the status of developed nations.

Population Control in Developing Nations

Since hunger in underdeveloped countries is basically a matter of too little growth in productivity compared with rates of population growth, control of the population growth rate has been one of the major concerns of many of these countries. Government-funded family planning clinics, legalized abortion, and public education programs about birth control are common means of fostering smaller family size. In some developing countries such as the People's Republic of China and Singapore, even stronger measures have been adopted.

One fourth of the human population, over one billion people, live in the People's Republic of China, and over half of those people are under 33 years of age (Tien, 1983). Both the absolute size of the Chinese population and the large percentage of the population that represents people of reproductive age make population control a major concern in China. A high fertility rate might well overcome China's ability to feed its population in the future, much less achieve the status of a developed nation. For these reasons, the Chinese government has taken more extreme measures than have many developing countries, and these measures appear to have been quite successful at reducing the fertility rate. One means of lowering the fertility rate is to delay the average age of marriage. The current legal age for marriage is 20 for women and 22 for men. However, the main efforts to reduce fertility involve direct intervention in family planning. As Article 53 of the revised 1978 constitution of China states, "The state advocates and encourages birth planning." Using newspapers, radio, and television, the government actively publicizes and encourages the goal of limiting births to one child per family. Bonuses, larger pensions, free health care for the child, priority in housing, and the promise of education and employment priorities for the child are all used as inducements for voluntary commitment to having only one child. County birth planning offices supply contraceptives and subsidize local health centers for IUD insertions, sterilizations, and abortions.

Peer pressure also is used to achieve the goal of one child per family in China. At the local level, the government has organized a system of fertility committees throughout the country. These committees meet with individuals and organize local meetings to create social pressure for conformity to government goals in family planning. Families are encouraged in community meetings to publicly commit themselves to having only one child, although—in deference to the strong value that Chinese peasants still place on sons—a second child is considered acceptable if the first is a daughter. The weight of public opinion is brought to bear on individuals who refuse to support the national goal of reduced population growth. A liberal policy on abortion and social pressure to terminate pregnancies after the second birth have reduced China's total fertility rate to only 2.1 children per family, a rate about half of what it was in 1970 and equivalent to that of developed countries.

Singapore, where 2.6 million people occupy a mere 200 square miles, is one of the three most densely populated countries of the world. The government provides free family planning services, including abortion and sterilization. Government policy is to encourage small families. Women receive maternity leave only for their first two children. The medical fees for the delivery of babies are greater for each successive child. Income tax exemptions apply only to the first two children. Subsidized housing is denied to large families. In 1983 the government began offering a cash payment equal to the average yearly income of a family in Singapore to any woman who was sterilized after her second child.

In developed countries where the costs of population growth have not been felt so strongly, it is difficult for many people to accept the degree to which the governments of China and Singapore are intervening in the reproductive lives of their citizens. These measures are more readily comprehended in light of the terrible costs that high fertility rates have had in slowing the process of economic development in much of the world. Remaining underdeveloped takes its toll, not only as an absence of the material luxuries associated with industrialization but also as hunger and high mortality rates.

Life expectancy at birth in the undeveloped countries is now 58 years, compared with 72 years in developed nations. In light of the advantages of successful development, similar strong governmental measures to control fertility rates may become more common in other parts of the developing world.

Summary

Industrialization has dramatically altered life in many nations, though some peoples continue to subsist by ancient foraging methods or simple hand cultivation. The indigenous cultures are becoming more and more scarce, either through adaptations to the dominant cultures that surround them or through forced takeovers of their ancestral lands and outright murder of the people. In more powerful cultures, industrialization has brought profound economic changes, population growth, concentration of population around cities, and both positive and negative effects on the quality of life. The majority of the world's people are affected by these trends but still live as peasants practicing small-scale food production for their own needs. Change in these peasant cultures comes slowly, but some are now cooperating to enhance their position in the world economy.

Key Terms and Concepts

indigenous people 273
acculturation 274
ethnocide 274
reservations 274
genocide 276
industrialization 276
developed country 277
underdeveloped country 277
developing country 277
peasants 280
feudal peasants 280
colonial peasants 280
pastoral and ranching areas 282

irrigated farmlands 283
large-farm (estate) areas 283
marginal and hill farming lands 283
intensive peasant smallholdings 284
frontier areas 284
labor reserve (remittance economy) areas 284
tenant or refugee farms 284
peri-urban squatter settlements 284
image of limited good 285
culture of poverty 285
applied anthropology 286
range management 287

Annotated Readings

Bernard, H. R., & Pelto, P. J. (Eds.). (1972). *Technology and social change*. New York: Macmillan. An important collection of case studies of the effects of the introduction of Western technology on a variety of cultures.

Bodley, J. H. (1975). *Victims of progress*. Menlo Park, CA: Cummings. A discussion of the destructive effects of contact with industrialized societies on traditional societies.

Geertz, C. (1963). *Agricultural involution: The processes of ecological change in Indonesia*. Berkeley, CA: University of California Press. An already classic study of cultural change and the interactions of technology and the agricultural habitat.

Goode, W. J. (1963). *World revolution and family patterns*. New York: Free Press. An examination of the influence of industrialization on the family.

Wolf, E. R. (1966). *Peasants*. Englewood Cliffs, NJ.: Prentice-Hall. A short but important introduction to the nature of peasant society.

Chapter 12

Contemporary American Culture

Traditionally, anthropologists have taken as their objects of study the cultures of the world's small-scale, technologically simple societies. Few have attempted to analyze the cultures of large-scale societies such as America.[1] By and large, anthropologists have tended to give priority to the study of simple societies because they represented a rapidly disappearing source of information about the human condition. Sociologists have studied social patterns in industrialized societies, but their interests generally have not centered on cultural questions, and far too little empirical fieldwork exists on American lifeways to develop an adequate model of American culture as a whole. Yet, if anthropology has any relevance to students for whom the introductory-level course will be their main exposure to the field, it lies in making their own cultural environment more meaningful. This chapter focuses on those aspects of American culture that seem most appropriate to the theme of this text and to the interests of university students, anthropology majors and non-majors alike.

American Social Organization

American society is composed of over 240 million people who live in cities of up to several million. These people are supported by an industrialized technology based primarily on fossil fuel burning and water-powered generators. About 40% of the population make up the civilian labor force of 96 million. Another 19 million are government workers. The American economy is productive enough that only about 30% of the labor force is involved in the production of goods, while the rest are service providers. Food is produced for the entire society by less than 3% of the labor force, a decline from 38% in 1900. America's high productivity has led to a relatively low demand for labor throughout most of its history. As a

---

Figure 12.1 *American Cities*
American culture is as diverse as its people and the places they live. Many people live in cities of up to several million.

---

1. For convenience, *America* will be used in this chapter to refer to the United States only, rather than to all the countries of North, Central, and South America.

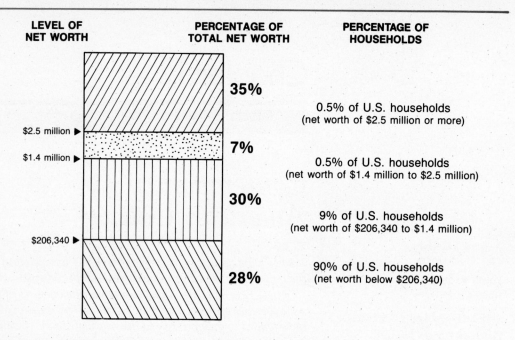

LEVEL OF NET WORTH	PERCENTAGE OF TOTAL NET WORTH	PERCENTAGE OF HOUSEHOLDS
	35%	0.5% of U.S. households (net worth of $2.5 million or more)
$2.5 million ▶	7%	0.5% of U.S. households (net worth of $1.4 million to $2.5 million)
$1.4 million ▶		
	30%	9% of U.S. households (net worth of $206,340 to $1.4 million)
$206,340 ▶		
	28%	90% of U.S. households (net worth below $206,340)

Note. From *Concentration of Wealth in the U.S.: Trends in the Distribution of Wealth Among American Families*, July, 1986, Washington, D.C.: Joint Economic Committee, Congress of the United States.

Table 12.1 *Distribution of Wealth in the United States*
While not formally stratified, most American wealth is concentrated in a small percentage of its population.

result of high productivity, the United States rarely has had an unemployment rate less than about 6% of the labor force except in time of war, and the unemployment rate for minorities often has risen above 10%.

Ideologically, Americans have not traditionally viewed their society as one made up of separate classes. Yet, as in other industrialized societies, the people of America do not all have equal access to the goods or services produced by its labor force. For instance in 1983, 5% of the United States population received 15.8% of the total income before taxes. American society, in other words, is socially stratified into classes (see Table 12.1). The American class system is somewhat ill-defined, in that the American ideology itself has traditionally denied its very existence as a formal structure. Polls have indicated that some 80% of Americans claim membership in the middle class. Interestingly, this figure includes both some persons who by technical standards would be considered members of the lower class and others who are technically of upper-class background. The failure of Americans to formally recognize that there are classes

within their social system has been made easier by a traditionally high level of mobility within the American class system.

An important measure of one's position within the American class system is one's occupation. The American economy is based primarily on market exchange. Rather than producing goods for direct exchange, most Americans are employed by someone else. In return, they are compensated with an income that they then exchange for the services and goods that they require. The size of their personal income depends largely, though not entirely, on the prestige ranking of their income-producing status (see Table 12.2).

The least prestigious and least well paid of the economic statuses are unskilled laborers. They usually are paid by the hour or by the quantity of goods that their work produces. Unskilled laborers often are hired for part-time or seasonal work such as food baggers at supermarkets, bus persons at restaurants, and farm laborers. Many of these jobs are held by young people who are not yet economically self-sufficient, by a disproportionate percentage of ethnic

Figure 12.2 *American Class System*
Americans are quick to deny that their democracy supports a class system, but ethnographic studies indicate that economically and socially such a system does exist.

minorities, and by migrant workers who travel from state to state for seasonal farm work.

Pink collar jobs are occupations traditionally held by women: waitress, sales clerk, file clerk, secretary, telephone operator, and grammar school teacher (see Table 12.3). There is some variation in the prestige and incomes associated with these jobs, but in the main they fall below average in both measures. This category of low-level human service and information processing jobs has been the fastest growing of the occupational categories since about 1950. Since World War II, tens of millions of jobs were opened up in this category. Since they were low-paid new jobs, rather than ones previously held by men, they were readily obtained by women without their being seen as competing with men for jobs (Harris, 1981).

Blue collar workers are manual laborers other than farm workers. Although they command little prestige, some of these statuses have access to above-average incomes due to the economic importance of the commodities and services that they control. Ex-

amples of blue collar workers are garbage collectors, dockhands, factory workers, taxicab and bus drivers, janitors, and supervisors of manual laborers.

White collar occupations are clerical workers, sales workers, technical workers, managers, and administrators. Their work is primarily the providing of services. Although many of these occupations are fairly prestigious and relatively well paid, over the years many white collar offices have become more and more like factories in the repetitive nature of the routine work.

Professionals are typically self-employed providers of services whose work generally requires a graduate-level university degree. Included in this category are the most prestigious nongovernmental occupations such as medical doctors, lawyers, scientists, and university faculty. These highly ranked positions, as well as highly ranked governmental positions, generally have been dominated by men (see Table 12.4).

Historically, the simplest means to climb to a higher position within the class system

Occupation	Score	Occupation	Score
Dentist	88.5	Stenographer	46.4
Mayor	84.2	Building superintendent	43.6
Electrical engineer	83.1	Automobile mechanic	41.2
Chemist	82.8	Dressmaker	39.6
Registered nurse	79.0	Librarian	39.5
Banker	77.1	Baker	39.1
Psychologist	73.7	Sales clerk	36.8
Army captain	60.6	Hairdresser	35.1
Insurance agent	58.1	Telephone operator	32.7
Child-care worker	56.0	Waiter/Waitress	31.8
High school teacher	55.1	Bus driver	28.8
Social worker	54.9	Miner	28.1
Plumber	54.6	Cashier	27.8
Secretary	53.0	Farm laborer	27.4
Firefighter	50.3		

Note. From ''Sex and Consensus in Occupational Prestige Ratings'' by B. Powell and J. A. Jacobs, 1983, *Sociology and Social Research, 67*(4), p. 400. Copyright 1983. Adapted by permission.

Table 12.2 *Occupations Ranked by Prestige in the United States*

All occupations	44.1%[a]
Managerial/professional	42.7%
Executive, administrative, managerial	35.6%
Teachers, college and university	35.2%
Teachers, except college and university	73.0%
Professional workers	49.1%
Technical/Sales/Administrative support	64.7%
Sales workers, retail and personal service	68.5%
Administrative support, including clerical	80.2%
Information clerks	90.1%
Service workers	60.6%
Personal service	80.9%
Protective service	13.2%
Crossing guards	73.3%
Precision production, craft, repair	8.4%
Operators, fabricators, laborers	25.4%
Farming, forestry, fishing	15.9%

Note. From *Professional Women and Minorities: A Manpower Data Resource Service* (Table 4-7, pp. 75-80) by B. M. Vetter and E. L. Babco, 1986, Washington, DC: Commission on Professionals in Science and Technology. Copyright 1986. Adapted by permission.

Note. [a]Figures show the percentage of female workers in these occupations.

Table 12.3 *Representation of Women in Occupations, 1985*

than one's parents had occupied was through the educational system, since higher-ranked occupations generally have required a higher level of education than have lower-ranked ones. Indeed, it is common for many employers in the United States to require an educational background in prospective employees that goes far beyond what is actually needed for the work itself. This system, in which education is strongly rewarded as a means to raising one's rank within the class system, keeps

	Men%	Women%
U.S. Population[a]	48.6	51.4
Office		
U.S. Senate[a]	98.0	2.0
U.S. House of Representatives[a]	99.5	0.5
U.S. Supreme Court	88.9	11.1
Governors[b]	96.0	4.0
State Legislators[a]	86.6	13.4
State Supreme Courts[b]	91.5	8.5

Note. [a]From *Statistical Abstract of the United States: 1986* (106th ed.) [Table No. 422, p. 249; Table No. 430, p. 253] by U.S. Bureau of the Census, 1985, Washington, DC: U.S. Government Printing Office. Copyright 1985 by U.S. Bureau of the Census.
Note. [b]From *State Elective Officials & the Legislature: 1985–86* (p. 1–126) by D. Gona (Ed.), 1986, Lexington, KY: The Council of State Governments. Copyright 1986 by The Council of State Governments.

Table 12.4 *Percentage of Men and Women Holding Political Positions in the United States, 1984*

Figure 12.3 *Geraldine Ferraro*
In 1984, Geraldine Ferraro became the first woman to run for the office of vice president of the United States.

potential workers in school for a longer period of time before they begin full-time work than might otherwise be the case. This has been one means by which the number of people in the labor pool, and therefore the unemployment rate, have been kept lower in the United States than they otherwise would have been.

Although opportunities for upward social mobility have been high in America, so have the chances of moving down in the occupational ranks. For instance, a decline in the demand for a product or service can make it impossible for a person who is qualified for a high-ranked occupation to obtain employment, and persons already employed may lose their positions. Thus, engineers who are educationally too specialized in their skills to move readily from one high-ranked position to another may find themselves bagging groceries, and recent university graduates may be forced to accept employment driving cabs. A great deal of personal anguish may accompany such downward shifts in social rank.

Power Relations

Just as Americans tend to deny the existence of ranked classes within their social

Crime Reported to Police	Canada[a]	United States[b]
Murder	9.1	2.7
Forcible rape	34.0	10.3
Robbery	239.0	110.7
Aggravated assault	289.0	511.2
Burglary	1,489.0	1,501.6
Larceny/Theft	3,085.0	4,099.5
Motor vehicle theft	459.0	353.2

Note. [a]From *Canada Yearbook 1985* (Table 20.3, p. 658; Table 20.5, pp. 658–659) Ottawa: The Minister of Supply and Services, Canada. Copyright 1985.

Note. [b]From "Crime in the United States, Annual" by U.S. Federal Bureau of Investigation, cited in *Statistical Abstract of the United States: 1986* (10th ed.) (p. 166) by U.S. Bureau of the Census, 1985, Washington, DC: U.S. Government Printing Office. Copyright 1985 by U.S. Bureau of the Census. Also from *Uniform Crime Reports,* September 11, 1983, and July 1, 1986.

Table 12.5 *Serious Crime Rates in the United States and Canada, 1982*

structure, they tend to see the power of their society as being the property of the democratic majority. Their value system favors grassroots political power, and they have traditionally viewed the federal government in negative terms. Politicians in general have been held in disdain as seekers after power; the expression "Politicians are all crooked" typifies this view. Political power is considered a necessary evil, and some political analysts claim that American voters most often cast their vote based on which candidate they oppose rather than on which they favor.

Americans view themselves as a peace-loving people who fight only when forced to. Nevertheless, the actual level of violence within the society is quite high. For instance, the homicide rate in the United States is among the highest in the world's industrialized nations. According to the annual *Uniform Crime Reports* of the FBI, the rate of murder and negligent homicide in the United States for 1984 was 79.5 per million people. This is over three times the rate among their culturally related Canadian neighbors to the north. In 1985, there were 18,976 murders in the United States. Other violent crimes also are frequent. For instance, there were 28,242 identified suicides in 1982, and it is estimated that there were 87,340 reported forcible rapes in the United States in 1985. Although Americans frequently complain that their judicial system is overly lenient with criminals, American courts convict a higher percentage of accused persons than do the courts of most other industrialized nations. Once convicted, American criminals are given and actually serve longer sentences than do their European counterparts. In 1984, there were 463,866 persons in American prisons.

Family

Americans often refer to the family as the basis of their society. In a society in which individuals must compete with one another for success, the family is one of the few relatively safe havens of close emotional ties and cooperation. However, the actual role of family in American society is minimal in contrast to the role of family in most other societies, and broken families are very common.

The limited role of the family. The American family has lost most social functions beyond the basic socialization of children and

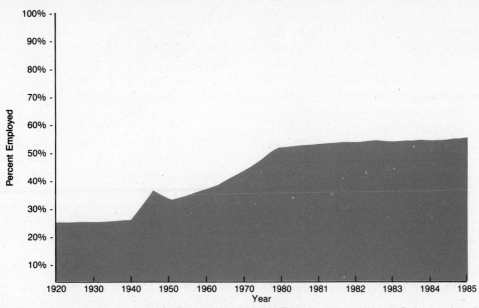

Figure 12.4 *Employment Rates of Women in the United States*
With the increase in contraception and the necessity to contribute economically to the family unit, over fifty percent of American women are employed outside the home.

the consumption of goods. Unlike families in peasant cultures, American families typically are not production units. With industrialization, home production declined, and the basic income of most Americans shifted to the nondomestic sphere.

The only economic function that most American families fulfill is that of consumption. In a sense, the American family could be defined as the group that eats together, but, since the rise of television, even this definition of the family might be invalid.

Even with industrialization, earlier American families often were held together by the presence of a mother whose work was home-centered. Before the development of effective contraceptive techniques, it was easier for the husband to seek employment outside the home than it was for the wife. Wives were likely to continue to bear children until about the age of 40, and most stayed home during their childbearing years. As the economic importance of domestic production declined, the American housewife was left in a dependent economic role. With increasingly effective birth control technology, the period of childbearing has declined from about 18 years in 1900 to about 6 years in 1980, and the average

number of children born to a couple is now less than 2. Today, due to economic necessity, over half of American women are employed outside the home.

Since labor in America is extremely specialized, children are likely to enter occupations different from those of their parents. The family therefore has ceased to play any important educational role beyond the early socialization of children. After they learn the basic skills of language and acquire their society's basic values, ideas, and customs from their family, children receive most of their formal education in adult life skills through state and private educational organizations. However, although children often enter occupations requiring different skills from those of their parents, their occupations are not likely to differ greatly in rank. The occupational choices of children, therefore, are influenced by their parents' occupations, income, and social status as mediated by such other factors as their place of residence and the quality of the schools available.

The American family is not typically a spiritual center for its members; religious ritualism within the family, where it occurs, is practiced as an extension of the rituals of a larger religious body that unites members of many family groups on the basis of a common religious ideology. It is not a center of authority, either. A complex state-level government monopolizes the right to exercise all legal force, so the American family is lacking in all governmental authority outside the governing of the family itself.

Fragmentation of families. Historically, the American family has been built around a norm of monogamous marriage—an exclusive, lifelong bond between one man and one woman. This ideal once fit into an extended family form, but industrialization has shrunk the family unit to the nuclear family, which is more readily adaptable to the demands of a highly mobile society. Different family members are not likely to find employment in the same place, and job changing has been frequent. Even the ideal of monogamous marriage has been influenced by the demands for social mobility. The increasing self-sufficiency of women has been paralleled by a rising divorce rate; the current average length of marriage is less than five years. Since 70 to 80% of divorced persons remarry, the American marriage system sometimes has been called serial monogamy, a form somewhere between strict monogamy and true polygamy.

The Life Cycle in America

In every society, we pass through the same age-related stages: birth, childhood, adolescence, perhaps marriage, old age, and death. But how we experience each one is strongly molded by our culture. Even in the United States, where rites of passage are minimal and socialization diffuse, we tend to experience the life cycle in ways that are unique to our culture.

Pregnancy and Childbirth

Like those of many other societies, American culture includes several traditional pregnancy taboos and admonitions. One of these is the idea of marking. According to this belief, children may be influenced by things that are done by or that happen to their mothers. For instance, birthmarks might be attributed to the mother's having eaten too many strawberries, raspberries,

or other red foods during the pregnancy. The most common expression of the concept of marking in the United States today is in admonitions to do things believed to influence the child in positive ways. For instance, a pregnant woman may hear that by spending time listening to classical music, reading good literature, and immersing herself in art she may predispose her child to similar pursuits. The concept of the marking of an unborn child by its mother parallels the idea that, after birth, mothers have the principal psychological influence on the development of the child and therefore usually receive greater credit or blame for what the child becomes.

Americans regard it as desirable for a woman to seek the services of a physician—most of whom are male in the United States—about two months into her pregnancy. This doctor will evaluate the health of the woman, check the progress of the pregnancy, and deliver the baby. Although some changes are occurring, for most Americans the preferred place for the delivery still is a hospital in the presence of the physician and one or more nurses. Only in recent decades have fathers been permitted in the delivery room. On entering the hospital, the woman spends several hours in a labor room. She is moved to a delivery room for the actual delivery and then to a hospital room for convalescence while the baby is cared for in a nursery. A few generations ago the convalescent period might have been several weeks long. Today it is usually no more than two days.

Due to the high costs of medical treatment and hospital costs, lower-income Americans do not follow the ideals outlined in the last paragraph with the same frequency as do members of the middle and upper classes. The last decade also has seen an increasing return to the less expensive system of delivery at home with the aid of a midwife. Many hospitals, in turn, are beginning to shift from the use of specialized labor and delivery rooms to the use of birthing rooms, which can save as much as half the hospital costs for a normal delivery. In this system the woman remains in the same room from labor through a convalescent period of up to 24 hours, and the child remains with the mother after the delivery.

Parents begin selecting a name for the child months before the birth. Most American families have no formal customary rules for selecting the name, such as a requirement to name the child after a particular relative, so the search for a name is largely a matter of the parents' agreeing on a name that "sounds good." Actually, this quest for an agreeable name involves finding two, since the sex of the child is not likely to be known in advance. To help them in this process, parents-to-be may even purchase a book of alphabetically arranged first names. Since the selection of the name is largely an aesthetic issue, the popularity of different names rises and falls over the generations much as do fashions in dress. Names like Blanche, Gertrude, Mildred, Helen, Edith, or Ada for girls and Edgar, Orville, Leonard, Albert, or Herbert for boys that were common among people born 75 years ago are uncommon today. Names are officially given without ceremony immediately after birth when the attending physician fills out a birth certificate to be filed in the county records. A religious naming ceremony may be conducted for the child a few weeks later.

Infancy and Childhood

After a period when breastfeeding was not common, it does appear to be increasing once again. Today 83% of mothers nurse their infants for at least six months, after which the percentage falls to the mid-forties. Most American mothers stop nursing their children far short of the several years that is common in many of the world's nonindustrialized cultures. Most Americans still deem it inappropriate for a mother to nurse her child publicly.

Americans socialize their children differently depending on the sex of the child. Symbolically, the color pink is associated with girls and blue with boys as appropriate for clothing and decorations of the baby's crib. It has been noted that mothers speak more to girl babies than to boys, and fathers tend to play in a rougher, more jostling fashion with their male children. Before six months of age, male babies are touched more frequently by their mothers than are

girls, but after six months of age the opposite is true. Boys are given less emotional support throughout the rest of their lives and learn rapidly that "Big boys don't cry." Instead of emotional support from others, they are encouraged to obtain pleasure from success in competition and in demonstrating skill and physical coordination. Girls are encouraged to take care in making themselves pretty, and their clothing is often designed more for eye appeal than for practicality in play. By and large, differences in the socialization of children reflect a stereotype of sex differences that views males as strong, active, unemotional, logical, dominant, independent, aggressive, and competitive and females as weak, passive, emotional, intuitive, supportive, dependent, sociable, status-conscious, shy, patient, and vain. In the past 20 years, stereotypes such as these have changed tremendously among university students, but there is little evidence that this is the case for American society at large.

Adolescence and Courtship

At 5 years of age, children are enrolled in school. Schooling is typically required by most states until the age of 16, which also is a common age for driving privileges to be obtained. There is no widespread practice of puberty rituals, and other adult rights and responsibilities, such as military service, voting rights, and the right to purchase alcoholic beverages, are acquired at different ages up to the age of 21. The absence of a clear-cut transition from childhood results in a great deal of uncertainty and turmoil about appropriate role behavior during adolescence.

During the teenage period, American adolescents explore their identities as social beings as they practice the skills necessary to achieve an independent adult status. Acceptance by their peers becomes extremely important, and adolescents begin to create a sense of independent functioning by adopting new values that are in harmony with their peer group and with the social milieu outside their family. This is a period of dating, in which adolescents begin to learn the skills of courtship and lay the foundations for their adult sexual iden-

Figure 12.5 *Romantic Love*
Romantic love as a basis for marriage is a highly regarded value in the United States, even though its ideal perpetuates the economic dependence of women on men.

tities. Although American ideals historically have required that both sex and pregnancy do not occur until after the marriage ceremony, the majority of both unmarried males and females experience sex by age 19. Tanfer and Horn (1985) found that in 1983 82% of unmarried women aged 20 through 29 had experienced sexual intercourse. For 1977, there were 700,000 adolescent pregnancies (Byrne, 1977). Many teenage pregnancies are aborted, but there also are many births before marriage. For instance, in 1985 there were 259,477 children born out of wedlock to women from 15 through 19 years of age. This represented 49.2% of all births to women of this age in that year.

Marriage

Americans are marrying later today than they were a generation ago. In 1982, the median age of males marrying for the first time was 24.1 years, and for females it was 22.3 years. In the American view, the ideal reason for marriage is love. The ideal of romantic love as a basis for marriage is perhaps nowhere else in the world so strongly supported. As Ralph Linton (1936), an anthropologist noted for his interpretations of American culture, observed over half a century ago:

> All societies recognize that there are occasional violent emotional attachments between persons of the opposite sex, but our present American culture is practically the only one which has attempted to capitalize on these and make them a basis for marriage. Most groups regard them as unfortunate and point out the victims of such attachments as horrible examples. Their rarity in most societies suggests they are psychological abnormalities to which our own culture has attached extraordinary value just as other cultures have attached extreme values to other abnormalities. The hero of the modern American movie is always a romantic lover just as the hero of the old Arab epic is always an epileptic. A cynic might suspect that in any ordinary population the percentage of people with a capacity for romantic love of the Hollywood type was about as large as that of persons able to throw genuine epileptic fits. However, given a little social encouragement either one can be adequately imitated without the performer admitting even to himself that the performance is not genuine. (p. 175)

Why is romantic love such an important ideal in the American courtship and marriage system? One factor, certainly, is the economic unimportance of the nuclear family as a unit of production in American society. As industrialization undermined the economic role of the extended family, the marital choices of children grew increasingly independent of parental authority. Emotional attraction has filled the void created by the declining role of parental decision making in the choice of mates. Romantic love as the basis of mate selection may be more prominent in the United States than elsewhere, but it certainly is not absent in other industrialized countries. Another factor in the maintenance of the ideal of romantic love between spouses appears to be the dependent economic status of women in countries where it is found. The romantic ideal stresses the role of women as objects of love, valued for their emotional, aesthetic, nurturing, and moral contributions to society rather than for their economic productivity and practical contributions to society outside the domestic sphere. Thus, the ideal of romantic love seems to play a role in perpetuating the economic dependence of women on men. This romanticism of women as love objects explains why, contrary to the popular American stereotype, it seems to be men who are the more romantic sex among Americans. Zick Rubin (1973) studied attitudes of dating couples at the University of Michigan and found that women were more likely than men to espouse practical issues over romantic considerations in spouse selection. The more pragmatic approach of women to marriage is not so surprising when one considers the higher income and broader economic participation in prestigious occupations that is enjoyed by men in the United States.

Just how does mate selection actually proceed? Several researchers suggest a model that involves a sequence of stages. First, proximity is an important factor. People are most likely to get together with those whom they are likely to encounter. Thus, in spite of their mobility, most Americans actually marry a partner who lives within a few miles of them. Ineichen (1979) found that almost 65% of a sample of 232 married couples lived in the same city before they married, most of them coming from the same area or adjacent areas of the city.

Initial attraction is likely to be based on superficial, easily observable characteristics such as physical attractiveness, dress, and evidence of social power and prestige. After meeting one another, compatibility of values and attitudes is especially important. Agreement on values such as religious, sexual, familial, and political values is a good predictor of the development of a stable relationship (Kerkhoff, 1962). Burgess and Wallin (1953) found that engaged couples were remarkably similar in their physical attractiveness, physical health, mental health, social popularity, race, religion, parents' educational levels, parents' incomes,

and the quality of their parents' marriages. Thus, similarity seems to be an important element in the attraction that leads to relationships.

The love ideal continues to shape relationships after marriage. Bean (1981) examined television soap operas for their portrayal of relationships within the family. Each weekday over 18 million Americans watch these dramatizations of human relationships even though the basic story lines are repeated over and over. According to Bean, "The triangle involving ties of love and marriage with various complications is the most frequently occurring plot" (p. 61). The American family is depicted in soap operas as composed of two sets of relationships: husband-wife and parent-child. Both are ideally composed of two and only two interacting units. That is, problems arise in either relationship if the interactions involve three persons, as when either husband or wife becomes involved with another person or when parents fail to relate to the child as a unit. Bean claims that according to the ideals held forth in soap operas,

> Each dyadic relationship should contain three basic ingredients. A man and a woman should be united by love, marriage, and sex. Parents and child should be united by blood, love, and nurturing. Love is an element in both relationships, but the love between parent and child is different from the love between husband and wife. The former is parental or familial love derived from the blood tie between parent and child, and the nurturing of a child by its parent. It has a beginning but no end. To stop loving your child would be unnatural in the worst sense of the word. The love between husband and wife is romantic love, the source of which is mysterious so that it may begin and may end suddenly. It just happens to people (one falls, not jumps). The two kinds of love are sharply differentiated and people who share familial love are prohibited from sharing romantic love by the incest taboo. (p. 70)

Illness

Americans predominantly espouse a secular medical model of illness rather than a spiritual model. This feature corresponds to the existence of an extensive system of health care that is based on a scientific view of illness. Secular medicine has been successful enough in combating disease to make the status of physician one of the most prestigious and well-paid in the American social system. In 1984, the average net income (that is, take-home pay after all expenses such as taxes and malpractice insurance) of an American medical doctor was $71,000 and surgeons, in particular, received an average of $152,000 after expenses. As of 1983, there were 520,000 medical doctors practicing in the United States. This means that there was one physician for about every 457 Americans in that year. In the same year, there were approximately 1,404,000 active registered nurses in the United States and another 3,322,000 auxiliary health workers such as nurse's aides, orderlies, attendants, and nonnursing health aides. As these figures suggest, health care is a major component of the American social and economic system. Without counting administrative personnel in hospitals, laboratory technicians, or paraprofessionals, nearly 1 in every 45 Americans is involved in the medical health care profession.

In 1984, there were 7,051 hospitals in the United States and approximately one and one third million beds for patients. Given the large number of patients who must be dealt with in the hospital setting, it is understandable that hospital rules, regulations, and procedures generally are designed for the benefit of the hospital personnel—to make their work more efficient and easy to do. Although the standardization of hospital routine may have an overall effect of improved efficiency in patient care, one by-product of such standardization is a depersonalization of the patient as an individual. A person entering treatment in a hospital setting undergoes a status change, a loss of the usual prestige and access to decision-making power accorded normal members of society (Goffman, 1961). Patients are expected to give up their normal autonomy and to passively accept hospital routine and treatment procedures. Information about their own case is available to them only at the physician's discretion. Howard Leventhal (1975), who has studied

patient reports of depersonalization, finds that American patients often experience themselves as objects or things rather than as people and that they feel psychologically isolated from other people.

Old Age and Death
In the United States, old age generally is thought of as beginning at 65 years, the traditional age of retirement from employment and the age of eligibility for old age social security benefits. With retirement comes a loss of many of the usual activities and social contacts that make life meaningful for the active person. This stage of the life cycle is the one most likely to be described as a time of loneliness and boredom. With retirement also comes a loss of the prestige and income associated with productive occupations. The low level of prestige and power associated with old age qualifies the aged in America for a minority status. Americans themselves are aware of the low rank of the aged and sometimes compare their own culture with other ways of life in which they believe the aged are accorded greater respect.

Death in America has been largely removed from the familial context by other social institutions that have taken over the management of the dying and the dead. Hospitals and nursing homes care for the terminally ill and insulate the surviving family members from much of the dying process. Americans are likely to die in either a hospital or a nursing home, often in isolation from their family members. Traditionally, doctors and nurses have tended to avoid telling terminal patients that they were dying. A specialized funeral industry exists to take care of the practical necessities preparatory to burial and to usher the survivors through the funeral and mourning process.

American Ideology

Despite its social diversity, the United States has not only a rather standardized approach to the life cycle but also a recognizable pattern of beliefs. Those explored here are religious ideology and the framework of American values and drives.

Religion in America

Americans tend to view the universe in mechanistic terms, and, historically, a scientific world view has been held central to their approach to everyday problems. The government recognizes no official religion, for the Bill of Rights of the United States Constitution guarantees a separation between church and state. Nevertheless, the American government traditionally has fostered religion in general, granting tax-exempt status to churches and their properties, while Americans as a people tend to view membership in a church, synagogue, or equivalent religious organization to be evidence of full allegiance to one's community. In early days, the church was often the center of local community life, and Americans still tend to participate in religious activities more frequently, for instance, than do most Europeans. Nearly half of Americans are likely to attend religious services at least once a month.

Currently 68% of Americans hold formal membership in a religion, and 40% attend religious services in a typical week (the Gallup Report, 1985, p. 13). Most belong to Christian churches, Protestant denominations being the most common. Judaism is America's most visible non-Christian religion, but one also finds Buddhists and Moslems in most American communities as well as adherents of several other religions, especially indigenous varieties of Christianity. Native American religion and organized witchcraft are found throughout the country, but these have entered the mainstream consciousness less well than have the other organized religions. About 5% of Americans espouse no religious belief, and another 5% who do assert a belief in God or a Universal Spirit express no preference for a particular religion (the Gallup Report, 1985, pp. 13, 50). Interestingly, the American tendency to emphasize membership and participation in religious organizations over religious belief is also found among nonbelievers: For instance the American Atheists have formed their own organizations.

Bellah (1967), a Harvard sociologist who has specialized in the study of religion, claims that the basic religious dimension of American life is a civil religion that coexists with the formally organized religions. The American civil religion is integrated into American social and political life and draws predominantly from Christianity and Judaism for its symbolism. Its God is the author of order, law, and morality and is actively involved in history, especially in American history, much as the God of ancient Israel. According to Bellah, the symbolism of American civil religion portrays America as the modern equivalent of the biblical Israel and the American Founding Fathers as the inspired prophets of American history. The Declaration of Independence, the Constitution, and Abraham Lincoln's Gettysburg Address are the three sacred documents of American civil religion. The first two grew out of the American Exodus from Europe, the symbolic Egypt from which God led people to the American Promised Land, which God set up as a light to all the world. Whereas Washington was the American Moses, Lincoln was the counterpart of Jesus, the wise and compassionate hero who counseled love of neighbor and whose life was taken by his enemies. Lincoln's Gettysburg Address, the New Testament of American sacred literature, is built around themes of death and rebirth such as "these honored dead," "conceived in liberty," and "a new birth of freedom." Bellah describes the sacred calendar of the American civil religion as consisting of Memorial Day, on which American communities honor their martyred dead, Thanksgiving Day, which integrates the family into the civil religion in a ceremonial feast of thanks to God for the bounties of American life, and the less overtly religious holidays of the Fourth of July, Veterans Day, and the birthdays of Washington and Lincoln. The recent addition of Martin Luther King's Birthday to U.S. holidays to symbolize and encourage interracial respect may be viewed as an extension of the American sacred calendar since Bellah originally set forth his idea.

American Drives and Values

As we saw in looking at the components of culture in general (chapter 3), every society holds certain concepts about how people should relate to each other and to the

Figure 12.6 *Allegiance*
Allegiance as a conforming force in society can be either positive or negative. The other side of patriotism and loyalty is ethnocentrism and sexism.

universe. But human behavior is characteristically symbolic and therefore subject to diverse interpretations. Scholars have commonly asserted that these value systems and the behavior they guide may coalesce into distinctive patterns (Kroeber, 1944). And in a society with as large a population as that of the United States, the broad generalizations that are necessary for the formulation of abstract values do not apply uniformly to all American subcultures, either past or present.

Nevertheless, there does seem to be a fair consensus in the writings of anthropologists and sociologists about the most important values that typify the dominant American way of life. These include emphasis on personal goal-directed effort, individualism, progress, freedom, equality, democracy, and an external conformity that is personally motivated by love of country, cooperation for the common welfare, a sense of personal morality and fair play, or the desire for social acceptance.

Although a great deal of agreement exists about the specific values that find their place in the American ideology, social scientists differ with one another in their efforts to find a pattern in American values. One attempt to reduce the complexity in the diverse list of values that have been ascribed to American culture is that of Henry (1963). Henry has suggested a distinction between what he calls drives and values. Drives are motives that people actually pursue, sometimes at great cost, rather than those to which they merely give lip service. Since it is in pursuit of their culture's drives that people invest their time and energy, drives represent the things that people value most strongly in the practical sense. They also are the source of stresses in life. What Henry calls values represent ideals that people long for but do not necessarily pursue. They are often opposites of drives, since they might give release from the stresses created by the pursuit of drives. Henry describes the roles of drives and values:

> Drives are what urge us blindly into getting bigger, into going further into outer space and into destructive competition; values are the sentiments that work in the opposite direction. Drives belong to the occupational world; values to the world of family and friendly intimacy. Drives animate the hurly-burly of business, the armed forces and all

Drives and Values in American Culture

SOCIAL TRAITS RESULTING FROM INDUSTRIALIZATION AND ROLE SPECIALIZATION	RESULTING DRIVES	SUBTYPES AND EXAMPLES OF DRIVES	COUNTER-BALANCING VALUES	EXAMPLES OF VALUES
Dependent status in employment ("self-alienation")	Conformity	*Allegiance* in-group sentiments; ethnocentrism; zenophobia; patriotism *Cooperation* obedience to authority; respect for law and office; opposition to boat-rocking and trouble-making *Equality* equality of opportunity; good citizenship; denial of class distinctions; mass education; democracy	Self-reliance	Freedom, autonomy, independence; the Marlborough Man; hero worship; preference for charismatic leaders; opposition to authority figures (politicians, etc.); desire for popularity; self-discovery; self-fulfilled meditation; favoring the underdog
Nonownership of products of own labor ("object alienation")	Work ethic (i.e., work is good in its own right, instead of in terms of its products)	*Optimism* future-orientation; desire for progress, improvement, getting ahead *Energy/Effort* effort-optimism; personal effort, vigor, and initiative; opposition to laziness and sensuality of youth *Purposefulness* purposeful recreation; pragmatic ingenuity; diligence; applied knowledge	Hedonism/ Pleasure/ Aesthetics	Spontaneity and "nowism"; pleasure, relaxation, existentialism; veneration of wisdom and maturity; Santa Claus; nostalgia for carefree days of youth; desire for loss of control, "letting one's hair down," "getting crazy," and being taken care of; reckless abandon
Insecure status ("social alienation")	Competitiveness	*Competition* competition in recreation, scorekeeping; oneupmanship; status climbing and desire for upward mobility; free enterprise system; multiple party system in government *Materialism* material acquisitiveness; profit motive; quest for luxuries; high standard of living; conspicuous consumption; "keeping up with the Joneses" *Mobility* physical mobility; expansiveness; desirability for change and novelty; American restlessness; wanderlust	Personable-ness	Generosity, charity, kindness; relaxation of interpersonal relationships; love; openness; honesty; resentment of quota-busting over-achievement and those in high office; desire for physical security; desire for simplicity; idyllic pastoral existence; myth of the Noble Savage; American familialism; nostalgia for "good old days," roots; desire for security, stability

Table 12.6 *The Relationship Between Drives and Values in American Culture*

those parts of our culture where getting ahead, rising in social scale, outstripping others, and merely surviving in the struggle are the absorbing functions of life. When values appear in these areas, they act largely as brakes, on drivenness. (p. 14)

At the time of his writing early in the 1960s, Henry, saw America as a culture driven by the needs for achievement, competition, profit, mobility, security, a higher standard of living, and expansiveness. American values—in effect, the things Americans long for as a result of being caught up by these drives—include such sentiments as love, kindness, quietness, contentment, fun, honesty, decency, relaxation, and simplicity.

Henry's drives may be understood as ideological reflections of the technologically and economically dictated means for achieving the necessities of life (see Table 12.6). Industrialization has created three prominent drives in American society: conformity, the work ethic, and competitiveness. These, colored by their counterbalancing values—self-reliance, fun, and personableness—can be seen as the basis of the distinctive pattern of American culture.

Conformity. All cultures impose a degree of conformity to socially determined norms, but all peoples do not value conformity to the same degree or become driven by their efforts to conform. The drive to conform is typical of large-scale industrialized societies because individuals in all walks of life are subordinated to rules, higher authorities, and powerful institutions whose goals often take precedence over the needs of individuals. Since most individuals in industrialized societies make their living by selling their labor as a commodity, income is partly contingent on conformity to the organizational and sometimes personal ideals by which supervisory personnel and management evaluate employees. Organizational efficiency is fostered by harmonious cooperation and "pulling together." Being "out of step," "rocking the boat," or "quota busting" are likely to be seen as forms of troublemaking precisely because they involve disruption of the routine of the group. One's economic security, personal prestige, and even status-linked rank are easily en-

dangered by too much nonconformity.

The drive for conformity motivated by the need for greater security is manifest in several ways: allegiance to the nation, to one's occupation, religion, ethnic group, and race; cooperation for the common welfare; and support for equality. The Americans' allegiance to others seems largely motivated by the wish to avoid public criticism. It includes the positive sentiments of patriotism, loyalty, and love of country, but it is here that one also finds the darker side of American drives: ethnocentrism, antipathies toward outsiders or foreigners, racism, and sexism. Under the general label of cooperation fall the American stresses on cooperation for the common welfare, respect and deference to rank and obedience to authority, and antipathies toward "radicalism," nonconformity, and "boatrocking." Americans also are driven to create greater equality for members of society. This aspect of their conformity drive stands in counterpoint to some of the frictions created by their in-group allegiances. The obligations of good citizenship include being a good neighbor and supporting equality of opportunity, participant democracy, and mass education.

Conformity in America, Germany, and Japan

Although America shares a drive for conformity with other cultures, especially with other industrialized nations, the specific influence that this drive has is tempered by various other factors, such as how formally or informally it is taught and how other drives and values modify the manifestations of conformity. German and Japanese cultures also emphasize conformity. Both differ from American culture in teaching this drive more explicitly and formally.

The traditional German emphasis on the importance of order in social life, orderliness in private life, and respect for authority and obedience are all summed up in the common expression, *Ordnung muss sein!* ("There must be order!"). The hero of traditional German literature was an individual who

Figure 12.7 *Conformity*
Some cultures value the ideal of conformity more than others. In military groups such as these Royal Canadian Mounted Police, A, conformity is obvious and necessary. Conformity may also be a more subtle value. These American teenagers, B, conform to a punk style of dress while supporting the idea of independence.

because of a personal flaw of character was unable to conform to the dictates of the social order and who was tragically doomed because of this flaw. All this explicit emphasis on the subordination of individual needs to the society's need for order is likely to strike the American as too intolerant of individual differences and too restrictive of individual freedom to be palatable. Americans, too, conform, but they learn this drive more informally and are less conscious of their conformity to their society's rules for living. Although it is a fact of life, their drive for conformity is overshadowed by their continual praise of the value of self-reliance. American conformity is more a result of their search for friendship, respect, social power, and income or of avoiding rejection than it is a formal recognition of the importance of social order for its own sake. Americans are much more likely than are Germans to describe their conformity as a simple by-product of their personal and inner-regulated morality or their desire to be good neighbors rather than as evidence of respect for the authority of society as a whole over their lives as individuals.

The Japanese, whom Germans have called "the Germans of the East," have a similarly formal emphasis on the importance of conformity to the rules of social life, but they place greater emphasis on the necessity of orders being imposed from above. At the same time, they express more ambivalence about this state of affairs. Like Americans, the Japanese stress the importance of competition and success, but their emphasis is on competition between groups rather than individuals. Loyalty to the team counts more heavily than the individual's ability to excel. Whiting (1979) has compared the Japanese and American approaches to baseball and reports a consistent Japanese willingness to sacrifice outstanding individual team members when their lack of cooperative team spirit threatened the sense of *wa*, or group harmony. Whiting summarizes the different feelings about individualism and cooperation in the two cultures:

> The U.S. is a land where the stubborn individualist is honored and where "doing your own thing" is a motto of contemporary society. In Japan, *kojin-shugi*, the term for individualism, is almost a dirty word. In place of "doing your own thing," the Japanese have a proverb: "The nail that sticks up shall be hammered down." It is practically a national slogan. (p. 60)

Self-reliance. The drives of conformity are counterbalanced by idealized values of self-reliance, expressed in praise of freedom,

liberty, grass-roots government, and independence. The value placed on autonomy includes the worship of heroes such as Daniel Boone, John Wayne, James Bond, Luke Skywalker, and Indiana Jones who embody the traits of rugged individualism, self-motivation, and self-reliance. The well-known American distaste for politics and the commonly held view that "All politicians are crooks" are expressions of antipathy for "the Establishment," the system of authority that requires conformity. Americans prefer to follow the political leaders who show charisma in handling themselves, thereby "rising above the office." The desire for popularity is a more personal expression of this same value, as is rooting for the underdog and the covert admiration that Americans tend to feel for the individual who stands up against great odds or successfully "bucks the system" (as illustrated in films such as *Fun With Dick and Jane*, *Dog Day Afternoon*, *Rage*, and *Death Wish*). The overcoming of impossibly powerful adversaries by a hero with great personal skill is perhaps the most common theme in American literature, and the great popularity of the James Bond movies in the 1960s and the Rocky and Rambo movies in the 1980s illustrates how long lived this value has been during a quarter century of great change.

Traditionally, the value of self-reliance has been especially emphasized for men. Women's status had less rank than did men's, and their roles as women were complementary to those of men. For instance, women featured in popular fiction generally have been adjuncts to men. Instead of seeking their own autonomy and independence, they usually have been portrayed as seeking love for and dependence on a man. There are increasing exceptions to this portrayal of women in the entertainment media, as women take an increasing role in American economic life. Similarly, a great deal of the feminist movement of the past two decades has been precisely focused on encouraging greater autonomy for women.

Francis Hsu (1961) believes that self-reliance in America is the central preoccupation from which all our other values arise. Hsu's self-reliance has as its primary psy-

Figure 12.8 *Work Ethic*
The American work ethic developed with industrialization. The aesthetic value of work was replaced with the need for production. These workers at an automobile assembly plant in Detroit were expected to perform a number of specialized tasks in a certain period of time.

chological manifestation the fear of dependence. He contrasts Chinese and American society in respect to the ideal of self-reliance:

> A man in traditional China where self-reliance was not an ideal may have been unsuccessful in his life. But suppose in his old age his sons were able to provide for him generously. Such a person not only was happy and content about it; he was likely also to beat the drums before all and sundry to let the world know that he had good children who were supporting him in a style to which he had never been accustomed. On the other hand, an American parent who has not been successful in life may derive some benefit from the prosperity of his children, but he certainly will not want anybody to know about it. In fact, he will resent any reference to it. At the first opportunity when it is possible for him to become independent of his children, he will do so.
>
> Therefore, even though we may find many individuals in traditional China and elsewhere who were in fact self-sufficient, and even though we may find individuals in America who are in fact dependent upon others, the important thing is that where self-reliance is not an ideal, it is neither promoted nor a matter of pride, but where it is an ideal, it is both. In American society the fear of dependence is so great that an individual who is not self-reliant is a misfit. "Dependent character" is a highly derogatory term, and a person so described is thought to be in need of psychiatric help. (p. 250)

Hsu argues that self-reliance is actually an impossible goal to achieve. Human society is based on mutual dependence on our fellow human beings, and no one can meet his or her technological, social, intellectual, or emotional needs in isolation. Therefore, Hsu believes that the American ideal of self-reliance creates contradictions that lead to insecurity in the lives of individuals: Self-reliance means impermanence in relationships and competition for status, which in turn requires conformity to organizations or peer groups. "In other words," Hsu explains, "to live up to their core value orientation of self-reliance, Americans as a whole have to do much of its opposite. Expressed in the jargon of science, there is a direct relationship between self-reliance and individual freedom on the one hand and submission to organizations and conformity on the other" (p. 250).

Figure 12.9 *Pleasure Seeking*
As a contrast to the work ethic of a generation ago, many people today value the existential philosophy of living for the moment and seeking pleasure in it.

The work ethic. An industrial technology leads to a high degree of labor specialization in which many individuals must work competitively to produce goods that they themselves do not own and that will be consumed by others. Under such circumstances, it is the labor itself that is rewarded, and work becomes a drive in its own right rather than simply the necessary means to create something of significant value to the worker. This work ethic may develop under other circumstances in societies with a nonindustrialized technology, but it would seem to be an inevitable drive wherever industrialization is prominent.

In normal day-to-day terms, it is work of a practical nature rather than work for work's sake that is likely to receive the greatest reward. Therefore, the work ethic is best understood as a drive that is more or less synonymous with a positive attitude toward pragmatic effort or accomplishment. The person who is well socialized for living in accordance with a work ethic will be optimistic, energetic, and purposeful. The specific evidences of a work ethic are manifestations of one of these three aspects.

Optimism is a positive expectation that the future is potentially better than the present state of affairs. In America one finds a traditional emphasis on progress, improvement, diligence, getting ahead, the expectation that children should grow up to be better and more successful than their parents, and the idea that, no matter how badly things are going, "Tomorrow is another day."

The emphasis placed on energy includes positive reactions to such traits as vigor, activity, personal effort, and initiative as well as negative responses to "laziness," passivity, and sensuality. In the opinion of Cora DuBois (1955) these traits form the underlying basis of the "cult of youthfulness" for which Americans are famous.

Where a work ethic is prominent, effort of any kind will be admired. But effort directed purposefully toward the achievement of specific ends will be more applauded than effort for which no clear purpose is evident. Purposefulness as an aspect of the work ethic is manifest in the national emphasis on pragmatism, ingenuity, inventiveness, and applied science and in the attitude that recreation, vacations, and other pleasurable activities should be undertaken because they are beneficial rather than for the sake of the pleasure itself. For instance, when I was a child, my father emphasized that meals should not be eaten for the pleasure of eating but because food is necessary so that one can work. He also insisted that the only good music is music with lyrics that convey a message. The value of purposefulness also was manifest in the attitude common among Americans of several generations ago that even sex should be for procreation and not merely for pleasure.

The idealized values that serve as brakes on these work ethic drives of future-oriented optimism, energetic effort, and purposefulness are nostalgia for the "good old days" (the presumably carefree, less hectic days of the past), relaxation, and fun. The latter is the value placed on spontaneity and the "Be here now" existential philosophy, the desire for enjoyment and pleasurable recreation, and the covert admiration for disaster-courting thrill-seekers.

Competitiveness. Along with conformity and the work ethic, competitiveness is the third major American drive. Like the others, its existence is inherent in an industrialized society. In such social systems, the products of labor usually are owned by someone other than the worker who produces them, and the working person generally is dependent on someone else for his or her livelihood. Since these conditions prevail in America, Americans must sell their labor as if it were a commodity. Economic statuses are insecure and dependent because

Figure 12.10 *Competition*
Competitiveness is a major drive in the American psyche manifesting itself in economic situations, social situations, and more recently, in sports.

they are organized around authority relationships and because holding them successfully is predicated on "selling oneself" effectively. It is the insecurity of American life that is the basis for the emphasis on the "spirit of competition."

Within the economic sphere, this drive manifests itself in the recurrent praise of the profit motive and the ideal of a free enterprise system, one in which economic competition is unhindered by noneconomic forces. Socially, the concept of enlightened self-interest is an attempt to reconcile the potential conflicts between drives of competition and drives of conformity, as noted by the French nobleman Alexis de Tocqueville (1969) over 100 years ago:

> In the United States there is hardly any talk of the beauty of virtue. But they maintain that virtue is useful and prove it every day. American moralists do not pretend that one must sacrifice himself for his fellows because it is a fine thing to do so. But they boldly assert that such sacrifice is as necessary for the man who makes it as for the beneficiaries. (p. 525)

Status climbing and upward social mobility are American drives that flow out of

Figure 12.11 *Relaxed Sociableness*
To counter the implicit hostility in competitiveness, many Americans have adopted a relaxed social attitude that has expressed itself in the popularity of discos and singles bars.

their competitive circumstances. The extreme emphasis on competition as a social good even carries over into the realm of relaxation and recreation. Even though Americans assert the idealized value that "It's not who wins the game that counts, but how you play the game," this statement is probably best understood as a wistful but unrealistic protestation against the practicalities of a way of life in which "Nice guys finish last." Americans continue to teach their children to keep score when playing games, a practice that the traditional Zuñi of the American Southwest would have eschewed as abhorrent.

American material acquisitiveness also must be seen as a manifestation of competitiveness. In a society in which, by Old World standards, the majority has never suffered from a lack of physical security or even luxury, materialism is best understood not as physical need but as a manifestation of the competitive desire to "keep up with the Joneses," that is, as evidence of one's competitive success. Social movement often is accompanied by physical mobility—the expansiveness of American society and the "Don't fence me in" restlessness of the American people that has been noticed so

frequently by foreign observers and so often appears as a theme of American literature and song.

The idealized values that counter the implicit conflict and potential hostility in competition include relaxed interpersonal relations, friendliness, frankness, love, kindness, decency, openness, and good sportsmanship. Charity and generosity also are valued as contrasts to the drive to make a profit. Simplicity, idealization of the idyllic pastoral life, and the myth of the noble savage are the drives of material acquisitiveness. American praise of family as the foundation of American society, nostalgia, and reminiscence for the "good old days" (in the sense of a wistful desire for stability and roots) may be seen as growing out of the stresses inherent in a way of life that emphasizes mobility and being "on the go."

The Changing Context of American Values and Drives

The difference between American values and drives and those emphasized in other industrialized societies may reflect the evolutionary adaptation of American society to its unique social and physical en-

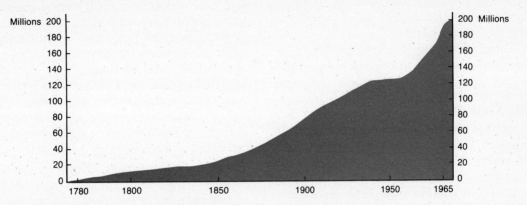

Note. From *Statistical Abstract of the United States: 1986* (106th ed.) [Table No. 1, p. 5] by U.S. Bureau of the Census, 1985, Washington, DC: U.S. Government Printing Office.

Figure 12.12 *Population Growth in the United States from 1780–1965*

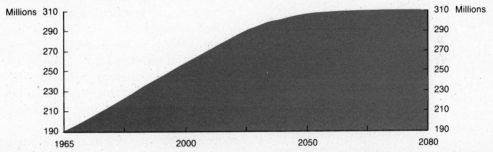

Note. From *Statistical Abstract of the United States: 1986* (106th ed.) [Table No. 1, p. 5] by U.S. Bureau of the Census, 1985, Washington, DC: U.S. Government Printing Office. Also from "Projections of the Population of the United States by Age, Sex and Race: 1983–2080" in *Current Population Reports: Population Estimates and Projections* (Series P - 25, No. 952) [Table 2, p. 30] by U.S. Bureau of the Census, 1984, Washington, DC: U.S. Government Printing Office.

Figure 12.13 *Projected Population Growth in the United States from 1965–2080*

vironments. Historically, America was one of the first societies in which the benefits of industrialization could be obtained by building a society to fit the growing technological apparatus rather than by trying to fit an industrialized economy into a pre-existing social order. In America, factories could be built to house the new tools instead of trying to fit equipment into the buildings of a previous generation, as was done in Europe. Cities grew up in a frontier society, and their form could be guided by technological and economic needs as they arose. In Europe, centuries-old cities that had grown up reflecting the needs of a pre-industrial age were a factor with which the new technology had to cope. America's backwater frontier status was therefore an advantage that made it possible to obtain the greatest social benefits from its developing way of life.

Population patterns. The population of the United States has been growing at an accelerating rate throughout most of its history (see Fig. 12.14). One important implication of this growth was what appeared to be an ever-expanding consumer market. This social condition encouraged technological growth and economic expansion. In the early phase of industrialization, the amazing material output of this new mode of production encouraged rapid population growth, since consumers were needed to use the goods that were manufactured. Much of this growth was accomplished through a rapid influx of immigrant consumer/workers. Yet, there are limits on the number of people who can be supported by any mode of production. The closer the limit is approached, the more that members of the growing population must compete with one another to obtain both jobs and access to products. The growing competition results in increasing costs in obtaining the necessities of life.

These increasing costs eventually must counterbalance the forces that induced the initial rapid population growth. At some point, the rate of growth begins to decelerate. In the United States, it took almost two centuries for this deceleration to begin. It was not until the early 1960s that the rate of American population growth stopped increasing. Since then, although it still is growing, it has been doing so at an ever-slowing rate. If this trend continues, it is estimated that the population of the United States will reach 310.8 million in 2080 (see Fig. 12.15). Most of the growth will occur by 2030 when the population will be about 304.8 million. After 2030 the growth rate will be relatively slow. If the growth rate were not to decelerate the competition for the goods produced would be so great that it would result in a decline in the standard of living of the population as a whole. Thus, it is likely that the total population will finally level off. Given these past population changes, current patterns, and projected changes, it is possible to consider the implications of population growth rates on American ideology during three phases of population growth: the initial period of accelerating growth, the current period of decelerating growth, and the projected period of nongrowth in the population.

The period of growth.   During the initial period of industrialization in the United States, the population was growing at a faster rate each decade. The internal consumer market seemed to offer unlimited potential for the expansion of sales. The same population growth represented a growing number of people in need of jobs, a further reason for expansion of industry. Under such circumstances it is no surprise that growth would be equated with progress, bigger with better, and material acquisitiveness with human nature. The traditional American value system and drives have their roots in the social conditions of this period.

The surplus output of the new industrial system made it possible to drain off some of the capital to expand the industrial

mechanism itself while still leaving enough to support the workers. Major public works projects such as highways, hydroelectric dams, airports, and mass public educational facilities could be financed by creating bills that would have to be paid back by future citizens. Since the population was growing at an accelerating rate, this meant that the costs of growth would be spread out more and more thinly with each year.

The period of transition.   Since the 1960s, however, important changes in American values have been developing. In the early 1960s, the economics of American life were changing in ways that led to a decline in the fertility rate. The cost of living was growing rapidly, affecting childrearing expenses. As the fertility rate fell, population growth decelerated. Middle-class families were finding it increasingly difficult to maintain their standard of living unless both spouses were employed. The divorce rate continued to grow tremendously during this period. During the 1960s the United States also was becoming more and more heavily involved in an unpopular foreign war.

The initial ideological response to these changing social circumstances took form during the political and social turmoil of the student and minority protests of the 1960s. During this period, many people noted the discrepancy between traditional drives and values and the current social circumstances. They formulated a new ideology—called the counterculture—with its own system of values and drives as a part of their opposition to the established social order. These counterculture values largely took the form of opposites of the traditional system.

Born in a period of intense political activism, the central counterculture drive was one that is necessary when people attempt to establish any new political movement: conformity to the ideas and practices of the new movement. Members of the counterculture were expected to be politically active in anti-war and "anti-Establishment" programs. These included a variety of symbolic shock tactics such as the adopting of radically new modes of dress, grooming, and language, and the espousal, at least verbally, of new and more permissive sexual customs. These behaviors had two important functions: (1) They were forms of political expression aimed at directly challenging customary, taken-for-granted symbols of conformity to the traditional social system; and (2) they simultaneously served as new symbols of group membership and cohesiveness. In the counterculture movement, failure to conform to the new group standards and failure to adopt an activist posture brought loss of esteem and personal distress.

As an offsetting value, the counterculture maintained the traditional American emphasis on self-reliance. But this established American value was spoken of in ways that contrasted with the usual ways of glorifying self-reliance. Counterculture self-reliance was described as noncompetitive individualism that rejected the traditional emphasis on acquisition of luxuries, rank within the established social order, and conformity to traditional morality.

Although the counterculture valued conformity and self-reliance, as did the mainstream culture, counterculture values did fundamentally diverge from those of the established value system in certain areas: (1) the rejection of materialism, monetary success, traditional education, pragmatic scientific rationality, efficiency, and cost-effectiveness as rationales for decisions, (2) an emphasis on sensory experiences and introspection as a source of knowledge in preference to abstract conceptual logic and objectivity, and (3) a quest for a return to harmony with nature as opposed to mastery over nature.

The period of stabilization. The counterculture was the initial awakening to the fact that traditional American values no longer fit the new social conditions. Nevertheless, its ideology was largely a reaction against the contemporary political and economic conditions of its day and not a true adjustment to the social conditions that have prevailed since the rate of population growth began to decline. As such, it was doomed to fall by the wayside as the mainstream American system values and drives gradually were adjusted to the problems of life when a society approaches the upper limits of its social and economic growth.

Following the 1960s these new values and drives began to impress themselves on the public consciousness. The changes that reflect these new values and drives have been described commonly, if not completely accurately, as a return to political conservatism, a reawakening of religious fundamentalism, and a reassertion of a practical interest in job security. Perhaps the major change within the American system of drives and values has been a shift within the work ethic away from the optimism drives—such as the traditional emphasis on progress, getting ahead, and the future—toward a greater drive for achieving security in the present. Before the 1970s the word *progress* was equated with change of almost any kind. America was one of the few places where, instead of being encouraged to grow up to be just like their parents, children were expected to learn more and achieve a higher standard of living than their parents had. This is no longer so. Now the goal of young adults is the much less expansive one of achieving economic security or of simply "making ends meet."

Probably the two most fundamental changes in American ideology that have resulted from the economic pressures of the sixties and seventies have been changes in ideas about the roles of men and women and changes in attitudes toward sex. The pre-sixties idea that a married woman should be economically dependent on a working husband has ceased to be feasible. It is not surprising, then, that not only has it become acceptable for women to seek employment, but Americans also increasingly view an economically productive life as essential to a woman's self-fulfillment as a person.

Childrearing is now extremely costly. A study by Minge (Harris, 1981, p. 94) estimates that it now costs almost $200,000 to raise a child through four years of college. It is certainly not surprising, then, that the average couple now has fewer than two children. The turn-of-the-century attitude that procreation was the only acceptable reason for sex is no longer tenable as the primary way in which Americans view their sexual lives. Increasingly, Americans are understanding sex primarily in the context

317

of pleasure rather than reproduction. This change is well illustrated by a study by Lewis and Brissett (1967) of marriage counseling texts published from 1947 through 1965. They found that in that period, a good sex life typically was described as something a couple could achieve if they worked at it hard enough. One text (Eichenlaub, 1963) in their study is quoted as saying:

> An ardent spur-of-the-moment tumble sounds very romantic. . . . However, ineptly arranged intercourse leaves the clothes you had no chance to shed in a shambles, your plans for the evening shot, your birth control program incomplete, and your future sex play under considerable better-be-careful-or-we'll-wind-up-in-bed-again restraint. (pp. 34–35)

Today, in contrast, the emphasis in most publications about human sexuality is on sensuality, pleasure, and enjoyment, rather than on technique.

The desire for economic security has shown itself in enrollment trends in American universities. Enrollments have shifted in the past decade away from the humanities, arts, and social sciences toward applied fields that offer a more secure promise of employment. On the job, workers are changing jobs less frequently than they used to, even within companies. The desire for a greater sense of security also may be seen in trends toward more conservative political views and in a reawakening of religious interests. Not only is the percentage of Americans today who are members of a church greater than it was a generation ago, but also the 1970s saw a resurgence of religious fundamentalism. There also is growing emphasis on secular ways of finding personal security, such as the seeking of self-knowledge, self-realization, and fulfillment through therapy.

The second major change in American drives has been within the drive for the acquisition of material goods. Although this drive is still with us, the role of conspicuous consumption—the acquisition and use of a surplus of goods as a way of competitively demonstrating one's success and prestige—is becoming less feasible for Americans. Instead, there is a growing emphasis on finding ways to conserve and extend the life of material goods. This trend is seen in such examples as the increasing popularity of smaller automobiles with greater gasoline mileage, the imposition of a 55-mile-an-hour maximum speed limit across the United States, the frequent discussion by the news media of ways in which conservation of energy and natural resources can be supported by citizens, the extension of tax credits for home insulation, the establishment of recycling centers in towns, and the passage of laws that require environmental impact studies before major building projects are undertaken.

If American population growth patterns continue, as has been predicted, stability rather than change will be the order of the day. Upward social mobility may be expected to become increasingly difficult as that stabilization is approached. The role of universities as a traditional means for upward mobility is likely to decline as the costs of a university education continue to grow beyond the means of more of the population. This process alone may insure that the most prestigious occupations with the American economy will become more or less self-perpetuating across generations: Those who can afford to support their children through a university education will be those whose income is great enough to do so by virtue of their own university degrees. For reasons of political tradition, Americans may remain resistant to any official recognition of classes. Nevertheless, it is unlikely that we will remain as successful during the coming half century as we have been in the past at denying the differences in income, power, and prestige that in fact exist within our society.

It may be argued that many of our problems as a society have been intimately linked to the rapid pace of change in American life throughout most of our history and that with stability may come a lessening of many of these problems. At the same time, however, a greater awareness of the effects of social, cultural, and subcultural differences on our way of life—a major concern of the field of anthropology—is likely to be crucial if a harmonious stability is to be achieved. Certainly, a more widespread recognition of the existence of social differences will make it more difficult to perpetuate the extremes of inequality that have long characterized U.S. society.

I will remind those of you who are not consoled by such thoughts that the very best of us these days are poor prophets, and the scenario of stability that I have sketched may not come to pass. The potentials embodied in new technologies such as computer communications and atomic or solar power—if they can be harnessed successfully for mass consumption—could bring about vast and beneficent changes in the lives of most Americans if they are ever developed to their full extent. Even more dramatic means for raising our standard of living as a society may yet be discovered. These as well as more tragic unpredictables, such as nuclear war, may circumvent the scenario that I have suggested as our most likely future. Yet, until those unpredictables become facts instead of mere possibilities, a course toward greater social stability appears to be the most likely continuing course of our internal social development in the coming half century.

External relations are another matter. As the effects of industrialization continue to spread around the world at the expense of technologically less complex ways of life, the cultures of the world are becoming more and more economically and politically interdependent. In this broader context, our future depends on what happens abroad as well as at home. Our relations with developing nations are likely to remain in a continuing state of flux as industrialization spreads and new power blocs and coalitions develop with the goal of insuring the political and economic self-interest of developing nations. How we shall fare in this process will depend largely on a recognition that our own national self-interest is not likely to be furthered in the long run by a narrowly ethnocentric view of the other cultures with which we share the world.

Summary

Despite Americans' typical belief that theirs is the best of all possible cultures, anthropological analysis of this society reveals many areas of actual or potential problems. In contrast to the American ideal of a classless society with equality of opportunity, the reality is a very unequal distribution of wealth and status that may stabilize or even become more distinct in the near future. In contrast to the ideal of a peace-loving people, the United States has a high rate of crime. Families, assumed to be the core of society, have little power and often are broken by divorce.

Nor do Americans inevitably handle life cycle changes with wisdom and sensitivity. Birth is being treated more personally than in the past, but socialization of boys and girls continues to perpetuate outdated stereotypes. Adolescents turn to their peer groups for socialization—and sex, with a high rate of teenage pregnancies. Marriages are occurring later than in the past—and breaking up sooner. Illness typically is treated according to a medical model, with the elderly placed in institutions to die.

In terms of ideology, the majority of Americans belong to some religious group or perhaps subscribe to the patriotic "civil religion." Driven by an emphasis on conformity, the work ethic, and competitiveness, Americans tend to balance these drives with contrasting values, such as love for fun, charity, and nostalgia for simpler times. These contrasting ideals developed as America's industrialization grew along with its population. But as the limits to growth are approached, the mainstream seems to be turning not toward the ideology of the counterculture but toward an emphasis on security rather than change and on conservative use of resources. During this present and predicted period of stability, changes in other cultures that are becoming industialized will inevitably and perhaps unpredictably affect us all.

Figure 12.14 *Population Stability*
New York City (pictured here) and San Francisco (pictured as the chapter opener) are likely to be affected by a decline in birthrate which began in the 1960s. If this trend continues, the result may be population stability which will influence social, economic, and cultural issues in the future.

Key Terms and Concepts

market exchange294
unskilled laborers 294
pink collar 295
blue collar 295
white collar 295
professionals 295
serial monogamy 300
marking 300
civil religion 305
drives 306

values 306
conformity 308
self-reliance 310
work ethic 312
optimism 312
energy 312
purposefulness 313
competitivenss 313
counterculture 316
conspicuous consumption 318

Annotated Readings

De Toqueville, A. (1945). *Democracy in America*. New York: A. A. Knopf.   Originally published in 1835, this classic description of American life was so insightful that it still rings true today.

Gorer, G. (1964). *The American people: A study in national character*. New York: W. W. Norton & Company.   The revision of a classic description of the United States written in 1947.

Harris, M. (1981). *America now: The anthropology of a changing culture*. New York: Simon and Schuster.   A provocative look at the effects of technological and economic change on American culture since World War II.

Hsu, F. L. K. (1983). *Rugged individualism reconsidered: Essays in psychological anthropology*. Knoxville, TN: University of Tennessee Press.   Comparisons of traditional Chinese and American cultures by an anthropologist who was born in China and lives today in the United States.

Jorgensen, J. G., & Truzzi, M. (1974). *Anthropology and American life*. Englewood Cliffs, N.J.: Prentice-Hall.   A useful collection of articles by anthropologists on American culture.

Schneider, D. M. (1968). *American kinship: A cultural account*. Englewood Cliffs, NJ: Prentice-Hall.   An important examination of the role of kinship in the United States.

Warner, W. L. (1953). *American life: Dream and reality*. Chicago: University of Chicago Press.   An early study by an anthropologist of life in a U.S. city.

West, J. (1945). *Plainville, U.S.A.*. New York: Columbia University Press.   One of the first descriptions by an anthropologist of life in a small U.S. town.

Glossary

Page references indicate where term is first defined.

absolute dating techniques for determining the age of a fossil or of material associated with it within a definable margin of error 27

acculturation the process in which one culture adapts to the influence of another culture by borrowing many of its traits 244, 274

achieved statuses social positions that one acquires by demonstrating the necessary role playing abilities 68

affective disorders mental disorders characterized by inadequate handling of one's own honor or self-esteem in role playing 175

affectlessness the complete control of emotion resulting in lethargy 169

agriculture the intensive working of land for food production through the use of tools and techniques such as the plow, irrigation, soil fertilization, and animal traction 56

alienation a dissociation of workers from ownership of the things they produce accompanied by feelings of powerlessness and boredom 269

alleles genes that occupy equivalent positions in a pair of chromosomes 22

allomorphs variants of a single morpheme that carry the same meaning but have different phonological structure 122

allophones phonetically variant forms of a single phoneme 121

altered state of consciousness a stress-induced trance state 180

American Sign Language (ASL) a system of hand gesture symbols used by hearing-impaired persons for communicating.

Although it is not a verbal system of symbols, ASL may be seen as a true nonverbal language, since it has its own grammar and vocabulary and is not simply a gestural copy of spoken language 116

amok a culture-specific hysterical disorder in which young men attack other people and destroy property 176

ancestral spirits the souls of ancestors who remain interested and involved in the affairs of their descendants 200

anger an emotional state during which another person is held responsible for one's own distress. Anger can substitute for anxiety, fear, guilt, grief, or shame in situations in which those emotions might otherwise be felt 169

anorexia nervosa a culture-specific obsessive-compulsive disorder characterized by an unrealistic appraisal of one's own body as overweight and by self-starvation 179

anthropological linguists cultural anthropologists who specialize in the study of communication, human languages, and the role of language in human social life 6

anthropomorphism using human qualities to explain the nonhuman realm; interpreting or acting toward the nonhuman realm as if it were human, especially as if it were able to respond to symbolic communication 197

antigenic distance the degree of difference between two animals as measured by the comparison of antiserum reactions against their serum proteins 31

anxiety a distressful subjective

awareness of stress; a general sense of powerlessness and foreboding without awareness of a specific danger 167

anxiety disorder a form of neurosis in which there is ritualistic expression of apprehension or panic without awareness of any specific danger 176

applied anthropology the attempt to use anthropological skills and insights to aid in the process of cultural development in nonindustrialized parts of the world or to aid in private and public policymaking 14, 286

archaeologists cultural anthropologists who study the material remains of earlier societies in order to reconstruct their cultures 5

arctic hysteria *amurakh* a culture-specific hysterical disorder that is characterized by compulsive imitation of sounds and gestures 176

art behavior that expresses the participants' feelings in a form that is intended to communicate those feelings. Like play, religion, and insanity, art may involve ritual behavior and altered states of consciousness—artistic reverie—in the artist and a sense of relief from anxieties 187

Aryans speakers of an early Indo-European language who immigrated into India about 1800 B.C. and brought an end to the native Indus Valley civilization 233

ascribed statuses social positions that one is assumed to occupy by virtue of the group into which one happens to be born—for instance, one's sex or race 68

association cortex the area of the cerebral cortex that coordinates information from various other parts of the brain 119

attitude a subjective reaction to an experience expressed in positive or negative terms 50

australopithecines popular term for the genus *Australopithecus*, the earliest known hominid genus, consisting of various species that lived from about 5 to 1 million years ago in various parts of Africa 31

Australopithecus afarensis the earliest known australopithecine species and currently the oldest known hominid ancestor of modern human beings, dating between 5.5 and 2.9 million years ago 31

Australopithecus africanus an australopithecine species that occupied South and East Africa from 2.9 to 1.3 million years ago and that possibly was ancestral to human beings 32

Australopithecus boisei an extremely robust australopithecine species that occupied East Africa between 2.2 and 1.1 million years ago. Like *robustus, boisei* is believed to have been a side branch of the evolutionary tree that has no modern descendants 33

Australopithecus robustus an australopithecine species, possibly descended from *Australopithecus africanus*, that occupied South Africa between 3 and 1.3 million years ago. Although *robustus* was a hominid, it generally is believed that this form was not ancestral to modern human beings but represented a line of hominids that became extinct 33

avunculocality the custom in which the newly married couple establishes residence with or near the groom's mother's brother 154

Aztec the dominant civilization of central Mexico at the time of the Spanish Conquest 237

band a seminomadic, kinship-based society with no full-time government, economically based on a foraging subsistence technology 250

Basic Law of Cultural Evolution the concept that increases in the production of energy through technological change is the primary cause of cultural evolution 246

basic vocabulary words for basic things expressed in all languages. Because such words are learned early in life and used with high frequency, they are more resistant to change than are words from other parts of a vocabulary 127

behavioral superstructure those behaviors most closely linked to a culture's ideology, including art, ritual, recreation, philosophy, science 58

beliefs the ideas people hold about what is factual or real 47

bilateral cross-cousin marriage (sister exchange) cross-cousin marriage in which a brother and sister marry cross cousins who are also brother and sister 149

bilateral descent tracing descent lines equally through males and females 136

bilocality (ambilocality) the custom in which a newly married couple may elect to set up residence with or near either the bride's or the groom's family 154

biological and psychological needs the needs for nutrition, reproduction, bodily comforts, safety, relaxation, movement, and growth 52

biological death death as measured by cessation of such organic functions as breathing, heartbeat, reaction to pain, or brain functioning 158

biological evolution cumulative change in the inherited characteristics of a species over successive generations 19

biostratigraphy a relative dating technique based on the association of fossil materials with fossil animals that previously were established to have occurred in a known sequence of fossil animals 28

bipedal locomotion walking on the hind legs with upright posture, which frees the hands for manipulating the environment 32

blue collar nonfarm manual labor occupations 295

bone-pointing a magical ritual for killing in which a sharp bone or stick is pointed at or ritually cast into the body of the intended victim 207

bound morphemes morphemes that can't stand as complete words 122

Brahmin the highest ranked Hindu caste, members of which are theoretically priests 71

brain stem the parts of the brain, except the cerebral hemispheres and cerebellum, that regulate involuntary processes such as breathing and heartbeat 119

bride price (progeny price) goods transferred from the groom's kin to the bride's to recompense them for her loss 152

bride service service performed by the groom for the family of the bride to recompense them for her loss 152

Broca's area the part of the cerebral cortex involved in organizing words into grammatical sequences 119

burin a chisel-like blade tool manufactured by early *Homo sapiens sapiens* and used for carving bone and ivory 40

carbon 14 dating an absolute dating technique for organic materials less than about 50,000 years old based on the known rate of decay of radioactive carbon 14 into nitrogen 27

caste a social class membership is determined by birth, so that an individual cannot legitimately change class membership by acquiring a new status 70

cerebellum the part of the brain below and behind the cerebral hemispheres of the brain that functions in the coordination of muscular activity 119

cerebral cortex the surface layer of the two large hemispheres of the brain that functions in the analysis of sensory experiences and initiates conscious action 119

Chan Chan the principal city of the Chimu empire 238

Chavin the northern Peruvian site of the earliest South American civilization 237

chief presiding political official of a chiefdom society or of a subdivision of a chiefdom society, whose legal authority extends in at least some areas over members of families other than his or her own 259

chiefdom a society, often of many villages, that has a government capable of coordinating social action within and between villages but in which governmental authority is balanced by the legal autonomy of families in many areas 226

chiefdom (rank society) a partially kinship-based society with a government that exercises authority in some areas of law over all families which are ranked with respect to each other 258

Chimu a Peruvian highland empire that built planned walled cities 238

chromosomes coiled, thread-like structures in plant and animal cells that are largely made up of the DNA responsible for inheritance 22

circumcision the surgical removal of the foreskin from the penis 146

city-states state-level societies in which each city is politically autonomous 228

civil religion a system of religious beliefs and values that is integrated into the broader, nonreligious aspects of society and is shared by its members regardless of their affiliation with formally organized religious organizations; in America, a system of largely Judeo-Christian religious symbolism within which the American political system is portrayed as divinely sanctioned and American society is viewed as God's modern chosen people. 305

civilization a culture characterized by a state government, large populations and economic specialists, social classes, draft labor and government-sponsored public works projects, markets and long-distance trade, an increased emphasis on residence location over family ties in determining social roles and usually, urban centers, writing, and mathematics 227

clan a kinship group whose members believe themselves to be descended from a common ancestor far enough in the past that they cannot trace their specific genealogical ties to one another 137, 255

class a broad, ranked stratum within society made up of unrelated families that have more or less equal power and prestige 70

closure the tendency to treat conceptual systems as if they were more complete than the incoming perceptual data 102

colonial peasantries peasant societies that were politically and economically dependent on a foreign state that perpetuated its economic exploitation of the peasant area by military domination 280

communal religions religions that include the performance of rituals by groups of lay practitioners as well as those by a shaman or individual 213

communication the transfer of information using objects and events to as signs or symbols transfer that information 105

competitiveness a central drive in American culture—fostered by the need to sell one's labor as a commodity—that emphasizes excelling over others 313

complementary statuses a pair of statuses, each of which have roles that are different from but compatible with the roles of the other 68

concepts mental models of experienced things, built from percepts 101

conformity a central drive in American culture, motivated by the obligation to defer to the authority of others in many areas of everyday life 308

conspicuous consumption the acquisition and use of a surplus of goods as a way of competitively demonstrating one's success and prestige 318

contagious magic ritual coercion of the supernatural realm by the use of the Law of Contagion 204

contextual cues culturally defined indicators such as setting, date, time of day, or the statuses of other persons present, that determine which roles are appropriate and which are inappropriate to play 72

Contrary Warrior a Cheyenne status that required the reversal of all normal behaviors, reserved for the bravest warriors 165

counterculture a movement of the 1960s that, in response to the increasing cost of living and the perceived nonresponsiveness of the established political environment to people's changing needs and goals, attempted to reformulate the American value system by inverting many traditional values 316

couvade a custom in which the husband acts as if he gives birth to his child 140

creationism the fundamentalist religious view that the Judeo- Christian scriptures are best interpreted from a highly literal point of view and as a valid source of scientific knowledge about the origins of the world and living things 218

cross cousins cousins who are related through parents who are brother and sister 149

cross-cultural comparison basing general conclusions about the nature of culture and its influence on society on the comparison of a diverse sample of cultures from many parts of the world, so that those conclusions will be generally valid for the human condition as a whole 9

cross-cultural research research that bases its conclusions from data drawn from many diverse ways of life rather than just one 4

cultural anthropologists anthropologists who specialize in the study of culture in general, or of specific cultures 4

cultural ecology the study of the ways in which cultures adapt to their specific habitats 14

cultural evolutionism the nineteenth-century emphasis on analyzing cultures in terms of their development through a series of stages from savagery to civilization 10

cultural relativism the principle that cultural traits are best understood in the context of the cultural system of which they are a part; the attempt to avoid the narrow bias of judging the value of a custom or entire culture on the basis of the values of one's own culture; the view that the meanings of behaviors are best understood when interpreted in terms of the culture of the actors 12, 61

culture a learned system of beliefs, feelings, and rules for living around which a group of people organize their lives; a way of life of a particular society 45

culture and personality the study of how a culture's child-rearing patterns influence the mental characteristics and values of a people 13

culture areas geographical areas in which different societies share a complex of cultural traits due to similar adaptations to their environmental zone and to the effects of diffusion of cultural traits through those societies 12

"culture-free" intelligence tests tests of intellectual skill that are written with few or no questions that pertain to a specific culture or subculture and that have directions that are equally easy to follow for people of all cultural backgrounds 90

culture of poverty an approach to life often found in situations of poverty in which actions are directed only to satisfying the needs of the present, by spending and consuming all income, because saving for the future seems futile 285

culture shock the loneliness and depression that is often experienced when one is in a foreign cultural setting 63

cultures ways of life, the rules for living that guide the customs of specific societies 5

Cuzco the capital city of the Inca empire 238

depression a mental disorder characterized by overt expression of a sense of personal worthlessness, failure, and sadness. In terms of role-playing, depression involves failure to make status-appropriate demands for honor 175

descent the concept of kinship connections between a child and one or both of his or her parent's kin 148

descent line the family line through which inheritance occurs 136

developed country an nation in which industrialization has become the primary basis of the economy 277

developing country an underdeveloped nation that is undergoing industrialization 277

deviant a person who has been labeled a rule violator by others for his or her role-playing errors 172

dialect a geographical or social subdivision of a language that differs systematically from other such subdivisions of the same language in its vocabulary, grammar, and phonology 130

diffusion the passage of a cultural traits such as customs, artifacts, and ideas from one society to another 12, 244

diffusionism the early twentieth-century approach to analyzing cultures that emphasized the historical reconstruction of the influences of one culture on another in contrast to the more general evolutionary perspective of earlier anthropologists 12

direct borrowing the adopting of a cultural trait by one society from another with relatively little change in form, as exemplified by traits acquired through trade or imitation 244

discovery the development of new insights and ideas 243

disease object an object such as a barbed stick or stone that is magically cast into the body of a victim to cause illness 206

divination the use of ritual to obtain answers to questions from supernatural sources 204

division of labor the rules that govern how the day-to-day work of life is divided among the holders of various statuses 69

DNA (deoxyribonucleic acid) a chemical substance that makes up the chromosomes and that carries the genetic code, or genotype, of individuals 22

domestic economy the reproductive, economic, and social behaviors that characterize life within the family or household 57

dominant an allele that is expressed in the phenotype even when it is paired with a different type of allele (called *recessive*, q.v.) 22

dowry a payment from the family of a bride to the family of her husband to compensate them for their acceptance of the responsibility of her support 152

Dravidians the native peoples of the Indus Valley who created the first civilization of India 233

drives the ideals that people actively pursue, sometimes at great cost, rather than those to which they merely give lip service 306

dryopithecines popular form of *Dryopithecus*, a genus of extinct hominoid that lived in Asia, Europe, and Africa from about 23 to about 14 million years ago and that are believed to be ancestral to both humans and apes 29

Dryopithecus africanus a 30- to 40-pound dryopithecine species that may be ancestral to either humans or chimpanzees 29

Dryopithecus fontani a European dryopithecine species that is similar to *Dryopithecus nyanzae* 29

Dryopithecus major a dryopithecine species that may be ancestral to modern gorillas 29

Dryopithecus nyanzae a dryopithecine species that may be ancestral to human beings 29

ecclesiastical religions religions that include not only individual, shamanic, and communal ritual practices but also a coordinating body of priests who perform rituals on behalf of congregations 214

emotion a pleasant or unpleasant subjective reaction to an experience, characterized by varying degrees of muscle tension and changes in respiration and heart rate 49

empiricism the viewpoint that conclusions should be based on careful observation and description, rather than on abstract theorizing 11

enculturation (socialization) the process by which children learn the customs, beliefs, and values of their culture 142

endogamy a rule requiring marriage within specified kinship categories or within other specified social or local groups to which one belongs 149

energy a positive American reaction—fostered by the work ethic—to such traits as vigor, activity, personal effort, initiative, and youthfulness 313

ensi a Sumerian city-state governor who headed the body of theocratic leaders as a kind of city manager 229

Era of Incipient Agriculture the period in which the first sedentary tribal societies developed by supplementing the collection of wild foods with some food domestication 267

Era of Regional Florescence the initial period of state government in the early civilizations when the political system was theocratic 267

ethnocentrism the attitude that one's own culture is the only good one and that other cultures are more inferior to one's own the more they differ from it 61

ethnocide the systematic destruction of a traditional way of life 274

ethnographers cultural anthropologists who spend prolonged periods living with and describing the cultures of specific peoples 5

ethnographies descriptions of the customs, beliefs, and values of individual societies 5

ethnologists cultural anthropologists who formulate general laws of culture based on the study of the ethnographies of many diverse societies 5

ethnomethodology the application of linguistic techniques to the study of the more conscious symbolic patterns of cultures 14

eureka experience a sense of intensified meaningfulness of experiences that sometimes occurs during an altered state of consciousness 181

exogamy a rule forbidding an individual from marrying a member of the kinship, residential, or other specified group to which he or she belongs 148, 256

extended family the form of family that includes two or more nuclear families and, often, their parents who reside together 156

external warfare warfare which is fought for prolonged periods in locations distant from the warriors' home with enemies who speak a foreign language and follow an alien way of life 92

face the positive social value that a person can contribute to a group; social standing 166

face-work interaction in which effort is directed to maintaining or returning behavior to roles considered appropriate for members of a group; efforts to maintain or reestablish face 167

family the group consisting of married persons, their children, and other relatives who reside with them 156

fear a distressful emotion characterized by concerns about inadequate power to protect oneself from specific danger 168

feelings subjective reactions to experiences as pleasant or unpleasant or as good or bad. Feelings include emotions, attitudes, and values 47

female infanticide the killing of female infants, a practice that is often associated with internal warfare 92

feudal peasantries preindustrialized societies in which peasant food producers pay rent or perform service for the privilege of farming lands owned by local aristocratic officials who have obligations to provide police and military protection, judicial services, and care for the peasants in times of hardship 280

fieldwork the basic tool of anthropological research in which information is gathered from the context in which it naturally occurs 7

fission-track dating an absolute dating technique for samples from 20 years to 4.6 billion years old based on counting the tracks left in certain minerals by the radioactive decay of uranium 238 27

Fissure of Rolando a vertical fold in the surface of the brain that separates the motor areas which control conscious muscle movement from corresponding areas which receive sensory information from various parts of the body 119

folklore the study of the traditional narratives or oral literature of a people and how it relates to the rest of their customs and artifacts 189

folktales (fairy tales) stories placed in a timeless setting and vague location that portray the basic dilemmas faced by members of a society 191

food domestication the intentional raising of plants and animals as food resources 222

foraging a subsistence technology based on gathering wild plant foods, hunting, and fishing 53, 222

formal learning learning that proceeds by admonition and correction of the learner's errors with emotional emphasis on the importance of behaving acceptably 143

Formative Era the period in which chiefdoms arose in various parts of the world 267

fraternal polyandry the form of polyandry in which the husbands are brothers 154

free morphemes morphemes that can stand as complete words 122

frigophobia (*pa-ling*) a culture-specific obsessive-compulsive disorder characterized by fear of loss of body heat 179

frontier areas areas opened to settlement by national governments that do not recognize the land claims of the indigenous population 284

function the contribution that any one cultural trait makes to perpetuating the unity, equilibrium, and adaptation of a way of life within its environment 12

functionalism the approach to analyzing cultures by examining the mechanics of society while it is in equilibrium, as opposed to the more historical emphasis of diffusionism or the developmental emphasis of evolutionism 12

funeral rite a rite of passage that formalizes the removal of an individual from the status of living member of the social group 159

ganzfeld phenomenon the inability to perceive when visual contrasts are not maintained 104

gene a distinct unit of a chromosome that controls the inheritance of biological traits 21

gene flow the transfer of genes from one population to another. Gene flow increases the genetic variability of the recipient population, thereby increasing its potential for surviving changing conditions in its environment 24

General Adaptation Syndrome the nonspecific changes that occur in the body as a result of stress, as it mobilizes itself to act against that stress 208

general evolution the process in which a culture becomes qualitatively more complex as it develops the technological means for harnessing new and greater amounts of energy 267

genetic drift random changes in the genes in a population caused by processes other than mutation or gene flow into the population 24

genocide the systematic extermination of a people 276

genotype the genetic traits of living things; the total genetic makeup of a species (compare phenotype) 21

glottochronology a technique for calculating the minimal length of time that two related languages have been diverging from a common ancestral language 130

grammar the analysis of the regular ways that the sounds of a language are combined to form meaningful utterances. Grammar includes morphology and syntax 121

grief a distressful emotion characterized by a sense of loss, failure, and personal worthlessness 169

group two or more individuals engaged in a common activity 67

group marriage the form of marriage in which two or more men are married to two or more women at the same time 155

guilt a distressful emotion characterized by remorse for having harmed another 169

hallucination a realistic-seeming experience—much like a vivid waking dream—that may include vision, hearing, the sense of touch, smell, and/or taste in the absence of external cause 181

hand-axes carefully made teardrop- or pear-shaped core tools of varying sizes manufactured by *Homo erectus* 36

Harappa one of the two great planned cities of the Indus Valley civilization 232

heredity biological inheritance 21

holistic emphasizing the full range of relations among parts of a system and the ways the operation of those parts helps to perpetuate the whole system 4

hominid popular form of

Hominidae, a *family* of bipedal primates including *Homo sapiens* and various fossil species that have more in common with *Homo sapiens* than with any other living primate 25

hominoid popular form of *Hominoidea*, a superfamily of primates including humans and apes, and the fossil species ancestral to both or that have more in common with both than with other living primate species 26

Homo erectus an early hominid believed to have been descended from *Homo habilis* who occupied Africa, Europe, and Asia from 1.5 million to 300,000 years ago and who is known to have controlled and used fire from at least half a million years ago 36

Homo habilis a hominid generally believed to have been descended either from *Australopithecus afarensis* or *Australopithecus africanus* who occupied South and East Africa between 2 and 1.5 million years ago and who manufactured the first known stone tools 35

Homo sapiens the species to which human beings belong, including contemporary humans and their ancestors possibly as early as Neanderthal 41

Homo sapiens neanderthalensis an early form of the human species descended from *Homo erectus* who occupied the Eastern Hemisphere from 125,000 to 40,000 years ago 38

Homo sapiens sapiens human beings of modern form, possibly descended from *Homo sapiens neanderthalensis*, found from about 40,000 years ago to the present 40

honor the ability to influence others without coercion or the threat of coercion 70

horticulture cultivation of crops using simple hand tools such as the hoe and digging stick and without fertilization of the soil, or crop rotation and often without irrigation 54, 255

household a group of people who share a common residence 156

hsieh-ping a culture-specific hysterical disorder that is characterized by tremor, disorientation, clouding of consciousness,

delirium, speaking in tongues, and hallucinations 177

Huangho River Valley (Yellow River Valley) the location of the earliest native Chinese civilization 233

Huari the first Peruvian empire based on warfare, trade, and imposition of religious beliefs on conquered peoples 238

Human Relations Area Files (HRAF) a research data pool containing information on over 1,000 cultures, each coded for the presence or absence of about 800 cultural and environmental traits 9

human soul the supernatural part of the human being that is believed to animate the human body during life or perpetuate the individual's memories or life-goals after death 200

hypochondriasis a form of neurosis in which the ritualistic expression of anxiety takes the form of preoccupation with physical health and the body or of unfounded beliefs that one is suffering from dire illnesses 176

hysteria a form of neurosis in which there is ritualistic avoidance of anxiety or ritualistic manipulation of others as a means of avoiding failure 175

ideal culture the ways people perceive their own customs and behaviors, often more a reflection of their feelings and ideals about what it should be rather than an accurate assessment of what it is 51

ideological communication communication that reaffirms people's allegiance to their groups and creates a sense of community by asserting its ideology 47

ideology the consciously shared beliefs and feelings that members of a society consider characteristic of themselves as a people 47, 246

image of limited good a fatalistic outlook common in situations of peasant poverty in which the drudgery of life is not believed to bring much reward, since the achievement of one person can only be accomplished at the expense of another 285

imitative magic ritual coercion of the supernatural realm by use of the Law of Similarity 203

Imperial Era of Cyclical Conquests the period of expansionist state government that followed the theocratic states of early civilizations 267

imu an hysterical disorder found among the Ainu of northern Japan characterized by automatic obedience or negativism and uncontrollable imitation of sounds and gestures 176

Inca the final and largest native Andean empire which ruled about six million subjects 238

incest taboo a rule that forbids sexual behaviors between designated kin, including but not limited to intercourse between parents and children and among siblings 144

indigenous people a people whose occupation of an area precedes the state political system that now controls that area and who have little or no influence within that political system 273

Indus Valley (Harappa) civilization the first civilization of India 232

industrialization the process of change from an economy based on home production of goods to one based on large-scale, mechanized factory production 276

industrialized agriculture the use of an industrialized technology and other techniques such as chemical soil fertilization to obtain high levels of food production per acre 57

industrialized state a society coordinated by a state form of political organization and economically supported by an industrialized system of food production 265

informal learning learning by imitation 143

insanity the process by which a person acquires and maintains the deviant master status of *residual rule breaker* 174

intensive peasant smallholdings areas of small, individually owned peasant farms in impoverished rural settlements with population densities equivalent to urban areas 284

internal warfare warfare in which the fighting is between peoples who share the same language and culture 92

International Phonetic Alphabet (IPA) a standard alphabet of nearly 100 sound symbols used by linguists throughout the world for writing phonetic transcriptions of languages 121

intimate distance the distance from their bodies that people reserve for those with whom they are intimate enough to permit casual touching 112

invention the act of combining preexisting cultural traits in new ways 244

IQ (Intelligence Quotient) ratio of a person's mental age to chronological age to determine intellectual potential 84

irrigated farmlands territories occupied and worked by peasants but owned by absentee landlords in which the productive land has sufficient water to make farming possible 283

jati an occupational subcaste in Hindu society 72

jokes humor that allows people to relieve tensions 191

kayak angst a culture-specific phobic disorder that is characterized by an inordinate fear of being at sea in a kayak 178

kindred a kinship group in a bilateral descent system that consists of the known relatives of a specific individual 137, 256

kinesics the study of the body movements that accompany speech as a component of communication 114

kinship group the individuals related to one another by ties of descent or by ties of marriage 148

koro a culture-specific anxiety disorder characterized by fear of death through loss of sexual essence 179

Kotash the site of the earliest Andean highland food domestication 237

Kshatriya the second most important of the Hindu castes, members of which were the traditional warrior-rulers, nobles, and landowners of society 71

latah a culture-specific hysterical disorder that is characterized by uncontrollable imitation of the actions and speech of others 176

La Venta the largest Olmec ceremonial center 235

labor reserve (remittance economy) areas peasant areas that have been impoverished by a drain of working-age laborers who have emigrated to urban areas to find employment 284

language a system of rules that govern the production and interpretation of speech 115

large farm (estate) areas lands owned by foreign corporations or governments and worked by peasant wage laborers who live in housing provided by the corporate or governmental owners 283

Law of Contagion the principle that things that have been in contact remain supernaturally in contact or that contact between things can be used to transfer *mana* from one to the other 204

Law of Cultural Dominance the concept that the technological capacity to harness the energy available in an environment is the major determinant of which culture will become socially and politically dominant within that environment 244

Law of Evolutionary Potential the concept that a culture's capacity to move from one general evolutionary stage to another varies inversely with the degree of its specific evolutionary adaptation to its environment 268

Law of Local Discontinuity of Progress the idea that the successive stages of general evolutionary change are not likely to occur in the same locality 268

Law of Similarity the principle that things that are similar to one another are spiritually identical, and can be used in rituals to influence a desired outcome 203

learning changes in behavior that result from interaction with the environment 101

legends stories about heroic characters involved in the creation of a society 190

levirate a rule that requires the kin of a deceased man to provide his widow with another husband, often one of the deceased man's brothers 151

life cycle the status changes from birth to death that are typical of a particular society 135

limbic system areas within the brain that deal with emotional experience 120

lineage a kinship group whose members can trace their lines of descent to the same ancestor 137, 255

linguistic relativity the idea that the characteristics of a language influence the way that its speakers think 123

lugal a Sumerian king or military commander-in-chief 229

magic the use of rituals that are believed to compel—as opposed to simply making requests of—the supernatural when performed correctly 203

maintenance system the parts of the economic and social structure of a society that determine its childrearing practices 164

mana supernatural power or force 196

manic episode a period of exhilaration and high activity that sometimes occurs in depression. It involves unrealistically high estimates of one's own honor, skill, or self-worth 175

marginal and hill farming lands peasant farming areas in which only hand farming techniques are feasible due to isolation, lack of sufficient water for irrigation, or the steepness of the land 283

market economy a form of distribution in which established places are used for the direct exchange of goods and services 262

market exchange a system of distribution for goods and services based primarily on the use of established locations for obtaining them 294

marking the idea that the behaviors of a woman during pregnancy may influence the physical or psychological characteristics of the unborn child 300

marriage a rite of passage that unites two or more individuals as spouses 148

Marxist anthropology the study of the effects of class conflict on social and cultural change 14

master status a social status that is noticed by others even when the contextual cues present do not call for the playing of its roles; a status that is its own contextual cue 73

matrilateral cross-cousin marriage marriage between a male and his mother's brother's daughter 151

matrilineality tracing descent lines through mothers 136

Maya the people of Guatemala, El Salvador, Honduras, and parts of Mexico whose civilization was stimulated by the Olmec 235

meta-communication system a system of communication that includes the capacity to communicate about itself 115

minority status a low ranked master status, commonly but incorrectly called a ''minority group'' 74

Moche the earliest Andean civilization to dominate several valleys 237

modal personality type the most common or typical pattern of personality traits in a particular society 164

mode of production the work practices by which people apply their subsistence technology within a particular environment 57

mode of reproduction the technology and practices operating within a particular social environment that influence the size of the society's population 57

Mohenjo-daro one of the two great planned cities of the Indus Valley civilization 232

moiety one of two basic complementary social subdivisions of a society 148, 256

molecular biology the study of the molecular structure of such things as hemoglobin, serum proteins, and DNA 31

monogamy the form of marriage in which one man and one woman are joined as husband and wife 154

monotheism the belief in a high god, a supreme being who either created the physical universe and other spiritual beings and rules over them or who at least maintains the order of the universe today 200

monotheistic religions ecclesiastical religions in which one god is supreme over all other gods or supernatural beings or in which all of the gods or supernatural beings are thought of as merely alternative manifestations of a single Supreme Being 214

morpheme the smallest meaningful sequence of sounds in a language 121

morphology the study of how phonemes are combined into the smallest meaningful units of a language 121

mutations changes in a gene or chromosome. Mutations are the basic source of all new variations within species and therefore the basis for evolution as a continuing process 23

myths beliefs usually told in stories about the origins of the supernatural realm, the universe, and human beings 189, 203

naming ceremony a rite of passage following birth at which the infant is declared a member of the human group by being given a name 141

natural selection the process whereby those members of a species that are better adapted to their environment contribute more offspring to succeeding generations than do other members so that the species gradually acquires those adapting traits that made some individuals more adapted than others 19

Neanderthal popular term for *Homo sapiens neanderthalensis*, (q.v.) 37

neocortex the evolutionarily younger surface portion of the human brain that controls the learning of conscious behaviors 101

neoevolutionism the contemporary approach to the study of how cultures evolve, placing emphasis on the diversity of processes and pathways followed by specific cultures 14

neofunctionalism the contemporary approach to studying the functional processes of cultural systems, with emphasis on the ways in which conflict may be one of the mechanisms by which cultural stability is maintained 14

neolocality the custom in which the newly married couple sets up residence in a new location apart from either of their families 154

neuroses mental disorders characterized by, and rituals expressing anxiety about, inadequate social power. (*singular,* neurosis) 175

nomes the farming communities of ancient Egypt 231

nonindustrialized state a society coordinated by a state form of political organization and economically supported by a labor-intensive, nonmechanized system of food production 265

nonkinship associations groups formed from members drawn from all parts of a community based on criteria other than kinship, such as age category or common interest, for the purpose of fulfilling specific responsibilities that affect the community as a whole 256

nonscientific beliefs beliefs that grow out of people's feelings 48

nonverbal communication all transfer of information other than with words. Nonverbal communication may include the use of such things as volume, pitch, tone of voice, and speed when speaking, as well as non-oral things such as gestures, posture, and use of space and time 110

nuclear family the form of family that consists only of married persons and their children 156

obsessive-compulsive neurosis a form of neurosis in which the ritualistic expression of anxiety about failure takes the form of make-work rituals 176

Olmec A people who lived on the Gulf of Mexico and developed what may have been the first civilization in the Americas 235

Olympian religions polytheistic eccclesiastical religions in which the gods or supernatural beings may be loosely ranked but in which no one of the supernatural beings is truly supreme over the others 214

optimism a positive American expectation—fostered by the work ethic—that the future is potentially better than the present 312

oracle bones bones used for divining by writing questions on them and then interpreting the patterns of cracks that develop from heating the bones 233

oral literature the myths, legends, folktales, stories, proverbs, riddles, and jokes that people pass from generation to generation by word of mouth in a nonliterate society 189

paleomagnetism a relative dating technique based on the established sequences of shifts in the earth's magnetic field 28

parallel cousins cousins whose parents are either two brothers or two sisters 151

participant observation the technique of cultural anthropology in which the researcher spends a prolonged period participating and observing subjects in their natural setting, as opposed to studying them in a laboratory setting 8

pastoral and ranching areas places occupied by low-density populations spread over large areas within which they make their living by the herding of livestock 282

pastoralism a subsistence technology based on animal husbandry 56, 257

patrilateral cross-cousin marriage marriage between a male and his father's sister's daughter 149

patrilateral parallel-cousin marriage (*bint 'amm*) marriage between a male and his father's brother's daughter 151

patrilineality tracing descent lines through fathers 136

peasants people who use nonindustrialized, labor-intensive techniques for producing food and who are politically and economically subordinate to a governing class of which they are not a part and with whom they have little influence 280

pebble tools cores of stone originally thought to have been made by australopithecines but now known to have been made by *Homo habilis* by knocking off a series of flakes, leaving a modified core with a sharp edge. Pebble tools manufactured about 2 million years ago represent the earliest known hominid tools. Currently it is de-

bated whether the primary tools being produced were the removed flakes or the remaining core 32

percepts the basic units of information about experienced things out of which concepts are built 102

peri-urban squatter settlements densely settled, legally unrecognized communities near rapidly growing cities occupied by peasants whose subsistence is based on extremely small farms, petty trading, casual work, gardening, and other services performed for citizens of the nearby cities 284

permissive societies tolerant of childhood sexual experimentation 143

personal distance the distance to which people adjust themselves when interacting with close friends 112

personality (psychological definition) a consistent pattern to an individual's behavior resulting from a more or less enduring set of inner forces; (anthropological definition) the pattern of an individual's behavior that results from the various social roles that an individual plays 163

phenotype the observable characteristics of living things (compare genotype) 21

phobia a form of neurosis in which there is ritualistic expression of fears of things not culturally defined as appropriate objects of fear 175

phone the smallest sound unit of a language 121

phoneme the smallest psychologically real unit of sound in a language 121

phonemic pertaining to the phonemes of a language. A phonemic transcription is a written record of speech that uses an alphabet composed of only one symbol for each phoneme of the language 121

phonetic pertaining to the smallest units of sound actually produced by speakers of a language. A phonetic transcription attempts to record all of the sounds consistently produced by the speakers of a language 121

phonology the study of the

rules that govern the production and the organization of the sounds of a particular language 120

physical (biological) anthropologists anthropologists who specialize in the study of the evolutionary origins of the human species, the relationships between the human species and other living primates, the physical variation within the human species today, and the relationships between human biology and our species's cultural capacities 6

pibloktoq a culture-specific hysterical disorder characterized by agitated attempts to flee the presence of other people 177

pink collar pertaining to service occupations that largely are held by women 295

play ritualized behavior attended by altered states of consciousness in which external things are experienced as if they were extensions of one's own fantasy. Unlike religion and mental illness, play does not involve a judgment that those experiences are objectively real 186

political economy the reproductive, economic, and social behaviors that are typical of life outside the family or household 57

polyandry the form of marriage in which one woman has more than one husband 154

polygyny the form of marriage in which one man has more than one wife 154

polytheism the belief in superior (but not supreme) gods, each of whom controls or rules over some major aspect of the universe 200

potassium-argon dating an absolute dating technique for materials between 100,000 and 4.6 billion years old based on the known rate of decay of radioactive potassium 40 into argon 40 27

power the ability to exercise coercion 70

practicing anthropology the application of anthropological knowledge, techniques, and skills to solving problems within the private economic sector 14

Pre-Agricultural Era the period of foraging bands 267

pregnancy rituals religious rules such as taboos designed to protect the unborn child and the mother during pregnancy and childbirth or admonitions to engage in acts believed to be a positive influence on the developing child 139

priests religious practitioners who perform rituals for the benefit of groups. Often, priests are full-time religious practitioners whose emphasis is on preserving the established ritual forms, rather than on inspiration and innovation in the application of their rituals 214

primary institutions the parts of social life related to childrearing, including the family and other primary care groups, feeding, weaning, care or neglect of children, sexual training, and subsistence patterns 164

primates popular form of *Primates*, an *order* of mammals to which humans, apes, monkeys, and prosimians belong 25

Principle of Stabilization the concept that as a culture becomes efficient at harnessing energy for society, the more expensive and difficult it becomes to implement new means of increasing efficiency 268

professionals self-employed, college-educated service providers 295

prosimians small tree-dwelling primates such as tarsiers, lemurs, and loris 28

"protective" legislation laws that are ostensibly intended to prevent the exploitation of women, but which in practice create social barriers against the full participation of women in social life outside the domestic sphere; for instance, many states in the U.S. have laws that prohibit the hiring of women into occupations that require the employee to lift more than 35 pounds 96

Proto-Germanic the ancestral language from which modern Germanic languages developed, including English, Dutch, German, Norwegian, Danish, and Swedish 126

Proto-Indo-European the ancestral language from which most of the contemporary languages of Europe, Iran, and India have developed 130

proverbs short statements, often inserted into conversations as admonitions, that embody the basic values of a culture 191

proxemics the study of how people structure the space around them when interacting with others 112

psychological anthropology the contemporary approach to the study of the relationships between personality and culture in which techniques such as statistical comparisons are used to validate ideas about those relationships 13

psychological death the process by which one subjectively prepares for impending biological death 158

puberty (adulthood) ritual a rite of passage that formalizes the change from the status of child to the status of adult 145

public distance the distance reserved for separating people whose interaction is not intended to perpetuate a social relationship 114

purposefulness a manifestation of the American work ethic that asserts the importance of goal-directed effort 313

quinoa a high-altitude grain that made possible the spread of agriculture into the Andes 237

quipu a knotted cord memory aid, used for record keeping in the Inca empire 239

race a rather arbitrary biological subdivision of the human species. The "races" of popular conception are most accurately understood to be culturally defined statuses rather than scientifically valid biological subdivisions 76

racial discrimination unequal social treatment of individuals based on their race 77

racism the belief that differences in the expected roles of members of different racial groups are based on the hereditarily controlled behavioral predispositions of those groups 77

ramapithecines popular form of *Ramapithecus*, a hominoid genus, possibly descended from the dryopithecines, that lived from 15 to 8 million years ago in

China, India, Europe, Kenya, and possibly Greece 30

range management planning for most effective use of land for raising livestock without depleting the environment 287

rank the relative importance of a status or group as measured by the amount of power and/or honor to which it is entitled 69

real culture culture portrayed in terms of the actually observable behaviors of a people 51

recessive an allele that is expressed in the phenotype only when it is paired with another allele of the same type 22

reciprocity sharing of surpluses with the understanding that the party receiving the gift will respond in kind in the future but with no explicit agreement about when and with what 251

reincarnation the belief that the soul of a human being may be repeatedly reborn into the human group to which it previously belonged or as an animal that may be symbolically associated with that group 200

relative dating techniques for determining whether the age of a fossil or group of fossils is greater than or less than the age of other fossils 27

religion beliefs concerning supernatural powers and beings and rituals designed to influence those beings and powers; a system through which people interpret the nonhuman realm as if it were human and seek to influence it through symbolic communication 195

reservations territories within a region controlled by a state political system that are set aside for the occupation of indigenous peoples 274

residual rules the miscellaneous, normally unspoken rules that people are expected to follow in order to avoid violating the pattern or style of behavior that permeates the rest of the culture 173

restrictive societies societies that do not accept childhood sexual experimentation 143

riddles entertaining mental puzzles that describe common things in novel ways 191

Rig-Veda the oldest surviving literature of the Aryans 233

rights of inheritance the legitimate claim of a child to property passed down the descent line on the death of a parent 148

rite of passage (life crisis rite) a ritual that formalizes a major change in social status 135

ritual behaviors, often performed in repetitive and stereotyped ways, that express people's anxieties by acting them out. May be an attempt to influence the supernatural realm to achieve greater control over the natural world 169

role the skills, abilities, and ways of acting towards others that belong to each status of a society 68

role conflict emotional discomfort and confusion experienced in situations in which conflicting contextual cues indicate that an individual should play the roles of more than one of his or her statuses 72

saka a culture-specific hysterical disorder that is characterized by repetition of actions or sounds believed to be a foreign language and loss of consciousness with body rigidity 177

scarification decorating the body by cutting designs in it and treating them with ashes or other material to insure that they will produce raised scars 146

schizophrenia a mental disorder characterized by residual rule breaking caused by difficulty in communicating an acceptable social identity. Schizophrenia may include hallucinations and ideas about reality that are greatly at odds with mainstream ideas 175

scientific beliefs beliefs that are based on the desire to solve the practical day-to-day problems of living 48

secondary institutions the institutions in social life that satisfy the needs and tensions created by the primary institutions, including especially taboo systems, religion, rituals, folk tales, and techniques of thinking 164

sedentarism living in permanent or semipermanent settlements 223

self-reliance a value central to America that emphasizes the importance of independence, autonomy of the individual, and the primacy of the individual over the group 310

semirestrictive societies accepting of childhood sexual experimentation so long as those involved follow established rules of etiquette and discretion 143

serial monogamy a marriage pattern in which individuals of either sex may have only one spouse at a given time, but through divorce and remarriage may have several spouses during their lifetime 300

serotonin a chemical produced in the brain during waking hours that inhibits the production of dreams or hallucinations 181

sexism the belief that differences in the sex roles of males and females are biologically determined 76

shamanic religions religions in which the only ritual specialist is the shaman and which contain only individual and shamanic ritual practices 212

shamans part-time religious practitioners who are believed to have access to supernatural power that may be used for the benefit of specific clients, as in healing or divining 209

shame (embarrassment) a distressful emotion characterized by a sense of personal ineptness resulting in damage to one's reputation 169

sign an object or event that represents another object or event because of a similarity between them or a tendency for the two to occur together in nature 106

signalized behavior normally symbolic behavior (especially speech) that has become more expressive of feelings and less indicative of the factual information it usually conveys 171

sin a form of taboo violation in which the rule breaker is thought of as morally responsible for the act 206

slash and burn cultivation a form of farming in which the land is prepared by cutting and burning the natural growth and in which several plots, in various stages of soil depletion, are worked in a cycle 55

sleep crawling a Samoan sexual practice in which an uninvited youth would enter a young woman's house with the intent of seduction 147

social death the point at which people respond to a person with the behaviors appropriate to one who is biologically dead 158

social distance the distance to which people adjust themselves when interacting in impersonal situations such as business transactions 114

social organization the relationships between the groups, statuses, and division of labor that structure the interaction of people within society 67, 246

social structure the part of social organization that is made up of groups and their relationships with each other 68

socialization the process of learning a culture and the role-playing skills necessary for social life 164

sorcerers practitioners of magical rituals that are done to harm others 211

sorcery the learned use of rituals to magically control the supernatural realm to achieve human goals 200

sororal polygyny the form of polygyny in which the wives are sisters 154

sororate a rule that requires the kin of a deceased woman to provide her widower with another wife, often one of the deceased woman's sisters 151

soul loss in primitive societies, the belief that the departure of the soul from the body, usually caused by a sudden fright, causes the body to weaken and die 206

spear-thrower a device invented about 40,000 years ago for increasing the leverage of the human arm when throwing a spear or dart 40

speciation the gradual divergence of two or more populations of a single species into separate species 25

species a population that can interbreed and produce fertile offspring 19

specific evolution the process in which a culture becomes bet-ter adapted to its specific environment by using the available energy more efficiently 267

speech an audible sequence of verbal symbols 115

speech motor area the part of the cerebral cortex that controls the production of speech sounds 120

spirit possession the control of a human being by a spirit that has entered his or her body. Spirit possession is often believed to cause disease or deviant behavior 206

spirit possession trance a trance in which individuals feel as if their behavior is under the control of one or more spirits that have entered their bodies 183

spirit travel trance a trance in which individuals experience themselves as leaving their bodies 183

states societies with centralized governments that monopolize the legal authority to use force 227, 262

status a culturally defined relationship that one individual may have with one or more other individuals; the position within a group that each member of that group holds 68

status pair two statuses that together form one of the relationships that may exist between people in a particular culture 68

status-appropriate roles the ways of behaving that are culturally defined as expected of an individual who holds a particular social status 165

stereoscopic vision the ability of the brain to perceive in three dimensions based on the different perspectives provided by each eye 28

stimulus diffusion the borrowing of the idea for a cultural trait by one society from another, with the implementation of that idea being more or less determined within the borrowing culture 244

stratigraphy a relative dating technique based on the sequence of fossil materials in various layers of earth 28

stress a physiological response to any demand characterized by the body's preparing itself for action 169

structural anthropology the application of a linguistic approach to analyzing meaningful systems in order to interpret the less conscious patterns of cultures 14

subsistence technology the tools and techniques by which people obtain food 53

Sudra the lowest of the Hindu castes, made up of farm artisans, servants, farmers, and laborers 71

Sumer the world's first civilization, which arose in southern Mesopotamia 228

supernatural that which transcends the natural, observable world 197

supernatural sanctions for violations of moral rules punishments for immoral acts by spiritual agencies as opposed to human agencies. In most societies, the enforcement of morality is a strictly human responsibility, rather than a religious preoccupation 200

survivals remnants of earlier social customs and ideas that can be used for reconstructing the evolutionary past of societies 11

susto (espanto, pasmo) a culture-specific anxiety disorder with some depressive features interpreted by the victim as caused by soul loss 179

symbol an object or event that represents another object or event only because of the agreement between people that it will 46, 106

symbolic anthropology the study of the most highly symbolic parts of culture, including myth, ritual, folklore, and the meaningful aspects of kinship as the basis for understanding the rest of social life and custom 14

symmetrical statuses a pair of statuses each of which has the same roles to play in respect to the other 68

syntax the study of the rules for combining morphemes into complete and meaningful sentences 122

Systema Naturae the book in which Carolus Linnaeus classified plants and animals into a hierarchical system based on their degree of similarity to one another 10

taboo a rule forbidding contact with sacred things, that is, with things containing *mana* 196

taboo violation the breaking of a supernatural rule, whether intentional or not. Taboo violations are often believed to be a cause of illness 206

technical learning learning that occurs when the logical rationales for specific ways of doing things—rather than emotional pressure to behave in that way—are given to the learner 143

technology tools and techniques through which human beings harness the energy available in their environment 53, 246

teknonymy the custom of referring to a person as the parent of their child rather than by their birth name 156

tenant or refugee farms farms worked by laborers who were dispossessed when the traditional system of mutual obligations between landowners and the tenant farmers was replaced by a system in which the farming is simply a paid labor 284

Tenochtitlan the island capital of the Aztec empire 237

Teotihuacan the capital city of the empire that superseded the Olmec colonies on the Mexican plateau. The civilization of Teotihuacan was viewed by later peoples of Mexico as the great Golden Age 235

the Fayum a lake region west of the Nile in which the earliest known Egyptian farming community existed 231

theocracy political rule by religious leaders 229

Toltec the militaristic civilization of central Mexico that superseded the civilization of Teotihuacan 237

traditional agriculture reliance on nonindustrialized tools and techniques such as the plow, animal traction, animal fertilizers, crop rotation, and irrigation to increase the productivity of cultivated land 56

tribe a semisedentary kinship-based society without a full-time government. Most tribal societies are economically based on a simple food domestication subsistence technology, either horticulture or pastoralism 255

Tula the capital city of the Toltec empire 237

underdeveloped country a nation with a largely nonindustrialized economy 277

unskilled laborers low-paid workers, including part-time or seasonal workers, who usually are paid by the hour or for the quantity of goods they produce 294

Untouchables the lowest status members of Hindu society who belonged to none of the traditional castes and who performed the ritually polluted tasks of life 71

uxorilocality (matrilocality) the custom in which a newly married couple is expected to set up residence with or near the bride's family 154

Vaisya the third Hindu caste, comprised of commoners 71

value a subjective reaction to experiences expressed in terms of good or bad, moral or immoral; the ideals that people

long for but do not necessarily pursue. Values are often opposites of drives 50, 306

virilocality (patrilocality) the custom in which a newly married couple is expected to set up their residence with or near the groom's family 152

voodoo death (magical death) death that occurs following a magical ritual performed to kill 207

Wernicke's area the part of the cerebral cortex involved in processing speech sounds 119

white collar pertaining to service-providing occupations such as clerical, sales, managerial, and administrative jobs 295

witchcraft the innate ability to influence supernatural forces to operate usually in ways that are harmful to others without the necessity of using rituals 200

witches persons believed to have the innate supernatural ability to harm others without the use of ritual 212

work ethic a central drive of American culture in which work is felt to be good in and of itself—a feeling fostered by an economic system in which individuals must work competitively to produce goods that they themselves do not own and that will be consumed by others 312

Y-5 tooth pattern a distinctive Y-shaped arrangement of fissures between 5 cusps on the molar teeth of apes, humans, and fossil dryopithecines 29

ziggurat a Sumerian step-pyramid that served as the base for a temple 228

Bibliography

Abercrombie, F. D. (1974). *Range development and management in Africa*. Washington, DC: Bureau for Africa, Agency for International Development.

Aberle, D. F. (1961). 'Arctic hysteria' and latah in Mongolia. In Y. A. Cohen (Ed.), *Social structure and personality: A casebook* (pp. 471-475). New York: Holt, Rinehart and Winston.

Aberle, D. F., Bronfenbrenner, U., Hess, E. H., Miller, D. R., Schneider, D. M., & Spuhler, J. N. (1963). The incest taboo and the mating patterns of animals. *American Anthropologist, 65*, 253-265.

Albert, E. M. (1964). Conflict and change in American values: A culture-historical approach. *Ethics, 74*, 272-279.

Altman, S. A. (1973). Primate communication. In G. A. Miller (Ed.), *Communication, language and meaning: Psychological perspectives* (pp. 84-94). New York: Basic Books, Inc.

Andrews, P., & Evans, E. (1979). The environment of *Ramapithecus* in Africa. *Paleobiology, 5*(1), 22-30.

Andrews, P., & Tobias, H. (1977). New Miocene locality in Turkey, and evidence on the origin of *Ramapithecus* and *Sivapithecus*. *Nature, 268*, 699-701.

Ausubel, D. (1961). Personality disorder is disease. *American Psychologist, 16*, 72.

Bagley, C. (1969). Incest behavior and incest taboo. *Social Problems, 16*, 505-519.

Barker-Banfield, G. J. (1983). The spermatic economy: A nineteenth century view of sexuality. In Dr. T. Altherr (Ed.), *Procreation or pleasure: Sexual attitudes in American history* (pp. 47-70). Malabar, FL: Robert E. Krieger Publishing.

Barnes, G. H., & Dummond, D. W. (Eds.). (1934). *Letters of Theodore Dwight Weld, Angelina Grimké Weld and Sarah Grimké: 1822-1844* (Vol. 1). New York: Appleton-Century.

Barry, H., III, Child, I. L., & Bacon, M. K. (1959). Relation of child training to subsistence economy. *American Anthropologist, 61*, 51-63.

Barth, F. (1954). Father's brother's daughter marriage in Kurdistan. *Southwestern Journal of Anthropology, 10*(1), 164-171.

Basedow, H. (1925). *The Australian aboriginal*. Adelaide: F. W. Preece and Sons.

Beals, A. M. (1974). *Village life in south India*. Chicago: Aldine.

Beals, A. M. (1980). *Gopalpur*. New York: Holt, Rinehart and Winston.

Bean, S. S. (1981). Soap operas: Sagas of American kinship. In S. Montague & W. Arens (Eds.), *The American dimension: Cultural myths and social realities* (pp. 61-75). Sherman Oaks, CA: Alfred Publishing Co.

Behnam, D. (1985). The Tunis conference. *Current Anthropology, 26*, 555-556.

Benedict, R. B. (1932). Configurations of culture in North America. *American Anthropologist, 34*, 1-27.

Benedict, R. F. (1934). *Patterns of culture*. Boston, MA: Houghton Mifflin.

Beyers, D. S. (1957). The Bering bridge—some speculations. *Ethnos, 1-2*, 20-26.

Binford, L. R. (1968). Post-Pleistocene adaptations. In L. R. Binford & S. R. Binford (Eds.), *New perspective in archaeology* (pp. 22-49). Chicago: Aldine.

Bird, C. (1973). *Born female: The high cost of keeping women down*. New York: David McKay.

Birdwhistell, R. L. (1970). *Kinesics and context: Essays on body motion communication*. Philadelphia, PA: University of Pennsylvania Press.

Bixler, R. H. (1981). Incest avoidance as a function of environment *and* heredity. *Current Anthropology, 22*, 639-654.

Blair, Z. S. (1981). *Black children/white children: Competence, socialization, and social structure*. New York: The Free Press.

Bloomfield, L. (1933). Dialect geography. In H. Hoijer (Ed.), *Language history* (pp. 321-345). New York: Holt, Rinehart and Winston, Inc.

Boas, F. (1940). Representative art of primitive people. In F. Boas, *Race, language and culture* (pp. 564-592). New York: Free Press. (Original work published 1916)

Boas, F. (1966). Introduction to the handbook of American Indian languages. In P. Holter (Ed.), *Introduction to the handbook of American Indian languages/Indian linguistic families of America north of Mexico* (pp. 20-22). Lincoln, NE: University of Nebraska Press.

Bogoras, W. (1907). *The Chukchee—religion*. (Memoirs of the American Museum of Natural History, No. 11, Part 2). New York: American Museum of Natural History.

Bonwick, J. (1884). *The lost Tasmanian race*. London: S. Low, Marston, Searle, and Rivington.

Boserup, E. (1977). *The condition of agricultural growth: The economics of agrarian change under population pressures*. Chicago: Aldine-Atherton.

Bourguignon, E. (1974). Culture and the varieties of consciousness. *Addison-Wesley Module in Anthropology* (No. 47). Reading, MA: Addison-Wesley Publishing.

Bourguignon, E., & Greenberg, L. (1973). *Homogeneity and diversity in world societies*. New Haven, CT: Human Relations Area Files.

Brace, C. L. (1967). *The stages of human evolution: Human and cultural origins*. Englewood Cliffs, NJ: Prentice-Hall.

Brace, C. L., & Montagu, A. (1977). *Human evolution: An introduction to biological anthropology*. New York: Macmillan.

Brain, C. K. (1970). New findings at Swartkrans australopithecine sites. *Nature, 225,* 1112-1119.

Brain, C. K. (1975). The bone assemblage from the Kromdraai australopithecine site. In R. Tuttle (Ed.), *Paleoanthropology: Morphology and paleoecology* (pp. 225-243). Chicago: Aldine.

Brown, J. (1963). A cross-cultural study of female initiation rites. *American Anthropologist, 656,* 837-853.

Buchsbaum, M. S. (1979). Tuning in an hemispheric dialogue. *Psychology Today, 12(8),* 100.

Bunzel, R. (1952). *Chichicastenango: A Guatemalan village (Monographs of the American Ethnological Society, 22).* New York: J. J. Augustin.

Byrne, D. (1977), A pregnant pause in the sexual revolution. *Psychology Today, 11 (2),* 67-68.

Burgess, F. W., & Wallin, P. (1953). Homogamy in social characteristics. *American Journal of Sociology, 49,* 109-124.

Cain, A. C. (1964). On the meaning of 'playing crazy' in borderline children. *Psychiatry, 27 (August),* 281-282.

Calder, J. E. (1874). Some accounts of the wars of extermination, and habits of the native tribes of Tasmania. *Journal of the Anthropological Institute of Britain and Ireland, 3.*

Caldwallande, T. C. (1958). Cessation of visual experience under prolonged uniform visual stimulation. *American Psychologist, 13,* 410.

Canady, H. G. (1936). The effect of 'rapport' on the I.Q.: A new approach to the problem of racial pyschology. *Journal of Negro Education, 5,* 209-219.

Cannon, W. B. (1942). Voodoo death. *American Anthropologist, 44,* 169-181.

Carniero, R. (1970). A theory of the origin of the state. *Science, 169,* 733-738.

Carniero, R. (1978). Political expansion as an expression of a principle of competitive exclusion. In R. Cohen & E. Service (Eds.), *Origins of the state* (pp. 205-233). Philadelphia, PA: ISHI.

Cassirer, E. (1944). *An essay on man: An introduction to a philosophy of human culture.* New Haven, CT: Yale University Press.

Caton-Thompson, G., & Gardner, E. W. (1934). *The desert Fayum* (Vols. 1-2) London: The Royal Anthropological Institute.

Chagnon, N. A. (1968). *Yąnomamö: The fierce people.* New York: Holt, Rinehart and Winston.

Chandler, J. T., & Platkos, J. (1969). *Spanish speaking pupils classified as educable mentally retarded.* Sacramento, CA: California State Department of Education, Division of Instruction.

Chang, Kwang-chih. (1977). *Archaeology of ancient China.* New Haven, CT: Yale University Press.

Chase, A. (1977). *Legacy of Malthus.* New York: A. Knopf.

Childe, V. G. (1950). The urban revolution. *Town Planning Review, 21(1),* 3-17.

Chomsky, N. (1965). *Aspects of the theory of syntax.* Cambridge, MA: The MIT Press.

Chomsky, N. (1971). Language acquisition. In J. P. B. Allen, & P. Van Buren (Eds.), *Chomsky: Selected readings* (pp. 127-148). London: Oxford University Press.

Clark, W. E. L. (1967). *Man-apes or ape-men?* New York: Holt, Rinehart and Winston.

Clements, F. E. (1932). *Primitive concepts of disease.* (Publications in American Archaeology and Ethnology, *32* [2].) Berkeley, CA: University of California Press.

Codere, H. (1950). *Fighting with property. (Monographs of the American Ethnological Society, 18).* New York: J. J. Augustin.

Coe, M. (1977). *Mexico.* New York: Praeger.

Coe, R. (1970). *The sociology of medicine.* New York: McGraw-Hill.

Cohen, W. (1957). Spatial and textural characteristics of the ganzfield. *American Journal of Psychology, 70,* 403-410.

Cohen, Y. A. (1964). *The transition from childhood to adolescence: Cross cultural studies in initiation ceremonies, legal systems, and incest taboos.* Chicago: Aldine.

Cohn, W. (1967). "Religion" in non-western culture? *American Anthropologist, 69,* 73-76.

Cooper, J. M. (1946). The Yahgan. In J. H. Steward (Ed.), *Handbook of South American Indians:, Vol. 1* (pp. 97-98). Washington, DC: Smithsonian Institution, Bureau of American Ethnology. Bulletin 143.

Coult, A. D. (1963). Causality and cross-sex prohibitions. *American Anthropologist, 65,* 266-277.

Coult, A. D., & Habenstein, R. W. (1965). *Cross tabulations of Murdock's world ethnographic sample.* Columbia, MO: University of Missouri Press.

The Council of State Governments. (1986). State elective officials & the legislature: 1985-86. Lexington, KY: Author.

Count, E. W. (1965). The biological basis of human society. *American Anthropologist, 60,* 1049-1085.

Critchfield, R. (1981). *Villages.* Garden City, NY: Doubleday Anchor Press.

Culbert, S. S. (Ed.). (1982). *The world almanac and book of facts.* New York: Newspaper Enterprise Association.

Czaplicka, M. A. (1914). *Aboriginal Siberia: A study in social anthropology.* Oxford, CT: Clarendon.

Dalton, G. (1969). Theoretical issues in economic anthropology. *Current Anthropology, 10,* 63-102.

D'Andrade, R. (1961). The anthropological study of dreams. In F. L. K. Hsu (Ed.), *Psychological anthropology* (pp. 296-332). Homewood, IL: Dorsey.

Dart, R. A. (1925). Australopithecus africanus: The man-ape of South Africa. *Nature, 115,* 195-199.

Darwin, C. (1967). *On the origin of species.* New York: Atheneum. (original work published 1859).

DeVore, P. (1965). Language and communication. In P. L. Devore (Ed.), *The origin of man* (pp. 77-77a). New York: The Wenner-Gren Foundation for Anthropological Research.

Dibble, C. E., & Anderson, A. J. O. (Trans.) (1950-1961). *Florentine codex: General History of the things of New Spain* (Vols. 1-12). Salt Lake City, UT: The School for American Research and the University of Utah.

Divale, W. (1972). Systematic population control in the middle and upper Paleolethic: Inferences based on contemporary hunters and gatherers. *World Archaeology, 4,* 222-243.

Divale, W. Chambaris, F., & Gangloff, D. (1976). War, peace and marital residence in pre-industrial societies. *Journal of Conflict Resolution, 20,* 57-78.

Divale, W., & Harris, M. (1976). Population, warfare and the male supremacist complex. *American Anthropologist, 78,* 521-538.

Dove, A. (1968, July 15). Taking the Chitling Test. *Newsweek,* 57-52.

Downs, J. F., & Bleibtreu, H. K. (1972). *Human variation: An introduction to physical anthropology*. Beverly Hills, CA: Glencoe Press.

DuBois, C. (1944). *People of Alor: A social psychological study of an East Indian island* (Vols. 1-2). Minneapolis, MN: University of Minnesota Press.

DuBois, C. (1955). The dominant value profile of American culture. *American Anthropologist, 57,* 1232-1239.

Dumont, L. (1970). *Homo heirarchicus*. Chicago: University of Chicago Press.

Durkheim, E. (1915). *The elementary forms of the religious life* (J. W. Swain, Trans.). London: Allen and Unwin. (Original work published 1912)

Eastwell, H. D. (1982). Voodoo death and the mechanism for dispatch of the dying in East Arnhem, Australia. *American Anthropologist, 84,* 5-18.

Edgerton, R. B. (1976). *Deviance: A cross-cultural perspective*. Menlo Park, CA: Cummings.

Eichenlaub, J. E. (1963). *The marriage art*. New York: Dial Press.

Eldridge, N., & Gould, S. J. (1972). Punctuated equilibria: An alternative to phyletic gradualism. In T. J. M. Schopf (Ed.), *Models in paleobiology* (pp. 82-115). San Francisco, CA: Freeman, Cooper.

Eliade, M. (1964). *Shamanism: Archaic techniques of ecstasy*. Princeton, NJ: Princeton University Press.

Ella, S. (1895). The ancient Samoan government. *Australasian Association for the Advancement of Science, 5.* Brisbane, Australia.

Ellwood, C. A. (1913). *Sociology and modern social problems*. New York: American Book.

Evans-Pritchard, E. E. (1976). *Witchcraft, oracles and magic among the Azande*. Oxford: Clarendon Press.

Fairservice, W. A., Jr. (1975). *The roots of ancient India*. Chicago: University of Chicago Press.

Fairservice, W. A. Jr. (1983). The script of the Indus Valley civilization. *Scientific American, 248*(3), 58-77.

Faron, L. C. (1961). *Mapuche social structure: Reintegration in a patrilineal society of central Chile*. Urbana, IL: University of Illinois Press.

Faron, L. C. (1964). *Hawks of the sun: Mapuche mortality and its ritual attributes*. Pittsburgh, PA: University of Pittsburgh Press.

Faron, L. C. (1968). *The Mapuche Indians of Chile*. New York: Holt, Rinehart and Winston.

Fischer, J. (1961). Art styles as cultural cognitive maps. *American Anthropologist, 63,* 80-84.

Fischer, J. (1972). Why do prospects fail to come up to expectations? *CENTO Seminar on Agricultural Planning* (pp. 106-113). Ankara, Turkey: Public Relations Division, Central Treaty Organization.

Flannery, K. V. (1971). The origins and ecological effects of early domestication in Iran and the Near East. In S. Struever (Ed.), *Prehistoric agriculture* (pp. 50-79). Garden City, NY: Natural History Press. (Original work published in Ucko, P. J., & Dimbleby, G. W. [1969]. *The domestication and exploration of plants and animals*. Chicago: Aldine)

Flannery, K. V. (1972). The cultural evolution of civilizations. *Annual Review of Ecology, 3,* 399-425.

Ford, C. S., & Beach, F. A. (1951). *Patterns of sexual behavior*. New York: Harper & Row.

Ford, E. B. (1964). *Ecological genetics*. London: Methuen & Co.

Fortune, R. (1932). Incest. *Encyclopedia of the Social Sciences, 7,* 620-622.

Fortune, R. F. (1963). *Sorcerers of Dobu: The social anthropology of the Dobu Islands of the Western Pacific*. New York: E. P. Dutton. (Original work published 1932)

Foster, G. (1965). Peasant society and the image of limited good. *American Anthropologist, 67,* 293-315.

Foulks, E. F. (1972). *The arctic hysterias of the north Eskimo* (No. 10). In Maybury-Lewis, (Ed.), *Anthropological Studies* Washington, DC: American Anthropological Association.

Fouts, R. S., Fouts, D. H., & Schoenfeld, D. (1984). Cultural transmission of a human language in a chimpanzee mother-infant relation. *Sign Language Studies, 42* (Spring), 1-17.

Fox, R. (1967). *Kinship and marriage: An anthropological perspective*. Baltimore, MD: Penguin Books.

Frazer, Sir James. (1910). *Totemism and exogamy* (Vols. 1-4). London: Macmillan.

Frazer, Sir James. (1922). *The golden bough: A study in magic and religion* (Vols. 1-12). New York: Macmillan. (Originally printed in 12 vols., London: Macmillan)

Freeman, D. (1983). *Margaret Mead in Somoa: The making and unmaking of an anthropological myth*. Cambridge, MA: Harvard University Press.

Freuchen, P. (1935). *Arctic adventure*. New York: Farrar and Rinehart.

Fried, M. H. (1967). *The evolution of political society: An essay in political anthropology*. New York: Random House.

Friedl, E. (1975). *Women and men: An anthropologist's view*. New York: Holt, Rinehart and Winston.

Frisch, R. (1975). Critical weights, a critical body composition, menarche and the maintenance of menstrual cycles. In E. Watts, F. Johnston, & G. Lasker (Eds.), *Biosocial interrelations in population adaptation* (pp. 309-318). The Hague: Mouton.

Frisch, R., & McArthur, J. (1974). Menstrual cycles: Fatness as a determinant of minimum weight for height necessary for their maintenance or onset. *Science, 185,* 949-951.

Gardner, B. T., & Gardner, R. A. (1969). Teaching sign-language to a chimpanzee. *Science, 165,* 664-672.

Gardner, B. T., & Gardner, R. A. (1970). Development of behavior in a young chimpanzee. In *Eighth summary of Washoe's diary*. Reno, NV: University of Nevada.

Gardiner, B. T , & Gardiner, R. A. (1971). Two-way communication with an infant chimpanzee. In A. Schries & F. Stollnitz (Eds.), *Behavior of nonhuman primates: Vol. 4*. New York: Academic Press.

Gardner, B. T., and Gardner, R. A. (1985). Signs of intelligence in cross-fostered chimpanzees, *Philosophical Transactions of the Royal Society of London, B 308,* 150-176.

Gibbs, J. L. (Ed.). (1965). *Peoples of Africa*. New York: Holt, Rinehart and Winston.

Gillin, J. P. (1955). Natural and regional cultural values in the U.S. *Social Forces, 34,* 107-113.

Gloucester, R. of. (1905). *Robert of Gloucester's chronicle—how the Normans came to England*. In O. F. Emerson, *A Middle English Reader* (pp. 203-210). New York: Macmillan.

Gobineau, A. de. (1967). *The inequality of human races* (A. Collins, Trans.). New York: Howard Fertig.

Goddard, H. H. (1913). The Binet tests in relation to immigration. *Journal of Psycho-Asthenics, 18,* 105-107.

Goddard, H. H. (1917). Mental tests and the immigrant. *Journal of Delinquency, 2,* 243-277.

Goffman, E. (1955). On face-work: An analysis of ritual elements in social interaction. *Psychiatry, 18,* 213-231.

Goffman, E. (1961). *Asylums.* New York: Anchor.

Goffman, E. (1967). *Interaction ritual: Essay on face-to-face behavior.* Garden City, NY: Doubleday.

Goleman, D. (1978). Why the brain blocks daytime dreams. *Psychology Today, 9*(10), 69-70.

Gould, S. J. (1981). *The mismeasurement of man.* New York: W. W. Norton.

Gregor, T. (1983). Dark dreams about the white man. *Natural History, 92*(1), pp. 8-14.

Grinnell, G. B. (1961). *The Cheyenne Indians: Their history and ways of life* (Vol. 2). New York: Cooper Square Publishers.

Gudschinsky, S. C. (1956). The ABC's of lexicostatistics (glotto-chronology). *Word, 12,* 175-210.

Gussow, Z. (1960). Pibloktoq (hysteria) among the polar Esikmo: An ethnopsychiatric study. In W. Muensterberger & S. Axelrad (Eds.), *The psychoanalytic studies of society* (Vol. 1). New York: International University Press.

Gussow, Z. (1963). A preliminary report of kayakangst among the Eskimo of West Greenland: A study in sensory deprivation. *International Journal of Social Psychiatry, 9,* 18-26.

Guthrie, S. (1980). A cognitive theory of religion. *Current Anthropology, 2,* 181-203.

Hall, E. (1959). *The silent language.* Greenwich, CT: Fawcett Publications.

Hammond, N. (Ed.). (1973). *South Asian archaeology.* Park Ridge, NJ: Noyes Press.

Harding, T. G. (1960). Adaptation and stability. In M. D. Sahlens & E. R. Service (Eds.), *Evolution and culture* (pp. 45-68). Ann Arbor, MI: University of Michigan Press.

Harner, M. (1977). The ecological basis of Aztec cannibalism. *American Ethnologist, 4*(1), 117-135.

Harré, R. (1984). *Personal being.* Cambridge, MA: Harvard University Press.

Harris, G. (1957). Possession 'hysteria' in a Kenya tribe. *American Anthropologist, 59,* 1046-1066.

Harris, M. (1968). *The rise of anthropological theory: A history of theories of culture.* New York: Thomas Y. Crowell.

Harris, M. (1974). *Cows, pigs, wars and witches: The riddle of culture.* New York: Random House.

Harris, M. (1979). *Cultural materialism.* New York: Thomas Y. Crowell.

Harris, M. (1981). *America now: The anthropology of a changing culture.* New York: Simon and Schuster.

Hayami, Y., & Kikuchi, M. (1981). *Asian village economy at the crossroads: An economic approach to institutional change.* Tokyo: University of Tokyo Press and Baltimore, MD: The Johns Hopkins University Press.

Hayes, K. J., & Nissen, C. H. (1971). Higher mental functions of a home-raised chimpanzee. In *Behavior of nonhuman primates.* A. M. Schrier & F. Stollnitz, (Eds.), (vol. 4, pp. 59-115). New York: Academic Press.

Heeren, J., Lindsay, D. B., & Mason, M. (1984). The Mormon concept of mother in heaven. *Journal for the Scientific Study of Religion, 23*(4), 396-411.

Hill, J. (1978). Apes and language. *Annual Review of Anthropology, 7,* 89-112.

Hoebel, E. A. (1949). *Man in the primitive world.* New York: McGraw-Hill.

Hofstadter, R. (1963). *Anti-intellectualism in American life.* New York: A. A. Knopf.

Hoijer, H. (1964). Cultural implications of some Navaho linguistic categories. In D. Hymes (Ed.), *Language in culture and society: A reader in linguistics and anthropology* (pp. 142-153). New York: Harper & Row.

Hollingshead, A. B., & Redlich, F. C. (1953). Social stratification and psychiatric disorders. *American Sociological Review, 18,* 163-169.

Holloway, R. L. (1970). Tools and teeth: Some speculations regarding canine reduction. *American Anthropologist, 69,* 63-67.

Honigmann, J. J., & Honigmann, I. (1965). *Eskimo townsmen.* Ottawa: University of Ottawa.

Hopkins, K. (1980). Brother-sister marriage in Roman Egypt. *Comparative Studies in Society and History, 22*(3), 303-354.

Hosken, F. P. (1980). Women and health: Genital and sexual mutilation of women. *International Journal of Women's Studies, 3*(1-3), 300-316.

Hsien, R. (1963). A consideration on Chinese concepts of illness and case illustrations. *Transcultural Psychiatry Research, 15,* 23-30.

Hsien, R. (1965). A study of the aetiology of koro in respect to the Chinese concept of illness. *International Journal of Social Psychiatry, 11,* 7-13.

Hymes, D. (1967). Models of interaction of language and social setting. *Journal of Social Issues, 23*(2), 8-28.

Ineichen, B. (1979). The social geography of marriage. In M. Cook & G. Wilson (Eds.), *Love and attraction.* New York: Pergamon.

Jacobs, B. L. (1978). Serotonin, the crucial substance that turns off dreams. *Psychology Today, 9*(10), 70-71.

Jacobson, T. (1946). *The intellectual adventure of ancient man.* Chicago: University of Chicago Press.

Jacobson, T. (1948). *Kingship and the gods.* Chicago: University of Chicago Press.

Jensen, A. R. (1969). How much can we boost I.Q. and scholastic achievement? *Harvard Educational Review, 39*(1), 1-123.

Johanson, D. C., & Edey, M. (1981). *Lucy: The beginnings of humankind.* New York: Simon and Schuster.

Johnson, P. (1979). *The civilization of ancient Egypt.* London: Weidenfeld and Nicholson.

Jolly, C. J. (1970). The seed eaters: A new model of hominid differentiation based in a baboon analogy. *Man, 5,* 5-26.

Kaplan, D. (1960). The law of cultural dominance. In M. D. Sahlins & E. R. Service (Eds.), *Evolution and culture* (pp. 69-92). Ann Arbor, MI: University of Michigan Press.

Kardiner, A. (1946). *The individual and his society.* New York: Golden Press.

Katz, J. J. (1972). *Semantic theory.* New York: Harper & Row.

Keller, H. (1954). *The story of my life.* Garden City, NY: Doubleday and Company.

Kellog, W. N. (1968). Communication and language in the home-raised chimpanzee. *Science 162,* 423-427.

Kemper, T. D. (1978). *A social interactional theory of emotions.* New York: John Wiley and Sons.

Kent, M. M., & Haub, C. (1985). *World population data sheet*. In E. M. Murphy *World population: Toward the next century*. Washington, DC: Population Reference Bureau.

Kenyon, K. (1957). *Digging up Jericho*. London: Ben.

Kerkhoff, A. C., & Davis, K. E. (1962). Values consensus and need complementary in mate selection. *American Sociological Review, 27,* 295-303.

Kettlewell, H. B. D. (1959). Darwin's missing evidence. *Scientific American, 200,* 48-53.

Kiev, A. (1972). *Transcultural psychology*. New York: Macmillan.

Kispert, R. J. (1971). *Old English: An introduction*. New York: Holt, Rinehart and Winston.

Klein, R. G. (1977). The ecology of early man in Southern Africa. *Science, 179,* 115-126.

Kluckhohn, C. M. and others (1951). Values and value orientation in the theory of action. In T. Parsons & E. A. Shills (Eds.), *Toward a general theory of action* (pp. 388-933). Cambridge, MA: Harvard University Press.

Kluckhohn, C. (1965). Recurrent themes in myth and myth-making. In A. Dundes (Ed.), *The study of folklore* (pp. 158-168). Englewood Cliffs, NJ: Prentice-Hall.

Koestler, A. (1964). *The act of creation*. New York: Macmillan.

Kolanda, P. (1978). *Castes in contemporary India*. Menlo Park, CA: Cummings.

Kolata, G. B. (1974). !Kung hunter-gatherers: Feminism, diet and birth control. *Science, 185,* 932-934.

Kramer, S. N. (1959). *History begins at Sumer*. Garden City, NY: Doubleday.

Krantz, G. S. (1961). Pithecanthropine brain size and its cultural consequences. *Man, 61,* 85-87.

Kroeber, A. L. (1944). *Configurations of culture growth*. Berkeley, CA: University of California Press.

Kroeber, A. L. (1948). *Anthropology*. New York: Harcourt, Brace and World.

Kroeber, A. L., & Kluckhohn, C. (1952). *Culture: A critical review of concepts and definitions*. Papers of the Peabody Museum of American Archaeology and Ethnology, 47, (November 1). (Reprinted by Random House, n. d.)

Krupke, D. F., & Lavie, P. (1975). Ultradian rhythms: The 90-minute clock inside us. *Psychology Today, 8*(11), 54-57.

Kübler-Ross, E. (1969). *On death and dying*. New York: Macmillan.

Lancaster, J. B. (1968). Primate communication systems and the emergence of human language. In P. C. Jay (Ed.), *Primates: Studies in adaptation and variability* (pp. 447-454). New York: Holt, Rinehart and Winston.

Langness, L. L. (1965). Hysterical psychosis in the New Guinea highlands: A Bena Bena example. *Psychiatry, 28,* 258-277.

Lappé, F. M., & Collins, J. (1977). *Food first: Beyond the myth of scarcity*. New York: Random House.

Leach, E. (1969). Virgin birth. In E. Leach, *Genesis as myth and other essays*. London: Jonathan Cape.

Leaf, M. (1971). Baking and roasting: A compact demonstration of a cultural code. *American Anthropologist, 73,* 267-268.

Leakey, L. S. B. (1961). New finds at Olduvai Gorge. *Nature, 189,* 649-650.

Leakey, L. S. B. (1962). A new lower Pliocene fossil primate from Kenya. *Annals and Magazine of Natural History, London, 13,* 689-696.

Leakey, R. (1973a). A new lower Pleistocene hominid from East Rudolf, Kenya, 1971. *Nature, 242,* 170-172.

Leakey, R. (1973b). Evidence for an advanced Plio-Pleistocene hominid from East Rudolf, Kenya. *Nature, 242,* 447-450.

Leakey, R. (1974). Further evidence of lower Pleistocene hominids from East Rudolf, North Kenya, 1973. *Nature, 248,* 653-656.

Lee, G. R., & Kezis, M. (1968). Family structure and the status of the elderly. *Journal of Comparative Family Studies, 10,* 429-443.

Lee, R. B. (1968). Population growth and the beginnings of sedentary life among the !Kung Bushmen. In B. Spooner (Ed.), *Population growth: Anthropological implications* (pp. 329-342). Cambridge, MA: MIT Press.

Lehmann, H. E. (1975). Schizophrenia: Clinical features. In A. M. Freedman, H. I. Kaplan, & B. J. Sadock (Eds.), *Comprehensive textbook of psychiatry-II* (Vol. 1, pp. 890-923). Baltimore, MD: Williams & Wilkins.

Leventhal, H. (1975). The consequences of depersonalization during illness and treatment: An information-processing model. In J. Howard & A. Strauss (Eds.), *Humanizing health care* (pp. 119-162). New York: Wiley-Interscience.

Lévi-Strauss, C. (1969). *The elementary structures of kinship*. Boston, MA: Beacon Press.

LeVine, R. (1973). *Culture, behavior and personality*. Chicago: Aldine.

Lewis, O. (1966). Culture of poverty. *Scientific American, 215,* 19-25.

Lieberman, P., Crelin, E. S., & Klatt, D. H. (1972). Phonetic ability and related anatomy of the new born and adult human, Neanderthal man, and the chimpanzee. *American Anthropologist, 74,* 287-307.

Linden, E. (1974). *Apes, men and language*. New York: Saturday Review Press and E. P. Dutton and Co.

Linton, R. (1936). *The study of man: An introduction*. New York: Appleton-Century-Crofts.

Li An-che. (1937). Zuñi: Some observations and queries. *American Anthropologist, 39,* 62-77.

Linnaeus, C. (1758). *Systema naturae per regna tria naturae secondum classes, ordines, species cum characteribus, differentiis, synonymis, locis*. Stockholm: Laurentii Salvii. (1956 photographic facsimile of the First Volume of the Tenth Edition. London: British Museum [Natural History])

Livingston, F. B. (1969). Genetics, ecology and the origins of incest and exogamy. *Current Anthropology, 10,* 45-61.

Llewellyn, K. N., & Hoebel, E. A. (1941). *The Cheyenne way*. Norman, OK: University of Oklahoma Press.

Lomax, A. (1968). *Folk song style and culture* (Publication No. 88). Washington, DC: American Association for the Advancement of Science.

Lomax, A., & Arensberg, C. M. (1977). A worldwide evolutionary classification of cultures by subsistence systems. *American Anthropologist, 18,* 659-708.

Ludwig, A. M. (1972). Altered state of consciousness. In C. T. Tart (Ed.), *Altered states of consciousness* (pp. 11-24). Garden City, NY: Doubleday. (Original work published 1966, *Archives of General Psychiatry, 15,* 215-234)

Lumsden, C., & Wilson, E. O. (1980). Gene-culture translation in the avoidance of sibling incest. *Proceedings of the National Academy of Sciences of the United States of America, 77*, 4382-4386.

Lumsden, C., & Wilson, E. O. (1981). *Genes, mind, and culture: The coevolutionary process.* Cambridge, MA: Harvard University Press.

MacNeish, R. S. (1964). The origins of new world civilization. *Scientific American, 21*(5), 29-37.

McCarley, R. W. (1978). Where dreams come from: A new theory. *Psychology Today, 12*(7), 15-20.

Malinowski, B. (1927). *Sex and repression in savage society.* London: Routledge and Keagan Paul.

Malinowski, B. (1929). *The sexual life of savages in north-western Melanesia: An ethnographic account of courtship, marriage and family life among the natives of the Trobriand Islands, British New Guinea.* New York: Harcourt, Brace & World.

Malinowski, B. (1939). The group and the individual in functional analysis. *American Journal of Sociology, 44*, 938-964.

Malinowski, B. (1955). *Magic, science and religion and other essays.* Garden City, NY: Doubleday. (Original work published 1925)

Mandelbaum, D. G. (1972). *Society in India.* Berkeley, CA: University of California Press.

Marett, R. R. (1909). *The threshold of religion.* London: Methuen.

Marler, P. (1965). Communication in monkeys and apes. In I. DeVore (Ed.), *Primate behavior: Field studies of monkeys and apes* (p. 544-584). New York: Holt, Rinehart and Winston.

Marriage: A garment of society. (1984). *Mahjubah, 3*(3), 16-19.

Martin, P. S. (1967). Pleistocene overkill. *Nature, 76*(10), 32-38.

Marx, K. (1961). *Economic and philosophic manuscripts of 1844.* Moscow: Foreign Language Publishing House.

Mead, M. (1928). *Coming of age in Samoa.* New York: Morrow.

Mead, M. (1950). *Sex and treatment in three primitive societies.* New York: Mentor.

Mellaart, J. (1964). A neolithic city in Turkey. *Scientific American, 210*(4), 94-105.

Mendel, G. (1959). Experiments in Plant Hybridization. In J. A. Peters (Ed.), *Classic papers in genetics* (pp. 1-20). Englewood Cliffs, NJ: Prentice-Hall.

Mendelssohn, K. (1974). *The riddle of the pyramids.* New York: Praeger.

Middleton, R. (1962). Brother-sister and father-daughter marriage in ancient Egypt. *American Sociological Review, 27*, 603-611.

Miller, S. N. (1974). The playful, the crazy and the nature of pretense. In E. Norbeck (Ed.), *The anthropological study of human play* (Rice University Studies 60 [3]), 31-52. Houston, TX: William Rice University.

Millon, R. (1973). *Urbanization at Teotihuacan, Mexico.* Austin, TX: University of Texas Press.

Minturn, L., & Lambert, W. W. (1964). *Mothers of six cultures: Antecedents of child rearing.* New York: Wiley.

Montagu, A. (1974). *Man's most dangerous myth: The fallacy of race.* Fair Lawn: Oxford University Press.

Morgan, L. H. (1851). *League of the /ho-de-no-sau-nee or Iroquois.* Rochester, NY: Sage and Brothers.

Morgan, L. H. (1977). *Ancient society.* New York: World.

Moris, J. (1981). *Managing induced rural development.* Bloomington, IN: International Development Institute.

Moscati, S. (1962). *The face of the ancient orient: A panorama of Near Eastern civilization in pre-classical times.* Garden City, NY: Doubleday.

Mounin, G. (1976). Language, communication, chimpanzees. *Current Anthropology, 17*, 1-21.

Müller, H. F. (1931). A chronological note on the physiological explanation of the prohibition of incest. *Journal of Religious Psychology, 6*, 294-295.

Munroe, R. L., Munroe, R. H., & Whiting, J. (1973). The couvade: A psychological analysis. *Ethos, 1*(1), 30-74.

Murdock, G. P. (1934). *Our primitive contemporaries.* New York: Macmillan.

Murdock, G. P. (1957). World ethnographic sample. *American Anthropologist, 59*, 664-487.

Murdock, G. P., Ford, C. S., Hudson, A. E., Kennedy, R., Simmons, L. W., & Whiting, J. W. (1981). *Outline of cultural materials* (5th ed.). New Haven, CT: Human Relations Area Files.

Murphy, J. M. (1976). Psychiatric labeling in cross-cultural perspective. *Science, 191*(4230), 1019-1028.

Murphy, R. F., & Kasdan, L. (1959). The structure of parallel cousin marriage. *American Anthropologist, 61*, 17-29.

Musil, A. (1928). *Manners and customs of the Rwala Bedouins.* New York: The American Geographical Society.

Naroll, R. (1973). Holocultural theory tests. In R. Naroll & F. Naroll (Eds.), *Main currents in cultural anthropology* (pp. 309-384). New York: Appleton-Century-Crofts.

Nassehi-Behnam, V. (1985). Change and the Iranian family. *Current Anthropology, 26*, 557-562.

National Center for Health Statistics, Vital and Health Statistics. (1963). *Divorce statistics analysis United States* (Series 21, No. 13, Table C). Washington, DC: U.S. Government Printing Office.

Nehmiah, J. C. (1975). Phobic neurosis. In A. M. Freedman, H. I. Kaplan, & B. J. Sadock (Eds.), *Comprehensive textbook of psychiatry-II* (Vol. 2, pp. 1247-1255). Baltimore, MD: Williams and Wilkins.

Newman, P. L. (1964). Wild man behavior in a New Guinea highlands community. *American Anthropologist, 66*, 1-19.

Noll, R. (1985). Mental imagery cultivation as a cultural phenomenon: The role of visions in shamanism. *Current Anthropology, 26*, 443-461.

Ohnuki-Tierney, E. (1969). Concepts of time among the Ainu of the northwest coast of Sakhalin. *American Anthropologist, 71*, 488-492.

Ohnuki-Tierney, E. (1972). Spatial concepts of the Ainu of the northwest coast of southern Sakhalin. *American Anthropologist, 74*, 425-457.

Olmstead, F. L. (1904). *A journey in the seaboard slave states in the years 1853-1854 with remarks on their economy* (Vol. 2). New York: Putnam.

Parker, S. (1962). Eskimo psychopathology in the context of Eskimo personality and culture. *American Anthropologist, 64*, 76-96.

Parsons, E. C. (1939). *Pueblo Indian religion.* Chicago: University of Chicago Press.

Patterson, F. (1978). Conversations with a gorilla. *National Geographic 154*(4), 438-465.

Peters, L. G., & Price-Williams, D. R. (1980). Towards an experiential analysis of shamanism. *American Ethnologist, 7,* 397-418.

Pilbeam, D. (1972). *The ascent of man.* New York: Macmillan.

Pilbeam, D. (1979). Recent finds and interpretations of Miocene hominoids. *Annual Review of Anthropology, 8,* 333-352.

Pilbeam, D., Meyer, G. E., & Badgley, C. (1977). New hominid primates from the Siwaliks of Pakistan and their bearing on hominid evolution. *Nature, 270,* 689-695.

Popov, A. A. (1936). *Tavgytsy: Matgerialy po ethnografi avamskikh i vedeyevskikh tavgytzevi.* Moscow and Leningrad: AN, Trudy Instituta Anthropologii i Ethnografii I, 5.

Poussaint, A. F. (1967, August 20). A Negro psychiatrist explains the Negro psyche. *The New York Times,* Section 6, pp. 52-80.

Powell, B., & Jacobs, J. A. (1983). Sex and consensus in occupational prestige ratings. *Sociology and Social Research 67*(4), 392-404.

Premack, A. J., & Premack, D. (1972). Teaching language to an ape. *Scientific American, 227,* 92-99.

Price-Williams, D. R. (n.d.). The waking dream in ethnographic perspective. In B. Tedlock (Ed.), *Dreaming: The anthropology and psychology of the imaginal.* Albuquerque, NM: University of New Mexico Press.

Price-Williams, D. (1985). On mental imagery and shamanism. *Current Anthropology, 26*(5), 656.

Putnam, C. (1967). *Race and reality: A search for solutions.* Washington, DC: Public Affairs Press.

Radcliffe-Brown, A. R. (1958). Taboo. In W. A. Lessa & E. Z. Vogt (Eds.), *Reader in comparative religion: An anthropological approach* (pp. 45-68). Evanston, IL: Row, Peterson.

Rambaugh, D. M. (1977). *Language learning by a chimpanzee: The Lana project.* New York: Academic Press.

Reynolds, P. C. (1968). Evolution of primate vocal-auditor communication systems. *American Anthropologist, 70,* 300-308.

Ribiero, D. (1971). *The Americas and civilization.* New York: Dutton.

Rist, R. (1970). Student social census and teacher expectations: The self-fulfilling prophecy in ghetto education. *Harvard Eductional Review, 40*(3), 411-451.

Rivers, W. H. R. (1901). *The Todas.* New York: Macmillan.

Rivers, W. H. R. (1914). *The history of Melanesian society.* Cambridge, MA: Cambridge University Press.

Rivers, W. H. R. (1926). *Psychology and ethnology.* New York: Harcourt, Brace and World.

Roberts, J., Arth, M. J., & Bush, R. R. (1959). Games in culture. *American Anthropologist, 61,* 597-605.

Roberts, J., & Sutton-Smith, B. (1962). Child training and game involvement. *Ethnology, 1,* 166-185.

Robinson, J. T. (1972). *Early hominid posture and locomotion.* Chicago: University of Chicago Press.

Rodney, W. (1972). *How Europe underdeveloped Africa.* London: Bogle-L'Ouverture Publications.

Rosenhahn, D. L. (1973). On being sane in insane places. *Science, 179,* 250-258.

Rossides, D. W. (1976). *The American class system.* Boston: Houghton Mifflin.

Roth, W. E. (1903). Superstition, magic and medicine. *North Queensland Ethnographic Bulletin 5.* Brisbane: G. A. Vaughn, Government Printer, Home Secretary's Department.

Rubel, A. J. (1960). Concepts of disease in Mexican-American culture. *American Anthropologist, 62,* 795-814.

Rubin, Z. (1973). *Liking and loving: An invitation to social pyschology.* New York: Holt, Rinehart and Winston.

Rukang, W. (1981). Where did humankind originate? *China Pictorial, 7,* 16-18.

Sahlins, M. D. (1960). The origins of society. *Scientific American, 203,* 76-89.

Sahlins, M. D. (1976). *Cultural and practical reason.* Chicago: The University of Chicago Press.

Sahlins, M. D., & Service, E. R. (1960). *Evolution and culture.* Ann Arbor, MI: University of Michigan Press.

Sapir, E. (1924). Culture, genuine and spurious. *American Journal of Sociology, 29,* 401-429.

Sapir, E. (1949). *Language: An introduction to the study of speech.* New York: Harcourt, Brace & World.

Sapir, E. (1970). Language. In D. G. Mandelbaum (Ed.), *Edward Sapir: Culture, language, and personality* (pp. 1-44). Berkeley, CA: University of California Press.

Sarich, V., & Wilson, A. (1967). An immunological time scale for hominid evolution. *Science, 158,* 1200.

Saussure, F. de. (1959). *Course in modern linguistics* (W. Baskin, Trans.). New York: The Philosophical Library.

Savage-Rumbaugh, E. S., Pate, J. L., Lawson, J, Smith, S. T., & Rosenbaum, S. (1983). Can a chimpanzee make a statement? *Journal of Experimental Psychology: General 112*(4) 457-492.

Savage-Rumbaugh, E. S., Rumbaugh, D. M., & Boysen, S. L. (1980). *American Scientist 68* 49-61.

Scheff, T. (1966). *Being mentally ill: A sociological theory* Chicago: Aldine.

Scott, J. C. (1976). *The moral economy of the peasant: Rebellion and subsistence in Southeast Asia.* New Haven, CT: Yale University Press.

Scott, R. (1969). *The making of blind men.* New York: Russell Sage Foundation.

Segall, M. H., Campbell, D. T., & Herskovits, M. J. (1966). *The influence of culture on visual perception.* Indianapolis, IN: Bobbs-Merrill.

Selye, H. (1976). *The stress of life.* New York: McGraw-Hill.

Service, E. R. (1962). *Primitive social organization: An evolutional perspective.* New York: Random House.

Service, E. R. (1971). *Cultural evolutionism: Theory in practice.* New York: Holt, Rinehart and Winston.

Service, E. R. (1975). *The origins of the state and civilization: The process of cultural evolution.* New York: W. W. Norton.

Service, E. R. (1978). *Profiles in ethnology.* New York: Harper and Row.

Sharp, L. (1952). Steel axes for stone age Australians. In E. H. Spicer (Ed.), *Human problems in technological change* (pp. 69-90). New York: Russell Sage Foundation.

Shepher, J. (1971a). *Self-imposed incest avoidance and exogamy in second generation kibbutz adults.* Unpublished doctoral dissertation, Rutgers University.

Shepher, J. (1971b). Mate selection among second generation kibbutz adolescents and adults: Incest avoidance and negative imprinting. *Archives of Sexual Behavior, 1,* 293-307.

Shepherd, G., & Shepherd, G. (1984). *A kingdom transformed: Rhetorical patterns with institutionalization of Mormonism.* Salt Lake City, UT: University of Utah Press.

Shoshtak, M. (1982). *Nisa: The life and words of a !Kung woman.* New York: Random House.

Sihler, A. L. (1973). Baking and roasting. *American Anthropologist, 75,* 1721-1725.

Singh, G. (1971). The Indus Valley culture. *Archaeology and Physical Anthropology in Oceania, 1*(2), 177-188.

Skinner, B. F. (1971). *Beyond freedom and dignity.* Toronto: Bantam Books.

Slotkin, J. S. (1947). On a possible lack of incest regulations in old Iran. *American Anthropologist, 49,* 612-617.

Soustelle, J. (1961). *Daily life of the Aztecs.* New York: Macmillan.

Stockwell, E. G., & Laidlaw, K. A. (1981a). *Third world: Problems and prospects.* Chicago: Nelson-Hall.

Stockwell, E. G., & Laidlaw, K. A. (1981b). *Third world development.* Chicago: Nelson-Hall.

Steward, J. H. (1938). Great-Basin sociopolitical groups. *Bureau of American Ethnology Bulletin 120.* Washington, DC: U.S. Government Printing Office.

Steward, J. H. (1949). Cultural causality and law: A trial formulation of the development of early civilizations. *American Anthropologist, 51,* 1-27.

Steward, J. H. (1955). *The theory of cultural change: The methodology of multilinear evolution.* Urbana, IL: University of Illinois press.

Stow, G. W. (1905). *The native races of South Africa: A history of the intrusion of the Hottentots and Bantu into the hunting grounds of the Bushmen, the aborigines of the country.* London: S. Sonnenschein.

Stuckert, R. P. (1966). Race mixture: The African ancestry of white Americans. In P. B. Hammond (Ed.), *Physical Anthropology and Archaeology: Selected Readings* (pp. 192-197). New York: Macmillan.

Sussman, R. (1972). Child transport, family size and the increase in human population size during the neolithic. *Current Anthropology, 13,* 258-267.

Swadesh, M. (1954). On the Penutian vocabulary survey. *International Journal of American Linguistics, 20,* 123-133.

Swadesh, M. (1955). Towards greater accuracy in lexicostatistic dating. *International Journal of American Linguistics, 21,* 121-137.

Swanson, G. E. (1960). *The birth of the gods: The origin of primitive beliefs.* Ann Arbor, MI: University of Michigan Press.

Szasz, T. (1970). *Ideology and insanity: Essays on the dehumanization of man.* Garden City, NY: Doubleday.

Tanaka, J. (1977). Subsistence ecology of the Central Kalahari !Kung. In R. B. Lee & I. Devore (Eds.), *Kalahari hunter gatherers* (pp. 99-119). Cambridge, MA: Harvard University Press.

Tanfer, K., & Horn, M. (1985). Contraceptive use, pregnancy and fertility patterns among single American women in their 20's. *Family Planning Perspective, 17*(1), 10-19.

Terrace, H. S. (1979). *Nim.* New York: Knopf.

Terrace, H. S., Pettito, L. A., Sanders, R. V., & Bever, T. G. (1979). Can an ape create a sentence? *Science, 206,* 891-902.

Terrace, H. S., Pettito, L., Sanders, R. J. & Bever, T. G. (1980). On the grammatical capacity of apes. In *Children's language* (Vol. 2. pp. 371-495). New York: Garner Press.

Thomas, A., Chess, S., & Birch, H. G. (1975). The origin of personality. In Thomas, A., Chess, S., & Birch, H. G. (Eds.), *Readings from Scientific American: Psychology in progress* (pp. 210-217). San Francisco, CA: W. H. Freeman

Tien, H. Y. (1983). China: Demographic billionaire. *Population Bulletin, 38*(2). Washington, DC: Population Reference Bureau.

Tonkinson, R. (1974). *The Jigalong mob: Aboriginal victors of the desert crusade.* Menlo Park, CA: Cummings.

Toth, N. (1985). The Oldowan reassessed: A closer look at early stone artifacts. *Journal of Archaeological Science, 12,* 101.

Turnbull, C. M. (1961). *The forest people: A study of the pygmies of the Congo.* New York: Simon and Schuster.

Turnbull, C. M. (1965). The Mbuti pygmy of the Congo. In J. L. Gibbs, Jr. (Ed.), *Peoples of Africa* (pp. 279-317). New York: Holt, Rinehart and Winston.

Tyler, E. B. (1871). *Primitive culture: Researches into the development of mythology, philosophy, religion, language, art and custom.* London: J. Murray.

Tyler, E. B. (1888). On a method of investigating the development of institutions; Applied to laws of marriage and descent. *Journal of the Royal Anthropological Institute, 18,* 245-269.

U.S. Bureau of the Census. (1984). Projections of the population of the United States by age, sex and race: 1985-2080. In *Current population reports: Population estimates and projections* (Series P-25, No. 952) (Table 2, p. 30). Washington, DC: U.S. Government Printing Office.

U.S. Bureau of the Census. (1985). *Statistical abstract of the United States: 1986* (106th ed.). Washington, DC: U.S. Government Printing Office.

U.S. Department of Labor, Employment and Training Administration. (1977). *Dictionary of occupational titles.* Washington, DC: U.S. Government Printing Office.

U.S. Federal Bureau of Investigation. (1983, September 11). *Uniform Crime Reports.* Washington, DC: U.S. Government Printing Office.

U.S. Federal Bureau of Investigation. (1986, July 1). *Uniform Crime Reports.* Washington, DC: U.S. Government Printing Office.

Van Gennep, A. (1960). *The rites of passage* (S. T. Kimball, Trans.). Chicago: University of Chicago Press.

Van Loon, F. H. G. (1926). Amok and latah. *Journal of Abnormal and Social Psychology, 21,* 434-444.

Vetter, B. M., & Babco, E. L. (1986). *Professional women and minorities: A manpower resource data service.* Washington, DC: Commission on Professionals in Science and Technology.

Walker, E. (1972). *The emergent Native Americans.* Boston, MA: Little, Brown.

Wallace, A. F. C. (1961). *Culture and personality.* New York: Random House.

Wallace, A. F. C. (1966). *Religion: An anthropological view.* New York: Random House.

Wallace, A. F. C. (1972 New Edition). Mental illness, biology, and culture. In F. L. K. Hsu (Ed.) *Psycho-*

logical anthropology. (pp. 363-402). Cambridge, MA: Schenkman.

Weber, M. (1947). *The theory of social and economic organization.* New York: The Free Press.

Weber, M. (1958). *From Max Weber: Essays in sociology* (H. H. Garth & W. Mills, Eds. and Trans.). New York: Oxford University Press.

Wertheimer, M. (1938). Laws of organization in perceptual forms. In W. D. Ellis, *A sourcebook of gestalt psychology* (pp. 73-88). New York: Farrar, Straus and Giroux.

Westermarck, E. A. (1922). *The history of human marriage* (5th ed. Vols. 1-3). New York: Macmillan.

Wheeler, Sir Mortimer. (1968a). *Early India and Pakistan* (rev. ed.). New York: Praeger.

Wheeler, Sir Mortimer. (1968b). *The Indus civilization.* Cambridge, MA: Cambridge University Press.

White, L. A. (1949). *The science of culture: A study of man and civilization.* New York: Grove Press.

White, L. A. (1959). *The evolution of culture.* New York: McGraw-Hill.

White, L. A. (1971). The expansion of the scope of science. The symbol: The origin and basis of human behavior. Energy and the evolution of culture. In L. A. White, *The science of culture: A study of man and culture* (pp. 363-393). New York: Farrar, Straus and Giroux.

Whiting, B. (1950). *Paiute sorcery (No. 15).* New York: Viking Fund Publications in Anthropology.

Whiting, J. W. M. (1959). Cultural and sociological influences on development. In *Growth and development of the child in his setting* (pp. 3-9). Baltimore, MD: Maryland Child Growth and Development Institute.

Whiting, J. W. M. (1964). Effects of climate on certain cultural practices. In W. H. Goodenough (Ed.), *Explorations in cultural anthropology: Essays in honor of George Peter Murdock* (pp. 175-195). New York: McGraw-Hill.

Whiting, J. W. M., & Child, I. L. (1953). *Child training and personality: A cross-cultural study.* New Haven, CT: Yale University Press.

Whiting, J. W. M., Kluckhohn, R., & Anthony, A. S. (1958). The function of male initiation ceremonies at puberty. In E. E. Maccoby, T. M. Newcomb, & E. L. Hartley, *Readings in social psychology* (pp.359-370). New York: Holt, Rinehart and Winston.

Whiting, R. (1979, September 25). You've gotta have 'Wa.' *Sports Illustrated,* pp. 60-71.

Wilson, M. H. (1951). Witch beliefs and social structure. *American Journal of Sociology, 56,* 307-313.

Winiarz, W., & Wielawski, J. (1936). Imu—A psychoneurosis occuring among Ainus. *Psychoanalytic Review, 23,* 181-186.

Witherspoon, G. (1977). *Language and art in the Navajo universe.* Ann Arbor, MI: University of Michigan Press.

Wittfogel, K. (1957). *Oriental despotism: A comparative study of total power.* New Haven, CT: Yale University Press.

Wittkower, E., & Fried, J. (1957). A cross-cultural approach to mental health problems. *American Journal of Psychiatry, 116,* 423-428.

Whorf, B. L. (1971a). Languages and logic. In J. B. Carroll (Ed.), *Language, thought and reality: Selected writings of Benjamin Lee Whorf* (pp. 233-245). Cambridge, MA: The MIT Press.

Whorf, B. L. (1971b). The relation of habitual thought and behavior to language. In J. B. Carroll (Ed.), *Language, thought, and reality: Selected writings of Benjamin Lee Whorf* (pp. 134-159). Cambridge, MA: The MIT Press.

Wolf, A. (1966). Childhood association, sexual attraction and the incest taboo: A Chinese case. *American Anthropologist, 68,* 883-898.

Wolf, A. (1969). Adopt a daughter-in-law, marry a sister: A Chinese solution to the problem of incest taboo. *American Anthropologist, 70,* 864-874.

Wolf, A. (1970). Childhood association and sexual attraction: A further test of the Westermarck hypothesis. *American Anthropologist, 72,* 503-515.

Wolf, E. (1964). *Anthropology.* Englewood Cliffs, NJ: Prentice-Hall.

Wolf, E. (1966). *Peasants.* Englewood Cliffs, NJ: Prentice-Hall.

Wolf, E. (1969). *Peasant wars of the twentieth century.* New York: Harper and Row.

Wright, G. D. (1954). Projection and displacement: A cross-cultural study of folk-tale aggression. *Journal of Abnormal and Social Psychology, 49,* 523-528.

Wu, R. (1981). Where did humankind originate? *China Pictorial, 7,* 16-18.

Yap, P. M. (1951). Mental illness peculiar to certain cultures: A survey of comparative psychiatry. *Journal of Mental Science, 97,* 313-327.

Yap, P. M. (1963). Koro or suk-yeong—An atypical culture-bound psychogenic disorder found in southern Chinese. *Transcultural Psychiatric Research, 1,* 36-38.

Yap, P. M. (1965). Koro: A culture-bound depersonalization syndrome. *British Journal of Psychiatry, 111,* 43-50.

Zelnick, M., & Kantner, J. (1977). Sexual and contraceptive experiences of young unmarried women in the United States, 1976 and 1971. *Family Planning Perspectives, 9,* 55-71.

Index

Page references in **bold** indicate glossary terms.

birth control, and peasant societies, 288, 289, 290
birthing rooms, 300
birthmarks, 300
Black English, 85
blue collar jobs, **295**
Blumenbach, Johann, 10
Boas, Franz, 11, 12, 59
bodily comforts, as cultural need, 52-53
body movements, as communication, 114-115
bone pointing, **207**, 208
Borah, Woodrow, 198
bound morpheme, **122**
bow and arrow, 40
Brahmin caste, 71
brain: structures of, 119-120
brain size: of australopithecines, 32-33; of *Homo erectus*, 36-37; of *Homo habilis*, 35; of Neanderthal, 37-38
brain stem, **119**
breastfeeding, 301; *see also*, nursing
bride price, **152**
bride service, **152**
Broca's area, grammatical function of, **119**, 120
burial practices, of Neanderthal, 39
burin, **40**

Cabral, Pedro, 276
calpulli, 263
cannibalism, 198
carbon 14 dating, **27**
caste, in India, **70**-71
Catal Hüyük, Turkey, 225, 226
cave art, of early *Homo sapiens*, 41
cave bear ceremony: among Ainus of Japan, 39; by Neanderthal, 39
Central America, early civilizations in, 228
cerebellum, **119**
cerebral cortex, **119**, 180
Chagnon, Napoleon, 63
chained reaction, 172
Chan Chan, **238**
Chanters for the Dead, 209
Chavin, **237**
Cherokee Indians: alphabet of, 245; and Trail of Tears, 274-276
Cheyenne Indians, and Contrary Warriors of, 165
chief, **259**
chiefdoms, 258-260; development of, **226**, 227; evolution of, 221
Chief Junaluska, 275
childbirth: in American culture, 300; in nomadic populations

vs. sedentarism, 223
childhood: and enculturation, 142-147; socialization, 164, 165
childrearing: in America, 317; and effect of culture on personality, 164, 165; and hysteria, 178; and maintenance system of a society, 164
children: effect of culture on personality of, 164, 165; and families, 156, 157; and primary institutions, 164; effect of socialization practices on, 164, 165
chimpanzees, language ability of, 116-119
Chimu, **238**
China: birth control in, 288-290; culture-specific disorders of, 177, 178; early civilizations in, 227, 228, 233; and value of self-reliance, 310, 311
chinampa, 263
chindi, 211
Chinese language, grammar of, 122
Christianity, 9; and Cherokee Indians, 274
chromosomes, **22**; and mutations, 23
Chuckchi, 54
circumcision: female, 90-91; and puberty rituals, **146**
cities, growth of, and industrialization, 278, 279
city-state, and Sumer, **228**
civilizations, characteristics of early, 227, 228
civil religion, **305**
clan, **137**, 255-257, 264
clan exogamy, 256
class: North American clothing as symbols of, 46; of statuses, **70**
class stratification, 263; in Aztec civilization, 264, 265; in early civilizations, 227, 233; in United States, 294-297, 318
closure, **102**
clothing, North American, as symbols of culture, 46
colonial peasants, and industrialization, **280**
colonial people, attempts at genocide against Native Americans, 276
communal hunting, cooperative, 251
communal religious, **213**
communication: human vs. nonhuman, 106-107; and the case of Helen Keller, 107-110; language as "open" system of, 115-131; nonverbal, 110-115; and schizophrenia,

175; and signalized behavior, 171; with signs and symbols, 105-110
competitiveness, American, **313**, 315, 316
complementary status, **68**
conception, 136-138
concepts, **101**-105
conformity: in America, **308**-310, 317; to belief system, 47-48; in Germany, 308-310; in Japan, 308, 310; vs. self-reliance, 310, 311, 317
conspicuous consumption, **318**
contagious magic, **204**
contextual cue, **72**
contraception, and peasants, 288
Contrary Warrior, **165**
counterculture, **316**
courtship, 301, 302; and premarital sex, 147; in Samoa, 147
cousin marriages, 149, 150, 151
couvade, and childbirth, **140**, 141
Coyote stories, 255
cranial capacity, *see* brain size
creation, hypothetical date of, 9
creationism, vs. science, 217, **218**
crime rate, in United States, 298
cross-breeding, experiment by Mendel with sweet pea plant, 22-23
cross cousin, **149**
cross-cousin marriages, **149**, 150, 151
cross-cultural comparison, **9**
cross-cultural research, **4**
cultural anthropologists, 4-6
cultural change: process of, 243-250; stages in history of, 267-269
cultural ecology, **14**
cultural evolutionism, **10**-11; neoevolutionism as rebirth of, 14
cultural relativism, **12**, 59, **61**-63
cultural systems, and anthropological view of personality, 163-193
culture, **45**-46; as adaptive systems, 52-59; conscious and unconscious beliefs of, 47; differences between, 59-65; extinction of, through acculturation, 274; ideal vs. real, 51; ideology of, 47-51; influence of, on perception, 103-104; effect of, on personality, 163-193; among Zuñi of United States, 51-52
culture and personality, as subfield of anthropology, **13**
culture areas, **12**

STAFF

Editor Mary Pat Fisher
Copy Editors Kathleen Burns and M. Marcuss Oslander
Production Manager Brenda S. Filley
Designers Jean Bailey, Charles Vitelli, and Whit Vye
Typesetter Libra Ann Cusack
Systems Coordinator Richard Tietjen
Art Editor Pamela Carley Petersen
Proofreader Diane Barker
Production Assistant Lynn Shannon
Illustrator Mike Eagle

This text was set in Palacio typeface on the Compugraphic MCS 8400.
Graphs and tables were rendered by Charles Vitelli.
The text was printed in narrow web offset lithography and bound by D.B. Hess,
Inc. at Woodstock, IL. The text paper is 50 lb. Penagra Gloss coated.
The cover material is 10 pt. Carolina coated one-side.